Dana Peterson · Vanessa R
Editors

2014

Handbook of LGBT
Communities, Crime,
and Justice

 Springer

8579973129

Editors
Dana Peterson
School of Criminal Justice
University at Albany
Albany, NY
USA

Vanessa R. Panfil
School of Criminal Justice
Rutgers University
Newark, NJ
USA

ISBN 978-1-4614-9187-3 (hardcover)   ISBN 978-1-4614-9188-0 (eBook)
ISBN 978-1-4939-1787-7 (softcover)
DOI 10.1007/978-1-4614-9188-0
Springer New York Heidelberg Dordrecht London

Library of Congress Control Number: 2013953251

Printed on acid-free paper

Springer is part of Springer Science+Business Media (www.springer.com)

Handbook of LGBT Communities, Crime, and Justice

"Trans people do exist" (Translar Vardir). Photo taken at the 2013 Pride Parade, Istanbul, Turkey. Printed with kind permission from Susan Pearce

Photographer: Susan Pearce

Foreword

In their *Handbook of LGBT Communities, Crime, and Justice*, Dana Peterson and Vanessa R. Panfil bring together a collection of scholarly works that represent a groundbreaking call to 'queer' criminology. The diverse range of research and academic discourse presented in their volume demonstrates our vital need to bring a queer lens to every dimension of the field—the causes and consequences of crime, violence, and victimization; criminal justice policy and practice; law and human rights; and each locally and globally. Heteronormativity permeates criminology and criminal justice; in nearly all of our theorizing, research, pedagogy, and practice, the field has been bound by assumptions about actors, acts, interactions, settings, and institutions that are normatively—and often invisibly—configured on the basis of a heterosexual social order.

Why does this matter? And why should *all* criminologists care? Simply, because the configurations and elisions on which our field is based distort how we *think* about crime and justice and—consequently as well as consequentially—what we *know* about crime and justice. Moreover, for those of us whose criminological research is coupled with the desire for our scholarship to contribute to social justice, the exclusion of LGBT communities fundamentally undermines the efficacy of these goals. My appreciation for this volume is thus both as a criminologist and as a feminist scholar who has spent my career negotiating the tensions between these overlapping facets of my academic identity. What better way to illustrate the need for a paradigm shift in criminology, then, than to reflect a queer mirror on my own research?

One salient example will do. In 2008, I published *Getting Played: African American Girls, Urban Inequality, and Gendered Violence*, a study that carefully investigated the ways in which entrenched racial segregation and economic inequalities in urban neighborhoods heighten young women's risks for gender-based victimization. I argued that these inequalities contribute to organizational properties within disadvantaged communities that facilitate gendered social processes conducive to violence against girls: male dominance of public spaces; masculine performances of aggression, sexual conquest, and the devaluation and mistreatment of women as status-enhancing; group loyalty, distrust of outsiders, and limited community scrutiny or intervention. My focus on the harmful consequences of the rewards young men receive for aggressive displays of heterosexual prowess reflects influential themes within feminist criminology, which seeks as one of its goals to problematize the crime-facilitative features of gender inequalities.

In fact, much of this work emerged as a result of the radical feminist efforts of second wave feminism in the mid-twentieth century, and was grounded in a critique of compulsory heterosexuality, including its impact on women's experiences of marriage, childrearing, housework, prostitution, and sexual violence. These concerns are infused in feminist criminology's theorizing about women's participation in crime, experiences of incarceration, desistance processes, and explanations for violence against women, among others. Radical feminism has of course faced fundamental critiques of its essentialist treatment of the category Woman, most notably by scholars and others who have interrogated its erasure of differences and called, instead, for intersectional approaches that recognize the interdependence of hierarchies of gender, race, class, age, and sexuality, among others, in systems of oppression. This epistemological stance informed my analysis in *Getting Played*, as I positioned young women's experiences of violence within the intersections of gender, race, and class, and their impact on heterosexual practices.

So where, then, did I go wrong? Whatever the limitations of radical feminist thought, its critique of compulsory heterosexuality emerged simultaneous with early gay rights activism and was forged by lesbian feminist thinkers. Of her famed essay "Compulsory Heterosexuality and Lesbian Existence," Adrienne Rich (2003) later explained that one of her goals was "to encourage heterosexual feminists to examine heterosexuality as a political institution which disempowers women" (p. 11). This is a challenge I certainly took seriously. Yet Rich also notes that she wrote the essay to "challenge the erasure of lesbian existence" in feminist scholarship (p. 11). Indeed, contemporary queer theorists, despite their epistemological and ontological distances from radical feminism, continue to interrogate the ways in which feminist attention to gender is—some claim inherently— "indentured to heteronormative conceptual models" (Jagone 2009, p. 165).

How might *Getting Played* look differently, then, if I interrogate its heteronormativity? For starters, when we interviewed young women and men, we indeed assumed that they were heterosexual, a common limitation in nearly all criminological research. What if we hadn't? Several examples provide insights into this question. When I moved from St. Louis, Missouri to Newark, New Jersey in 2010, I learned of two incidents (among countless others, I'm sure) that reflected back to me the crucial limitations of this research. In 2003, 15-year-old African American Sakia Gunn and several friends were sexually propositioned by two adult men while at a bus stop in downtown Newark. This was a familiar scenario described regularly by the young women we interviewed, who consistently identified such encounters as a primary source of fear, risk, and anxiety in their communities. I detailed the double binds they faced in negotiating such interactions safely, but with the assumption that these negotiations occurred in the context of shared heterosexual positions. In Sakia Gunn's case, she rebuffed the men by identifying herself as a lesbian. Her rejection was unequivocal, as she declared herself outside the boundaries of the men's heterosexual "game." One of them then fatally stabbed her. And though he was convicted of manslaughter, aggravated assault, and bias intimidation, the incident received little publicity, locally or nationally (see Logan 2011).

Three years later, a group of young African American lesbians, also from Newark, were in Greenwich Village when they, too, were accosted and sexually harassed by a man on the streets. The New Jersey 7, as they came to be known, fought back, and bystanders in the vicinity jumped in to defend them as well. In the chaos that followed their harasser was stabbed, though not fatally. And while the actual perpetrator has never been identified, the *New York Post* headline cried "ATTACK OF THE KILLER LESBIANS." Four of the New Jersey 7 were convicted of felony and gang assault (despite *no* evidence of gang involvement, save their presence in the company of *friends*). One—Patreese Johnson—remains incarcerated. Upon their conviction, *The New York Daily News* headline read "Lesbian wolf pack guilty," with the reporter seemingly gleeful to report that "four tough lesbians from New Jersey were reduced to crying convicts" (Martinez 2007; see Logan 2011 for a discussion). In *Getting Played*, I theorized about how victim blaming processes blocked young women's access to justice when they were victimized; yet the racialized sexual identities of the New Jersey 7, read through a fundamentally heterosexist lens, didn't simply prevent the success of their claims of victimization, but led to their criminalization.

That both of these incidents occurred while I worked on *Getting Played* makes them no more tragic and outrageous. But it does give them particular salience for me, as they provide a stark reminder of both the crucial limitations of my research, and the imperative for the paradigm shift that Peterson and Panfil's *Handbook* calls for. Indeed, our assumption that the youths we interviewed were heterosexual resulted in missed opportunities for better understanding how and when young women were aggressively targeted by their heterosexual male peers, including the roles that sexual identity and gender presentations played, and how these also shaped young women's negotiations of risk and safety. Moreover, because we brought a heterosexual lens to our interviews, the LGB youth who were surely included in our sample were not provided a safe space to fully share such experiences and their perspectives on them, resulting in an analysis that was incomplete because it was based on partial stories, edited for the ears of the interviewers' presumptions.

Yet these examples are just one way to think about the limitations of *Getting Played*. Vanessa R. Panfil's pathbreaking research on gay gang- and crime-involved young men provides another lens through which to view the masculinity constructions I interrogated; her work complicates the linkages between the tough personas that I and others have traced to heterosexual masculinity and violence against women. Instead, she spoke with numerous gay young men of color in urban communities who not only construct masculine identities based on the embrace of competence in violence, but often utilize these performative skills to defend against anti-gay harassment and threats of violence (Panfil 2013; see also this volume). Indeed, *Getting Played* included interviews with young men who were critical of the aggressive heterosexual practices of some of their male peers; had we not assumed all of the young men we spoke with were heterosexual, I could have investigated the extent to which such variations mapped onto young men's sexual identities, and also expanded my conceptualization of gender-based violence. Notably, we also assumed that the youth we interviewed fit neatly on a male/female gender binary. The recent brutal murder of Cemia Acoff, a transgender young woman of color in suburban Cleveland, and the disturbing news coverage graphically describing her as an "oddly dressed man" (Caniglia 2013), points to additional critical layers missing from my analysis as a result of the heteronormative conceptual model I employed.

My detailed interrogation of *Getting Played* is not an exercise in self-flagellation. Instead, my goal has been to use my own research to illustrate what's lost— theoretically, empirically, pedagogically, and in our efforts to affect policy and practice—when criminology fails to investigate the heterosexual grounds on which our conceptual models are largely built, and fails to consider the experiences of LGBT communities. And I hope my efforts lead other scholars to follow suit. As the diversity of scholarship in the *Handbook of LGBT Communities, Crime, and Justice* reveals, the impact of a criminology that has been 'queered' is far reaching, and will strengthen how we understand crime and justice. "The normativity of the heterosexual male body has acted to structure the discourses of" criminology, criminal justice, "law and public policy" (Peel and Thomson 2009, p. 430), as many feminist scholars have noted (see Britton 2000). While its own tensions and fissures are well articulated in this volume—providing an important and critical roadmap for those wishing to better understand its complex debates and potentials—there is no doubt that the emergence and embrace of queer criminology is imperative.

Newark, USA   Jody Miller
                                                                 Rutgers University

References

Britton, D. M. (2000). Feminism in criminology: Engendering the outlaw. *The Annals of the American Academy of Political and Social Science, 571*, 57–76.

Caniglia, J. (2013). Oddly dressed body found in Olmsted Township pond identified. Retrieved from http://www.cleveland.com/metro/index.ssf/2013/04/body_of_oddly_dressed_man_foun.html

Jagose, A. (2009). Feminism's queer theory. *Feminism & Psychology, 19*(2), 157–174.

Logan, L. S. (2011). The case of the "killer lesbians." *The Public Intellectual.* Retrieved from http://thepublicintellectual.org/2011/07/18/the-case-of-the-killer-lesbians/

Martinez, J. (2007). Lesbian wolf pack guilty: Jersey girl gang gets lockup in beatdown. Retrieved from   http://www.nydailynews.com/news/ny_crime/2007/04/19/2007-04-19_lesbian_wolf_pack_guilty.html

Miller, J. (2008). *Getting played: African American girls, urban inequality, and gendered violence.* New York, NY: Oxford University Press.

Panfil, V. R. (2013). *Socially situated identities of gay gang- and crime-involved men.* Ph.D. Dissertation, University at Albany (SUNY), New York.

Peel, E., & Thomson, M. (2009). Editorial introduction: Lesbian, gay, bisexual, trans and queer health psychology: Historical developments and future possibilities. *Feminism & Psychology,* *19*(4), 427–436.

Rich, A. C. (2003). Compulsory heterosexuality and lesbian existence (1980). *Journal of Women's History, 15*(3), 11–48.

Acknowledgments

The editors would like to extend our sincere and deepest appreciation to the following:

Our editor at Springer, Katie Chabalko, who not only reached out to us about putting together this collection, but guided and encouraged us along the way.

A number of scholars doing work in these areas who, although they were not able to contribute chapters, took time to connect us with other scholars and spread the word about the *Handbook*. We are also indebted to the pioneers who helped lay the groundwork for this volume by pursuing research with LGBT populations long before it was politically or academically safe.

Our contributing authors, who not only provided the opportunity to share their important work through this volume, but who provided that work in a timely manner, were responsive to our suggestions, and were a pleasure to work with.

Everyone around the world committed to improving the lives and experiences of LGBT people and to those scholars, especially emergent scholars, who are queering criminology.

Contents

Part I Introduction and Overview of LGBT Communities, Crime, and Justice

1 Introduction: Reducing the Invisibility of Sexual and Gender
Identities in Criminology and Criminal Justice   3
Dana Peterson and Vanessa R. Panfil

2 "Queering Criminology": Overview of the State of the Field   15
Jordan Blair Woods

Part II LGBT Communities, Crime, and Victimization

3 Bias Crimes Based on Sexual Orientation and Gender
Identity: Global Prevalence, Impacts, and Causes   45
Rebecca L. Stotzer

4 Marking 35 Years of Research on Same-Sex Intimate
Partner Violence: Lessons and New Directions   65
Adam M. Messinger

5 The LGBT Offender   87
Jeffery P. Dennis

6 When They Tell You Who You Are: Lesbian Resistance
to the Policing of Multiple Identities 103
Dominique E. Johnson

7 "I Will Fight You Like I'm Straight": Gay Gang- and
Crime-Involved Men's Participation in Violence 121
Vanessa R. Panfil

**Part III   LGBT Communities and Juvenile and Criminal
            Justice Systems**

8   **Pleasures, Perversities, and Partnerships: The Historical
    Emergence of LGBT-Police Relationships**   149
    Angela Dwyer

9   **Intersections of Gender and Sexuality in Police Abuses
    Against Transgender Sex Workers in Sri Lanka**   165
    Andrea J. Nichols

10 **Policing the Lesbian and Gay Community: The Perceptions
    of Lesbian and Gay Police Officers**   183
    Roddrick Colvin

11 **Lesbian, Gay, and Bisexual Youth Incarcerated
    in Delinquent Facilities**   207
    Joanne Belknap, Kristi Holsinger and Jani S. Little

12 **Gender Integration in Sex-Segregated U.S. Prisons:
    The Paradox of Transgender Correctional Policy**   229
    Jennifer Sumner and Valerie Jenness

13 **LGBT Issues and Criminal Justice Education**   261
    Kevin Cannon, P. Ann Dirks-Linhorst, P. Denise Cobb,
    Florence Maatita, Dawn Beichner and Robbin Ogle

Part IV   LGBT Communities, Law, and Justice

14 **Rethinking the "World Polity" Perspective on Global
    Sodomy Law Reform**   283
    Neil Cobb

15 **LGBT Movements in Southeast Europe: Violence, Justice,
    and International Intersections**   311
    Susan C. Pearce and Alex Cooper

16 **The Death Penalty as Genocide: The Persecution
    of "Homosexuals" in Uganda**   339
    Christina DeJong and Eric Long

17 **Presumptive Criminals: U.S. Criminal Law
    and HIV-Related Aggravated Assaults**   363
    Ari Ezra Waldman

**18 Define "Sex": Legal Outcomes for Transgender Individuals
in the United States** 387
Alexis Forbes

**19 Bullying of LGBT Youth in America: Prevalence,
Effects, and Government Responses** 405
Sarah Warbelow and Ty Cobb

Part V   LGBT Communities, Crime, and Public Health

**20 Examining Dating Violence and Its Mental Health
Consequences Among Sexual Minority Youth** 431
Tameka L. Gillum and Gloria T. DiFulvio

**21 The Queer Delinquent: Impacts of Risk and Protective
Factors on Sexual Minority Juvenile Offending in the U.S.** 449
Meredith Conover-Williams

**22 Diversity at the Margins: The Interconnections Between
Homelessness, Sex Work, Mental Health, and Substance Use
in the Lives of Sexual Minority Homeless Young People** 473
Tyler Frederick

**23 A State of Exception: Intersectionality, Health,
and Social Exemption** 503
Ryan A. Levy

Part VI   Future Directions and Concluding Thoughts

24 What's Queer About Queer Criminology? 531
Matthew Ball

**25 Hardly Queer, or Very Queer Indeed? Concluding Thoughts
about the *Handbook of LGBT Communities,
Crime, and Justice*** 557
Vanessa R. Panfil and Dana Peterson

Glossary-Defining Terms and Acronyms 563

About the Editors 567

Index 569

Contributors

Matthew Ball Queensland University of Technology, Brisbane, QLD, Australia; Durham University, Durham, UK

Dawn Beichner Illinois State University, Normal, IL, USA

Joanne Belknap University of Colorado, Boulder, CO, USA

Kevin Cannon Southern Illinois University Edwardsville, Edwardsville, IL, USA

Neil Cobb University of Manchester, Manchester, UK

P. Denise Cobb Southern Illinois University Edwardsville, Edwardsville, IL, USA

Ty Cobb Human Rights Campaign, Washington, DC, USA

Roddrick Colvin John Jay College of Criminal Justice, New York, NY, USA

Meredith Conover-Williams Humboldt State University, Arcata, CA, USA

Alex Cooper Central European University, Budapest, Hungary

P. Ann Dirks-Linhorst Southern Illinois University Edwardsville, Edwardsville, IL, USA

Christina DeJong Michigan State University, East Lansing, MI, USA

Jeffery P. Dennis Wilkes University, Wilkes-Barre, PA, USA

Gloria T. DiFulvio University of Massachusetts Amherst, Amherst, MA, USA

Angela Dwyer Queensland University of Technology, Brisbane, QLD, Australia

Alexis Forbes John Jay College of Criminal Justice, New York, NY, USA

Tyler Frederick Toronto Center for Addiction and Mental Health, Toronto, ON, Canada

Tameka L. Gillum University of Massachusetts Amherst, Amherst, MA, USA

Kristi Holsinger University of Missouri Kansas City, Kansas City, MO, USA

Dominique E. Johnson Beam Youth Collaborative, Philadelphia, PA, USA

Valerie Jenness University of California Irvine, Irvine, CA, USA

Ryan A. Levy University at Albany, Albany, NY, USA

Jani S. Little University of Colorado, Boulder, CO, USA

Eric Long University of Maryland, College Park, MD, USA

Florence Maatita Southern Illinois University Edwardsville, Edwardsville, IL, USA

Adam M. Messinger Northeastern Illinois University, Chicago, IL, USA

Jody Miller Rutgers University, Newark, NJ, USA

Andrea J. Nichols St. Louis Community College Forest Park, St. Louis, MO, USA

Robbin Ogle University of Nebraska at Omaha, Omaha, NE, USA

Vanessa R. Panfil Rutgers University, Newark, NJ, USA

Susan C. Pearce East Carolina University, Greenville, NC, USA

Dana Peterson University at Albany, Albany, NY, USA

Rebecca L. Stotzer University of Hawai'i, Mānoa, HI, USA

Jennifer Sumner Seattle University, Seattle, WA, USA

Ari Ezra Waldman New York Law School, New York, NY, USA

Sarah Warbelow Human Rights Campaign, Washington, DC, USA

Jordan Blair Woods UCLA School of Law, Los Angeles, CA, USA; University of Cambridge, Cambridge, UK

Part I
Introduction and Overview of LGBT Communities, Crime, and Justice

Chapter 1
Introduction: Reducing the Invisibility of Sexual and Gender Identities in Criminology and Criminal Justice

Dana Peterson and Vanessa R. Panfil

Abstract In this chapter, the *Handbook* editors provide an overview of the volume. They discuss what led to this collection of papers that deconstruct the heteronormativity of Criminology and Criminal Justice (CCJ); their goals in producing this volume for CCJ so that LGBT people are better understood and better served; and the organization and content of the *Handbook*. Each of the chapters is briefly described and tied to the overarching goals and themes of the *Handbook*.

Keywords LGBT · Lesbian · Gay · Bisexual · Transgender · Trans* · Queer · Criminology · Criminal justice · Queer criminology · Essentializing · Theory · Research · Practice · Heteronormative · Heterosexism · Identity · Agency

Individuals who are lesbian, gay, bisexual, and/or transgender (LGBT) have been largely absent in criminological and criminal justice (CCJ) theorizing and research. That is, although they are likely *present* in research samples, their sexual and/or gender identities are not interrogated as salient characteristics, as these are likely not even recognized at all. As a number of the authors in this *Handbook* detail, much of the research that has been conducted with LGBT individuals has examined their experiences as victims of intimate partner violence or bias/hate crimes, or, when their participation in criminal activity is discussed, it is often framed in terms of sexual deviance and sex work. The current state of the CCJ research therefore provides too narrow a view of the issues that students, scholars, and practitioners need to understand in order to appropriately address and respond

D. Peterson (✉)
School of Criminal Justice, University at Albany, 135 Western Ave., DR 219,
Albany, NY 12222, USA
e-mail: dpeterson@albany.edu

V. R. Panfil
School of Criminal Justice, Rutgers University, Center for Law and Justice,
123 Washington Street Room 579B, Newark, NJ 07102, USA
e-mail: vanessa.panfil@rutgers.edu

D. Peterson and V. R. Panfil (eds.), *Handbook of LGBT Communities,*
Crime, and Justice, DOI: 10.1007/978-1-4614-9188-0_1,
© Springer Science+Business Media New York 2014

to LGBT populations and to improve their situations and treatment in justice systems globally. It is our goal with this volume to bring together the scant and scattered scholarly work, including much original research, that can inform CCJ about LGBT communities' experiences with regard to crime commission, crime victimization, juvenile and criminal justice systems, law and policy, public health, and human rights, in order to provide a more coherent and comprehensive awareness and understanding. With this volume, we also seek to identify and rectify educational, training, service, policy, and legal gaps in knowledge.

We want to acknowledge very explicitly at the outset of this volume our recognition that the acronym "LGBT" does not capture all of the gender, sexual, and/ or political identities with which individuals discussed in the *Handbook* might identify. However, our intention is that the use of this acronym is an umbrella term, short-hand if you will, meant to encompass any and all individuals who identify themselves in ways that are within and outside of the narrow "LGBT" acronym and categorizations. Several authors in the *Handbook* (see chapters by Ball; Frederick; Johnson; Woods) take up discussion of the limiting and essentializing nature of such categorizations, and by no means do we intend our shorthand to contribute to or perpetuate the practice of forcing individuals into what become quite heterogeneous "homogenous" categories and that leave out many individuals completely. We therefore take this opportunity to remind the reader that gender and sexuality, and their intersections, are complex, fluid, and individual, and that our use of "LGBT" represents not just lesbian, gay, bisexual, and/ or transgender individuals, but the full complement of gender- and sexual- (and intersecting gender X sexual) identities. Thus, we further explicitly acknowledge (as do a number of the authors) intersectional identities; that is, persons are not defined and do not define themselves in terms of only their sexual and gender identities, but also in terms of their race, ethnicity, culture of origin, socioeconomic status, and so on. These "characteristics," and persons' experiences based upon them, are not merely additive but intersectional and multiplicative. We therefore note that while the *Handbook* is framed around just a few facets of identity, this is not to the exclusion of other identities, but rather only to bring awareness of gender and sexual identities to the forefront. Indeed, structural factors in the lives of queer people such as race, socioeconomic status, and region may themselves complicate hegemonic notions of sexual and gender identity.

How the Volume Came to be and Other Queer Tales

The most proximal impetus for this collection emerged from the 2011 annual meeting of the American Society of Criminology (ASC), held in Washington, DC. The second author had experienced previous difficulty in placement of her research with queer youth populations on ill-fitting panels; the panels were hodge-podge collections with no thematic thread, or organizers made assumptions about the nature of the work. For example, one year she was placed on a panel with scholars of youth sexual violence (though those words appeared in her presentation, they were certainly not in that order!). It seemed criminologists were befuddled with just what to do with such work (and, even finding an appropriate "topic area," pre-defined by conference organizers, to which to submit an abstract was a challenge). We decided instead that she should organize her own panel and invite authors doing work on similar topics; thus was entered onto the conference program the panel entitled "The Role of Identity in LGBT Individuals' Responses to Violence," chaired by the first author and with papers presented by the second author (on gay gang- and crime-involved young men's use of violence to respond to anti-gay harassment), by Andrea Nichols and Jody Miller (on intersectional identities and experiences of Sri Lankan nachchi[1] sex workers), and by Laura S. Logan (on queer women's resistance to street harassment). These papers highlighted that, while experiences of violence and the construction and negotiation of identity apply to all people, the individuals in these studies experience them from particular places, from intersections of sexual orientation and gender identity that structure their experiences of and responses to victimization. Further, the authors demonstrated that, relevant to CCJ, certain aspects of violence cannot be understood, and violence prevention efforts mounted, unless the roles of sexual orientation and gender identity, within the context of societal heterosexism, are taken into account. These salient intersections, we (and others) argue, must be examined and understood in diverse disciplines and not limited to places like women's studies programs, queer studies programs, urban studies, and so on; CCJ can provide an interdisciplinary context that brings these perspectives together—provided we open our eyes to the issues.

Importantly, the panel attracted the attention of an Editor at Springer Publishing, who contacted the first author[2] to inquire whether we would be interested in submitting a book prospectus on the topic of the panel. As evidenced by the existence of this *Handbook*, we jumped at the opportunity, not just to further work about LGBT individuals' responses to violence (highlighting their agency), but to bring together for CCJ a collection of work dealing with a range of issues about LGBT people and their interactions with legal systems and, even more broadly, integrating perspectives of justice, health, and human rights in hopes, ultimately, of improving theory, research, and practice in all of these areas, globally. That a well-known publisher of criminological and criminal justice titles was interested in promoting this work was a welcome sign and an indicator of shifts within CCJ that are beginning to "allow space" for consideration of these issues.

---

[1] Nachchi are biological males who embrace feminine identities, celebrate aspects of their maleness, and who are sexually attracted to other males; thus, they are both "transgender" and "gay" (see Nichols, this volume; and Miller and Nichols (2012). Identity, sexuality, and commercial sex among Sri Lankan nachchi. *Sexualities, 15*, 554–569.).

[2] The first author was known to the Springer editor through a contribution of a co-authored (with Dena C. Carson) chapter to an edited book (*Youth Gangs in International Perspective: Tales from the Eurogang Program of Research*, edited by Finn-Aage Esbensen and Cheryl L. Maxson) published by Springer in 2012.

These shifts are evident in other ways as well, in CCJ scholarship and practice. For example, in addition to providing a thematic "home" for papers that would have ended up on potpourri panels, connecting scholars with an interest in queering criminology, and providing the impetus for this *Handbook*, that 2011 ASC conference panel continues to pay other big dividends, having created (or perpetuated) ripples that continue to grow and spread. To name a few of the advances just since that meeting (and not to downplay all the advances to queer criminology that have preceded these): A chance encounter in the conference center hallway between the first author and Christine Galvin-White from Arizona State University resulted in the creation of a "Queer CCJ" listserv (https://lists.asu.edu/cgi-bin/wa?A0=QUEERCCJ), fostering additional connections and sharing of information, research, and events; scholars who made connections at that meeting continue to organize LGBT thematic panels and roundtables at annual ASC meetings; a number of *Handbook* authors, along with other scholars from the U.S. and Canada, presented papers at an April 2013 symposium, "Explorations in Justice: Gender, Sexuality, and Violence," hosted by the University at Albany School of Criminal Justice as part of their ongoing "Justice and Multiculturalism in the 21st Century" project (http://www.albany.edu/justiceinstitute/); and, several *Handbook* authors and other scholars are contributing to a special issue (March 2014) of *Critical Criminology* entitled "Queer/ing Criminology: New Directions and Frameworks," edited by Matthew Ball, Carrie L. Buist, and Jordan Blair Woods.

On the practice side, we note a few recent advancements within the U.S. (though not to the exclusion of advances worldwide) that indicate shifts in the federal perspective. The U.S. Department of Justice's National Institute of Corrections, for example, has developed online resources about offenders who are LGBT for corrections agencies (http://nicic.gov/LGBTI), and the federal Office of Juvenile Justice and Delinquency Prevention has hosted a webinar series and training to promote understanding of LGBT youth and improve justice system responses for LGBT youth in custody (https://www.nttac.org/index.cfm?event=trainingCenter.traininginfo&eventID=10). We are excited to see these movements in scholarship, policy, and practice, and we hope this *Handbook* helps to further our collective goals.

Goals of the *Handbook*

Criminological and criminal justice research has typically been heteronormative, assuming traditional sex-based gender roles and heterosexual orientation. "Nonnormative" sexual orientation, gender identity, and/or gender expression remain relatively unrecognized and certainly under-examined. What has resulted, both from the narrow scope of research and from the "heterosexualization" of the fields of criminology and criminal justice, is failure to understand and respond to the unique challenges that LGBT-identified individuals face. Although contemporary scholars have explored these challenges in a growing victimization literature, very little research is focused on LGBT individuals' patterns of offending (beyond, largely, sex work) and their experiences with the law, police, courts, and correctional institutions. Consequently, there are very few insights that can be gleaned for crime prevention and intervention policies and programs; as well, this dearth of knowledge means that LGBT youth and adults are currently underserved by the law and by juvenile and criminal justice systems worldwide. Importantly, the focus on LGBT individuals' victimization and human rights abuses has overlooked the important fact of agency; that is, members of LGBT communities are not passive victims without voice and choice. They (we) are (it should go without saying) fully-realized human beings who think, feel, act, and react. They are victims, they are offenders, they are victims and offenders, and—lest we forget—they are themselves justice system actors (police officers, lawmakers, judges, attorneys, and so forth). To overlook these facts is to deny justice, in all its forms.

This *Handbook* intends to help rectify these deficiencies by presenting as thorough as possible a treatment of these under-explored issues in one interdisciplinary and international volume that is useful for scholars, students, and practitioners alike. The discussions within this *Handbook* of issues pertinent to LGBT communities are intended to raise awareness ('for better or for worse,' we suppose, a point that we and others raise) and break down preconceived notions about people who are LGBT, to reduce fear and discomfort, to open conversations, and to stimulate positive changes in education, theory, research, and practice. We hope that educators will integrate LGBT topics into their CCJ curricula and raise these issues in classroom discussions and assignments, to prepare CCJ students for their work with diverse populations. We hope that legislatures in each and every country take steps to create laws that protect LGBT people and to repeal laws that discriminate against or harm them. We hope that scholars around the world test existing theories for their applicability in understanding and predicting crime and victimization and construct new theories to account for the unique experiences and influences that lead LGBT people to crime and victimization. We encourage critical- and forward-thinking by researchers and practitioners to address the needs and improve treatment of LGBT people in justice systems worldwide, and we hope that these chapters provide insights that can be shared across multiple country contexts.

In the advancement of justice, it is not just multiple intersections of identity that should be taken into account, but also the multiple methods, disciplines, and perspectives that inform our knowledge and practice. Some of the *Handbook* chapters are theoretical discussions, some are reviews of research, law, or social movements, and some are original research from authors using different qualitative and quantitative methodologies. In addition, although we certainly do not claim to provide a complete accounting of these issues worldwide (and, most of the chapters are U.S. based), a number of different countries are represented (i.e., authors are drawn from different countries, but also issues/experiences from different countries around the world are described in various chapters). Finally, as with CCJ in general, the contributors to the volume represent a variety of perspectives from a multitude of disciplines (i.e., anthropology; CCJ, justice studies, law, and legal practice; psychology; public health; public management/ public policy; social work; sociology; women's, gender, and/or sexuality studies). Among these contributors are established scholars in CCJ whose work has now turned attention to issues of sexual orientation and gender identity; scholars who have engaged their entire careers in gender and sexuality studies; and, importantly, emerging CCJ scholars who have begun their careers by integrating the study of SOGI within their CCJ work and are boldly blazing the path—it is these emerging scholars in particular who will come to be known as the "pioneers of queer criminology." It is with enthusiasm and optimism for the possibilities of a CCJ paradigm shift that we now describe the specific content of this *Handbook*.

Organization of the *Handbook*

It is difficult to categorize the chapters of this *Handbook* into specific "sections" or under larger topical umbrellas, since many of the issues discussed in most of the chapters easily cross over the boundaries we have artificially created for the purposes of organization. Indeed, our multidisciplinary and multinational approach, in addition to the complexity of the issues, necessarily means that neat categorizations are impossible. And, in fact, the competing desire for and resistance to categorization is an important theme in a number of the chapters. With these caveats in place, we turn to an overview of the six organizing sections and the 25 chapters that make up this volume (and we hope readers have taken the opportunity already to read the Foreword).

Part I: Introduction and Overview of LGBT Communities, Crime, and Justice

This section provides an overview of the issues covered throughout the *Handbook*'s chapters, making the case for their importance, including underscoring the dearth of research that can inform practice. Part 1 contains two chapters, the first of which you are now reading. In Chap. 2, Jordan Blair Woods provides an overview of the state of "queer criminology," highlighting the lack of treatment of LGBT individuals and issues in CCJ theoretical and empirical discourse, outside of conceptualizations of sexual deviance, and arguing for their comprehensive inclusion in theorizing about the causes of crime and in examinations of experiences with crime and justice systems. Woods also cautions us, however, in moving forward, so that in our efforts to bring attention to them, we do not to further stigmatize people who are LGBT. This is salient point underscored by a number of the *Handbook* authors (e.g., Ball; Johnson; Panfil).

Part II: LGBT Communities, Crime, and Victimization

Chapters in this section review or present research on LGBT individuals' experiences as victims and, importantly, as perpetrators of crime. In the first chapter of this section (Chap. 3), Rebecca L. Stotzer provides a global overview of SOGI-based bias crime, discussing prevalence (and the limitations of current data that prevent a fuller accounting of this type of crime victimization), the health and social consequences of experiencing crime based on one's sexual orientation and/ or gender identity, and explanations for the occurrence of SOGI-motivated bias crime. In Chap. 4, Adam Messinger takes an historical and contemporary look at same-sex intimate partner violence (IPV) to highlight what is known and yet unknown about prevalence, causes, and outcomes in order to highlight important avenues for future research and practice in addressing this oft-hidden problem, including avoidance of heteronormativity in victims' services provision. Chapter 5 by Jeffery P. Dennis traces historical portrayals, in research and media, of gay men (and, to a lesser extent, lesbians) as villains to their contemporary absence except as victims, despite their presence among the offending population. Dennis is among the authors in the *Handbook* who demonstrate that ignoring LGBT individuals as offenders is to ignore their agency and full personhood. The next two chapters in this section illustrate this agency. Dominique E. Johnson (Chap. 6) uses the case of a lesbian gang formed in reaction to school-based homophobic bullying as a jumping-off point to discuss lesbian (and LGBT) resistance to surveillance, social control, and categorization that strips and essentializes identity. Vanessa R. Panfil (Chap. 7) next highlights gay men's agency in an illuminative discussion of gay gang- and crime-involved young men's uses of violence, including as a vehicle to resist anti-gay harassment and violence. The chapters in this section present a fuller range of LGBT persons' experiences and behaviors than is commonly depicted, and each chapter increases awareness and provides guidance for future research and practice to improve crime and victimization prevention and intervention approaches.

Part III: LGBT Communities and Juvenile and Criminal Justice Systems

Within this section is research on interactions between LGBT communities and justice systems. These chapters provide baseline understanding and offer direction for better treatment of LGBT individuals by police, courts, and corrections agents and administrators. Angela Dwyer (Chap. 8) traces the historically strained and sometimes hostile relationships between law enforcement and LGBT communities, revealing troughs and peaks over time and both pain and partnership at various instances. The next two chapters provide an example each of the pain and partnership aspects, respectively. The dark or painful side of police relationships with LGBT communities is starkly demonstrated by Andrea J. Nichols (Chap. 9), who gives voice to nachchi sex workers in Sri Lanka who suffered a multitude of abuses at the hands of police, based on both their gender identity and sexual orientation. On the partnership side, as a means to improve police-community relationships and better serve communities, many police departments have implemented community-oriented policing (COP) strategies. Roddrick Colvin (Chap. 10) questions whether these contemporary moves to implement COP (and increase the diversity of police forces to better represent community populations) result in more effective relationships with LGBT communities, especially when gay and lesbian officers police their own communities.

The next two chapters address correctional settings that fail to adequately serve the needs of LGBT individuals housed therein. The treatment and programmatic desires and needs of LGB youth housed in U.S. juvenile facilities were found to differ from those of non-LGB youth in research by Joanne Belknap, Kristi Holsinger, and Jani S. Little (Chap. 11), yet these different service needs were largely unmet. Their work provides evidence as to why corrections officials should not only recognize, but support LGB youth in juvenile facilities. Chapter 12 presents Jennifer Sumner and Valerie Jenness's thorough review of U.S. correctional policies and practices that fail to account for the presence and needs of transgender individuals housed in correctional facilities that are based on the sex binary of male and female. Lack of attention to the fact that sex-segregated facilities are multi-gendered means that transgender persons face discrimination, harassment, victimization, and de-humanization. Rounding out this section is an important chapter that provides insights into another key avenue for improving treatment of LGBT individuals by justice system actors: undergraduate CJ students as future CJ practitioners. Cannon and colleagues Dirks-Linhorst, Cobb, Maatita, Beichner, and Ogle (Chap. 13) reveal that CJ students hold more negative attitudes about LGBT individuals, compared to other college students. These authors stress the importance of and provide guidance for including LGBT content in CJ curricula, in order to prepare students for the diverse populations with whom they will work in their chosen careers.

Part IV: LGBT Communities, Law, and Justice

Chapters in this section recognize the changing global legal landscape, with attention to laws and policies affecting LGBT communities and various movements undertaking the fight for human rights and justice for all the world's citizens. Neil Cobb (Chap. 14) challenges the world polity perspective through analysis of global efforts to either repeal or fortify laws against same-sex sexual behavior, as illustrated in four case examples, including Uganda. Cobb argues that beyond growing global consensus, based on diffusion of Western sexual culture, about the necessity of repealing "anti-sodomy laws," the roles of conflict and local social movements need also be considered. Such local (yet globally-networked and

-supported) movements are the focus of the next chapter (Chap. 15), in which Susan C. Pearce and Alex Cooper vividly detail the resistance, violence, and hope that has accompanied LGBT organizing and events across eight Southeast European countries preparing for entry into the European Union. Chapter 16 also further addresses issues raised by Cobb's Chap. 14, as Christina DeJong and Eric Long delve into the specifics of and history that lead to the proposal of Uganda's "Anti-Homosexuality" (or "Kill the Gays") Bill. These authors argue that the progression of actions taken against LGBT persons in Uganda mirrors the event progression that has resulted in genocide of particular groups in other countries. All of these authors call, in various ways, for greater involvement and support from the international community for more equitable treatment of LGBT persons under the law.

Even in countries that have repealed "anti-sodomy laws," however, potential for and actual harm and discrimination persists. Ari Ezra Waldman's (Chap. 17) legal analysis reveals the flaws in relatively recent laws to criminalize transmission of HIV (ostensibly to stem the tide of AIDS). Waldman unpacks the use of aggravated assault statutes, juxtaposing the discriminatory use of generalized knowledge against specific medical realities to demonstrate heterogeneity in the HIV positive population that should be, but is not, taken into account in U.S. jurisdictions. In Chap. 18, Alexis Forbes exposes the myriad ways in which transgender persons continue to experience discrimination under U.S. law in areas such as employment, housing, marriage, and child custody, and, for transgender youth, in school, at home, and in foster care. Lack of equal protection and experiences of discrimination have a multitude of adverse consequences for transgender people, which further support calls for equal justice under the law. In the final chapter in this section (Chap. 19), Sarah Warbelow and Ty Cobb detail the harmful effects of SOGI-based bullying experienced by LGBT youth in schools and the patchwork of U.S. state and federal laws that attempt to address it. While these efforts are encouraging, much remains to be done to make schools a safer place and to protect LGBT youth.

Part V: LGBT Communities, Crime, and Public Health

This section brings together work that recognizes the intersections between Criminology, Criminal Justice, and Public Health. Increasingly, crime has been viewed from a public health perspective, not only epidemiologically, but in terms of the interplay between certain kinds of criminally defined behaviors and their public health consequences. As well, proclamations of health as a basic human right underscore the overlaps between health and justice. Although we have included certain *Handbook* chapters specifically in this section, issues of public health are also clear in chapters contained in other sections—including, but not limited to, negative health and mental health consequences of LGBT victimization, bullying, harassment, and discrimination; unaddressed health and mental health needs of LGBT inmates; overt mental and physical abuses by justice system actors, to name a few. In this section, then, we take the opportunity to explicitly highlight ways in which criminal justice and public health researchers and practitioners might come together to better address needs of LGBT populations.

Often-times, and as demonstrated throughout this *Handbook*, the specific experiences of LGBT people go unrecognized and unaddressed. Tameka L. Gillum and Gloria T. DiFulvio's research (Chap. 21) exposes the mental health consequences (including depression and PTSD) of dating violence experienced by sexual minority youth, and critiques the existing heteronormative dating violence prevention and healthy relationships programs in schools, as well as victims' services. In Chap. 20, Meredith Conover-Williams uses data from a nationally representative sample of U.S. adolescents to compare sexual minority youth to their majority peers and finds that sexual minority youth experience a greater number of risk factors (and fewer protective factors) in their lives and that these factors in large part explain their greater involvement in offending behaviors, especially (but not limited to) sex work. As Tyler Frederick (Chap. 22) describes, LGBT individuals' involvement in sex work is often preceded by trauma and homelessness experienced as a result of their LGBT identities and co-occurs with other risky behaviors such as drug use. However, joining other authors in this *Handbook*, Frederick argues that the role of agency or choice, even if it is constrained choice, should not be overlooked and that categorizations such as "homeless young LGBT people" (or even "LGBT people") impede understanding because such categories are not, in fact, homogenous and they fail to capture the dynamic and lived experiences of a full range of humanity. Along these same lines, Ryan A. Levy (Chap. 23) encourages us to consider how multiple intersections of identity serve to exclude individuals from, for example, HIV/AIDS treatment and to increase systemic violence. Levy offers a way forward to better understand individuals' full identities and needs through anthropological ethnographic analysis. This author's advocating of queer critical ethnography of sexuality (and cautioning about essentializing LGBT persons) leads nicely into the first chapter of the concluding section, tying in with Matthew Ball's examination of the meanings and goals of "queer criminology."

Part VI: Future Directions and Concluding Thoughts

In this final section, Matthew Ball (Chap. 24) critiques the varied meanings of "queer criminology," provides a vision for what queer criminology might entail in the future, and presents and reiterates appropriate cautions relating to categorizing and counting LGBT people as the field moves forward. In so doing, Ball re-caps a number of important issues and themes raised throughout the *Handbook* and makes explicit ties back to Jordan Blair Woods's introductory chapter on the state of queer criminology. A concluding chapter by the editors (Vanessa R. Panfil and Dana Peterson, Chap. 25) summarizes the key issues of the *Handbook* through the lens of existing critiques and provides recommendations for theory, research, and practice.

Closing Considerations

While this single volume is intended to be as comprehensive as possible and international in nature in order to introduce readers to key issues of concern, we acknowledge wholeheartedly that we have just scratched the surface and also that other issues of import have necessarily been left out. Some of these issues, just to name a few, are the use of "corrective rape" in a number of countries to "cure" lesbianism; the U.S. military's enactment and then repeal of its Don't Ask, Don't Tell (DADT) policy; the recent U.S. Supreme Court ruling that a key section of the federal Defense of Marriage Act (DOMA) is unconstitutional, effectively striking down the power of the Act; the roles of sexual orientation and gender identity in criminal court outcomes; and LGB adults' experiences in correctional settings. As well, the experiences of LGBT individuals in a host of countries and societies not included in this *Handbook* deserve recognition.

There is danger in this work and the challenges are many. For example, there is an inherent tension between the need for theory-building (e.g., Woods) and basic knowledge (e.g., Messinger; Stotzer) and the negative consequences that can come from such illumination (e.g., Ball; Johnson). Illustrative of this is the ostensibly simple, yet complex question of measurement, a question taken up by a number of the authors: how should we measure sexual orientation and gender identity, given their complex, fluid, and interactional nature, and should we "measure" these at all? We encourage readers, as you take this work forward, to consider carefully the cautions outlined by a number of the authors.

We close our introduction with the humble acknowledgement that the issues raised in this *Handbook* are not "new," as scholars in fields other than CCJ as well as scholars scattered within CCJ have dedicated years of their efforts to them. Accordingly, although this volume may be the first of its kind in CCJ, we do not claim to be the first to raise these issues; rather, we see this *Handbook* as a way to raise our collective voices in order better to be heard.

Chapter 2
"Queering Criminology": Overview of the State of the Field

Jordan Blair Woods

Abstract This chapter provides an overview of the treatment of sexual orientation and gender identity issues and LGBTQ populations in the field of criminology. The chapter advances three main points. First, it argues that there is very little data on LGBTQ people's experiences of crime, both in terms of victimization and offending. Second, the overwhelming majority of criminological engagement with sexual orientation and gender identity occurred prior to the 1980s, and discussed these concepts insofar as assessing whether "homosexuality"—a term that was often employed to describe non-heterosexual sexualities and gender non-conforming identities/expressions—was or was not a form of criminal sexual deviance. Third, to date, there is little to no theoretical engagement with sexual orientation and gender identity in each of the four major schools of criminological thought: biological, psychological, sociological, and critical. I argue that these three points are a reflection of the historical and continuing stigma of the sexual deviance framework on the treatment of sexual orientation and gender identity concepts, and LGBTQ people in the field. This chapter makes a call to "queer criminology," which in my view, requires overcoming the sexual deviance framework and reorienting criminological inquiry to give due consideration to sexual orientation and gender identity as non-deviant differences that may shape people's experiences of crime and experiences in the criminal justice system more generally.

Keywords Crime data · Criminological theory · Gender identity · Intersectionality · Offending · Queer · Race · Sexual deviance · Sexual orientation · Sodomy laws · Victimization

J. B. Woods (✉)
Williams Institute, UCLA School of Law, Los Angeles, CA, USA

Institute of Criminology, University of Cambridge, Cambridge, UK

405 Hilgard Avenue, Box 951476 Los Angeles, CA 90095, USA

e-mail: jw567@cam.ac.uk

D. Peterson and V. R. Panfil (eds.), *Handbook of LGBT Communities, Crime, and Justice*, DOI: 10.1007/978-1-4614-9188-0_2,
© Springer Science+Business Media New York 2014

Introduction

The inception of modern criminology is often traced to the 1870s, when a group of Italian physicians began to apply the scientific method to study crime and criminal offenders. Since then, criminology has developed into a vibrant and diverse field that utilizes biological, psychological, sociological, and critical methods. This chapter provides an overview of criminologists' engagement with lesbian, gay, bisexual, transgender, and queer (LGBTQ) populations; sexual orientation and gender identity concepts; and queer theories. The extent of this engagement can be summarized in three short words: Not very much.

The criticism that the field of criminology has distorted or ignored particular social groups is not new. For decades, feminists have called attention to the neglect and damaging stereotyping of women in criminological theory and research (Gelsthorpe and Morris 1990; Heidensohn 1985; Messerschmidt 1997; Smart 1977). Criminologists have also criticized the field for its inadequate treatment of class and race/ethnicity (Phillips and Bowling 2003; Quinney 1977; Rusche and Kirchheimer 1968 [1939]; Taylor et al. 1973). These trailblazers took it upon themselves to construct spaces within the field that recognized, and attempted to further the understanding of, specific social groups as criminological subjects. In spite of this progress, LGBTQ populations have remained largely neglected and misrepresented in the field.

This chapter makes a call to "queer" criminology. In so doing, I advocate for greater inclusion of LGBTQ perspectives, concepts, and theories in the field. This call requires reorienting the focus of criminological inquiry to give due consideration to the relationship between sexual orientation/gender identity differences and victimization and offending.

At the onset, I recognize that it is impossible to provide a complete summary of the criminological treatment of sexual orientation and gender identity in a single chapter. Consequently, there are areas of criminological theory and research that are not discussed in this overview. That being said, this overview goes beyond merely stating the obvious—that criminologists have largely mistreated and ignored sexual orientation and gender identity issues and LGBTQ populations—by identifying and discussing three key themes.

First, there is very little data on LGBTQ people's experiences of crime. As the chapter explains, there is almost no data on LGBTQ offenders or LGBTQ-headed families. Moreover, the bulk of LGBTQ-inclusive criminological research from the past four decades has focused almost exclusively on bias crime/bullying and intimate partner violence (Peterson and Panfil, this volume). Although these growing bodies of research have been instrumental in increasing knowledge about certain aspects of LGBTQ people's experiences of crime, their applicability is limited because they focus on narrow areas of victimology. Consequently, there is a need for criminologists to investigate the diversity of circumstances under which LGBTQ people experience and commit crime.

Second, the overwhelming majority of criminological engagement with sexual orientation and gender identity occurred prior to the 1980s, and discussed these concepts insofar as assessing whether "homosexuality"—a term primarily used to describe non-heterosexual sexualities and gender non-conforming identities/ expressions—was a type of criminal (or non-criminal) sexual deviance. The nature of this engagement was a reflection of the stigma attached to homosexuality and LGBTQ people in Western legal, social, and political spheres. Anti-sodomy and sexual psychopath laws had central roles in these prior criminological discussions. These discussions also often included damaging characterizations of LGBTQ people as criminals, psychopaths, and perverts (see too, Dennis, this volume).

Third, there is little to no theoretical engagement with sexual orientation and gender identity in each of the four major schools of criminology: biological, psychological, sociological, and critical. This lack of engagement raises concerns about whether existing criminological methods and theories apply to the experiences of LGBTQ people today, and whether queer criminologists can and should modify them to address sexual orientation and gender identity. It also raises key questions about the role of queer theories—which have been virtually excluded from criminological theories—to inform those modifications and to create new criminological frameworks. These themes parallel prior and ongoing discussions among feminist scholars about the propriety of working within existing criminological frameworks to provide a complete understanding of the relationship between gender and crime (Cain 1990). Whether queer criminologists must challenge criminological frameworks at their core to provide a comprehensive and nuanced understanding of the relationship between sexual orientation, gender identity, and crime is an important and debatable question.

The combination of these three key themes gives rise to a core argument, which I label the *homosexual deviancy thesis*, and is summarized as follows: Prior to the 1970s, LGBTQ people in Western countries were often labeled as criminals, psychopaths, sinners, and perverts (Sarbin 1996). The *homosexual deviancy thesis* argues that the field of criminology has historically facilitated, reinforced, and left these deviant misconceptions of LGBTQ people intact (Woods 2013). This thesis has two elements, which I label the *deviance-centered element* and the *invisibility element*. The *deviance-centered element* applies to discussions of sexual orientation, gender identity, and LGBTQ populations in the field until about the 1970s. It argues that these discussions contained the degrading characterizations of LGBTQ people described above. Although some criminologists disagreed with these characterizations, the discipline as a whole engaged with sexual orientation and gender identity insofar as determining whether being lesbian, gay, bisexual, or transgender was or was not a form of deviancy itself. The *invisibility element* applies to criminological discussions of sexual orientation, gender identity, and LGBTQ populations after the 1970s until today. The element argues that after the 1970s—when sodomy laws largely lost force in Western countries, and especially the United States, through repeal and lack of enforcement—discussions of sexual orientation, gender identity, and LGBTQ populations virtually disappeared from criminological theory and research. Studies on bias crime/bullying and intimate partner violence are notable exceptions. As a result of the historical distortion and more recent exclusion of LGBTQ populations from criminological theory and research, there is very little understanding of how sexual orientation and gender identity might shape the causes of crime today.

In making a call to "queer" criminology, my point of view in this chapter is rooted in the present state of the treatment of sexual orientation and gender identity in the field, which is subject to (and hopefully will) change in the future. My core argument is that in light of this present state, one central goal of queer criminology must be to advance the field beyond the sexual deviance framework to consider how sexual orientation and gender identity/expression as non-deviant differences—in combination with other differences, such as race/ethnicity, class, and religion—may influence victimization, involvement in crime, and experiences in the criminal justice system more broadly (Woods 2014). In short, the lingering stigma of sexual deviance that still attaches to LGBTQ people in the field is a reflection that criminology is behind the times in its treatment of sexual orientation and gender identity. The availability of identity-based and critical deconstructionist paradigms illustrates the variety of alternatives that criminologists may adopt to engender a shift away from the sexual deviance framework—the basic point is that this shift is, and has been, long overdue.

Crime Data on LGBTQ Populations in the United States

Existing official crime statistics, victim surveys, and self-report surveys provide a very limited glimpse of LGBTQ people's victimization and offending because they exclude sexual orientation and gender identity as key variables (but see, e.g., Johnson, this volume, who offers cautions regarding LGBTQ people's inclusion in "big data"). The main source of official crime data in the United States is the Uniform Crime Report (UCR), which is based on data reported by over 17,000 law enforcement agencies. The UCR includes data on four categories of violent crime (murder, forcible rape, robbery, and aggravated assault) and four categories of property crime (burglary, larceny-theft, motor vehicle theft, and arson). In expanded data, the UCR breaks down murder offenses based on the race (White, Black, other race, unknown race), sex (male, female), and age of the victims and the offenders. Sexual orientation and gender identity are omitted from the expanded data, and sex constructs are based on binary conceptions of biological sex. The UCR also includes data on the number of arrests for twenty-eight specific offenses.[1] In other expanded data, the UCR breaks down these arrests for various

---

[1] These offenses include murder and non-negligent manslaughter, forcible rape, robbery, aggravated assault, burglary, larceny-theft, motor vehicle theft, arson, other assaults, forgery and counterfeiting, fraud, embezzlement, stolen property (buying, receiving and possessing), vandalism, weapons (carrying and possessing), prostitution and commercial vice, sex offenses (except forcible rape and prostitution), drug abuse violations, gambling, offenses against the family and children, driving under the influence, liquor laws, drunkenness, disorderly conduct, vagrancy, all other offenses (except traffic), suspicion, and curfew and loitering law violations.

geographic localities based on the age, sex (male, female), and race (White, Black, American Indian or Alaskan Native, Asian or Pacific Islander) of the arrestees. Sexual orientation and gender identity are also omitted from this expanded data.

The only mention of sexual orientation in the UCR appears in a separate report on bias crime, which records the number of bias crime incidents, offenses, victims, and known offenders based on "sexual orientation bias" (anti-male homosexual, anti-female homosexual, anti-homosexual, anti-heterosexual, anti-bisexual). Bias-motivation codes for gender identity were added very recently (in 2012) to the bias crime report, but data are not yet available.

One limitation of official crime data is that many crimes are not reported to the police. Crime victimization surveys are useful because they have the potential to capture both reported and unreported crime. The National Crime Victimization Survey (NCVS), conducted jointly by the U.S. Department of Justice and the U.S. Census Bureau, is the largest ongoing victim survey in the United States. The NCVS is based on a nationally representative sample of about 40,000 households (approximately 70,000–75,000 people). The households are included in the sample for three years, and the participants are interviewed twice a year about their victimization experiences with violent and property crimes. The NCVS asks participants demographic questions about age, marital status (married, widowed, divorced, separated, never married), sex (male, female), race (Hispanic, White, Black/African American, American Indian/Alaska Native, Asian, Native Hawaiian/Other Pacific Islander, Other—Specify), and income.[2] Sexual orientation and gender identity are omitted from these demographic questions. These concepts only appear in a series of questions about bias crimes. In those questions, the respondents can answer whether they believed that they were victims of a bias crime, whether they perceived the crime to be motivated by their "gender" or "sexual orientation," and whether the incident took place near a gay bar or at a Gay Pride March.[3] Although Bureau of Justice statisticians report that the NCVS has included statistics on crimes motivated by "gender or gender identity bias" since 2010 (Sandholtz et al. 2013), the operationalization of this construct makes it

---

[2] Questions involving demographic characteristics are part of the NCVS Basic Screen Questionnaire, which is a separate document from the NCVS Crime Incident Report, which asks about the criminal incidents themselves. The point made here is based on the latest released version of the NCVS Basic Screen Questionnaire (covering July 2008 through December 2009).

[3] In the latest released version of the NCVS Crime Incident Report (covering July 2008 through December 2009), Question 161 reads: "Do you have any reason to suspect the incident just discussed was a hate crime or crime of prejudice or bigotry?" The participants can then answer yes/no. Question 162 reads: "Do you suspect that the offender(s) targeted you because of..." 162(e) states "your gender" and the participants can check yes/no/don't know. 162(f) states "your sexual orientation" and the participants can check yes/no/don't know. Question 165 asks about the evidence that made participants suspect that the incident was a hate crime or crime of prejudice or bigotry. 165(a) asks: "Did the incident occur on or near a holiday, event, location, gathering place, or building commonly associated with a specific group (for example, at the Gay Pride March or at a synagogue, Korean church, or gay bar)?" The participants can then answer yes/no/don't know.

difficult to distinguish crimes motivated by gender from crimes motivated by gender identity and/or expression. The NCVS questionnaire only asks whether respondents believe that they have been targeted because of their "gender," and the most recent edition of the NCVS survey manual defines "gender" explicitly as "male or female."

In addition to official crime statistics and victim surveys, some criminologists and researchers in other fields have conducted research on specific types of LGBTQ criminal victimization. The majority of this research focuses on bias crime (Berrill 1990; Berrill and Herek 1990; Carragher and Jay 2002; D'Augelli and Grossman 2001; Herek 1989, 2009; Herek and Berrill 1992; Herek et al. 1997, 1999, 2002; Meyer 2010; Stotzer 2008, 2009). Research on LGBTQ people's experiences of intimate partner violence (Ard and Makadon 2011; Burke et al. 2002; Cruz 2003; Greenwood et al. 2002; Hester and Donovan 2009; Island and Letellier 1991; Letellier 1994; Leventhal and Lundy 1999; Margolies and Leeder 1995; McClennen 2005; McClennen et al. 2002; Messinger 2011; Murray and Mobley 2009; Oriel 2012; Renzetti and Miley 1996; Waldner-Haugrud et al. 1997) and bullying (Berlan et al. 2010; Birkett et al. 2009; Darwich et al. 2012; Hong and Garbarino 2012; Russell et al. 2011) have also become more common. Moreover, researchers in other fields have documented prevalent rates of substance abuse in LGBTQ communities (Carpiano et al. 2011; Cabaj 1992; Chesney et al. 1998; Halkitis and Parsons 2002; Halkitis et al. 2001, 2003; Hospers and Kok 1995; Leigh and Stall 1993; McKirnan and Peterson 1989; Morales and Graves 1983; Ostrow and Shelby 2000; Stall and Leigh 1994; Stall and Wiley 1988; Woody et al. 1999).

Advocating for greater inclusion of sexual orientation and gender identity in crime data raises challenging questions about how to define sexual orientation and gender identity constructs—a theme that parallels debates in the field over how to define other characteristics, such as race/ethnicity and class, in criminological research (Georges-Abeyie 1984; Hinch 1983). It also raises ethical questions about the government monitoring of LGBTQ people and whether it is more appropriate to use particular methods when conducting criminological research to respect LGBTQ people's privacy.

Although these inquiries invite careful consideration in future research, the omission of sexual orientation and gender identity from crime data is concerning for at least three reasons. First, this omission has resulted in little to no baseline statistics on how crime influences the lives of LGBTQ people in obvious and non-obvious ways, both in terms of victimization and offending. Second, because crime statistics influence budgetary decisions for criminal justice programs, the omission of LGBTQ populations from crime data may inhibit governments at the local, state, and federal levels from implementing and/or funding programs that address the specific needs of LGBTQ victims and offenders. Third, this omission may also perpetuate a lack of engagement with sexual orientation and gender identity in criminological theory. A vast amount of criminological theory has been influenced by three propositions involving individual/group differences and crime: (1) men commit more, and more serious crime, than women; (2) racial and ethnic minorities in poor urban neighborhoods commit a disproportionate amount of crime; and (3) crime rates peak during adolescence and then decline rapidly until the late-twenties, when those rates level off. The omission of sexual orientation and gender identity from crime data prevents criminologists from exploring how these general propositions differ when applied to LGBTQ populations, and also inhibits them from discovering and problematizing any comparable propositions that involve LGBTQ people.

The Treatment of LGBTQ Populations in Major Criminological Theories

Early Biological Perspectives on Crime

I have argued that the treatment of sexual orientation and gender identity in early biological theories of crime was the product of Western societal changes during the second half of the twentieth century (Woods 2013). Before then, homosexuality was viewed as a series of abominable acts as opposed to a distinct identity (Weeks 1981). As city spaces and populations became increasingly mobile from rapid industrialization and urbanization, a diversity of sexual and gender non-conforming behaviors became more visible in the public sphere (Bullough 1979; Weeks 1979). Because Victorian ideology restricted the government from maintaining a large role in regulating private sexual conduct, middle-class society turned to medical experts to resolve moral dilemmas and to generate new definitions of sexual normalcy (Hamowy 1977; Greenberg 1988).

A science of sexology emerged under these circumstances. As sexologists studied homosexuality in greater detail, societal conceptions of homosexuality shifted from abominable committed acts to an individual biological characteristic (Foucault 1979; Greenberg 1988). German and French doctors Johann Ludwig Casper (1852) and Ambroise Tardieu (1857) advanced the first suggestions that homosexuality was congenital. Less than a decade later, German jurist Karl Heinrich Ulrichs articulated the first comprehensive medical conception of homosexuality (Herrn 1995; Kennedy 1997). Soon after, a number of prominent physicians, including Westphal, Benkert, Ellis, Carpenter, and Hirschfeld, advanced the view that homosexuality was biologically innate and a "natural" feature of human sexuality. Many of these physicians, with intentions of improving the social and legal status of homosexuals, characterized homosexuality as an innate biological feature (Greenberg 1988). Other late-nineteenth century physicians, however, combined medical advancements with emerging theories of degeneracy to situate homosexuality outside the realm of sexual normalcy (Charcot and Magnan 1882; Féré 1899; Forel 1905; Krafft-Ebing 1965 [1886]; Moll 1891; Moreau 1887; Tarnowski 1886). Austrian psychiatrist Richard von Krafft-Ebing (1965 [1886]) advanced the most influential of these positions in his popular work *Psychopathia Sexualis*. Although Krafft-Ebing later changed his position to argue that homosexuality was a harmless and natural variant of human sexuality, his early positions defined heterosexuality as the biological norm and ostracized homosexuals as a class of biological degenerates (Makari 2008).

Evolving conceptions that homosexuality was something people *were*, as opposed to something that people *did*, were present in early biological theories of crime, including the popular works of Cesare Lombroso (Woods 2013). Lombroso embraced principles of biological determinism to argue that crime was a natural phenomenon rooted in the physical constitutions of individuals, and assumed that external physical features mirrored internal moral states (Gibson and Rafter 2006). Influenced by Darwin's theory of evolution, Lombroso utilized Darwin's concept of "atavism" to describe criminals as biological throwbacks to a lesser-evolved, more primitive human (Lombroso 2006 [1878]). Although early biological theories of crime are now viewed as antiquated, two important themes emerge from Lombroso's writings that demonstrate the multidimensional stigma attached to LGBTQ people in early biological perspectives on crime. First, homosexual men ("pederasts") emerged as a distinct type of "insane criminal" marked by inferior pathology. In the first edition of his popular work *Criminal Man*, Lombroso (2006 [1876]) identified "pederasts" based on physical attributes, mannerisms, and clothing that failed to conform to gender norms. He viewed pederasts as odd and strange. In later editions, Lombroso (2006 [1889]) incorporated Krafft-Ebing's conception of homosexuality as a sexual inversion to classify pederasts as a type of "insane criminal." His statement that "sexual inversion...often shapes the person's entire psychology" (2006 [1886], p. 273) reflects how emerging late-nineteenth-century conceptions of homosexual identity infiltrated into early modern criminological writings to stigmatize homosexuals as a distinct class of criminals.

Second, the patriarchal sexual ideology of late-Victorian society shaped Lombroso's treatment of female sexual intimacy between women. Lombroso characterized women as the "weaker sex" (2006 [1878], p. 128) with "weak and delayed" sexualities (Lombroso and Ferrero 2004 [1893], p. 171). He invoked principles of biological determinism to argue that women's biology prevented them from having a pronounced sense of eroticism, which in his view caused lesbianism to be uncommon. Lombroso described lesbianism as a form of "sexual perversion" (Lombroso and Ferrero 2004 [1893], p. 176), but he did not view lesbianism as a distinct type of criminal identity. Although Lombroso acknowledged a connection between prostitution and lesbianism, his conception of female sex criminality was largely shaped by societal demands on women to uphold gendered expectations. For instance, female adultery was one of the main female sex crimes that Lombroso discussed in his writings, which society then defined as a married woman having sexual relations with a man who was not her husband (Warnke 1999).

Psychological Perspectives on Crime

The history of the relationship between LGBTQ populations and the psychological and psychiatric professions is marked with tension. From the 1950s until the 1970s, homosexuality was widely understood as a mental illness in the professions (Bayer 1981; Kitzinger and Coyle 2002). This pathological view was reinforced by the inclusion of homosexuality as a mental disorder in the American Psychiatric Association's Diagnostic and Statistical Manual of Mental Disorders (DSM) from 1952 until 1973.

Psychoanalytic and psychopathological perspectives on crime developed before the 1980s showcased the debate over whether homosexuality should be considered a crime, mental illness, both, or neither. Psychoanalytic perspectives, which originated from the work of Sigmund Freud, displayed more favorable attitudes towards homosexuality. A cohort of psychoanalytic criminologists advocated strongly against the criminalization of homosexuality based on Freud's (1905, 1911) characterization of homosexuality as a non-harmful and natural variation of psychosexual development (Alexander and Staub 1931 [1929]; Friedlander 1947). Even in these more favorable writings, however, psychoanalytic criminologists resisted embracing non-conforming sexual and gender non-conforming behaviors in youth. Relying on Freud's concept of sublimation, these criminologists argued that children's inclinations to engage in non-conforming sexual or gender behaviors could, and should, be altered during the early stages of psychosexual development through proper education and programming (Aichorn 1935; Alexander and Staub 1931 [1929]; Friedlander 1947).

More hostile attitudes towards homosexuality appeared in psychopathological perspectives on crime, which focus on mental illness. Freud's position on homosexuality prevailed in the psychiatric profession until the 1940s, when a group of researchers engendered a major shift in the profession that homosexuality and gender non-conformity were mental illnesses that could, and should, be cured (Bergler 1956; Bieber 1962; Rado 1940; Socarides 1968). As pathological conceptions of homosexuality and gender non-conformity gained force, they shaped the treatment of LGBTQ people within the legal and political spheres. The clearest example of this treatment was the wave of "sexual psychopath laws" that swept across the United States from the late-1930s until the early-1970s. Between 1946 and 1959, twenty-nine states enacted such laws, which often provided for the indefinite commitment of LGBTQ people into psychiatric facilities (Eskridge 2008). In addition, ten states created special government commissions to investigate the problem of sex crimes and sexual psychopathy (Freedman 2006). Although these committees investigated homosexuality to varying degrees, the simple fact that homosexuality itself fell within the scope of sex crime research demonstrated the influence of pathological conceptions of homosexuality on the treatment of LGBTQ people in criminological research and the criminal justice system more broadly at the time.

During the mid-1970s, pathological conceptions of homosexuality lost force in the psychiatric profession. Homosexuality was removed from the DSM manual in 1973, and twenty-one U.S. states repealed their sexual psychopath laws during the 1960s and early 1970s (largely as a result of adopting the American Law Institute's Model Penal Code). Two factors contributed to this shift. First, an increasing body of empirical research, especially from the behaviorist perspective, discounted the notion that homosexuality was a disease (Ford and Beach 1951; Hooker 1956, 1957, 1958; Kinsey 1948, 1953; Szasz 1970). Second, gay and lesbian organizations—including the Mattachine Society and the Daughters of Bilitis—started to gain political influence and advance the social status of gays and lesbians in the United States. Official publications sponsored by early gay and lesbian organizations, such as the *Mattachine Review*, provided a public forum for emerging research that discounted orthodox pathological conceptions of homosexuality. The advocacy approach of gay and lesbian political organizations took a more radical turn during the 1960s, as demonstrated by the popular Stonewall Riots of 1969. These more radical followers prioritized combating the "gay is sick" stigma, and protested frequently at psychiatric professional meetings to eliminate that stigma (Barnhouse 1977).

Even after pathological conceptions of homosexuality lost force, some forensic psychiatrists continued to stress the connection between homosexuality and sexual criminality. In 1984, for instance, British forensic psychiatrists collaborated to release a co-edited volume on forensic psychiatry (Craft et al. 1984). While the investigators did not characterize homosexuality as a criminal status *per se*, they stressed that "the lifestyle of males with homosexual preferences may inevitably put them at risk of contravening the law" (Craft et al. 1984, p. 65). The investigators also emphasized that "[w]hile psychiatrists and others may disagree about the deviancy of homosexual activities, the law is quite clear that boys, young men and indeed the public at large, should be protected against 'unnatural acts'" (Craft and Craft 1984, p. 403). These statements show that the stigma of the sexual deviancy framework persisted in forensic psychiatric perspectives even during the late-twentieth-century.

Other major psychological perspectives on crime that gained popularity after the 1970s, when anti-sodomy and sexual psychopath laws lost force, largely omit discussions of sexual orientation and gender identity. Personality trait theories, for instance, focus on the structural components of the human personality. Three models of personality have been widely used to study crime: (1) Eysenck's (1977) Psychoticism-Extraversion-Neuroticism (PEN) model, (2) Tellegen's (1985) three-factor (T-3) model, and (3) Costa and McCrae's Five Factor Model (FFM) (McCrae and Costa 1990). With the exception of Eysenck, each of these personality theorists neglected sexual orientation and gender identity in developing their models; criminologists who later tested and refined these models also neglected these concepts. When briefly discussing homosexuality in his criminological application of the PEN model, Eysenck (1977, p. 77) recognized that societies differed in terms of whether it was criminalized, stating that it was "a crime in some American states but not in Germany." Eysenck (1977, p. 35) also acknowledged that "[i]f homosexuality is a crime in England but not in France, then criminologists would be engaged in quite different pursuits on the two sides of the Channel. This, they argue, is absurd." These statements reflected the changing legal attitudes towards homosexuality, but their focus centered on homosexuality as a disputed type of deviance.

Moreover, sexual orientation and gender identity are largely omitted from developmental and life course (DLC) theories of crime, which focus on the development of criminal and antisocial behavior during a person's life span. DLC theories gained popularity in the 1990s, and rely mostly on longitudinal research (Catalano et al. 2005; Farrington 2003, 2005, 2006, 2010; Hawkins and Catalano 1992; Hawkins et al. 2003, 2008; Lahey and Waldman 2005; Lahey et al. 2006, 2008; Laub and Sampson 2001, 2003; LeBlanc 1997, 2005, 2009; LeBlanc and Frechette 1989; Moffitt 1993, 2006; Moffitt et al. 2001, 2002; Sampson and Laub 1993, 1995, 2003, 2005, 2009; Thornberry 2005; Thornberry et al. 2009; Thornberry and Krohn 2001, 2005; Thornberry et al. 2003; Wikström 2005, 2010). DLC theories exclude sexual orientation and gender identity as demographic constructs, but often include constructs that capture other demographic differences, including age, socioeconomic status, sex (male/female), and race/ethnicity. Many discussions of sexual behavior and gender within DLC theories also assume that their subjects are heterosexual and/or have gender identities that conform to binary conceptions of biological sex.

In fairness, it is possible that a small number of LGBTQ subjects in the longitudinal studies that form the basis of existing DLC theories motivate the omission of sexual orientation and gender identity. We do not know, however, what proportion of the participants in those studies identify as LGBTQ. This omission might also have been influenced by a lack of recognition that being LGBTQ was a non-deviant, demographically relevant difference when the bulk of those longitudinal studies were designed from the 1960s until the 1980s. Regardless, the omission of sexual orientation and gender identity from DLC theories raises questions over their unique applicability to the experiences of LGBTQ people today, especially given that LGBTQ youth are coming out in greater numbers and at earlier ages (Fein-Zachary and Lacava 2008; Shilo and Savaya 2011).

Sociological Perspectives on Crime

The origins of modern sociology are typically traced to the late nineteenth- and early twentieth-century writings of Durkheim, Marx, and Weber that sought to explain the process of modernization and its influence on Western social life (Healey 2001; Hughes et al. 2003; Morrison 2006). In spite of the emerging conceptions of "modern homosexual identity," each of these key thinkers neglected sexual orientation and gender identity (and sex/gender more broadly) in their writings (Plummer 2000; Seidman 1996). One major factor contributing to the neglect of sexual orientation and gender identity from early Classical theories of sociology is that theorists likely viewed these concepts as individual conditions that had no bearing on social structure or organization (McIntosh 1968; Seidman 1996).

Given this context, it is unsurprising that sexual orientation and gender identity are neglected in most social structure theories of crime—the first of two major categories of sociological perspectives on crime. Social structure theories view structural conditions of society such as poverty, unemployment, racism, and poor education as key determinants of crime. Sexual orientation and gender identity are largely omitted from the conceptual development and empirical testing of each of the three main types of social structure theories: (1) social disorganization theories (Lowenkamp et al. 2003; Park and Burgess 1921, 1925; Sampson and Groves 1989; Shaw and McKay 1931, 1942, 1969; Veysey and Messner 1999), (2) anomie and strain theories (Agnew 1992, 2006; Merton 1938, 1957; Messner and Rosenfeld 1994), and (3) subcultural theories (Cloward and Ohlin 1960; Cohen 1955, 1966; Miller 1958; Wolfgang and Ferracuti 1967). Sexual orientation and gender identity bore the stigma of sexual deviancy the few times they were discussed. In developing his subcultural theory, for instance, Cohen characterized homosexuality as a form of "sexual immorality" (1955, p. 22) and described homosexuals as a "community of deviants" who had "in common a propensity to some activity that is stigmatized and penalized by the larger society" (1966, pp. 86–87). Consequently, there is a need for macro-level sociological investigations of crime that characterize and discuss homophobia and transphobia as structural conditions of society (Woods 2014).

Most sociological-criminological engagement with sexual orientation and gender identity has operated at the micro-level in the second category of socio-logical perspectives on crime—social process theories. Social process theories view criminality as a function of the socialization process and the interactions that people have with different social institutions, including peer groups, families, and schools (Siegel 2011). Consistent with the homosexual deviancy thesis, social process theories of crime have focused largely on the ways in which socialization processes sustain homosexuality as a pattern of sexual deviance.

Social learning theories, which view crime as learned behaviors, have mostly characterized homosexuality as a form of sexual deviance learned and sustained through environmental interactions. For instance, in articulating his "differential-reinforcement" theory, Jeffery (1965, p. 295) stressed that "[t]he homosexual selects a male rather than a female as the sex object because of his past conditioning in the sexual area." Moreover, Akers (1973) viewed homosexual subcultures as a mechanism of reinforcement for homosexuals to continue engaging in their deviant sexual patterns. More recent social learning criminological studies published after anti-sodomy and sexual psychopath laws lost force omit any discussion of sexual orientation and gender identity concepts (e.g., Akers 1998).

Social control theories, which focus on why people refrain from committing crime, also discussed homosexuality insofar as characterizing it as a form of sexual deviance. For instance, Reiss's (1961) popular sociological study examined a specific form of male prostitution in which adult homosexual males ("queers") hired delinquent youth hustlers ("peers") for sexual services. Reiss concluded that norms within the youths' peer groups defined sexual transactions in ways that inhibited the peers from viewing themselves as sexual deviants. This conclusion reflected the established stigma against homosexuals as sexual deviants in society at the time. Similarly, in articulating his drift theory, Matza (1964) described homosexuality as a type of deviance, and characterized homosexual subcultures as types of deviant subcultures that reinforced the behavior of its members. Later social control theories developed after anti-sodomy and sexual psychopath laws lost popularity in the United States omit discussions of LGBTQ populations entirely (Gottfredson and Hirschi 1990; Hagan 1988; Hirschi 1969).

Critical Perspectives on Crime

Critical perspectives on crime have barely engaged with critical queer theories. The sexual deviancy framework has also governed most discussions of sexual orientation and gender identity in this school of criminological thought (Woods 2014).

The dominance of the sexual deviancy framework in early critical perspectives on crime is showcased in societal reaction and labeling of crime, which examine the process by which societies come to define certain behaviors and people as deviant (Siegel 2011). These theories came to the fore of criminology during the 1950s and 1960s, when sociologists drew upon the interactionist framework of George Herbert Mead (1934) to study deviance. Lemert (1951) used the "homosexual" as an example of a deviant status, and identified homosexuality as a type of deviance sustained through associations of people with similarly deviant sexual preferences. Moreover, in his popular book, *Outsiders*, Becker (1963, p. 30) stressed that the homosexual "makes deviance as a way of life" and "organizes his identity around a pattern of deviant behavior." Becker also identified "the homosexual community" as an "organized deviant group" (p. 38). The only popular societal reaction and labeling theory developed after the 1980s was John Braithwaite's (1989) "shaming reintegration theory."[4] Braithwaite's sole mention of homosexuality was governed by the sexual deviancy framework. In his view, most crimes in contemporary societies were supported by a strong social consensus, but a small number of victimless crimes were not supported by an

---

[4] In the year that Braithwaite released his theory, Western Australia decriminalized homosexuality under the Law Reform (Decriminalization of Sodomy) Act of 1989. However, decriminalization laws had been enacted previously in other areas of Australia. For instance, South Australia became the first Australian jurisdiction to decriminalize sodomy in 1972. In 1976 and 1980, some aspects of homosexual behavior were decriminalized in Australian Capital Territory and Victoria. In 1983, Northern Territory decriminalized homosexual acts between men in 1983, and New South Wales in 1984 (Bull et al. 1991).

overwhelming consensus. Braithwaite identified homosexuality as an example of a crime in the latter category, which demonstrates the lingering stigma of the sexual deviancy framework.

In other areas of critical criminology, there is little to no engagement with LGBTQ populations or sexual orientation and gender identity concepts. Consider social conflict theories, which view the norms embodied in the criminal law as reflections of the values of dominant social groups. Social conflict theories largely omit considerations of sexual orientation and gender identity, despite the fact that LGBTQ political organizations were gaining national prominence when the bulk of these theories were developed from the late-1950s until the late-1970s (Dahrendorf 1959, 1968; Sellin 1938; Turk 1966, 1969, 1971; Vold 1958; Vold and Bernard 1979, 1986). The sexual deviance framework framed the few discussions of homosexuality in social conflict perspectives. For instance, the second edition of *Theoretical Criminology*, released after Vold's death, characterized the "battle for gay rights" as a battle in which "two groups are attempting to define each other as deviants" (Vold and Bernard 1979, p. 279). The same edition also mentioned that "[o]pponents of 'gay rights'… want homosexuals to be officially recognized as deviants… and proponents of gay rights want official recognition that those who practice such discrimination are deviants" (Vold and Bernard 1979, p. 278).

Further, radical (Marxist) perspectives on crime also largely omit sexual orientation and gender identity concepts, which might be explained by the broad exclusion of sexuality and gender in Marx's writings (Bonger 1916; Chambliss 1984, 1988; Quinney 1970, 1974a, b, 1977). The few discussions of homosexuality in popular radical perspectives emerged in the context of the debate over the criminalization of homosexuality (Chambliss 1984, 1988; Quinney 1970). To date, there is no comprehensive radical analysis of crime that considers how sexual orientation and gender identity relate to capitalist production or the occurrence of crime in capitalist societies. This gap in the literature further supports the need for macro-level analyses of crime that engage with sexual orientation and gender identity differences.

Few feminist criminological perspectives have focused on the experiences of queer and transgender women, but there has been greater engagement with sexual orientation and gender identity in this area of criminology. Generally, this engagement has taken two forms. First, some feminist perspectives have drawn attention to specific areas of LGBTQ victimization, including sexual harassment (MacKinnon 1979) and bias crime (Messerschmidt 1993; Stanko 1990). This research has been useful in advancing the understanding of LGBTQ people's experience of crime, but their scope is limited to specific areas of victimization. Second, some feminist perspectives have articulated a need to deconstruct a heterosexist social order that subordinates LGBTQ people (Collier 1998; Messerschmidt 1993). Although perceptive, these calls have remained at a highly abstract level and invite more detailed consideration.

In the 1990s, a new trend in feminist criminology emerged that focused on the role of men and their performance of masculinity in offending (Collier 1998; Messerschmidt 1993). As Messerschmidt (1993, p. 14) explains, this enterprise focuses on "men as men and boys as boys." Although this area of criminology has provided meaningful insight into how gender norms are socially constructed, it has largely focused on deconstructing the "heterosexual male" offender. Consequently, this enterprise has yet to further the understanding of how gender norms may lead LGBTQ people, and LGBTQ people who identify as male in particular, to commit crime (though see Panfil, this volume). It also does not provide much insight into how race, class, and religious differences may intersect with sexual orientation and gender identity to shape motivations for offending (see also Johnson, this volume).

Left-realism emerged in the United Kingdom during the 1980s in response to the law and order criminal justice policies of Conservative Prime Minister Margaret Thatcher (Kinsey et al. 1986; Lea and Young 1984; Matthews and Young 1986; Taylor et al. 1973; Young 1986). Left realists criticized criminological frameworks for being overly abstract and impractical under the new conservative administration, and rejected the notion of Marxist criminologists that members of the working class were concerned with crimes of the rich. Left realists called for practical solutions to address crime, which in their view disproportionately affected working-class people.

In calling for this shift, early left-realist perspectives ignored LGBTQ people. The few included discussions of homosexuality focused on whether homosexuality was a form of deviance (Pearson 1975; Taylor et al. 1973). One plausible reason for the omission of LGBTQ populations in early left-realist perspectives is that left realists attempted to explain changes in crime rates. The instruments used to measure crime rates then excluded, and largely continue to exclude, sexual orientation and gender identity as demographic constructs. Therefore, early left realism may serve as an example that shows how the omission of sexual orientation and gender identity in crime data drives the neglect of LGBTQ populations in criminological theory. More recent left-realist perspectives still largely omit sexual orientation and gender identity, but some authors have briefly discussed anti-gay bias crimes and essentialism in recognizing homosexual identity and subcultures in late modernity (Young 1999; Young and Matthews 1992).

Moving Forward: "Queering" Criminology

This overview has demonstrated a need for theoretical and empirical advancements to bring the experiences of LGBTQ people out of the shadows in the field of criminology. Executing an enterprise to "queer" criminology, however, is not as simple as it might seem, and raises a number of complex questions, including: What should be the goals of such an endeavor? Should queer criminology provide guidance on the assumptions that criminologists make about sexual orientation and gender identity? What methodological implications does queer criminology have for criminological research? Although queer criminologists will confront these questions and identify new ones in the future, I conclude this overview by discussing some of these questions that may pose potential obstacles to building momentum for a queer criminological enterprise.

One potential challenge stems from conflicting definitions of the term "queer" itself. Although academics and community activists disagree over its precise meaning, the term "queer" has been generally used in two ways (also see discussion by Ball, this volume, regarding "queer" meanings). First, "queer" has been used as an umbrella term to describe persons who assume an array of defined sexual orientation and gender identity categories, including "gay," "lesbian," "bisexual," and "transgender" (Jargose 1996). Second, the term "queer" has been used to challenge and subvert phenomena that are viewed as stable and determined. Based on this view, "queer" can debunk the notion that sex, gender, and sexuality are essential and fixed identity concepts. "Queer" may also challenge the stability of concepts, methods, and assumptions of conventional social science research (Plummer 2005).

The tension between these two definitions poses a potential catch-22 situation: On the one hand, if queer criminology accepts the first meaning of the term "queer," then it risks being void of critical introspection. Queer criminology may draw attention to the exclusion of LGBTQ populations within criminological research, but also perpetrate the subordination of individuals with sexual orientations and gender identities who do not identify with, or fit within, accepted definitions of lesbian, gay, bisexual, and transgender terms (see also, this volume, Ball; Johnson). On the other hand, if queer criminology accepts the second meaning of the term "queer," then it risks diluting demographically-relevant social differences to the extent that it may discount the experiences of people who identify with, and experience marginalization on the basis of, those differences.

Individual criminologists may prefer identity-based over deconstructionist paradigms, or vice versa. As a discursive space in the field, however, I argue that queer criminology should encourage research under identity-based *and* deconstructionist paradigms. On the surface, this position may seem internally inconsistent. In my view, however, embracing both lines of research facilitates a tension that is both productive and meaningful. Regarding identity-based approaches, many LGBTQ people view sexual orientation and/or gender identity as central features of their lives—in addition to race/ethnicity, class, and religion (see, for example, Panfil, this volume). Criminological research that includes constructs capturing sexual orientation and gender identity differences can assist in explaining how those differences may shape LGBTQ people's experiences of crime, both in terms of victimization and offending (e.g., Conover-Williams, this volume). Scholars and advocates have criticized mainstream lesbian and gay social movements for perpetuating their own forms of marginalization based on gender, class, and race (Chasin 2001; Hutchinson 2000; Spade and Currah 2008; see too, this volume, Ball; Johnson). Deconstructionist paradigms can help to identify which individuals do and do not receive recognition in criminological research that utilizes identity-based models of sexual orientation and gender identity. In challenging basic assumptions about the organization of sexual orientation and gender identity, queer theories can further problematize how sexual orientation and gender identity is conceptualized in criminological research that uses traditional social science methods. Therefore, embracing the tensions that arise from contested meanings of the term "queer" builds diversity in the discourse on the criminologically-relevant experiences that are shaped by sexual orientation and gender identity.

Although the enterprise of queer criminology attempts to bring sexual orientation and gender identity issues to the fore of criminological inquiry, it cannot neglect how intersecting differences of race, gender, class, and religion shape LGBTQ people's experiences of crime, both in terms of victimization and offending (Woods 2014). These intersections can cause a queer woman of color to experience marginalization on the basis of her sexuality and a transgender woman of color to experience marginalization on the basis of her gender identity in different ways than a white gay man experiences marginalization on the basis of his sexuality (Pharr 1977; Smith 1993). This observation is especially valuable given the dearth of criminological research on queer women, transgender individuals, and LGBTQ people of color. Critical race scholarship—especially theories of intersectionality (Crenshaw 1991)—offer valuable frameworks to investigate intersections of race/ethnicity, class, age, religion, sexual orientation, and gender identity in criminological contexts. Encouraging intersectionality approaches in the queer criminological enterprise assists in capturing the range of LGBTQ people's experiences of crime, and inhibits it from becoming an exclusive criminal justice movement for economically well-off, white, gay men. Other criminological areas, especially those that focus on particular social groups, can also gain from queer criminological perspectives that embrace intersectional approaches. For instance, engagement with queer criminological perspectives could assist criminology scholars and criminal justice practitioners in those other areas to recognize and to address the needs of particular subsets of LGBTQ victims and offenders in sensitive and effective ways.

The call to "queer" criminology also raises important questions about the assumptions that criminologists should make about the nature of sexual orientation and gender identity. One of the largest controversies involving these concepts is whether sexual orientation and gender identity are social constructions, innate biological characteristics, or a combined product of environmental and biological factors (Stein 1992). The moral and political implications of the nature-nurture debate are immense. Social constructivist explanations of sexual orientation and gender identity discount the view that being LGBTQ is an immutable sickness or an innate manifestation of biological degeneracy. However, rooting the causes of sexual orientation and gender identity in patterns of socialization might facilitate the use of aversion therapies to "cure" LGBTQ people. The implications of the biological view are just as great. If scientists discovered that sexual orientation and gender identity had biological origins, then governments might be more willing to grant full legal protections to LGBTQ people on the basis that sexual orientation and gender identity are "immutable characteristics." Grounding sexual orientation and gender identity in biology, however, might inspire eugenics practices and enable parents to prevent their newborn children from being LGBTQ. Many scholars believe that both biological and societal factors are relevant, and advocate for the full equality of LGBTQ people regardless of ontological and epistemological considerations.

The nature-nurture debate raises challenges to "queer" criminology because of the incredible diversity of theories and methods in the field. Some criminologists emphasize biological, psychological, or sociological factors exclusively in their explanations of crime, whereas other criminologists emphasize a combination of one or more of these factors. If queer criminology takes a particular position on the nature-nurture debate, then it risks isolating entire schools of criminological thought. Again, this does not imply that individual criminologists should refrain from making specific assumptions about the nature of sexual orientation and gender identity. But as a discursive space, queer criminology should provide room for a diversity of evidence-based assumptions to thrive, and to come into conflict or complement one another. Such diversity can enable criminologists to think critically about why they hold specific assumptions about LGBTQ people, and combat assumptions about sexual orientation and gender identity in the field that are grounded in outdated conceptions of LGBTQ people as sexual deviants.

Perhaps the greatest challenge of queer criminology is engendering a shift within the field that enables criminologists to engage with sexual orientation and gender identity in ways that do not further stigmatize LGBTQ people. Careful attention to nuance and tone is essential for queer criminology to be successful. A stigma still attaches to being LGBTQ today, and drawing attention to LGBTQ people's experiences of crime, especially in terms of offending, runs the risk of further marginalizing people on the basis of sexual orientation and gender identity, as well as race and class. Queer criminology must equip criminologists with the tools to explore how various circumstances shape LGBTQ people's experiences of crime without inherently labeling them as victims, or as criminals, on account of their sexual orientations and gender identities. This task is not easy given that the treatment of LGBTQ people in the field of criminology has been shaped largely by their perceived statuses as criminal sexual deviants.

Acknowledgments Thank you to Loraine Gelsthorpe and Caroline Lanskey—and most especially to Michael Rice—at the Institute of Criminology at the University of Cambridge for their support and comments in helping me to develop these ideas. I am also appreciative of the useful suggestions of Dana Peterson and Vanessa Panfil.

References

Agnew, R. (1992). Foundation for a general strain theory of crime and delinquency. *Criminology, 30*(1), 47–87.

Agnew, R. (2006). General strain theory: Current status and directions for further research. In F. T. Cullen, J. P. Wright, & K. R. Blevins (Eds.), *Taking stock: The status of criminological theory—Advances in criminological theory* (pp. 101–123). New Brunswick, NJ: Transaction.

Aichhorn, A. (1935 [1925]). *Wayward youth.* E. Bryant, J. Deming, M. O'Neil Hawkins, G. J. Mohr, E. J. Mohr, H. Ross, & H. Thun (Trans.). New York, NY: Viking.

Akers, R. L. (1973). *Deviant behavior: A social learning approach* (1st ed.). Belmont, CA: Wadsworth Publishing Company, Inc.

Akers, R. L. (1998). *Social learning and social structure: A general theory of crime and deviance* (1st ed.). Boston, MA: Northeastern University Press.

Alexander, F. & Staub, H. (1931 [1929]). *The criminal, the judge and the public.* New York, NY: Macmillan.

Ard, K. L., & Makadon, H. J. (2011). Addressing intimate partner violence in lesbian, gay, bisexual, and transgender patients. *Journal of General Internal Medicine, 26*(8), 930–933.

Barnhouse, R. T. (1977). *Homosexuality: A symbolic confusion.* New York, NY: The Seabury Press.

Bayer, R. (1981). *Homosexuality and American psychiatry: The politics of diagnosis.* New York, NY: Basic Books.

Becker, H. (1963). *Outsiders.* New York, NY: Free Press.

Bergler, E. (1956). *Homosexuality: Disease or way of life.* New York, NY: Hill and Wang.

Berlan, E. D., Corliss, H. L., Field, A. E., Goodman, E., & Austin, S. B. (2010). Sexual orientation and bullying among adolescents in the growing up today study. *Journal of Adolescent Health, 46*(4), 366–371.

Berrill, K. T. (1990). Anti-gay violence and victimization in the United States: An overview. *Journal of Interpersonal Violence, 5*(3), 274–294.

Berrill, K., & Herek, G. M. (1990). Primary and Secondary Victimization in anti-gay hate crimes. *Journal of Interpersonal Violence, 5*(3), 401–413.

Bérubé, A. (1990). *Coming out under fire: The history of gay men and women in World War II.* New York, NY: Free Press.

Bieber, I., Dain, H. J., Dince, P. R., Drellich, M. G., Grand, H. G., & Gundlach, R. H., et al. (1962). *Homosexuality: A psychoanalytic study of male homosexuals.* New York, NY: Basic Books.

Birkett, M., Espelage, D. L., & Koenig, B. (2009). LGB and questioning students in schools: The moderating effects of homophobic bullying and school climate on negative outcomes. *Journal of Youth and Adolescence, 38*(7), 989–1000.

Bonger, W. (1916). *Criminality and economic conditions.* Boston, MA: Little, Brown, and Co.

Braithwaite, J. (1989). *Crime, shame and reintegration.* Cambridge, UK: Cambridge University Press.

Bull, M., Pinto, S., & Wilson, P. (1991). Homosexual law reform in Australia. *Trends & Issues in Crime and Criminal Justice, 29,* 1–10.

Bullough, V. L. (1979). *Homosexuality: A history.* New York, NY: New American Library.

Burke, T. W., Jordan, M. L., & Owen, S. S. (2002). A cross-national comparison of gay and lesbian domestic violence. *Journal of Contemporary Criminal Justice, 18*(3), 231–257.

Cabaj, R. P. (1992). Substance abuse in the gay and lesbian community. In J. Lowinson, P. Ruiz, & R. Millman (Eds.). *Substance abuse: A comprehensive textbook* (2nd ed., pp. 852–60). Baltimore, MD: Williams and Wilkins.

Cain, M. (1990). Towards transgression: New directions in feminist criminology. *International Journal of the Sociology of the Law, 18*(1), 1–18.

Carpiano, R. M., Kelly, B. C., Easterbrook, A., & Parsons, J. T. (2011). Community and drug use among gay men: The role of neighborhoods and networks. *Journal of Health and Social Behavior, 52*(1), 74–90.

Carragher, D. J., & Rivers, I. (2002). Trying to hide: A cross-national study of growing up for non-identified gay and bisexual male youth. *Clinical Child Psychology Psychiatry, 7*(3), 457–474.

Casper, J. L. (1852). Über Nothsucht und Päderastie und deren Ermittelung seitens des Gerichtsarztes. *Vierteljahrschrift für gerichtliche und öffentliche Medicin, 1,* 21–78.

Catalano, R. F., Park, J., Harachi, T. W., Haggerty, K. P., Abbott, R. D., & Hawkins, J. D. (2005). Mediating the effects of poverty, gender, individual characteristics, and external constraints on antisocial behavior: A test of the social development model and implications for developmental life-course theory. In D. P. Farrington (Ed.), *Integrated developmental life-course theories of offending* (pp. 93–123). New Brunswick, NJ: Transaction.

Chambliss, W. J. (Ed.). (1984). *Criminal law in action.* New York, NY: Wiley.

Chambliss, W. J. (1988). *Exploring criminology.* New York, NY: Macmillan.

Charcot, J. & Magnan, V. (1882). Inversion du sens génital. *Archives de Nurologie, 3*, 53–60 and *4*, 296–322.

Chasin, A. (2001). *Selling out: The gay and lesbian movement goes to market.* New York, NY: Palgrave.

Chesney, M., Barrett, D., & Stall, R. D. (1998). Histories of substance abuse and risk behavior: Precursors to HIV seroconversion in homosexual men. *American Journal of Public Health, 88*, 113–116.

Cloward, R. A., & Ohlin, L. E. (1960). *Delinquency and opportunity: A theory of delinquent gangs.* Glencoe, IL: The Free Press.

Cohen, A. K. (1955). *Delinquent boys: The culture of the gang.* New York, NY: The Free Press.

Cohen, A. K. (1966). *Deviance and control.* Englewood Cliffs, NJ: Prentice Hall.

Collier, R. (1998). *Masculinities, crime and criminology: Men, heterosexuality and the criminal(ised) other.* London, UK: SAGE.

Craft, A., & Craft, M. (1984). Treatment of sexual offenders. In M. Craft & A. Craft (Eds.), *Mentally abnormal offenders* (pp. 403–416). London, UK: Butler and Tanner Ltd.

Craft, A., Craft, M., & Spencer, M. (1984). Sexual offences: Intent and characteristics. In M. Craft & A. Craft (Eds.), *Mentally abnormal offenders* (pp. 60–87). London, UK: Butler and Tanner Ltd.

Crenshaw, K. (1991). Mapping the margins: Intersectionality, identity politics, and violence against women of color. *Stanford Law Review, 43*, 1241–1299.

Cruz, J. M. (2003). "Why doesn't he just leave?": Gay male domestic violence and the reasons victims stay. *The Journal of Men's Studies, 11*(3), 309–323.

D'Augelli, A. R., & Grossman, A. H. (2001). Disclosure of sexual orientation, victimization, and mental health among lesbian, gay, and bisexual older adults. *Journal of Interpersonal Violence, 16*(10), 1008–1027.

Dahrendorf, R. (1959). *Class and class conflict in industrial society.* Stanford, CA: Stanford University Press.

Dahrendorf, R. (1968). *Essays in the theory of society.* Stanford, CA: Stanford University Press.

Darwich, L., Shelly, H., & Waterhouse, T. (2012). School avoidance and substance use among lesbian, gay, bisexual, and questioning youths: The impact of peer victimization and adult support. *Journal of Educational Psychology, 104*(2), 381–392.

Eskridge, W., Jr. (2008). *Dishonorable passions: Sodomy laws in America, 1861–2003.* New York, NY: Viking Press.

Eysenck, H. J. (1977). *Crime and personality.* London, UK: Routledge and Kegan Paul.

Farrington, D. P. (2003). Key results from the first 40 years of the Cambridge study in delinquent development. In T. P. Thornberry & M. D. Krohn (Eds.), *Taking stock of delinquency: An overview of findings from contemporary longitudinal studies* (pp. 137–183). New York, NY: Klumer/Plenum.

Farrington, D. P. (2005). The integrated cognitive antisocial potential (ICAP) theory. In D. P. Farrington (Ed.), *Integrated developmental and life-course theories of offending* (pp. 73–92). New Brunswick, NJ: Transaction.

Farrington, D. P. (2006). Building developmental and life-course theories of offending. In F. T. Cullen, J. P. Wright, & K. R. Blevins (Eds.), *Taking stock: The status of criminological theory* (pp. 335–364). New Brunswick, NJ: Transaction.

Farrington, D. P. (2010). Life-course and developmental theories in criminology. In E. McLaughlin & T. Newburn (Eds.), *The Sage handbook of criminological theory* (pp. 249–269). Thousand Oaks, CA: SAGE Publications.

Fein-Zachary, V. J., & LaCava, L. (2008). LGBT couples and families with children. In H. J. Makadon, K. H. Mayer, J. Potter, & H. Goldhammer (Eds.), *The Fenway guide to lesbian, gay, bisexual, and transgender health* (pp. 100–134). East Peoria: Versa Press.

Féré, C. (1899). *L'instinct sexuel: Evolution et dissolution*. Paris, FR: Félix Alcan.

Ford, C. S., & Beach, F. A. (1951). *Patterns of sexual behavior*. New York, NY: Harper and Brothers.

Forel, A. H. (1905). *Die sexuelle Frage: Eine naturwissenschaftliche, psychologische, hygienische und soziologische Studie für Gebildete*. Munich, Germany: E. Reinhardt.

Foucault, M. (1979). *The history of sexuality, volume 1: An introduction*. London, UK: Allen Lane.

Freedman, E. B. (2006). *Feminism, sexuality and politics: Essays*. Chapel Hill, NC: University of North Carolina Press.

Freud, S. (1905). Three essays on the theory of sexuality. *Standard edition, 7*, 125–245.

Freud, S. (1911). Psychoanalytical notes on the autobiographical account of a case of paranoia (Dementia Paranoides). *Standard edition, 12*, 1–82.

Friedlander, K. (1947). *Psycho-analytic approach to juvenile delinquency*. London, UK: Routledge and Kegan Paul.

Gelsthorpe, L., & Morris, A. (Eds.). (1990). *Feminist perspectives in criminology*. Milton Keynes, UK: Open University Press.

Georges-Abeyie, D. (1984). Definitional issues: Race, ethnicity, and official crime victimization statistics. In D. Georges-Abeyie (Ed.), *The criminal justice system and blacks* (pp. 5–19). New York, NY: Clark Boardman.

Gibson, M., & Rafter, N. H. (2006). Editor's Introduction. In M. Gibson & N. H. Rafter (Eds.), *Criminal man* (pp. 1–41). Durham, NC: Duke.

Gottfredson, M. R., & Hirschi, T. (1990). *A general theory of crime*. Stanford, CA: Stanford University Press.

Greenberg, D. F. (1988). *The construction of homosexuality*. Chicago, IL: University of Chicago Press.

Greenwood, G. L., Relf, M. V., Huang, B., Pollack, L. M., Canchola, J. A., & Catania, J. A. (2002). Battering victimization among a probability-based sample of men who have sex with men. *American Journal of Public Health, 92*(12), 1964–1969.

Hagan, J. (1988). *Structural criminology*. Cambridge, UK: Polity Press.

Halkitis, P., & Parsons, J. T. (2002). Recreational drug use and HIV risk sexual behavior among men frequenting urban gay venues. *Journal of Gay and Lesbian Social Services, 14*, 19–38.

Halkitis, P., Parsons, J., & Stirratt, M. (2001). A double epidemic: Crystal methamphetamine use and its relation to HIV prevention among gay men. *Journal of Homosexuality, 41*, 17–35.

Halkitis, P., Parsons, J., & Wilton, L. (2003). An exploratory study of contextual and situational factors related to methamphetamine use among gay and bisexual men in New York City. *Journal of Drug Issues, 33*, 413–432.

Hamowy, R. (1977). Medicine and the crimination of sin: "Self-abuse" in 19th century America. *Journal of Libertarian Studies, 1*(3), 229–270.

Hawkins, J. D., & Catalano, R. F. (1992). *Communities that care*. San Francisco, CA: Jossey-Bass.

Hawkins, J. D., Smith, B. H., Hill, K. G., Kosterman, R., Catalano, R. F., & Abbott, R. D. (2003). Understanding and preventing crime and violence: Findings from the Seattle Social Development Project. In T. P. Thornberry & M. D. Krohn (Eds.), *Taking stock of delinquency: An overview of findings from contemporary longitudinal studies* (pp. 255–312). New York, NY: Kluwer/Plenum.

Hawkins, J. D., Brown, E. C., Oesterle, S., Aurthur, M. W., Abbott, R. D., & Catalano, R. F. (2008). Early effects of communities that care on targeted risks and initiation of delinquent behavior and substance use. *Journal of Adolescent Health, 43*, 15–22.

Healey, J. F. (2001). Sociology and society: How does sociological theory help us interpret the world? In Y. W. Bradshaw, J. F. Healey, & R. Smith (Eds.), *Sociology for a new century* (pp. 41–74). London, UK: Fine Forge Press.

Heidensohn, F. (1985). *Women and crime*. London, UK: Macmillan Press.

Herek, G. M. (1989). Hate crimes against lesbians and gay men: Issues for research and policy. *American Psychologist, 44*(6), 948–955.

Herek, G. M. (2009). Hate crimes and stigma-related experiences among sexual minority adults in the United States: Prevalence estimates from a national probability sample. *Journal of Interpersonal Violence, 24*(1), 54–74.

Herek, G. M., & Berrill, K. (1992). *Hate crimes: Confronting violence against lesbians and gay men*. Newbury Park, CA: Sage.

Herek, G. M., Gillis, J. R., Cogan, J. C., & Glunt, E. K. (1997). Hate crime victimization among lesbian, gay, and bisexual adults: Prevalence, psychological correlates, and methodological issues. *Journal of Interpersonal Violence, 12*(2), 195–215.

Herek, G. M., Gillis, J. R., & Cogan, J. C. (1999). Psychological sequelae of hate crime victimization among lesbian, gay, and bisexual adults. *Journal of Consulting and Clinical Psychology, 67*(6), 945–951.

Herek, G. M., Cogan, J. C., & Gillis, J. R. (2002). Victim experiences in hate crimes based on sexual orientation. *Journal of Social Issues, 58*(2), 319–339.

Herrn, R. (1995). On the history of biological theories of sexuality. *Journal of Homosexuality, 28*(1–2), 31–56.

Hester, M., & Donovan, C. (2009). Researching domestic violence in same-sex relationships—A feminist epistemological approach to survey development. *Journal of Lesbian Studies, 13*(2), 161–173.

Hinch, R. (1983). Marxist criminology in the 1970s: Clarifying the clutter. *Crime and Social Justice, 19*, 65–73.

Hirschi, T. (1969). *Causes of delinquency*. Berkeley, CA: University of California Press.

Hong, J. S., & Garbarino, J. (2012). Risk and protective factors for homophobic bullying in schools: An application of the social-ecological framework. *Educational Psychology Review, 24*(2), 271–285.

Hooker, E. (1956). A preliminary analysis of group behavior of homosexuals. *Journal of Psychology, 42*, 217–225.

Hooker, E. (1957). The adjustment of the male overt homosexual. *Journal of Projective Techniques, 21*, 18–31.

Hooker, E. (1958). Male homosexuality in the Rorschach. *Journal of Projective Techniques, 22*, 33–54.

Hospers, H. J., & Kok, G. (1995). Determinants of safe and risk-taking sexual behavior among gay men: A review. *AIDS Education and Prevention, 7*, 74–95.

Hughes, J. S., Sharrock, W. W., & Martin, P. J. (2003). *Understanding classical sociology: Marx, Weber, Durkheim* (2nd ed.). London, UK: SAGE.

Hutchinson, D. L. (2000). Out yet unseen: A racial critique of gay and lesbian legal theory and political discourse. In R. Delgado & J. Stefanicic (Eds.) *Critical race theory: The cutting edge* (2nd ed., pp. 325–333). Philadelphia, PA: Temple University Press.

Island, D., & Letellier, P. (1991). *Men who beat the men who love them: Battered gay men and domestic violence*. Binghamton, NY: Haworth Press.

Jagose, A. (1996). *Queer theory: An introduction*. New York, NY: New York University Press.

Jeffery, C. R. (1965). Criminal behavior and learning theory. *Journal of Criminal Law, Criminology, and Police Science, 56*(3), 294–300.

Kennedy, H. (1997). Karl Heinrich Ulrichs: First theorist of homosexuality. In V. Rosario (Ed.), *Science and homosexualities* (pp. 26–45). New York, NY: Routledge.

Kinsey, A. C., Pomeroy, W. B., & Martin, C. E. (1948). *Sexual behavior in the human male*. Philadelphia, PA: Saunders.

Kinsey, A. C., Pomeroy, W. B., Martin, C. E., & Gebhart, P. H. (1953). *Sexual behavior in the human female*. Philadelphia, PA: Saunders.

Kinsey, R., Lea, J., & Young, J. (1986). *Losing the fight against crime*. Oxford, UK: Basil Blackwell.

Kitzinger, C., & Coyle, A. (2002). Introducing lesbian and gay psychology. In A. Coyle & C. Kitzinger (Eds.), *Lesbian and gay psychology: New perspectives* (pp. 1–29). Oxford, UK: Blackwell.

Krafft-Ebing, R. von (1886 [1965]). *Psychopathia Sexualis* (F. S. Klaf, Trans.). New York, NY: Arcade.

Krafft-Ebing, R. von (1886 [2006]). *Psychopathia sexualis*. (F. J. Rebman, Trans.). New York: Kessinger.

Lahey, B. B., & Waldman, I. D. (2005). A developmental model of the propensity to offend during childhood and adolescence. In D. P. Farrington (Ed.), *Integrated developmental and life-course theories of offending* (pp. 15–50). New Brunswick, NJ: Transaction.

Lahey, B. B., Loeber, R., Waldman, I. D. & Farrington, D. P. (2006). Child socioemotional dispositions at school entry that predict adolescent delinquency and violence. *Impuls: Tidsskrift for Psykologi, 3*, 40–51.

Lahey, B. B., Applegate, B., Chronis, A. M., Jones, H. A., Williams, S. H., Loney, J., et al. (2008). Psychometric characteristics of a measure of emotional dispositions developed to test a developmental propensity model of conduct disorder. *Journal of Clinical Child and Adolescent Psychology, 37*, 794–807.

Laub, J. H., & Sampson, R. J. (2001). Understanding desistance from crime. In M. Tonry (Ed.), *Crime and Justice* (Vol. 29, pp. 1–69). Chicago, IL: University of Chicago Press.

Laub, J. H., & Sampson, R. J. (2003). *Shared beginnings, divergent lives: Delinquent boys to age 70*. Cambridge, MA: Harvard University Press.

Lea, J., & Young, J. (1984). *What is to be done about law and order?* (2nd ed.). London, UK: Pluto Press.

LeBlanc, M. (1997). A generic control theory of the criminal phenomenon: The structural and dynamic statements of an integrated multilayered control theory. In T. P. Thornberry (Ed.), *Developmental theories of crime and delinquency* (pp. 215–285). New Brunswick, NJ: Transaction.

LeBlanc, M. (2005). An integrated personal control theory of deviant behavior: Answers to contemporary empirical and theoretical developmental criminology issues. In D. P. Farrington (Ed.), *Integrated developmental and life-course theories of offending* (pp. 125–163). New Brunswick, NJ: Transaction.

LeBlanc, M. (2009). The development of deviant behavior, and its self-regulation. *Monatsschrift fur Kriminologie und Strafrechtsreform (Journal of Criminology and Penal Reform), 92*, 117–136.

LeBlanc, M., & Frechette, M. (1989). *Male criminal activity from childhood through youth*. New York, NY: Springer.

Leigh, B., & Stall, R. (1993). Substance use and risky sexual behavior for exposure to HIV. *American Psychologist, 48*, 1035–1045.

Lemert, E. (1951). *Social pathology*. New York, NY: McGraw-Hill.

Letellier, P. (1994). Gay and bisexual male domestic violence and victimization: Challenges to feminist theory and responses to violence. *Violence and Victims, 9*(2), 95–106.

Leventhal, B., & Lundy, S. E. (Eds.). (1999). *Same-sex domestic violence: Strategies for change*. Thousand Oaks, CA: Sage Publications, Inc.

Lombroso, C. (2006 [1876, 1878, 1884, 1889, 1896-97]), *Criminal man* (M. Gibson & N. H. Rafter, Trans.). Durham, NC: Duke University Press.

Lombroso, C. & Ferrero, G. (2004 [1893]). *Criminal woman, the prostitute, and the normal woman* (M. Gibson & N. H. Rafter, Trans.). Durham, NC: Duke University Press.

Lowenkamp, C. T., Cullen, F. T., & Pratt, T. C. (2003). Replicating Sampson and Groves's test of social disorganization theory: Revisiting a criminological classic. *Journal of Research in Crime and Delinquency, 40*(4), 351–373.

MacKinnon, C. (1979). *Sexual harassment of working women: A case of sex discrimination*. New Haven, CT: Yale University Press.

Makari, G. (2008). *Revolution in mind: The creation of psychoanalysis*. New York, NY: HarperCollins Publishers Inc.

Margolies, L., & Leeder, E. (1995). Violence at the door: Treatment of lesbian batterers. *Violence Against Women, 1*(2), 139–157.

Matthews, R., & Young, J. (Eds.). (1986). *Confronting crime*. London, UK: Sage.

Matza, D. (1964). *Delinquency and drift*. New York, NY: Wiley.

McClennen, J. (2005). Domestic violence between same-gender partners: Recent findings and future research. *Journal of Interpersonal Violence, 20*(2), 149–154.

McClennen, J. C., Summers, A. B., & Vaughan, C. (2002). Gay men's domestic violence: Dynamics, help-seeking behaviors, and correlates. *Journal of Gay and Lesbian Social Services, 14*(1), 23–49.

McCrae, R. R., & Costa, P. T. (1990). *Personality in adulthood*. New York, NY: Guilford Press.

McIntosh, M. (1968). The homosexual role. *Social Problems, 16*(2), 182–192.

McKirnan, D. J., & Peterson, P. L. (1989). Alcohol and drug use among homosexual men and women: Epidemiology and population characteristics. *Addictive Behaviors, 14*, 545–553.

Mead, G. H. (1934). *Mind, self, and society: From the standpoint of a social behaviorist*. C. W. Morris (Ed.). Chicago, IL: University of Chicago Press.

Merton, R. (1938). Social structure and anomie. *American Sociological Review, 3*(5), 672–682.

Merton, R. (1957). *Social theory and social structure*. Glencoe, IL: The Free Press.

Messerschmidt, J. W. (1993). *Masculinities and crime: Critique and reconceptualization of theory*. Lanham, MD: Rowman and Littlefield.

Messerschmidt, J. W. (1997). *Crime as structured action: Gender, race, class, and crime in the making*. Thousand Oaks, CA: Sage.

Messinger, A. M. (2011). Invisible victims: Same-sex IPV in the National Violence Against Women Survey. *Journal of Interpersonal Violence, 26*(11), 2228–2243.

Messner, S. F., & Rosenfeld, R. (1994). *Crime and the American dream*. Belmont, CA: Wadsworth.

Meyer, D. (2010). Evaluating the severity of hate-motivated violence: Intersectional differences among LGBT hate crime victims. *Sociology, 44*(5), 980–995.

Miller, W. B. (1958). Lower class culture as a generating milieu of gang delinquency. *Journal of Social Issues, 14*(3), 5–19.

Moffitt, T. E. (1993). Adolescence-limited and life-course-persistent antisocial behavior: A developmental taxonomy. *Psychological Review, 100*, 674–701.

Moffitt, T. E. (2006). Life-course persistent and adolescent-limited antisocial behavior. In D. Cicchetti & D. J. Cohen (Eds.), *Developmental psychopathology: Risk, disorder, and adaptation* (Vol. 3, pp. 570–598). New York, NY: Wiley.

Moffitt, T. E., Caspi, A., Rutter, M., & Silva, P. A. (2001). *Sex differences in antisocial behaviour: Conduct disorder, delinquency, and violence in the Dunedin longitudinal study*. Cambridge, UK: Cambridge University Press.

Moffitt, T. E., Caspi, A., Harrington, H., & Milne, B. J. (2002). Males on the life-course-persistent and adolescence-limited antisocial pathways: Follow-up at age 26 years. *Development and Psychopathology, 14*(1), 179–207.

Moll, A. (1891). *Die konträre sexualempfindung*. Berlin, Germany: Fischer.

Morales, E. S., & Graves, M. S. (1983). *Substance abuse: Patterns and barriers to treatment for gay men and lesbians in San Francisco*. San Francisco, CA: San Francisco Department of Public Health.

Moreau, P. (1887). *Des aberrations du sens génétique*. Paris, FR: Asselin.

Morrison, K. (2006). *Marx, Durkheim, Weber: Formations of modern social thought*. London, UK: SAGE.

Murray, C. E., & Mobley, A. K. (2009). Empirical research about same-sex intimate partner violence: A methodological review. *Journal of Homosexuality, 56*(3), 361–386.

Oriel, K. (2012). Intimate partner violence in same-sex relationships. In R. S. Fife & S. Schrager (Eds.), *Family violence: What health care providers need to know* (pp. 65–74). Sadbury, MA: Jones and Bartlett Learning.

Ostrow, D., & Shelby, D. (2000). Psychoanalytic and behavioral approaches to drug-related sexual risk-taking: A preliminary conceptual and clinical integration. *Journal of Gay and Lesbian Psychotherapy, 3*, 123–139.

Park, R. E. & Burgess, E. W. (1969 [1921]). *Introduction to the science of sociology* (3rd ed.). Chicago, IL: University of Chicago Press.

Park, R.E. & Burgess, E.W. (1967 [1925]). *The city*. Chicago, IL: University of Chicago Press.

Pearson, G. (1975). Misfit sociology and the politics of socialization. In I. Taylor, P. Walton, & J. Young (Eds.), *Critical criminology* (pp. 147–166). London, UK: Routledge and Kegan Paul.

Pharr, S. (1977). *Homophobia: A weapon of sexism*. Berkeley, CA: Chardon Press.

Phillips, C., & Bowling, B. (2003). Racism, ethnicity and criminology: Developing minority perspectives. *British Journal of Criminology, 43*(2), 269–290.

Plummer, K. (2000). Mapping the sociological gay: Past, presents and futures of a sociology of same sex relations. In T. Sandfort, J. Schuyf, J. W. Duyvendak, & J. Weeks (Eds.), *Lesbian and gay studies: An introductory, interdisciplinary approach* (pp. 46–60). London, UK: SAGE.

Plummer, K. (2005). Critical humanism and queer theory: Living with the tensions. In N. K. Denzin & Y. S. Lincoln (Eds.), *The SAGE handbook of qualitative research* (3rd ed., pp. 357–373). Thousand Oaks, CA: Sage.

Quinney, R. (1970). *The social reality of crime*. Boston, MA: Little, Brown, and Co.

Quinney, R. (1974a). *Criminal justice in America*. Boston, MA: Little, Brown, and Co.

Quinney, R. (1974b). *Critique of legal order: Crime control in capitalist society*. Boston, MA: Little, Brown, and Co.

Quinney, R. (1977). *Class, state, and crime: On the theory and practice of criminal justice*. New York, NY: Longman.

Rado, S. (1940). A critical examination of the concept of bisexuality. *Psychosomatic Medicine, 2*, 459–467.

Reiss, A. J. (1961). The social integration of queers and peers. *Social Problems, 9*(2), 102–120.

Renzetti, C. M., & Miley, C. H. (Eds.). (1996). *Violence in gay and lesbian domestic partnerships*. Binghamton, NY: Haworth Press.

Rusche, G. & Kirchheimer, O. (1968 [1939]). *Punishment and social structure*. New York, NY: Columbia University Press.

Russell, S. T., Ryan, C., Toomey, R. B., Diaz, R. M., & Sanchez, J. (2011). Lesbian, gay, bisexual, and transgender adolescent school victimization: Implications for young adult health and adjustment. *Journal of School Health, 81*(5), 223–230.

Sampson, R., & Groves, W. B. (1989). Community structure and crime: Testing social disorganization theory. *American Journal of Sociology, 94*(4), 774–802.

Sampson, R. J., & Laub, J. H. (1993). *Crime in the making: Pathways and turning points through life*. Cambridge, MA: Harvard University Press.

Sampson, R. J., & Laub, J. H. (1995). Understanding variability in lives through time: Contributions of life-course criminology. *Studies on Crime and Crime Prevention, 4*, 143–158.

Sampson, R. J., & Laub, J. H. (2003). Life-course desisters? Trajectories of crime among delinquent boys followed to age 70. *Criminology, 41*, 555–592.

Sampson, R. J., & Laub, J. H. (2005). A general age-graded theory of crime: Lessons learned and the future of life-course criminology. In D. P. Farrington (Ed.), *Integrated developmental and life-course theories of offending* (pp. 165–181). New Brunswick, NJ: Transaction.

Sampson, R. J., & Laub, J. H. (2009). A life-course theory and long-term project on trajectories of crime. *Monatsschrift fur Kriminologie und Strafrechtsreform (Journal of Criminology and Penal Reform), 92*, 226–239.

Sandholtz, N., Langton, L. & Planty, M. (2013). *Hate crime victimization, 2003-2011*. Special report NCJ 241291: U.S. Department of Justice, Office of Justice Programs, Bureau of Justice Statistics. Last retrieved May 12, 2013 from http://www.bjs.gov/content/pub/pdf/hcv0311.pdf.

Sarbin, T. R. (1996). The deconstruction of stereotypes: Homosexuals and military policy. In G. M. Herek, J. Jobe, & R. Carney (Eds.), *Out in force: Sexual orientation and the military* (pp. 177–196). Chicago, IL: University of Chicago Press.

Seidman, S. (1996). Introduction. In S. Seidman (Ed.), *Queer theory/sociology* (pp. 1–30). Oxford, UK: Blackwell.

Sellin, T. (1938). *Culture conflict and crime.* New Jersey: Social Science Research Council.

Shaw, C. R., & McKay, H. D. (1931). *Social factors in juvenile delinquency: Report on the causes of crime to the Wickersham Commission* (Vol. 2). Washington, DC: Government Printing Office.

Shaw, C. R., & McKay, H. D. (1942). *Juvenile delinquency and urban areas.* Chicago, IL: University of Chicago Press.

Shaw, C. R. & McKay, H. D. (1969). *Juvenile delinquency and urban areas* (rev. ed.). Chicago, IL: University of Chicago Press.

Shilo, G., & Savaya, R. (2011). Effects of family and friend support on LGB youths' mental health and sexual orientation milestones. *Family Relations, 60*(3), 318–330.

Siegel, L. J. (2011). *Criminology* (11th ed.). Belmont, CA: Wadsworth.

Smart, C. (1977). *Women, crime and criminology: A feminist critique.* London, UK: Routledge.

Smith, B. (1993). Homophobia: Why bring it up? In H. Abelove, M. Barale, & D. Halperin (Eds.), *The lesbian and gay studies reader* (pp. 99–102). New York, NY: Routledge.

Socarides, C. W. (1968). *The overt homosexual.* New York, NY: Aronson.

Spade, D., & Currah, P. (2008). Introduction to the special issue: The state we're in: Locations of coercion and resistance in trans policy, Part 2. *Sexuality Research and Social Policy, 5*(1), 1–4.

Stall, R. D., & Leigh, B. (1994). Understanding the relationship between drug or alcohol use and high-risk sexual activity for HIV transmission: Where do we go from here? *Addiction, 89,* 131–134.

Stall, R., & Wiley, J. (1988). A comparison of alcohol and drug use patterns of homosexual and heterosexual men: The San Francisco Men's Health Study. *Drug and Alcohol Dependence, 22,* 63–73.

Stanko, E. A. (1990). *Everyday violence: How women and men experience sexual and physical danger.* London, UK: Pandora.

Stein, E. (Ed.). (1992). *Forms of desire: Sexual orientation and the social constructionist controversy.* New York, NY: Routledge.

Stotzer, R. L. (2008). Gender identity and hate crimes: Violence against transgender people in Los Angeles County. *Sexuality Research and Social Policy, 5*(1), 43–52.

Stotzer, R. L. (2009). Violence against transgender people: A review of United States data. *Aggression and Violent Behavior, 14*(3), 170–179.

Szasz, T. S. (1970). *Ideology and insanity.* New York, NY: Doubleday.

Tardieu, A. (1857). *Étude médico-légale sur les attentats aux mœurs [Medico-legal studies of offences against morals].* Paris, FR: Librairie JB Baillière et Fils.

Tarnowski, B. (1886). *Die krankhaften erscheinungen des geschlechtsinnes: Eine forensisch-psychiatrische studien.* Berlin, Germany: Hirschwald.

Taylor, I., Walton, P., & Young, J. (1973). *The new criminology: For a social theory of deviance.* London, UK: Routledge and Kegan Paul.

Tellegen, A. (1985). Structures of mood and personality and their relevance to assessing anxiety with an emphasis on self-report. In A. H. Tuma & J. D. Maser (Eds.), *Anxiety and the anxiety disorders* (pp. 681–706). Hillsdale, NJ: Lawrence Erlbaum Associates.

Thornberry, T. P. (2005). Explaining multiple patterns of offending across the life course and across generations. *Annals of the American Academy of Political and Social Science, 602,* 156–195.

Thornberry, T. P., & Krohn, M. D. (2001). The development of delinquency: An interactional perspective. In S. O. White (Ed.), *Handbook of youth and justice* (pp. 289–305). New York, NY: Plenum.

Thornberry, T. P., & Krohn, M. D. (2005). Applying interactional theory to the explanation of continuity and change in antisocial behavior. In D. P. Farrington (Ed.), *Integrated developmental and life-course theories of offending* (pp. 183–209). New Brunswick, NJ: Transaction.

Thornberry, T. P., Lizotte, A. J., Krohn, M. D., Smith, C. A., & Porter, P. K. (2003). Causes and consequences of delinquency: Findings from the Rochester Youth Development Study. In T. P. Thornberry & M. D. Krohn (Eds.), *Taking stock of delinquency: An overview of findings from contemporary longitudinal studies* (pp. 11–46). New York, NY: Kluwer/Plenum.

Thornberry, T. P., Freeman-Gallant, A., & Lovegrove, P. J. (2009). Intergenerational linkages in antisocial behavior. *Criminal Behaviour and Mental Health, 19,* 80–93.

Turk, A. T. (1966). Conflict and criminality. *American Sociological Review, 31*(3), 338–352.

Turk, A. T. (1969). *Criminality and legal order.* Chicago, IL: Rand McNally and Company.

Turk, A. (1971). *Legal sanctioning and social control.* Washington, DC: Government Printing Office.

Veysey, B. M., & Messner, S. F. (1999). Further testing of social disorganization theory: An elaboration of Sampson and Groves's "community structure and crime". *Journal of Research in Crime and Delinquency, 36*(2), 156–174.

Vold, G. B. (1958). *Theoretical criminology.* New York, NY: Oxford University Press.

Vold, G. B., & Bernard, T. J. (1979). *Theoretical criminology* (2nd ed.). New York, NY: Oxford University Press.

Vold, G. B., & Bernard, T. J. (1986). *Theoretical criminology* (3rd ed.). New York, NY: Oxford University Press.

Waldner-Haugrud, L. K., Gratch, L. V., & Magruder, B. (1997). Victimization and perpetration rates of violence in gay and lesbian relationships: Gender issues explored. *Violence and Victims, 12*(2), 173–184.

Warnke, G. (1999). *Legitimate differences: Interpretation in the abortion controversy and other public debates.* Berkeley, CA: University of California Press.

Weeks, J. (1979). *Coming out: Homosexual politics in Britain, from the nineteenth century to the present.* London, UK: Quartet Books.

Weeks, J. (1981). *Sex, politics, and society: The regulation of sexuality since 1880.* New York, NY: Longman.

Wikström, P.-O. H. (2005). The social origins of pathways in crime: Towards a developmental ecological action theory of crime involvement and its changes. In D. P. Farrington (Ed.), *Integrated developmental and life-course theories of offending* (pp. 211–245). New Brunswick, NJ: Transaction.

Wikström, P.-O. H. (2010). Situational action theory. In F. T. Cullen & P. Wilcox (Eds.), *Encyclopedia of criminological theory.* Thousand Oaks, CA: Sage.

Wolfgang, M. E., & Ferracuti, F. (1967). *The subculture of violence: Towards an integrated theory in criminology.* London, UK: Tavistock Publications.

Woods, J. B. (2013). The birth of modern criminology and gendered constructions of homosexual criminal identity. *Journal of Homosexuality* (forthcoming).

Woods, J. B. (2014). Queer contestations and the future of a "queer" criminology. *Critical Criminology: An International Journal* (special issue on "Queer/ing criminology: New directions and frameworks") (forthcoming).

Woody, G. E., Donnell, D., Seage, G. R., Metzger, D., Marmor, M., Koblin, B. A., et al. (1999). Non-injection substance use correlates with risky sex among men having sex with men: Data from HIVNET. *Drug and Alcohol Dependence, 53*(3), 197–205.

Young, J. (1986). The failure of criminology: The need for radical realism. In R. Matthews & J. Young (Eds.), *Confronting crime* (pp. 4–30). London, UK: Sage.

Young, J. (1999). *The exclusive society: Social exclusion, crime and difference in late modernity.* Thousand Oaks, CA: SAGE.

Young, J., & Matthews, R. (Eds.). (1992). *Rethinking criminology: The realist debate.* London, UK: Sage.

Part II
LGBT Communities, Crime, and Victimization

Chapter 3
Bias Crimes Based on Sexual Orientation and Gender Identity: Global Prevalence, Impacts, and Causes

Rebecca L. Stotzer

Abstract This chapter highlights the high rates of sexual orientation and/or gender identity (SOGI) motivated bias crimes faced by LGBT people around the world. Research consistently demonstrates that the prevalence of SOGI-motivated bias crimes is distressingly high, the consequences of this type of violence and harassment are particularly severe, and that the risk factors for victimization are often beyond the control of the victim/s. Given the unique differences between sexual orientation-motivated and gender-identity motivated bias crimes, the unique features of these separate forms of bias are discussed. This chapter also explores existing theories that attempt to explain how and why bias crimes occur, examining individual, interpersonal, and sociocultural explanations for SOGI-motivated bias crimes.

Keywords Bias crimes · Corrective rape · Levin & McDevitt's typology of bias crime perpetrators · Gay pride parades · Gayborhoods · Indigenous people · Internalized homophobia · LGBT homicides · Office for Democratic Institutions and Human Rights (ODIHR) · Organization for Security and Cooperation in Europe (OSCE) · "Peter meter" study · Sex workers · Well-being

Violence against LGBT people is a global issue. Some countries have elected to address this violence, along with other types of prejudice-motivated violence, by passing bias or "hate" crime laws. Despite differences in definitions across jurisdictions, the Organization for Security and Cooperation in Europe (OSCE) and the Office for Democratic Institutions and Human Rights (ODIHR) outline two basic features of bias crimes: (1) there has been a base offense (e.g., vandalism, assault, etc.), and (2) that bias was a motive for the crime. This means that "the

R. L. Stotzer (✉)
Myron B. Thompson School of Social Work, University of Hawai'i, Mānoa,
1800 East–West Road, Henke Hall Room 227, Honolulu HI 96822, USA
e-mail: rstotzer@hawaii.edu

D. Peterson and V. R. Panfil (eds.), *Handbook of LGBT Communities, Crime, and Justice*, DOI: 10.1007/978-1-4614-9188-0_3, © Springer Science+Business Media New York 2014

perpetrator intentionally chose the *target* of the crime because of some *protected characteristic…*" and that unlike victims of other types of crime, bias crime victims "are selected on the basis of *what* they represent rather than *who* they are" (OSCE/ODIHR 2009, p. 16–17). The majority of countries *have not* addressed SOGI-motivated violence through the enactment of bias crime laws. As of 2008, only 12 of the 56 OSCE participating countries had legislation that addressed sexual orientation bias (Human Rights First 2008). Nations have also chosen to cover different social identity statuses. Race, ethnicity, and nationality are frequently covered social categories, while sexual orientation and gender identity (SOGI) are less frequently included (OSCE/ODIHR 2009). Although bias crime statutes may not be a culturally appropriate response for all countries, enacting these laws has frequently led to better data collection and monitoring of SOGI-motivated violence.

The purpose of this chapter is to discuss available evidence of SOGI-motivated violence around the world. For the purpose of this chapter, bias crime as a concept is discussed, including evidence from those nations that do not have formal bias crime statutes, but that have conducted surveys about bias-motivated crimes. This chapter will include data available about prevalence, impacts to victims and their communities, information about perpetrators, and the potential causes of bias crimes. Given the nature of existing research and legal infrastructure, most empirical studies have been conducted in Europe, the United States, Canada, Australia, and New Zealand. However, whenever possible, research on the global nature of SOGI-motivated violence will be included. Also given the limited nature of available evidence, since systematic research on SOGI-motivated violence has only been conducted since the late 1980s, most research discussed in this chapter was gathered since 1995. This naturally limits the available information to a limited cohort of LGBT people and does not reflect the SOGI-motivated violence prior to the redefinition of prejudice-motivated crime as bias crime. This limitation also does not allow for a nuanced discussion of how risk, consequences, and explanations for bias crime may change over time, despite evidence that looking more closely at cohorts of LGBT people and their peers is an increasingly critical area of research (Martin and D'Augelli 2009). This chapter can only offer a snapshot of the current evidence of SOGI-motivated violence. However, historic violence prior to the emergence of the bias crime concept has been documented in other sources (e.g., Fone 2000).

Prevalence of SOGI-Motivated Violence

Before beginning any discussion of prevalence of SOGI-motivated violence, issues with data collection efforts should be acknowledged. One of the most significant issues in current attempts to research bias crime is the significant lack of reliable and accurate data. This data challenge is due in no small part to the justifiable reluctance of LGBT people to report their experiences of violence to police based on routine maltreatment at the hands of law enforcement officials. In a study of transphobia in the European Union, the vast majority of transgender respondents reported that they were not confident in the response of the police (Turner et al. 2009). Across the globe, reporting rates are distressingly low: 75 % of the victims of homophobic hate crime in the UK (Dick 2008), 60 % in Sweden (Swedish National Council for Crime Prevention [SNCCP] 2012), and 90 % in Germany (MANEO 2007) did not report acts of homophobic violence to the police. Among the crime types least reported, 97 % were harassment and/or insults, but a number of physically violent crimes were also not reported, including 56 % of crimes involving bodily harm, and 31 % of those crimes that involved grievous bodily harm (MANEO 2007).

Other factors related to whether or not victims will go to police is their belief that their complaint will be taken seriously and whether or not the perpetrators will be punished (i.e., Herek et al. 2002; MANEO 2007), similar to the reasons why people do not report rape, domestic violence, and other stigmatized crimes. Unfortunately, this has not been the case for many LGBT victims. One transgender respondent said, "After an assault I reported I was not given the opportunity to make a statement or even given a crime number... so they did not treat the assault as a crime. I felt they either thought I deserved the attack because I am transsexual or I brought the attack on myself because I am transsexual" (Turner et al. 2009). In South Africa, Black South African lesbians and transgender men reported that police rarely prevented violence or promoted feelings of safety for them, and often taunted them, their family members, and friends (Human Rights Watch 2011). There has been little research into arrests and prosecutions of bias crime perpetrators and their prosecution. In the United Kingdom for the year 2009–2010, the Crown Prosecution Service received cases with 1,373 defendants of homophobic and transphobic bias crimes, and prosecuted 76 % of them, with an 82 % success rate (Williams 2012). This was similar to race-motivated offenses, in which 84 % of defendants were prosecuted, though in both cases how many of these were successful prosecutions of the base crime (e.g., assault) versus the aggravating circumstance (e.g., race or sexual orientation) is unclear. Byers et al. (2009) found in the 2001 National Prosecutor's Survey in the U.S. that bias crimes were under-prosecuted, while other research in the U.S. has suggested that bias crimes are referred for prosecution at rates similar to other types of crime (Jenness and Grattet 2004; Phillips 2009).

Despite this scarcity of consistent and reliable reporting to official law enforcement sources, data available from governments, public interest groups, and community surveys have found that SOGI-motivated bias crimes are particularly violent, prevalent, and harmful to victims compared to other types of crime. Given the frequently stigmatized nature of LGBT identities, often these populations are hard to reach and "hidden." Thus, sampling has been a consistent issue in the surveying efforts, with most surveys utilizing convenience samples collected through colleges or universities, or through LGBT centers and programs (see, too, discussion by Messinger, this volume). This inherently leads to bias in the "type" of LGBT person who is included, and most clearly excludes those who are less clearly identified, less able/willing to access resources, and/or isolated. Studies have also faced measurement issues, most problematically being the definition of "LGBT." This is most often measured by how people self-identify, sexual practices, or sexual desires, but evidence suggests that these three types of inclusion criteria generate very different results (e.g., Gates 2012). Also included in measurement issues is the nature of defining bias crimes themselves. Most frequently, questions ask about experiences of certain acts (e.g., being physically attacked, having property destroyed, being verbally harassed) without sufficient evidence to determine if this incident would rise to the level of prosecutable "crime" by current legal standards. Thus, many surveys of LGBT violence reflect bias "incidents" rather than bias "crimes."

Despite these methodological limitations, research in the last few decades has demonstrated consistent evidence of LGBT people facing significant discrimination, harassment, and violence. Although sharing similar etiology, sexual orientation and gender identity bias crimes have been found to be quantitatively and qualitatively different, and thus will be discussed separately.

Bias Crimes Based on Sexual Orientation

A limited number of countries have specific law enforcement bias crime tracking and reporting. For example, in 2010 there were 1,470 crimes motivated by sexual orientation reported to police in the United States (FBI 2011), and 218 in Canada (Dowden and Brennan 2012). Of these, crimes based on sexual orientation were particularly violent, with over 50 % of crimes in the U.S. and 65 % of crimes in Canada reported to police containing elements of physical violence (such as murder, assault, or sexual assault). In addition, crimes based on sexual orientation that were reported to U.S. and Canadian law enforcement officials were also more likely to have resulted in physical injury (Dowden and Brennan 2012; FBI 2011) while Sweden officials reported more unlawful threat and non-sexual molestation (47 %) compared to violent crime (22 %; SNCCP 2012). However, official data are often cited as being at best a severe undercount of bias-motivated crimes in any jurisdiction (e.g., Wolf Harlow 2006).

Although official sources often report lower levels of crime than non-governmental sources, reports by NGOs, government surveys, and academic research tell a similar story. In the United Kingdom, the Stonewall Survey found that one in eight lesbian or gay people have been victims of bias crimes in the last year and one out of every six of those crimes was a physical assault (Dick 2008). In Ireland, 80 % of LGBT people reported experiencing verbal abuse and 25 % reported physical abuse because of their sexual orientation or gender identity (Mayock et al. 2009). In the only national probability sample of LGBT people, Herek (2009) found that 25 % of self-identified LGBT people in the United States reported being victims of crime or attempted crime motivated by sexual orientation. Japan does not have bias crime laws, but 20.5 % of LGBT respondents in an online survey in Japan reported that they had experienced gay bashing (DiStefano 2006). Finally, Katz-Wise and Hyde (2012) performed a meta-analysis on over 300 studies of 18 countries which included over half a million people who self-identified as sexual minorities. Although they did not distinguish between bias-motivated and non-bias motivated violence among 24 measures of victimization experiences, they found that LGB people report significantly more violence than heterosexuals (Katz-Wise and Hyde 2012). Taken together, these studies suggest high rates of prejudice-motivated violence targeting lesbian, gay, and bisexual men and women across different regions and utilizing a variety of research methodologies.

Sexual orientation-motivated bias crime characteristics. Sexual orientation-based bias crimes in Sweden (Roxell 2011; SNCCP 2012) and the United States (Herek et al. 1997; Kuehnle and Sullivan 2001) were more likely to be violent than non-bias motivated crimes, and violent crimes frequently happened in public places and were perpetrated by strangers. In Germany, a survey of 24,000 gay and bisexual youths and adults in 2006/2007 revealed that almost 40 % of those questioned had experienced bias-motivated violent acts in the past 12 months, most incidents involved multiple perpetrators, and over 70 % of perpetrators were strangers to the victims (MANEO 2007). Although non-bias crimes often involve a perpetrator who is a stranger as well, bias crimes have strangers as perpetrators in far greater proportions than non-bias crimes (Levin and McDevitt 1993), just as they are more likely to involve multiple perpetrators than non-bias crimes. In Sweden, 45 % of offenders had at least one prior conviction (not necessarily hate-related; Roxell 2011), as did those in Johannesburg, South Africa (Reid and Dirsuweit 2002), suggesting that perpetrators were crime "generalists" rather than bias crime "specialists."

In one of the few studies that compares anti-gay bias related homicides to general homicides of men, scholars in New South Wales, Australia, found that gay homicides were more likely to involve one victim with multiple perpetrators, to involve victims 50 years old and older, to be perpetrated by a friend or acquaintance, more likely to involve a knife, blunt object, or hands and feet (as opposed to a shooting), and more likely to occur in the street or an open space than heterosexual male homicides (Mouzos and Thompson 2000). A similar study comparing anti-LGB homicide and non-bias homicides in the U.S. found that anti-LGB homicides were mostly committed by young men, less likely to involve a gun, and more likely to be committed in a group (Gruenewald 2012). Taken together, these studies suggest that bias crimes based on sexual orientation are likely to be particularly violent, to disproportionately happen in public places, to be committed by strangers who have a history of prior criminal activity, and to have perpetrators acting as a group.

Differences between men and women in sexual orientation-motivated bias crime. In many places around the globe, gay men have been found to be more frequent victims of sexual orientation-motivated physical violence than lesbians or bisexuals, including in the United States (Herek 2009; NCAVP 2012), Mexico

(Ortiz-Hernández and Torres 2005), Sweden (Roxell 2011), Britain (Dick 2008), and Hong Kong (Stotzer and Lau 2012). In 2011, the Swedish National Council for Crime Prevention (2012) in a mix of police reports and survey results found that over 850 crimes based on sexual orientation had happened in Sweden, and that gay men are victims of bias crimes twice as often as lesbians. In the United States, gay men have also been found to be 2.6 times more likely to be victims of physical violence than lesbians (Stotzer 2012). Additional research suggests that men are more likely to be alone and assaulted by a stranger in the UK while lesbians are more likely to be with their partner and/or children (Dick 2008), and that lesbians are more likely than gay men to be sexually assaulted by a family member (Rose and Mechanic 2002). Gay men are more likely to be victimized in public places that are "gay-identified" while lesbians are more likely to be victimized in private settings in the U.S. (Comstock 1991). However, some have suggested that different rates of SO-motivated victimization among men may be due to methodological issues in the ways that men and women respond to questions about violence (e.g., Faulkner 2006) rather than differences in men's and women's experiences of violence.

The issue of differences between men and women becomes even more complicated when comparing lesbians and gay men to bisexual men and women. However, the unique experiences of bisexuals are severely understudied. Studies often lump lesbian/bisexual women and gay/bisexual men together, providing information about SOGI-motivated violence risk for men and women, but not for gay/lesbians separate from bisexuals. The studies that have separated bisexuals have demonstrated mixed results. For example, Herek et al. (2009) found that lesbians, bisexual men, and bisexual women all reported similar rates of victimization, while gay men reported the highest rates of bias-motivated crime and attempted crime in their national probability sample of the United States. In contrast, in an earlier study in California, Herek et al. (1999) found that being a sexual minority man was more related to victimization than being a sexual minority woman, but that bisexual men reported similar victimization (27 %) as gay men (28 %), which was more than lesbians (19 %) or bisexual women (15 %). Still another study of sexual orientation minority men (Huebner et al. 2004) found no differences between gay and bisexual men in verbal harassment or discrimination, but more bisexual men reported experiencing anti-gay physical violence (8.2 %) than did gay men (4.1 %). Particularly in light of the emerging evidence that bisexuals face even greater risk than lesbians or gay men for a variety of negative mental health outcomes and overall well-being (Jorm et al. 2002), increased research on the role of different types of sexual orientation in sexual orientation-motivated bias crimes is needed.

Risk factors for sexual orientation-motivated bias crime. Visibility is an important component of SO-motivated violence. Because sexual orientation is concealable (it is not associated with specific phenotypes), individuals looking to gay bash need signs to determine someone's sexual orientation. For example, there are numerous documented cases of people taunting, threatening, and assaulting participants or spectators at gay pride parades (e.g., in Bulgaria, Croatia, Czech Republic, Estonia, Hungary, Latvia, Moldova, Poland, Romania, the Russian

Federation, Slovenia; Human Rights First 2008). Being "out of the closet" and more strongly affiliated with LGBT-organizations have also been found to be related to reports of experiencing violence (Waldner and Berg 2008). However, some research has found although the highest *counts* of SOGI-motivated bias crimes were in gayborhoods and other gay-identified areas, poverty, density of businesses, and other economic factors were better predictors of *rates* of SOGI-motivated bias crimes rather than LGB-residential density/concentration (Stotzer 2010). This suggests that bias crimes may be highest not only where targets are concentrated, but also where they are *available* and *identifiable.*

There is also some evidence that "stereotypical" gay men (who act femininely) or lesbians (who act manly) may provoke the most animosity (Lehavot and Lambert 2007) compared to those who are more "straight-acting." This coincides with research that suggests people whose sexual identity "shows" reported higher levels of sexual orientation-motivated violence than those whose sexual orientation was not as clear (Tiby 2001). Multiple studies have also found that racial/ethnic minority LGBT people may be more at risk of bias crime victimization (e.g., Dick 2008; NCAVP 2012; Nel and Judge 2008) including particularly vulnerable racial/ethnic minorities such as indigenous peoples (Lampinen et al. 2008; Mason 1997). However, there is also evidence that racial/ethnic minorities are less likely than racial/ethnic majority group members to report bias crime of any type, including bias crimes based on sexual orientation (Zaykowski 2010). Thus, determining the intersectionality of identities and the ways in which race/ethnicity and sexual orientation interact is a critical area in need of future research.

Bias Crimes Based on Gender Identity

Violence against transgender people across the globe has also been found to be persistent and severe, but even more poorly researched or documented than SO-motivated crimes. Non-governmental sources have provided the best evidence to date of the violence against transgender people. For example, a study of transphobic bias crimes among over 2,500 transgender people across the European Union found that 70 % of respondents reported experiencing some type of verbal or physical violence because of their gender identity (Turner et al. 2009). The majority of these incidences were verbal harassment, but 7 % reported being victims of GI-motivated physical assault and 2 % GI-motivated sexual assault. Among 253 transgender people in Australia and New Zealand, 19 % reported that they had been physically attacked because of their gender identity (Couch et al. 2007). In a systematic review of violence against transgender people in the United States reported in community assessments, official police reports, and social service agencies' reports, Stotzer (2009) found that studies generally reported that between 25 and 50 % of respondents had been victims of GI-motivated physical attacks, roughly 15 % reported being victims of sexual assault/rape, and over 80 % had reported being victims of verbal abuse motivated by their gender identity. In addition, existing research suggests that transgender people suffer from bias-motivated violence at rates even higher than LGB people (e.g., Browne and Lim 2008; Idaho Tobacco Prevention and Control Program 2004; Turner et al. 2009), including being at heightened risk of being murdered (NCAVP 2012).

Gender identity-based bias crime characteristics. Given the limited availability of research on violence against transgender people, identifying clear GI-bias crime characteristics is an ongoing challenge. In a review of research on GI-motivated violence in the United States, there was no clear consensus on perpetrators—the evidence showed a wide variety of responses, including family members, strangers, colleagues, even friends (Stotzer 2009). There is also evidence across Europe that transwomen (as opposed to transmen) are more at risk of experiencing GI-motivated violence (Turner et al. 2009), which has also been found in the U.S. (Stotzer 2008), though that evidence has been mixed (Stotzer 2009). Bias crimes based on gender identity frequently occur in public areas such as streets, sidewalks, parking lots or garages, or while in transit on a bus, train, or in a taxi (Gorton 2011). Similar to bias crimes based on sexual orientation, perpetrators tend to be male (Stotzer 2008) and to have a high frequency of multiple perpetrators involved in the crime.

Risk factors for gender identity-based bias crimes. In the United States, NGOs have found that racial/ethnic minority MTF transgender people are at particular risk of victimization compared to other LGBT people, and at particular risk of being murdered (NCAVP 2012). Visibility also appears to be an important predictor of violence: only 27 % of transgender people in the United Kingdom who chose to live in their acquired gender permanently had *not* experienced any type of verbal or physical harassment (Whittle et al. 2007). Violence against transgender people seems to be particularly high when engaged with sex work (Betron and Gonzalez-Figueroa 2009; Stotzer 2009; see too Nichols, this volume), although the violence based on gender identity is difficult to clearly disentangle from the violence motivated by status as sex workers. For example, among 304 transvestis engaged in sex work in Brazil, 91 % reported that they had experienced homophobia, and 61 % were victims of violence (Martins et al. 2013). In a study of 474 transgender women in Thailand, 26.4 % had experienced sexual coercion at some point in their lives (Guadamuz et al. 2011), which was a statistically significant higher rate than MSM (19.4 %) or male sex workers (12.2 %). Similar to sexual orientation-motivated crimes at gay pride parades around the globe, sex work increases visibility, and thus increases the probability of gender identity motivated violence. Less is known about transgender people who either live in a second or third gender part time (such as cross-dressers or drag kings/queens), or those who transition fully into another sex (such as post-operative transsexuals) who "pass" more readily and who may no longer consider themselves transgender.

Impacts of SOGI-Motivated Violence on Well-Being

SOGI-motivated bias crimes are clearly prevalent, violent, and can have significant impacts on the lives of victims, as well as on their friends, families, and communities. For example, research among transgender people has found that experiencing gender identity-motivated abuse was related to an increase in depressive symptoms (Couch et al. 2007; Rotondi et al. 2011), increased sexual risk behaviors (Nuttbrock et al. 2013), increased symptoms of anxiety (Lombardi 2007), and increased suicidal ideation, suicide attempt, and substance abuse (Testa et al. 2012). Experiencing sexual orientation-motivated verbal harassment or bullying has been found to increase suicide risk among Japanese gay, bisexual, or questioning men (Hidaka and Operario 2006), increase depression among gay men and lesbians in Guateng, South Africa (Polders et al. 2008) and affect the overall mental health of gays and lesbians in Chile, including increasing rates of depression and perceptions of hostility, and decreasing psychological well-being (Gómez and Barrientos Delgado 2012). In Canada, 33 % of two spirit men reported being gay bashed (Monette et al. 2001), and in Australia, reports of sexual assaults against indigenous gay men and transgender people have been cited as having significant impacts on identity development, particularly among indigenous youth in rural areas (Lee 1998).

People who have experienced bias crimes have been found to be more angry and fearful, less inclined to think of people as being benevolent, to express more depressive symptoms, and to feel more at risk in the future than those who had experienced a similar crime without the bias motive (Herek et al. 1999). There is also preliminary evidence of gender differences in the experience of bias-motivated violence. Stotzer and Lau (2012) found that in Hong Kong, gay/bisexual men experienced more SO-motivated violence than lesbian/bisexual women, but that women had higher rates of internalized homophobia ("the gay person's direction of negative social attitudes toward the self, leading to a devaluation of the self and resultant internal conflicts and poor self-regard"; Meyer and Dean 1998, p. 161). In a study of Dutch LGBs, Kuyper and Fokkema (2011) found that experiencing homonegativity had different impacts for gays/lesbians compared to bisexuals, such that bisexuals' mental health was more significantly impacted by their experiences. This evidence suggests that regardless of location, experiencing SOGI-motivated violence is related to psychological and behavioral impacts that can further impair the health and well-being of LGBT people.

Research has also found that experiencing bias crime, or fearing bias crime victimization, can cause LGBT people to alter their behavior in significant ways. The crux of these strategies was to (a) not be recognizable as an LGBT person, and (b) to limit interactions with potential perpetrators. In every survey in every country that asked questions about perceived safety, all reported that LGBT persons engaged in a variety of behavior modifications. This finding was consistent for LGB people: The British Crime Survey found that SO-motivated bias crime victims were more likely to avoid certain areas (Dick 2008). Tiby (2001) found that victims of sexual orientation-motivated bias crime in Stockholm were far more likely than victims of non-SO-motivated crime to employ safety strategies such as avoiding "looking gay," avoiding buses or subways, avoiding showing affection to their partner in certain spaces, and avoiding alcohol consumption in public. Faulkner (2006) found that in Canada, data were unclear whether women experienced the same amount or less victimization than men, but that lesbian/bisexual women reported greater changes to their behaviors to avoid future victimization. Behavior modification to decrease risk of victimization was also true among transgender people: Transgender respondents in Australia and New Zealand also say that fear for their safety causes them to modify their behaviors (Couch et al. 2007) and in the UK, transgender people were more likely than LGBs to say that they avoided going out at night and avoided public displays of affection (Browne and Lim 2008).

Less research has focused on how victimization has impacted the family, friends, and communities of LGBT people. Meyer and Dean (1998) highlight how experiences of stigma, devaluation, and even violence can lead to increased levels of internalized homophobia. This internalized homophobia in turn was associated with decreases in likelihood of being partnered and reporting more sex problems, suggesting that bias crimes can impact relationships. A study of transgender people in the Midwestern United States also found that among those who reported experiencing gender-identity related abuses, 45 % reported that this experience had either damaged or ended a relationship with a significant other (FORGE 2005).

The knowledge that visibility of SOGI identity increases risk also impacted the willingness to, and methods by which, LGBT people engaged in political activity in their communities (Levitt et al. 2009). A study that researched LGBT people in U.S. states that were considering LGBT civil rights legislation found perceived increased safety risk related to visibility, and LGBT people and their families demonstrated higher levels of psychological distress than those people and families in states not debating LGBT civil rights issues (Arm et al. 2009; Rostosky et al. 2009). In the Ukraine, many transgender people reported not participating in any social or political activity for fear of being identified and subsequently victimized (Insight 2010).

Bias crimes have also been found to impact the community that a victim represents (e.g., Boeckmann and Turpin-Petrosino 2002) and the larger community. In a study of seven different groups (e.g., Asians, people of Jewish faith, LGBT people, etc.) who were surveyed about how they felt when they heard about bias crimes in their community, participants reported similar responses to those who are directly victimized, namely fear/vulnerability, shock, anger, and a sense of their groups' inferiority (Perry and Alvi 2011). These impacts extend beyond the LGBT communities; Silverschanz et al. (2008) found that among college students, those who reported hearing more derogatory language targeting LGBT people reported worse psychological and academic outcomes. This impact was detected amongst LGBT people, but *also heterosexual people*, suggesting that expressions of bias impact everyone in a community, not just those who are the target of abuse or violence.

Explaining SOGI-Motivated Bias Crimes

Given the lack of consistent governmental tracking, research on bias crimes has primarily focused on cataloging prevalence and unique characteristics. This focus on problem description has resulted in accusations that bias crime research is problematically atheoretical (Perry 2001, 2003). As stated by Perry, "in the absence of empirical information about bias-motivated violence, it is difficult to construct conceptual frameworks. Without the raw materials, there is no foundation for theorizing" (2003, p. 16). Most attempts to explain SOGI-motivated bias crimes have come out of the U.S. due to their comparatively early entry into data collection efforts. Therefore, it must be kept in mind that these explanations are necessarily culturally bound and may not explain SOGI-motivated bias crimes around the globe. Beyond the impact and importance of culture, it is also important to note that most attempts at explaining SOGI-motivated bias crimes have in fact examined data specific to LGB people. Information about transgender people has been largely absent from the process of testing hypotheses that explain the causes of SO-versus GI-related bias crimes.

One of the earliest attempts to understand the reasons why bias crimes occurred was the creation of a typology of perpetrators, developed by Levin and McDevitt (1993; and later McDevitt et al. 2002) on bias crimes in general, not LGBT bias crimes in particular. They found that the majority of bias crimes were not perpetrated by "mission-oriented" perpetrators (those in hate or supremacist groups). Instead, they found that the majority of crimes were committed by young people, typically men, looking for a "good time" and a way to interact and gain esteem among their peers (those they called "thrill-seekers"). They also found that some bias crimes were committed based on a need to "defend" something that was changing (such as the definition of marriage) or some perception of lost turf (such as loss of heterosexual power or patriarchy). Other crimes could be explained as retaliation for perceived wrongs (such as attacks on Muslim Mosques post-9/11). This typology provided a framework for many attempts to match the causes of bias crimes, and can be divided into three main approaches: (1) individualistic explanations, (2) interpersonal explanations, and (3) sociocultural explanations.

Individualistic Explanations

One of the more in/famous theories about why people victimize LGBT people is based on the theory that the perpetrators are attempting to suppress their own homosexual desire by assaulting the object of their "inappropriate" affection. This theory was stimulated in part by the "peter meter" study (Adams et al. 1996), which measured the turgidity of participants' penises when exposed to a variety of stimuli, including homosexual pornography. Interestingly, those that had the top scores in rating their homophobia and negative affect toward homosexuals also had the highest turgidity ratings, suggesting sexual arousal.

Another theory to explain SOGI-motivated bias crime is to link bias crimes with personal prejudices, attitudes, homophobia, or transphobia, similar to Levin and McDevitt's typology conceptualization of a "mission" oriented bias crime offender. For example, in a study of hate crime perpetrators in general, Dunbar (2003) found that those perpetrators who exhibited more signs of bias also demonstrated more planning, and were more interested in attaining a sense of social dominance than monetary/personal gain from their crime. Parrott and Peterson (2008) also found that those with high levels of sexual prejudice had an increased likelihood of past acts of anti-gay aggression. However, psychological research has demonstrated repeatedly that attitudes rarely predict behavior, and in this case, homophobia has not generally been found to explain aggressive behavior as effectively as other factors (such as anger proneness, gender role beliefs, and/or concerns around masculinity), or homophobia in combination with those other factors, such as a man who has high anger proneness, is homophobic, and has concerns about his ability to demonstrate his masculinity (e.g., Franklin 2000; Parrott et al. 2008). Other individual explanations have suggested that fears of appearing feminine (e.g., Parrott et al. 2008), low autonomy (van der Meer 2003), distorted cognitions about social realities (Sun 2006), and having anger issues (Parrot 2009; Rayburn and Davison 2002) may play a role in determining who, where, and when SOGI-motivated bias crimes occur.

Interpersonal Explanations

Interpersonal explanations have offered the most concrete explanations for Levin and McDevitt's "thrill-seeking" perpetrators. Franklin (2000) surveyed six different community colleges to learn about sexual orientation-motivated bias crime perpetrators in the San Francisco area of the United States. She found that in this community sample, 10 % of the sample admitted to physically assaulting or threatening people whom they believed were lesbian, gay, or bisexual, and another 23.5 % reported verbally abusing those they perceived as LGB, despite relatively positive attitudes overall toward LGB people. More specifically, *peer dynamics* was reported as the primary reason why people offended, followed by anti-gay ideology, then thrill-seeking. In a study of "gay bashers" in the Netherlands, van Der Meer (2003) found that bashers were predominantly young men who saw gay bashing in front of other men as a means of achieving a masculine status. Because masculinity is more fragile in many cultures than femininity, violence against LGBT people can be considered a form of group performance (Bufkin 1999) to engage in, earn, and demonstrate masculinity and heterosexuality (Perry 2001). In fact, a strong desire to prove masculinity to friends has been found to be associated with more frequent perpetration of anti-gay aggression (Parrott and Peterson 2008). However, these theories of demonstrating masculinity are based largely in a Western conception of appropriate gender roles for men and women. More research is needed to understand the different experiences of men and women (and in particular bisexuals) in regard to SOGI-motivated bias crimes, and how cultural expectations of gender role enactment play a role in bias crime. More research is also needed to tease apart how these forces might explain the high rates of physical violence based on gender identity compared to sexual orientation.

Conversely, rather than performing one's own gender/sexuality, emerging research suggests that some SOGI-motivated bias crimes are utilized to correct unwanted behavior in others. This research suggests that gay men are targeted to "teach them to be real men" while women are targeted to "correct" a woman's sexual orientation and make them available for men (Daley et al. 2007; Human Rights Watch 2011). In interviews conducted by Human Rights Watch in South Africa with Black South African lesbians, anti-lesbian crimes were endorsed by their community, and that men who rape lesbians (also called "corrective rape") are treated "like heroes. They applaud them … [they] are free and threaten to repeat what they did to [my friend] and do the same to every lesbian" (Human Rights Watch 2011, p. 29).

Although often called "hate crimes," some researchers have argued that perpetrators are not "haters," but are enacting a more subtle interaction between (a) societal messages that devalue and scapegoat certain members of society, and (b) a culture's strict rules about patriarchy, appropriate gender roles and expectations for men and women (and subsequent homophobia) that create an environment ripe for victimizing LGBT people (e.g., Herek 1992). Franklin (1998, p. 7), in her study of bias crime perpetrators, said that "I came to conceptualize the violence not in terms of individual hatred but as an extreme expression of … cultural stereotypes and expectations regarding male and female behaviours … a learned form of social control of deviance rather than a defensive response to personal threat." In fact, there is increasing evidence that perpetrators feel they are acting on behalf of society and have tacit approval (Human Rights Watch 2011; van der Meer 2003). Even in "gay-friendly" countries there is evidence that gender and sexuality norms are powerful forces; situational factors such as peer pressure can trigger negative responses even among those people who espouse tolerant attitudes (Buijs et al. 2011).

Sociocultural Explanations

Sociopolitical, sociocultural factors, and the desire to maintain systems of oppression have also been proposed as explanations for SO-motivated (and more infrequently GI-motivated) bias crimes, but have been infrequently tested. Van Dyke et al. (2001) found in the United States that political opportunity structure, such as the presence of anti-LGBT laws (e.g., sodomy laws) and a conservative legislature, significantly increased the number of sexual orientation-motivated bias crimes. Conversely, they also found that locations that had more protective legislation (e.g., pro-gay civil rights legislation) and more openly gay legislators also reported a higher number of sexual orientation-motivated bias events than those areas without protective legislation or openly gay legislators.

Beyond sociopolitical explanations, socioeconomic factors, such as unemployment rates and other indicators of economic hardship (such as poverty rates) have been linked to sexual orientation-motivated bias crime rates. Alden and Parker (2005) found that attitudes in different cities in the U.S. had a significant impact on the rate of sexual orientation-motivated bias crimes, but through a morality mechanism (people seeing sexual minorities as immoral) rather than gender role ideology (gay/lesbians as failing to live up to gender role expectations) mechanism. They also found that as gender inequality (measured as the difference in incomes between men and women) *decreased*, sexual orientation-motivated bias crimes *increased*. The offered explanation was that when men are in positions of economic power, they did not need to demonstrate their masculinity through violence in order to prove their dominance.

Finally, scholars have suggested that cultural values and explanation of gendered behavior can influence the prevalence of, and ways in which, LGBT people are accepted or denigrated in society. For example, scholars from Asia have proposed that there is less evidence of SOGI-motivated violence in Confucian countries because prejudice against LGBT people is not deeply rooted in religious doctrine, but instead may be seen as a challenge to family integrity (e.g., Chou 2001; Martin 2000). Thus, sexuality and gender variance are not worthy of public derision and annihilation, but are matters of shame and "losing face" (e.g., Liu and Dang 2005; Tang et al. 1997). Similarly, Zanghellini (2013) found that the greater degree of western colonial influence in Hawaii lead to more restrictive policies and denigration of LGBT people than in Tahiti where the colonial influence was less strong and indigenous conceptions of sexuality and gender remained. In another example, many Latino cultures that place value on *machismo* and men having a need for penetrative sex, effeminate men who engage in receptive anal sex may bear the consequences of homophobia more than those in the penetrative role (e.g., Jarama et al. 2005; Sandfort et al. 2007; see also Nichols's discussion of Sri Lanka, this volume). This small sample of studies suggests that culture impacts prejudice and its expressions but is still poorly understood. More research is needed to understand how these larger cultural values across the globe influence SOGI-motivated violence, in prevalence as well in overall characteristics.

Summary of Causes for Bias Crimes

Limited by current data collection efforts, it is challenging to determine if any of these explanations, individualistic, interpersonal, or sociocultural, offers more compelling explanatory power for SOGI-motivated bias crimes. Franklin (1998) suggested that rather than having one causal factor, bias crimes are best viewed as being explained by multiple determinism. In all likelihood, some combination of these factors—perpetrators with certain psychological needs who have an opportunity to target victims sanctioned by society while reinforcing sociocultural norms and systems of oppression—best explains the prevalence, characteristics of, and impact of SOGI-motivated bias crimes.

Discussion and Conclusion

This chapter highlights the high rates of prejudice-motivated violence faced by LGBT people around the world, demonstrating that official counts and surveys from a variety of sources indicate that SOGI-motivated violence is a common occurrence. This means that in addition to any other type of non-bias-motivated violence that LGBT people may face, they face this additional burden of being targets for bias-motivated violence. Though only some nations have chosen to label these SOGI-motivated acts of violence and harassment as "bias crimes," research demonstrates that bias-motivated violence is harmful to victims and their communities. This finding is particularly troubling given that while many countries are moving toward protections for LGBT people, others have increased their persecution of LGBT people. Beyond the scope of this paper are the nations that still criminalize same-sex sexual activity between consenting adults, and the distressing number who punish this contact with death (Ottosson 2009; see too, in this volume, Cobb; DeJong and Long; Pearce and Cooper). While the drive to adopt bias crime laws appears to have slowed down around the globe, the growing number of *nations* that actively persecute LGBT people challenges the definition of bias crimes as something perpetrated by *citizens* alone.

Despite cultural and legal differences in defining bias crimes, clear similarities in SOGI-motivated violence are emerging, although additional research is needed to uncover how culture is related to the ways that prejudice is manifested as well as punished. Crimes motivated both by sexual orientation and gender identity show a high frequency of crimes of physical violence committed by groups of strangers in public places. Limited information on GI-motivated bias crimes suggests that transgender individuals may face even higher levels of violence than LGB people. Visibility (being identifiably LGBT), as well as availability of victims (being out in public), also appear to be key factors in bias crime perpetration. SOGI-motivated bias crimes have also been found to be harmful to direct victims, other LGBT people, their friends and families, as well as their communities as a whole (heterosexuals and LGBT alike). Studies also suggest that rather than one overarching theory to explain all SOGI-motivated bias crimes, an approach that addresses the multiple reasons why bias crimes occur may provider a stronger explanation. This is supported by evidence of individual reasons such as a need to defend against one's own sexual inclinations, interpersonal reasons such as the need for peer approval and proving one's masculinity, and larger sociocultural explanations such as political and economic power. However, these explanations are limited by geography, since most studies have been conducted in occidental countries, and time, since most studies have been conducted only in the last few decades. As research improves, more studies need to examine differences by geography, culture, and time to fully understand the nature of SOGI-motivated bias crimes.

Research into SOGI-motivated violence has improved in the last 30 years, but challenges still remain. The integrity and quality of data collection is an ongoing issue for governments and non-government bodies alike. Although these numerous studies have provided information about sexual orientation-motivated violence against lesbians and gay men, data and theories specific to bisexual or transgender people are significantly lacking. There has also been little research into whether or not bias crime laws are the only legislative option, or if there are other culturally appropriate choices that governments can make to protect people from the harms of SOGI-motivated violence. In particular, there has been little research into prevention and even fewer policies passed that address a more comprehensive approach to prevention strategies rather than focusing on punishment. However, research should continue that contributes to the goal of increased safety for LGBT people around the world.

References

Adams, H. E., Wright, L. W. J., & Lohr, B. A. (1996). Is homophobia associated with homosexual arousal? *Journal of Abnormal Psychology, 105*(3), 440–445.

Alden, H. L., & Parker, K. F. (2005). Gender role ideology, homophobia and hate crime: Linking attitudes to macro-level anti-gay and lesbian hate crimes. *Deviant Behavior, 26*(4), 321–343.

Arm, J. R., Horne, S. G., & Levitt, H. M. (2009). Negotiating connection to GLBT experience: Family members' experience of anti-GLBT movements and policies. *Journal of Counseling Psychology, 56*(1), 82–96.

Betron, M., & Gonzalez-Figueroa, E. (2009). *Gender identity, volence, and HIV among MSM and TG: A literature review and a call for screening.* Washington, DC: Futures Group International, USAID/Health Policy Initiative, Task Order 1.

Boeckmann, R. J., & Turpin-Petrosino, C. (2002). Understanding the harm of hate crime. *Journal of Social Issues, 58*(2), 207–225.

Browne, K., & Lim, J. (2008). *Count me in too: LGBT Lives in Brighton & Hove.* Retrieved from http://www.brighton.ac.uk/cupp/images/stories/projects/c-k-e/LGBTU/CMIT_Safety_Report_ Final_Feb08.pdf.

Bufkin, J. L. (1999). Bias crime as gendered behavior. *Social Justice, 26*(10), 155–176.

Buijs, L., Hekma, G., & Duyvendak, J. W. (2011). As long as they keep away from me: The paradox of antigay violence in a gay-friendly country. *Sexualities, 14*(6), 632–652.

Byers, B. D., Warren-Gordon, K., & Jones, J. A. (2009). Predictors of hate crime prosecutions: An analysis of data from the National Prosecutor's Survey and state-level bias crime laws. *Race & Justice, 2*(3), 203–219.

Chou, W. (2001). Homosexuality and the cultural politics of Tongzhi in Chinese societies. *Journal of Homosexuality, 40*, 27–46.

Comstock, G. D. (1991). *Violence against lesbians and gay men.* New York, NY: Columbia University Press.

Couch, M, et al. (2007). *Tranznation: A report on the health and wellbeing of transgender people in Australia and New Zealand.* Victoria, Australia: Australian Research Centre in Sex, Health, & Society. LaTrobe University.

Daley, A., Solomon, S., Newman, P. A., & Mishna, F. (2007). Traversing the margins: Intersectionalities in the bullying of lesbian, gay, bisexual and transgender youth. *Journal of Gay and Lesbian Social Services, 19*(3/4), 9–29.

Dick, S. (2008). *Homophobic hate crime: The Gay British Crime Survey 2008.* Stonewall. Retrieved from http://www.stonewall.org.uk/.

DiStefano, A. (2006). *Report on violence involving sexual minorities in Japan: Summary and recommendations from the JLGBT Study: 2003–2004 (English version).* San Francisco, CA: Institute for Global Health, University of California.

Dowden, C., & Brennan, S. (2012). Police-reported hate crime in Canada, 2010. *Component of Statistics Canada, catalogue no. 85–002-x, Juristat.*

Dunbar, E. (2003). Symbolic, relational, and ideological signifiers of bias-motivated offenders: Toward a strategy of assessment. *American Journal of Orthopsychiatry, 73*(2), 203–211.

Faulkner, E. (2006). Homophobic sexist violence in Canada: Trends in the experiences of lesbian and bisexual women in Canada. *Canadian Woman Studies/Les Cahiers De La Femme, 25*(1/2), 154–161.

Federal Bureau of Investigation. (2011). *Hate crime statistics, 2010.* Retrieved from http://www.fbi.gov/ucr.

Fone, B. (2000). *Homophobia: A history.* New York, NY: Picador.

FORGE (For Ourselves: Reworking Gender Expression). (2005). *Transgender sexual violence project.*

Franklin, K. (1998). Unassuming motivations: Contextualizing the narratives of antigay assailants. In G. Herek (Ed.), *Stigma and sexual orientation: Understanding prejudice against lesbians, gay men, and bisexuals* (pp. 1–23). Thousand Oaks, CA: Sage.

Franklin, K. (2000). Antigay behaviors among young adults: Prevalence, patterns, & motivators in a noncriminal population. *Journal of Interpersonal Violence, 15*(4), 339–362.

Gates, G. (2012). LGBT identity: A demographer's perspective. *Loyola of Los Angeles Law Review, 45,* 693–714.

Gómez, F., & Barrientos Delgado, J. E. (2012). Efectos del prejuicio sexual en la salud mental de gays y lesbianas, en la ciudad de Antofagasta, Chile. *Sexualidad, Salud, y Sociedad—Revista Latinoamericana, 10,* 100–123.

Gorton, D. (2011). *Anti-transgender hate crimes: The challenge for law enforcement.* Boston, MA: The Anti-Violence Project of Massachusetts.

Grant, J. M., Mottet, L. A., Tanis, J., Harrison, J., Herman, J. L., & Keisling, M. (2011). *Injustice at every turn: A report of the National Transgender Discrimination Survey.* Washington, DC: National Center for Transgender Equality and National Gay and Lesbian Task Force.

Gruenewald, J. (2012). Are anti-LGBT homicides in the United States unique? *Journal of Interpersonal Violence, 27*(18), 3601–3623.

Guadamuz, T. E., Wimonsate, W., Varangrat, A., Phanuphak, P., Jommaroeng, R., Mock, P. A., et al. (2011). Correlates of forced sex among populations of men who have sex with men in Thailand. *Archives of Sexual Behavior, 40*(2), 259–266.

Herek, G. M. (1992). *Hate crimes: Confronting violence against lesbians and gay men.* Newbury Park, CA: Sage.

Herek, G. M. (2009). Hate crimes and stigma-related experiences among sexual minority adults in the United States: Prevalence estimates from a national probability sample. *Journal of Interpersonal Violence, 24,* 54–74.

Herek, G. M., Cogan, J. C., & Gillis, J. R. (2002). Victim experiences in hate crimes based on sexual orientation. *Journal of Social Issues, 58*(2), 319–339.

Herek, G. M., Gillis, R., & Cogan, J. C. (1999). Psychological sequelae of hate crime victimization among lesbian, gay, and bisexual adults. *Journal of Consulting and Clinical Psychology, 67,* 945–951.

Herek, G. M., Gillis, J. R., Cogan, J. C., & Glunt, E. K. (1997). Hate crime victimization among lesbian, gay, and bisexual adults: Prevalence, psychological correlates, and methodological issues. *Journal of Interpersonal Violence, 12*(2), 195–215.

Hidaka, Y., & Operario, D. (2006). Attempted suicide, psychological health and exposure to harassment among Japanese homosexual, bisexual, or other men questioning their sexual orientation recruited via the internet. *Journal of Epidemiology and Community Health, 60,* 962–967.

Huebner, D. M., Rebchook, G. M., & Kegeles, S. M. (2004). Experiences of harassment, discrimination, and physical violence among young gay and bisexual men. *American Journal of Public Health, 94*(7), 1200–1203.

Human Rights First. (2008). *Violence based on sexual orientation and gender identity bias.* Retrieved from http://www.humanrightsfirst.org/our-work/fighting-discrimination/2008-hate-crime-survey/2008-hate-crime-survey-lgbt/i-violence-based-on-sexual-orientationand-gender-identity-bias/

Human Rights Watch. (2011). *"We'll show you you're a woman": Violence and discrimination against black lesbians and transgender men in South Africa.* Retrieved from http://www.hrw.org/reports/2011/12/06/well-show-you-youre-woman

Idaho Tobacco Prevention and Control Program. (2004). *LGBT Health Assessment Survey.* Idaho Department of Health and Welfare.

Insight. (2010). *Situation of transgender persons in the Ukraine: Research Report.* Kyiv, Ukraine.

Jaram, S. L., Kennamer, D., Poppen, P. J., Hendricks, M., & Bradford, J. (2005). Psychosocial, behavioral, and cultural predictors of sexual risk for HIV infection among Latino men who have sex with men. *AIDS and Behavior, 9,* 513–523.

Jenness, V., & Grattet, R. (2004). *Policing hate crime in California.* Berkeley, CA: California Policy Research Center.

Jorm, A. F., Korten, A. E., Rodgers, B., Jacomb, P. A., & Christensen, H. (2002). Sexual orientation and mental health: Results from a community survey of young and middle-aged adults. *British Journal of Psychiatry, 180,* 423–427.

Katz-Wise, S., & Hyde, J. S. (2012). Victimization experiences of lesbian, gay, and bisexual individuals: A meta-analysis. *Journal of Sex Research, 49*(2–3), 142–167.

Kuehnle, K., & Sullivan, A. (2001). Patterns of anti-gay violence: An analysis of incident characteristics and victim reporting. *Journal of Interpersonal Violence, 16*(9), 928–943.

Kuyper, L., & Fokkema, T. (2011). Minority stress and mental health among Dutch LGBs: Examination of differences between sex and sexual orientation. *Journal of Counseling Psychology, 58*(2), 222–233.

Lampinen, T. M., Chan, K., Anema, A., Miller, M. L., Schilder, A. J., Schechter, M. T., et al. (2008). Incidence of and risk factors for sexual orientation-related physical assault among young men who have sex with men. *American Journal of Public Health, 98*(6), 1028–1035.

Lee, G. (1998). *The National Indigenous Gay and Transgender Project: Consultation report and sexual health strategy.* New South Wales, Australia: Australian Federation of AIDS Organizations.

Lehavot, K., & Lambert, A. J. (2007). Toward a greater understanding of antigay prejudice: On the role of sexual orientation and gender role violation. *Basic and Applied Social Psychology, 29*(3), 279–292.

Levin, J., & McDevitt, J. (1993). *Hate crimes: The rising tide of bigotry and bloodshed.* New York, NY: Plenum.

Levitt, H. M., Ovrebo, E., Anderson-Cleveland, M. B., Leone, C., Jeong, J. Y., Arm, J. R., et al. (2009). Balancing dangers: GLBT experience in a time of anti-LGBT legislation. *Journal of Counseling Psychology, 56*(1), 67–81.

Liu, J., & Ding, N. (2005). Reticent poetics, queer politics. *Inter-Asia Cultural Studies, 6,* 30–55.

Lombardi, E. (2007). Substance use treatment experiences of transgender/transsexual men and women. *Journal of LGBT Health Research, 3*(2), 37–47.

MANEO. (2007). Gewalterfahrungen von schwulen und bisexuellen jugendlichen und männern in Deutshland. Retrieved from http://www.maneo.de/.

Martin, F. (2000). Surface tensions: Reading production of Tongzhi in contemporary Taiwan. *GLQ: A Journal of Lesbian and Gay Studies, 6,* 61–86.

Martin, J. I., & D'Augelli, A. R. (2009). Timed lives: Cohort and period effects in research on sexual orientation and gender identity. In W. Meezan & J. I. Martin (Eds.), *Handbook of research with lesbian, gay, bisexual, and transgender populations.* New York, NY: Routledge.

Martins, T. A., Kerr, L. R. F. S., Macena, R. H. M., Mota, R. S., Carneiro, K. L., Gondim, R. C., & Kendall, C. (2013). *Travestis,* an unexplored population at risk of HIV in a large metropolis of northeast Brazil: A respondent-driven sampling survey. *AIDS Care: Psychological and Socio-medical Aspects of AIDS/HIV, 25*(5), 606–612.

Mason, G. (1997). Sexuality and violence: Questions of difference. In C. Cunneen & D. Fraser (Eds.), *Faces of hate: Hate crime in Australia* (pp. 97–114). New South Wales, Australia: Hawkins Press.

Mayock, P., Bryan, A., Carr, N., & Kitching, K. (2009). *Supporting LGBT Lives: A study of the mental health and well-being of lesbian, gay, bisexual, and transgender people*. Ireland: Gay and Lesbian Equality Network (GLEN) and BeLonG to Youth Service.

McDevitt, J., Levin, J., & Bennett, S. (2002). Hate crime offenders: An expanded typology. *Journal of Social Issues, 58*(2), 303–317.

Meyer, I. H., & Dean, L. (1998). Internalized homophobia, intimacy, and sexual behavior among gay and bisexual men. In G. M. Herek (Ed.), *Stigma and sexual orientation: Understanding prejudice against lesbians, gay men, and bisexuals* (pp. 160–186). Thousand Oaks, CA: Sage.

Monette, L., Albert, D., & Waalen, J. (2001). *Voices of two-spirited men: A survey of aboriginal two-spirited men across Canada*. Toronto, Canada: 2-Spirited People of the First Nations.

Mouzos, J., & Thompson, S. (2000). Gay-hate related homicides: An overview of major findings in New South Wales. *Trends and Issues in Crime and Criminal Justice, No. 155*. Retrieved from http://aic.gov.au/.

National Coalition of Anti-Violence Programs. (2012). *Hate violence against lesbian, gay, bisexual, transgender, queer, and HIV-affected communities in the United States in 2011*. Author: Washington, D.C.

Nel, J. A., & Judge, M. (2008). Exploring homophobic victimisation in Gauteng, South Africa: Issues, impacts, and responses. *Acta Criminologica, 21*(3), 19–36.

Nuttbrock, L., Bockting, W., Rosenblum, A., Hwahng, S., Mason, M., Macri, M., & Becker, J. (2013). Gender abuse, depressive symptoms, and HIV and other sexually transmitted infections among male-to-female transgender persons: A three-year prospective study. *American Journal of Public Health, 103*(2), 300–307.

Organization for Security and Cooperation in Europe (OSCE) and Office for Democratic Institutions and Human Rights (ODIHR) (2009). *Hate crime laws: A practical guide*. Retrieved from http://www.osce.org/odihr/36426?download=true.

Ortiz-Hernández, L., & Torres, M. I. G. (2005). Efectos de la violencia y la discriminación en la salud mental de bisexuals, lesbianas, y homosexuals de la Ciudad de México. *Cadernos de Saúde Publica, 21*(3), 913–925. Retrieved from http://www.bvsde.paho.org/.

Ottosson, D. (2009). *State-sponsored homophobia: A world survey of laws prohibiting same sex activity between consenting adults*. The International Lesbian, Gay, Bisexual, Trans and Intersex Association. Retrieved from http://ilga.org/historic/Statehomophobia/ILGA_State_Sponsored_Homophobia_2009.pdf.

Parrott, D. J. (2009). Aggression toward gay men as gender role enforcement: Effects of male role norms, sexual prejudice, and masculine gender role stress. *Journal of Personality, 77*(4), 1137–1166.

Parrott, D. J., & Peterson, J. L. (2008). What motivates hate crimes based on sexual orientation? Mediating effects of anger on antigay aggression. *Aggressive Behavior, 34*, 306–318.

Parrott, D. J., Peterson, J. L., Vincent, W., & Bakeman, R. (2008). Correlates of anger in response to gay men: Effects of male gender role beliefs, sexual prejudice, and masculine gender role stress. *Psychology of Men & Masculinity, 9*(3), 167–178.

Perry, B. (2001). *In the name of hate: Understanding hate crimes*. London, UK: Routledge.

Perry, B. (2003). Where do we go from here?: Researching hate crime. *Internet Journal of Criminology, 3*, 45–47.

Perry, B., & Alvi, S. (2011). 'We are all vulnerable': The *in terrorem* effects of hate crimes. *International Review of Victimology, 18*(1), 57–71.

Phillips, N. (2009). The prosecution of hate crimes: The limitations of the hate crime typology. *Journal of Interpersonal Violence, 24*, 883–905.

Polders, L. A., Nel, J. A., Kruger, P., & Wells, H. L. (2008). Factors affecting vulnerability to depression among gay men and lesbian women in Gauteng, South Africa. *South African Journal of Psychology, 38*(4), 673–687.

Rayburn, N. R., & Davison, G. C. (2002). Articulated thoughts about antigay hate crimes. *Cognitive Therapy and Research, 26*(4), 431–447.

Reid, G., & Dirsuweit, T. (2002). Understanding systemic violence: Homophobic attacks in Johannesburg and its surrounds. *Urban Forum, 13*(3), 99–126.

Rotondi, N. K., Bauer, G. R., Travers, R., Travers, A., Scanlon, K., & Kaay, M. (2011). Depression in male-to-female Ontarians: Results from the Trans PULSE Project. *Canadian Journal of Community Mental Health, 30*(2), 113–133.

Rose, S. R., & Mechanic, M. B. (2002). Psychological distress, crime features, and help-seeking behaviors related to homophobic bias incidents. *American Behavioral Scientist, 46*, 14–26.

Rostosky, S. S., Riggle, E. D. B., Horne, S. G., & Miller, A. D. (2009). Marriage amendments and psychological distress in lesbian, gay, and bisexual (LGB) adults. *Journal of Counseling Psychology, 56*(1), 56–66.

Roxell, L. (2011). Hate, threats, and violence: A register study of persons suspected of hate crimes. *Journal of Scandinavian Studies in Criminology & Crime Prevention, 12*, 198–225.

Sandfort, T. G. M., Melendez, R. M., & Diaz, R. M. (2007). Gender nonconformity, homophobia, and mental distress in Latino gay and bisexual men. *Journal of Sex Research, 44*, 181–189.

Silverschanz, P., Cortina, L. M., Konik, J., & Magley, V. (2008). Slurs, snubs, and queer jokes: Incidence and impact of heterosexist harassment in academia. *Sex Roles, 58*, 79–101.

Stotzer, R. L. (2008). Gender identity and hate crimes: Violence against transgender people in Los Angeles County. *Sexuality Research and Social Policy, 5*(1), 43–52.

Stotzer, R. L. (2009). Violence against transgender people: A review of United States data. *Aggression and Violent Behavior, 14*, 170–179.

Stotzer, R. L. (2010). Seeking solace in West Hollywood: Sexual orientation-based hate crimes in Los Angeles County. *Journal of Homosexuality, 57*, 986–1002.

Stotzer, R. L. (2012). *Comparison of hate crime rates across protected and unprotected groups - An update.* Los Angeles, CA: Williams Institute.

Stotzer, R. L., & Lau, H. S. (2013). Violence based on sexual orientation in Hong Kong. *Asia Pacific Law and Policy Journal, 14*, 84–107.

Sun, K. (2006). The legal definition of hate crime and the hate offender's distorted cognitions. *Issues in Mental Health Nursing, 27*, 597–604.

Swedish National Council for Crime Prevention. (2012). *Hate Crime 2011: Statistics on police reported offences with an identified hate crime motive.* Brå report No 2012:7.

Tang, C. S., Lai, F. D., & Chung, T. K. H. (1997). Assessment of sexual functioning for Chinese college students. *Archives of Sexual Behavior, 26*, 79–90.

Testa, R. J., Sciacca, L. M., Wang, F., Hendricks, M. L., Goldblum, P., Bradford, J., & Bongar, B. (2012). Effects of violence on transgender people. *Professional Psychology: Research and Practice, 43*(5), 452–459.

Tiby, E. (2001). Victimization and fear among lesbians and gay men in Stockholm. *International Review of Victimology, 8*, 217–243.

Turner, L., Whittle, S., & Combs, R. (2009). *Transphobic hate crime in the European Union.* Press for Change. Retrieved from http://www.ucu.org.uk/.

van der Meer, T. (2003). Gay bashing—A rite of passage? *Culture, Health, and Sexuality, 5*(2), 153–165.

Van Dyke, N., Soule, S. A., & Widom, R. (2001). The politics of hate: Explaining variation in the incidence of anti-gay hate crime. *The Politics of Social Inequality, 9*, 35–58.

Waldner, L. K., & Berg, J. (2008). Explaining antigay violence using target congruence: An application of revised routine activities theory. *Violence and Victims, 23*(3), 267–287.

Whittle, S., Turner, L., & Al-Alami, M. (2007). *Engendered penalties: Transgender and transsexual people's experiences of inequality and discrimination.* The Equalities Review. Retrieved from http://www.pfc.org.uk/pdf/EngenderedPenalties.pdf.

Williams, N. (2012). *Hate crime.* CIVITAS Institute for the Study of Civil Society. Retrieved from http://www.civitas.org.uk/crime/factsheet-hatecrime.pdf.

Wolf Harlow, C. (2006). *Hate crime reported by victims and police.* NCJ: Bureau of Justice Statistics Special Report, 209911.

Zanghellini, A. (2013). Sodomy laws and gender variance in Tahiti and Hawai'i. *Laws, 2*, 51–68.

Zaykowski, H. (2010). Racial disparities in hate crime reporting. *Violence and Victims, 25*(3), 378–394.

Chapter 4
Marking 35 Years of Research on Same-Sex Intimate Partner Violence: Lessons and New Directions

Adam M. Messinger

Abstract In 35 years of scholarship, a great deal of valuable information has come to light about same-sex intimate partner violence (SSIPV). The literature reveals many similarities between SSIPV and opposite-sex IPV (OSIPV), including rates of IPV, relative rates of forms of IPV, directionality of physical violence, patterns of control that keep victims silent and trapped, and outcomes for victims. At the same time, theories have been challenged and adapted, and a number of unique aspects of SSIPV have emerged, many revolving around issues pertaining to perceived, experienced, and internalized heterosexism. Considerable gaps have been found to still exist in SSIPV research methodology, prevention and intervention, victim resources, and legal avenues of protection. In reviewing this literature, it is clear that, while much has been gained in knowledge of SSIPV that can and should be put into practice, much important work still needs to be done by scholars, service providers, and policymakers to help make society safer for lesbian, gay, and bisexual people and all sexual minorities.

Keywords Partner violence · Domestic violence · Same-sex · Sexual orientation · Gay · Lesbian

Intimate partner violence (IPV)—verbal abuse, controlling behaviors, physical violence, or sexual violence between current or former intimate partners—is a major public health concern with serious consequences for victims (Wallace 2005; see too Gillum and DiFulvio, this volume). In absolute number of cases, opposite-sex IPV (OSIPV) is more common in the United States than same-sex IPV (SSIPV; for example, see Messinger 2011), not surprising given that the majority of Americans identify as heterosexual (Gates 2011). This statistical reality along with the stereotype that SSIPV is not as serious as OSIPV (e.g., Sorenson and Thomas 2009; Younglove et al. 2002) may help explain why the literature on and

A. M. Messinger (✉)
Northeastern Illinois University, 5500 North St. Louis Ave., Chicago, IL 60625, USA
e-mail: a-messinger@neiu.edu

D. Peterson and V. R. Panfil (eds.), *Handbook of LGBT Communities,*
Crime, and Justice, DOI: 10.1007/978-1-4614-9188-0_4,
© Springer Science+Business Media New York 2014

services for SSIPV are noticeably less robust than those for OSIPV. However, in reviewing the past 35 years of research on SSIPV—its prevalence, dynamics, and victim resources—two points become immediately apparent: SSIPV is just as serious as OSIPV, and there is much more work still to be done to help ensure the safety of lesbian, gay, and bisexual (LGB) people and all sexual minorities.

Prevalence

SSIPV scholarship dates back as early as 35 years ago (Diamond and Wilsnack 1978), with the pioneering books on SSIPV appearing in the 1980s and 1990s with Lobel's (1986) *Naming the Violence: Speaking Out About Lesbian Battering*, Island and Letellier's (1991) *Men Who Beat the Men Who Love Them: Battered Gay Men and Domestic Violence*, and Renzetti's (1992) *Violent Betrayal: Partner Abuse in Lesbian Relationships*. Since that point, a great deal of research has been conducted to estimate the scope of the problem.

Relative Prevalence of Forms of SSIPV

Research shows that, as with OSIPV, the forms of SSIPV that are most common are psychological SSIPV (typically measured as a combination of verbal abuse and controlling behaviors), followed by physical SSIPV, followed by sexual SSIPV (Bimbi et al. 2007; Freedner et al. 2002; Greenwood et al. 2002; Halpern et al. 2001, 2004; Messinger 2011; Turrell 2000; Walters et al. 2013; for exceptions, see Blosnich and Bossarte 2009 and NCAVP 2012).

Psychological IPV occurs in the lifetimes of somewhere between just under one-fifth (Bradford et al. 1994; NCAVP 2012) to as high as 83 % of sexual minorities (Turrell 2000). Physical IPV occurs in the lifetimes of around a third of LGB persons (Turrell 2000; for current and recent physical IPV prevalence rates, see Bimbi et al. 2007; NCAVP 2012). Sexual IPV victimization is experienced by 5 % of LGB people (NCAVP 2012; Greenwood et al. 2002), although rates among sexual minority women are considerably higher than among sexual minority men (Walters et al. 2013). There are approximately seven times as many partner homicides in male same-sex relationships as in female same-sex relationships (Puzone et al. 2000).

Relative Prevalence of SSIPV and OSIPV

Among nationally representative probability samples estimating adult IPV among sexual minorities, the 2010 *National Intimate Partner and Sexual Violence Survey* (NISVS) arguably presents the most reliable estimates, given that it is 10–15 years more recently collected than most other nationally representative studies of its kind and given that it employs a broader definition of an intimate relationship than many studies, capturing both cohabitating and non-cohabitating relationships. According to NISVS, while self-identified lesbian and bisexual women are more likely to experience IPV than heterosexual women and while bisexual men are more likely to experience IPV than heterosexual men, gay men experience similar rates of IPV to heterosexual men (Walters et al. 2013). Thus, with the exception of gay men where rates are comparable to rates for heterosexual men, adult sexual minorities appear to be at greater risk of IPV than heterosexuals. Most older data with adult nationally representative probability samples reveals a similar pattern, with the exception that *all* sexual minorities—whether defined by self-identity or relationship history—are shown in these studies to be at a heightened risk, including gay men (Cameron 2003; Messinger 2011; Tjaden and Thoennes 2000; Tjaden et al. 1999). One additional study (Hughes et al. 2010) showed considerable differences from the rest—while self-identified lesbian and bisexual women were at greater risk of physical IPV victimization than heterosexual women, heterosexual men were at greater risk than not only gay but also bisexual men—but this departure in findings may be in part explained by methodological limitations. More specifically, this particular study is not methodologically comparable to the aforementioned studies given that its survey more narrowly measured physical IPV with such value-laden item wording as "attacked," "beaten," and "badly" (Hughes et al. 2010).

Conversely, among adolescents, analyses of the nationally representative probability sampled *National Longitudinal Study of Adolescent Health* (Add-Health) determined that, as compared to adolescents with an exclusively opposite-sex relationship history, adolescents with an exclusively same-sex relationship history were at similar risk of physical IPV but at lower risk of psychological IPV (Halpern et al. 2001, 2004). Compared to other studies with similarly representative samples, AddHealth represents the most comprehensive picture of adolescent IPV because it utilizes the well-established Conflict Tactics Scale (CTS; Straus and Gelles 1986), which measures IPV solely in terms of tactics used and received that occur in a conflict. While IPV victimization could be defined more narrowly to ensure "play fighting" is omitted, doing so runs the risk of excluding valid IPV victims. Unlike with AddHealth, such narrowed IPV definitions limit the utility of other large-scale studies of adolescent SSIPV. For example, one such study of adolescent SSIPV only categorized violence as IPV if the respondent was willing to identify as being "hurt" as a direct result of the violence (Massachusetts Department of Education 2006), a problematic requirement not only because IPV does not always result in injury but also because whether respondents interpret the outcomes of IPV as injury can be subjectively influenced by a number of factors such as gender identity (see Miller and White 2003). Likewise, another study of adolescent SSIPV required that, to be termed an IPV victim, the respondent must have experienced violence during a fight initiated by the partner (Rhodes et al. 2009), despite research indicating that initiation of a fight is often defined very differently by respondents, with some interpreting "initiation" as the respondent being the first to use physical violence in a fight and others interpreting it as the respondent starting a verbal argument which then results in the partner physically attacking the respondent (see Olson and Lloyd 2005). Lastly, one study of adolescent SSIPV defined IPV as violence that a respondent's partner used "on purpose" (Kann 2011), thereby requiring a subjective interpretation of motivations that may be impacted by whether respondents perceive their partner's violence as justified, beyond the partner's control, or reciprocated. Each of these three studies (Kann 2011; Massachusetts Department of Education 2006; Rhodes et al. 2009) found that, unlike in AddHealth, LGB adolescents are at an elevated risk of *all* forms of IPV. Nonetheless, the narrow definitions of IPV employed by these three studies potentially exclude a variety of IPV victims, suggesting that AddHealth's findings in turn represent the most accurate available data on adolescent SSIPV.

Relative Prevalence of SSIPV and OSIPV among Bisexuals

Few studies have explored whether bisexuals and those with a history of both same-sex and opposite-sex relationships are more likely to experience IPV in a same- or opposite-sex relationship. Research on adults suggests that their opposite-sex partners are most likely to perpetrate physical IPV (Balsam et al. 2005; Messinger 2011; Walters et al. 2013) and psychological IPV (Messinger 2011; Walters et al. 2013), but not sexual IPV (Messinger 2011). Conversely, one study found that, for both adolescent males and females, self-identified bisexuals were just as likely to experience IPV in same- and opposite-sex relationships (Freedner et al. 2002). It is unclear whether these discrepancies in findings are due to the age differences in the samples or are artifacts of methodological distinctions such as sampling design.

Prevalence of Bidirectional Versus Unidirectional SSIPV

Evidence suggests that about half of SSIPV relationships involve *bidirectional* IPV, in which both partners engage in IPV tactics (Kelly et al. 2011; Renner and Whitney 2010). Although no analyses to date have compared the relative directionality of OSIPV and SSIPV, a review of 50 directionality studies on predominantly OSIPV determined that 58 % of those involved in IPV are involved in bidirectional IPV (Langhinrichsen-Rohling et al. 2012), thus suggesting that bidirectional IPV occurs at similar rates in opposite- and same-sex relationships. Whether bidirectional IPV typically entails two "abusers" or a victim using violence in self-defense is debated in the OSIPV literature (see Anderson 2005). A similar debate and supporting evidence have not yet been adequately developed in the SSIPV literature, inhibiting informed interpretations of physical SSIPV directionality data.

Dynamics

A variety of aspects of SSIPV relationships have been examined by scholars that are detailed below, including the intergenerational transmission of violence, sequencing of abuse, gender performance, substance abuse, power differentials, reasons victims stay, and outcomes.

Intergenerational Transmission of Violence

Socialization into violence-condoning attitudes by exposure to violence in the family is associated with experiencing an OSIPV relationship in adulthood (Wallace 2005). LGB people are more likely than heterosexuals to experience and witness violence in general and to experience child abuse (Balsam et al. 2005; Russell et al. 2001), so it is perhaps not surprising that several studies have found that witnessing aggression between family members (Lie et al. 1991) and experiencing child abuse (Craft and Serovich 2005; Fortunata and Kohn 2003) is associated with IPV among LGB persons.

Sequencing of Abuse

Regarding the temporal sequencing of abuse in SSIPV relationships, research suggests that the first physically violent incident typically does not occur until well into these relationships (Merrill and Wolfe 2000), and, after it occurs, violence frequency often escalates over time (Glass et al. 2008; McClennen et al. 2002; Renzetti 1992). Beyond physical violence, it is unclear when other forms of IPV typically emerge over the course of SSIPV relationships. Little is also known about the sequence of events that immediately precede and follow a specific abusive incident, and the research that does examine this focuses on testing the applicability of Walker's (1979) cycle of violence theory to SSIPV. The cycle of violence is described by Walker (1979) as a recurring cycle of three phases over the course of an OSIPV relationship: a tension-building phase, a physically violent incident, and a honeymoon phase in which apologies and promises of change are made by the abuser (Walker 1979). Walker (1979) and others (for example, see Dutton 2009) have pointed out that the interview data used to initially develop this theory showed the complete cycle to be applicable to only a minority of the small unrepresentative sample, calling into question whether the cycle is common in OSIPV relationships. A number of small studies have found this cycle to be applicable to some same-sex relationships (Cruz 2003; Johnson 2005; McClennen et al. 2002; Merrill and Wolfe 2000). That said, it is unclear what proportion of physically violent SSIPV relationships follow this cyclical pattern of abuse and what alternate temporal sequences of abuse, if any, typify other physically violent as well as non-physically-violent SSIPV relationships.

Gender Performance

Feminist IPV theory contends that the performance of "hegemonic masculinity" (Connell 1987)—culturally prominent masculinity norms including being in control and aggressive—in the context of a patriarchal society enables and encourages men to acquire dominance in intimate relationships with women (Dobash and Dobash 1992; Haraway and O'Neil 1999). Many posit that feminist IPV theory is invalid because it excludes SSIPV (for example, see Island and Letellier 1991; Merrill 1996). Others contend that, while feminist IPV theory is inapplicable to SSIPV, it may still apply to OSIPV if gender performance varies by sex and sexual orientation (Bograd 1999; Craft and Serovich 2005). Indeed, LGB individuals often do not perform stereotypical heterosexual gender roles in relationships and, like heterosexuals, exhibit a broad range of gender performances (Peplau et al. 1996).

That said, research is mixed on the general forms of gender performed most often in SSIPV relationships, with contradictory findings suggesting that either hegemonic masculinity (McKenry et al. 2006; Oringher and Samuelson 2011), the simultaneous lack of hegemonic masculinity and lack of stereotypical heterosexual femininity (Kelly and Warshafsky 1987), or no aspect of gender (Balsam and Szymanski 2005) is associated with SSIPV. One study of 109 sexual minority youths suggested that SSIPV may also be associated with strain emerging from the gender performance of a partner shifting over the course of a relationship as well as strain emerging from disagreements over whether same-sex partners should be performing stereotypical heterosexual gender roles (Gillum and DiFulvio 2012).

Substance Abuse

A known predictor of OSIPV perpetration (see Wallace 2005), substance abuse has been similarly linked to SSIPV perpetration (see Kelly et al. 2011; Lewis et al. 2012) as well as more severe SSIPV (McClennen et al. 2002). Kelly et al. (2011) theorize that the pharmacological effects of alcohol and illicit drugs may increase aggression and likelihood of perpetration among abusers and, at the same time, may be intentionally consumed by abusers to more easily justify to themselves and their victims the abuse either they have recently perpetrated or are about to perpetrate. Substance abuse is also a known correlate of being a SSIPV victim (Kelly et al. 2011; McClennen et al. 2002; Stall et al. 2003), acting for some as a coping mechanism.

Power Differentials

McLaughlin and Rozee (2001) note that the underlying IPV predictor in feminist IPV theory is power differences. Around 40 % of both male and female same-sex couples self-label as not fully egalitarian (Landolt and Dutton 1997; Peplau and Chochran 1980), and lack of egalitarianism in relationships is associated with SSIPV (Eaton et al. 2008; Landolt and Dutton 1997). Power imbalances in same-sex relationships can stem from a variety of sources, including issues pertaining to labor, dependency, outness, heterosexism, and HIV status.

Power differentials: Labor. As in OSIPV (e.g., Macmillan and Gartner 1999), differences in partner income are associated with SSIPV (see Peplau et al. 1996). Additionally, a study of 284 lesbians noted that triggers for verbal and physical SSIPV can include work and unemployment, division of household labor, and the spending of money (Lockhart et al. 1994).

Power differentials: Dependency. SSIPV may also be associated with the relative dependency of partners (Peplau et al. 1996). McClennen and colleagues (2002) suggest that, particularly, female same-sex relationships often involve "lesbian fusion"—isolation from society and dependency on one's intimate partner—and IPV may result when one partner becomes more autonomous. Some research does indeed find that high levels of fusion and dependency are associated with SSIPV (Miller et al. 2001) and greater frequency and severity of SSIPV (McClennen et al. 2002; Renzetti 1992). Research is mixed on whether greater dependency by the perpetrator or the victim best predicts SSIPV (see Poorman and Seelau 2001; Renzetti 1992).

Power differentials: Outness. One study of 272 lesbian and bisexual women found openness or "outness" about their sexual orientation with society was unassociated with IPV (Balsam and Szymanski 2005). That said, greater outness is associated with stronger emotional and psychological well-being, whereas less outness can isolate partners and inhibit their addressing relationship problems (see Balsam and Szymanski 2005). Additionally, some abusers may threaten to out an LGB victim to prevent the victim from leaving (see Kulkin et al. 2007). Conversely, some closeted abusers may actively deter SSIPV victims from forming friendships, coming out of the closet, and openly discussing their relationship with others out of fear that doing so could entail outing the abuser's sexual orientation (Donovan and Hester 2008; Walters 2011), effectively acting to silence the victim. Other abusers have been noted to question their victims' sexual orientation status as a means of control (Borenstein et al. 2006).

Power differentials: Heterosexism. LGB persons are at an elevated risk of violence victimization (Balsam et al. 2005; Russell et al. 2001) and discrimination (Badget and Frank 2007) in society. Balsam (2001) theorizes that maltreatment of LGB people is due to *heterosexism*, an institutionally-reinforced, society-wide elevation of heterosexual people over LGB people (Balsam 2001). *Minority stress* has been defined as stress for LGB people that results from experiences with and fear of heterosexism, acceptance of socially learned heterosexist beliefs (i.e., *internalized heterosexism*), and a low degree of outness. Some abusers may attempt to cope with minority stress through SSIPV perpetration (Balsam and Szymanski 2005; Bartholomew et al. 2008; Brooks 1981; Carvalho et al. 2011). It has also been theorized that victims with high degrees of internalized heterosexism may perceive themselves to be "defective" and thereby deserving of being abused (Balsam and Szymanski 2005, p. 260).

Power differentials: HIV status. Men who have sex with men are at greater risk of contracting HIV and AIDS than other men (Relf et al. 2004). Being HIV-positive predicts SSIPV victimization (Greenwood et al. 2002; Houston and McKirnan 2007; NCAVP 2012; Stall et al. 2003) and bidirectional SSIPV (Bartholomew et al. 2008). This association may be facilitated by a variety of factors. Whether or not safe sex practices are used with an HIV-positive partner can be wielded by abusers as a tool of control: victims often fear and experience SSIPV retaliation if they request safer sex practices (Gielen et al. 2000; Heintz and Melendez 2006), SSIPV abusers often lie about whether or not they are using protection (Heintz and Melendez 2006), and many victims are forced by an HIV-positive SSIPV abuser to have sex without protection (Craft and Serovich 2005). Anecdotal evidence suggests some HIV-positive abusers purposely infect victims to make the victims less desirable to perceived romantic competition (Letellier 1996). Possible barriers to leaving that are unique for HIV-positive victims include relying emotionally and financially on the abuser for care, fear of not finding another partner wanting to date and take care of an HIV-positive person, and the abuser threatening to reveal the victim's HIV status to others. Conversely, victims of HIV-positive abusers may feel guilt over leaving a medically ailing abuser (see Bartholomew et al. 2008; Craft and Serovich 2005; Letellier 1996).

Reasons Victims Stay

Victims stay in SSIPV relationships for a host of reasons, including hope that the abuser will change, loyalty and love for the abuser, fear that no one else will love them, fear of additional harm, financial dependence, a lack of access to help-giving resources, the abuser's attempts to reconnect with the victim, and fear of reinforcing negative stereotypes of LGB people and their relationships (Cruz 2003; Merrill and Wolfe 2000). Two other factors—isolation and not recognizing abuse—also play important roles in keeping victims in relationships.

As with OSIPV, isolation facilitates the continuation of SSIPV. For example, female SSIPV frequency is highest for victims with no female friends (Stevens et al. 2010), and, for those with friends, because local LGB communities can be small, victims often share friends with abusers, thereby inhibiting help-seeking (Borenstein et al. 2006). Similarly, many in SSIPV relationships stay with abusers out of fear that one else could love them (Cruz 2003; Gillum and DiFulvio 2012; Merrill and Wolfe 2000), a fear enhanced by concerns that there are fewer dating options for LGB persons (Gillum and DiFulvio 2012).

Additionally, victims often remain with abusers because of an inability to recognize SSIPV. It is well-documented that many SSIPV victims have trouble recognizing that their relationship is abusive (Bornstein et al. 2006; Cruz 2003; Gillum and DiFulvio 2012; Hassouneh and Glass 2008; Island and Letellier 1991; Merrill and Wolfe 2000). This can be facilitated by two factors. First, it may be perceived that society portrays IPV as exclusively the domain of opposite-sex relationships (Gillum and DiFulvio 2012; McLaughlin and Rozee 2001) and that—owing to gender stereotypes that women are inherently non-aggressive, women's violence is not impactful, and men are inherently physically strong enough to protect themselves—same-sex relationships are always peaceful (Donovan and Hester 2010; Hassounch and Glass 2008). Second, a perceived lack of media images of same-sex relationships may result in LGB persons not knowing what a healthy same-sex relationship entails (Borenstein et al. 2006; Donovan and Hester 2010).

Outcomes of SSIPV

SSIPV is associated with a number of negative sequelae for victims (see Burke and Follingstad 1999). These include substance abuse (Kelly et al. 2011; McClennen et al. 2002; Stall et al. 2003), mental health issues (Stall et al. 2003; see, too, Gillum and DiFulvio, this volume), and injury (Dolan-Soto 2000; NCAVP 2012). Furthermore, lesbian and bisexual female IPV victims are more likely to report negative outcomes than heterosexual female IPV victims (Walters et al. 2013). Potentially compounding these conditions for victims, LGB members of society are at a heightened risk of health problems like substance abuse (see Kelly et al. 2011; Lewis et al. 2012) eating disorders, and suicidal ideation (Massachusetts Department of Education 2006).

Helping Victims

SSIPV victims often perceive there to be limited resources tailored to them (Al-husen, Lucea, and Glass 2010) and may be told by abusers that they will encounter heterosexism from IPV victim service providers (Dolan-Soto 2000). As a result, victims may be deterred from seeking out formal help-giving sources like shelters, IPV agencies, law enforcement, and the courts (Bornstein et al. 2006; Glass et al. 2008). Unfortunately, there are a number of reasons to conclude that resources are indeed limited for SSIPV victims.

Absence of Formal Help-Giving Resources

Many needed IPV help-giving resources are either non-existent or not tailored to
SSIPV (see, too, in this volume, Gillum and DiFulvio's discussion of resource
deficiencies for adolescents experiencing same-sex dating violence). For instance,
unlike with OSIPV, no SSIPV-specific prevention and education programs have
been evaluated (Murray et al. 2006), and the only SSIPV perpetrator treatment
model to be described and evaluated (Margolies and Leeder 1995) is outdated and
used a small all-lesbian sample. Counseling services specialized in SSIPV victimization is not widely available throughout the U.S. (Jablow 2000), and one study
indicated that SSIPV victims perceived domestic violence hotlines to be among the
least helpful sources to turn to (McClennen et al. 2002). A study of 213 IPV agencies
randomly sampled from a national database of 1,980 IPV agencies found that most
services assessed were provided to sexual minority women but that several services
were provided by only one to two-thirds of the agencies to sexual minority men, such
as shelter services, safe homes, transitional housing, and group mental health services (Hines and Douglas 2011). Though female SSIPV victims can access shelters
designed for female OSIPV victims, such shelters may not successfully screen for
female SSIPV abusers (Aulivola 2004; Borenstein et al. 2006) and may house
heterosexist OSIPV victims who do not believe SSIPV victims are truly victims
deserving of the limited space available at shelters (Borenstein et al. 2006). Perhaps
not surprisingly then, in a survey of 3,930 IPV victims, 87 % of whom were sexual
minorities, it was found that 62 % of victims seeking shelter were denied (NCAVP
2012). Service providers suggest an increase is needed in LGB-specific outreach,
staff training, and services (NCVC and NCAVP 2010).

Lack of funding appears to be one of the factors driving this trend. A recent
study of 648 IPV victim service providers concluded that limited funding prevented the creation of services and outreach tailored to SSIPV victims (NCVC and
NCAVP 2010), and previous research has documented fears of funding cuts from
private and government donors should an agency choose to become more inclusive
of SSIPV (Donnelly et al. 1999; Renzetti 1996). Renzetti (1996) suggests an
additional factor may be at play: some service providers may intentionally provide
few SSIPV-targeted services and LGB community-based advertising of services
due to SSIPV victims rarely utilizing such agencies, but perhaps, in an ironic twist
evidenced in the literature (see Alhusen et al. 2010), a key reason many SSIPV
victims do not contact these agencies is that the agencies are not providing tailored
services and advertising.

Heterosexism Among Service Providers

Beyond the absence of services, heterosexist attitudes have been documented
among service providers, acting as an additional barrier to help-seeking by SSIPV

victims. For example, studies have found that crisis center and shelter staff view SSIPV as less serious than OSIPV (Basow and Thompson 2012; Brown and Groscup 2009). Law enforcement typically are not trained to handle SSIPV (Tesch et al. 2010), may incorrectly base the decision of who to arrest on gender stereotypes (Hassouneh and Glass 2008), in some instances verbally abuse SSIPV victims (Dolan-Soto 2000), and tend to hold more negative views of LGB persons than heterosexuals (Bernstein and Kostelac 2002). LGB people may also fear (Freedberg 2006) and encounter (Harrison and Silenzo 1996) negative reactions when coming out to health professionals, creating a barrier to SSIPV disclosure with health care providers.

Legal Barriers

Regarding legal barriers for SSIPV victims, prior to the 2003 U.S. Supreme Court ruling in *Lawrence v. Texas*, male SSIPV victims risked being arrested for sodomy if they sought help from law enforcement (Aulivola 2004). While sodomy laws have been struck down, other major legal barriers still exist. As of 2012, Montana and South Carolina did not allow SSIPV victims to get civil orders of protection, which—unlike the criminal protection orders available to SSIPV victims in all states—can be easier to acquire, more quickly implemented, and are not contingent upon pressing criminal charges (ABA 2009; WomensLaw.org 2012a, b). This is an improvement from just 14 years earlier, when SSIPV victims were excluded from accessing civil orders of protection in six states (NCAVP 1998). Such states excluding SSIPV from their definitions of domestic violence may exclude victims from access to additional protections in criminal cases, such as higher bail and stronger penalties for abusers (Aulivola 2004).

Finally, at the federal level, protection for SSIPV victims was only recently awarded in 2013 after a nearly two-decade journey. The 1995 federal Violence Against Women Act (VAWA) addressed the problems of domestic violence, sexual violence, and stalking by providing extensive funding for prosecution of these crimes, additional training to criminal justice agencies and law enforcement working with victims, the establishment of the National Domestic Violence Hotline, and funding for both new government offices handling these issues as well as existing organizations like shelters. The Act also criminalized IPV that involves an abuser crossing state lines or a victim being forced to cross state lines, criminalized interstate stalking, required all states and territories to recognize a state court's order of protection, allowed victims to provide testimony in VAWA detention hearings, and in VAWA cases required full restitution be paid by a guilty perpetrator to cover victim losses related to the crime such as physical and mental health costs, temporary housing, childcare costs, lost income, costs incurred in obtaining an order of protection, and attorney fees. The Act was reauthorized and expanded by Congress in 2000 and in 2005, and the 2005 Act expired in 2011 pending additional reauthorization (Fine 1998; Meyer-Emerick 2001;

WhiteHouse.gov 2012). Although VAWA has always used gender neutral terminology, given the history of the law, its title, and its narrow definition of domestic violence, some questioned its applicability to SSIPV (Potoczniak et al. 2003). Despite a 2010 memorandum by the U.S. Department of Justice stating that the criminal-legal aspects of VAWA should be extended to SSIPV victims (U.S. Dept. of Justice 2010), in 2011, a congressional battle ensued over whether to include SSIPV victims in the VAWA reauthorization: Senate Bill 1925 was inclusive of SSIPV victims while the House's H.R. 4970 was not (NCAPV 2012). After the Senate bill was ultimately approved by Congress, on March 7, 2013, President Obama signed into law a version of VAWA that is the first ever to be specifically inclusive of SSIPV victims (Calmes 2013). It remains unclear how the reauthorization will impact funding for the expansion of services, outreach, and service provider training regarding SSIPV.

Future Directions

The past three and a half decades of scholarship on SSIPV have revealed a serious public health threat: IPV is as likely if not more likely to occur in same-sex relationships and among LGB individuals as compared to in opposite-sex relationships and among heterosexuals, power differentials that characterize many OSIPV relationships reappear and may be augmented in SSIPV, and many victims feel trapped and face severe health outcomes. Beyond the intergenerational transmission of violence, a number of factors relating to heterosexism—such as partner outness and minority stress—appear to play key roles in fueling SSIPV. This literature suggests several future directions for research methodologies, research topics, and policy improvements.

Future Research Methodologies

Throughout the history of this literature, a number of methodological issues have arisen. In addition to methodological quandaries inherent in IPV research more generally (e.g., how to measure IPV and its components, how to capture the context and motivations of IPV, etc.; for a review of methodological issues in IPV research, see Anderson 2005, and Burke and Follingstad 1999), researchers also have had to tackle two serious methodological problems specific to SSIPV: defining and sampling the population.

Defining the population. Arguably one of the most unique aspects of SSIPV is the impact of heterosexism on it: as discussed in this chapter, heterosexism can affect the risk of IPV perpetration, the risk of victimization, and the availability of victim resources for sexual minorities. That said, the literature has not yet assessed whether sexual minorities experience stigma and barriers to resources solely in same-sex relationships or also in opposite-sex relationships. Thus, a key dilemma is whether to define the population by the sex or sexual orientation of partners.

In turn, the research literature is divided into studies defining the target population as those ever involved in a same-sex IPV relationship (e.g., Halpern et al. 2004; Messinger 2011) and studies defining the target population as sexual minorities ever involved in an IPV relationship regardless of whether it was a same- or opposite-sex relationship (e.g., Hughes et al. 2010; Rhodes et al. 2009). Few publications in the literature have simultaneously reported upon same-sex IPV and sexual minority IPV (IPV relationships with at least one sexual minority partner; for a rare exception, see Kann 2011), and no study to date has assessed the sexual orientation of respondents' partners. To determine how the sex and sexual orientations of partners interact, it is highly recommended that future research measures both sex and sexual orientation of both the respondent and the respondent's partners. Additionally, IPV research should explore beyond binary biological sex to be inclusive of the intersex and trans* communities.

Relatedly, researchers must take care in the measurement of sexual minority status. Competing definitions include self-identifying as a sexual minority, romantic-sexual attraction to at least the same sex, and romantic-sexual behaviors and relationships with at least the same sex (Meyer and Wilson 2009; see, too, discussions in this volume by Johnson; Stotzer; Woods). These aspects of sexual orientation do not always neatly align for individuals, and they can shift over time (Moradi et al. 2009). For example, in a survey of 521 adolescents at an LGB youth rally, 19 % of self-identified lesbian women and 7 % of self-identified gay men reported having been an IPV victim of an *opposite-sex* abuser, suggesting that current self-identified sexual orientation is not equivalent to behaviorally-based sexual orientation (Freedner et al. 2002). It is therefore recommended that future research assess the many aspects of sexual orientation—self-identity, attraction, behavior, and relationships—to gain a more complete picture of how sexual orientation affects IPV.

Sampling the population. With regards specifically to survey research, in the interest of quickly and inexpensively locating eligible respondents, most researchers of SSIPV recruit respondents from LGB-centric venues like gay pride parades. Some researchers have endeavored to enhance representativeness specifically of this out and community-connected portion of the LGB population by randomly selecting LGB-centric venues and organizations from a comprehensive listing categorized by venue type (e.g., Meyer et al. 2008). Representativeness of selected venues can be further enhanced by what is referred to as time–space sampling. With this approach, times and days of the week are randomly selected for recruitment at selected venues, and the same percentage of present venue members is recruited each time to ensure that the proportions of the sample recruited from various times and days are the same proportions in the venue overall (see Meyer and Wilson 2009).

Although providing valuable insights into the types of sexual minorities who frequent LGB-centric venues, scholars note that such venues represent only a particular segment of the LGB population (e.g., those with a greater degree of outness, politically active, young) and thus may present only a partial picture of SSIPV (see Greenwood et al. 2002). Scholars have raised the same limitation regarding sampling from IPV-centric venues such as shelters or service-providing agencies, wherein individuals who visit such venues likely only represent a skewed portion of the SSIPV victim population, the majority of whom do not access such venues (see Anderson 2005). Instead, greater representativeness of the LGB population can be obtained from *probability sampling* by finding a non-LGB-centric, non-IPV-specific locale, collecting a complete list of member contact information, randomly selecting members from the list to recruit, and asking recruited members a screening question to identify their LGB status for study participation or analysis eligibility (see Burke and Follingstad 1999; Meyer and Wilson 2009).

That said, because only a small portion of the general population has experienced same-sex relationships or a relationship involving a sexual minority, very large numbers of heterosexuals will need to be screened in the process of ultimately arriving at a sample of the target population large enough for statistical analysis. For many researchers, this process is too lengthy and expensive to be feasible. For example, the Urban Men's Health Study (UMHS) randomly sampled and called *53,050 phone numbers* across four gay-centric neighborhoods in order to acquire a sample size of 915 MSMs, or men who have sex with men (Greenwood et al. 2002). Arguably even such extensive efforts to obtain representativeness can still be problematic when they entail sampling from LGB-centric neighborhoods—as was the case with the UMHS—where residents may differ in substantial ways (e.g., degree of outness) from those who reside in other neighborhoods (Meyer and Wilson 2009). While sampling from non-LGB-centric neighborhoods would avoid this bias, the ratio of screened to study-eligible individuals would be even greater than the already alarmingly high ratio for the UMHS. Existing nationally representative probability sampled studies without a neighborhood-based bias are feasible in part because they do not screen out individuals based on sexual orientation, but they are not without their own limitations, as they tend to include too few LGB persons or those with a history of same-sex relationships to conduct sophisticated analyses on SSIPV (see Greenwood et al. 2002). Regardless of what sampling design is utilized, it is important for researchers to consider methods that will improve population representativeness wherever possible to strengthen the appropriateness of applying their study conclusions to the broader LGB population.

Future Research Topics and Policy Implications

Based on this review of the literature, scholars should consider exploring several under-studied research topics. In particular, future research should address what role, if any, does gender performance by partners play in SSIPV perpetration and victimization, what motivates IPV in bidirectional SSIPV relationships, and what are the unique dynamics of IPV for bisexual, intersex, and trans* persons in opposite-sex and same-sex relationships? Additionally, to date, there has been very little research conducted on SSIPV outside of the United States, with rare exceptions including research on Canada (St. Pierre and Senn 2010), China (Mak et al. 2010), Cuba (Santaya and Walters 2011), the United Kingdom (Hester and Donovan 2009), and Venezuela (Burke et al. 2002). Given that the degree of acceptance for sexual minorities both socially and legally varies widely across societies, experiences of SSIPV should be examined outside of the context of the U.S.

With regards to policy, concerns over the lack of resources and heterosexism among service providers have prevented many SSIPV victims from seeking help and have been used as a tool by SSIPV abusers to deter victims from seeking help. Clearly, additional services, training, and legal reform are needed, but, just as importantly, with many SSIPV victims having difficulty recognizing abuse, targeted advertising and outreach is needed to raise awareness in the broader LGB community about the nature of SSIPV and the services that are available to victims.

Conclusions

Research on SSIPV has come a long way in 35 years, as has public recognition of the problem and resources available for victims. However, it is equally clear that a great deal of work still needs to be done by scholars, service providers, and policymakers to ensure the safety and well-being of LGB people living in what McClennen (2005) refers to as a double closet, silenced not only by their abusers but also by their fears that they may live in a heterosexist society that refuses to help them.

Acknowledgments The author greatly appreciates the generosity and expertise of Dr. Claire Renzetti in reviewing an early draft and providing valuable insights for revision.

References

Alhusen, J. L., Lucea, M. B., & Glass, N. (2010). Perceptions of and experience with system responses to female same-sex intimate partner violence. *Partner Abuse, 1*(4), 443–462.

American Bar Association (2009). *Domestic Violence Civil Protection Orders (CPOs) by state.* Retrieved December 2012 from www.americanbar.org/content/dam/aba/migrated/domviol/pdfs/dv_cpo_chart.authcheckdam.pdf

Anderson, K. L. (2005). Theorizing gender in intimate partner violence research. *Sex Roles, 52,* 853–865.

Aulivola, M. (2004). Outing domestic violence affording appropriate protection to gay and lesbian victims. *Family Court Review, 42,* 162–177.

Badget, M. V. L., & Frank, J. (Eds.). (2007). *Sexual orientation discrimination: An international perspective.* London, UK: Routledge.

Balsam, K. F. (2001). Nowhere to hide: Lesbian battering, homophobia, and minority stress. *Women and Therapy, 23*(3), 25–37.

Balsam, K. F., Rothblum, E. D., & Beauchaine, T. P. (2005). Victimization over the life span: A comparison of lesbian, gay, bisexual, and heterosexual siblings. *Journal of Consulting and Clinical Psychology, 73*, 477–487.

Balsam, K. F., & Szymanski, D. M. (2005). Relationship quality and domestic violence in women's same-sex relationships: The role of minority stress. *Psychology of Women Quarterly, 29*, 258–269.

Bartholomew, K., Regan, K. V., White, M. A., & Oram, D. (2008). Patterns of abuse in male same sex relationships. *Violence and Victims, 23*(5), 617–636.

Basow, S. A., & Thompson, J. (2012). Service providers' reactions to intimate partner violence as a function of victim sexual orientation and type of abuse. *Journal of Interpersonal Violence, 27*(7), 1225–1241.

Bernstein, M., & Kostelac, C. (2002). Lavender and blue: Attitudes about homosexuality and behavior towards lesbians and gay men among police officers. *Journal of Contemporary Criminal Justice, 18*, 302–328.

Bimbi, D., Palmadessa, N., & Parsons, J. (2007). Substance use and domestic violence among urban gays, lesbians and bisexuals. *Journal of LGBT Health Research, 3*(2), 1–7.

Blosnich, J. R., & Bossarte, R. M. (2009). Comparisons of intimate partner violence among partners in same-sex and opposite-sex relationships in the United States. *American Journal of Public Health, 99*(12), 2182–2184.

Bograd, M. (1999). Strengthening domestic violence theories: Intersections of race, class, sexual orientation, and gender. *Journal of Marriage and Family Therapy, 25*(3), 275–289.

Bornstein, D. R., Fawcett, J., Sullivan, M., Senturia, K. D., & Shiu-Thornton, S. (2006). Understanding the experiences of lesbian, bisexual and trans survivors of domestic violence: A qualitative study. *Journal of Homosexuality, 51*(1), 159–181.

Bradford, J., Ryan, C., & Rothblum, E. (1994). National Lesbian Health Care Survey: Implications for mental health care. *Journal of Consulting and Clinical Psychology, 62*, 228–242.

Brooks, V. R. (1981). *Minority stress and lesbian women*. Lexington, MA: D.C. Health.

Brown, M. J., & Groscup, J. (2009). Perceptions of same-sex domestic violence among crisis center staff. *Journal of Family Violence, 24*, 87–93.

Burke, L. K., & Follingstad, D. R. (1999). Violence in lesbian and gay relationships: Theory, prevalence, and correlational factors. *Clinical Psychology Review, 19*, 487–512.

Burke, T. W., Jordan, M. L., & Owen, S. S. (2002). A cross-national comparison of gay and lesbian domestic violence. *Journal of Contemporary Criminal Justice, 18*, 231–256.

Calmes, J. (2013, March 7). Obama signs expanded anti-violence law. *The New York Times*. Retrieved from http://thecaucus.blogs.nytimes.com/2013/03/07/obama-signs-expanded-anti-violence-law/

Cameron, P. (2003). Domestic violence among homosexual partners. *Psychological Reports, 93*, 410–416.

Carvalho, A. F., Lewis, R. J., Derlega, V. J., Winstead, B. A., & Viggiano, C. (2011). Internalized sexual minority stressors and same-sex intimate partner violence. *Journal of Family Violence, 26*, 501–509.

Connell, R. W. (1987). *Gender and power*. Stanford, CA: Stanford University Press.

Craft, S. M., & Serovich, J. M. (2005). Family-of-origin factors and partner violence in the intimate relationships of gay men who are HIV positive. *Journal of Interpersonal Violence, 20*, 777–791.

Cruz, J. M. (2003). "Why doesn't he just leave?": Gay male domestic violence and the reasons victims stay. *Journal of Men's Studies, 11*, 309–323.

Diamond, D. L., & Wilsnack, S. C. (1978). Alcohol abuse among lesbians: A descriptive study. *Journal of Homosexuality, 4*(2), 123–142.

Dobash, R. E., & Dobash, R. P. (1992). *Women, violence, and social change*. Boston, MA: Routledge Kegan Paul.

Dolan-Soto, D. (2000). *Lesbian, gay, transgender and bisexual (LGTB) domestic violence in New York City.* The New York City Gay and Lesbian Anti-Violence Project.

Donnelly, D. A., Cook, K. J., & Wilson, L. A. (1999). Provision and exclusion: The dual face of services to battered women in three deep South states. *Violence Against Women, 5*(7), 710–741.

Donovan, C., & Hester, M. (2008). 'Because she was my first girlfriend, I didn't know any different': Making the case for mainstreaming same-sex sex/relationship education. *Journal of Sex Education, 8*(3), 277–287.

Donovan, C., & Hester, M. (2010). 'I hate the word "victim"': An exploration of recognition of domestic violence in same sex relationships. *Social Policy & Society, 9*(2), 279–289.

Dutton, M. A. (2009). Update of the "Battered Woman Syndrome" critique. *VAW.net* Retrieved from http://www.vawnet.org/Assoc_Files_VAWnet/AR_BWSCritique.pdf

Eaton, L., Kaufman, M., Fuhrel, A., Cain, D., Cherry, C., Pope, H., & Kalichman, S. C. (2008). Examining factors co-existing with interpersonal violence in lesbian relationships. *Journal of Family Violence, 23*, 697–705.

Fine, D. M. (1998). The Violence Against Women Act of 1994: The proper federal role in policing domestic violence. *Cornell Law Review, 84*, 252–303.

Fortunata, B., & Kohn, C. S. (2003). Demographic, psychosocial, and personality characteristics of lesbian batterers. *Violence and Victims, 18*, 557–568.

Freedberg, P. (2006). Health care barriers and same-sex intimate partner violence: A review of the literature. *Journal of Forensic Nursing, 2*(1), 15–25.

Freedner, N., Freed, L. H., Yang, W., & Austin, S. B. (2002). Dating violence among gay, lesbian, and bisexual adolescents: Results from a community survey. *Journal of Adolescent Health, 31*, 469–474.

Gates, G. J. (2011). *How many people are lesbian, gay, bisexual, and transgender?* Los Angeles, CA: The Williams Institute.

Gielen, A. C., McDonnell, K. A., Burke, J. G., & O'Campo, P. (2000). Women's lives after an HIV-positive diagnosis: Disclosure and violence. *Maternal and Child Health Journal, 4*(2), 111–120.

Gillum, T. L., & DiFulvio, G. (2012). "There's so much at stake": Sexual minority youth discuss dating violence. *Violence Against Women, 18*(7), 725–745.

Glass, N., Perrin, N., Hanson, G., Bloom, T., Gardner, E., & Campbell, J. C. (2008). Assessing risk for repeat violence in abusive female same-sex relationships. *American Journal of Public Health, 98*(6), 1021–1027.

Greenwood, G. L., Relf, M. V., Huang, B., Pollack, L. M., Canchola, J. A., & Catania, J. A. (2002). Battering victimization among a probability-based sample of men who have sex with men. *American Journal of Public Health, 92*, 1964–1969.

Halpern, C. T., Oslak, S. G., Young, M. L., Martin, S. L., & Kupper, L. L. (2001). Partner violence among adolescents in opposite-sex romantic relationships: Findings from the National Longitudinal Study of Adolescent Health. *American Journal of Public Health, 91*, 1679–1685.

Halpern, C. T., Young, M. L., Waller, M. W., Martin, S. L., & Kupper, L. L. (2004). Prevalence of partner violence in same-sex romantic and sexual relationships in a national sample of adolescents. *Journal of Adolescent Health, 35*, 124–131.

Haraway, M., & O'Neil, J. (Eds.). (1999). *What causes men's violence against women?.* London, UK: Sage.

Harrison, A., & Silenzio, V. (1996). Comprehensive care of lesbian and gay patients and families. *Primary Care, 23*(1), 31–46.

Hassouch, D., & Glass, N. (2008). The influence of gender-role stereotyping on women's experiences of female same-sex intimate partner violence. *Violence Against Women, 14*(3), 310–325.

Heintz, A. J., & Melendez, R. M. (2006). Intimate partner violence and HIV/STD risk among lesbian, gay, bisexual and transgender individuals. *Journal of Interpersonal Violence, 21*, 193–208.

Hester, M., & Donovan, C. (2009). Researching domestic violence in same-sex relationships: A feminist epistemological approach to survey development. *Journal of Lesbian Studies, 13*(2), 161–173.

Hines, D. A., & Douglas, E. M. (2011). The reported availability of U.S. domestic violence services to victims who vary by age, sexual orientation, and gender. *Partner Abuse, 2*, 3–30.

Houston, E., & McKirnan, D. (2007). Intimate partner abuse among gay and bisexual men: Risk correlates and health outcomes. *Journal of Urban Health, 84*, 681–690.

Hughes, T., McCabe, S. E., Wilsnack, S. C., West, B. T., & Boyd, C. J. (2010). Victimization and substance use disorders in a national sample of heterosexual and sexual minority women and men. *Addiction, 105*(12), 2130–2140.

Island, D., & Letellier, P. (1991). *Men who beat the men who love them: Battered gay men and domestic violence*. Binghamton, NY: Haworth Press.

Jablow, P. M. (2000). Victims of abuse and discrimination: Protecting battered homosexuals under domestic violence legislation. *Hofstra Law Review, 28*, 1095–1145.

Johnson, J. J. (2005). Same-sex domestic violence: Testing the cycle theory of violence. *Dissertation Abstracts International, 66*, 556.

Kann, L., Olsen, E. O., McManus, T., Kinchen, S., Chyen, D., Harris, W. A., & Wechsler, H. (2011). *Sexual identity, sex of sexual contacts, and health-risk behaviors among students in grades 9–12—Youth Risk Behavior Surveillance, selected sites, United States, 2001-2009*. MMWR Early Release, Vol. 60, i–133.

Kelly, B. C., Izienicki, H., Bimbi, D. S., & Parson, J. T. (2011). The intersection of mutual partner violence and substance use among urban gays, lesbians, and bisexuals. *Deviant Behavior, 32*, 379–404.

Kelly, C. E., & Warshafsky, L. (1987). *Partner abuse in gay male and lesbian couples*. Paper presented at Conference for Family Violence Researchers, Durham, NC.

Kulkin, H. S., Williams, J., Borne, H. F., de la Bretonne, D., & Laurendine, J. (2007). A review of research on violence in same-gender couples: A resource for clinicians. *Journal of Homosexuality, 53*(4), 71–87.

Landolt, M. A., & Dutton, D. G. (1997). Power and personality: An analysis of gay male intimate abuse. *Sex Roles, 37*, 335–359.

Langhinrichsen-Rohling, J., Misra, T. A., Selwyn, C., & Rohling, M. L. (2012). Rates of bi-directional versus uni-directional intimate partner violence across samples, sexual orientations, and race/ethnicities: A comprehensive review. *Partner Abuse, 3*(2), 199–230.

Letellier, P. (1996). Twin epidemics: Domestic violence and HIV infection among gay and bisexual men. *Journal of Gay and Lesbian Social Social Services, 4*(1), 69–81.

Lewis, R. J., Milletich, R. J., Kelley, M. L., & Woody, A. (2012). Minority stress, substance use, and intimate partner violence among sexual minority women. *Aggression and Violent Behavior, 17*, 247–256.

Lie, G.-Y., Schilit, R., Bush, J., Montagne, M., & Reyes, L. (1991). Lesbians in currently aggressive relationships: How frequently do they report aggressive past relationships? *Violence and Victims, 6*, 121–135.

Lobel, K. (1986). *Naming the violence: Speaking out about lesbian battering*. Seattle, WA: Seal Press.

Lockhart, L. L., White, B., Causby, V., & Isaac, A. (1994). Letting out the secret: Violence in lesbian relationships. *Journal of Interpersonal Violence, 9*, 469–493.

Macmillan, R., & Gartner, R. (1999). When she brings home the bacon: Labor-force participation and the risk of spousal violence against women. *Journal of Marriage and the Family, 61*, 947–958.

Mak, W. W. S., Chong, E. S. K., & Kwong, M. M. F. (2010). Prevalence of same-sex intimate partner violence in Hong Kong. *Public Health, 124*(3), 149–152.

Margolies, L., & Leeder, E. (1995). Violence at the door: Treatment of lesbian batterers. *Violence Against Women, 1*(2), 139–157.

Massachusetts Department of Education. (2006). *2005 Massachusetts Youth Risk Behavior Survey results*. Boston, MA: Author.

McClennen, J. C. (2005). Domestic violence between same-gender partners: Recent findings and future research. *Journal of Interpersonal Violence. 20*, 149–154.

McClennen, J. C., Summers, A. B., & Vaughan, C. (2002). Gay men's domestic violence: Dynamics, help-seeking behaviors, and correlates. *Journal of Gay and Lesbian Social Services, 14*(1), 23–49.

McKenry, P. C., Serovich, J. M., Mason, T. L., & Mosack, K. (2006). Perpetration of gay and lesbian partner violence: A disempowerment perspective. *Journal of Family Violence, 21*, 233–243.

McLaughlin, E. M., & Rozee, P. D. (2001). Knowledge about heterosexual versus lesbian battering among lesbians. *Women and Therapy, 23*(3), 39–58.

Merrill, G. S. (1996). Ruling the exceptions: Same-sex battering and domestic violence theory. In C. M. Renzetti & C. H. Miley (Eds.), *Violence in gay and lesbian domestic partnerships* (pp. 9–22). New York, NY: Haworth Press.

Merrill, G. S., & Wolfe, V. A. (2000). Battered gay men: An exploration of abuse, help seeking, and why they stay. *Journal of Homosexuality, 39*(2), 1–30.

Messinger, A. M. (2011). Invisible victims: Same-sex IPV in the National Violence Against Women Survey. *Journal of Interpersonal Violence, 26*, 2228–2243.

Meyer, I. H., Schwartz, S., & Frost, D. M. (2008). Social patterning of stress and coping: Does disadvantaged status confer excess exposure and fewer coping resources? *Social Science and Medicine, 67*, 368–379.

Meyer, I. H., & Wilson, P. A. (2009). Sampling lesbian, gay, and bisexual populations. *Journal of Consulting Psychology, 56*(1), 23–31.

Meyer-Emerick, N. (2001). *The Violence Against Women Act of 1994: An analysis of intent and perception.* Westport, CT: Praeger Publishers.

Miller, D. H., Greene, K., Causby, V., White, B. W., & Lockhart, L. L. (2001). Domestic violence in lesbian relationships. *Women and Therapy, 23*, 107–127.

Miller, J., & White, N. A. (2003). Gender and adolescent relationship violence: A contextual examination. *Criminology, 41*, 1207–1248.

Moradi, B., Mohr, J. J., Worthington, R. L., & Fassinger, R. E. (2009). Counseling psychology research on sexual (orientation) minority issues: Conceptual and methodological challenges and opportunities. *Journal of Counseling Psychology, 56*(1), 5–22.

Murray, C., Mobley, A., Buford, A., & Seaman-DeJohn, M. (2006). Same-sex intimate partner violence: Dynamics, social context, and counseling implications. *Journal of LGBT Issues in Counseling, 1*(4), 7–30.

National Center for Victims of Crime and the National Coalition of Anti-Violence Programs. (2010). *Why it matters: Rethinking victim assistance for lesbian, gay, bisexual, transgender, and queer victims of hate violence & intimate partner violence.* Washington, D.C. & NYC: Native American Press.

National Coalition of Anti-Violence Programs. (2012). *Lesbian, gay, bisexual, transgender, queer and HIV-affected intimate partner violence, 2011.* New York, NY: Author.

National Coalition of Anti-Violence Programs. (1998). *Annual report on lesbian, gay, bisexual, transgender domestic violence.* New York, NY: Author. Retrieved December 2012 from http://www.mincava.umn.edu/documents/glbtdv/glbtdv.html#idp37094432

Olson, L. N., & Lloyd, S. A. (2005). "It depends on what you mean by starting": An exploration of how women define initiation of aggression and their motives for behaving aggressively. *Sex Roles, 53*, 603–617.

Oringher, J., & Samuelson, K. W. (2011). Intimate partner violence and the role of masculinity in male same-sex relationships. *Traumatology, 17*(2), 68–74.

Peplau, L. A., & Cochran, S. D. (1980). *Sex differences in values concerning love relationships.* Paper presented American Psychological Association conference, Montreal, Canada.

Peplau, L. A., Veniegas, R. C., & Campbell, S. M. (1996). Gay and lesbian relationships. In R. C. Savin-Williams & K. M. Cohen (Eds.), *The lives of lesbians, gays, and bisexuals: Children to adults* (pp. 250–273). Fort Worth, TX: Harcourt Brace College Publishers.

Poorman, P. B., & Seelau, S. M. (2001). Lesbians who abuse their partners: Using the FIRO-B to assess interpersonal characteristics. *Women and Therapy, 23*(3), 87–105.

Potoczniak, M. J., Murot, J. E., Crosbie-Burnett, M., & Potoczniak, D. J. (2003). Legal and psychological perspectives on same-sex domestic violence: A multisystemic approach. *Journal of Family Psychology, 17*, 252–259.

Puzone, C. A., Saltzman, L. E., Kresnow, M. J., Thompson, M. P., & Mercy, J. (2000). National trends in intimate partner homicide: United States, 1976–1995. *Violence Against Women, 6*(4), 409–426.

Relf, M. V., Huang, B., Campbell, J., & Catania, J. (2004). Gay identity, interpersonal violence, and HIV risk behaviors: An empirical test of theoretical relationships among a probability-based sample of urban men who have sex with men. *Journal of the Association of Nurses in AIDS Care, 15*, 14–26.

Renner, L. M., & Whitney, S. D. (2010). Examining symmetry in intimate partner violence among young adults using socio-demographic characteristics. *Journal of Family Violence, 25*, 91–106.

Renzetti, C. M. (1992). *Violent betrayal: Partner abuse in lesbian relationships*. Newbury Park, CA: Sage.

Renzetti, C. M. (1996). The poverty of services for battered lesbians. *Journal of Gay and Lesbian Social Services, 4*(1), 61–68.

Rhodes, S. D., McCoy, T. P., Wilkin, A. M., & Wolfson, M. (2009). Behavioral risk disparities in a random sample of self-identifying gay and non-gay male university students. *Journal of Homosexuality, 56*(9), 1083–1100.

Russell, S. T., Franz, B. T., & Driscoll, A. K. (2001). Same-sex romantic attraction and experiences of violence in adolescence. *American Journal of Public Health, 91*(6), 903–906.

Santaya, P. O. T., & Walters, A. S. (2011). Intimate partner violence within gay male couples: Dimensionalizing partner violence among Cuban gay men. *Sexuality and Culture, 15*(2), 153–178.

Sorenson, S. B., & Thomas, K. A. (2009). Views of intimate partner violence in same- and opposite-sex relationships. *Journal of Marriage and Family, 71*, 337–352.

Stall, R., Mills, T. C., Williamson, J., Hart, T., Greenwood, G., Paul, J., et al. (2003). Association of co-occurring psychosocial health problems and increased vulnerability to HIV/AIDS among urban men who have sex with men. *American Journal of Public Health, 93*, 939–942.

St. Pierre, M., & Senn, C. Y. (2010). External barriers to help-seeking encountered by Canadian gay and lesbian victims of intimate partner abuse: An application of the barriers model. *Violence and Victims, 25*(4), 536–552.

Stevens, S., Korchmaros, J., & Miller, D. (2010). A comparison of victimization and perpetration of intimate partner violence among drug abusing heterosexual and lesbian women. *Journal of Family Violence, 25*, 639–649.

Straus, M. A., & Gelles, R. J. (1986). Social change and change in family violence from 1975 to 1985 as revealed by two national surveys. *Journal of Marriage and Family, 48*, 465–479.

Tesch, B., Bekerian, D., English, P., & Harrington, E. (2010). Same-sex domestic violence: Why victims are more at risk. *International Journal of Police Science & Management, 12*(4), 526–535.

Tjaden, P., & Thoennes, N. (2000). *Extent, nature, and consequences of intimate partner violence: Findings from the National Violence Against Women Survey*. Washington, DC: National Institute of Justice/Centers for Disease Control and Prevention.

Tjaden, P., Thoennes, N., & Allison, C. (1999). Comparing violence over the life span in samples of same-sex and opposite-sex cohabitants. *Violence and Victims, 14*, 413–425.

Turrell, S. C. (2000). A descriptive analysis of same-sex relationship violence for a diverse sample. *Journal of Family Violence, 15*, 281–293.

U.S. Dept. of Justice. (2010). *Whether the criminal provisions of the Violence Against Women Act apply to otherwise covered conduct when the offender and victim are the same sex: Memorandum opinion for the acting deputy attorney general*. Washington: GPO.

Walker, L. E. (1979). *The battered woman*. New York, NY: Harper Perennial.

Wallace, H. (2005). *Family violence: Legal, medical, and social perspectives* (4th ed.). Boston, MA: Pearson Education.

Walters, M. L. (2011). Straighten up and act like a lady: A qualitative study of lesbian survivors of intimate partner violence. *Journal of Gay and Lesbian Social Services, 23,* 250–270.

Walters, M. L., Chen, J., & Breiding, M. J. (2013). *The National Intimate Partner and Sexual Violence Survey (NISVS): 2010 findings on victimization by sexual orientation.* Atlanta, GA: National Center for Injury Prevention and Control, Centers for Disease Control and Prevention.

WhiteHouse.gov. (2012). *Factsheet: The Violence Against Women Act.* Retrieved from http://www.whitehouse.gov/sites/default/files/docs/vawa_factsheet.pdf

WomensLaw.org. (2012a). *Know the laws: Montana: Orders of Protection.* Retrieved from womenslaw.org/laws_state_type,phpid=544&state_code=MT&open_id=all&lang=en

WomensLaw.org. (2012b). *Know the laws: South Carolina: Orders of Protection.* Retrieved from womenslaw.org/laws_state_type,phpid=584&state_code=SC&open_id=all&lang=en

Younglove, J. A., Kerr, M. G., & Vitello, C. J. (2002). Law enforcement officers' perceptions of same sex domestic violence: Reasons for cautious optimism. *Journal of Interpersonal Violence, 17,* 760–772.

Chapter 5
The LGBT Offender

Jeffery P. Dennis

Abstract Criminological and cultural discourses concerning LGBT persons as criminals are traced from the 1880s through the 1980s, when "gay criminal" gave way to the "gay victim." The contemporary absence of LGBT persons from criminology, except as victims, is addressed through several studies that determine LGBT and heterosexual offenders differ.

Keywords Criminology · Criminal offenders · Film · Heterosexism · Homophobia · Juvenile delinquency · Prisons · Television

It is problematic to write a chapter on the LGBT person as criminal offender, since for over 100 years, LGBT people were framed as the villains of every story and the culprits of every crime. Today the model of the gay criminal, forced by an intrinsically criminogenic same-sex desire to commit atrocities, has been discounted as irrational and bigoted, a relic of the homophobic past. However, the model of the gay victim, forced by an intrinsically victimizing same-sex desire to endure hate crimes, assaults, and sundry injustices, requiring the paternal intervention of heterosexual big brothers, is still alive and well, and informs much of contemporary scholarship and popular discourse. Both models derive from a heteronormative dismissal of same-sex desire, behavior, and identity, transforming LGBT persons into aliens, outsiders, and potential enemies. Both are equally destructive. This chapter will trace the history of the gay criminal and the gay victim, and suggest a third model, of LGBT persons as potential citizens and potential offenders.

J. P. Dennis (✉)
Department of Sociology, Wilkes University, 84 West South Street,
Wilkes-Barre PA 18701, USA
e-mail: jefferypdennis@yahoo.com

D. Peterson and V. R. Panfil (eds.), *Handbook of LGBT Communities,*
Crime, and Justice, DOI: 10.1007/978-1-4614-9188-0_5,
© Springer Science+Business Media New York 2014

The First Gay Criminals

Prior to the nineteenth century, there were few gay criminals, because, as many scholars have argued, there was little concept of a separate LGBT identity. Same-sex behavior was known, and certain individuals were acknowledged as having a primary or exclusive interest in the same-sex, but they were not perceived as belonging to a special type of being, nor did such interest make people especially prone to criminality (Jordan 1998). Dante placed sodomites next to murderers in the Seventh Circle of Hell, not because they were prone to murder, but because both groups "did violence" to the state by killing and refusing to have children, respectively (Boswell 1994). In Colonial North America, people convicted of sodomy were punished and then re-introduced into society, as if they had committed theft or desecrated the Sabbath, certainly not as if they were innately criminal (Katz 2007).

Not coincidentally, essentialist discourses concerning the "homosexual" and "the criminal" arose at the same moment of history, during middle years of the nineteenth century, in response to the same political and cultural forces, such as the rationalization of industry and the anonymity of urban life (see in this volume, Ball; Woods). While Lombroso was attempting to distinguish criminal types by their physical and physiognomic traits, and Quetelet by their psychosocial precursors, Richard von Krafft-Ebing and Havelock Ellis were attempting to identify and describe the types of "sexual inverts" (Groombridge 1999; Oosterhuis 2000; Tomsen 1997). Both criminologists and sexologists hoped that by isolating the deviant "type," they could relieve the everyday citizen from ever being troubled by criminal thoughts or deviant desires.

But even after the types of the invert and the criminal were isolated, tabulated, medicalized, and psychoanalyzed, they were rarely connected; during the last decades of the nineteenth century and the first decades of the twentieth, inverts were rarely ascribed an innate criminality, or criminals sexual deviance. Lombroso attributes "sex crimes" such as sodomy and prostitution to a lack of noncriminal sexual outlets, and otherwise assumes that the criminal has a "normally constituted" sexual identity (Leon 2011, p. 28). Similarly, Moran (1998) analyzes the notorious 1895 trial of playwright Oscar Wilde through conflicting attempts to name what precisely was being tried: a criminal act ("gross indecency") or a criminal identity.

During the first decade of the twentieth century, there was little public fear of inverts (soon renamed "homosexuals"). Usually they were tolerated as harmless eccentrics, as jokes. Few articles on "the problem of homosexuality" appeared in the scholarly journals of Britain, the United States, or Germany through the 1920s. In Hollywood, a hint—or double-dose—of androgyny in a Franklin Pangborn or a Jack Benny actually enhanced his popularity. As long as they maintained a heteronormative façade, perhaps being seen at parties on the arms of ladies or submitting to a studio marriage, William Haines could live openly with his lover, and Errol Flynn and Clark Gable could bed male partners with abandon (Faderman 2006, pp. 33–48).

There were thriving gay and lesbian communities in Hollywood and Harlem, in Paris and Berlin, with night spots, private parties, open expressions of romantic interest, open homoromantic unions (Miller 1995).

But the rumors of war brought the era of the "harmless eccentric" to a close. In 1937, U.S. Federal Bureau of Investigation (FBI) head J. Edgar Hoover declared "War on the Sex Criminal," by which he meant the "homosexual," and psychiatrists began careful examination of the inmates of prisons and psychiatric hospitals to see how closely linked the twin "evils" of same-sex desire and criminality might be. They found a strong causal link, at least in gay men (lesbians remained mostly tragic figures). They proclaimed, with increasing urgency as they waited out the Blitz in England and awaited the War in the U.S., that "homosexuality" was not an in-joke or a lascivious wink, but a dangerous disease, threatening body, mind, and soul (Bergler 1944; Hamilton 1939; Liebman 1944; Wuff 1942). "Homosexual psychopaths" did not confine themselves to depraved sexual acts; they were compelled to commit the most atrocious acts of rape and murder, not to mention seductions to produce more of their kind. Obviously they could not safely live among citizens. An alarum had been raised, and as Leon (2011) states, for the next 20 years, the "sexual psychopath" or the "sex fiend" was the chief bogeyman of both psychiatric and popular literature, the most significant factor in dividing the world into good/evil, civilized/uncivilized, healthy/depraved, and citizen/criminal (Corber 1997, pp. 23–30; Kimmel 1996, pp. 221–260; Terry 1999, pp. 329–342).

Drawing on their new awareness of the "homosexual," especially the male, as innately criminal, scholars began some rather feverish speculations about the cause of "homosexuality." The suggestions ranged from the inane to the ridiculous. Physicians suggested either autoeroticism or estrogen poisoning in the womb, and offered as evidence the thin, willowy frames, soft, hairless faces, long fingers, and high-pitched voices of gay asylum inmates. Psychiatrists and criminologists countered with Oedipal fixations, lack of early religious training, and absent or smothering mothers (or fathers). Sociologists suggested lack of social controls, lack of moral training, criminal subcultures, drug addiction, and simple evil (Ellis 1945; Greene and Johnson 1944; Moore 1945).

Sometimes the "homosexual" became even more important, not merely a criminal, but the only criminal. During the late 1930s and 1940s, criminology was informed by social disorganization theory, in which entire neighborhoods became criminogenic due to their transient populations (by which they meant ethnic minority and immigrant), who spurned gender roles and flaunted a subculture of "masculine women and feminine men" (Blumer 1937; Hawley 1944). During the 1950s, when family environment took precedence, criminologists interrogated juvenile delinquents for same-sex behavior in their life histories. Well into the 1970s, case studies of criminals commonly included "homosexual experience," often as a casual aside, as if such experience was expected, and case studies of "homosexuals" commonly included a laundry-list of minor criminal offenses, such as shoplifting and petty thefts, disorderly conduct, vagrancy, loitering, drug abuse, and vandalism.

In 1954, psychiatrist Charles E. Smith tried to understand the link between gay identity and crime: he compared 100 gay male prisoners in federal prisons with their presumably nongay counterparts (Smith 1954). He found, understandably, that the most common gay-related offenses were sodomy and postal law violations (attempting to use the U.S. mail to arrange sexual liaisons). The gay prisoners committed homicide, rape, and assault far less often than heterosexual prisoners; Smith explained that they were weak and feminine, not up to such macho crimes. They committed car theft, forgery, and robbery more often than heterosexual prisoners, Smith explained that these are usually impulsive crimes, and "homosexuals" were impulsive, excitable, and unable to exercise good judgment. Thus, the gay criminal was not prodigiously evil, doing bad things for the sheer joy of being bad; he had a pecuniary motive. His psychosis only increased his risk.

More commonly, the gay criminal was a fairy tale bogeyman, lurking in the shadows, waiting for an opportunity to kill and destroy. He was even more terrifying than the child molesters of the later "stranger danger" hysteria, because he could transform as well as destroy: the "normal" could turn gay with remarkable ease, even by hearing the word "homosexual." Thus, as Carpenter (2012, p. 6) states, U.S. federal policy of the period worried about the problem of a single "pervert" infecting an entire government office, and eventually the entire government. In 1958, the homophile organization One, Inc. won a major victory when the Supreme Court ruled that the word "homosexual" could be used in print; it would not, in itself, "deprave the weak-minded" (the most common test of obscenity at the time).

States adopted policies of containment and erasure, banning "immoral" plays, films, and books. In some cities, it was illegal for "known homosexuals" to purchase alcoholic beverages, gather in public places, and rent apartments. "Sexual outlaws" were forbidden from entering the U.S. (Eskridge lists many state laws and local ordinances 1999, pp. 328–384). Every state proscribed sexual acts, usually vaguely defined, plus such crimes as "indecent behavior," "contributing to sexual indecency," and "exposing a juvenile to immorality." In 1955, the Indiana Supreme Court heard the case of two men who were sitting in a parked car, arrested not for engaging in any physical contact but of "homosexual intent," and decided that intent was proscribed, even in the absence of activity (Carpenter 2012, p. 18). Moran (1995) notes that the Wolfenden Report, published in Britain in 1957, recommended the revocation of sodomy laws because the committee could not decide how to classify an act as "homosexual": what if a person engaged in a heterosexual or non-sexual act with "homosexual intent?" This expansion of the criminality of same-sex desire and behavior reflected the increasing perception of "gay" as universally malevolent, and led to the ongoing gay-coding of the fictional villain.

The Gay Villain

During the late 1930s and 1940s, novelists and movie and radio writers took note of the new link between gay and criminal identities, and when they wanted an adequately creepy villain, they began drawing upon the stereotypic mannerisms of "inversion." The Hayes Code (1930) forbade open explications of "sexual perversion" in movies, but it did not prohibit a mincing gait, a trembling voice, a leer, an air of sophistication and decadence, preferably with an actor who was tall, thin, and willowy, with the long face and long fingers of the homosexual pheno-type promoted by criminologists. A gay-coded villain appeared in the comic strip *Terry and the Pirates* as early as 1936 (Dennis 2012); during the 1940s, the type became popular, and then practically universal. Film noir offered Joe Cairo (Peter Lorre), the mincing, weak-willed gunsel in *The Maltese Falcon* (1941), and Johnny (Glenn Ford), passive boyfriend to Ballin (Joe Macready) in *Gilda* (1946). In thrillers, Alfred Hitchcock presented amoral gay murderers in *Rope* (1948) and *Strangers on a Train* (1951). Many critics have noted the homoerotic subtexts in gangster films; according to Richard Dyer (1993, p. 52), it was characterized by anguish, malaise, a loss of psychological bearings, and "a nebulous and poly-morphous" eroticism, or as Shadoian notes in homophobic contempt, "a tinge of abnormality" (1977, p. 72).

The type of the gay villain remained popular for the next 50 years, and shows no sign of abating. James Bond movies have run the superspy against a huge assortment of gay-vague "sexual misfits"—or not so gay-vague, as the transvestite Spectre agent in *Thunderball* (1965) or the hand-holding Mr. Witt and Mr. Kidd in *Diamonds are Forever* (1971). In *Skyfall* (2012), Javier Bardem camps it up as an openly bisexual villain.

Juvenile media was no exception. Disney gave us long-faced, sophisticated, gay-coded villains in everything from *Peter Pan* (1953) to *Aladdin* (1992), and the gastrophile Anton Ego in *Ratatouille* (2007). On the Cartoon Network, *The Powerpuff Girls* (1998–2005) had the preteen superheroes face off against a swishing, falsetto-voiced devil in a pink tutu, black leather boots, and a pink boa. He was known only as Him, the masculine pronoun emphasizing his gay-coded gender-transgression.

The First Gay Victims

During the 1940s and 1950s, criminologists and psychiatrists occasionally evoked crime victimization as a significant risk of adopting an "active homosexual life-style." LGBT people placed themselves in danger of extortion and blackmail from either heterosexuals or their own compatriots who threatened to reveal their "shameful secret" to the world. They assumed the risk of assault and murder when they chose to align themselves with a criminal demimonde (Rupp 1970). Often they actively sought out violent victimization, reifying a desire to be punished for their wrongdoing. Guy Hocqueghem evoked "the intimate, ancient, and very strong bond between the homosexual and his murderer" (quoted in Altman 1983, p. 65). This explanation for gay victimization remained strong in mass media for many years: in *Midnight Cowboy* (1969), a gay client welcomes an assault by hustler Joe Buck, stating that he deserves it; and in *Cruising* (1980), a serial killer moves easily through Manhattan's gay community because many of his victims desire and welcome death.

During the 1950s, the fledgling gay press began to publicize "gay bashing," heterosexual assaults on LGBT persons as a form of recreation (D'Emilio 1983). Reports increased dramatically with the rise of the Gay Rights Movement in the 1970s, both because LGBT persons were experiencing a sense of empowerment, and because their increased visibility sparked antigay hostility (Ireland 1979; Rofes 1978). Criminologists continued to blame the victim. D. J. West stated, "*of course* homosexuals who put themselves in compromising positions are in danger of attack...from ordinary young delinquents whose exuberant aggression finds an outlet in the sport of 'queer-bashing'" (1977, p. 204; italics mine). What did you expect when you stayed out too late, cruised in sleazy bars, and made lewd propositions to straight people (Saghir and Robins 1980; Sangarin and MacNamara 1975)?

By the end of the 1970s, however, the image of the "homosexual" prowling city streets, seeking to seduce straight people, was fading away, replaced by a new image of gay ghettos, subcultures completely distinct from the mainstream, shadowy zones on the margins of "normal society." Police departments in big cities marked off gay neighborhoods for special patrolling, and geographers evoked "forbidden fruitlands" (pun probably intended) where "activities, normally considered illegal, such as gambling, prostitution, and overt homosexual behavior, cluster" (Weightman 1981, p. 107; Zukin 1995; see, also, in this volume Dwyer; Johnson; Nichols).

In these shadow zones, safely isolated from heterosexuals, LGBT people remained both criminals and victims, robbing, assaulting, and blackmailing their compatriots, and in turn being robbed, assaulted, and blackmailed. Maghan and Sangarin (1983, pp. 160–161) argue that "crime-prone people commit their illegal acts where the opportunity is offered...the victim turned offender finds a ready target in his own backyard, neighborhood, or bedroom. So it is with homosexuality."

Beginning in the mid-1980s, AIDS and the association of gay people with contagion accelerated the number and severity of cases of antigay violence. A proliferation of local antiviolence projects, some of which established coalitions with Jewish and African-American antiviolence watchdogs, led to extensive lobbying and several influential pieces of state and federal legislation, such as the Hate Crime Statistics Act (1990) and the Violent Crime Control and Law Enforcement Act (1994). In 1989 and 1991, Gary Comstock (1991) published the results of the first national survey of hate crime victimization among gay men and lesbians; in 1990, a special issue of *The Journal of Interpersonal Violence* was devoted to antigay hate crimes, and later published in book form. Many other articles on antigay hate crimes appeared in the 1990s (e.g., Berk et al. 1992; Herek 1992).

AIDS also impacted the criminological literature. Discourses about gay criminality faded into silence by the mid-1990s (thousands of people dying in hospices can hardly be responsible for all of the evil in the world). Instead, hundreds of articles and books made LGBT persons victims: of AIDS, antigay violence, domestic violence, hate crimes, job discrimination, harassment, and oppression. Same-sex desire and behavior were still linked with death, dying, pain, and misery, but with a lack of agency as the LGBT person was buffeted about by a cruel fate.

From Villain to Victim on TV

We can trace the shift from villain to victim by investigating mass culture, especially television and film. The first specifically identified gay character on American network television appeared in a 1971 episode of the sitcom *All in the Family,* and during the next 20 years, many television programs included gay characters in individual episodes, especially comedies that aspired to be hip or dramas that aspired to be "gritty and realistic." Table 1.1, based on my own research project, tabulates the individual episodes of American television programs in which LGBT persons were portrayed as victims (of crime, serial killers, gay-bashing or AIDS), as villains (criminal offenders or otherwise evil), or other ("coming out," experiencing noncriminal harassment).

Note that comedies presented LGBT persons overwhelmingly as "other," neither victims nor villains, as usually problems for the straight characters to solve. But in dramas, the 1970s were informed by LGBT villains, usually murderers. A Presidential cabinet nominee kills his lover and his sister to prevent them from outing him. A coin collector who is involved with both a man and a woman tries to murder them both. A lesbian murders her lover. A transvestite slashes women (because he cannot really be a woman, and he is jealous).

The percentage of dramatic series portraying villains dropped substantially during the 1980s, from 54.5 to 38.5 %, and again in the 1990s, to 17.5 %. The villains also became more gender-transgressive, more overtly drawing upon heterosexual audience fears of the feminine. Transvestites murdered as a symptom of their "identity confusion," or because they felt threatened by their "other personality," however that would work.

We see a similar pattern in film. While the sophisticated, vaguely feminine gay male villain and vaguely butch, predatory lesbian remained popular villains through the 1980s and 1990s, it became more common to feature extreme "gender confusion," suggesting that not all LGBT persons are villains, just those who transgress gender conventions. Novel attempts at sex-reassignment occur in

Table 1.1 Depictions of LGBT persons on American prime time television, 1970–1999

	Drama			Comedy		
	1970s	1980s	1990s	1970s	1980s	1990s
Victim (%)	30.3	27.9	42.1	12.9	7.1	21.5
Villain (%)	54.5	38.5	17.5	3.2	10.7	4.5
Other (%)	18.2	33.6	40.4	83.9	82.1	75.5
n	33	39	57	36	34	66

Silence of the Lambs (1991), where Buffalo Bill is making himself a suit of female skin to wear, and more recently in *The X-Files: I Want to Believe* (2008), in which a man is grafting his male lover's head onto a woman's body.

The percentage of dramatic portrayals of LGBT persons as victims on television remained stable from the 1970s to the 1980s, declining from 30.3 to 27.9 %, but the type of victimization changed, from being murdered by serial killers to contracting AIDS. In the 1990s, the percentage increased to 42.1 %, but the number of AIDS victims declined sharply; now LGBT people were victimized almost exclusively by homophobic violence.

The Gay Victim and Criminology

Though it is nicer to be assumed a victim than a criminal, discourses of gay victims eliminates their agency and separates them from the normal, "everyday" world where crime is rare, an unwelcome intrusion from outside. LGBT persons still occupy "forbidden fruitlands," except now instead of lurking in the shadows, they have become the prey of those who lurk. As a result, LGBT people have been all but erased from criminology (see, too, discussions in this volume by Ball; Panfil; Woods).

In the fall of 2012, I conducted a keyword search of "gay," "homosexual," "LGBT," and "sexual orientation" in articles published in professional criminology journals between 2000 and 2012, and found over 300 studies of LGBT persons as victims of hate crimes, domestic violence by their partners, and oppressive laws and legal systems. There were a dozen or more studies of same-sex practices in prison, but they were usually framed as forms of domination or sexual release among heterosexual men in an exclusively heterosexual environment (e.g., Alarid 2000). There were studies of LGBT offenders in the domains of prostitution, pedophilia, and other sex crimes. But I found no articles that discussed LGBT persons as offenders in non-sexual crimes, suggesting that criminologists, students, and the world tend to believe that only heterosexuals are ever arrested for vandalism, weapons offenses, or disorderly conduct, or perhaps that only heterosexuals exist at all outside the narrow confines of sex crimes (see too, Panfil, this volume). As confirmation, I scanned the indexes of ten popular criminology textbooks, and found LGBT persons mentioned only in outdated statements about sodomy laws and lists of the targets included in FBI Hate Crime Reports.

The impact of heterosexist erasure on those LGBT individuals who are introduced into the criminal justice system is severe. As Irvine notes (2010), juveniles in juvenile detention, always assumed to be heterosexual, are given advice about heterosexual courtship and marriage, enrolled in homophobic faith-based programs, and punished severely for gender transgressions (see too Belknap, Little, and Holsinger's chapter on LGB youth in juvenile facilities, this volume). My research into prison populations suggests that gay male prisoners are substantially more likely than heterosexual prisoners to be assaulted and to suffer from many medical problems, such as heart disease and diabetes. Gay female prisoners are more likely than heterosexual prisoners to suffer from emotional problems and drug addiction, and to require psychiatric hospitalization.

It would be more profitable to interpret and understand LGBT persons as neither innate villains nor innate victims, but as capable of the entire gamut of human activity, capable of being both law-abiding citizens and criminals. The historical and cultural milieu of the LGBT experience, such as growing up with parents who are generally not gay and often homophobic, may produce a different trajectory into criminality, and a different configuration of crimes than we see among heterosexuals.

The LGBT Offender

The most promising theoretical framework for beginning a study of the LGBT offender is not queer theory, which is more concerned with broad issues of marginalization and exclusion, but conflict theory, which originated in Marxist studies of class differences in crime (but read Ball's and Woods's perspectives, this volume). According to conflict theory, groups in each society compete for social, political, and economic capital, or wealth, power, and prestige. Members of "dominant" groups (majority races, religions, social classes, and sexual identities) have adequate capital to universalize their norms: teach them in schools, legislate them into law, promote them in mass media. They then justify the social inequality by labeling "subordinate" groups (minority races, religions, social classes, and sexual identities) deviant: uncivilized, violent, illogical, barbaric, overly sexual or asexual, superstitious, duplicitous, trivial, emotional, and so on (Collins 2010; Dahrendorf 1959).

Members of subordinate groups tend to experience increased surveillance by both the police and the general population, so they are observed and challenged more often for engaging in criminal acts, and even borderline acts; talking loudly on the street may pass unnoticed if you are white, but result in a disorderly conduct arrest if you are black. They are thus likely to experience a disproportionately large number of police stops and arrests (Barak et al. 2010; Reiman 2009). For instance, in 2010 African-Americans constituted about 13 % of the U.S. population but 41 % of arrests for violent crimes, 32 % for serious property crimes, 41 % for disorderly conduct, and 72 % for gambling (FBI 2011).

However, the disproportion is not merely a matter of biased perception. Conflict theory also states that members of subordinate groups objectively commit more crimes. First, they internalize stereotypes, reasoning that if teachers, the police, and other authority figures believe them to be bad, they must be bad. Second, they can hardly be expected to have a strong attachment to social institutions responsible for their ongoing oppression. Third, they may respond to their low economic capital by engaging in "self-help" (Collins 2010).

Conflict theory can apply to LGBT offenders in three ways, depending on how LGBT persons are viewed by onlookers, and how they respond to ongoing oppression. This suggests three hypotheses.

Hypothesis 1: LGBT identities function like racial identities, with visible identity markers and an increased sense of danger or fear in onlookers. In this case, LGBT criminal behavior should begin early, with problem behaviors and status offenses in early adolescence as a means of escaping homophobic harassment and fitting in with heterosexual peers. LGBT persons should also experience a stronger involvement in criminal subcultures as they look for alternative avenues to social capital. In addition, they should be arrested and adjudicated more often than heterosexuals, especially for highly visible offenses like disorderly conduct.

Hypothesis 2: LGBT identities function like gender, with visible identity markers but a decreased sense of danger or fear in onlookers. Although men constitute a dominant group, with high levels of political, social, and economic capital, they are arrested far more often for most offenses than women. Some gender theorists attribute this reverse gap to the special nature of gender-based oppression: women are stereotyped as weak, nurturing, and harmless, much less of a threat than men (Britton 2011). Thus, they are under less surveillance; a woman talking loudly on the street is unlikely to be arrested. When they do commit crimes, the authorities assume that they have been influenced by a man, so they receive less severe punishment (Merlo and Pollock 2005). If LGBT people, and especially gay men, tend to be perceived as weak, harmless, and laughably inept rather than threatening, then they should have a lower rate of criminality, and their general trajectories into criminal activity should closely resemble those of heterosexuals of similar races and social classes.

Hypothesis 3: LGBT identities function like religion, with few visible identity markers, and therefore no additional surveillance. Religion is largely invisible to outsiders, unless you are wearing a visual marker of religious status, like a Star of David or a hijab. But adherents of religions with recognizable identity markers tend to belong to ethnic minorities, so any surveillance they receive is probably due to their race or ethnicity, not to their religion. We also find little difference in either self-reports or arrest/adjudication rates between dominant and subordinate religious groups. For instance, Smith and Faris (2002) found that Protestant and Roman Catholic juveniles were equally likely or slightly more likely than Jewish juveniles to self-report fighting, stealing, and vandalism; and in their study of German youth, Brettfeld and Wezels (2003) found no difference in self-reports between religious and non-religious Muslims and non-religious Christians. This hypothesis states that individuals are commonly identified as LGBT only if they make a specific statement, if they express gender-transgressive traits, if they are wearing gay symbols (a pink triangle, a lambda, a gay pride flag), if they are engaging in same-sex affection at that moment, or if they are seen patronizing a gay establishment. Otherwise, heteronormativity dictates that strangers, acquaintances, and friends will invariably assume that they are heterosexual. Indeed, many LGBT individuals attempt to minimize harassment by "passing," pretending to be heterosexual in public situations. If they cannot be identified, they cannot be placed under more surveillance, although minority stress can still lead to "acting out," an increase in the proportion of criminal offenses (Epstein 1996).

LGBT Delinquents

Most research conducted during the last decade on LGBT persons as criminal offenders has occurred with juvenile populations. Regarding the incidence of criminality, Garnette and colleagues (2011) found that 13 % of male incarcerated youth were gay, and 23 % of females were lesbian, somewhat larger than the gay/lesbian population of 5–10 %. Another 3 % were heterosexual, but harassed due to gender nonconformity. This suggests an increased surveillance and increased intervention of LGBT youth.

In a study of self-reports of juveniles not involved with the juvenile justice system, Hunter (2004) found that lesbians were significantly more likely than heterosexual girls to self-report minor, serious, and violent offenses. However, gay male juveniles had an increased incidence only of minor violations; they were less likely than heterosexual male juveniles to engage in violent offenses, and equally likely to engage in serious non-violent offenses. Since self-reports are based on incidence rather than surveillance, this suggests an internalization of gender-transgressive stereotypes, especially for the youth who are likely to identify as LGBT at an early age.

Soto (2007) looked at factors increasing delinquency risk for gay/lesbian youth (see too Conover-Williams, this volume). Some deterring factors, such as having a high GPA, are similar to those we see with youth in general. Others, such as having gay-positive parents, have no parallel among heterosexuals, and sometimes the effect is reversed: having a boyfriend or girlfriend deters gay/lesbian youth but increases risk for heterosexual youth. Both parental acceptance and a romantic partner tend to enhance the juvenile's attachment to the LGBT subculture, thus decreasing antisocial behavior.

The Gay/Lesbian Prisoner

Since few studies of LGBT adult offenders have been conducted for many years, I conducted a preliminary study of gay/lesbian inmates in state and federal prisons, using the 2004 National Inmate Survey. The lack of classification was a significant hurdle. Although race, age, and gender are asked on every level of the adjudication process, sexual orientation is not. The 2007 National Inmate Survey was the first official criminal justice survey to specifically ask the sexual orientation of prisoners; unfortunately, it did not ask other necessary background variables.

In the 2004 survey, several questions allowed for an admission of same-sex romantic partners. Respondents were asked, "in the month before your arrest, was anyone living with you?" Other surveys conflated "boyfriend" and "girlfriend" into a single response, or instructed researchers to select the "appropriate" term for the respondent's sex, assuming that all prison inmates were necessarily heterosexual; but these surveys did not, thus allowing male respondents to state that they had been living with a boyfriend, and female respondents, with a girlfriend. Similarly, respondents could mention same-sex partners in response to the question: "After you are released, who do you intend to live with?"

Certainly there was a huge amount of informal pressure placed on the inmate to exclude same-sex boyfriends/girlfriends, or to subsume them under the category "unrelated friend/nonrelative." Nevertheless, 249 women and 134 men disclosed that they had been living with same-sex partners, or intended to live with them upon their release. I coded them as "gay" or "lesbian," aware that this designation might not match the fluidity of desire, behavior, and identity (for discussions of these issues, see chapters in this volume by Frederick; Johnson; Messinger; Woods).

But who should the group of partnered gay men and lesbians be compared with? The general prison population would include an unknown number of single gay inmates. Most gay people in the United States cannot marry, so they tend to perceive a live-in partnership as an equivalent. Therefore I compared them to the prisoners who lived with or planned to live with an opposite-sex partner (2128 women and 5826 men). They were coded as "heterosexual," again with an awareness of the potential fluidity in their identities. There was no way to distinguish bisexual and transgender persons.

In the U.S. there are about 11 million cohabitating couples, 89 % heterosexual, 6 % gay male, and 5 % lesbian (Bureau of the Census 2011). However, gay men comprised 2.3 % of the sample, and lesbians 11.7 %. This suggests a smaller proportion of gay men and a larger proportion of lesbians involved in the criminal justice system, suggesting a reversal of surveillance similar to the male/female gender gap in Hypothesis #2: gay men perceived as weak and passive, lesbians as dangerous.

Gay men were significantly more likely than heterosexual men to be in prison for public order offenses, such as disorderly conduct, which require police observation and are thus susceptible to the demonization of subordinate groups. They were less likely than heterosexual men to be in prison for violent offenses such as robbery, assault, and homicide. With lesbians, the pattern was reversed, more violent and fewer public order offenses than heterosexual women. This suggests the internalization of stereotypes in Hypothesis 2. Gay men, internalizing stereotypes of weakness and passivity, may be less likely to consider violent crime as an option than heterosexual men working to maintain a façade of hegemonic masculinity (Messerschmidt 1993; but see Panfil, this volume). Similarly, lesbians, perceived as strong, aggressive, and "dominant," are more likely to consider violent crime as an option than heterosexual women.

Several differences in the life histories of the gay/lesbian inmates suggested significantly different trajectories into crime. During adolescence, heterosexual male inmates were more likely to have friends who used drugs (71.1 % versus 53.2 %) and damaged property, but gay male inmates were more likely to have friends who committed more serious offenses, such as auto theft, burglary, and robbery. When their friends engaged in delinquent behavior, 90.2 % of gay men and 80.2 % of heterosexual men joined in (chi square 2.8, p = 0.008). Gay men also began their criminal activity at an earlier age than heterosexual men. The tendency to have friends who engaged in more, and more serious, criminal offenses may be the result of trying to "fit in" with heteronormative society by selecting the most aggressive associates possible. Soto (2007) found similar results in the study of gay/lesbian juveniles; having heterosexual friends was a significant predictor of delinquency. Again, Hypothesis 2 is suggested.

Conclusion

Even these few studies reveal that not all criminals are heterosexual; a significant percentage of those individuals involved in the criminal justice system are LGBT. They also reveal that LGBT offenders differ from heterosexual offenders in the nature and extent of their criminality, the types of crimes they engage, and their childhood and adolescent trajectory into crime. Much more research needs to be done in this area, both to facilitate crime prevention efforts and to ameliorate the treatment of LGBT delinquents and adult arrestees and prisoners. However, first the discipline of criminology must acknowledge that LGBT persons are neither innate villains nor innate victims, but have the full human capacity to engage in prosocial, antisocial, positive, negative, heroic, self-serving, noble, and despicable acts.

References

Alarid, L. T. (2000). Sexual orientation perspectives of incarcerated bisexual and gay men: The county jail protective custody experience. *Prison Journal, 80*(1), 80–95.

Altman, D. (1983). *The homosexualization of America*. Boston: Beacon Press.

Barak, G., Leighton, P., & Flavin, J. (2010). *Class, race, gender, and crime: The social realities of justice in America*. Lanham, MD: Rowman and Littlefield.

Bergler, E. (1944). Eight prerequisites for the psychoanalytic treatment of homosexuality. *Psychoanalytic Review, 31*, 253–286.

Berk, R., Boyd, E., & Hamner, K. (1992). Thinking more clearly about hate-motivated crime. In G. Herek & T. Berrill (Eds.), *Hate crimes* (pp. 123–143). Newbury Park, CA: Sage.

Blumer, H. (1937). Social disorganization and individual disorganization. *American Journal of Sociology, 42*(6), 871–877.

Boswell, J. (1994) Dante and the Sodomites. *Dante Studies, 112*, 63–76.

Brettfeld, K., & Wezels, P. (2003). *Muslime in Deutschland*. Berlin: Bundesministerium des Inneren.

Britton, D. (2011). *The gender of crime*. Lanham, MD: Rowman and Littlefield.

Bureau of the Census. (2011). *Working paper on the change in cohabitating couples from 2009 to 2010*. Washington, DC: Bureau of the Census.

Carpenter, D. (2012). *Flagrant conduct: The story of Lawrence v. Texas*. New York, NY: Norton.

Collins, R. (2010). *Conflict sociology: A sociological classic updated*. Boulder, CO: Paradigm Publishers.

Comstock, G. D. (1991). *Violence against lesbians and gay men*. New York, NY: Columbia University Press.

Corber, R. J. (1997). *Homosexuality in cold war America: Resistance and the crisis of masculinity*. Durham, NC: Duke University Press.

Dahrendorf, R. (1959). *Class and conflict in industrial society*. Stanford, CA: Stanford University Press.

D'Emilio, J. (1983). *Sexual politics, sexual communities: The making of a gay and lesbian movement, 1940–1970*. Chicago, IL: University of Chicago Press.

Dennis, J. (2012). Gay content in newspaper comics. *Journal of American Culture, 35*(4), 304–314.

Dyer, R. (1993). Homosexuality and film noir. In R. Dyer (Ed.), *The matter of images* (pp. 52–72). New York, NY: Routledge.

Ellis, A. (1945). The sexual psychology of human hermaphrodites. *Psychosomatic Medicine, 7*, 108–125.

Epstein, D. (1996). Keeping them in their place: Heterosexist harassment, gender, and the enforcement of heterosexuality. In L. Adkins & J. Holland (Eds.), *Sexualizing the social* (pp. 181–196). London, UK: Macmillan.

Eskridge, W. (1999). *Gaylaw: Challenging the apartheid of the closet*. Cambridge, MA: Harvard University Press.

Faderman, L., & Gay L.A. (2006). *A history of sexual outlaws, power politics and Lipstick Lesbians*. New York, NY: Basic Books.

Federal Bureau of Investigation. (2011). *Crime in the United States, 2010*. Washington, DC: Federal Bureau of Investigation.

Garnette, L., Irvine, A., Reyes, C., & Wilber, S. (2011). Lesbian, gay, bisexual and transgender (LGBT) youth and the juvenile justice system. In F. T. Sherman & F. H. Jacobs (Eds.), *Juvenile justice: Advancing research, policy, and practice* (pp. 156–173). Hoboken, NJ: Wiley.

Green, E. W., & Johnson, L. G. (1944). Homosexuality. *Journal of Criminal Psychopathology, 5*, 467–480.

Groombridge, N. (1999). Perverse criminologies: The closet of Doctor Lombroso. *Social and Legal Studies, 8*(4), 531–548.

Hamilton, D. M. (1939). Some aspects of homo-sexuality in relation to total personality development. *Psychiatric Quarterly, 13*, 229–244.

Hawley, A. (1944). Ecology and human ecology. *Social Forces, 42*(4), 398–405.

Herek, G. M. (1992). The social context of anti-gay violence: Notes on cultural heterosexism. In G. Herek & T. Berrill (Eds.), *Hate crimes* (pp. 89–104). Newbury Park, CA: Sage.

Hunter, J. (2004). Developmental pathways in youth sexual aggression and delinquency. *Journal of Family Violence, 19*(4), 233–242.

Ireland, D. (1979). The new homophobia: Open season on gays. *Nation, 229*, 207–210.

Irvine, A. (2010). "We've had three of them": Addressing the invisibility of lesbian, gay, bisexual and gender non-conforming youths in the juvenile justice system. *Columbia Journal of Gender and the Law, 19*(3), 675–701.

Jordan, M. L. (1998). *The invention of sodomy in Christian theology*. Chicago, IL: University of Chicago Press.

Katz, J. (2007). *The invention of heterosexuality*. Chicago, IL: University of Chicago Press.

Kimmel, M. (1996). *Manhood in America*. New York, NY: Free Press.

Leon, C. S. (2011). *Sex fiends, perverts, and pedophiles: Understanding sex crime policy in America*. New York, NY: NYU Press.

Liebman, S. (1944). Homosexuality, transvestism, and psychosis. *Journal of Nervous and Mental Disease, 99*, 945–958.

Maghan, J., & Sangarin, E. (1983). Homosexuals as victimizers and victims. In D. MacNamara & A. Karman (Eds.), *Deviants: Victims or victimizers?* (pp. 147–162). Beverly Hills, CA: Sage.

Merlo, A., & Pollock, J. (2005). *Women, law, and social control*. Boston, MA: Allyn and Bacon.

Messerschmidt, J. W. (1993). *Masculinities and crime*. Lanham, MD: Rowman and Littlefield.

Miller, N. (1995). *Out of the past: Gay and lesbian history since 1869*. New York, NY: Vintage.

Moran, L. (1995). The homosexualization of English law. In D. Herman (Ed.), *Legal inversions* (pp. 3–28). Philadelphia, PA: Temple University Press.

Moran, L. (1998). Oscar Wilde: Law, memory, and the proper name. In L. J. Moran, D. Monk, & S. Beresford (Eds.), *Legal queries: Lesbian, gay and transgender legal studies* (pp. 10–25). London, UK: Cassell.

Moore, T. V. (1945). The pathogenesis and treatment of homosexual disorders. *Journal of Personality, 14*, 47–83.

Oosterhuis, H. (2000). *Stepchildren of nature: Krafft-Ebing, psychiatry, and the making of sexual identity*. Chicago, IL: University of Chicago Press.

Reiman, J. (2009). *The rich get richer and the poor get prison: Ideology, class, and criminal justice*. Upper Saddle River, NY: Prentice-Hall.

Rofes, E. (1978). Queer bashing. *Gay Community News* (Aug 12), 8–11.

Rupp, J. C. (1970). Sudden death in the gay world. *Medical Science and the Law, 10*, 189–191.

Saghir, M., & Robins, E. (1980). Clinical aspects of female homosexuality. In J. Marmor (Ed.), *Homosexual behavior* (pp. 280–295). New York, NY: Basic Books.

Sangarin, E., & MacNamara, D. E. (1975). The homosexual as a crime victim. *International Journal of Criminology and Penology, 3*(1), 13–25.

Shadoian, J. (1977). *Dreams and dead ends: The American gangster film*. New York, NY: Oxford University Press.

Smith, C. E. (1954). The homosexual federal offender: A study of 100 cases. *Journal of Criminal Law, Criminology, and Police Science, 44*(5), 582–591.

Smith, C., & Faris, R. (2002). *Religion and American adolescent delinquency, risk behaviors, and constructive social activities*. Chapel Hill, NC: National Study of Youth and Religion.

Soto, D. (2007). *Sexual orientation, gender, and adolescent involvement in delinquency*. (Unpublished doctoral dissertation). Bowling Green State University, Bowling Green, OH.

Terry, J. (1999). *An American obsession: Science, medicine, and homosexuality in modern society*. Chicago, IL: University of Chicago Press.

Tomsen, S. (1997). *Was Lombroso a queer? Criminology, criminal justice, and the heterosexual imaginary*. Sydney, Australia: Hawkins Press, Australian Institute of Criminology.

Weightman, B. (1981). Commentary: Towards a geography of the gay community. *Journal of Cultural Geography, 1*, 106–112.

West, D. J. (1977). *Homosexuality re-examined*. Minneapolis, MN: University of Minnesota Press.

Wuff, M. (1942). A case of male homosexuality. *International Journal of Psycho-Analysis, 23*, 112–120.

Zukin, S. (1995). *The culture of cities*. Malden, MA: Blackwell.

Chapter 6
When They Tell You Who You Are: Lesbian Resistance to the Policing of Multiple Identities

Dominique E. Johnson

Abstract Lesbian resistance to the policing of their multiple identities provides an important example of agency in the era of big data. Revisiting an earlier article about the lesbian gang Dykes Taking Over (DTO) as an example of lesbian resistance now 10 years later, this chapter presents their experiences with systems of control in school as tactics for resistance to the biopower inherent in these data regimes. As extensions of the panopticon and yet another expression of the carceral society (Foucault 1995, 2003), the experiences of DTO indicate that these data are used to control populations, not to liberate them. These themes are investigated in context of intersectionality, resistance to surveillance, bullying in schools, and the implications of data regimes operating as organizing forces in activist contexts. Arguing that the use of big data presents a critical dilemma where identities are verified and presented as a finite number of choices, communities such as the greater LGBT community will lose agency in self definition if they organize around these identities to the exclusion of others. Challenging the invisibility imposed on multiplicative being will be a necessary act so that self identification will not become a practical impossibility in this new future.

Keywords Lesbian · Surveillance · Gangs · Policing · Data · Quantitative methodology · Intersectionality

A portion of this chapter was originally published in Johnson (2007) and is reprinted here by permission of Taylor & Francis Ltd, http://www.tandf.co.uk/journals. An earlier version of this chapter was presented as "Critical Dilemmas and Methodological Regimes: Toward a Genealogy of an Empirical Borderland" at the Foucault Society Symposium in New York City.

D. E. Johnson (✉)
Beam Youth Collaborative, 345 Pine Street, Philadelphia, PA 19107, USA
e-mail: djohnson@beamyouth.org

It first appeared in our school last year. I didn't know what it was, I thought it was somebody's initials and I asked the school police, "Who is DTO?" They looked at me like I was crazy…. "Who is this kid who is signing his initials on our wall?" The school police said this stands for "Dykes Taking Over." Ms. Johnson, Principal (WYBE-TV 2002).

It is no surprise that some young lesbians might form gangs, both preemptively and in retaliation to harassment. Dykes Taking Over (DTO), referenced above, is just one example of a lesbian student gang in the United States (Johnson 2007). This chapter builds on an earlier article about DTO and the social context of this lesbian student gang now a decade after it first came to the attention of the greater public in Philadelphia, Pennsylvania. DTO is used for illustrative purposes in this chapter as opposed to serving as its central focus. Specifically, DTO serves as an example to expand the previous discussion to consider the experiences of other young lesbians of color. The chapter focuses especially on the implications of how new technologies of recognition, most notably big data, might be a force for further marginalization in the education and criminal justice systems and a manifestation of biopower in these contexts. The panoptic quality of our twenty-first century life and the power inherent in the process of being validated by it creates a landscape that is potentially defining and redefining who and what we are, who is and who is not. This necessitates a careful questioning of these practices and the related goals of wanting to join this developing quantitative matrix.

The political ramifications of gathering big data in the new century are explored in this chapter as they relate to intersectionality, resistance to surveillance, bullying in schools, and the implications of data regimes operating as organizing forces in activist contexts (see also Ball, this volume, for additional critiques). This chapter argues that the use of big data presents a critical dilemma where identities are verified by their existence though data alone, establishing a finite number of choices. Communities such as the LGBT community will then organize around these identities to the exclusion of others. The borderlands of identity will only continue into the future if we are able to imagine these borderlands through the process of self definition. Lesbian resistance to the policing of multiple identities, like the resistance of DTO, lays this groundwork to challenge the invisibility imposed on intersectional identities and life in the borderlands. The implications of proceeding without critical resistance are also discussed.

The section "Lesbian Youth in Resistance" discusses lesbian youth as agents of resistance in context of their lived experiences. The section "Critical Dilemmas: Intersectionality and the Quantitification of Identities" considers intersectionality and the challenges of visibility in this new era of quantifying identities. The section "Lesbians in the Queer Landscape of the Borderlands" focuses on the borderlands of big data and the exercise of biopower in control of lesbian identities and bodies. The section "Policing Lesbian Gangs: Negotiating Multiple Identities and Challenging Invisibility" revisits DTO as an example of lesbian resistance now 10 years later. The section "Queer Recognition in Methodological Regimes" explores the drive to seek recognition in the quantitative matrix, followed by a conclusion that asks if self identification will be a practical impossibility in this new future.

Lesbian Youth in Resistance

Since DTO first emerged over 10 years ago, lesbian youth continue to experience homophobia along multiple dimensions in their schools and communities, from both their peers and the adults in their lives. They also endure injustice in the streets from law enforcement, particularly when they are together in public as a group. Statistics indicate that 90 % of LGBTQ teens (versus 62 % of non-LGBTQ teens) have been verbally or physically harassed or assaulted because of their perceived or actual appearance, gender, sexual orientation, gender expression, race/ethnicity, disability, or religion (Berlan and Austin 2007). But no national data on the experiences of violence among lesbian youth, particularly lesbian youth of color, is yet available.

Additionally, the masculine female adolescent is largely ignored in the gender binary-reinforcing research literature on both girls (Artz 1999; Barnett and Rivers 2006; Pepler et al. 2004; Pipher 1994; Simmons 2002; Wiseman 2002) and boys (Kindlon and Thompson 2000; Pollack 1988; Tyre 2006; Weaver-Hightower 2003). The fact that many gender nonconforming young women identify as lesbians contributes to the escalation of this discrimination (Rehder 2001; Rich 1980). The research that is available describes the significant sex discrimination and discrimination based on gender expression endured by young lesbians in school, both from peers and school personnel (Ma'ayan 2003). Despite this, young lesbians resist the policing of their identities and bodies and assert a place for themselves in their schools and communities.

But what happens when this lesbian resistance now operates in the context of big data? The new trend of big data allows for panoptic surveillance of aspects of life beyond traditional surveillance techniques. These data technologies surpass street cameras and gather data into large sets that allow recognition of individuals and sorting into groups. Data science is an emergent field of inquiry and by many accounts we are in a new age, marked by technological sophistication and this ever-increasing and vast data infrastructure. Data is increasingly global and without borders. Big data is now affecting the ways in which intersectional identities might also be reified within specific cultures and nations. These notions of identity in turn might eschew the importance of the socio-historical contexts from which they emerged. Interpreting intersectional identities from big data will require an understanding of larger contexts in which individuals are situated. The very process of collecting, cleaning, and interpreting big data could in fact render any such context invisible. Lesbian resistance to the policing of identities and bodies and their life claimed in the borderlands of identity provide a much needed example to explore in this new data-rich terrain.

Critical Dilemmas: Intersectionality and the Quantification of Identities

Young lesbians of color have always navigated life in the borderlands. Sakia Gunn, an African-American 15-year-old, was murdered at a Newark bus stop in 2003. A 29-year-old man tried to convince her and her friends to enter his vehicle, presumably with the intent to initiate a sexual encounter; they told him they were lesbians (Johnson 2006). Calling Sakia a dyke, he grabbed her and stabbed her in the chest. Young Black lesbians who identify as aggressives, like Sakia Gunn, demonstrate the purposeful use of this word as an identity marker (Moore 2006). Since Sakia Gunn's murder, young Black lesbians continue to endure street harassment and violence because of their sexuality, race, and gender presentation. Members of the Lesbian Seven from Newark, New Jersey are still incarcerated. The last of these women will be released from prison in August 2013, having spent 7 years in a New York correctional facility after being convicted of assaulting a man after he threatened to rape them when they rebuffed his sexual advances on a street in the West Village of New York City. The seven women, friends with Sakia Gunn, acted in self-defense and a fight broke out, resulting in their arrests and subsequent trials for four of the women on charges of gang assault (which, in New York State is assault committed by two or more persons, who may or may not be a "gang"). The longest sentence received was 11 years. Groups of young lesbians of color are still policed as gangs whether or not they actually are members of a gang (Johnson 2007). Anti-lesbian violence remains a defensible act in society. Sometimes the gay panic defense is argued, where a person is assaulted for "making sexual overtures" (Patton 2000, p. 149). Lesbian threat is also deployed, often like the gay panic defense, where lesbian bashers might argue they were physically threatened. But the lesbian refusal of sexual advances (harassment) is an assault on the male lesbian basher's masculinity, and this threat plays into the fear of the lesbian body and specifically the masculine lesbian body.

Too often this violence becomes the dominant frame that society uses to define young lesbian identity. With very few exceptions research has also been very silent on these issues, particularly the gender presentation and expression of Black lesbians. Moore's (2006) breakthrough article argued that there are various physical representations of gender in Black lesbian communities that are related to a conscious decision as to how to present oneself to the world and to prospective romantic partners in particular. This presentation of self through gender expression comes into play not only in gender role expectations in interpersonal relationships but also in expectations for social interaction and in building African-American lesbian communities. In addition, Moore (2006) presented an historical framework for understanding these relationships between gender presentation and community, rooted deeply in the Black lesbian identities emerging from Black lesbian feminism.

More recent research sought to establish a framework for understanding how to quantitatively express Black lesbian identities. Bowleg's (2008) ground-breaking article ("When Black + Lesbian + Woman ≠ Black Lesbian Woman") boldly shaped this terrain. Her examination of the dilemmas faced when encountering additive models of identity in the methodology of intersectional identities began an important conversation. It can no longer be assumed that traditional methods and measurements capture the interdependent experiences of life at all its intersections in the borderlands. Bowleg's (2008) work allows us to push further in order to question whether identities are neither multiplicative nor additive but simultaneous, and should be measured accordingly in quantitative data collection.

In this way, every individual in a dataset can be represented by an equation involving both additive and multiplicative functions. Clearly, Bowleg's ideas illuminate the central assumption that identity, when conceived as additive (Black + Lesbian + Woman), fails to represent the multiplicative praxis of being critical race feminist theorist Wing (1991) describes (Black × Lesbian × Woman) and to capture simultaneous, intersectional identity construction. It also obscures within-group variance and potentially makes implementing intersectional analyses all the more difficult. Interpretation of data according to this new framework becomes all the more important if intersectional identities are to survive this quantification of identity.

Bowleg builds on the solid foundation of Black Feminist Thought and feminist methodology to chart a course that might begin to negotiate the borderlands between critical theory, qualitative research, and quantitative postmodern empiricism. Collins (2000) was among the first to articulate the conception of multiplicative identities as a force of oppression in the matrix of domination. And Harding's (1998) discussion of borderlands epistemologies asserted the need for innovative thinking in how we design research so as to better reflect the lived experiences of women. Because of this work, intersectionality is now increasingly accepted as an analytical paradigm.

Yet critical dilemmas still pose necessary challenges to transforming long-standing conceptualizations of what it is to do quantitative research that also engages in intersectional analyses in particular. Foucauldian approaches to the relationships between truth and power remind us that expanding conceptualizations of quantitative research using queer engagements is a radical intervention. Application of queer theoretical perspectives and the use of postmodern queer empirical frameworks are just two emerging models for research (Johnson and Lugg 2011). These interventions can expand our understanding of social lives as reflected in quantitative datasets and the methods used in analyzing them, producing a critical, theoretically informed method. This expansion of theoretical possibilities poses a critical dilemma for empirical research resistant to change. And this critical dilemma poses a necessary challenge to expand our conceptualizations of what it is to do quantitative research.

Ironically, investigation of the role of quantitative data in the construction, maintenance, and representation of social identities reveals that one identity is almost always privileged over any others and intersectional identities are silenced and/or repressed. For example, that Black + Lesbian + Woman has been granted status as truth, as opposed to Black × Lesbian × Woman, reveals the power inherent in being able to name the relationships between multiple, intersecting identities. Yet the intersections of gender, race, ethnicity, class, and sexuality frame some of the most important questions addressing the languages and experiences of identity. Young lesbians are practicing a radical identity politics of self-definition against those who would tell them who they are. Whether it is in a group of friends, a gang like DTO, or as individuals, they resist the policing of their identities and bodies by schools, law enforcement, and society's other institutions as they challenge the invisibility imposed on their multiplicative being.

Lesbians in the Queer Landscape of the Borderlands

In this era of surveillance, Foucault's panopticon could suggest that young women have the benefit of constant surveillance from the observation of the police, security cameras, and other people. The failure of others to intervene in this panoptic observation, however, could indicate that those who transgress norms experience punishment and discipline toward their normalization (Foucault 1995). Instead of intervention on their behalf, there is a willingness to persecute young lesbians of color, particularly when they are from working class or poor communities. What is more, their friendship groups are assumed to be dangerous, sometimes misunderstood as gangs when they are not. This reveals the racist and homophobic realities faced by these women in their life contexts.

For example, the West Village piers in New York City have historically been a place for young LGBT youth of color to meet, spend time among their peers, and create a space they can call their own. As the gentrification of the Village increased, the piers were shut down. Some have yet to be developed. LGBT youth would effectively be trespassing to regain access to a longstanding space they once made their own. The membership-based organization Fierce (fiercenyc.org) continues to sponsor campaigns to reclaim part of the piers for an LGBT youth center, advocates against police harassment of LGBT youth, and educates youth about these issues in New York City. The Village Hudson River waterfront is now a developed public park that operates as a pseudo-private space. For example, only certain people—particularly those with children—can be admitted to this park to watch the city's Fourth of July fireworks. But late in June every year, this park becomes a major site of police intervention in the lesbian community.

Given the significance of the piers in the past, this park is a main meeting area for groups of friends during New York City's pride events every June. According to my 2012 field observations, the experiences of women of color on the West Village piers, particularly after the parade, are yet further examples of the policing endured by young lesbians. Their experiences of harassment by the New York Police Department (NYPD) at pride, present mainly for the purpose of providing necessary crowd control as pedestrians enter the Village for parties and celebrations, are largely ignored by the larger LGBT community. The park itself is largely closed except for small pathways on the sidewalks in which revelers are penned between police barricades. There is very little freedom of movement and accessibility to streets is based on appearances only. The largely white, affluent residents of this part of the Village are granted more sidewalk access after discussion with police, whereas access to these public spaces is denied to the young women based on their race, gender, and sexuality. They are outsiders in a historically LGBT neighborhood, under severe surveillance, controlled by those presumably charged with protecting them during this time of celebration.

Lesbian bodies and their movements were controlled. Video documentarians are present to chronicle instances of police harassment and violence, yet they continue to occur. When arrests are made or lesbians are pulled aside for questioning, the police visibly use excessive force. Additionally, groups of friends are cast with suspicion, perhaps as gangs, whether or not they really are a gang. And verbal altercations, no matter the severity, are immediately treated by police as fighting.

When these women are in fact involved with violence, the enforcement they experience is severe. Young women—especially women of color—experience harsher penalties for violence. For example, Gastic and Johnson (2013) used Massachusetts's school safety and discipline records to describe that while females are less likely than males to be cited for fighting and also less likely than males to receive an out-of-school suspension, when they are punished, they face significantly longer required absences from school than their male counterparts. On average, these women are barred from their schools for one additional day. Under no circumstances, and for no subgroups of students studied, were female students found to receive lighter sentences than males for fighting at school. This work is consistent with the relevant literature on feminist criminology (Britton 2000; Burgess-Proctor 2006; Chesney-Lind 2006), youth justice research focusing on the experiences of girls (Gelsthorpe and Sharpe 2006) in intersectional contexts of race and gender (Guevara et al. 2006; Moore and Padavic 2010), on patriarchy and gender role expectations in juvenile-police interactions (see Nanda 2012; Sherman 2012; and the special 2012 symposium issue of the *UCLA Law Review*, generally), and in juvenile court processing (Carr et al. 2008; Freiburger and Burke 2011; Kempf-Leonard and Sample 2000).

The relationships between masculinity, homophobia, and violence as discussed in the research literature have only minimally considered these experiences among female adolescents. A previous article (Johnson 2007) discussed the African-American lesbian gang, DTO, as an example of a student-initiated strategy for dealing with homophobic bullying in an urban American school district. A series of alleged incidents of same-sex sexual harassment by these gang members on heterosexual students was reported in the local television and print media. These students were reacting, perhaps preemptively and in retaliation to, homophobia in their schools, particularly from their peers. Lesbian threat was used by these young women to reestablish a power differential after they experienced bullying based on their sexuality and gender expression. They formed gangs under the DTO names and used same-sex sexual harassment of other students as a weapon against homophobia and a means by which they could assert themselves in their

masculinities, not unlike their male peers who experience same-sex bullying and/
or harassment and use anti-female sexual harassment to assert their masculinity
(Johnson 2007).

Policing Lesbian Gangs: Negotiating Multiple Identities and Challenging Invisibility

DTO first came to media attention through the city's most notable newspaper, the
Philadelphia Inquirer, in a sensationalized February 2004 article, "They're 'Out'
at School and Tension is In." It describes the hostilities between heterosexual
female and openly lesbian public high school students. According to the article,
"[a]ccusations of intimidation have surfaced on both sides: from lesbians who say
they are being harassed and from heterosexual girls who say they have been
grabbed and bothered" (Snyder 2004, para 3). Students reported knowing of
conflicts between lesbian and straight girls up to as many as 5 years earlier. A
principal at one of the high schools where DTO members attended stated,
"...students had complained that lesbians were 'brushing up against [them],
watching [them] in the bathrooms, gathering in corners, and talking about [them]'"
(Snyder 2004, para 15).

In an attempt to address the harassment, the principal, who was eventually
moved to a central district office position, held an all-female student assembly.
Instead of calling private meetings between DTO members and the students
involved in the harassment, she held this school-wide gathering about DTO actions
because, she argued, the entire school knew about the confrontations. Many lesbian
students and LGBT community members thought this event unjustly singled out the
lesbian students at the school by labeling them as sexual predators (Johnson 2007).

School district response began to align more with the media's continuing
dominant frame of lesbian gang members as sexual predators. In contrast, LGBT
community representatives, including some of the social service providers to
LGBTQ youth communities, focused on the homophobia LGBTQ students endure
while in school. Although the community did not discuss DTO members' behavior
as activist, its major frame argued that the students were reactive (Johnson 2007).

Meanwhile, having heard enough concerns about the issue, the district promised
to provide training for teachers, administrators, aides, school police, and other staff
members about gay and lesbian issues in the spring term of the school-year. Further,
the school district's Chief Executive Officer (CEO) declared that sexual harassment
and consensual activity between female students are "all unacceptable." He went
on to state: "Consensual sexual activity isn't going to be tolerated in the schools
either–same-sex or opposite-sex" (Johnson 2007; Snyder 2004, para 7).

Although the media coverage framed these incidents as sexual harassment,
LGBT community members saw them as, at best, sensationalized and, at worst,
fabricated by nervous parents and fanned by an overzealous local news media.

Instead, these community members believed the lesbian students' behavior was the result of a lack of programs and services available for LGBTQ youth (Johnson 2007). They, too, may have speculated about the disproportionate attention and/or response given to these instances of female-initiated same-sex sexual harassment compared to those which are male-initiated and heterosexual.

When revisiting DTO as an example of a lesbian youth gang, intersections of gender, race, ethnicity, class, and sexuality frame several major ongoing questions. Thinking about the experiences of violence and homophobic harassment DTO members endured requires an expanded reading of the link between adolescent female masculinity, homophobia, and violence. Masculinity, more specifically normative masculinity, is traditionally defined by traits and behaviors that include fighting and dominant relationships with girls (Klein 2006). For women who bully other women and use sexual harassment as a means of proving their masculine power, these actions might serve to reinforce the very hierarchies of power which threatened them via homophobia (Foucault 1995; Klein 2006). These framings provide little possibility for aggression outside of male behavior and relegate masculinity solely to the domain of young men.

Any discussion of DTO should emphasize the agency among these LGBTQ youth and respect the various ways they resist and challenge homophobic bullying in their lives. At the same time, same-sex attracted youth, girls and young women included, have the potential to be bullies. This aggression could be in the name of creating support networks or subverting and resisting (hetero)normative gender identities (Leck 2000) and anti-gay abuse through the female reproduction of male gender hierarchies in the performance and enforcement of bullying behaviors. The actions of DTO provide a unique set of circumstances through which to examine the functional and dysfunctional coping strategies for homophobic bullying that young people develop, partly because student-initiated strategies might be the only ones available to them in many U.S., especially urban, schools. The same-sex sexual harassment of other students might have been a means by which DTO members asserted themselves in their masculinities.

These responses to DTO did not consider that the gang was a student-initiated strategy for dealing with homophobic bullying. However, the local LGBT community—represented by community-based organizations, gay city government liaisons, and community business leaders—did contend that these young women's behaviors were the result of a lack of school-based and after school programs and services available for LGBTQ youth. They were also a response to school policies and a school climate that tolerated or even supported anti-lesbian hostilities.

Additionally, DTO reflects a powerfully different vision of the anxiety-fueled crisis in American masculinity (Stein 2005), in which girls' academic success and advancement are presumed to play a role. Although Weaver-Hightower (2003, 2005) and Davis (2001a, b) have convincingly argued for the recognition of diverse masculinities, particularly those of African-American boys, DTO members posed a threat to this hegemonic masculinity and to Black masculinities in particular. They demonstrated through their actions that aggressive masculinity is not the sole property of men and a powerful weapon to combat harassment.

These masculine young women were feared constantly by other students. They were not seen as acting out in self-defense as masculine women. Neither was any expression of same-sex sexuality for heterosexual men's enjoyment. Thus, while aggression might be seen as a masculine behavior, it has been viewed as solely a male behavior. And paradoxically, left to their own devices, some LGBTQ youth contribute to an unsafe institutionalized school environment for others in order to obtain a zone of safety for themselves. In spite of everything, both educational and political leaders have yet to address the reality that a safe environment for LGBTQ youth often does not exist in urban schools and communities. Furthermore, this may actually contribute to an increasingly hostile school climate.

The complexity of the issue (including the homophobic bullying, harassment, lack of safety, and double standard of the consequences for their actions as lesbians) should not, by any means, obscure the fact that members of DTO were sexually harassing their peers. In the case of DTO, student gangs form because they experience homophobic bullying and the school district fails to protect them. The choice of these women to use sexual harassment and bullying to restore the power differential, however, can and should be seen as a separate issue.

The issue is further complicated by the realities that this restoration of personal safety is left to the students to carry out themselves because of the failure of the schools to act on their behalf. The students then endured even more homophobia as a result of the increased level of attention their behavior received. The attribution of their behavior to their sexuality—as opposed to their aggression, disrespect, and objectification of their female classmates and the double standard for young men engaging in the exact same behavior without similar consequences—underpinned this increase in anti-lesbian hostility.

Many administrators, teachers, and staff members equate consensual same-sex affection with nonconsensual same-sex harassment, as did the CEO of the school district DTO members attended (Snyder 2004). School-based resistance to lesbian students mostly operates outside and despite a greater LGBT community. When DTO members sexually harassed other female students, it forced school officials to acknowledge *same-sex* sexual harassment as legitimate sexual contact. It is a distressing commentary that this might be among the first times the school officials have considered same-sex sexuality as legitimate or that African-American lesbian students exist at all.

Queer Recognition in Methodological Regimes

The question of whether or not those with intersectional identities exist is becoming increasingly important in the emerging world of big data and the imperative to be counted among it. But members of DTO did not assert a hygienic identity, fitting cleanly within the boundaries of how dominant structures define queerness or a queer person. Theirs is multiplicative, intersectional, and context-dependent. But data is hygienic. It is a means by which an order is imposed onto a complex world.

In so doing, it oversimplifies the complexities of lived experience, particularly for those who claim multiple identities in the intersectional borderlands.

The landscape of very recent and very intense interest in data has implications not just for social scientists but for society and its institutions. It certainly has implications for individuals in everyday life. But it is also an indication that we have been in the process—for some time now—of creating a digital infrastructure that is as real a human experience as someone has in any physically built environment. Technologies used both by individuals (e.g., Facebook) and by governments (e.g., surveillance software and hardware) are ever-expanding, with basic cell phones producing sizeable amounts of data every day that is mined by both private and public entities. This is the landscape of big data, and it remains to be seen if it will be a queer space in any way.

There are dilemmas when considering whether or not to enter this emergent data regime. Foucault might have called it a quantitative matrix. It is a landscape that is potentially defining and redefining who and what we are, who is and who is not. This necessitates a careful questioning of these practices via a queer perspective that illuminates the borderlands of this new big data terrain. But this interrogation has barely had an opportunity to begin. Lincoln and Cannella (2004, p. 1) warned of the potential dangers of "methodological conservatism and governmental regimes of truth," and exposed the role of early postmodern theorists in further deciding what counts as truth.

Before the greater LGBT community continues to eagerly seek recognition in this new space, the complexities of how to negotiate multiple identities when challenging invisibility in this quantitative matrix should be addressed. The fluid space of queerness illuminates challenges and dilemmas of seeking to enter the matrix, and allows an opportunity to question whether to enter this matrix at all. This is especially the case as more and more data is collected as a means to administer our educational and criminal justice systems.

Indeed, big data is all around us in this new century. For example, government education and crime databases are increasingly sophisticated. Beyond government data, the data produced and collected from Google searches, cloud computing, Facebook and Twitter posts, and Siri requests are being mined for a variety of purposes, from global business development to public health to marketing. Government at both the state and federal level, major corporations like Intel and AIG, and federal agencies such as the U.S. National Science Foundation are leading (and funding) a number of notable big data projects for opening and mining federal datasets in partnership with leading U.S. research universities, from University of California, Berkeley to the Massachusetts Institute of Technology (MIT).

These public/private partnerships are the new vanguard to unlocking the potential hidden in all this data. For example, the State of Massachusetts recently partnered with Intel and MIT in collaboration on a big data project that will be a foundation to what Massachusetts Governor Patrick hopes is the establishment of the state as a "big data hub." And this trend is also emerging in the myriad data compiled into the government's datasets. The United States Federal government and the World Bank recently partnered to present the second international conference on open government data. The topics discussed included the intersection of big data and open data and the need for investing in a public data infrastructure.

This emergent governmental data regime is immediately normative in our current era. The desire to be included in it is also something largely left unquestioned. Approaching it from a Foucauldian perspective, it is a matrix where new realities and truths are made and remade. By definition, a matrix is something within or from which something else originates, develops, or takes form. This new data infrastructure has the power to verify truth. A matrix is also a mold from which imprinted copies are made and a mathematical field where equations are developed and balanced. This new methodological regime is one where being counted within the data is the means by which people identify who and what they are.

The mainstream gay and lesbian social movement has for some time sought visibility in this new data-centered and driven regime. Scherer (2010) describes this search for new queer paradigms as one where new normativities emerge. When nonconforming LGBT people seek to be counted among the normative community, they are denied inclusion, invisible in this new reality. Scherer (2010) argues that the transgender community and the invisibility of intersexuality are but two examples of this policing of identity that erases identities from LGBT existence. Investigation of the role of quantitative data in the construction, maintenance, and representation of social identities reveals that one identity is almost always privileged over any others and intersectional identities are silenced and/or repressed. Yet, the lure of being counted among the data as a recognized category of identity has convinced the mainstream movement to be hygienic in what defines queerness or a queer person in the new century.

Impossible Futures?

The panoptic quality of our data-rich twenty-first century life and the power inherent in the process of being validated by it makes the use of Foucault's ideas indispensible in this effort. Foucault's (2003) work on regimes of verification (or "veridiction") and the carceral society (1995) provide useful tools for engaging both the risks and opportunities that arise from seeking to enter the quantitative matrix. It also provides a foundation for a queer critique of the desire for this systemic recognition in this new quantitative methodological regime. Where we are in the data structure (i.e., how we are quantified) has increasingly more power to define us than we ourselves do. By seeking this recognition in the system we are relenting to the definitions created for, not by, us. We will be told who we are.

This use of power through technology is not an entirely new phenomenon and Foucault's framework proved extremely prophetic. The control of populations through biopower reveals the life or death nature of many of these governmental regimes. From the use of IBM data machines by Nazi Germany in World War II to the drones currently flying overhead, data has been and continues to be collected and analyzed as a basis for deciding who is allowed to live and who is to die. Of course, one can live in this new data-dependent era without officially existing.

For example, the Institute of Education Sciences (of the U.S. Federal Department of Education) does not include LGBT youth in its data collection. The IES is the major source of data about the education of American youth and the schools they attend. Yet, according to the data, LGBT students do not exist. And when other government datasets are considered, more questions emerge: Do LGBT crime victims exist? What about LGBT criminals? And LGBT teachers? Further, most governmental data systems do not allow for the existence of a person who claims multiple identities. The critical dilemma, then, becomes how to count what or who does not exist. But when you exist *and* you can be counted, there will likely be unintended consequences. Among the most concerning of these negative consequences might be the diminished agency LGBT youth have in claiming their own identities and having those identities respected by the greater community. The LGBT community could further fracture as a result, with a very small group of people in privileged positions in the political movement making decisions about which identities are true and which are to be silenced. Marginalized communities stand to risk losing the most in this new reality, a future of impossible identities.

There is no universal census of LGBT Americans to know more definitively how many LGBT people there are in the United States. The Williams Institute at UCLA School of Law (Gates 2011) and Gallup (Gates and Newport 2011) among others have used quantitative means to try to answer this question. Not counting LGBT identity as an aspect of personhood does limit the ability of governmental agencies to work to identify and then eliminate inequities, such as health disparities. For example, the United States Department of Health and Human Services (HHS) recently announced that sexual orientation measures would be included for the first time in the Federal government's National Health Indicators Survey (NHIS) in 2013. Gender identity measures are currently being tested for addition at an unspecified time in the future. And in late 2013, the Department of Education quietly began the process to include a measure of some form of LGBT identity in their national datasets. The seduction of being recognized and verified by the matrix is becoming too great for the LGBT community to resist but it is a dilemma too important to ignore.

Grundy and Smith (2007) describe this dilemma as the inherent tension operating in queer politics today. Traditional activist knowledges are being subverted by the imperative to be counted and verified by social science methodological regimes. Grundy and Smith discuss the emergence of an orientation among LGBT activists to engage in social science as a form of claiming identity and articulating policy goals. This is, of course, a reaction to the growth of big data and policy-making based on evidence from these datasets. The Task Force (National Gay and Lesbian Task Force), GLSEN (Gay, Lesbian, and Straight Education Network), the Williams Institute at the University of California, Los Angeles School of Law, and increasingly the Human Rights Campaign (HRC) are major players in this policy field. They have all directed more resources to the use of statistical analyses in articulating LGBT experiences and lives. In fact, over the past decade more and more of this work is done in-house by dedicated, paid staff.

Grundy and Smith's (2007) compelling article, now over 5 years old, proved very prophetic. They argued that this new imperative to seek validation and recognition in the quantitative matrix was not without struggle. LGBT activists were all too aware of the limits of existing social science methodologies in articulating queer realities in all of their diversity. Ultimately, Grundy and Smith concluded that the activists adopted the methodological regimes that privilege normative LGBT identities. In so doing they were reinforcing these as truths (Foucault 2003). There are certainly implications for citizenship, or who counts in U.S. society, from these vigorously adopted tactics.

The ever-increasing desire for and dependence on using quantitative data to verify LGBT existence has indeed shaped LGBT political activism in profound ways in recent years (Grundy and Smith 2007). All trends indicate that this will continue without much critical discussion as to its consequences, particularly for those with intersectional identities. Questions remain unaddressed: Should the LGBT community proceed with this data agenda if we are already aware of its inabilities to capture our lives as we actually live them? What if the data say we are something that does not actually represent who we know ourselves to be, in all of our diversity? What do we give up by so actively pursuing inclusion in this quantitative matrix? The negative consequences could be many and are largely unexplored, but certainly the agency to define ourselves is among them.

The potential unintended consequences that might arise when using data about LGBT people have particular implications for youth in schools and the justice system. With the hygienic categorization of the data systems already in place, LGBT youth are being denied the opportunity and agency of self identification unless they resist these very strong social forces. Young lesbians like those who resist police intervention at the Village piers and those members of DTO who asserted their identities and rightful place in their schools challenge accepted hierarchies, binaries, and hegemonies. They provide us with ways to challenge the methodological regime and to insist on the inclusion of queer space in the data infrastructure if we decide to proceed. The potential to map the terrain of this new queer space might even be found in these examples of resistance.

The resistance of lesbians in the policing of their multiple identities provides an important example of another set of possibilities. Investigating the dynamics of quantitative data on the body/person and on lived experience requires a specific focus on how the quantitative matrix of data embodies a structure of social control and surveillance. Their experiences with systems of control would no doubt make resistance to further control and classification a viable and perhaps necessary option. Given their experiences in their schools, young lesbians like the members of DTO would certainly understand the biopower inherent in these data regimes. An extension of the panopticon and yet another expression of the carceral society, data is used to control populations, not liberate them (Foucault 1995, 2003).

When they tell you who you are by establishing a finite number of choices, the future becomes more impossible to imagine outside of this system of verification.

When this definition of identity becomes truth, communities will organize around it. The borderlands of identity at the beginning of this new century will only continue into the future if we are able to imagine these borderlands through the process of self definition. Lesbian resistance to the policing of multiple identities lays this groundwork to challenge the invisibility imposed on multiplicative being. Like DTO, challenging invisibility in this new landscape will require us to articulate who we are on our own terms. Otherwise, we will exist on the terms of others and they—not us—will have the power to tell the truth of who we are.

References

Artz, S. (1999). *Sex, power, and the violent school girl*. New York, NY: Teachers College Press.

Barnett, R., & Rivers, C. (2006). The boy crisis—fact or myth? *Teachers College Record*. Retrieved October 10, 2006, from http://www.tcrecord.org.

Berlan, E., & Austin, B. (2007). *Gay and lesbian teens face more bullying*. Poster presented at the Society for Adolescent Medicine Annual Meeting, Denver, Colorado.

Bowleg, L. (2008). When black + lesbian + woman ≠ black lesbian woman: The methodological challenges of qualitative and quantitative intersectionality research. *Sex Roles, 59*(5–6), 312–325.

Britton, D. M. (2000). Feminism in criminology: Engendering the outlaw. *Annals of the American Academy of Political and Social Science, 571*, 57–76.

Burgess-Proctor, A. (2006). Intersections of race, class, gender, and crime: Future directions for feminist criminology. *Feminist Criminology, 1*(1), 27–47.

Carr, N. T., Hudson, K., Hanks, R. S., & Hunt, A. N. (2008). Gender effects along the juvenile justice system: Evidence of a gendered organization. *Feminist Criminology, 3*(1), 25–43.

Chesney-Lind, M. (2006). Patriarchy, crime, and justice: Feminist criminology in an era of backlash. *Feminist Criminology, 1*(1), 6–26.

Collins, P. (2000). *Black feminist thought* (2nd ed.). New York, NY: Routledge.

Davis, J. (2001a). Black boys at school: Negotiating masculinities and race. In R. Majors (Ed.), *Educating our black children: New directions and radical approaches* (pp. 169–182). London, UK: Taylor and Francis.

Davis, J. (2001b). Transgressing the masculine: African American boys and the failure of schools. In B. Mayeen & W. Martino (Eds.), *What about the boys? Issues of masculinity in school* (pp. 140–153). Buckingham, England: Open University Press.

Foucault, M. (1995). *Discipline and punish*. New York, NY: Vintage.

Foucault, M. (2003). *Society must be defended*. New York, NY: Picador.

Freiburger, T. L., & Burke, A. S. (2011). Status offenders in the juvenile court: The effects of gender, race, and ethnicity on the adjudication decision. *Youth Violence and Juvenile Justice, 9*(4), 352–365.

Gates, G. J. (2011). *How many people are lesbian, gay, bisexual, and transgender?* Retrieved July 29, 2013, from http://williamsinstitute.law.ucla.edu/wp-content/uploads/Gates-How-Many-People-LGBT-Apr-2011.pdf.

Gates, G. J. & Newport, F. (2011). *Special report: 3.4% of U.S. adults identify as LGBT*. Retrieved July 29, 2013, from http://www.gallup.com/poll/158066/special-report-adults-identify-lgbt.aspx.

Gastic, B., & Johnson, D. (2013). Girl fight: Race, gender, and school discipline in Massachusetts. Manuscript submitted for publication.

Gelsthorpe, L., & Sharpe, G. (2006). Gender, youth crime, and justice. In B. Goldson & J. Muncie (Eds.), *Youth crime and justice* (pp. 47–62). London, UK: Sage Publications.

Grundy, J., & Smith, M. (2007). Activist knowledges in queer politics. *Economy and Society, 36*(2), 294–317.

Guevara, L., Herz, D., & Spohn, C. (2006). Gender and juvenile justice decision making: What role does race play? *Feminist Criminology, 1*(4), 258–282.

Harding, S. (1998). *Is science multicultural?* Bloomington, IN: Indiana University Press.

Johnson, D. (2006). LGBTQ students in urban schools: Sexuality, gender, and school identities. In D. Armstrong & B. McMahon (Eds.), *Inclusion in urban educational environments: Addressing issues of diversity, equity, and social justice* (pp. 137–152). Greenwich, CT: Information Age.

Johnson, D. (2007). Taking over the school: Student gangs as a strategy for dealing with homophobic bullying in an urban public school district. *Journal of Gay and Lesbian Social Services, 19*(3–4), 87–104.

Johnson, D., & Lugg, C. A. (2011). Queer theories in education. In S. Tozer, B. Gallegos, A. Henry, M. B. Greiner, & P. Groves-Price (Eds.), *Handbook of research in the social foundations of education* (pp. 233–243). New York, NY: Routledge.

Kempf-Leonard, K., & Sample, L. L. (2000). Disparity based on sex: Is gender-specific treatment warranted? *Justice Quarterly, 17*(1), 89–128.

Kindlon, D., & Thompson, M. (2000). *Raising Cain: Protecting the emotional life of boys*. New York, NY: Ballantine.

Klein, J. (2006). Cultural capital and high school bullies: How social inequality impacts school violence. *Men and Masculinities, 9*(1), 53–75.

Leck, G. (2000). Heterosexual or homosexual: Reconsidering binary narratives on sexual identities in urban schools. *Education and Urban Society, 32*, 324–348.

Lincoln, Y. S., & Cannella, G. S. (2004). Dangerous discourses: Methodological conservatism and governmental regimes of truth. *Qualitative Inquiry, 10*(1), 5–14.

Ma'ayan, H. (2003). Masculine female adolescents at school. *Equity and Excellence in Education, 36*, 125–135.

Moore, L. D., & Padavic, I. (2010). Racial and ethnic disparities in girls' sentencing in the juvenile justice system. *Feminist Criminology, 5*(3), 263–285.

Moore, M. (2006). Lipstick or timberlands? Meanings of gender presentation in black lesbian communities. *Signs: Journal of Women in Culture and Society, 32*(1), 113–139.

Nanda, J. (2012). Blind discretion: Girls of color and delinquency in the juvenile justice system. *UCLA Law Review, 59*(6), 1502–1539.

Patton, C. (2000). Tremble, hetero swine! In M. Warner (Ed.), *Fear of a queer planet* (pp. 143–177). Minneapolis, MN: University of Minnesota Press.

Pepler, D., Madsen, K., Webster, C., & Levene, K. (Eds.). (2004). *The development and treatment of girlhood aggression*. Rahway, NJ: Lawrence Erlbaum.

Pipher, M. (1994). *Reviving Ophelia: Saving the selves of adolescent girls*. New York, NY: Penguin.

Pollack, W. (1988). *Real boys: Rescuing our sons from the myths of boyhood*. New York, NY: Random House.

Rehder, T. (2001). Discussion and expression of gender and sexuality in schools. *Georgetown Journal of Gender and the Law, 2*, 489–509.

Rich, A. (1980). Compulsory heterosexuality and lesbian existence. *Signs, 5*, 631–660.

Scherer, B. (2010). Introduction: Queering paradigms. In B. Scherer (Ed.), *Queering paradigms* (pp. 1–6). Oxford, UK: Peter Lang.

Sherman, F. T. (2012). Justice for girls: Are we making progress? *UCLA Law Review, 59*(6), 1584–1628.

Simmons, R. (2002). *Odd girl out: The hidden culture of aggression in girls*. San Diego, CA: Harcourt.

Snyder, S. (2004, February 8). They're 'out' at school, and tension is in. *Philadelphia Inquirer*. Retrieved April 26, 2007, from http://www.bridges4kids.org/articles/2-04/PhillyInq2-8-04.html.

Stein, A. (2005). Make room for daddy: Anxious masculinity and emergent homophobias in neopatriarchal politics. *Gender and Society, 19,* 601–620.

Tyre, P. (2006). The trouble with boys. *Newsweek.* Retrieved September 25, 2006, from http://www.msnbc.com/id/10965522/site/newsweek/.

Weaver-Hightower, M. (2003). The "boy turn" in research on gender and education. *Review of Educational Research, 73,* 471–498.

Weaver-Hightower, M. (2005). Dare the school build a new education for boys? *Teachers College Record.* Retrieved July 5, 2006 from http://www.tcrecord.org.

Wing, A. (1991). Brief reflections toward a multiplicative theory and praxis of being. *Berkeley Women's Law Journal, 6,* 181–201.

Wiseman, R. (2002). *Queen bees and wannabees: Helping your daughter survive cliques, gossip, boyfriends and other realities of adolescence.* New York, NY: Crown.

WYBE-TV (2002, Spring). Tolerance project: Quotes from the series 2. Retrieved April 27, 2007 from http://www.wybe.org/programs/toleranceproject/behind/behind2.html.

Chapter 7
"I Will Fight You Like I'm Straight": Gay Gang- and Crime-Involved Men's Participation in Violence

Vanessa R. Panfil

Abstract Despite extensive criminological literature on violence and victimization, the portrait of gay men's involvement is unclear. Literature exists on gay men as victims of intimate partner violence and anti-gay bias crimes, but there is very little on gay perpetrators of violence. In this chapter, I seek to critically interrogate existing assumptions and address this lack of coverage. I utilize in-depth, semi-structured interviews with 53 gay gang- and crime-involved men to discuss their participation in violence under a variety of contexts to provide a descriptive picture of their varied uses of violence. Although their uses of violence are largely consistent with the extant literature, their experiences as gay men are often central to their justifications for violence. I also explore the links between violent victimization and violence perpetration. My data suggest that negative experiences such as neighborhood violence, homophobic bullying in schools, and anti-gay harassment all play roles in respondents' decisions to utilize violence; however, this violence did not always serve to prevent their future victimization.

Keywords Gay · Gang · Violence · Crime · Homophobic bullying · Anti-gay harassment · Agency · Masculinity · Stereotypes · Victims · Intimate partner violence · Interviews

V. R. Panfil (✉)
School of Criminal Justice, Rutgers University, Center for Law and Justice, 123 Washington Street Room 579B, Newark, NJ 07102, USA
e-mail: vanessa.panfil@rutgers.edu

D. Peterson and V. R. Panfil (eds.), *Handbook of LGBT Communities, Crime, and Justice*, DOI: 10.1007/978-1-4614-9188-0_7,
© Springer Science+Business Media New York 2014

Introduction

"Just cuz you're straight, I'm not gonna back down."—Jeremy

"I don't know why they think gay people cain't fight."—Imani

"I will fight you like I'm straight."—Johnny

Jeremy, Imani, and Johnny are gay men who are willing to use violence to address disrespect, to "fight back" against anti-gay harassment, and to retaliate against rival gangs, among other reasons. The extant criminological literature suggests a variety of ways individuals, particularly men, utilize and justify violence. For example, violence can be used to defend the self or others from violence or the threat of violence, and to gain or maintain masculine status (e.g., Anderson 1999; Bourgois 1996; Connell 2005; Decker 1996; Matza 1964; Presser 2003). These and other criminological studies have examined the uses of and justifications for violence among a variety of groups, including inner-city Black and Latino men, gang members, incarcerated men, juvenile delinquents, and men in general. However, these studies assume a heterosexual man (Collier 1998), and therefore cannot examine the ways violence is utilized and justified by men who identify as gay. Similarly, only one study of gang members uncovered any information about gay gang members and their uses of violence (Totten 2000). Extant criminological literature focuses on gay men as *victims* of anti-gay bias crimes (Herek 2009; Herek et al. 1997; Kuehnle and Sullivan 2001) or intimate partner violence (Greenwood et al. 2002; Merrill and Wolfe 2000), but gives virtually no attention to gay men as perpetrators of violence.

This study is uniquely situated to fill these gaps in knowledge. The in-depth, semistructured interviews I analyze in this chapter are data collected as part of a study on the intersection of masculinity and sexuality in the lives of gay gang- and crime-involved men. It is the first study that explicitly seeks to explore the ways gay men who are also members of gangs or involved in criminal activity (or both) use and justify violence. Accordingly, in this chapter, I explore the following questions: Under what contexts do they engage in violence? What are their reasons for engaging in violence? In so doing, I also explore the roles prior victimization has played in their decisions to engage in violence. By shedding light on gay men's uses of violence, this chapter challenges existing criminological and popular assumptions about who engages in interpersonal (and often public) violence and why.

Violence: Answered and Unanswered Questions

What Purposes Does Violence Serve for Perpetrators?

In light of its negative social and legal consequences, why might anyone engage in violence? For men across many racial, socioeconomic, and geographic communities, aggression and physical toughness confer masculine status (Connell 2005; Mahalik et al. 2003; Messerschmidt 1993), especially when other opportunities to gain masculine status, such as employment, are blocked or absent (Anderson 1999; Gibbs and Merighi 1994; Majors and Billson 1993; Oliver 1994). Thus, violence can be enacted to address disrespect and to defend "masculine ideals" such as honor and reputation (Bandura et al. 1996; Matza 1964), especially if one's masculinity is explicitly challenged by another male (Messerschmidt 2000) through insults or intimidation. Furthermore, and especially among urban populations, violence serves as a conflict resolution strategy when formal systems of intervention, such as police and school administrators, have failed (Anderson 1999; Ferguson 2000; Rios 2011). Self-defense, both of the physical body and of the reputation, is also served through the commission of violence, as is the defense of others. Perpetrators view targets of their defensive violence as appropriate or deserving victims for initiating the conflict (Hochstetler et al. 2010; Katz 1988; Presser 2003; Sykes and Matza 1957).

For men involved in certain forms of crime, such as drug selling or gang activity, violence can provide perpetrators with both intrinsic and extrinsic benefits. Those involved in underground economies may use violence not only to obtain tangible goods, but to construct "badass" street personas that aid in their business dealings (Katz 1988). The lack of legal avenues for recourse produces additional motivation for them to respond violently to customers and competitors in order to collect debts, exact revenge, or give themselves an advantage (Bourgois 1996; Jacobs 2000; Wright and Decker 1997). Within the gang context, violence can be used to respond to threats, either to the safety of members or to turf and economic interests; as a vehicle to join and/or leave the gang; to gain status; and in retaliation for violence committed against group members by rival groups. Given these varied uses of violence, gang members describe violence as a central feature of their gang experience (Decker 1996; Decker and Van Winkle 1996). Involvement in gangs and other illicit pursuits is linked not only with violence perpetration, but also violent victimization (Peterson et al. 2004; Taylor et al. 2007; Thornberry et al. 2003).

What Do We Know About Gay Men's Involvement in Violence?

The criminological literature on violence says very little about gay-identified men who perpetrate violent crimes, except for those who batter their partners (Craft and Serovich 2005; McKenry et al. 2006; Regan et al. 2002; Toro-Alfonso et al. 2004;

Waldner-Haugrud et al. 1997). However, most criminological literature on same-sex intimate partner violence (IPV) actually focuses on the *victim's* experiences, such as victims' likelihood of seeking help or resources, reasons for staying in the relationship, and their decisions to report the abuse (Greenwood et al. 2002; Kuehnle and Sullivan 2001; McClennen et al. 2002; Merrill and Wolfe 2000). While it is important to gain knowledge about gay men's victimization experiences, men who identify as batterers are rarely interviewed unless they are also victims of IPV. Cruz (2003) states that it may be more useful to the victim for us to ask, "Why does the batterer do it?" However, Cruz's research, like other existing sources, asks why gay men stay in relationships with batterers. Studies have avoided gathering narrative data on gay men who identify as perpetrators of intimate partner violence, or on any sort of violence, for that matter.

In a manner similar to the intimate partner violence literature, much research exists on gay men's victimization by perpetrators of anti-gay bias crimes and has likewise focused on patterns of reporting to the police, the characteristics of the crimes, and the damaging psychological symptoms experienced after the attacks (Herek et al. 1997; Kuehnle and Sullivan 2001), but not on responses to the violence as it is occurring. That is, the literature includes no information on whether or not gay men "fight back" against their attackers. This remains true despite evidence that some groups of young lesbian women do fight back, with violence, against anti-lesbian bullying, street harassment, and violent victimization (Johnson 2008; Logan 2011). Fighting back has even been encouraged by radical LGBT rights groups, such as the early-1990s Queer Nation. They protested sharp increases in anti-LGBT violence with banners that read "Dykes and Fags Bash Back!" (Carriles 2011). In their literature, they explicitly *encouraged* queer persons to "Bash Back" (Queer Nation 1990). These sources would suggest that at least some men who are under attack because of their sexuality are willing to fight back, but research has not explored male victims' physical resistance strategies or responses to the attacker during anti-gay bias crimes.

This issue of whether or not LGBT people actively resist their victimization also plagues the large literature on LGBT youths' experiences with homophobic bullying, by focusing on consequences such as negative school outcomes and increased depression, suicidality, and substance use (e.g., Birkett et al. 2009; Bontempo and D'Augelli 2002; Espelage et al. 2008). While an interdisciplinary literature, it is located largely in disciplines other than criminology and criminal justice, such as sexuality, psychology, or public health journals. A similar argument can be made for the aforementioned studies on gay victims of intimate partner violence and bias crimes. Although victims' experiences are worthy avenues for exploration, these limited foci do not provide a complete picture of gay individuals' experiences with violence. This, coupled with the lack of cross-disciplinary research, means that theoretically significant connections are not being made. For example, we know very little about the links (if any) between homophobic bullying victimization and delinquent outcomes, despite evidence in the criminological literature that school bullying victimization is associated with delinquent behavior, gang membership, and violence (Carbone-Lopez et al. 2010; Cullen et al. 2008; McGee et al. 2011; Ttofi et al. 2012).

Furthermore, and perhaps related to homophobic bullying victimization, research suggests sexual minority youth are more likely to engage in fighting and weapons carrying than their peers (Button et al. 2012; CDCP, 2011; Russell et al. 2001); however, the extent to which these acts are defensive in nature is unclear. Only a "handful" of the thousands of students represented in Kosciw and colleagues' (2010, p. 37) study of LGBT youth in schools mentioned "resorting to physical retaliation to deal with victimization" (which the authors describe as "disturbing"), but small samples of queer youth also produce a number of respondents who report doing so (see, for example, Grossman et al. 2009). This calls into question the alleged rarity of such responses.

However, despite what seems like a logical connection between homophobic bullying and gang membership, there is virtually no scholarly research on gay gang-involved men; the only source that can shed any light on gay-identified gang members suggests they participate in gay-bashing incidents to construct masculine personas and conceal their sexual orientations from their gangs (Totten 2000). While insightful, this study uncovered information about only a few gay gang members, none of whom were 'out' to their gangs. It is unclear how else their non-normative sexual identity factored into their violence perpetration. Miller (2002) argues that an investigation into responses to structural or situational exclusion, as well as attention to intersections, such of those of gender and sexuality, are necessary to provide a more dynamic portrait of agency.

If, in fact, there is so much more to know, why don't we know it? As I discuss elsewhere (Panfil 2014a), depictions of gay men are absent from our discipline's enormous body of research on violence perpetration (despite being such an obvious home for this sort of work) for several interrelated reasons. These include: prevailing popular cultural stereotypes that represent gay men as effeminate, nonthreatening pacifists; sociopolitical concerns regarding progress towards LGBT equality; and assumptions of active offenders' heterosexuality by criminologists. Regarding this last point, violence, gang membership, and certain crimes have been gendered as masculine. For example, the violence literature reviewed herein has included many examples of how men enact violence to perform traditional scripts of masculinity (see also Collier 1998); gangs are regarded as hypermasculine groups (Peterson and Panfil 2014); and illegal pursuits such as street robbery are regarded, by criminologists and by perpetrators themselves, as essentially "masculine games" (e.g. Katz 1988; Miller 1998). Because of prevailing popular stereotypes, gay men are not seen as normatively gendered and thus have been excluded from inquiry. Even the title of this chapter, a quote from a respondent, suggests that only straight (heterosexual) men are seen to possess the capacity for violence or fighting dexterity. Because they are represented solely as passive victims of bias crimes, intimate partner violence, or homophobic bullying without any attention to their roles as perpetrators, gay men are regarded as lacking agency. That is, they are seen to lack both *choice* and *power*, and to possess little ability to control the situation (also see Panfil 2014a; and for related discussions in this volume, Dennis; Woods). Based on the extant literature, it seems likely that their experiences with previous victimization or discrimination are integrally related to their decisions to enact violence.

Current Study

Utilizing in-depth interviews from a sample of 53 gay gang- and crime-involved men, this study seeks to explicitly address the dearth of empirical evidence on gay men's involvement in violence. To do so, I will discuss their uses of violence under a variety of circumstances and their motivations for engaging in such violence. I explicitly engage with and challenge existing literature by discussing respondents' violence within several scenarios: for self-defense or the defense of others; in the context of romantic relationships; to address disrespect; as a regular part of gang life; and to combat anti-gay harassment on the streets and in schools. My data show that gay men do engage in violence, often for reasons they feel very strongly about, and refuse to be the passive victims the literature or cultural stereotypes might suggest. In fact, prior victimization plays roles in their decisions to enact violence. It is to my study's methods that I now turn.

Methods and Sample

Sampling Strategy

I recruited 53 respondents by utilizing a snowball sampling design, in which willing participants refer additional participants to the researcher. Snowball sampling is a common methodology to access underground populations (Lofland et al. 2006). I sampled in Columbus, Ohio, which is the only city where I had connections to gay gang- and crime-involved men. I obtained the initial group of eligible participants by contacting men previously known to me when I lived in Columbus, during which time I volunteered for and utilized services of several LGBT advocacy organizations. I also approached noneligible (gay, but not gang/crime-involved) individuals who had connections to eligible participants and asked them to speak to their friends on my behalf in the same manner in which I asked eligible participants to refer friends. I even accessed social networking websites such as MySpace to view user profiles and then contact men whose profiles suggested gang membership or involvement in criminal activity. These varied recruitment strategies allowed me to tap into different friendship networks (and gangs) and interview a diverse group of respondents. This sample includes men in gangs with a variety of structures, including all-gay gangs.

Interviews

I asked a series of screening questions to confirm eligibility before beginning each interview. Gay identity[1] and either gang membership or involvement in criminal activity, determined through self-nomination, made a man eligible to participate. Participants also had to be at least 18 years of age, primarily for reasons related to human research subjects protections.

I conducted in-depth interviews, which allow respondents to speak for themselves without researchers imposing artificial concepts or categories on them (Becker 1967; Wright and Bennett 1990). I asked each participant about his background, his relationships and sexual identity, his gang and/or criminal experiences, his experience with the criminal justice system, and what it meant for him to 'be a man,' among other topics. The interview instrument is unique to this study, but includes some questions used in prior research that have been adapted or borrowed verbatim for use in this study (Copes and Hochstetler 2006; Edin and Kefalas 2005; Esbensen 2003; Miller 2001, 2008). I also drew inspiration from my own lived experience as a queer person and the many conversations I have had over the past decade with other self-identified LGB individuals. My indigenous knowledge (Holstein and Gubrium 1995) of gay culture, gang/criminal justice system argot, and Columbus's geography helped me to ask follow-up questions that tapped concepts or experiences to which other researchers might not be attuned and to gain rapport with my respondents. Because my sex, race, or education level could have discouraged them from sharing certain details of their lives with me, our shared experience helped respondents to feel the social differences between us were not so great because I, in a way, spoke their language. As a result, interviews were very conversational in nature.

I conducted the interviews between November 2009 and January 2012.[2] Respondents chose to be interviewed in such locations as their homes, a private meeting room at a public library, a park, and my car. Respondents were paid 15 dollars for the interview and reimbursed for gas, bus, or parking expenses, if they had to travel for the interview. Interviews lasted between approximately 45 min and 2 h and 45 min, were audio recorded with consent, and were then transcribed verbatim. Names contained herein are pseudonyms; each respondent came up with

---

[1] Although some men told me during the interview that they occasionally date or have sex with women and would identify as bisexual, they were still eligible for the study if they self-identified as gay at the outset of the interview, regardless of whether they identified as gay, bisexual, or as some other term that suggested sexual minority status. For parsimony, I refer to my respondents as "gay" men, but understand the arguments against collapsing the fluidity of sexual identification into tidy categories for researchers' or readers' convenience (see in this volume, for example, Ball; Johnson; Levy; Woods).

[2] I also spent additional time with participants to better understand their lives. As this chapter does not utilize data from fieldnotes, I do not discuss my fieldwork; however, over 225 h of fieldwork were completed.

a "code name" that was not an existing nickname or street name. Many chose common first names, but others chose stylized names such as M6, Batman, and Hurricane.[3]

Method of Analysis

After the interviews were transcribed, I then analyzed the data using an inductive approach (Glaser and Strauss 1967), which allows themes to emerge from the data. Because I conducted all of the interviews, I had an idea of some of the major themes before I began coding. I used a basic word processing program to code the data. I coded transcripts in their entirety for every mention of violence, but will only present several of the main themes here.

The majority of the examples presented in this chapter originated from several separate, nonconsecutive questions on the interview instrument. These include: (1) What was school like for you? (2) Can you tell me a little bit about your past relationships? (3) Have you ever physically fought because someone called you a fag or a faggot? and (4) What kinds of things do you [and your gang] do together? Because interviews were transcribed and coded on an ongoing basis that was concurrent with data collection, I kept emerging themes in mind while in the field and attempted to delve deeper into those topics during subsequent interviews. For example, the question regarding fighting due to being called a fag or faggot was not on the original interview instrument, but I began to regularly ask it after this theme was present in many of my early interviews. Similarly, no questions on the interview instrument were intended to explicitly tap intimate partner violence or homophobic bullying/harassment in schools; these themes simply arose in respondents' narratives and I asked follow-up questions to gain detail. This is further evidence of the inductive quality not only of qualitative coding, but of qualitative research more generally.

---

[3] Several pseudonyms were changed after the interviews when I realized the respondent had given me an existing nickname, part of his real name, or a name extremely close to his real name. If I could not contact the respondent to select a new name, I attempted to capture the 'feel' of the original code name. Because I was granted a waiver of signed informed consent, the code name is the only name attached to any of their responses. I also obtained a Confidentiality Certificate from the U.S. National Institute of Health. This Certificate protects my respondents from being prosecuted for anything they tell me, and protects me from being forced to turn over notes and transcripts or from being subpoenaed to testify against them in any court proceeding. At the start of the interview, I also gave participants a list of referrals for various LGBT-centered services, including counseling, suicide prevention, alcohol/drug treatment, and HIV/STI testing.

Sample Characteristics

At the time of the interview, 52 participants lived within Columbus's metropolitan statistical area (MSA), and one lived directly north of Columbus's MSA in a very small town. They ranged in age from 18 to 28, with an average age of 21.5. The majority (89 %) were men of color. Forty-eight respondents identified as a member or an affiliate of a gang, crew, clique, set, posse, or organization at some point in their lives. The remaining five men had also engaged in repeated criminal activity as part of a group, but denied their groups were gangs. Table 7.1 presents additional information regarding the sample characteristics.

Table 7.1 Descriptive characteristics of sample (n = 53)

Mean age (Range: 18–28)	21.5
Race	
Black/African-American	77 %
White	11 %
Latino	2 %
Biracial	9 %
Country/state of origin other than Ohio	42 %
Parents are immigrants	9 %
Immigrated to the USA with parents	4 %
Employment status	
Employed (legally or off-books)	45 %
Unemployed	49 %
Receiving Supplemental Security Income (SSI) benefits	6 %
Education	
High school/High school equivalency or some college	75 %
In high school at time of interview	17 %
Less than high school; not enrolled	8 %
Fathered children	19 %
HIV status	
HIV positive	11 %
HIV negative	87 %
Unsure	2 %
Gang membership	91 %
Gang-involved at time of interview—mean age	21.4
Gang joining—mean age	16.2
Average length of time in gang, in years	4.0
History of CJ contact	
Arrested	77 %
Incarcerated (Range: 2 days–8 years)	55 %
Foster care (Range: 3 months–13 years)	28 %

Findings

When "You've Gotta Knock Somebody Out": Circumstances for Justifiable Violence

Regardless of the scenario, many of the incidents of violence mentioned by respondents were accompanied with justifications or rationalizations for the violence. Justifications included self-defense or the defense of others, infidelity, dishonesty, disrespect, and retaliation. Even the respondents who reported little involvement in violence appreciated these justifications. Kevin acknowledged that sometimes, "lines are crossed, and you've gotta knock somebody out." In this section, I discuss some of the major themes to which respondents attributed their violence.

Self-defense and the defense of others. Violence in order to defend self or others was overwhelmingly supported by respondents. Being threatened, hit, or shot at first was always an acceptable reason to respond with equal force. To this effect, a common refrain I heard regarding when a respondent would fight back was, "If you put your hands on me." Fighting back in self-defense has long been a legally- and socially-recognized justification for violence, but persons involved in delinquency and crime may define "self-defense" broadly to suit their own interests (Sykes and Matza 1957). Indeed, respondents sought to defend against attacks not only to their physical bodies, but to their identities and reputations. Specifically, anti-gay harassment and threats of violence were seen as assaults on a man's masculinity and sexual identity, and were deemed worthy of a violent response. Several men explicitly used the phrase "defending my honor" to refer to the actions they took. In these scenarios, defense of masculine honor and reputation were also linked to perceived disrespect. It is to these instances of "fighting back" against anti-gay harassment that I will return to later in the chapter.

Also theoretically important to the study of gay men's violence is the fact that several respondents formed identities around their willingness to defend individuals who were unable or unwilling to properly defend themselves. Brian told me that he initially started fighting while in a juvenile facility in order to defend his "projects," by which he meant: "the mentally challenged," "younger gays," and anyone who was otherwise "vulnerable" or "weak." He said that because he had been bullied his entire life, he "just can't stand to see someone getting picked on." He suggested, "I didn't like to fight, but whenever I got angry, and someone pissed me off, I didn't hold back, and I would definitely fight to defend what was right or what was mines." Brian's willingness to intervene in order to defend others resulted not only in several years added on to his time in a juvenile facility, but also in an incarceration as an adult. On his way home from work one night, he saw someone being seriously beaten by a large group of men. He drew a legally registered gun, took aim from inside his car, and shot two of the assailants. Despite committing two aggravated assaults, he served only 30 days in jail on these charges and attributes the leniency to what were, in essence, mitigating circumstances. Specifically, he defended someone who was outnumbered and at risk of serious or fatal injury. The use of the handgun shows the extremes to which Brian is willing to go to in order to defend what is "right."

Brian was not the only one to have these inclinations. Max also said he will fight for those who would not or could not defend themselves, and against those who pick on "the downtrodden." As an adult, he often defended his gay friends from anti-gay harassment. His protective behaviors started early:

> Like, when I was younger younger, like in elementary [school], I've gotten in trouble before, for... Kickin' this boy in the head, and he hit his head on a rock, but they was jumpin' this little boy, this little white boy, just because he was a little white boy. We was in [my neighborhood], and it was a couple of black dudes that just moved in, and they were doin', like, beatin' him up on the mulch and all that stuff at the bus stop, and I pushed him down and I kicked him in his head! [...] Like, [the boy getting beaten up] was really, like, a crybaby, and it made me feel so bad, because they were really over there, he was screamin', turnin', he was red, like, it's snow outside and everything, like... "Why do y'all got him on the ground like that?" It just enraged me, and I got upset, and it just happened. They don't have to be gay, but I don't like for people to fuck with the downtrodden. [...] If they're already down, why keep putting them further down, you know?

The "rage" described by Max was echoed by other respondents, who used similar terms to denote the anger or explosive episodes they experienced just prior to engaging in violence they saw as righteous. M6 reported that he had "moral anger like a son of a bitch" for men who chose to pick on others substantially smaller than themselves. Fighting smaller men was not "fair" and furthermore, he mentioned that it carried no honor. Despite being a member of a prison gang, he was disgusted by inmate politics, wherein "50" members of a racial group might attack one member of another group. He called this practice "lame" and "soft."

In light of the existing literature regarding gay men's status as victims, the willingness to defend the self from violence is illuminating; the willingness to defend others violently when no real threat is posed to the 'defender' is even more surprising. Furthermore, the desire to defend others is paradoxical considering the fact that my respondents are gang- and crime-involved. That is, one might wonder why men who have committed crimes against members of the public would want to defend anyone from violence. Although respondents' prohibitions against bullying and fighting dirty were inconsistent and often very context-specific, no one took any pride in "bullying" another person and thus all felt the need to justify their behavior, so as not to be counted among the bullies of the world. Masculine norms such as those of physical toughness (Connell 2005; Mahalik et al. 2003; Messerschmidt 1993) would not be served by fighting smaller, weaker, or outnumbered persons, but by besting the person who does.

Intimate matters. The vast majority of criminological research on gay perpetrators of violence has focused on those men who commit intimate partner violence (IPV); explanations for why men batter their partners include aggressive conflict resolution styles, experiencing domestic violence in their families of origin, and perpetrators' concerns regarding challenges to their control of their intimate partners (McKenry et al. 2006; Toro-Alfonso et al. 2004). However, because the majority of research on same-sex IPV has focused on victims instead of offenders, these motivations are not well-understood and receive inconsistent support in the literature. My study's data also fail to provide a coherent picture of the nature of same-sex IPV, as the majority of violent incidents discussed at length in the interviews were *not* among intimate partners.

With these caveats in mind, there were instances of serious intimate partner violence reported to me, which were often provided as one example of a larger pattern of violence. For example, Silas claimed he ran over his "abusive" boyfriend with a car; Eric attempted to strangle his boyfriend with a cell phone charger and "beat him up pretty badly" when he discovered him at a local motel with another man; Reese bit and took "a chunk" out of his boyfriend's chest during a fight. Silas, Eric, and Reese all reported that they experienced ongoing, often mutual IPV in these long-term relationships. Although the specific motives for each incident varied, these three men and others suggested their relationship violence stemmed from infidelity, dishonesty, and/or jealousy.

These issues also caused fights between respondents and those whom they either suspected of or knew were cheating with their partners. Lying to someone, especially when confronted about a particular transgression, was taken as a sign of disrespect to the partner and to the relationship. This exchange with Reese is illustrative:

Reese: Okay, the first time [I was arrested as an adult] was because this little chump was in my [ex-]boyfriend's face. [...] He was in his face constantly, you know, like flirting or whatever, and he was so-called straight. So one day I pulled up, and no one expected me to pull up, everyone thought I was out with my friends, and they was in the parking lot, and I saw the boy reach over and kiss my boyfriend, so then I confronted both of them right after it happened, and they both denied it, so [the boyfriend] owned a bar at the time, so I went downstairs and I started drinking. It was just like, irritating me even more and more thinking about it, and I just called the boy outside, and I was like, "Look dude," I was like, "Be truthful with me, or me and you are gonna fight," and he was like, "Dude, I don't know what the hell you're talking about, I'm not gay." "Okay, why'd you reach in and kiss my boyfriend then if you're not gay?" Well, then he continued to lie to me and I had a beer bottle in my hand, and it made me so mad that I just cracked [him] in the forehead with it, and he ran and called the cops like a little bitch.

VP: Okay, so why is he a bitch for calling the cops on you after that?

Reese: Because he shouldn't have kissed my boyfriend!

VP: Okay, so was it more that he kissed your boyfriend or that he lied to you?

Reese: Both!

VP: If he had come out there and said, "I kissed your boyfriend, I'm sorry..."

Reese: No, no, I would've went in there and tried to fight him!

VP: Oh, your boyfriend?

Reese: Yeah! So, either way I was gonna fight that night.

Presumably because the other man would not come clean and admit his mistake(s), Reese continues to mark him as less than a man by first introducing him as a "little chump," referring to him repeatedly as a "boy," and then as a "little bitch." He reported instances of fighting other men whom he suspected of flirting or sleeping with his boyfriend in an attempt to encourage his partner's fidelity. Brian also shared this desire to keep what was 'his':

> The majority of [my fights during my 7 years in a juvenile facility] were over people that I was dating in there, you know, a lot of people like to try to come in and steal that person from you, and I'm the kind of person, I don't fight for show, I fight to protect what's my mine, and I am very territorial, very protective, and a very jealous person, so when I'm dating someone, I will not stand, I will not allow someone to stand in my way.

Although these examples suggest that complex influences such as infidelity, dishonesty, alcohol, and episodic anger contribute to respondents' enactment of violence regarding intimate matters, motives for these incidents certainly speak to concerns regarding the control of an intimate partner. Interestingly, Oz suggested that these concerns were inherent in same-sex relationships:

> I know, to me, it feels like in homosexual relationships, feelings are way stronger, like… Feelings are way stronger, it's really intense, you tend to fight more, than I think in a straight relationship. You know, it's… Cuz you know, you don't wanna lose that person. Two males bein' together, they're gonna fight, you know?

Consistent with this assumption, several other men went so far as to say they enjoyed the ability of male same-sex couples to get "rough" with each other. These sentiments suggest support for normative conceptions of masculinity, which may actually contribute to IPV perpetration (McKenry et al. 2006; though see Messinger, this volume).

Disrespect as recurrent theme. An underlying motivation for many of the fights described by respondents was the desire to address perceived disrespect. Especially in the urban context where respect is the currency of the street, much status is to be lost when one is "dissed" (Anderson 1999). As has been illustrated by these examples, disrespect is perhaps an amorphous concept that applies to many forms of poor social behavior. These include challenging someone's honor or reputation, calling someone a fag/faggot, being unfaithful to a romantic partner, and lying. Relatedly, gossip was another motivation for fights. For example, Bob described the origin of many of the ongoing conflicts at a popular gay club:

> Boys. […] He said she said umm, just drama. […] [J]ust about really their boyfriends talkin' to somebody else, and it was a lot of unfaithfulness, and just, that was in like, the gay relationships. Umm, and they wanted to fight that person or this person said somethin' about me, or lied on me, or, uhh what else? Really like, petty stuff, where […] they be talkin' about each other, and they'll then get mad of course, and argue, you know, start fightin' or something.

Jealousy, gossip, and immaturity even caused members of some gangs to fight with each other, but they usually "got over it." Tony said members of his clique would fight with each other or with rival cliques over "lil stuff that get us aggravated and annoyed." While in the moment, respondents felt that these encounters required action, but they also admitted afterwards that these fights were unimportant by using terms like "petty" or "little stuff." Respondents described many other fights with disrespect at the core of the problem, some which started as fairly innocuous events, such as accidentally bumping into another person or being asked about a prior romantic partner. Although these were not judged to be nearly as serious as anti-gay harassment, threats to personal safety, or the potential loss of an intimate partner, they still necessitated a response, which could then escalate to physical violence.

The explainable, but not justifiable. Although I have focused primarily on physical fights and/or assaults, other categories of violent crimes exist. These include homicides, rapes, and robberies. I did not ask any respondent if he had ever committed a homicide or a rape, and no one freely offered that he had. However, many had engaged in robberies, often in connection to other delinquent or illegal pursuits, such as gang membership or selling drugs or sex. With very few exceptions, respondents did not typically try to argue that this violence was justifiable. Rather, they focused on the immediate reasons for committing these crimes, such as wanting money, goods, or drugs. When they did argue it was justifiable, they suggested these items were owed to them for goods or services rendered. Secondary motivations also included revenge for other wrongs committed. However, for many respondents, their involvement in these offenses was virtually indistinguishable from their histories of gang involvement, as these activities were often engaged in with their gangs. It is to the larger topic of gang violence to which I now turn.

Gang Violence

Consistent with prior research (e.g., Decker 1996), respondents' narratives suggested that violence is a defining feature of gang membership. For some, their knowledge of neighborhood violence or gang activity was precisely the reason they joined. However, a chance of encountering gang violence became a guarantee upon joining for almost all of the gang-involved men in the sample.

Just over half of the men in primarily heterosexual gangs reported an initiation ritual for at least one of their crews, all of which included violence. Thus, their initiation into gang violence began immediately with their initiation into gang membership. One such ritual was being "jumped in," wherein existing gang members hit the recruit for a designated period of time. Sometimes, recruits were allowed to fight back. Another violent initiation ritual involved assaulting and/or robbing someone, especially someone who the OGs (Original Gangsters) or other higher-ups in the gang wanted to retaliate against. Boog likened this to military rank: as a "foot soldier," a new recruit serves the interests of the gang by robbing the "adversary" of the OG. Brad echoed this language when describing how he joined and moved up in his gang:

Uhh, just bein' a soldier. Uhh, crashin' out on people. They'd be like, "Hey, dude owes money and he ain't paid, go get 'em," so I'd go beat 'em up, or fight 'em. [...] Whatever they wanted me to do, I just kept doin' it, and as the years went on, I just got to my spot.

In addition to solidifying gang members' ties to each other and meting out fear and retaliation to other crews, these rituals helped to prove that the new recruit was tough and allowed existing gang members to gauge whether he possessed useful skills. For example, Jayden "earned his stripes" (another military reference) by fighting with members of other crews; Brandon "went around fightin' random people" to show he could fight and be "down" with his gang; Spiderman suggested that he was allowed to fight back during his gang's violent initiation ritual because the other members wanted "to see where your skills is, to see if you're really down for the clique."

Although much of gang members' time was spent in law-abiding activity, fighting other crews was also of concern. For men in primarily heterosexual gangs, much of this violence was to defend their neighborhood ("hood" or "turf") or their group membership:

Jayden: Might fight with other gangs, there is another gang out there that they fight with. [...] I guess just bein' in the same neighborhood and claimin' this [gang], and they claimin' that [gang], and they just be fightin', like, they'll throw up they hood, and then somebody else throw up [their hood], and then they just wanna fight, yeah. It be like that. [...] Like, hoods, cuz that's what it's by now, ain't nobody like, "Oh, Bloods, Crips," no, it goes by hoods, you feel what I'm sayin'?

DJ: [We would fight with] other neighborhoods, if we didn't like how you was comin' at us. Or, if we ain't like you period, we would fight you.

This defense of the neighborhood group extended even beyond the boundaries of the neighborhood:

Rocc: It's called reppin', you know? We were out, like, if we were out at [a festival], or whatever, like, everybody was together, everybody wore they color, and we were goin' out lookin' for fights, brawls, you know? Hit somebody in red, dodge out [leave], like, everything before the police came. It was kinda like a game, you know?

It also transcended beyond rival crews; nongang affiliated ("random") people were sometimes targets of violence:

Toby: [We'd] play Knockout. [...] Knockout, basically, is like goin' to another neighborhood, and randomly walkin' around the neighborhood, whoever you see, just punch 'em. And then run, and just keep doin' it. Over and over and over again, no matter who it is.

Elijah: [My brother and I] had to do the dirty work. Like the beatin' somebody up if they know they don't belong in the [neighborhood], or just beatin' a random person up as they walkin' down the street.

Perhaps especially telling regarding the ubiquity of violence in gang life is gang members' transformations of violence into a source of entertainment; as "play" or a "game."

Men in primarily gay gangs also had physical confrontations with rival crews and other members of the public, especially those who harassed them for being gay. However, these fights (and the gay gangs) were not often centered around neighborhoods. They more often involved issues of reputation and respect; jealousy, gossip, and "drama" were the undertones of many of these fights. As was previously mentioned, although respondents tended to describe the reasons for these fights as "petty," the fights often still resulted in serious injuries, legal ramifications, and ongoing retaliatory violence.

"Tit for tat": Boog's experience with gang violence. The cycle of violence and violence's entrenched status within gangs can be further exemplified with an extended example. At the time of his interview, Boog had been seriously gang-involved for over 10 years and had spent a combined total of 8 years in prison for violent offenses. He reported seeing gangs and violence in the neighborhood as a child, and even being attracted to that aspect of gang life as an adolescent:

> I was excited with the more violence, the more people, the better off, I just wanted to make trouble. I feel like, my feelings, I wasn't getting love [from my family], so I didn't want nobody to be happy in my life, you know, nobody. [...] I mean, my friends, my brothers, the gangs, they showed love. Whether it's the wrong kind of love, it's the love you need at that time.

Boog had an idea of the violence that awaited him in the gang: His older brother "didn't live to see 18" because he had been murdered, shot twice in the head. Regarding gang involvement in violence, he suggested, "If you gon' live by it, you gon' die by it, that's the rule."

Boog had to commit a violent (retaliatory) offense to join the gang and then continued engaging in violence with the gang in order to respond to threats. In his narrative, he made efforts to convey that the targets of this violence were "particular" individuals who were somehow deserving. He described jumping, shooting, and/or robbing individuals who came into his project "repping" (representing) another project, who were enemies of his gang's OG as part of his initiation, who had harmed a fellow gang member, who had shot at him first, or who were also involved in the drug trade. He noted that because these people were also in "the game," they were acceptable targets. Beyond that, the risk of being formally punished was low because they had no legal recourse, and the potential payoffs were considerable:

> [Because] you knew they had money, you knew they had dope, and all the other stuff was bonus. So they, they always gonna give you something. You know, my thing in robbing, why rob somebody that's only gonna have $100 or $200, and they too many consequences after the fact if you get caught. [...] Yeah, go for drug dealers, who they gonna call? The police and tell them? "Oh, I just got robbed for my drugs and..." Okay.

Of his estimated ten arrests, Boog stated that "most of them was [for] violent crimes." He received a five-year prison sentence for shooting his accomplice (his best friend and a fellow gang member) when a post-crime money distribution went wrong. What started out as a hand fight escalated to trading gunfire. In a telling turn of phrase, Boog says he shot this man in "self-defense" because, as he put it, "I felt like it was either him or me."

Boog explained that the gang afforded him some level of protection on the street, in reform school, and in prison, but in order to maintain the protection that the gang offered him, he had to engage in violence. Sometimes this was at the behest of the OG, but usually it was to protect his fellow gang members. In return, he was the victim of violence, but he alleged that he would have been hurt more if he did not claim membership. When asked if he was able to avoid being victimized in prison, he replied:

> I mean, as far as assaulted, no. As far as jumped on, no. As far as being raped and things, yes. Yes, just because of what I claim. And that's what most people get into the game for, is protection anyway, you know what I mean? Because if you do something to me, it gonna always be a response, if you did something to my brother, there gonna be a response, you know, tit for tat. [...] Yes, it afforded me a lot of, a lot of protection. You know, I can say more, do a little bit more, because it's basically about power, you know?

He also noted that he still cannot visit his home state and old neighborhood without fearing for his safety, or without actually being victimized. Although he was still peripherally involved with a Blood set in Columbus at the time of the interview, he reported that he not only did not engage in violence anymore, but that he viewed himself as more guarded and less social as a result of his continued viewing of and engagement in violence over the course of his lifetime.

Boog's narrative illustrates the complex cycle of victimization and violence many men in gangs experience. Paradoxically, he joined his first gang in reform school for protection before ever being victimized, but became a victim of violence as a result of his involvement. Rios (2011, p. 55) refers to this as the "gang double bind": Inner-city boys of color fight to prevent their future victimization, but their involvement in violence only leads to more potential for victimization. Similarly, Darius suggested that because his family "wasn't there" for him, he had to join a gang to preserve his safety: "I didn't have nobody, so it was like, if I did get into it wit somebody, I was gettin' jumped on." Although he joined to protect himself from fights, his gang membership initiated him into deadly violence. In his sophomore year of high school, Darius sustained serious head injuries after being pistol-whipped in a gang fight, during which one of his fellow gang members was killed. Toby also joined a gang to prevent neighborhood trials:

> Because, we was new to the neighborhood, and basically, that's the only way they was gonna basically accept us livin' there. I didn't wanna have to every day get up and fight everybody in the neighborhood. I just decided to join.

His "jumping in" ritual consisted of being "beat up" by his gang's members for about ten minutes, during which he was able to fight back. He then also became involved in serious violence with his crew, and sustained his own stabbing injuries, also resulting in visible scars. On this note, several other men including Darius mentioned or showed me scars they had obtained in gang fights.

Consistent with prior research, many respondents described violence as an integral part of their gang experience, especially as a way to deal with threats, either to their personal safety, or to their group membership. Accordingly, they justified much of their violence as a necessary part of gang life, both on the streets and while incarcerated. The willingness to engage in violence on behalf of the gang or its members is both a sign of loyalty and a way to secure protection for himself when trouble comes his way. Respondents were also willing to engage in violence in order to defend themselves and others against a different kind of trouble: anti-gay harassment. I will now discuss their responses to this harassment.

Responding to Anti-gay Harassment with Violence

While the criminological literature focuses on gay men as victims of bias crimes and an analogous body of literature focuses on LGBT youths' experiences with homophobic bullying in schools, an unexplored area is their active responses to victimization. Although research suggests some LGBT youth do fight back against their harassers in school (Grossman et al. 2009; Johnson 2008; Kosciw et al. 2010), these instances remain largely unexplored. The present study is uniquely situated to explore the circumstances under which respondents chose to fight back against anti-gay harassment, and why.

Over two-thirds of the men in my study physically fought with another person due to anti-gay harassment, threats of violence, and/or actual violence. Fights occurred in schools and school yards; public places, such as clubs or community festivals; and even in juvenile and adult correctional facilities. Most men who had fought back had done so several times, sometimes well over ten times: Derrick estimated over 20 such fights; Brandon, over 30.

Respondents asserted that being called "punk," "bitch," or "sissy" did not bother them nearly as much being called "fag" or "faggot." An assault on one's masculinity implied in the use of *bitch* or *punk* was offensive, but an assault on one's masculinity *and* sexual orientation implied in the use of *faggot* could rarely be ignored. Because of its explicit attack on identity, the use of *fag* as an insult was considered to be "derogatory," "offensive," "hurtful," and a "low blow"; Casper suggested that only "low-lifes" use it. Jeremiah explained:

> So, you could call me a bitch, you can call me out my name, duh duh duh, I don't care, but when you call me a faggot, I know wut chu mean by that, and that's just as bad as calling me a nigger, or, that's the lowest you could go. That's you resortin' to your bottom pit, so I feel like once you call me that, I'ma resort to my bottom, and my bottom is wit my hands.

Fag/faggot was most often described as "disrespectful." Thus, responses to anti-gay harassment were deemed necessary to reclaim the masculine status that has been challenged when a man is disrespected and harassed for being gay. Messerschmidt (2000, p. 13) notes that normative masculine resources such as fighting can be marshaled to "correct" scenarios wherein a man has been subordinated by another.

Despite these visceral reactions to the words fag/faggot, an anti-gay insult alone was typically insufficient to spark a physical altercation. Usually there was some form of escalation, such as coupling the slur with another wrong or an aggressive delivery, but more often there was a series of successive, escalatory steps. The most common response to a harasser was first a verbal one, such as asking the individual to repeat the comment, clarify it, or to say it "to my face." All of these strategies were intended to cause the aggressor to capitulate and essentially withdraw the insult, which would end the conflict. When this happened, it served to reinforce respondents' self-perceptions of respectable masculinity, and suggested that the aggressor himself was lacking in that department:

> Max: Once they see that you're not a punk, that you're gonna say somethin' back, they back off, they do. People do. It happens that way a lot. [...] Because most people when you say something to 'em, they back down. [...] I'm gonna stay and defend myself until it's over. Because I'm not a fag, your dad is! Like, that's how I am!

> Elijah: I'd be like, "You just got punked by a fag. So who's the fag?" And I'll leave it there, and then they'll feel stupid, because you just called me so many fags, look at chu now! You just got punked by the fag.

However, if the harasser continued to be disrespectful or aggressive, respondents said they would "take it to the next level" by invading the harasser's space or throwing the first punch. In these scenarios, fighting only at "the next level" (after escalation) allowed respondents to maintain that they were *defending* their gay identities instead of stirring up unnecessary trouble. For example, Batman denied he was a "bully"; Johnny denied he was "an initial fight-starter"; Hurricane denied he was "the type to pick the fight"; and Bird denied he was "a violent person."

Respondents engaged in these fights for various reasons, as evidenced herein. In defending themselves and others from anti-gay harassment, they proved the masculine status that was assumed to be lacking. Respondents were well aware of cultural stereotypes regarding gay men; namely, that they were weak, passive, and would not defend themselves. They were pleased to defy these negative stereotypes:

> Derrick: I'm not scared of no straight person, if you gon' come at me, I'm still a boy at the end of the day. It don't matter like, how gay I am, how gay I might be, I can still fight a straight dude.

> Marcus: [T]hey wouldn't expect it, cuz they'd be like, "Oh, he's gay." Forget, underestimatin' me, forgettin' that I *am* still a boy. And then they're like, shocked, like, "Oh!"

In essence, respondents utilized normative markers of masculinity such as physical toughness and fighting dexterity to defend a non-normative (and thus stigmatized) sexual identity.

With these fights, respondents also sought to curtail future harassment. They supposed that losing a fight to a "faggot" would prevent aggressors from harassing other gay people. Jeremy suggested, "[I]f you get yo ass whooped, now you gon' be lookin' like, 'Okay. I just got my ass whooped by a fag, so maybe I should think about it!'" Steve's choice to severely beat his harasser was motivated by one goal: "[I] made sure he never called one of us a faggot again." ATL asserted that only after gay people defied existing stereotypes and fought back would they be taken seriously: straight classmates will learn that "faggots fight too, they'll defend theyself too." Drawing from his own experience with homophobic bullying in schools, Darius summed it up concisely: "[T]hey don't respect gay people, cuz they think gay people are not gonna take up for theirself, but when you take up for yourself and do stuff for yourself, then you see the respect." These assertions are consistent with Anderson's (1999, p. 10) claims regarding inner-city violence management strategies: "repeated displays of 'nerve' and 'heart' build or reinforce a credible reputation for vengeance that works to deter aggression and disrespect" (though see Stewart et al. (2006), for empirical evidence to the contrary).

This notion of "building a reputation" to curtail future anti-gay harassment was especially critical for gay youth like ATL and Darius who sought to prevent future homophobic victimization in their schools. LGBT youth report high levels of verbal and physical homophobic harassment in schools, as well as low levels of teacher intervention in these incidents (Kosciw et al. 2012). The men in my study reported a general dislike of school not because of the work, but because of classmates who constantly teased them. Concerns about being a target of homophobic bullying were amplified when respondents moved schools or moved up in grade. For example, when Jeremiah was asked how many times he thought he had fought over someone calling him a fag, he suggested seven times, which directly corresponded to the number of schools he had attended. He added:

> But once you fight one person at the school over it, they don't do it no more. Like, not wit me, anyway, they didn't. They left me alone. So it always takes, like, it depends, like, every time I switched schools, it took for me to fight at least one person.

In contrast, Hurricane did not fight initially, but was able to build a reputation over time:

> After I started getting taunted enough, I opened up my mouth and started speakin' up for myself, like, "No, you got me fucked up!" (laughs) But, it didn't get better until I got into high school, because by the time I had got into high school, 6th, 7th, and 8th grade, I had built my reputation, so everybody that I was in middle school with transferred to the high school that I went to or whatnot.

In a telling comment regarding his own fights with students who called him a faggot, Nate asserted that he felt like he "had to get them back" for using a "rude and disrespectful" word. Nate's comments succinctly represent the shared sentiment that actively responding to anti-gay harassment was *necessary* to address disrespect and curtail future harassment. Repeated homophobic bullying, which attacks an individual's masculinity and sexuality, coupled with a lack of teacher intervention and low social support, produces additional, direct motivation for gay youth to fight back. For additional information regarding how school-based homophobic bullying and harassment contributed to respondents' decisions to fight back in school and/or join gangs, see Panfil (2014b).

One additional note is necessary. These findings are in direct contrast to the only other study that uncovered the violent behavior of a handful of gay gang members. The gay gang members in Totten's (2000) study engaged in gay-bashing incidents to construct masculine identity and conceal their sexual orientation, whereas my respondents protect themselves and others from anti-gay harassment and bullying *in order to* construct masculine identity and proudly assert their sexual identity. In fact, the harassment of other members of LGBT communities was regarded, on some level, as a personal attack.

Discussion and Conclusion

In this chapter, I have detailed many circumstances under which a sample of 53 gay gang- and crime-involved men engage in violence, and for what reasons. Some motivations, such as self-defense, seeking to control an intimate partner, or as a necessary part of gang life, were consistent with extant literature. Others, such as "fighting back" to combat anti-gay harassment on the streets and in schools, have been largely unexplored in the literature. Consistent with extant literature's suppositions regarding the relationships between victimization and offending, respondents' prior victimization or fear of victimization contributed to their willingness to engage in violence. Their narratives indicate they refuse to be the passive victims the literature or cultural stereotypes might suggest.

Furthermore, evidence that gay men are active members of gangs or that they violently defend themselves in general may alone be surprising to some scholars, considering the relative lack of attention to queer populations in criminological research. My findings contribute to further revelations. For example, respondents have referred to violence as a behavior they have engaged in many times; as something they "had" to do; as escalating from mere verbal provocation; as punishment for other nonviolent infractions such as infidelity; as a regular part of gang life; and even as entertainment or a "game." In light of potential sociopolitical gains towards LGBT equality, some might argue that gay men's violence is better left unsaid; I, however, am not one of them (Panfil 2014a). To deny that LGBT persons engage in violence and crime is to ignore their lived experiences, to deny that they have agency, and to lose opportunities for analyses that could inform prevention and intervention efforts (Panfil 2014a; though, for a critique of this last claim, see in this volume Ball; Johnson).

The characteristics of my sample also permit some qualifications regarding "gay men's violence." My respondents are a fairly high-risk group of men with long histories of violence, crime, and gang involvement. That is, my sample is of gay men who are, by definition, involved in these behaviors. Their decisions to join gangs and/or engage in violence were also made against a backdrop of prior victimization, such as neighborhood violence or familial neglect. Both violence and gang membership arise from nearly identical risk factors (Esbensen et al. 2009; Peterson and Morgan 2014); thus, it is unclear whether individuals who do not possess these risk factors and are otherwise uninvolved in gangs/violence would be willing to actively defend themselves from an anti-gay physical attack, let alone justify a violent response to broader attacks on their masculinity or sexuality. The requisite questions simply have not been asked. My respondents' behaviors were also heavily influenced by the fact that they were 'out,' or open about their sexuality. This likely explains the stark contrast between my findings and Totten's (2000) findings regarding gay gang members' engagement in gay-bashing scenarios, partially to conceal their own sexual interests. I cannot speak to the experiences of men who are not out. Finally, the vast majority of my respondents are young men of color in an urban area, so these findings may not be applicable to all gang- and/or crime-involved men, especially if such men are demographically different than the sample studied herein (such as white, middle-aged men who live in rural areas).

This research has helped shed light on a previously understudied area, that of gay men's participation in violence. I encourage all scholars, but especially criminologists, to critically interrogate existing assumptions regarding LGBT persons and their (non)involvement in crime, violence, and gangs. Only then will we gain insight on how to better understand and serve queer populations.

Acknowledgments This study was supported in part by two awards from the University at Albany's Initiatives for Women. I also thank Dana Peterson for her helpful comments on an earlier draft of this chapter.

References

Anderson, E. (1999). *Code of the street: Decency, violence, and the moral life of the inner city.* New York, NY: W. W. Norton and Company.

Bandura, A., Barbaranelli, C., Caprara, G. V., & Pastorelli, C. (1996). Mechanisms of moral disengagement in the exercise of moral agency. *Journal of Personality and Social Psychology, 71,* 364–374.

Becker, H. S. (1967). Whose side are we on? *Social Problems, 14,* 239–247.

Birkett, M., Espelage, D. L., & Koenig, B. (2009). LGB and questioning students in schools: The moderating effects of homophobic bullying and school climate on negative outcomes. *Journal of Youth and Adolescence, 38,* 989–1000.

Bontempo, D. E., & D'Augelli, A. R. (2002). Effects of at-school victimization and sexual orientation on lesbian, gay, or bisexual youths' health risk behavior. *Journal of Adolescent Health, 30,* 364–374.

Bourgois, P. (1996). *In search of respect: Selling crack in El barrio.* Cambridge, UK: Cambridge University Press.

Button, D. M., O'Connell, D. J., & Gealt, R. (2012). Sexual minority youth victimization and social support: The intersection of sexuality, gender, race, and victimization. *Journal of Homosexuality, 59,* 18–43.

Carbone-Lopez, K., Esbensen, F.-A., & Brick, B. T. (2010). Correlates and consequences of peer victimization: Gender differences in direct and indirect forms of bullying. *Youth Violence and Juvenile Justice, 8,* 332–350.

Carriles, F. (2011, January 26). The 90s: Queer Nation and the Lesbian Avengers. *A portrait of queer America.* Retrieved from http://lgbtqamerica.blogspot.com/2011/01/90s-queer-nation.html.

Centers for Disease Control and Prevention. (2011). *Sexual identity, sex of sexual contacts, and health-risk behaviors among students in grades 9–12: Youth Risk Behavior Surveillance, selected sites, United States, 2001–2009.* Atlanta, GA: Department of Health and Human Services, MMWR Early Release 60.

Collier, R. (1998). *Masculinities, crime, and criminology.* London, UK: Sage.

Connell, R. W. (2005). *Masculinities* (2nd ed.). Berkeley, CA: University of California Press.

Copes, H., & Hochstetler, A. (2006). "Why I'll talk": Offenders' motives for participating in qualitative research. In P. Cromwell (Ed.), *In their own words: Criminals on crime* (4th ed., pp. 19–28). Los Angeles, CA: Roxbury.

Craft, S. M., & Serovich, J. M. (2005). Family-of-origin factors and partner violence in the intimate relationships of gay men who are HIV positive. *Journal of Interpersonal Violence, 20*, 777–791.

Cruz, J. M. (2003). "Why doesn't he just leave?" Gay male domestic violence and the reasons victims stay. *Journal of Men's Studies, 11*(3), 309–323.

Cullen, F. T., Unnever, J. D., Hartman, J. L., Turner, M. G., & Agnew, R. (2008). Gender, bullying victimization, and juvenile delinquency: A test of general strain theory. *Victims and Offenders, 3*, 331–349.

Decker, S. H. (1996). Collective and normative features of gang violence. *Justice Quarterly, 13*, 243–264.

Decker, S. H., & Van Winkle, B. (1996). *Life in the gang.* Cambridge, UK: Cambridge University Press.

Edin, K., & Kefalas, M. (2005). *Promises I can keep: Why poor women put motherhood before marriage.* Berkeley, CA: University of California Press.

Esbensen, F. (2003). *Evaluation of the Gang Resistance Education and Training (G.R.E.A.T.) Program in the United States, 1995–1999.* 2nd ICPSR version. Ann Arbor, MI: Inter-university Consortium for Political and Social Research.

Esbensen, F.-A., Peterson, D., Taylor, T. J., & Freng, A. (2009). Similarities and differences in risk factors for violent offending and gang membership. *The Australian and New Zealand Journal of Criminology, 42*, 310–335.

Espelage, D. L., Aragon, S. R., Birkett, M., & Koenig, B. W. (2008). Homophobic teasing, psychological outcomes, and sexual orientation among high school students: What influence do parents and schools have? *School Psychology Review, 37*, 202–216.

Ferguson, A. A. (2000). *Bad boys: Public schools in the making of black masculinity.* Ann Arbor, MI: University of Michigan Press.

Gibbs, J. T., & Merighi, J. R. (1994). Young black males: Marginality, masculinity, and criminality. In T. Newburn & E. Stanko (Eds.), *Just boys doing business?: Men, masculinities, and crime* (pp. 64–80). London, UK: Routledge.

Glaser, B. G., & Strauss, A. L. (1967). *The discovery of grounded theory: Strategies for qualitative research.* Chicago, IL: Aldine.

Greenwood, G. L., Relf, M. V., Huang, B., Pollack, L. M., Canchola, J. A., & Catania, J. A. (2002). Battering victimization among a probability-based sample of men who have sex with men. *American Journal of Public Health, 92*, 1964–1969.

Grossman, A. H., Haney, A. P., Edwards, P., Alessi, E. J., Ardon, M., & Howell, T. J. (2009). Lesbian, gay, bisexual and transgender youth talk about experiencing and coping with school violence: A qualitative study. *Journal of LGBT Youth, 6*, 24–46.

Herek, G. M. (2009). Hate crimes and stigma-related experiences among sexual minority adults in the United States: Prevalence estimates from a national probability sample. *Journal of Interpersonal Violence, 24*, 54–74.

Herek, G. M., Gillis, J. R., Cogan, J. C., & Glunt, E. K. (1997). Hate crime victimization among lesbian, gay, and bisexual adults: Prevalence, psychological correlates, and methodological issues. *Journal of Interpersonal Violence, 12*, 195–215.

Hochstetler, A., Copes, H., & Williams, J. P. (2010). "That's not who I am": How offenders commit violent acts and reject authentically violent selves. *Justice Quarterly, 27*, 492–516.

Holstein, J. A., & Gubrium, J. F. (1995). *The active interview.* Thousand Oaks, CA: Sage.

Jacobs, B. A. (2000). *Robbing drug dealers: Violence beyond the law.* New York, NY: Aldine.

Johnson, D. (2008). Taking over the school: Student gangs as a strategy for dealing with homophobic bullying in an urban public school district. *Journal of Gay and Lesbian Social Services, 19*(3/4), 87–104.

Katz, J. (1988). *Seductions of crime: Moral and sensual attractions in doing evil.* New York, NY: BasicBooks.

Kosciw, J. G., Greytak, E. A., Bartkiewicz, M. J., Boesen, M. J., & Palmer, N. A. (2012). *The 2011 National School Climate Survey: The experiences of lesbian, gay, bisexual, and transgender youth in our nation's schools.* New York, NY: GLSEN.

Kosciw, J. G., Greytak, E. A., Diaz, E. M., & Bartkiewicz, M. J. (2010). *The 2009 National School Climate Survey: The experiences of lesbian, gay, bisexual, and transgender youth in our nation's schools.* New York, NY: GLSEN.

Kuehnle, K., & Sullivan, A. (2001). Patterns of anti-gay violence: An analysis of incident characteristics and victim reporting. *Journal of Interpersonal Violence, 16,* 928–943.

Lofland, J., Snow, D., Anderson, L., & Lofland, L. H. (2006). *Analyzing social settings: A guide to qualitative observation and analysis* (4th ed.). Belmont, CA: Wadsworth/Thomson.

Logan, L. S. (2011). Gender, race, sexuality, and street harassment: Media and the case of the Killer Lesbians. Paper presented at the annual meeting of the American Society of Criminology, Washington, D.C.

Mahalik, J. R., Locke, B., Ludlow, L., Diemer, M., Scott, R. P. J., Gottfried, M., & Freitas, G. (2003). Development of the Conformity to Masculine Norms Inventory. *Psychology of Men and Masculinity, 4,* 3–25.

Majors, R., & Billson, J. M. (1993). *Cool pose: The dilemmas of black manhood in America.* New York, NY: Lexington.

Matza, D. (1964). *Delinquency and drift.* New York, NY: Wiley and Sons.

McClennen, J. C., Summers, A. B., & Vaughan, C. (2002). Gay men's domestic violence: Dynamics, help-seeking behaviors, and correlates. *Journal of Gay and Lesbian Social Services, 14*(1), 23–49.

McGee, T. R., Scott, J. G., McGrath, J. J., Williams, G. M., O'Callaghan, M., Bor, W., & Najman, J. M. (2011). Young adult problem behaviour outcomes of adolescent bullying. *Journal of Aggression, Conflict, and Peace Research, 3,* 110–114.

McKenry, P. C., Serovich, J. M., Mason, T. L., & Mosack, K. (2006). Perpetration of gay and lesbian partner violence: A disempowerment perspective. *Journal of Family Violence, 21,* 233–243.

Merrill, G. S., & Wolfe, V. A. (2000). Battered gay men: An exploration of abuse, help seeking, and why they stay. *Journal of Homosexuality, 39*(2), 1–30.

Messerschmidt, J. W. (1993). *Masculinities and crime: Critique and reconceptualization of theory.* Lanham, MD: Rowman & Littlefield.

Messerschmidt, J. W. (2000). *Nine lives: Adolescent masculinities, the body, and violence.* Boulder, CO: Westview.

Miller, J. (1998). Up it up: Gender and the accomplishment of street robbery. *Criminology, 36,* 37–66.

Miller, J. (2001). *One of the guys: Girls, gangs, and gender.* New York, NY: Oxford University Press.

Miller, J. (2002). The strengths and limits of 'doing gender' for understanding street crime. *Theoretical Criminology, 6,* 433–460.

Miller, J. (2008). *Getting played: African-American girls, urban inequality, and gendered violence.* New York, NY: New York University Press.

Oliver, W. (1994). *The violent social world of black men.* San Francisco, CA: Jossey-Bass.

Panfil, V. R. (2014a). Better left unsaid? The role of agency in queer criminological research. *Critical Criminology.*

Panfil, V. R. (2014b). Gay gang- and crime- involved men's experiences with homophobic bullying and harassment in schools. *Journal of Crime and Justice.* doi: 10.1080/0735648X.2013.830395.

Peterson, D. & Morgan, K. A. (2014). Sex differences and the overlap in youths' risk factors for onset of violence and gang involvement. *Journal of Crime and Justice.* doi: 10.1080/0735648X.2013.830393.

Peterson, D. & Panfil, V. R. (2014). Street gangs: The gendered experiences of female and male gang members. In R. Gartner and W. McCarthy (Eds), *The Oxford Handbook on gender, sex, and crime*. New York, NY: Oxford University Press.

Peterson, D., Taylor, T. J., & Esbensen, F. (2004). Gang membership and violent victimization. *Justice Quarterly, 21*, 793–815.

Presser, L. (2003). Remorse and neutralization among violent male offenders. *Justice Quarterly, 20*, 801–825.

Queer Nation. (1990). History is a weapon: The Queer Nation manifesto. Retrieved from http://www.historyisaweapon.com/defcon1/queernation.html.

Regan, K. V., Bartholomew, K., Oram, D., & Landolt, M. A. (2002). Measuring physical violence in male same-sex relationships: An item response theory analysis of the Conflict Tactics Scales. *Journal of Interpersonal Violence, 17*, 235–252.

Rios, V. M. (2011). *Punished: Policing the lives of Black and Latino boys*. New York, NY: New York University Press.

Russell, S. T., Franz, B. T., & Driscoll, A. K. (2001). Same-sex romantic attraction and experiences of violence in adolescence. *American Journal of Public Health, 91*, 903–906.

Stewart, E. A., Schreck, C. J., & Simons, R. L. (2006). "I ain't gonna let no one disrespect me": Does the code of the street reduce or increase violent victimization among African American adolescents? *Journal of Research in Crime and Delinquency, 43*, 427–458.

Sykes, G. M., & Matza, D. (1957). Techniques of neutralization: A theory of delinquency. *American Sociological Review, 22*, 664–670.

Taylor, T. J., Peterson, D., Esbensen, F.-A., & Freng, A. (2007). Gang membership as a risk factor for adolescent violent victimization. *Journal of Research in Crime and Delinquency, 44*, 351–380.

Thornberry, T. P., Krohn, M. D., Lizotte, A. J., Smith, C. A., & Tobin, K. (2003). *Gangs and delinquency in developmental perspective*. Cambridge, UK: Cambridge University Press.

Toro-Alfonso, J., & Rodriguez-Madera, S. (2004). Domestic violence in Puerto Rican gay male couples: Perceived prevalence, intergenerational violence, addictive behaviors, and conflict resolution skills. *Journal of Interpersonal Violence, 19*, 639–654.

Totten, M. D. (2000). *Guys, gangs, and girlfriend abuse*. Peterborough, Canada: Broadview.

Ttofi, M. M., Farrington, D. P., & Lösel, F. (2012). School bullying as a predictor of violence later in life: A systematic review and meta-analysis of prospective longitudinal studies. *Aggression and Violent Behavior, 17*, 405–418.

Waldner-Haugrud, L. K., Gratch, L. V., & Magruder, B. (1997). Victimization and perpetration rates of violence in gay and lesbian relationships: Gender issues explored. *Violence and Victims, 12*, 173–184.

Wright, R., & Bennett, T. (1990). Exploring the offender's perspective: Observing and interviewing criminals. In K. L. Kempf (Ed.), *Measurement issues in criminology* (pp. 138–151). New York, NY: Springer-Verlag.

Wright, R. T., & Decker, S. H. (1997). *Armed robbers in action: Stickups and street culture*. Boston, MA: Northeastern University Press.

Part III
LGBT Communities and Juvenile and Criminal Justice Systems

Chapter 8
Pleasures, Perversities, and Partnerships: The Historical Emergence of LGBT-Police Relationships

Angela Dwyer

Abstract Relationships between LGBT people and police have been turbulent for some time now, and have been variously characterized as supportive (McGhee 2004) and antagonistic (Radford et al. 2006). These relationships were, and continue to be, influenced by a range of political, legal, cultural, and social factors. This chapter will examine historical and social science accounts of LGBT-police histories to chart the historical peaks and troughs in these relationships. The discussion demonstrates how, in Western contexts, we oscillate between historical moments of police criminalizing "homosexual perversity" and contemporary landscapes of partnership between police and LGBT people. However, the chapter challenges the notion that it is possible to trace this as a lineal progression from a painful past to a more productive present. Rather, it focuses on specific moments, marked by pain or pleasure or both, and how these moments emerge and re-emerge in ways that shaped LGBT-police landscapes in potted, uneven ways. The chapter concludes noting how, although certain ideas and police practices may shift towards more progressive notions of partnership policing, we cannot just take away the history that emerged out of mistrust and pain.

Keywords LGBT · Police · History · Sodomy · Criminalisation · Perversion · Partnership · Diversity · Police mistreatment · Sexual deviance · Mistrust · Community policing · Police liaison · Sexual diversity training · LGBT police recruitment · Homosexuality · Professionalization · Accountability · Entrapment · Politics · Victimization · Same-sex affection · Medical knowledge · Religious knowledge · Masculinity · Violence · Harassment · Arrests · Collaboration · Public inquiries · State security · Diagnostic and Statistical Manual (DSM) · Police culture · Hate crime legislation · Disclosure · Wolfenden Report · Homophobia ·

A. Dwyer (✉)
School of Justice, Queensland University of Technology, Gardens Point Campus, X Block, 2 George Street, Brisbane, QLD 4001, Australia
e-mail: ae.dwyer@qut.edu.au

D. Peterson and V. R. Panfil (eds.), *Handbook of LGBT Communities, Crime, and Justice*, DOI: 10.1007/978-1-4614-9188-0_8,
© Springer Science+Business Media New York 2014

149

Homophobic attitudes · Surveillance · Fines · Prison · Harvey Milk · Comptons
Cafeteria · Stonewall Riots · Admiral Duncan bombings · Mardi Gras · Solidarity ·
White Night riots · Death penalty · Hard labor

Introduction

The history of police interactions with LGBT communities is one fraught with
contradiction and tension. Knowing this history is important to understanding
police-LGBT relations in the present, but these historical moments are not necessarily neatly recounted. Historical narratives emerging from research literature
seem to be anchored in a conception of LGBT-police relations as negative and
painful. Accounts focus on LGBT policing in history as though pleasurable,
productive experiences were almost non-existent, as policing interactions were
shaped by the association of LGBT people with perversion and sexual deviance.
Commentators speak about the abundance of mistrust between police and LGBT
communities in the past. However, even though mistrust no doubt emerged from
the criminalization of homosexuality and gender diversity, for instance, it does not
appear as clear-cut as historical accounts suggest.

Interestingly, things do not seem to be any more obvious in contemporary
contexts. Commentators note how LGBT-police relations have shifted in contemporary times due to police professionalization and community policing (see,
e.g., Colvin, this volume). Again, there is little doubt police-LGBT relationships
have progressed somewhat, with an evident police move away from regulating
same sex intimacies as perverse. Commentators now suggest police are fostering
partnerships with LGBT people in an attempt to make policing practices more
accountable, human rights focused, and supportive (Tomsen 2009). Even so, there
are moments in contemporary times that are reminiscent of past pains experienced
by LGBT people who had interactions with police (see, e.g., Nichols, this volume).

What is less clear is whether negative accounts of past LGBT-police relations
dominate because of almost exclusively negative interactions between police and
LGBT people in the past. We know little about whether this landscape may have
been shaped by a lack of official documentation of positive interactions or indeed a
broader censorship of LGBT-police interactions by police and government
authorities. Contemporary policing organizations now often utilize police media
units to ensure that news circulating about police remains positive (McGovern and
Lee 2010). To suggest we have seen a marked historical shift from policing
perversion to police now partnering with LGBT people, however, would also be
erroneous and simplistic. Contemporary contexts of police-LGBT interactions are
far more complex than this. For example, while the New South Wales Police Force
is known in Australia for its dedicated approach to improving relationships
between police and LGBT communities, and indeed having a dedicated contingent
of full uniform police march every year in the Mardi Gras parade, there were
claims of police brutality amongst the officers from New South Wales that

patrolled the Mardi Gras in 2013 (Rubensztein-Dunlop 2013). This hints at the complexity of these relationships and how, in a climate of partnership, the less familiar historical narratives of negative policing can re-emerge (Dwyer and Hotten 2009). Any history of these relations therefore needs to challenge simplistic historical narratives that suggest we have reached a more productive contemporary end point.

Drawing on secondary social science and queer historical accounts, this chapter therefore charts a potted history and focuses instead on the different factors which influenced LGBT-police relationships. It draws on a Foucauldian lens to "help us see that the present is just as strange as the past, not to help us see that a sensible or desirable present has emerged" (Kendall and Wickham 1999, p. 4). This historical approach takes into consideration, for instance, how police-LGBT relationships have been censored by police themselves (Moran 1996), or how they have been censored by government-sanctioned laws that police have to enforce (as is the case with the current "gay gag" laws in Russia—Hermant 2013). With a focus on the social, cultural, political, and economic factors, it shows how narratives of policing perversity do not just mark the past but can also creep into contemporary accounts of LGBT-police relationships.

The chapter initially brings together the patchwork of historical accounts of how police focused on LGBT people as perverse and the types of policing that happened. The chapter then moves to accounts discussing how police operate now more through partnership models of engagement with LGBT people. The chapter concludes to highlight the tenuous nature of accounts of policing LGBT people in a contemporary climate of perpetually renewed political landscapes and makes suggestions for future research and ways to improve LGBT-police practices.

Policing Perverse Pleasures: Historically Painful Moments of LGBT-Police Relations

Historical accounts of policing of LGBT people reflect how this meant policing "perversion" (Chauncey 1994; D'Emilio 1983; Willett 2008), as perversion was firmly linked with sexuality in nineteenth century medical and sexological texts (Schaffner 2012; see, too, in this volume Dennis; Woods). Forms of same-sex desire were targeted by medical and psychological practitioners as perversion needing treatment (Meem et al. 2010), and this filtered through to the policing of non-procreative sexual activities as perversions requiring careful legal regulation (Guerra 2010; Smaal and Moore 2008). These ideas were informed heavily by religious ideas about the sinfulness of sexual pleasure (Herman 1997), and discussions suggest police provided the cornerstone mechanism at which these activities could be governed.

Commentators seem to point up how police regulated 'perversion' by targeting LGBT bodies in public and private spaces, from day to day harassment in public spaces (Rosen 1980) through to more serious forms of violence (Comstock 1991).

They engaged in 'sting' operations where police would entrap gay men by mimicking gay bodily comportment (Dalton 2007) in public sex spaces and they raided LGBT friendly bars, nightclubs, balls, and bathhouses on a regular basis (Disman 2003; Jennings 2007; Jivani 1997; Wotherspoon 1991). Police would also take bribes from LGBT bars and nightclubs to ensure that business continued in these areas and the safety of the patrons frequenting these clubs was assured (Stein 2012; Stryker 2008; Wotherspoon 1991). Most disturbing was how police would also engage in explicitly targeted violence against LGBT people (Comstock 1991), with some reported cases of men being shot by police simply because they were gay (Altman 1971). Even a person whose dress contradicted her/his biological sex was considered to be perverting normality and would be subject to legal sanctions and police mistreatment (Faderman 1991; see also Nichols, this volume). These historical narratives demonstrate that perversions of sexuality and gender were not tolerated by police and this led to significant pain and criminalization amongst LGBT people.

Historical accounts show that, even as victims, police responded to LGBT people through a lens of perversion. Police often did not respond to these victims, minimized the seriousness of their victimization, blamed the victims for their experiences, and harassed them when they sought police assistance (Comstock 1991). With the criminalization of same-sex sex, kissing, hand holding, and dancing, it appears that most interactions between LGBT people and police ended not only with some form of criminal sanction. Victims were often further victimized by police actions (Dodge 1993), as police used a broad discriminatory approach legitimized by medical and political knowledges and social and religious attitudes of the time.

Social and cultural factors undoubtedly shaped police regulation of LGBT people, and especially medical ideas and religious ideologies. These knowledges worked in collaboration with legal knowledge to ensure LGBT people were marginalized and their way of life was controlled (LeVay 1996), something which further bolstered homophobic attitudes in the general public. For instance, it was more difficult to challenge police treatment of LGBT people in history when the leading diagnostic manual used by psychologically-focused health professionals (the *Diagnostic and Statistical Manual*) listed homosexuality as a "sociopathic personality disturbance" (Stein 2012, p. 49) in the 1950s. Assuming that same-sex desire and cross-dressing in any form were medical abnormalities to be fixed further legitimized the at best harassing, and at worst violent, treatment of LGBT people not only by friends, family, and strangers, but also police (Feinberg 1996). As one American lesbian woman recounts her experiences with police in the 1950s, "[t]hey would ask if I was a man or a woman. They could arrest a woman for impersonating a man, so you had to be sure you were wearing three pieces of women's clothes" (Faderman 1991, p. 185). Any person who blurred the gender binary in any sense was considered a serious threat not only to general public normality, but also to state security (Johnson 2004). By the 1960s in Australia, for example, it was standard practice to medically treat homosexuality as a "potentially curable disease" (Wilson 2008, p. 148) using aversion therapies such as psychosurgery, drugs that paralyze, and electro shock therapies. Combined with public ignorance about AIDS and gay men (Ames 1996), treating LGBT people like this further supported the efforts of religious groups seeking to shape laws to exclude LGBT people from public life (Herman 1997). Historical accounts therefore leave no doubt that medical actions shored up public and government support for policing LGBT people as perverts.

Queer histories show how police targeted LGBT people as perverts with some fervor, with governments ordering police inquiries into homosexuals in public service organizations (Johnson 2004). There is no doubt police acted as *agents provocateur* that incited and initiated homosexual acts to entrap gay men (Moran 1996; Wotherspoon 1991). Estimates of arrest of LGBT people in the United States reveal this clearly: "from 1946 to 1965 there were approximately 1,000–4,000 annual sodomy arrests based on consensual adult same-sex sex" (Stein 2012, p. 49). Police even engaged in covert surveillance of same sex sexual activities in private residences, showing their increasing eagerness to detect same-sex sex in action. Australian Detectives, for example, watched two men have anal sex in their private flat behind closed doors with the light off from the vantage point of "a stepladder leaning against the wall of the flat, peering through a hole they had bored through the fibro, eight feet up the bedroom wall" (Moore 2001, p. 128). It seemed police were willing to do anything to catch LGBT perversion in action, and these police actions were increasingly painful for LGBT people. However, at times there was a pleasurable, homoerotic flavor to these actions as a comment by a Detective during one investigation suggests: "I was feeling quite good myself watching you" (Moore 2001, p. 129). Policing "perverts" moved some police to experience pleasure, with police surveillance blurring the divide between voyeurism and work (Smaal 2012).

Histories of LGBT justice show that legislative frameworks legitimized invasive and discriminatory police actions in public and private spaces. Anal sexual penetration, known in the statutes as sodomy, was an act criminalized in most international historical contexts (LeVay 1996; Gunther 2009; Nussbaum 2010; Rydstrom and Mustola 2007; see also, this volume, Cobb; DeJong and Long). Although these laws applied to both homosexual and heterosexual people, the laws were most commonly applied to gay men. In Australia, for instance, a country which inherited the British legal system at the time of British colonization, sodomy was considered "a crime so abominable that even its mention was improper before Christian people" (Smaal and Moore 2008, p. 68). Even though male to male sexual activity was commonplace at this time (Smaal and Moore 2008), there were multiple ways that same sex sexual interactions were defined as offenses by police. "[C]rimes against nature, cross-dressing, disorderly conduct, indecency, lewdness, loitering, sodomy, solicitation, vagrancy, and other sexual offenses" (Stein 2012, p. 34) were all applied to same sex intimacies and received punishments like fines, hard labor, imprisonment, and the death penalty in the 1800s (Bongiorno 2012). What charge a person received was determined by police, demonstrating clearly to publics of the time that LGBT perversion deserved concerted police regulation.

Masculinized cultures of police affirmed the status of LGBT people as perverse (Bernstein and Kostelac 2002; Tomsen 2009). Policing was defined by a certain idea of masculinity and maintaining that at all costs. Anything that digressed from this norm was strongly admonished by the police establishment. A number of studies demonstrate the harassment that gay men and lesbian women were subject to as officers in police services across the world (Buhrke 1996; Burke 1993; Colvin 2012; Leinen 1993). This is not to suggest, however, that police did not engage in same-sex sexual contact. Examples from early colonial Australia evidence that police engaged in same-sex sexual activities, but these pleasures were barely documented (Smaal 2012). What was clear, though, was that these officers were typically denigrated by other police officers (Buhrke 1996; Burke 1993; Hayes and Dwyer 2011), and, according to one police officer, they produced "a form of exaggerated machismo to hide what they are" and protect themselves from harassment (Leinen 1993, p. 3). Male to male sexual activity breached the boundaries of this machismo, at the center of which is the understanding that male bodies are "unbroken and powerful, protected from penetration and any emasculating desire" (Tomsen 2009, p. 22). Thus, regulating men who partook in pleasure with other men was a priority in police organizations in history and harassment of gay police officers was commonplace (Buhrke 1996), and something gay officers themselves were compelled to engage in to avoid detection by other police.

Historical accounts seem to paint a bleak and unjust picture of LGBT-police interactions, but there were many productive, pleasant moments. Stryker (2008), for instance, discusses how one of the greatest allies of trans* people in San Francisco in the United States was a police officer, Elliot Blackstone, who managed the National Transsexual Counseling Unit established in the 1960s as part of his role in community policing. More typically, though, it was painful events in LGBT history that motivated a more productive response from police. For instance, significantly traumatic LGBT-police interactions lead to uprisings which shaped the growth of a political movement of LGBT solidarity not only in the United States (Stein 2012; Stryker 2008), but also the United Kingdom (Jivani 1997) and later in Australia (Carbery 1995). Police raids on LGBT patrons at the Stonewall Inn in 1969 in the United States, and the violent riots of LGBT people which ensued, are widely discussed by historians as some of the most unjust, painful police interactions in history. What is more interesting, though, is how LGBT people drew great pleasure and empowerment from moments like throwing bricks at police during the Stonewall uprisings.

These confusing moments of pain and pleasure with police inspired significant shifts in consciousness, as was evidenced in the police raid of Comptons Cafeteria in San Francisco in 1966 (Stryker 2008). Police raids on this establishment were common, but 1966 marked the year that patrons fought back rather than passively receiving police harassment, leading to violence between patrons and police and arrests of patrons. Police actions against LGBT people marching in the first gay and lesbian solidarity march in Sydney, Australia, in 1978 led to a series of uprisings culminating in a historic meeting between the Gay Solidarity Group and then Premier and Police Minister Neville Wran, where he was presented with 57 questions about how a Mardi Gras turned into police violence (Carbery 1995). These powerful moments perhaps culminated with the White Night riots in San Francisco in 1979 where LGBT people responded violently to the lenient sentence of David White. White was a highly conservative former police officer and San Francisco politician who assassinated Harvey Milk (an openly gay politician) and George Moscone (then-Mayor who supported Milk) in San Francisco in 1979 (D'Emilio 1993). Riots like these evidenced some of the earliest flash points in history when LGBT people began to explicitly challenge police practices (Stein 2012) and demand that changes be made. Out of pain and pleasure came a focus on shifting police relationships away from a focus on LGBT perversion so that victims as well as offenders would seek police assistance (Baird 1997; Willett 2008).

Policing Partnerships: Contemporary Moments of LGBT-Police Relations

When peak bodies like the American Civil Liberties Union (ACLU) (Stein 2012), and landmark decisions like the recommendations from the Wolfenden Report in the United Kingdom (McGhee 2004), began to support the idea that LGBT people were human beings with human rights, police could see that discriminatory police interactions were no longer appropriate. Although we do not know about the impact these shifts had on police or even public sentiment, passing key legislative frameworks demonstrated government seriousness about stopping violence against LGBT people, particularly legislation that mandated the collection of data about hate crimes motivated by sexuality or gender diversity (like the *Hate Crime Statistics Act of 1990* in the United States). Key points of change like this motivated the take up of new partnership-oriented approaches (Bartkowiak-Theron 2011) that were being demanded as a form of police work conducted in collaboration with LGBT people, government and non-government organizations, and community groups. Shifts towards partnership policing did not emerge as a response to LGBT unrest alone as this collided with more generalized demands for police professionalization and accountability. These policing modes were taken up by police services as early as the 1960s in the United States (Palmiotto 2011), and as late as the mid-1980s in the Australian policing context (Fleming 2011). Whatever the motives, it was clear that police could no longer legitimately cause pain to LGBT people.

Interestingly, though, some commentators note that professionalization and partnership building were not necessarily motivated by unrest about the painful policing of perversion meted out by police. For instance, the process of professionalization of the San Francisco Police readily demonstrates that courts were increasingly unsatisfied with policing efforts that were not based in evidence of illegal activities, and instead were based in allegations focused on 'immoral acts' (Agee 2006). Police and governments in San Francisco would seek to close down bars patronized by gay men on the basis of 'immoral acts,' but these cases were rejected by justice officials demanding evidence of illegal activity rather than immorality alone. These moments erupted unevenly and challenged the legitimization of policing work that happened with LGBT people.

These shifts were further propelled by pocketed moves in public social and cultural attitudes that began to recognize LGBT people as people with human rights. This was legitimized at the highest level of medical authority when homosexuality was removed as a disorder from the *Diagnostic and Statistical Manual* in 1973 (Meem et al. 2010). Homophobia amongst police officers was increasingly less tolerated by police organizations, although it did not disappear. Even very recent research suggests we have some way to go before this is achieved in some American contexts (Bernstein and Kostelac 2002). However, certain historical moments were suggestive of movements away from homophobia in the general public, which may have influenced the same movement in police. For example, in the year following the controversial *Bowers v. Hardwick* (1986) decision in the United States (where the Supreme Court upheld the constitutionality of sodomy laws on the basis that sodomy was immoral), upwards of 500,000 people protested in Washington, D.C. (Stein 2012), demonstrating that LGBT rights had a lot of support amongst heterosexual people too. The lessening of homophobia among the general public and police, combined with demands for police professionalization, meant there was increasing dissatisfaction with the idea that LGBT people were perverse and needed police control. In addition, increasing pleasure was being drawn from the collective empowerment experienced amongst LGBT people.

Some of the most painful historical moments in LGBT lives also shifted police responses towards partnership. In the United Kingdom, the bombing of the Admiral Duncan in 1999 in Soho, London, spurred police in London to improve police procedures for supporting LGBT people in London (Forsyth, A. personal communication, April 13, 2012). The inquiry into the police raid of the Tasty Nightclub in Melbourne, Australia, in 1994 publicized the inappropriate techniques used by police, including: inappropriate language; lengthy police searches because patrons outnumbered police available for conducting searches; inconsistent searching techniques; lack of respect for privacy; lack of glove changes by officers between searches; and lack of female officers to search female patrons (Groves 1995). Fillichio (2006, p. 57) notes how a "federal grand jury indicted an MPD (Metropolitan Police Department in Washington, D.C.) lieutenant…for blackmailing (known as 'fairy shaking') men he believed to be living double lives: married and gay" in 1995. Less than positive media coverage of these events increasingly led police organizations to embrace partnerships with LGBT people and provide more supportive and sensitive policing as a result.

The take up of police-LGBT partnerships was, however, increasingly patchy and disparate, depending on the location in which the changes were occurring. A good example of this is the Australian context wherein change has been unevenly spread across the landscape rather than following any immediate chronological or geographical progress. The first major research on LGBT hate crime in Australia was conducted by, and in cooperation with, Australian police services in certain states (Tomsen 2009). These research outcomes spurred police to establish new recruit training and collaborative anti-violence projects like the one between the New South Wales (NSW) Police Force and ACON (an LGBT community health organization). This work encourages LGBT people to report violence and provides education campaigns about violence against LGBT communities and in same-sex partnerships. Police reporting measures are being improved regularly to ensure the best possible statistical data on these forms of violence (Berman and Robinson 2010). However, this is not uniform in all states of Australia, with only some states (like New South Wales—Thompson 1997) investing time and funds into maintaining these processes, and other states, where a more politically conservative government has now been elected (such as Victoria), defunding police support for LGBT people (particularly the police liaison program—Noonan 2012). Accounts of these histories demonstrate that changes like these can be motivated by a single person working from the 'grassroots' in a police station (Stryker 2008), or alternatively are happening because of changes made at the highest levels of police hierarchy (Nixon and Chandler 2012). Thus, the accounts of these changes demonstrate they have been contingent and shaped by social and political climates of the time.

Partnership policing approaches demanded shifts in how police thought about LGBT people, requiring a substantial change in police culture. Partnering well with LGBT people meant having police officers who respected LGBT people, as well as having gay and lesbian police officers who felt respected and supported by police organizations. This was a formidable task set in motion in two key ways: sexual diversity training of officers; and employing LGBT people as police. These were actioned sporadically across different locations and contexts, and at different times, and were met with significant resistance. Sexual diversity training programs have been used since the late 1970s to ameliorate homophobic attitudes of officers, but they have sometimes been criticized heavily. Stewart (1997, p. 334) suggests these programs have "simply structured sexual orientation as part of a laundry list of protected classes with no specific information or intervention attempted" and fail to address the simplicities of what police recruits "want to know" about LGBT people. These forms of training were used in conjunction with diversifying police services through the targeted recruitment of LGBT people (Blair 1999). Some police organizations distinctly targeted LGBT people for recruitment, such as the program that London Metropolitan Police are now using to recruit trans* people, as well as having a police association dedicated to trans* people. When these forms of recruitment originally began, there was a significant influx of openly gay and lesbian people who joined police organizations, but genuine partnerships were often tempered by continued harassment of these officers in police workplaces (Buhrke 1996). This indicated that partnerships between police and LGBT people were emerging and were producing better outcomes, even if these were inconsistent and sometimes met with resistance.

LGBT-police partnerships also came in the very popular form of police liaison officers. In this model, police officers are trained with specific knowledge of LGBT issues so that they can appropriately and sensitively support LGBT people who are victimized to ensure they gain a supportive police experience (Bartkowiak-Theron 2012). These duties were, and still are, done in conjunction with other general police duties. Despite this approach being taken up by police organizations across the world (Wertheimer 1997), only limited research has examined their effectiveness (Cherney and Chui 2011), with some research concluding that LGBT people engage even less with police liaison officers than they do with general police (Berman and Robinson 2010). It is very much taken for granted that police liaison programs have been one of the most important ways of building better relationships between LGBT people and police (Dwyer and Ball 2013).

LGBT-Police Partnerships: A Pointed Future?

Seeing the gay, lesbian, and bisexual police officers of the San Francisco Police Department share their personal experiences of homophobia in a video to let young LGBT people know "It Gets Better" (http://www.itgetsbetter.org/) clearly represents a historical shift away from policing perversion. This form of explicit support of LGBT people by a police organization would have been almost unheard of 100 years ago. However, it is clear this cannot be categorized as linear historical progress towards a more liberated, productive end point—the discursive terrain is more complex than this (Tomsen 2009). The legacy of historical experiences can linger, for instance, with "many lesbian and gay male New Yorkers remember[ing] the police harassment and violence that occurred on a regular basis before the state's sodomy statues were declared unconstitutional in 1980" (Wertheimer 1997, p. 234). More importantly, the landscape of LGBT policing continues to oscillate in light of new political, moral, social, cultural, and economic responses to LGBT people. The peaks and troughs of conservative politics perpetually reshape how policing happens with LGBT people (Herman 1997), with sometimes very successful police partnerships with LGBT people literally losing political support overnight (Noonan 2012).

Police still have interactions with LGBT people which cause pain for LGBT people in Western contexts (Amnesty International 2006; Dwyer 2011, 2014), even if police support of LGBT people means more victims are coming forward and criminal prosecutions of perpetrators are increasing (Tomsen 2009). The unacceptable police practices that happened during the raid of the Tasty Nightclub, for instance, happened after the decriminalization of same-sex sexual acts in Victoria (Bull et al. 1991). This suggests that decriminalization is not enough to shift police attitudes and culture. The police brutality claims leveled at the New South Wales Police Force happened alongside an exemplary police liaison program for LGBT communities. This suggests that partnership policing cannot in itself overcome the issues which influence this landscape. Accounts in the United States still reflect how police conduct can be "disrespectful, rude…engaging in harassment, denying services to victims…[and] acting as the actual perpetrators of anti-LGBT verbal harassment, intimidation, and physical assault" (Wolff and Cokely 2007, p. 12). Thus, accounts demonstrate one thing is certain: there is room for improvement with LGBT-police relationships in a contemporary context. More importantly, the level of trust that LGBT communities have in police is remarkably fragile, especially at a time when anti-gay comments are commonly heard in many contexts (Dickter 2012). As reflected in narratives of sexual prejudice at gay and lesbian tourism events (particularly Sydney Mardi Gras), LGBT people continue to be viewed by some members of the public as "feminizing and unsettling" in a way that creates a "deep uneasiness" amongst males in particular (Tomsen 2009, p. 39). This highlights the considerable work that lies ahead for shifting social attitudes in ways that move beyond a momentary suspension of prejudice against LGBT people (Tomsen and Markwell 2009) so that police practices may be reshaped to enable better future outcomes for LGBT people. What this might look like in the future and how this ought to happen are key questions we are yet to address.

Moving Forward in an Ever-Shifting LGBT-Police Landscape

Historical and social science accounts demonstrate that police services in Western contexts have moved beyond the painful, homophobic policing practices evidenced in history. However, they also demonstrate how complex the nexus between LGBT communities and police actually is. Seemingly regressive moments of policing can randomly emerge in ways that are antithetical to the contemporary policing partnership climate. Ruminating on the historical moments of LGBT policing makes it possible to understand how we may well be investing in "a sensible and desirable present" (Kendall and Wickham 1999, p. 4) with LGBT-police relations which is unachievable and out of our control. It is clear that at any moment, the present could become unfamiliar as moments reminiscent of the past re-emerge, and we may never be able to separate LGBT-police relations in history—the fragile trust in the present may be inextricably linked with the mistrust of the past.

Intersecting with these shifts in police practice with LGBT people are multiple factors that we need to know more about, and there are some things which police can initiate themselves. For instance, we can explore further the factors that inform the conduct and attitudes of individual police officers. What and how officers think about LGBT people at all levels of police hierarchy are uncomfortable questions that require additional answers. We can also further investigate the factors that prevent gay and lesbian police from disclosing their sexuality in police workplaces, as there are recent examples of research where gay male police officers are unwilling to be interviewed due to concerns about disclosure in police workplaces (Hayes and Dwyer 2011). This implies that we need to know more about how masculinized police culture features in these complicated relations, something which has been noted as difficult to change (Chan 2007). We could also be asking additional questions about the extent to which partnership policing models have informed street level police work (Tomsen 2009). Police organizations may well have policies in place, like the explicit guidelines regulating how police must interact with trans* people in their work (Los Angeles Police Department 2012; Queensland Police Service 2011), but this may not actually filter down into day-to-day interactions with LGBT people in public spaces. There are risks in doing research on police attitudes because it could show police organizations to be homophobic. However, although police organizations may want to manage their public image (McGovern and Lee 2010), these issues must be examined, and this is only made possible with police organizations willing to provide access to police officers.

There are, of course, also factors which influence LGBT-police relations that are beyond the control of police and LGBT communities alike. The volatility of the legislative landscape needs to be addressed in this respect; for example, although police in the United States are compelled to respond appropriately to, and record instances of, LGBT hate crime, this is not necessarily a legislative requirement in other parts of the world (Tomsen 2009). Legislation that requires police to record statistics about hate crimes motivated by sexual orientation or gender diversity is something which could be more consistently applied, as most jurisdictions in Australia, for instance, do not record these details. More importantly, legislation that discriminates against LGBT people can be passed on the whim of a government seeking to appease conservative constituents, and police must give effect to these laws even if discriminatory. Ultimately, officers have discretion in deciding whom to arrest under these laws, but they are also subject to pressures from government and their employers to be seen to be doing something with this legislation. However, discretionary decision making is just that—an individual decision making process and something that police might be further trained to use in situations where legislation directly contravenes the human rights of LGBT people. Furthermore, historical narratives indicate the need to elaborate how discretionary decision making processes impact upon LGBT-police relationships, as well as upon LGBT police officers (Colvin 2012). These types of change are difficult to control due to shifts in political climates (Herman 1997), which indicates the need to legislate them at a level that cannot be influenced by political decision making. In addition, masculinized police culture still requires significant reform if police decision making is going to produce better outcomes for LGBT people in street-level police work.

It is clear there is no silver bullet here, as there are many competing forces at play. Even so, elaborating the issues above and informing the highest levels of government and policing with the results may go some way to producing more sustainable LGBT-police relationships. Consistent government responses would also assist, should antithetical moments of policing emerge to disrupt the partnerships that have been forged. Supporting the position of LGBT people at the highest levels of governing bodies, whether part of police services or not, can only demonstrate to other more localized authorities (such as school) that an unwavering, non-discriminatory approach is required if the rights and freedoms of LGBT people are to be adequately protected.

References

Agee, C. (2006). Gayola: Police professionalization and the politics of San Francisco's gay bars, 1950–1968. *Journal of the History of Sexuality, 15*(3), 462–527.

Altman, D. (1971). *Homosexual: Oppression and liberation.* Sydney, NSW: Angus and Robertson.

Ames, L. J. (1996). Homo-phobia, homo-ignorance, homo-hate: Heterosexism and AIDS. In E. D. Rothblum & L. A. Bond (Eds.), *Preventing heterosexism and homophobia* (pp. 239–252). Thousand Oaks, CA: Sage Publications.

Amnesty International. (2006). *Stonewalled—still demanding respect: Police abuses against lesbian, gay, bisexual and transgender people in the USA.* London, UK: Amnesty International Publications.

Baird, B. (1997). Putting police on notice: A South Australian case study. In G. Mason & S. Tomsen (Eds.), *Homophobic violence* (pp. 118–131). Annandale, NSW: The Hawkins Press.

Bartkowiak-Theron, I. (2012). Reaching out to vulnerable people: The work of police liaison officers. In I. Bartkowiak-Theron & N. Asquith (Eds.), *Policing vulnerability.* Annandale, NSW: Federation Press.

Bartkowiak-Theron, I. (2011). Partnership policing for policing organisations. In P. Birch & V. Herrington (Eds.), *Policing in practice* (pp. 180–204). South Yarra, VIC: Palgrave MacMillan.

Berman, A., & Robinson, S. (2010). *Speaking out: Stopping homophobic and transphobic abuse in Queensland.* Bowen Hills, QLD: Australian Academic Press.

Bernstein, M., & Kostelac, C. (2002). Lavender and blue: Attitudes about homosexuality and behavior toward lesbians and gay men among police officers. *Journal of Contemporary Criminal Justice, 18*(3), 302–328.

Blair, J. (1999, September 7). Quietly, police are making largest effort in US to add gay officers (p. 1). *New York Times.*

Bongiorno, F. (2012). *The sex lives of Australians: A history.* Collingwood, VIC: Black Inc.

Buhrke, R. A. (1996). *A matter of justice: Lesbians and gay men in law enforcement.* New York, NY: Routledge.

Bull, M., Pinto, S., & Wilson, P. (1991). *Homosexual law reform in Australia. Trends and issues in Criminal Justice, no. 29.* Canberra: Australian Institute of Criminology.

Burke, M. E. (1993). *Coming out of the blue: British police officers talking about their lives in 'the job' as lesbians, gays and bisexuals.* London, UK: Cassell.

Carbery, G. (1995). *A history of the Sydney Gay and Lesbian Mardi Gras.* Parkville, VIC: Australian Lesbian and Gay Archives Inc.

Chan, J. (2007). Making sense of police reforms. *Theoretical Criminology, 11*(3), 323–345.

Chauncey, G. (1994). *Gay New York: Gender, urban culture, and the making of the gay male world, 1890–1940.* New York, NY: Basic.

Cherney, A., & Chui, W. H. (2011). The dilemmas of being a police auxiliary—An Australian case study of police liaison officers. *Policing, 5*(2), 180–187.

Colvin, R. A. (2012). *Gay and lesbian cops: Diversity and effective policing.* Boulder, CO: Lynne Rienner Publishers.

Comstock, G. D. (1991). *Violence against lesbians and gay men.* New York, NY: Columbia University Press.

Dalton, D. (2007). Policing outlawed desire: 'Homocriminality' in beat spaces in Australia. *Law and Critique, 18*, 375–405.

D'Emilio, J. (1983). *Sexual politics, sexual communities: The making of a homosexual minority in the United States, 1940–1970*. Chicago, IL: University of Chicago Press.

D'Emilio, J. (1993). Gay politics and community in San Francisco since World War II. In L. D. Garnets & D. C. Kimmel (Eds.), *Psychological perspectives on lesbian and gay male experiences* (pp. 59–79). New York, NY: Columbia University Press.

Dickter, C. L. (2012). Confronting hate: Heterosexuals' responses to anti-gay comments. *Journal of Homosexuality, 59*(8), 1113–1130.

Disman, C. (2003). The San Francisco bathhouse battles of 1984. *Journal of Homosexuality, 44*(3), 71–129.

Dodge, K. S. (1993). 'Bashing back': Gay and lesbian street patrols and the criminal justice system. *Law and Inequality, 11*, 295–368.

Dwyer, A. (2014). 'We're not like these weird feather boa–covered AIDS-spreading monsters': How LGBT young people and service providers think riskiness informs LGBT youth-police interaction. *Critical Criminology: An International Journal* (special issue on "Queer/ing criminology: New directions and frameworks").

Dwyer, A. (2011). 'It's not like we're going to jump them': How transgressing heteronormativity shapes police interactions with LGBT young people. *Youth Justice, 11*(3), 203–220.

Dwyer, A. & Ball, M. (2013). GLBTI police liaison services: A critical analysis of existing literature. *Changing the way we think about change: Shifting boundaries, changing lives*. Refereed Conferencing Proceedings of the Australian and New Zealand Critical Criminology Conference, Tasmania, Australia.

Dwyer, A. & Hotten, J. (2009). 'There is no relationship': Service provider staff on how LGBT young people experience policing. *The Future of Sociology*, Refereed Conference Proceedings of The Annual Conference of The Australian Sociological Association, Canberra, Australia.

Faderman, L. (1991). *Odd girls and twilight lovers: A history of lesbian life in twentieth-century America*. New York, NY: Penguin Books.

Feinberg, L. (1996). *Trans gender warriors: Making history from Joan of Arc to Dennis Rodman*. Boston, MA: Beacon Press.

Fillichio, C. A. (2006). The new beat. *The Public Manager*, 56–59.

Fleming, J. (2011). Community policing: The Australian connection. In J. Putt (Ed.), *Community policing in Australia*. Research and Public Policy Series 111. Canberra, ACT: Australian Institute of Criminology.

Guerra, L. (2010). Gender policing, homosexuality, and the new patriarchy of the Cuban Revolution, 1965–1970. *Social History, 35*(3), 268–289.

Groves, M. (1995). Not so tasty. *Alternative Law Journal, 20*(3), 123–127.

Gunther, S. (2009). *The elastic closet: A history of homosexuality in France, 1942-present*. Hampshire, England: Macmillan.

Hayes, S., & Dwyer, A. (2011). Queer cops in Queensland: Exploring LGBT narratives in the Queensland Police Service. In B. Scherer & M. Ball (Eds.), *Queering paradigms II: Interrogating agendas* (pp. 277–293). Oxford, UK: Peter Lang.

Herman, D. (1997). *The antigay agenda: Orthodox vision and the Christian right*. Chicago, IL: University of Chicago Press.

Hermant, N. (2013, February 21). Russia backs law banning homosexual 'propaganda'. *ABC News*. Retrieved from http://www.abc.net.au/news/2013-01-26/russia-backs-law-banning-homosexual-propaganda/4485354.

Jennings, R. (2007). *A lesbian history of Britain: Love and sex between women since 1500*. Westport, CT: Greenwood World Publishing.

Jivani, A. (1997). *It's not unusual: A history of lesbian and gay Britain in the twentieth century*. Bloomington, IN: Indiana University Press.

Johnson, D. K. (2004). *The lavender scare: The Cold War persecution of gays and lesbians in the Federal Government*. Chicago, IL: University of Chicago Press.

Kendall, G., & Wickham, G. (1999). *Using Foucault's methods*. London, UK: Sage.

Leinen, S. (1993). *Gay cops*. New Brunswick, NJ: Rutgers University Press.

LeVay, S. (1996). *Queer science: The use and abuse of research into homosexuality*. Cambridge, MA: The MIT Press.

Los Angeles Police Department. (2012). *Police interactions with transgender individuals*. Retrieved from http://learningtrans.files.wordpress.com/2012/04/lapd-transgender-policies.pdf.

McGhee, D. (2004). Beyond toleration: Privacy, citizenship and sexual minorities in England and Wales. *The British Journal of Sociology, 55*(3), 357–375.

McGovern, A., & Lee, M. (2010). Copy[ing] it sweet: Police media units and the making of news. *Australian and New Zealand Journal of Criminology, 43*(3), 444–464.

Meem, D. T., Gibson, M. A., & Alexander, J. F. (2010). *Finding out: An introduction to LGBT studies*. Thousand Oaks, CA: Sage.

Moore, C. (2001). *Sunshine and rainbows: The development of gay and lesbian culture in Queensland*. St Lucia, QLD: University of Queensland Press.

Moran, L. (1996). *The (homo)sexuality of law*. London, UK: Routledge.

Nixon, C. & Chandler, J. (2012). *Fair cop: Christine Nixon*. Melbourne, VIC: Melbourne University Press.

Noonan, A. (2012). GLLO unit dissolved. *Star Observer*. Retrieved from http://www.starobserver.com.au/news/2012/03/02/gllo-unit-dissolved/73063.

Nussbaum, M. C. (2010). *From disgust to humanity: Sexual orientation and constitutional law*. Oxford, UK: Oxford University Press.

Palmiotto, M. J. (2011). *Community policing: A police-citizen partnership*. New York, NY: Routledge.

Queensland Police Service. (2011). *Good practice guide for interaction with transgender clients*. Brisbane, QLD: Queensland Police Service. Retrieved from http://www.police.qld.gov.au/Resources/QPS/specialist/OSC/cscpb/documents/Good%20Practice%20Guide%20Interaction%20with%20Transgender%20Clients%20V12.pdf.

Radford, K., Betts, J., & Ostermeyer, M. (2006). *Policing, accountability and the lesbian, gay and bisexual community in Northern Ireland*. Belfast, Ireland: Institute for Conflict Research.

Rosen, S. A. (1980). Police harassment of homosexual women and men in New York City 1960–1980. *Columbia Human Rights Law Review, 12*, 151–190.

Rubensztein-Dunlop, S. (2013, March 6). Police investigate Mardi Gras brutality claims. *ABC News*. Retrieved from http://www.abc.net.au/news/2013-03-06/claims-of-police-brutality-at-mardi-gras-parade/4554958.

Rydstrom, J., & Mustola, K. (2007). *Criminally queer: Homosexuality and criminal law in Scandinavia, 1842–1999*. Amsterdam, Netherlands: Aksant Academic Publishers.

Schaffner, A. K. (2012). *Modernism and perversion: Sexual deviance in sexology and literature, 1850–1930*. Hampshire, England: Palgrave Macmillan.

Smaal, Y. (2012). *"Indecent and indecorous" behaviour: Police and sex between men in turn-of-the century Queensland*. Paper presented at the Homosexual Histories Conference, Brisbane, QLD.

Smaal, Y., & Moore, C. (2008). Homophobia in *Fin De Siecle* colonial Queensland. In S. Robinson (Ed.), *Homophobia: An Australian history* (pp. 63–85). Leichardt, NSW: Federation Press.

Stein, M. (2012). *Rethinking the gay and lesbian movement*. New York, NY: Taylor and Francis.

Stewart, C. (1997). Sexual orientation training in law enforcement agencies. In J. T. Sears & W. L. Williams (Eds.), *Overcoming heterosexism and homophobia: Strategies that work* (pp. 326–338). New York, NY: Columbia University Press.

Stryker, S. (2008). *Transgender history*. Berkeley, CA: Seal Press.

Thompson, S. (1997). Hate crimes against gays and lesbians: The New South Wales Police response. In G. Mason & S. Tomsen (Eds.), *Homophobic violence* (pp. 132-146). Leichardt, NSW: Federation Press.

Tomsen, S. (2009). *Violence, prejudice and sexuality*. New York, NY: Routledge.

Tomsen, S., & Markwell, K. (2009). Violence, cultural display, and the suspension of sexual prejudice. *Sexuality and Culture, 13*, 201–217.

Wertheimer, D. M. (1997). Treatment and service interventions for lesbian and gay male crime victims. In G. M. Herek & K. T. Berrill (Eds.), *Hate crimes: Confronting violence against lesbians and gay men* (pp. 227–240). Newbury Park, CA: Sage.

Willett, G. (2008). From 'vice' to 'homosexuality': Policing perversion in the 1950s. In S. Robinson (Ed.), *Homophobia: An Australian history* (pp. 113–127). Leichardt, NSW: Federation Press.

Wilson, E. (2008). 'Someone who is sick and in need of help': Medical attitudes to homosexuality in Australia, 1960–1979. In S. Robinson (Ed.), *Homophobia: An Australian history* (pp. 148–171). Leichardt, NSW: Federation Press.

Wolff, K. B., & Cokely, C. L. (2007). To protect and serve? An exploration of police conduct in relation to the gay, lesbian, bisexual, and transgender community. *Sexuality and Culture, 11*, 1–23.

Wotherspoon, G. (1991). *City of the plain: History of a gay sub-culture.* Sydney, NSW: Hale and Iremonger.

Chapter 9
Intersections of Gender and Sexuality in Police Abuses Against Transgender Sex Workers in Sri Lanka

Andrea J. Nichols

Abstract The academic discourse focusing on intersections of sexual orientation and gender in the victimization experiences of transgender individuals is limited, particularly in the victimization directed toward transgender people by law enforcement. Through inductive analysis of 24 in-depth interviews and three focus groups with male-to-female transgender ("nachchi") sex workers in Sri Lanka, police mistreatment was examined to show how police abuses reflected the intersectional nature of transgender victimization. Findings indicated that police simultaneously targeted the main components of nachchi identity—feminine gender expression and homosexuality—in their victimization of the nachchi. Police abuses directed toward the nachchi included verbal, physical, and sexual abuse as well as inequality in the police response to nachchi's victimization and criminality.

Keywords Nachchi · Gender defined models of sexuality · Transgender · Sex work · Police abuse

Literature that focuses on intersections of gender and sexuality suggests that violence directed at one's gender or sexuality targets not each of these in isolation, but concurrently (Kulick 1998; Mason 2002; Miller 2002). Mason (2002) maintained that individuals embody and express multiple identities, and victimization parallels the confluence of these identities. Research specifically investigating

This chapter is adapted from an article originally published by SAGE: Nichols, A.J. (2010). Dance ponnaya, dance! Police abuses against transgender sex workers in Sri Lanka. *Feminist Criminology*, vol. 5, 2: pp. 195–222. DOI: 10.1177/1557085110366226. http://fcx.sagepub.com/content/5/2/195.full.pdf+html.

A. J. Nichols (✉)
Sociology Department, St. Louis Community College Forest Park,
5600 Oakland Avenue, St. Louis, MO 63110, US
e-mail: anichols@stlcc.edu

D. Peterson and V. R. Panfil (eds.), *Handbook of LGBT Communities,
Crime, and Justice*, DOI: 10.1007/978-1-4614-9188-0_9,
© Springer Science+Business Media New York 2014

victimization directed toward the feminine gender identity of male-bodied individuals who are also gay is limited. This chapter examines the experiences of gay male-bodied individuals who embraced a feminine gender identity and worked in the sex industry in Sri Lanka ("nachchi"). Drawing from a case study of transgender sex workers in Sri Lanka, where same-sex sexuality is gendered in such a way that only feminine-identified gay men are culturally labeled as homosexual, the current research illustrates how the components of gender and sexual orientation intersect to produce unique victimization directed toward transgender sex workers in the context of police abuses.

This chapter is based upon 24 in-depth interviews and interviews from three focus groups with male-to-female transgender ("nachchi") sex workers in Colombo, Sri Lanka. Nachchi sex workers primarily engaged in street-level sex work, and there is one road in Colombo in particular that they were known to frequent. Two Sri Lankan field researchers did both the contacting and the interviews. Initial contacts were made with individual nachchi by field researchers while the nachchi were working on the streets. From here, snowball sampling was used to expand the sample. This technique allowed access to sex workers who would otherwise have been difficult to contact due to the hidden nature of both their sex work and homosexuality, as both are illegal in Sri Lanka. All participants were interviewed by Sinhala-speaking research assistants. Participation in interviews was completely voluntary and each respondent was assured of confidentiality. Pseudonyms were used for all of the participants and names were changed at the time of the interview so no identifying information remained. The interviews were transcribed and translated into English, and were re-checked for accuracy.

The analysis was an inductive process that began by exploring the details and specifics of the interview data to discover important patterns and themes through open coding. When a recurring theme of police interactions was found in the transcripts, the transcripts were further explored using selective coding. The research design and interview questions guided the selective coding of the data. Questions regarding police included (a) "Have you ever been caught by police?"; (b) "Have you ever gone to the police for help?"; (c) "Have you ever been to jail?"; (d) "Do you have any problems from police?"; and (e) "Do you have help from police?" The responses to the questions were rich with detail. A general pattern of police abuse was found in almost all of the interviews, and there were few accounts of interactions with police that were not abusive. Exceptions included a case where a respondent had developed a love relationship with an officer and a few brief statements that there were also good police. Cases of abuse were then explored further and categorized by different types of abuse, which included monetary, physical, verbal, and sexual abuse as well as inequality in police response and forced gendered behavior.

Interlocking Systems of Oppression: Sexuality and Gender in Sri Lanka

Constructions of sexuality and gender vary cross culturally; in Sri Lanka, constructions of gender and sexuality are conflated. Effeminate males who have a same-sex sexual preference are labeled as homosexual, while their masculine male sexual partners are not. Such constructions of gender and sexuality are similar to those found in Bolivia, Brazil, and the Philippines (Johnson 1998a; Kulick 1998; Manalansan 2003; Whitham 1992; Wright and Wright 1997). In gender defined models of sexuality, masculine partners uphold masculinity in both their penetrating role and expression of masculine gender identity. As such, masculine men are not labeled as gay within cultures that maintain this gender defined model of sexuality, and they are not stigmatized. In contrast, partners who express gender in ways that are culturally labeled as feminine are labeled as homosexual and are stigmatized, as is the case with Sri Lankan nachchi. This double standard is apparent beginning in adolescence, where nachchi are targeted as sexual outlets for their peers as well as adult males, and throughout nachchi's adulthood, where they are arrested for prostitution or homosexuality and their masculine partners are not (Miller and Nichols 2012). While male-to-male sex is legally and culturally stigmatized, it is generally only the feminine nachchi who are punished. While publicly male-to-male sex is illegal and strongly condemned in Sri Lanka, privately, male-to-male sexual contact is relatively common (Jayasundara 2000; Miller 2002; Silva et al. 1998). Silva et al. (1998) found nearly two-thirds of men reported having engaged in male-to-male contact at some point in their lives. Further, according to the Kinsey Institute (2009), Sri Lankan boys often engage in mutual masturbation, thigh sex, and oral and anal sex. When men pass adolescence and get married, they are expected to "give up" male-to-male sexual relations. In Sri Lanka, virginity is highly valued for women (Kinsey Institute 2009); as a result, gender segregation occurs in adolescence. This separation of boys and girls and the unavailability of female partners may result in relatively high rates of male-to-male sexual experiences (Jayasundara 2000; Kinsey Institute 2009; Miller 2002; Silva et al. 1998). Yet, constructions of sexuality in Sri Lanka are such that men are usually not considered homosexual and consequently stigmatized unless they are feminine as well. These gay men expressing femininity can be described in Western conceptualizations as transgender.

The academic discourse on transgender studies among queer theorists has been subject to much debate, primarily between scholars who wish to label and examine transgender identities in largely dichotomous terms, and those who wish to move beyond such dichotomous labels. The latter support the use of "transgender" as an "umbrella" term used to describe any sex/gender coupling (including gender identity, sexual orientation, and embodiment) falling outside of a hetero-normative male/female binary. The umbrella use of the term is intended to recognize the fluidity of gender, to oppose rigid definitions, and to move away from binary representations of gender. Agustín (2007, p. 70) stated, "Outsiders who insist on imposing set categories forget that there is gender identity, but also gender play and experimentation." Similarly, Namaste (2000) described the fluidity of gender, and suggested that by labeling identities, such identities are limited and ignore variations within groups as well as outside them. Ignoring realities of cultural constructions of masculinities and femininities and the impact on transgender people marginalizes their experiences within a gendered culture, and removes individuals from the context of their lived experiences. Further, Mason (2002) stated that not only is the academic discourse surrounding gender largely removed from the context of lived experiences, but from realities of intersecting identities, and the impact of such identities *on* lived experiences. (For additional discussion of the issues of categorical labeling, see in this volume Frederick; Johnson; Messinger; Woods.) Contextual ethnographic work that does ground research within the cultural contexts in which it takes place is still generally expressed in binary representations of gender and does not maintain an intersectional perspective (Luibhéid 2004; Mason 2002). With these concerns in mind, the label transgender is used throughout this chapter as an umbrella term, intentionally broad so as to be inclusive, but grounded in contextual analysis through detailed presentation of nachchi identity and experiences.

In Sri Lanka, such transgender individuals, who often take part in a subculture involving sex work, call themselves *nachchi* or *pons*. The nachchi are gay effeminate males who walk and speak like women, and situationally dress and accessorize like women as well. Yet, they take pride in their male sexual functioning and desire for men as well as their feminine gender identity and expression (see Miller and Nichols 2012). Some of the respondents believed they had been women in their previous lifetimes, and that their feminine gender identity resulted from karma. The respondents felt they were like women in their minds, mannerisms, and behaviors, but had a man's body and sexual functioning. Lahiru explained his nachchi identity:

> ...So we [nachchi] like to be like women. So from some karma, from the last birth, we have become like this. So, we go like women, we talk, Miss [the interviewer] must realize I talk also like woman, no... we have male qualities [body]...but the voice, face. Yes, that is different, yes. Like women. Otherwise everything is like men.

Other nachchi indicated the same sentiment, that they were feminine, and sexually attracted to men. They also indicated a preference for activities such as dressing like women, cooking, and fashion. The nachchi described shaving their eyebrows, wearing dresses, carrying purses, and wearing make-up, although most did so situationally. In a culture that defines these things as feminine, the definition of transgender is applicable.

Sri Lankan society stigmatizes both gender transgression and cross dressing (Wijewardene 2007). Generally the nachchi cross dress, and their identity as nachchi is largely defined by gender transgression (Kinsey Institute 2009). Nachchi identity is also defined by their sexual desire for masculine men. This further complicates stigmatization of the nachchi, as homosexuality is illegal and culturally condemned. Homosexuality was made a criminal offense under the

British colonial rule in 1883 and currently exists under Penal Code 365A (Gujarat 2004). Under this code, homosexuality is punishable by 12 years in jail, but until recently, the law was rarely enforced (Gujarat 2004; Kinsey Institute 2009). Largely due to the rise in sex tourism in Sri Lanka, the criminal justice system has begun to enforce this penal code more, with a rise in arrests and convictions of homosexual male sex workers (Fernando 2002). Legal contexts of homosexuality in Sri Lanka exacerbate the victimization of nachchi sex workers. Researchers have found that law and cultural stigma are used by some Sri Lankan police officers to harass, rape, assault, and blackmail the nachchi (Kinsey Institute 2009; Miller 2002; Price 1998). Nachchi in the current study described experiencing verbal abuse, physical abuse, forced bribes and theft, failure to protect, inequality in punishment, false accusations, forced gender behavior, and sexual abuse by police. Narrative illustrations of such police abuses are described in detail below, including the ways victimization was directed at nachchi's transgender identity.

Police Abuses

Verbal Abuse

The verbal abuse that nachchi experienced consisted of name calling that specifically focused on the nachchi's femininity and sexuality. "Ponnaya" is derogatory slang for transvestites, very effeminate males, or males who are weak in their relationships with women. "Ponnaya" is also used to imply that nachchi are not able to sexually function like "real" men and is seen by nachchi as insulting to both their gender and sexual identity. The nachchi indicated that police called them "ponnaya" to deliberately insult and denigrate them. Lakshith described a general account of this:

> Now even if they [police] see you in the road... they pass saying ..."Ponnaya, ponnayo, what are you doing?" this and that, yes, "Ponnaya get in the jeep." So [police] say this and that and insult [us] in filth, remand [jail us] for no reason. That is why. Now the police of course can't stand us. That much we are bitter to them, we also can't stand them. We're so disgusting to them. From that [I] get scared.

This example of verbal abuse includes name calling relating to intersections of their sexual orientation and femininity by using the word "ponnaya." Almost all of the respondents reported verbal abuse by police, predominately by being called "ponnaya" both in the course of their sex work and outside of their sex work. Moreover, verbal abuse often accompanied other abuses. For example, Lalith described a general account of verbal abuse crossing lines with physical abuse:

> Most harassment to us is from the police. From the police and from the thug kollo [men]. They call us, "Kella, [Girl] Baba [Baby], Chuti [Little One], where are you going?" and throw stones at us. Major harassment, that is the thing.

When used by the police, in this context, calling to nachchi in words used to refer to girls was meant to insult, and was another form of verbal abuse used by police officers.

Physical Abuse

The majority of the nachchi reported physical abuse by police, often occurring in tandem with verbal abuse. They primarily described being hit, beaten, or having stones thrown at them by police. Physical abuse occurred both in jail and on the street while the nachchi were engaging in sex work or soliciting for clients, but notably, physical abuse by police also occurred outside of their sex work. The following example illustrates physical abuse by police while Kusum was not working but simply going out to buy something from the store:

> From the police also we have plenty of harassment. Even if you just go to the road to buy something, sometimes they would take us and would hit and all and would send us back [from jail] next morning, there are times like that.

When asked what happens when the police come, Chaminda responded:

> The thuggish police beat us badly. They beat us badly and shame us and put us in places where we would get shamed and... they drag us and take us just the way they drag prostitutes, they drag us in the road and take us.

Notably, Chaminda stated that the nachchi are treated like female sex workers, but Kusum indicated an additional component of abuse because they are beaten outside of their sex work for being nachchi. Like verbal abuse, physical abuse sometimes accompanied the other forms of abuses, such as rape, forced bribes, failure to protect, and verbal abuse. In addition, the nachchi described being regularly subjected to routine theft and police extortion of bribes.

Forced Bribes and Theft

A majority of respondents described police extorting bribes in exchange for avoiding arrest. The nachchi also stated that money was routinely stolen from them on police rounds. Police were described as opportunists, extortionists, and thieves. Respondents stated that they are vulnerable to theft and forced bribes by police not only because of the illegality of their sex work and homosexuality but also because it is known that the nachchi are carrying cash received from clients. Susil suggested that police see the nachchi as an opportunity to make easy money. "They try to get money from us. That is to take money. They expect that." Nachchi have few alternatives; if they refuse to give a bribe, they will be arrested and have to pay a fine for engaging in sex work. Indrajith expanded on the various forms of forced bribes, including luxury items in addition to money:

> The police of course are just trash. Take our money and scold us. Now when we go with a customer, [police] would take 2000–3000 [rupees][1] from him and insult us calling us "pons." They insult us, scold us and take our money and go. If not things like that they say, "Bring an arrack bottle [hard liquor]." Say, "Bring a chicken." We earn about 100–200, so giving that, can you do [buy] those [expensive items] no? So because of things like that the police of course are very [morally] weak. A lot of trouble from the police.

Many of those interviewed noted that they always carried enough to cover a bribe if they got caught engaging in sex work. This delineates the normative nature of giving bribes, as nachchi would not carry bribe money if extortion was not expected. When asked about self-protection from the law, Viraj replied, "I do things like this, I take money… (because) if they catch (us), (we) have to give… a bribe. Bribes only they take." Most of those interviewed described not only forced bribery/extortion, but theft as well. Viraj described theft as routine: "Now if I get caught to police people, they check pockets and all and take everything" and noted that "police people are the madavi kariyo (no good people/bullies) only." Viraj described the inability to save money because "the police people will snatch it away… Even if we find two hundred (rupees) a police person will come (and take it)." Respondents reported that if they were arrested, they would not go home with any money in their pockets. Whatever they came in with, the day's earnings would be appropriated regardless of the fine for sex work. While police forced bribes and robbed them, the police also failed to provide police assistance when nachchi were victimized by those in the community. Thus, police were their victimizers, and also provided little recourse for the victimization that the nachchi experienced.

Failure to Protect

Some nachchi described being denied the same quality of service or any service at all because of their transgender identity. The majority of respondents who went to the police to report some form of victimization described having police services refused. When asked about going to the police for help, Jayantha responded: "The police do not accept our entries, no…If we run to the police, they will say 'get out ponnaya'." When asked the same question, Malith described a similar incident:

> Now so we go in the night and kollo [men] take us and beat us and take our money and gold jewelry and we report that to the police but no action is taken. They tell us, "Hah hah, get out. Get out!" and chase us.

A few respondents who reported to the police described that the police blamed them for their victimization. For example, when asked about experiencing harassment, Suranjith stated:

> Yes, you get in the road… people with no proper manners. They are the kind of people who mostly come like that and harass. So sometimes, they take you and get what they

---

[1] The exchange rate to U.S. dollars was approximately 80 rupees to one USD.

want fulfilled [rape][2] and then beat you. They beat you and snatch what you have in your hand or pull what you are wearing, so there are a lot of criminals like that… so that is why we are scared a lot also no. Now to go in the road in the night also, we are very scared, we are scared because you face problems like that. So even if you go to the police, you don't get any help from the police … "What were you doing in the road? Why were you all in the road?" Like that they ask.

In addition, reporting victimization to police can put the nachchi at risk for further victimization and exploitation. Raju described going in to report a crime, and being forced to have sex with two of the officers.

It's like this, something was stolen from my brother's house, and when I went to the police for that, two officers who were in the jeep called me. "If you don't stay [have sex] we will lock you up," they said.

Inequality in the police response to the nachchi's victimization exemplified a system that did not serve the interests of nachchi nor offer them protection; instead, nachchi described a system that served to exploit and victimize them. As the above quote delineates, the nachchi experienced this discrimination not only because they were sex workers, but also for complaints outside of their work in the sex industry. This is important, because while male and female sex workers generally experience inequality in the police response to their victimization, nachchi experience this outside of their sex work as well, indicating a transgender identity as a source of this inequality in police response.

When asked if ever harassed, Indrajith described being beaten by men in the community, raped multiple times, and sustaining eye injuries requiring surgery. Indrajith was asked if the police helped, and responded:

Normally incidents, police, police of course don't take notice. When you go to the police, they say "So it's because y'all also do something you get beaten, no," …Those people [perpetrators] are also scared no… Those people, when we go to the police they also talk insultingly to us… We go to the police and they [perpetrators] give some number of 500, 1,000 rupee notes, then they [the police] will take their side. Don't take our side. They don't care two hoots about us.

In this example, bribery is associated with police failing to protect the nachchi. Respondents described multiple forms of inequalities in police response that went beyond police trading bribes to ignore their complaints. Moreover, interviewees indicated that not only are the nachchi likely victims of crime without recourse because they are at the bottom of the social hierarchy, but they are also likely scapegoats for crime.

---

[2] Sex and violence were often discussed in somewhat vague terms, in keeping with colloquial Sinhala speech patterns. This is a common feature of Sanskrit and Pali derived from South Asian languages (Puri 1999).

False Accusations

Many nachchi stated that they believed their arrest for crimes they did not commit was related to their transgender identity. A majority of respondents claimed to have been the victim of a false accusation. They would be identified as nachchi, whether they were working or not, and falsely accused of crime. When asked about experiences with police, Malith described a situation of false accusation:

> Yes, I have got caught to the police about twice. To tell you the truth one time I was on the beach, my life was in a difficult situation and I did not know what to do and I went to the beach and was thinking and when I got up, I was taken on suspicion [of prostitution]. And [they have] written false accusation in the books, that is, "Was intending to solicit and that is why we brought this one," like that they wrote false accusations, told me to sign them, they took me in by force...At that time I asked, "What did I do that is so shameful? I was on the beach minding my own business. You all don't know the problems I have, I was seated minding my own business, other than that I did not do anything that you all accuse me of doing. You all do this to innocent people like that making false accusations." I fought with them saying whether it's right. To tell you the truth, the police harass us a lot. When they find out we are like this, homosexuals, they harass us a lot. How many things are happening in the country–there are thugs, murderers, looters. They stay, still don't go after them. We are just homosexuals, what are they to do to us? Even the police have been told of how many things [that] are going on in the country. [They] don't bother about those. Without going after [those crimes], they are chasing these homosexuals in the road. Make false accusations about them and put them in court. To tell the truth.

Mustafa described another incident involving false accusations of theft while with a client in a car parked on the beach:

> When we were parked, some group of kollo came and took that Sir's purse. Then that Sir told the police that I was also involved in it. I didn't even know anything about it. Saying I was involved in it, they beat me and all and put me in prison.

Mustafa served 2 years for the offense. Mustafa's example demonstrates a false accusation and the law taking the side of the accusers for a crime that involved theft, not sex work. It demonstrates a bias against the nachchi, in this case with the serious consequence of incarceration for a crime not committed. In the first case, the false accusations occurred when Malith was not working. Because the nachchi identifiably embody femininity, they are easily recognized as transgender. The false accusations are directed at the nachchi not only for their sex work, as in the case of female sex workers, but for their transgender identity combined with homosexuality as well.

Inequality in Punishment

According to laws prohibiting prostitution in Sri Lanka, both prostitutes and clients are committing a crime; however, transgender sex workers described being arrested or fined when caught on the job while clients were less likely to be punished, and if they were punished, it was likely to take the form of minor fines or coerced bribes. Findings indicate that in some cases, officers extorted money from both clients and nachchi sex workers, but none of the sex workers described incidents in which a client was arrested or brought in on charges. Dinuth was asked if any client had ever been caught by police. Dinuth replied:

> That day they didn't have [arrested clients]. Took nachchi like us. There were more than seven, took all of us. Why, because Colombo gets thieves. Snatch chains and rings. [They] thought we were mostly people like that.

This example shows inequality in police response in tandem with false accusation, based on their nachchi identity. Police assumed they were thieves because of their nachchi identity. Yet, their clients were let to go. Jayantha described being caught by police, while the client was let go:

> I went to the streets and that was a day when I earned well.... Go wearing make-up and stay [had sex] and after that, I was caught... that was the last deal. Caught me when I was in the vehicle... two police officers put me in the vehicle and took me.... The first dirty scummy thing they did was... that Sir in the vehicle [the client]was allowed to go and I was taken in... Because of the dirty thing done, then that person also must be produced to court, no? I went because that man came, no? I didn't go by force, wave the hand and get in, no? I got in because I was asked to get in.

In this example, Jayantha points out that sex work would not occur without demand, but it is nachchi sex workers who are brought in while clients are not.

Forced Gendered Behavior

In addition to experiencing inequality in arrest, Jayantha also described being forced to take part in feminine gender behavior in the morning following his arrest, in the incident described above.

> [While] I was in police [custody]... A lot of injustice was done by the police to me. I was wearing a dress, keeping breasts, with long hair. I was like a woman that day...In the morning they put the radio on and told me to dance... Told me to dance for those [songs], I still danced for whatever way I could. [Police] came to squeeze these of mine [breasts]. Did like this, did nonsense...

Many nachchi described similar situations in which police forced them to display feminine gender behavior. Outside of the legal system, many nachchi described dancing, singing, sweeping, sewing, serving tea, dressing brides for their weddings, and other behaviors they saw as feminine as a part of their preferred activities and a part of their identities. Yet, while the nachchi generally enjoyed doing these activities in their homes and in their communities, they described feeling humiliated when officers forced them to do it. The context of the behaviors was different; in times where they freely performed and enjoyed "feminine" activities, it was seen by the nachchi as positive. However, when police forced them to do it while simultaneously verbally and physically abusing them, it was described as a degrading experience. In over one-third of cases, nachchi described having been brought in on charges, and then forced to sweep, sing, dance, clean uniforms and shoes, cook, and arrange and prepare tea. This form of police behavior is gendered, as the nachchi were identified as transgender by their dress and accessories and forced by the police to take part in what are considered traditionally feminine behaviors in Sri Lanka, while simultaneously being condemned for performing these behaviors. Respondents indicated that forced gendered behavior was a form of demeaning abuse with the intent of humiliation. Viraj was jailed on charges of prostitution, and described an incident with police involving forced gender behavior: "I'm very scared of policemen of course… They straight away tell… 'Go sing a song! sweep!' Talk to us like dogs." Lahiru noted that nachchi sex workers are treated differently than female prostitutes when they are forced to do these gendered behaviors, indicating a unique configuration of abuse based on transgender identity/embodiment and sexuality:

> The prostitutes have more freedom than us. That's because they are women. We of course are mostly taken for a joke. To do ridiculous things [forced gender behavior] and for various, various things. At times we get really fed up. "Why in the name of god are we like this, and things are like this?" and we feel angry inside. There is like a sadness that comes. That is what I can say.

In some cases, forced gendered behavior was accompanied by verbal abuse, primarily by the use of the derogatory term *ponnaya*. For example, Ranil stated that they are also verbally abused when they are forced to do these things by police:

> The police…disturb you- come and crack jokes, so put you in a difficult situation only. So that is they insult [you] really badly, tell to dance, tell "Dance!", "How did y'all give [the ass]," they ask, "how did y'all do [have sex]," they ask, "how do y'all suck the Sirs," so those [things] only [they say]. Listen to those [questions] plenty of times and after giving answers to those only, in the end they remand and put [us] in prison also.

This example shows forced gendered behavior occurring in tandem with sexual verbal abuse, specifically targeting their homosexuality in the verbal references to oral and anal sex. In other cases, forced gendered behavior co-occurred with sexual abuse and rape. For example, in a focus group setting, Viraj stated:

> Once the police saw me and took me, took me and told us to sweep the police [office], to sing and to dance, so I danced and all. So that is how, like sometimes take you and take advantage [he described then being forced to have sex with the officer].

As this example and the next section shows, the majority of respondents reported that officers went beyond such verbal abuses and forced gendered behavior to perpetrate sexual coercion and violence as well.

Sexual Abuse

While police condemned and punished nachchi sex workers for their profession and sexual orientation, over half of the respondents described police engaging in sexual encounters with them. These encounters included sexual bribes, coerced sexual activity, individual rape, and group rape. Those interviewed stated that sexual coercion occurred in the road, in jail, and in prison, both in the course of their sex work and when they were not working. Ranil described rape by police as a normative occurrence:

> They look at us like animals, that is like they have found a prey like. They need to take us like that, so ... when they see us, they fight over each other and get things done [e.g. sex] from us...

The mildest form of sexual abuse described by the sample included coerced sexual acts. Some respondents reported being forced to masturbate officers, provide oral sex, and engage in sexual acts with other nachchi while the officer watched. Nalin illustrated an example of forced masturbation with another nachchi sex worker in the street by police:

> [The police] have caught [us], when we were in the park, while we were behaving [working]... police told ... [another nachchi sex worker] to take my one [penis], and told me to take [the other nachchi sex worker's] one. ... After watching, told us to run and kicked us and left us...So they also must like to watch us doing it no, and we did it, so what else to do?

Jayantha gave a description of forced oral sex while in jail: "One day in the night a jailer came and... when I was in the cell, he told me to take it to the mouth." Sexual bribery was also described by respondents as a "trade" for dropping charges. Lahiru described a trade of oral sex when not carrying bribe money:

> We always keep some money at least a hundred [rupees] with us and go. Why because police catch... Either we give them a hundred and escape or stay with them and either suck their thing or do backside and escape. Anyway even in daylight we can't go anywhere or they just catch us. Or they just keep us in police [custody] like that and stay with us...They have stayed with us, the police officers. The days we don't take [bribe] money, we suck.

Lahiru's example reflects multiple police abuses, including concurrently being identified as nachchi through feminine dress. Lahiru indicated that this also occurred when not working.

> We can't go in the road, the police call us ponnaya. We do get caught to police sometimes, but if we stay [have sex] with people in the police we don't get produced [to court]. It's as if the police are ashamed... They hit the kollo [clients] two three times and send them off and take us in...They take us and so we stay [have sex] with them and so they don't produce us to jails.

Respondents described having little alternative but to comply with a request for sexual services by the police. In some cases, refusal of sexual services resulted in false accusation, arrest, and rape. Mustafa exemplified this dynamic:

> So that SI mahaththaya [policeman], when I was coming back after going in the night told me to get in the jeep. I didn't get in. I told "Sir, Did I do anything wrong? I didn't do a wrong; I can't get in the jeep like that." The police threatened me, "You will know, you are the only one [nachchi] who refused to get into my jeep, you will know what I will do to you," he said. It is a week later only they took me during the day and did that thing [rape]...

Mustafa described getting written up and fined under a false accusation by this officer in addition to rape for refusal of services:

> I went to boil some pickle and fish, while going to boil; halfway the jeep came and picked me up. Took me and later filed a case against me telling I was selling seal arrack, [liquor] and other things. Later I was fined 8,000 [rupee].

While female sex workers also generally report sexual abuse and violence, Mustafa was not engaging in any sex work or illegal activity at that point, indicating that the profession is not the only source or justification by police for exploitation. Simply being identifiably effeminate increases vulnerability to victimization. In this way, nachchi's experiences with sexual abuse both parallel and differ from that of female sex workers.

In addition to acts of sexual coercion by individual officers, rape involving multiple officers was experienced by almost one-third of those interviewed. Police engaged in group rape of nachchi, often referred to as "polin daanawa" or "polin gahanawa" by participants. Nalin described a situation involving rape by multiple police officers: "Three from the police did that one day, taking me. Yes, three of them stayed [rape] and each one stayed twice." Some of the respondents believed that female sex workers were less likely to have acts of sexual violence involving anal and oral sex perpetrated against them. Marcus suggested this dynamic in the following excerpt, describing what happened after arrest:

> Have stayed with 10, 15 of them. [They] torture us in every way and send us. That is, taking to the mouth, fucking the ass, do everything there is to do to us. Those things they can't do to the women: fuck the ass, give it to the mouth. Give it the mouth, do various things like that and we escape. We can't say "Can't."… They strip us stark naked and about 15 people come and do to us. We just bear it up and wait…

In some cases it appears that rape of nachchi by police officers may be informally institutionalized. This interpretation is indicated by nachchi respondents who described places that are known to be specifically used for raping nachchi sex workers brought in on charges of prostitution or homosexuality. Lahiru stated that the room commonly used for strip searching arrestees in one police station is used for rape by multiple officers:

> Inside the police [station]…They have these separate sections to remove clothes and all. So if there are five [officers on duty], all five won't come, some don't like no. So upstairs there is clothes room, so [they] take [us] to that. Sometimes [we] have to stay with two.

When asked what Lahiru meant by staying with two, Lahiru stated,

> One's suck, the other's … [Interviewer: Doing to] Yes. At such times we don't like to do, but by force, so they must have some desire no… At such times, go with fear in mind, and somehow only try to come out.

Lahiru also indicated that different police stations treated nachchi differently. Comparing two districts in Colombo, Lahiru stated:

> Sometimes when they catch [us] they ask us to do some work, like sweep… Police [at this station] also stay [have sex] [but] not so much. If there are ten, all ten won't come. They

understand the pain. About two would come and do. After that again in early morning.
Like that, like that they do. Like that give [us] breaks and do. [The other station] is not like
that, all come together. If there are four, three come at the same time. Have to stay with
two...Again another two would come.

Lahiru was also asked if women were treated like this as well: "I have not heard of
them doing like that to women, of course." Sadun described a situation of a friend,
also a nachchi, involving group rape by 37 officers on the first day.

> There are ones who are taken to the court no, those men's desires are more Mahaththaya
> [for men, i.e., homosexual]. When their desires are more like that, now if it's a court house
> near Colombo area of course you get big toilets [bathrooms]. Put you in an uncomfortable
> situation like that, beat you and polin daawana [group rape]. A friend of mine called
> Aruna, got caught to the police...Aruna got caught and now this. I'm telling something
> that happened. [Aruna] went to the prison and paid a 500 rupee fine and I took [Aruna] out.
> Then [Aruna] couldn't sit even on the ground... Had tortured that much. First day, 37
> people have come. All of them. So backside, had given to the backside only. Given to the
> mouth. When [Aruna] said can't, they had beaten. Lips were swollen, face was swollen.

The first line of Sadun's quote indicates that nachchi are specifically identified as
homosexual, and then particularly targeted for rape. Homosexuality appeared to be
a source of victimization, albeit according to the gender defined model of
homosexuality found in Sri Lanka. While female sex workers in general also
report rape and group rape, nachchi may be experiencing rape directed at their
homosexuality in tandem with feminine gender identity, in addition to their
lowered status as sex workers.

Discussion

The nachchi's descriptions of abuses perpetrated by police illustrate the intersectional nature of victimization involving sexual orientation and gender. While
some abuses parallel those of female sex workers, the nature of the transgender sex
workers' abuses is in some cases directed at their transgender identity and
homosexuality, and heightened in some instances. This claim is substantiated by
two main points. First, findings show that nachchi experience police abuses both
inside and outside of their sex work, suggesting transgender identity as a primary
source of stigma. In addition, the violence directed at them due to their homosexuality does not occur in isolation; it occurs in tandem with their feminine
gender identity according to the culturally constructed gender defined model of
homosexuality. As such, the abuses transgender sex workers face are unique and
multifaceted. The nachchi are not victimized solely in the context of sex work or
homosexuality, or even both of these elements combined. It is the addition of a
feminine gender identity/transgender identity to these elements that precipitates
their victimization by police. The victims specifically indicate being identified as
nachchi by their feminine behavior, cross dressing, and homosexuality while
experiencing various abuses, which is consistent with previous research (Kulick

1998; Miller 2002; Wright and Wright 1997) that finds transgender individuals are at a heightened risk of victimization due to the visibility of their stigmatized transgender identity.

Homosexuality, in isolation, is not condemned in nachchi's experiences with police. It is the *cultural construction* of homosexuality in Sri Lanka, in that male-to-male contact must be concurrent with femininity to equate nachchi identity and consequential victimization. While police are engaging in male-to-male sexual contact, and men in general may engage in male-to-male contact in Sri Lanka (Miller 2002; Silva et al. 1998), it is the feminine nachchi that are the targets of victimization by police–not clients, police, or other members of the community engaging in male-to-male sex. This contributes to and supports prior intersectional literature that explores how gender shapes violence directed at sexual orientation (Mason 2002). Further, it is similar to research in Latin America and the Philippines, in which the insertive partners in sex preserve masculinity and are not stigmatized, while their penetrated partners are perceived as feminine and are consequently stigmatized (Johnson 1998a, b; Kulick 1998; Manalansan 2003). These findings are consistent with a small body of research that finds the experiences of gay male sex workers who are feminine are different from the experiences of gay male sex workers who are masculine (Kulick 1998; Wright and Wright 1997). This suggests that sexual orientation-based violence does not necessarily occur in isolation, but is also shaped by gender. Individuals who are homosexual and feminine may find that intersections of gender and sexual orientation form a dynamic of dual oppression (Franklin 2004; see too Stotzer, this volume). Male-to-female transgender sex workers may be stigmatized not only for their homosexuality, but their feminine gender identity and expression as well (Kulick 1998; Mason 2002; Miller 2002; Wright and Wright 1997).

Moreover, the *nature* of the nachchi's abuse is distinct, not only in the way their gender identity is specifically addressed by the police in the course of their abuse, but the abuses themselves are gendered. In the case of forced gendered behavior, for example, making nachchi sing, sweep, dance, cook, and serve tea in addition to cleaning shoes and uniforms—feminine behaviors in Sri Lanka—is a clear indication of the gendered nature of their victimization. It shows how intersections of gender and sexuality are combined in a particular manifestation of abuse. Prior literature does not show similar actions being inflicted on female or male sex workers. In fact, no academic articles on sex work could be located that referenced this type of abuse from police, suggesting a unique form of victimization experienced by transgender sex workers based on their feminine gender identity. They are forced to do "women's work" in a demeaning fashion.

In addition, homosexuality and gender as a dual source of victimization is indicated by widespread use of the insult "ponnaya," which references both the nachchi's gender and sexuality simultaneously. Herek (2004) maintains that the rejection of anything feminine is a defining factor of masculinity. For example, McCann et al. (2009) point out that homophobic language and misogynistic language are intertwined with names that are used to label homosexual men. The research findings in the current study support this claim and demonstrate the intersectional nature of verbal abuse used against the transgendered nachchi through the use of the insult "ponnaya." While prior research indicated male and female sex workers also experience verbal abuse, the verbal abuse transgender individuals experience directly targets both their sexuality and feminine gender identity.

Physical abuse of the nachchi by police generally paralleled the abuse inflicted on female and male sex workers (Sangram 2002; Thukral and Ditmore 2003). Yet, in the nachchi's experiences, the verbal abuse was frequently concurrent with physical abuse that insulted the victims' transgender identity. Further, nachchi victims experienced physical abuse by police outside of their sex work. Respondents specifically reported being identified as transgender by police, and police physically abusing them for that reason. Thus, the nachchi also reported additional physical abuse which targeted their transgender identity both in the course of and outside of their sex work.

Nachchi suggest that inequality in arrest patterns may be heightened by a transgender identity and homosexuality because if the nachchi are caught in the course of their sex work or outside of their sex work, they may be charged not just with prostitution but homosexuality as well. Homosexuality, transgender identity, and sex work all shape the nachchi's experiences with arrest patterns. The main premise of the intersectional literature is supported by the current research findings: that multiple identities intersect to inform individual experiences.

Police officers' failure to protect the nachchi is parallel to that of the experiences of male (Scott et al. 2005) and female sex workers (Fairstein 1993; Sanchez 2001), in that complaints to police related to the nachchi's sex work were generally dismissed. Yet, this dynamic may be heightened for the nachchi. The nachchi are refused help because they are sex workers, but the current research findings show their complaints outside of the sex industry are also ignored and condemned, in part, because the nachchi are easily recognized outside of their sex work by their feminine attire and accessories. The findings also indicate that the nachchi's lack of recourse goes further in some cases, including instances of rape and other forms of victimization, although the rape of female sex workers and coerced sex acts by police are also noted in prior research (Kempadoo and Doezema 1998; Miller 1997). However, the nachchi are recognized and victimized even when they are not working and their complaints have nothing to do with the sex industry. As such, findings indicate the nachchi's transgender identity *as well as* their illegal sex work is a basis for victimization. Findings support the notion that gender, in this case *trans*gendering, is a basis for victimization.

The nachchi are seen as "fair game" because of their stigmatized status; therefore, they are vulnerable in terms of rape and forced sex acts. There is some evidence that male sex workers are not as likely to be victimized as transgender or female sex workers (Dennison-Hunt 2007; Farley 1998). Group rape of female prostitutes by police has been documented (Jenkins 2000), but group rape of male sex workers has not, although it may be due to the overall lack of research in this area. The current findings document group rape of transgender sex workers by police. Notably, the cultural construction of homosexuality includes femininity, or transgendering, in Sri Lanka. Nachchi are raped because of the stigma attached to their feminine gender identity and embodiment combined with their sex work. Findings show that nachchi are identified as homosexual, and they are raped for this reason as well, indicating a form of abuse directed at nachchi's multiple identities as sex workers, homosexuals, and transgender individuals. This finding is consistent with Mason's (2002) claim that multiple identities interact to produce unique victimization targeting those identities.

Conclusion

The aim of this research was to explore the intersections of gender and sexual orientation in transgender victimization, and to highlight the police victimization of nachchi. Femininity and homosexuality in tandem are stigmatized in Sri Lanka, and the resulting victimization by police paralleled this relationship. Defining oppression within a vacuum of only gender, or sexual orientation, or embodiment is too simplistic. Individuals express intersecting identities, and consequently, oppression is experienced differently. This chapter illustrated the intersectional nature of victimization of transgender individuals by police. Excerpts from interviews with transgender sex workers show how constructions of gender and sexuality in Sri Lanka interact to produce unique configurations of abuses in which the violence is directly misogynistic *and* homophobic in nature.

Acknowledgment Thanks to Jody Miller for providing access to this data and for her advice in preparing this manuscript.

References

Agustin, L. (2007). *Sex at the margins*. London, UK: Zed Books.
Dennison-Hunt, S. (2007). *The SW5 project*. London, UK: UK Network of Sex Work Projects.
Fairstein, L. A. (1993). *Sexual violence: Our war against rape*. New York, NY: William Morrow & Co.
Farley, M., & Barkan, H. (1998). Prostitution and post traumatic stress disorder. *Women and Health, 27*, 37–49.
Franklin, K. (2004) Enacting masculinity: Antigay violence and group rape as participatory theater. *Sexuality Research and Social Policy, 1*, 25–40.
Fernando, C. (2002). *Women and children as victims of crime: The Sri Lankan perspective*. Japan: Asian Crime Prevention Foundation.
Gujarat, G. (2004, July 9). Sri Lanka's gays join south Asian fight for rights. *Sodomy Laws*. Retrieved from http://www.glapn.org/sodomylaws/world/sri_lanka/slnews011.htm.
Herek, G. (2004). Beyond "homophobia": Thinking about sexual prejudice and stigma in the twenty-first century. *Sexuality Research and Social Policy, 1*, 1–24.
Jayasundara, D. (2000). *Clients' motives and justifications for visiting sex workers in Sri Lanka*. San Francisco, CA: Paper presented at the Annual Meeting of the American Society of Criminology.
Jenkins, C. (2000). *Female sex worker HIV prevention projects: Lessons learned from Papua New Guinea, India and Bangladesh*. Geneva, Switzerland: UNAIDS Best Practice Collection.

Johnson, M. (1998a). Remembrances identity, cultural transformation and transgendering in the southern Philippines. *International Journal of Comparative Race and Ethnic Studies 2*, 116–132.

Johnson, M. (1998b). Global desiring and translocal loves: Transgendering and same sex sexualities in the southern Philippines. *American Ethnologist, 25*, 695–711.

Kempadoo, K., & Dozema, J. (1998). *Global sex workers: Rights, resistance and redefinition.* New York, NY: Routledge.

Kinsey Institute. (2009). *The continuum complete: International encyclopedia of sexuality.*

Kulick, D. (1998). *Travesti.* Chicago, IL: University of Chicago Press.

Luibhéid, E. (2004). Heteronormativity and immigration scholarship: A call for change. *GLQ: A Journal of Lesbian and Gay Studies, 10*, 227–235.

Manalansan, M. (2003). *Global divas. Filipino gay men in the diaspora.* Durham, NC: Duke University Press.

Mason, G. (2002). *Spectacle of violence.* London, UK: Routledge.

McCann, D., Minichiello, V., & Plummer, D. (2009). Is homophobia inevitable? Evidence that explores the constructed nature of homophobia, and the techniques through which we unlearn it. *Journal of Sociology, The Australian Sociological Association, 45*, 201–220.

Miller, J. (1997). Victimization and resistance among street prostitutes. In P. A. Adler & P. Adler (Eds.), *Constructions of deviance* (pp. 500–515). Belmont, CA: Wadsworth.

Miller, J. (2002). Violence and coercion in Sri Lanka's commercial sex industry: Intersections of gender, sexuality, culture and the law. *Violence Against Women, 8*, 1044–1073.

Miller, J., & Nichols, A. (2012). Gender identity, sexuality, and commercial sex among Sri Lankan nachchi. *Sexualities, 15*, 554–569.

Namaste, V. (2000). *Invisible lives: The erasure of transsexual and transgender people.* Chicago: University of Chicago, IL Press.

Price, S. (1998). Gays hopeful law will be changed. *South China Morning Post.*

Puri, J. (1999). *Women, body, and desire in postcolonial India.* New York, NY: Routledge.

Sanchez, L. (2001). Gender troubles: The entanglement of agency, violence, and law in the lives of women in prostitution. In C. Renzetti & L. Goodstein (Eds.), *Women, crime, and criminal justice* (pp. 60–76). Los Angeles, CA: Roxbury Publishing.

SANGRAM. (2002). Rehabilitation: Against their will? Of veshyas, vamps, whores and women: Challenging preconceived notions of prostitution and sex work. *Point of View and VAMP, 1*, 2.

Scott, J., Minichiello, V., Marino, R., Harvey, G., & Jamieson, M. (2005). Understanding the new context of the male sex work industry. *Journal of Interpersonal Violence, 3*, 320–342.

Silva, K. T., Sivayoganathan, C., & Lewis, J. (1998). Love, sex and peer activity in a sample of youth in Sri Lanka. In S. T. Hettige (Ed.), *Globalization, social change and youth* (pp. 24–43). Colombo, Sri Lanka: German Cultural Institute.

Thukral, J., & Ditmore, M. (2003). *Revolving door: An analysis of street-based prostitution in New York City.* USA: Urban Justice Center.

Whitham, F. (1992). Bayot and callboy: Homosexual-heterosexual relations in the Philippines. In S. Murray (Ed.), *Oceanic homosexualities* (pp. 231–248). London, UK: Garland Publishing.

Wijewardene, S. (2007). But no one has explained to me who I am now: "Trans" self-perceptions in Sri Lanka. In S. E. Wieringa, E. Blackwood, & A. Bhaiya (Eds.), *Women's sexualities and masculinities in a globalizing Asia* (pp. 101–116). New York, NY: Palgrave Macmillan.

Wright, T., & Wright, R. (1997). Bolivia: Developing a gay community: Homosexuality and AIDS. In D. J. West & R. Green (Eds.), *Sociolegal control of homosexuality* (pp. 101–123). New York, NY: Plenum Press.

Chapter 10
Policing the Lesbian and Gay Community: The Perceptions of Lesbian and Gay Police Officers

Roddrick Colvin

Abstract This exploratory research conducted in the U.S. examines the workplace views and shared perceptions of lesbian and gay police officers about community policing. Using survey responses from 134 officers and 3 focus group sessions, advantages and disadvantages are identified for lesbian and gay officers and the communities and departments they service. While representative community policing is valued, officers report that cultural competence for officers and good police skills—regardless of sexual orientation—are the most important factors for being an effective officer.

Keywords Community policing · Lesbian police officer · Gay police officer · Shared perceptions in the workplace · Liaison officers · Hate crimes · Law enforcement · Diversity

Introduction

Community policing is a collaborative approach for the delivery of police services. It represents an acceptance that the community served has an active and legitimate role in the successful resolution of crime and social order problems, and these partnerships with the community and its members can be much more effective than traditional policing strategies. Central to the implementation of community policing throughout the United States has been the diversification of the police department personnel. The basic premise has been that in order to better serve the public, the police department needs to be representative of the communities in its jurisdiction. Thus, departments across the United States have attempted to improve

R. Colvin (✉)
Department of Public Management, John Jay College of Criminal Justice, City University of New York, 524 West 59th Street, New York, NY 10019, USA
e-mail: rcolvin@jjay.cuny.edu

D. Peterson and V. R. Panfil (eds.), *Handbook of LGBT Communities, Crime, and Justice*, DOI: 10.1007/978-1-4614-9188-0_10, © Springer Science+Business Media New York 2014

recruitment, retention, and promotion of minorities, including, but not limited to women, people of color, people who are gay or lesbian, and bilingual officers (Sklansky 2006). Although most departments have not been successful in achieving parity, many departments are significantly more diverse than they were 20 years ago. For example, in 2010, the New York City Police Department (NYPD) for the first time had a majority of rank-and-file police officers come from minority communities (El-Ghobashy 2011). With 53 % of police officers from minority communities, the department—at least in terms of race—reflected the City of New York as a whole.

This chapter explores North American-based lesbian and gay police officers in the context of community policing and their shared perceptions about their work as police officers. Like women and racial minorities, integration into the police ranks for lesbian and gay police officers has not been without its challenges. Traditionally, lesbian and gay police officers 'served in silence' and remained closeted, or were out to only a few about their sexual orientations, for fear of being subjected to discrimination and harassment (Colvin 2012; Leinen 1993). However, with the adoption and implementation of community–based policing, passage of local and state nondiscrimination employment laws, changes in social norms, and citizen demands for more representative police departments, more officers are able to serve openly (Colvin 2012). Thus today we can ask, what are the workplace views and shared perceptions of lesbian and gay police officers in the context of community policing? I hypothesize that officers will report better working relationships within the LGBT community, given that they are from that community. Second, I hypothesize that the diversity and cultural competence that these officers bring to the police ranks will make them more effective officers when serving members of the LGBT community who come into contact with the criminal justice system. Third, as a measure of acceptance, I hypothesize that lesbian and gay officers will report high-quality professional relationships with colleagues in their departments. Before presenting analyses of these hypotheses, I first review the relevant policing literature, focusing on gay and lesbian police officers, community policing, the emotional labor of police work, policing in LGBT communities, and measuring community policing outcomes and shared workplace perceptions.

Literature Review

Police Departments in the United States

According to the U.S. Department of Justice (2010), there are over 700,000 uniformed police officers and nearly 15,000 police departments in the United States. Variations from one department to the next are many. At one end are professional departments with diverse police forces that match the demographics of the communities they serve. A prime example of this type of department is the NYPD. In 2010, 53 % of NYPD officers on patrol (22,000) were racial minorities (black, Asian, or Latino), a close match to the 55 % racial-minority composition of New York City (El-Ghobashy 2011; U.S. Census Bureau 2011). In other cases, police departments have minority officers, but the departments themselves are not demographically representative of the communities they serve (Weisburd et al. 2001). For example, more than half of the residents of the City of Boston are people of color, yet only 31 % of the Boston Police Department consists of people of color (Jeromski 2012). Even in smaller communities, police workforce representativeness is rare. For example, Providence, Rhode Island is comprised of 45.5 people of color, yet its police department is 80 % white and 93 % male (Kasdan 2006). While the demographics of a police department rarely match those of its community, efforts (sometimes legally mandated) are under way to remediate this situation; meanwhile, officers in these environments are often trained how to professionally respond to and interact with various constituencies within the larger community (Kasdan 2006). Although the efficacy of diversity training has been challenged, the efforts of these departments are often undertaken in consultation with the various communities served.

At the other end of the spectrum are the "traditional" police agencies, whose personnel engage in classic law enforcement functions (rapid response to calls for service, arrest, and follow-up investigations) and rarely focus on community involvement, representative police service, or strategic planning to prevent crime. This latter department is less frequent as more and more communities adopt community policing programs (Wilson et al. 2009).

Although New York City is highlighted as an example of a representative police force, the size of a police department is not necessarily an indicator of its diversity, professionalism, or training. There are large police departments with generous resources that have low public support, low police morale, and minimal diversity professional training (Sege 2012). Conversely, many smaller police departments have led the U.S. in efforts to diversify and professionalize policing, and to garner public support (Torres and Stefkovich 2009). Most police departments in the United States, however, lie between these two extremes. Although models for planned change are being implemented at many departments across the country, the process is lengthy and requires incremental shifts from one policing generation to the next. As part of these incremental shifts and increasing diversity of police departments throughout the U.S., a greater number of openly gay men and lesbians are documented among the police ranks, though their integration has not been without trial.

Lesbians and Gay Men in Policing

During the past two decades, researchers have approached the topic of lesbian and gay people in law enforcement from a number of different angles, from research on dual identity and disclosure to shared workplace perceptions among gay and lesbian officers and perceptions of gay and lesbian officers by their heterosexual counterparts. Earlier research focused on the idea that being "homosexual" (associated with deviancy) and being a police officer represented dual—often conflicting—identities. Thus, scholars attempted to understand how officers reconciled a "deviant" behavior with their law enforcement role as regulators of deviance (Buhrke 1996; Leinen 1993). These studies—based on interviews— spawned interesting research about the mental health, productivity, ability to cope, and self-acceptance of lesbian and gay police officers (Herek 2003).

The issue of disclosure of sexual orientation in the workplace is related to the idea of dual identity, and a number of studies have considered the factors that affect when or if police officers reveal their sexual orientation on the job (Buhrke 1996; Leinen 1993; Miller et al. 2003). The idea of dual identity originated in the psychology literature and suggests that people split their identity as a coping mechanism to operate in different environments. In this understanding, officers split their "gay" identity from their "police" identity. The general consensus is that lesbians and gay men in law enforcement are under tremendous pressure to conform to prevailing law enforcement hetero-normative stereotypes, and that each lesbian and gay officer must determine the costs and benefits of disclosing her or his sexual orientation at work. An individual's decision might include personal considerations such as physical safety, organizational considerations such as social isolation, or institutional considerations such as evaluation, promotion, and assignments. When the benefits exceed the costs, lesbians and gay men are more likely to disclose their sexual orientation. Of course, officers do not always have the option of managing disclosure at work. Like other workplace environments, police officers—regardless of sexual orientation—are sometimes "outed" at work as lesbian or gay. When the officer is in fact lesbian or gay, this situation requires the officer to reevaluate the costs and benefits and act accordingly. How an officer responds might include exhibiting homophobic actions, dating a person of the opposite sex, or revealing her or his sexual orientation as lesbian or gay.

Recent research has focused on the shared perceptions of target populations in the workplace. The idea of shared perceptions builds on the notion that individual perceptions are often communicated to other people both inside and outside the organization. If a group of employees share a negative perception about management, these employees might be less committed to the organization, and this attitude might impact the organization's efficiency and effectiveness. For example, female police officers who share a perception that women are not evaluated fairly, and thus are less likely to be promoted, may be less motivated to engage in police work with full commitment. Conversely, when officers have positive shared perceptions, their commitment and motivation will be greater, which can translate into improved efficiency and effectiveness for the organization (Colvin 2012). The individual's perceptions and experiences are also shaped by his or her membership in a specific group (Bolton 2003). Such experiences and perceptions of the law enforcement workplace have been considered for a number of specific groups, including for racial minorities (Alex 1969; Bolton 2003; Essed 1991; McCluskey 2004), by race and gender (Edgar and Martin 2004; Holder et al. 2000), and by sexual orientation (Colvin 2009). More recent works have examined the shared perceptions and work experiences of officers with multiple group memberships and the interactive effects with these identities. For example, Hassell and Brandl (2009) explore the roles of race, sex, and sexual orientation and their effects on workplace stress.

Finally, valuable research has been conducted that considers the effects of lesbian and gay inclusion in the law enforcement environment (Belkin and McNichol 2002; Miller et al. 2003; Myers et al. 2004). Research on the attitudes and beliefs of heterosexual officers about their lesbian and gay counterparts continues to grow (Bernstein and Kostelac 2002; Lyons et al. 2008). Existing literature on attitudes and beliefs about lesbian and gay people suggested that familiarity with lesbian and gay people is highly correlated with positive perceptions of lesbian and gay people (Lewis 2006). That is to say, knowing gay and lesbian people reduces animus toward them. Some of the most comprehensive research on inclusion and familiarity has been conducted in the context of integrating lesbians and gay men into the military (Belkin and McNichol 2002). Although not perfectly analogous to police forces, the armed forces are also highly cohesive, formerly segregated, and majority-male organizations and thus offer a good perspective on the potential challenges inherent in developing more inclusive police departments (Belkin and McNichol 2002; Koegel 1996). Finally, another line of research examines the extent of this development of inclusive police agencies as part of the move toward community policing, with expectations of improvements in community representation and service.

Community Policing

According to the U.S. Department of Justice (2009, p. 1), community policing is "a philosophy that promotes organizational strategies which support the systematic use of partnerships and problem-solving techniques, to proactively address the immediate conditions that give rise to public safety issues such as crime, social disorder, and fear of crime." Community policing is understood as a joint effort between law enforcement and a community it serves to best determine the policing needs of the community. Groups and individuals—including government agencies, nonprofit organizations, businesses, local media, and community members—all have partnerships with the police, which encourage responsiveness and make communities safer.

Police departments in the United States began experimenting with this new philosophy of policing in the 1980s. These departments tried to engage community members to jointly address recurring crime and disorder issues through proactive or problem-solving efforts (Diamond and Weiss 2009). These diffused efforts to change the nature of policing were codified at the federal level in 1994 through the Violent Crime Control and Law Enforcement Act. As a result of federal support, over 80 % of the United States population is served by a law enforcement department practicing community policing (U.S. Department of Justice 2011).

Also, central to the idea of a community policing model is the idea of a representative police force. A basic premise and driving influence behind a representative force is the idea of representative bureaucracy. The theory of representative bureaucracy suggests that a demographically diverse public sector workforce will lead to policy outcomes that reflect the interests of all groups represented, including historically disadvantaged communities (Bradbury 2004). Implicit in this idea is the expectation that minority public servants, in particular, will have similar attitudes to minority citizens on issues of critical import and relevance, and those attitudes, in turn, will influence policy decisions (Bradbury 2004). In the case of policing and representativeness, the same logic applies. With minority representation on the force, more informed and community supported policing decisions will be made. As the U.S. Department of Justice (2009, p. 32) noted, a more diverse police force serves a number of purposes: (1) helps officers arrive at a broader array of solutions; (2) develops balanced, relevant, and culturally sensitive responses to community problems and incidents; (3) enhances mutual understanding between the department and the community; (4) reduces stereotyping on the part of the community and the police, and; (5) inspires members of under-represented groups to trust and support the police.

There is little empirical data to support the U.S. Department of Justice's (2009) assertion. Although there are some general statements that women and minority officers express more optimism about community policing, others have found no significant association between gender and/or race and attitudes toward community-based policing (Lord and Friday 2008). An important factor to consider as this work moves forward is "emotional labor" in police work and its role in perceptions and experiences of minority officers, including those who are gay and lesbian, who engage in community police work.

Emotional Labor and Police Work

Beyond examining the effectiveness of community policing on communities and community relations, is the more concrete and systematic research on emotional labor and its impact on police officers' work. As Scott et al. (2003) noted, police officers are regularly confronted with noncooperative community members, including suspects and victims. As a consequence, police officers engage in emotional labor on a daily basis. Emotional labor can be described as the employee's management of feelings, in order to create an observable display in accordance with situational demands (Hochschild 2003). Display rules can usually be derived from an organization's policy, stating which emotions the department considers appropriate to show to clients. In the case of policing, crime victims and offenders are important clients to be serviced. In order to make a professional appearance and reach organizational goals, police officers may need to suppress their felt emotions (for example, anger toward a suspect) or display emotions that are not felt (for example, sadness or regret). This state of discrepancy between felt and displayed emotions is called emotional dissonance, which is considered to be detrimental to the officer's long-term mental wellbeing (Ashfort and Humphrey 1993; Bakker and Heuven 2006). Most emotional labor research shows that the general construct of emotional dissonance is related to emotional exhaustion and depersonalization (Hochschild 2003; Kruml and Geddes 2000; Zapf 2002). Previous research on emotion regulation emphasizes the negative social and detrimental health effects of suppressing emotions. Suppression of emotions may disrupt communication and heighten stress levels, which makes police work even more difficult to attend to (Butler et al. 2003; Richards and Gross 1999, 2000). As Herek (2009) noted, given the detrimental health effects of the general construct of emotional dissonance, it is important to broaden these insights by taking the effect of suppressing emotions into account (Glomb and Tews 2004). This is because suppression of certain emotions can be more detrimental for individual wellbeing than suppression of other emotions. The potential role of emotional labor in gay and lesbian police officers' community policing work is taken up later.

Policing in Lesbian and Gay Communities

Lesbian and gay communities have a history of being both over- and under-policed. This historical relationship has present-day implications for contemporary relationships between these LGBT communities and local police agencies.

In terms of over-policing, relations between lesbian and gay communities and the police have historically been fraught with contention (Williams and Robinson 2004; see, too, Dwyer, this volume), due to the uneven and inequitable policing extended to these communities. Across the United States, police officers have often been seen as the active "enforcers" of laws primarily affecting lesbian and gay people, given their harassment of patrons at local gay bars and their arrests of people (mostly men) allegedly engaged in "lewd behavior" (Buhrke 1996; Leinen 1993). Such harassment and arrests have been driven mostly by officers' homophobia. Early research in the 1960s showed that lesbians and gay men were ranked as the second most disliked group by a sample of New York police officers (Niederhoffer 1967), and this outcome was replicated and validated almost a decade later (Fretz 1975). Although societal norms are rapidly changing, even contemporary research suggests that "homosexuals" are the third most disliked group in the United States, after atheists and Muslims (Edgel et al. 2006). The occupational culture of police officers can instill negative attitudes about minority individuals, especially those identifying as lesbian or gay (Leinen 1993). These negative attitudes have contributed to discrimination, harassment, and, in some cases, brutalization of lesbian and gay people (Miller et al. 2003).

In contrast, under-policing is the failure to provide a satisfactory level of policing for communities and victims of crime (Mike and Childs 2002; see, too,

Dwyer, this volume). Under-policing has also negatively affected community relations. Herek (1998, 2004) argued that the low reporting of antigay hate crimes—and the high number of such crimes that go unsolved—result not just from lack of interest on the part of the police, but also from the fact that such crimes are sometimes committed by police officers themselves (see too, Nichols, this volume). Community members thus often perceive the police as being antigay, and fear both primary and secondary victimization by officers (Comstock 1989; V. Codling, personal communication, 2009). Davis (1992) and Mitchell (1992) found that lesbian and gay people who approached the police for help tended to receive a negative reception, including a lack of interest in their reports of victimization.

This tumultuous relationship made effective policing in the lesbian and gay community virtually impossible. It seriously limited police efforts to monitor and investigate hate crimes, same-sex domestic violence, and drug-related activities. For the most part, lesbian and gay people refused to report crime or to aid police in any substantive way. The unbalanced policing of lesbian and gay populations, the perceived disinterest in complaints from lesbian and gay people, and the high level of police-perpetrated antigay hate crimes combined to create an atmosphere of harassment and intimidation (for additional discussion, see in this volume Dwyer; Nichols).

In contrast to these past models of policing, community policing focuses on building relationships between community members and officers, once police accept that all communities—including lesbian and gay communities—have "a legitimate, active role to play in the policing process" (White and Perrone 2005, p. 29). This "legitimate" role is vastly different from the policing model of the past. Whereas traditional models endow police officers and departments with the power to enforce the law, the community policing model requires a collaborative process to decide how compliance with laws will be achieved. In this scenario, arrest and prosecution may not be the most effective, efficient, or equitable approach. Furthermore, this new role suggests that police departments will be better able to serve a community when the composition of the police force reflects the composition of that community. Thus, lesbian and gay people have a right to be an active part of the departments that serve their community. Police departments in the past allowed themselves to homogenize, and this lack of diversity had a direct effect on the ability of police departments to meet their mission (Colvin 2012).

Measurable Outcomes of Community Policing

Understanding the outcomes of community policing can be a challenging task. Despite the increased use of community policing, expected outcomes, common objectives, and valid measures remain elusive when assessing the impact of this model. This is especially the case when attempting to assess impact on minority officers, especially lesbian and gay officers. Many departments continue to use performance measures based on other models of policing, including levels of crime and fear, numbers of arrests and citations, and staffing levels (Alpert et al. 2001).

Much of what we do know about community policing comes from case studies of various jurisdictions around the United States (Scott et al. 2003; Trojanowicz et al. 1990). These case studies are diverse in their objectives and in their perspectives on community policing. Collectively, however, they provide much-needed information about community policing—particularly about the places where it has been implemented, its stated purposes, its strategic and structural components, the obstacles encountered in its implementation, and occasionally its outcomes (Kerley and Benson 2000; Kurki 2000). For example, Lombardo et al. (2010) explore the largest community policing effort in the United States, the Chicago Alternative Policing Strategy (CAPS), with an emphasis on understanding the change in community satisfaction as a result of the strategy. They found that communities that had implemented CAPS had more favorable perceptions of the police compared to non-CAPS communities.

Unfortunately, the diversity of/and variation among the case studies make it difficult to identify more universal patterns of success or failure in community policing. Furthermore, the nature of case studies makes developing consistent performance measures all but impossible. One difficulty is not knowing precisely what is to be measured (Fielding and Innes 2006). When community policing is operationalized, it can range from neighborhood-watch programs to problem-oriented policing to zero-tolerance approaches. This makes meaningful comparison among the programs problematic.

Despite these challenges, some appropriate measures for outcomes of community policing have emerged. Of course, traditional measures, including reduction in crime and fear, are appropriate for most law enforcement efforts. These performance measures have historical and political roots, and thus police departments tend to be most comfortable with them. But other measures—for example, community processes (community organization, cohesion, and cooperative security), community satisfaction, and community trust—also seem intuitively appropriate to evaluating community policing's successes and failures (Kerley and Benson 2000). These community-oriented measures, unlike traditional measures, are much more ambiguous, and lack the historical and political influence that police departments have grown accustomed to.

One of our best, and under-utilized, sources of information on the community policing of lesbian and gay communities comes from lesbian and gay officers themselves. While traditional measures of police performance remain important for understanding the essential work of law enforcement, new measures that reflect the unique role of police officers in community policing are needed. Scholars are beginning to survey different aspects of this type of police work in the field, but we can already see the important effects that community policing can have on minority or marginalized communities. Community policing efforts can lead to greater connectedness and increased trust on both sides and ultimately improve both the life of the community and the effectiveness of policing (Colvin 2012).

Gathering Officer Experiences and Perceptions

As mentioned previously, shared perceptions among employees in the workplace can have a profound effect on an organization. These shared perceptions often originate from the individual experiences of employees. An employee who feels that s/he has been unfairly treated in the organization might share her/his dissatisfaction with a sympathetic coworker. The coworker may repeat the story to another employee, who might in turn repeat it to a third. Before long, many employees know the story—understand it as fact—and react accordingly. Their reactions can include uncertainty, loss of work satisfaction, on-the-job distraction, and reduced motivation. In the worst-case scenarios, employees can impede the organization's performance or subvert its mission. Thus, organizations that fail to monitor and respond to the shared perceptions and experiences of employees risk failure. It therefore seems worthwhile to examine gay and lesbian police officers' perceptions of community policing in gay and lesbian communities as a means of informing police agencies not only about the perceived effectiveness of such efforts, but also the shared perspectives of officers who "represent" those communities and whether increased diversity within the police force achieves the intended goals of improved representation and service.

The remainder of this chapter describes a study that gathered data about the shared perceptions and experiences of lesbian and gay police officers in the context of community policing. The aggregated survey data give us a good picture of their work environment and their workplace perceptions. These data, coupled with focus group discussions, will provide a more complete understanding of both community policing and shared perceptions. No doubt, challenges still remain for lesbian and gay officers, but if they share the perception that policing also provides benefits, then organizational failures are less likely. The survey data were originally collected from officers during the 2009 International Conference of Gay and Lesbian Criminal Justice Professionals in New York City. These survey data were supplemented by three focus group discussions in New York (2) and Washington, DC (1) conducted in 2011.

Methodology

Survey of Lesbian and Gay Officers

The survey represents an effort to better understand the work environment in which lesbian and gay people in North American (largely U.S.) police departments operate. The design of the survey instrument was based on surveys conducted for previous studies focusing on the shared perceptions of other minority groups in law enforcement—blacks and women (Bolton 2003). The instrument was pretested with the help of the New York City Gay Officers Action League (GOAL NY), a professional support organization, and Law Enforcement Gays and Lesbians International (LEGAL International), an umbrella organization for local lesbian and gay law enforcement professional associations.

The final instrument was completed in March 2009 and administered at the thirteenth annual International Conference of Gay and Lesbian Criminal Justice Professionals, held in New York City, New York from June 23 to 28 of that year. According to the hosting committee, the conference drew about 300 participants from twenty-two U.S. states, Canada, and Puerto Rico, representing over thirty police departments (T. Duffy, personal communication, June 28, 2009). The majority of the officers were from the Northeast region, with New York City representing over a third of the attendees.

The four-page survey included three major components:

1. Questions capturing social-demographic data about the officers and their status in law enforcement.
2. Questions eliciting the officers' perceptions, as lesbian and gay officers, about their workplace environment. Officers were asked about barriers or obstacles, as well as access points or openings, to equal employment opportunities—for example, whether or not they received their first-choice assignment.
3. Questions focusing on elements of work specific to the law enforcement environment, including questions about workplace relationships with external and internal entities.

The anonymous survey was administered over a two-day period at the conference on the campus of John Jay College of Criminal Justice, where a separate area was set up specifically to administer the survey. Conference attendees were reminded about the survey data at each major gathering of officers at the conference, including plenary sessions, guest lectures, and meals. Officers' reaction to the survey was generally positive, although administration of the survey competed for the attention of officers during the short break and against other conference-related tables.

The results presented here are drawn from surveyed officers' responses to five statements of agreement. Each response was on a 5-point scale of strongly agree, agree, neutral, disagree, and strongly disagree. The statements were:

1. I have a good relationship in the *non-gay* community in which I serve.
2. I have a good relationship in the *gay* community in which I serve.
3. Lesbian and gay officers are more effective than non-gay officers when working with gay suspects/prisoners.
4. I have good relationships with my non-gay coworkers, supervisors, and subordinates (if applicable).
5. My job advancement opportunities are the same as non-gay officers.

The first three questions were designed to gather the officers' views on working with and in the communities. These questions are assumed to capture the views of police officers post-community policing. The fourth and fifth questions attempt to measure officers' shared perceptions of the workplace and how 'integrated' officers felt in relation to other officers. Although explicit questions about the work environment and community policing were not asked, the theme of the questions, combined with the focus groups' responses, provide us with a good perspective on lesbian and gay officers, their work, and their relationships with communities served.

Focus Groups Sessions with Lesbian and Gay Officers

In addition to the survey, three focus group sessions were conducted. Two focus group sessions were conducted with the NY Gay Officers Action League (GOAL NY). This group meets weekly at the Gay and Lesbian Community Center in New York City. One focus group session was planned and executed in April 2011. Another focus group was planned and executed in May 2011. For both sessions, announcements about the sessions were made at the two preceding meetings, and an e-mail reminder was sent out one week preceding. Volunteers were invited to participate with a goal of 5–7 officers in each session. There were 5 and 7 participants in each session, respectively, for a total of 12 participants. The 12 participants were self-selected. Since GOAL NY does not release statistical or demographic data about the organization, it is not known if the participating officers were representative of the organization (T. Duffy, personal communication, May, 2011).

The third focus group session consisted of lesbian and gay police officers in Washington, DC who were part of the city's special liaison unit for the gay and lesbian community. Formerly the Gay and Lesbian Liaison Unit (GLLU), in 2009, this unit was transformed from a community-based, proactive unit to become a citywide unit, responding to the lesbian and gay community in a more traditional liaison unit capacity. A meeting was arranged for officers available to meet after hours at the Washington Gay and Lesbian Community Center. Five of the twelve members of the special liaison unit attended the May 2011 focus group session.

For each session, police officers were asked general questions about their work-lives as openly lesbian and gay officers. The questions were designed to give officers an opportunity to explore issues and come to consensus or an agreed upon perception about certain issues or topics. There were some common questions and themes used in each session. Specifically, each group was asked:

1. Are there advantages and/or disadvantages of having gay and lesbian people in law enforcement?
2. Do you think lesbian and gay officers and staff are more effective when working with lesbian and gay community residents or on community-specific issues?
3. Can you tell me about 'typical or atypical incidents' of miscommunication or misunderstanding in dealings with gays and lesbians in the community?
4. Describe the effects of lesbian and gay recruiting on the police department?

   Each of these questions was designed to provide more context to survey
questions asked previously. Each session was 90 min and was audio recorded. The
audio recordings were then transcribed and keywords were used to conduct content
analysis—related to community policing—for this research.

Results

Table 10.1 shows the demographic information of 134 officers out of 300 who
completed the survey. This is a response rate of 45 %. While it is difficult to assess
with certainty whether the respondents are representative of the conference, law
enforcement, or the general population, a prima facie review of the race and
educational attainment data indicates a close match to the general population (U.S.
Department of Commerce 2010). Additionally, the high response rate suggests that
a good cross section of the conference population was surveyed. In term of police
departments, the respondents are more diverse than the police population. This is
most evident with 30 % of the respondents being female. According to the 2008
Census of State and Local Law Enforcement Departments (CSLLEA) and the
2007 Law Enforcement Management and Administrative Statistics (LEMAS)
survey, women comprise about 12 % for the police force. Additionally, the surveys find that about 25 % of the sample's police officers are of a racial minority,
which corresponds to the national averages. Finally, with 48 % of respondents
reporting undergraduate or advanced degrees, they are better educated than most
officers (Rydberg and Terrill 2010).

Table 10.1 Demographic information about respondents

	Number of officers	Percentage of officers
Gender		
Female	40	30
Male	94	70
Race		
Black/African-American	12	9
Hispanic	20	15
White/Non-Hispanic	97	72
Mixed	4	3
No answer/Other	1	1
Education—Completed		
High school	20	15
Community college	42	31
Undergraduate	40	30
Graduate	24	18
No answer	9	12

$N = 134$. Numbers were rounded and may equal more or <100

Table 10.2, like Table 10.1, provides demographic information about the offi-cers who completed the survey, but highlights the sexual orientation-related demographic information. Not surprisingly, the majority of officers identified as gay or lesbian (97 %), and 82 % considered themselves out to everyone in their lives—friends, family, and coworkers. Respondents' relationship status was interestingly divided: 48 % were single and 38 % reported being in a relationship (including state sanctioned domestic partnerships, marriages, and civil unions, and informal non-state relationships). Thirteen percent report some other relationship status.

Table 10.3 shows how officers responded to the statements of agreement about their relationships with the community. Interestingly, while almost 70 % of police officers responded positively that they have good relations in the straight com-munity, only 60 % report the same for the gay community. In terms of providing service and support to lesbians and gay people in the criminal justice system (as suspects or prisoners), only about 40 % responded affirmatively. This means that the vast majority do not believe that they are better equipped than non-gay officers to work with these members of the criminal justice community.

Table 10.3 also shows the responses officers gave regarding their work envi-ronments. When asked about relationships with coworkers, 71 % of officers responded positively. However, only 48 % of lesbian and gay officers believe that they have the same job advancement opportunities as other officers. The first response and the second response appear to contradict each other in terms of explaining the work environment or climate in police departments.

Table 10.2 Sexual orientation demographic information about respondents

	Number of officers	Percentage of officers
Sexual Orientation		
Lesbian/Gay	130	97
Straight	0	0
Other	4	3
Relationship Status		
Single	64	48
Recognized partnership (marriage, civil union, domestic partnership)	38	28
Relationship	14	10
Other	18	13
Level of 'Outness'		
Out to everyone	110	82
(Friends, family, and at work)	16	12
Out to friends and family	8	6
Out only to select people	0	0
Not out	0	0

$N = 134$. Numbers were rounded and may equal more or <100

Table 10.3 Responses to more effective policing

	Number who 'strongly agreed' and 'agreed'	Percent
I have a good relationship in the *non-gay* community in which I serve.	93	69
I have a good relationship in the *gay* community in which I serve.	81	60
Lesbian and gay officers are more effective than non-gay officers when working with gay suspects/prisoners.	52	39
I have good relationships with my non-gay coworkers, supervisors, and subordinates (if applicable)	95	71
My job advancement opportunities are the same as non-gay officers.	64	48

$N = 134$. Numbers were rounded and may equal more or <100

The content analysis of the focus groups can help us to better understand the aggregated results of the survey. The focus group sessions totaled 4.5 h of discussion. The transcribed documents totaled about 75 pages of dialog. Table 10.4 shows the common words and phrases found in the transcripts. The word "community" was used most frequently, yet the concept of "community policing" was not commonly invoked.

In terms of the working within the lesbian and gay community, the police officers had several views that highlight the challenges they face. Some of the comments include:

> ...You can become a point of contact, because you become so well entrenched within your own community, and you become so well-trusted ...because you are the one person who is constantly getting results from the people with whom you're working with, then you become the main point of contact and then you are inundated with telephone calls, you're inundated with letters, you're inundated with emails ...if you go out socially, you're having a quiet drink at the bar and someone taps you on your shoulder and says 'can I just,'...

> I think, quite clearly, what we need to do in the training is insure that we set the expectation with the [gay] victim, wherever it may be, as to what your role is, and, at some point, there will be weaning off of that relationship...once they get a hold of you, people won't contact the police. And sometimes this is a, you know, there's been any sort of contact with police. There's still a bit of society there that thinks you don't want the police involved, right across the board.

Table 10.4 Key word count from focus group sessions

	Word count
Community	251
Community policing	2
Liaison	57
Hate crimes	100
Sexual orientation	12

I think it can be detrimental, to be fair, because the gay community can be considered to be very gossipy and incestuous, and because it's a close-knit community...sometimes to actually know that the individual is within the same community can be of its detriment. You want someone who is removed. That, yes, still understands, but won't—someone's concern is always confidentiality. And it's always ensuring that the confidentiality is there and remains throughout. And sometimes people don't feel that, or they may question that. And if someone is involved within the same community as, there could be potential where questions, problems, and concerns could be raised outside of. And so, I would say, actually, it would be more of a hindrance to have someone who's within the same community rather than an advantage.

Because sometimes it can be a barrier, because sometimes they would try and hit on you depending on what part of the community they're from. Sometimes it can be an advantage, because they know you have a true understanding of, perhaps, what they've been through or what they're lifestyle is. I don't think there's an advantage of it being there, but in some circumstances...they will have an affinity where you actually do understand what they talking about...

Lesbian and gay officers appear to have conflicting roles in the LGBT community. Their roles as out police officers appear to afford them little anonymity in the community, and on occasion cause conflicts of interest. Officers appear to resent having to be police officers, even when off-duty in the community.

When asked about lesbian and gay officers' effectiveness with members of the community who are in the criminal justice system (victims, suspects, and perpetrators), the officers across the sessions confirmed the survey data. None of the officers in the sessions thought that lesbian and gay officers were more effective than others. They said:

Not necessarily. I think they might have a better understanding of the issues, but I don't think you'd necessarily work more effectively.

...as for being more effective, I don't think so at all. It doesn't make me more effective. I just might know a bit more about the community and things like that. But as for effective skills, it's just up to the officer.

I think we got some very competent police officers. And I think to have such police officers, it doesn't matter what your sexual orientation is. They're very professional, and they want to do a really, really good job ...

You're in a professional job, and getting the right result at the end of it. That's a very powerful message, not just internally to the organization, but to our community...actually, the message across the board is: we want to get it right, irrelevant of whether they're gay, they're heterosexual, or whatever. The message is: you matter.

...it depends on your skills as a police officer. It's not what your sexuality is...it's how you are effective in your job.

> I think the same way that an African-American officer can come into a domestic scene where it's two, Caucasian, gay males and be effective by using him using his head and having some training and background .... and anything else...He can be just as effective. There are areas where you're not going to be as effective. Sometimes people do need to see that familiar face or someone that's like them that maybe they feel like they can have this understanding with. But me being a lesbian doesn't make me more effective with lesbians.

As the data suggest, being an effective police officer is not contingent on personal characteristics. While being lesbian or gay might be helpful in a situation, it is not believed to be essential when working with LGBT people who come into contact with the criminal justice system.

The focus group sessions did not provide much insight in terms of why officers perceived good relations with colleagues in the force, nor did the sessions provide insights on the low perception of equal advancement opportunities. In the case of the former, these numbers could be highly correlated with the questions about working as police officers in gay and non-gay communities. In both cases, there are high levels of agreement about the nature of work with others.

Discussion

The survey data suggest that lesbian and gay police officers have better relationships with the general (non-gay communities) they serve. The focus group responses appear to confirm and explain why fewer officers report good relations with the gay community. Based on the focus group responses, community members and police officers themselves often muddle their role of police officer and their role of community member, unable to split their dual identities into that of "police officer" and "lesbian" or "gay man." Officers often feel too close to the community. As members of a small community, they are more visible as community members within the LGBT community. One respondent suggested this muddled role can compromise police effectiveness. The officer suggested that members of the community might contact the lesbian and gay officers directly instead of using established procedures for contacting the police. This issue appears to be common among officers serving in liaison positions, and is not exclusive to gay liaison officers. Family liaison officers, sexual assault liaison officers, and many others, report being contacted about issues beyond the scope of their liaison role (Colvin 2012). In these cases, a community member has formed a bond with the officer because of her or his close and personal service. A similar situation can arise when a lesbian or gay officer is supporting, for example, a gay-related hate crime victim. In such scenarios, lesbian and gay police officers may experience emotional dissonance; however, like their various liaison counterparts, they are proscribed in the responses they can display when engaged with community members who are in difficult situations. In the case of the lesbian/gay hate crime victim, the police officer may feel anger toward the perpetrator. However, the police officer would have to suppress those feelings, since anger would not be an appropriate emotion for the officer.

This interaction appears to contrast the experiences of other minority police officers, namely African-American officers. While African-American officers have noted strained relationships within the African-American community served, the strain is a different form. Based on the data presented here, lesbian and gay officers are viewed favorably in the community, and they are expected to work on behalf of the community. Some African-American police officers report being accused of switching allegiance to support the police over the community (Bolton 2003). Thus, the assumption is that they will work in favor of formal institutions of social control and to the detriment of the community. Prior research has both confirmed (Moskos 2008) and refuted (Weitzer 2005) the claim that African-American residents view African-American police officers as disloyal to the community. The common thread shared between African-American and lesbian/gay police officers is the less than ideal working environment than one would assume resulting from working with members of their own communities.

Despite negative perceptions of working within one's own community, officers reported a good working relationship with the non-gay community and with other people in law enforcement. In terms of better relationships in the non-gay community, respondents might be reacting to the conditions they experience when serving the larger LGBT community. In this case, the officers are from the community and have some—but less than average—level of separation between personal life and work life. Within the non-gay community, there is no level of extra support, empathy, or understanding expected. This environment also reduces the level of emotional dissonance that can result from the nature of the work and organizational expectations (Ashfort and Humphrey 1993). The space between the community and officers makes enforcing the law less of a personal action and more of a professional or work-related action. This more positive perspective may also come from less social interaction with members of non-gay communities when officers are not working. As one focus group member suggested, it not uncommon to be approached in a social setting—like a bar—by a lesbian or gay community member, and be presented with a police-related problem. Such an incident is less likely to occur outside of the LGBT community.

As well, officers report good relationships with coworkers, supervisors, and subordinates. The high level of agreement (70 %) for this perception suggests that work environment—in terms of interpersonal relationships—is satisfying for lesbian and gay officers. The data suggest a stronger affiliation to their identity as police officer than to their identity as a lesbian or gay person. Taken at face value, police acculturation appears to be a stronger influencing factor than other factors. This high level of agreement is in contrast to the perception of equal advancement opportunities. Here, just under 50 % of the respondents thought they have equal advancement opportunities. It is not exactly clear why promotional opportunities are perceived as less available. One theory is that out lesbian and gay police officers—like other minority officers—are usually assigned to areas that are not routes to promotion, for example, specialized units, like homicide or narcotics. In the case of women, they are 12 % of the uniformed workforce, but are over-represented in training and liaison positions (Colvin 2012). A similar phenomenon might be occurring with lesbian and gay officers. Instead of being assigned to prestigious units, they are recruited to serve in training, recruitment, liaison, and other "people-focused" (instead of crime-focused) units.

Most intriguing was the low level of agreement that lesbian and gay officers were more effective than non-gay officers in dealing with members of the gay community. A prima facia review of these data would suggest that this is counter to the idea of community policing. An essential component of this approach to policing assumes that officers from the community bring a unique perspective or cultural competence to the forces, and that this improves the ability of the force to meet its mission. However, a closer look at the focus group responses reveals important additional perspectives. The officers appear to draw a distinction with respect to the function of policing. The knowledge, skills, and abilities that an officer possesses are more important than her/his demographic background. Competent officers will be able to work with victims, suspects, and perpetrators regardless of sexual orientation, race, religion, or other factors. One officer suggested that shared demography might help, but that the skills of the police officer were more important. This notion harks back to the idea of being a police officer first, and everything else second. Scholars who have studied other minorities have discussed the socialization of police officers so that this identity supersedes others, like race or gender (Alex 1969; Bolton 2003; Essed 1991; McCluskey 2004), race *and* gender (Holder et al. 2000), and sexual orientation (Colvin 2009). The current data suggest that the majority of lesbian and gay officers responding did not find sexual orientation central to being a good police officer, even in the context of community policing within the LGBT community. This shared perception reinforces the feeling of good relationships with other members of the law enforcement community. If sexual orientation or other personal characteristics are not the driving measure for determining or assessing police competence, then we should not expect variations based on personal characteristics as related to police work.

Conclusion

This exploratory research examines data about community policing and the shared perceptions of lesbian and gay police officers. One of the core assumptions of community policing is that the representativeness of the police force in community policing would produce better interactions with and service to those communities. The survey data and focus group responses suggest that the situation is more complicated for minority officers from minority communities. This seems to be highlighted for lesbian and gay officers in smaller communities. In these situations, lesbian and gay officers are split between their identities as officers and as members of the community they serve. Additionally, members of the community may confuse their roles as liaison officers with their membership in the community. This suggests some limitations for community policing and the degree to which police officers can become integrated into local communities of which they are a part. The responses in the focus group support this idea, and suggest that effective policing can and should happen regardless of the personal demographics of the officer. While lesbian and gay officers endorsed the idea of competent police officers regardless of sexual orientation or these demographics, these officers should be competent in police practices as well as culturally competent to serve and support the diversity that exists in the entire community.

Acknowledgments I would like to acknowledge and thank the Gay Officers Action League (GOAL) and Law Enforcement Gays and Lesbians International (LEGAL) for providing access to officers at the annual conference, and to the three focus groups who met with me to discuss the lives of police officers.

References

Alpert, G. P., Flynn, D., & Piquero, A. R. (2001). Effective community policing performance measures. *Justice Research and Policy, 3*(2), 79–94.

Alex, N. (1969). *Black in blue: A study of the Negro policeman*. New York, NY: Appleton-Century Crofts.

Ashforth, B. E., & Humphrey, R. H. (1993). Emotional labor in service roles: The influence of identity. *Academy of Management Review, 18*(1), 88–115.

Bakker, A. B., & Heuven, E. (2006). Emotional dissonance, burnout, and in-role performance among nurses and police officers. *International Journal of Stress Management, 13*(4), 423.

Belkin, A., & McNichol, J. (2002). Pink and blue: Outcomes associated with the integration of open gay and lesbian personnel in the San Diego Police Department. *Police Quarterly, 5*(1), 63–95.

Bernstein, M., & Kostelac, C. (2002). Lavender and blue: Attitudes about homosexuality and behavior toward lesbians and gay men among police officers. *Journal of Contemporary Criminal Justice, 18*(3), 302–328.

Bolton, K, Jr. (2003). Shared perceptions: Black officers discuss continuing barriers in policing. *Policing: An International Journal of Police Strategies and Management, 26*(3), 386–399.

Bradbury, M. D. (2004). Un-packing the theory of representative bureaucracy. Retrieved May 1, 2013, from http://athenaeum.libs.uga.edu/handle/10724/7349

Buhrke, R. (1996). *A matter of justice: Lesbians and gay men in law enforcement*. New York, NY: Routledge Press.

Butler, E. A., Egloff, B., Wlhelm, F. H., Smith, N. C., Erickson, E. A., & Gross, J. J. (2003). The social consequences of expressive suppression. *Emotion, 3*(1), 48.

Colvin, R. (2009). Shared perceptions among lesbian and gay police officers: Barriers and opportunities in the law enforcement work environment. *Police Quarterly, 12*(1), 86–101.

Colvin, R. A. (2012). *Gay and lesbian cops: Diversity and effective policing*. Boulder, CO: Lynne Rienner Publishers.

Comstock, G. D. (1989). Victims of anti-gay/lesbian violence. *Journal of Interpersonal Violence, 4*(1), 101–106.

Davis, J. (1992, May). *Identifying acute post-traumatic stress disorder (PTSD) in disaster victims and emergency responders*. San Diego, CA: Disaster Management Training Seminar.

Diamond, D., & Weiss, D. M. (2009). *Advancing community policing through community governance: A framework document*. U.S. Department of Justice, Department of Community Oriented Policing Services.

Edgar, K., & Martin, C. (2004). *Perceptions of race and conflict: Perspectives of minority ethnic prisoners and of prison officers.* Home Office, Research, Development and Statistics Directorate.

Edgell, P., Gerteis, J., & Hartmann, D. (2006). Atheists as "other": Moral boundaries and cultural membership in American society. *American Sociological Review, 71*(2), 211–234.

El-Ghobashy, T. (2011). Minorities gain in NYPD ranks. *The Wall Street Journal.* Retrieved March 23, 2011 from http://online.wsj.com/article/SB1000142405274870441510457606302323002420.html

Essed, P. (1991). *Understanding everyday racism: An interdisciplinary theory.* Newbury, CA: Sage Publications.

Fielding, N., & Innes, M. (2006). Reassurance policing, community policing and measuring police performance. *Policing and Society, 16*(2), 127–145.

Fretz, B. R. (1975). Assessing attitudes towards sexual behaviors. *The Counseling Psychologist, 5*(1), 100–106.

Glomb, T. M., & Tews, M. J. (2004). Emotional labor: A conceptualization and scale development. *Journal of Vocational Behavior, 64*(1), 1–23.

Hassell, K. D., & Brandl, S. G. (2009). An examination of the workplace experiences of police patrol officers: The role of race, sex, and sexual orientation. *Police Quarterly, 12*(4), 408–430.

Herek, G. M. (1998). *Stigma and sexual orientation: Understanding prejudice against lesbians, gay men, and bisexuals.* Newbury, CA: Sage Publications.

Herek, G. M. (2000). The psychology of sexual prejudice. *Current Directions in Psychological Science, 9*(1), 19–22.

Herek, G. M. (2003). Evaluating interventions to alter sexual orientation: Methodological and ethical considerations. *Archives of Sexual Behavior, 32*(5), 438–439.

Herek, G. M. (2004). Beyond "homophobia": Thinking about sexual prejudice and stigma in the twenty-first century. *Sexuality Research and Social Policy, 1*(2), 6–24.

Herek, G. M. (2009). Sexual stigma and sexual prejudice in the United States: A conceptual framework. In D. A. Hope (Ed.), *Contemporary perspectives on lesbian, gay, and bisexual identities* (pp. 65–111). New York, NY: Springer.

Herek, G. M., Jobe, J. B., & Carney, R. M. (Eds.). (1996). *Out in force: Sexual orientation and the military.* Chicago, IL: University of Chicago Press.

Hochschild, A. R. (2003). *The managed heart: Commercialization of human feeling, with a new afterword.* Berkeley, CA: University of California Press.

Holder, K. A., Nee, C., & Ellis, T. (2000). Triple jeopardy: Black and Asian women police officers' experiences of discrimination. *International Journal of Police Science and Management, 3*(1), 68–87.

Jeromski, A. (2012). Yancey holds explosive hearing on lack of racial diversity in city of Boston departments; Few people of color in top spots. *Open Media Boston.* Retrieved May, 2012, from http://openmediaboston.org/node/2474

Kasdan, A. (2006). Increasing diversity in police departments: Strategies and tools for human rights commissions and others. *Human Rights Commissions and Criminal Justice.* Retrieved May 1, 2012, from http://www.hks.harvard.edu/var/ezp_site/storage/fckeditor/file/pdfs/centers-programs/programs/criminal-justice/ExecSessionHumanRights/increasing_police_diversity.pdf

Kerley, K. R., & Benson, M. L. (2000). Does community-oriented policing help build stronger communities? *Police Quarterly, 3*(1), 46–69.

Koegel, P. (1996). Lessons learned from the experience of domestic police and fire departments. In G. M. Herek, J. B. Jobe, & R. M. Carney (Eds.), *Out in force: Sexual orientation and the military* (pp. 157–176). Chicago, IL: University of Chicago Press.

Kruml, S. M., & Geddes, D. (2000). Exploring the dimensions of emotional labor: The heart of Hochschild's work. *Management Communication Quarterly, 14*(1), 8–49.

Kurki, L. (2000). Restorative and community justice in the United States. *Crime and Justice, 22*(1), 235–303.

Leinen, S. (2012). *Black police, white society.* New York, NY: NYU Press.

Leinen, S. H. (1993). *Gay cops*. New Brunswick, NJ: Rutgers University Press.

Lewis, G. (2006). *Who knows gay people and what impact does it have on attitudes toward homosexuality and gay rights*. Presentation at the annual meeting of the American Political Science Association, Philadelphia, PA.

Lombardo, R. M., Olson, D., & Staton, M. (2010). The Chicago Alternative Policing Strategy: A reassessment of the CAPS program. *Policing: An International Journal of Police Strategies and Management, 33*(4), 586–606.

Lord, V. B., & Friday, P. C. (2008). What really influences officer attitudes toward COP? The importance of context. *Police Quarterly, 11*(2), 220–238.

Lyons, P. M., DeValve, M. J., & Garner, R. L. (2008). Texas police chiefs' attitudes toward gay and lesbian police officers. *Police Quarterly, 11*(1), 102–117.

McCluskey, C. (2004). Diversity in policing. *Journal of Ethnicity in Criminal Justice, 2*(3), 67–81.

Miller, S. L., Forest, K. B., & Jurik, N. C. (2003). Diversity in blue: Lesbian and gay police officers in a masculine occupation. *Men and Masculinities, 5*(4), 355–385.

Mike, S., & Childs, P. (Eds.). (2002). *British cultural identities*. New York, NY: Routledge.

Mitchell, D. B. (1992). Contemporary police practices in domestic violence cases: Arresting the abuser: Is it enough? *The Journal of Criminal Law and Criminology, 83*(1), 241–249.

Moskos, P. (2008). *Cop in the Hood*. Princeton, NJ: Princeton University Press.

Myers, K. A., Forest, K. B., & Miller, S. L. (2004). Officer friendly and the tough cop: Gays and lesbians navigate homophobia and policing. *Journal of Homosexuality, 47*(1), 17–37.

Niederhoffer, A. (1967). *Behind the shield: The police in urban society* (pp. 103–151). New York, NY: Doubleday.

Richards, J. M., & Gross, J. J. (1999). Composure at any cost? The cognitive consequences of emotion suppression. *Personality and Social Psychology Bulletin, 25*(8), 1033–1044.

Richards, J. M., & Gross, J. J. (2000). Emotion regulation and memory: The cognitive costs of keeping one's cool. *Journal of Personality and Social Psychology, 79*(3), 410.

Rydberg, J., & Terrill, W. (2010). The effect of higher education on police behavior. *Police Quarterly, 13*(1), 92–120.

Scott, J. D., Duffee, D. E., & Renauer, B. C. (2003). Measuring police-community coproduction: The utility of community policing case studies. *Police Quarterly, 6*(4), 410–439.

Sege, A. (2012). Police to overhaul ranking system. *The Globe*. Retrieved on May 1, 2013, from http://www.boston.com/news/local/massachusetts/articles/2012/08/09/boston_police_department_planning_new_promotion_system_to_spur_diversity/

Sklansky, D. A. (2006). Not your father's police department: Making sense of the new demographics of law enforcement. *The Journal of Criminal Law and Criminology, 96*(3), 1209–1243.

Torres, M. S., & Stefkovich, J. A. (2009). Demographics and police involvement implications for student civil liberties and just leadership. *Educational Administration Quarterly, 45*(3), 450–473.

Trojanowicz, R. C., & Bucqueroux, B. (1990). *Community policing: A contemporary perspective*. Cincinnati, OH: Anderson Publishing Company.

U.S. Census Bureau. (2011). *2010 Census Data*. U.S. Census Bureau. Retrieved March 23, 2012 from http://2010.census.gov/2010census

U.S. Department of Justice. (2009). *Law Enforcement Recruitment Toolkit: COPS/IACP leadership project*. Retrieved May 1, 2013, from http://www.cops.usdoj.gov/pdf/vets-to-cops/e080921223-RecruitmentToolkit.pdf.

U.S. Department of Justice. (2010). *About Crime in the U.S. (CIUS)*. Retrieved July 1, 2012 from http://www.fbi.gov/ucr/cius2011/index.html

Weisburd, D., Greenspan, R., Hamilton, E. E., Bryant, K. A., & Williams, H. (2001). *The abuse of police authority: A national study of police officers' attitudes*. Washington, DC: Police Foundation.

Weitzer, R., & Tuch, S. A. (2005). Racially biased policing: Determinants of citizen perceptions. *Social Forces, 83*(3), 1009–1030.

White, R. D., & Perrone, S. (2005). *Crime and social control: An introduction.* Australia and New Zealand: Oxford University Press.

Williams, M. L., & Robinson, A. L. (2004). Problems and prospects with policing the lesbian, gay and bisexual community in Wales. *Policing and Society, 14*(3), 213–232.

Wilson, J., Dalton, E., Scheer, C. & Grammich, C. A. (2009). *Police recruitment and retention for the new millennium: The state of knowledge.* Center on Quality Policing, RAND: CA. Retrieved on May 1, 2013, from http://cops.usdoj.gov/Publications/101027321_Police-RecruitmentRetention.pdf

Zapf, D. (2002). Emotion work and psychological well-being: A review of the literature and some conceptual considerations. *Human Resource Management Review, 12*, 237–268.

Chapter 11
Lesbian, Gay, and Bisexual Youth Incarcerated in Delinquent Facilities

Joanne Belknap, Kristi Holsinger and Jani S. Little

Abstract The incarcerated population of both youth and adults has long been characterized as disproportionately male, of color, and poor, compared to their numbers in the community (non-incarcerated individuals). When sexual minority status (SMS) or sexual identity has been addressed, it has typically been to sensationalize, demonize, and pathologize incarcerated SMS youth and adults. Our research is the only existing study, of which we are aware, that documents the representation of SMS youth among incarcerated youth. In this state-wide study of 404 girls and boys incarcerated in Ohio, we found it significant that SMS incarcerated youth tended to want more treatment/counseling than their non-SMS counterparts, particularly sexual and physical abuse counseling. There were far fewer differences in these youth based on SMS in terms of their desires for programs that were not treatment/counseling, and in all of these cases, the non-SMS youth wanted the programs more than the SMS youth. The findings stress the need to acknowledge incarcerated youths' needs that may be accentuated by SMS.

Keywords Lesbian · Gay · Bisexual · Sexual identity · Sexual minority status (SMS) · Juveniles · Delinquents · Incarcerated · Labeling theory · General strain theory · Counseling

J. Belknap (✉)
Sociology Department, University of Colorado, 327 UCB, Boulder, CO 80309-0327, USA
e-mail: Joanne.Belknap@colorado.edu

K. Holsinger
Department of Criminal Justice and Criminology, University of Missouri–Kansas City, 5215 Rockhill Road, Kansas City, MO 64110-2499, USA
e-mail: holsingerk@umkc.edu

J. S. Little
Computer and Research Services Director Institute of Behavioral Science, University of Colorado, 483 UCB, Boulder, CO 80309-0483, USA
e-mail: Jani.Little@colorado.edu

D. Peterson and V. R. Panfil (eds.), *Handbook of LGBT Communities, Crime, and Justice*, DOI: 10.1007/978-1-4614-9188-0_11,
© Springer Science+Business Media New York 2014

Introduction

In the mid-1990s, the first two authors conducted qualitative focus groups across Ohio with incarcerated girls. The focus group study was funded by monies distributed from the U.S. *Office of Juvenile Justice and Delinquency Prevention* (OJJDP) to the Columbus, Ohio *Office of Criminal Justice Services* (OCJS) to identify what was then referred to as the "gender-specific needs" of delinquent girls. The focus group study resulted in two publications (Belknap et al. 1997; Belknap and Holsinger 1997), and also laid the groundwork for a subsequent large, state-wide, anonymous, quantitative survey of girls and boys incarcerated in Ohio to identify "gender-specific needs." This large study that included boys as well as girls was also funded by OJJDP monies distributed through OCJS and resulted in numerous publications (Belknap and Holsinger 2006; Belknap et al. 2012; Holsinger 2003; Holsinger and Holsinger 2005).

A major part of both our qualitative focus group and quantitative survey studies was to examine prior trauma and abuse as potential pathways to offending or being labeled offenders. Research at that time, and far more since,[1] identified prior trauma as a risk factor for subsequent offending (e.g., Arnold 1990; Dodge et al. 1990; Gilfus 1993; Widom 1989). We[2] also wanted to identify the incarcerated youths' self-reported needs regarding what would help them while they were incarcerated. While we were conducting the focus group research with the girls in the mid-1990s, we were struck with comments made by a couple of the staff members, about the incarcerated girls "who think they are lesbians but aren't." When we asked why they thought this, they said that when girls are incarcerated and away from boys they wrongly start thinking they are lesbians. We found it curious that it did not seem to occur to those staff members that the girls might actually be lesbians and that (even if the girls were not lesbians) staff were communicating to the girls, through their comments, that being a lesbian was wrong. We began to wonder about the presence, histories, and current institutional experiences of the sexual minority status (SMS) youth incarcerated in these institutions. Therefore, in addition to extensive survey items designed to address both trauma/victimization and offending histories of these youth so that we could make sex comparisons, we added an item to measure SMS, to make comparisons between SMS and non-SMS ("straight" or "heterosexual" youth). To our surprise, the extensive trauma/victimization items (including sexual, physical, and emotional/psychological child abuses) were not a concern of the Internal Review Boards for either our university or the state Department of Youth Services, but both were very resistant to us collecting SMS data in this anonymous survey of

---

[1] Belknap and Holsinger (2006); Gaarder and Belknap (2002); McDaniels-Wilson and Belknap (2008).

[2] The "we" in the history and method used in the study refers to the first two authors (Joanne Belknap and Kristi Holsinger). Since designing the study, and collecting and entering the data, we began to work with the third author (Jani Little).

incarcerated youth. After a significant amount of negotiation with both of these review boards indicating that we believed these youth likely had unique histories and needs, we were finally given approval to measure SMS simply as: "I would describe my sexual orientation as: (1) heterosexual/straight, (2) homosexual/gay/lesbian, or (3) bisexual." Thus, a limitation of our study is that we do not have information regarding transgender youth or other SMS youth whose identities may not fit within the three category item we used on the survey.

A Review of the Literature

Historically, the most common research on SMS and offending narrowly focused on the deviant nature of SMS, including seemingly voyeuristic examinations of the sexual behaviors amongst incarcerated women and girls (e.g., Giallombardo 1966; Ward and Kassebaum 1965; and see Hensley et al. 2002, for a review of these homophobic and racist accounts of incarcerated girls' SMS from 1913 to 1951). Although some scholars have suggested that lesbians may be more likely than straight women/girls and gay men/boys (with other characteristics held constant) to be labeled and detained as criminal or delinquent, this research is more anecdotal than empirical (Faith 1993; Fishbein 2000; Rafter and Stanko 1982; Robson 1992). The handful of studies that are an exception to this are summarized at the end of this literature review section.

Two theories are useful to guide the research on how youths' SMS might be related to their offending. First, *general strain theory* purports to examine how racism, sexism, and classism can be risks for youthful offending (e.g., Agnew 1985, 1992; Broidy 2001; Broidy and Agnew 1997), and hypothesizes that whether individual youth respond to strains by offending depends on their self-esteem, support systems, and personalities (Agnew 1992). Second, *labeling theory* is related to Schur's (1984) suggestion that being treated as a "deviant" may be more related to what "kind of person" someone is than her or his actual behavior. More specifically, labeling theory is concerned with both risk factors for being labeled delinquent/criminal and the effects of being labeled delinquent/criminal (e.g., Becker 1963; Erikson 1962; Kitsuse 1962; Lemert 1951). Stated alternatively, labeling theory posits that all else equal, youth marginalized by their race and/or class are more likely to be identified (labeled) as delinquents than their White and wealthier peers. Furthermore, discriminatory labeling has an added impact in that once labeled "delinquent" or "offender," it is difficult to lose this label, and it can become a self-fulfilling label. For example, a youth wrongly arrested, charged or convicted of a crime s/he did not do, may decide "I'm already being treated as a delinquent, so I might as well be one."

Although far too infrequently recognized, Suzanne Pharr's 1988 book *Homophobia: A Weapon of Sexism* (republished in 1997) should be considered a classic in identifying the strain of growing up gay, lesbian, or bisexual. Since *Homophobia* was first published, many others have documented the serious harm that homophobia and heterosexism can have on SMS youth (e.g., Bontempo and D'Augelli 2002; D'Augelli 2002; D'Augelli and Patterson 1995; DuRant et al. 1998; Huebner et al. 2004; Hunter 1990; Pilkington and D'Augelli 1995). A considerable amount of research indicates that compared to their non-SMS counterparts, SMS youth are at significantly greater risk of non-sexual physical attacks (e.g., Corliss et al. 2009; D'Augelli 2002; D'Augelli and Patterson 1995; Grossman et al. 2006; Huebner et al. 2004; Hunter 1990; Saewyc et al. 1998; Walls et al. 2010), verbal/emotional abuse or harassment (e.g., Corliss et al. 2009; D'Augelli and Patterson 1995; Huebner et al. 2004; Pilkington and D'Augelli 1995), and sexual abuse (e.g., Corliss et al. 2009; Finlinson et al. 2008; Fishbein 2000; Garofalo et al. 2006; Grossman et al. 2006; Pathela and Schillinger 2010; Saewyc et al. 1998), and these abuses are typically attributed to their SMS identity. In addition to abuse victimization, and likely related to these abuse traumas, SMS youth are more at risk than non-SMS youth for drug and alcohol (ab)use (e.g., Birkett et al. 2009; Russell and Joyner 2001; Salomonsen-Sautel et al. 2008; Walls et al. 2010); running away and homelessness (e.g., Garofalo et al. 2006; Nesmith 2006; Salomonsen-Sautel et al. 2008, Walls et al. 2010); and poorer mental health/ depression (e.g., Birkett et al. 2009; D'Augelli 2002; Russell and Joyner 2001; Salomonsen-Sautel et al. 2008; Walls et al. 2009, 2010). SMS youths' more-compromised mental health and depression is further supported by research findings that, relative to their non-SMS peers, SMS are more likely to report suicidal thoughts, plans, and attempts (e.g., Balsam et al. 2005; Birkett et al. 2009; Bontempo and D'Augelli 2002; Corliss et al. 2009; D'Augelli 2002; McDaniel et al. 2001; Russell 2003; Russell and Joyner 2001; Thompson and Light 2011; Walls et al. 2009) and additional self-harming behaviors, such as "cutting" and other self-mutilation (e.g., Alexander and Clare 2004; Balsam et al. 2005; Corliss et al. 2009; Scourfield et al. 2008; Walls et al. 2010). Notably, Corliss and her colleagues' (2009) large study on adult SMS women's self-reports of their childhood maltreatment and youthful suicide attempts found that the younger she was when she identified as SMS, the more likely the (then) girl was to both be abused as a child and to attempt suicide.

Reports on the higher suicide ideation, attempts, and completion of SMS relative to straight youth has encountered some controversy (e.g., Anhalt and Morris 1998; Cover 2005; Savin-Williams 2001a, b), with criticisms about excessive portrayals of SMS youth as depressed and suicidal. However, an extensive review concludes that "numerous studies spanning the past quarter century have used varied designs and methods in multiple settings and have consistently demonstrated that sexual minority youth are among those most likely to report suicidality (suicidal thoughts, plans, and attempts)" (Russell 2003, p. 1241). However, a small qualitative study of SMS youth argues that current-day SMS youth have more positive experiences in coming out, with more non-gay peer networks (Eccles et al. 2003). This study suggests that SMS youths' experiences around coming out and their SMS identities have likely improved significantly in more recent years, where SMS is becoming far more accepted. For example, many states in the U.S. have passed same-sex marriage rights and President Barack Obama is the first U.S. president to advocate for the legalization of same-sex marriages nationwide. However, this does not mean that bigotry and discrimination against SMS youth and adults has stopped, just as racism did not end with the passage of civil rights legislation.

To date, both general strain and labeling theories have focused almost exclusively on race, class, and gender as potential strains and labels, respectively, and virtually ignored SMS as a potential strain for delinquency or a potential risk for being labeled "delinquent." It is certainly possible, perhaps likely, that sexual minority youth are responded to differently by the criminal legal system (e.g., police and courts) than their non-SMS (straight) counterparts. Additionally, it is possible that SMS may be gendered and raced in terms of strains for delinquency and responses by the criminal legal system (i.e., labeling). For example, SMS youth may be more likely than straight youth to "do gender" in a way that is contrary to their biological sex (see Striepe and Tolman 2003). Given that offending is associated with masculinity, if girls' SMS includes a greater likelihood of "doing gender" in a way that is perceived as more "masculine," then it is quite possible that SMS girls are viewed/labeled as more delinquent than straight girls for the same behaviors. Simultaneously, the opposite may hold true for boys: If SMS boys are perceived as less masculine than non-SMS boys, and/or have a greater propensity of "doing gender" in a way that is perceived as more feminine, they may be less likely than non-SMS boys to be viewed as offenders (see also Panfil, this volume; but see Dennis, this volume, for historical portrayals in film and TV of effeminate men as criminal). Research also reports differential criminal legal responses to youth depending on their sex and race (e.g., Chauhan et al. 2010; Leiber 1994), indicating that an examination of SMS as a potential strain or label must account for how sexual identity intersects with sex (and sexism) and race (and racism).

The limited research on SMS and offending is primarily about drug and alcohol use. Notably, in GST, Agnew (1992) identified drug use and other offenses as a way to cope with the bad feelings resulting from strains. The research on drug/alcohol use by SMS individuals consistently reports overall higher rates among these youth than their straight counterparts (Garofalo et al. 2006; Rostosky et al. 2003; Wilsnack et al. 2008). One study found that bisexual youth are more likely to report substance use and substance abuse than straight or gay/lesbian youth (Russell et al. 2002).

A 2006 study of male-to-female transgender youth found that many had turned to sex work (prostitution, stripping, dancing) in attempts to gain financial stability or even food, but this placed them at a high risk of arrest and incarceration. In that study, 67 % of these transgender youth had a history of arrest and 37 % had a history of incarceration (Garofalo et al. 2006). Himmelstein and Brückner's (2011) recent analysis of the 1994–1995 National Longitudinal Study of Adolescent Health data examined how SMS was related to the following sanctions: being expelled from school, stopped by the police, arrested as a juvenile or adult, and convicted or plead guilty in juvenile or adult court. They found a trend for youth who had an attraction to or relationship with a same-sex peer to disproportionately report all of the sanctions except school expulsion and adult arrest, and this trend was stronger for SMS girls/young women than SMS boys/young men (Himmelstein and Brückner 2011).

Method for Our Study

The current study was based on a 15-page anonymous self-report survey, designed by the first two authors and distributed in 1998 and 1999 to youth incarcerated in Ohio's twelve Department of Youth Services' (DYS) delinquent institutions. Unlike existing surveys of delinquent youth, we included a measure of SMS: "I would describe my sexual orientation as: (1) heterosexual/straight, (2) homosexual/gay/lesbian, or (3) bisexual." In addition, the survey collected data on other demographic measures (e.g., race, education, sex), victimization/trauma, family, education, self-esteem, mental health, personalities and attitudes, and offending (including drug and alcohol use) histories. All 163 of the girls incarcerated at Scioto Village and Freedom Center (the two residential correctional facilities for girls in the state) were included, as well as a random sample of 350 of the approximately 850 boys incarcerated in the ten DYS facilities across the state. The youth were brought to large rooms by DYS staff where the research staff explained the study, and emphasized that participation was voluntary, no identifiers would be on the surveys, only research staff had access to surveys, and the surveys would be stored and findings written in a manner to maintain participants' anonymity. All 163 girls participated in the study and completed usable surveys. Of the 350 boys, 290 were given the opportunity to take part in the study (60 were excluded due to being ill or in trouble, and we were not allowed to re-contact them), 281 participated in the study, and of these, 241 surveys were usable. However, of the completed surveys, 11 girls and 29 boys did not answer the SMS item. Thus, of the 163 girls in the facilities (all of whom were sampled), 93.3 % ($n = 152$) had usable surveys with SMS data; and 252 boys returned completed surveys with SMS data, representing 29.6 % of the roughly 850 boys incarcerated in Ohio DYS and 86.9 % of the 290 incarcerated boys who had the opportunity to take part in the study. This chapter, then, is based on 404 (152 girls' and 252 boys') surveys of youth incarcerated in Ohio. (For a more detailed account of the data sampling and collection refer to Belknap and Holsinger 2006, and Belknap et al. 2012). In a previous publication (Belknap et al. 2012), we reported that among the incarcerated African American youth, girls (14 %) and boys (12 %) were equally likely to skip (not answer) the SMS item, but that among the incarcerated White youth, boys (10 %) appeared more likely than girls (4 %) to skip this item. However, *all* of the American Indian and bi- and multi-racial youth, regardless of sex, answered the SMS item, perhaps because there is less stigma for SMS among American Indians, and perhaps because bi- and multi-racial youth are already "border crossing" in living with their multiple racial identities (see Anzaldúa 2007).

In our previous publication on SMS and these incarcerated youth, we focused on whether SMS was related to the youths' abuse histories, family experiences, school experiences, mental health, attitudes, personality, self-esteem, parenting, and substance use (Belknap et al. 2012). After summarizing our previous findings on the representation of SMS and victimization self-harming self-reports (Belknap et al. 2012), we will focus on the quantitative survey findings, heretofore unpublished, regarding the SMS youths' wishes for programs, education, and services/treatment compared to the non-SMS youths' program wishes, among these incarcerated youth. Finally, we will report some of the comments the youth wrote on the open-ended parts of our survey that are related to SMS.

Regarding the new findings described in this chapter, toward the end of the survey, youth were presented with 18 possible treatment/services, programs/training, and education options. For each option, participants were asked whether they had already participated or were currently participating in the program (received), had not participated in the program but would like to (desired), or had not participated and had no desire to participate in that program. For the purposes of this chapter, the 18 options, listed in Fig. 11.1, were divided into treatment/counseling (more psychological/mental health in nature and reported in Table 11.2) and programs (e.g., training, skill-building, reported in Table 11.3). Finally, we wanted to determine how SMS impacted the incarcerated youths' service and programs options when controlling for sex and race/ethnicity. Table 11.4 reports these findings using logistic regression, where we made the service/program options dichotomous (instead of three categories). Specifically, if youth reported either that s/he received or desired a service/program, these were recoded as yes (1), and if youth reported not receiving and having no interest in a program, these were recoded as no (0).

Findings from Our Study on Incarcerated Ohio Youth

Summary of Previously-Reported Findings on SMS Youth in Our Study

Before we report the findings comparing SMS and non-SMS incarcerated youths' desired programs, treatment and education, it is useful to recap what we found in our prior research on these data concerning the representation of SMS youth among an incarcerated population, and how this representation is gendered and raced (from Belknap et al. 2012). Furthermore, our prior article found that, consistent with community (non-incarcerated) youth, the SMS youths in our study were significantly more likely to report both abuse victimizations and self-harming behaviors than their non-SMS counterparts (Belknap et al. 2012).

First, Table 11.1 and Figs. 11.2 and 11.3 include the representation of SMS youth in this sample of incarcerated youth (from findings reported in Belknap et al. 2012).

Fig. 11.1 Survey options for received and desired treatment and programs

A. Treatment/Counseling

1. Drug and alcohol treatment

2. Sex offender treatment

3. Sexual abuse counseling

4. Physical abuse counseling

5. Emotional abuse counseling

6. Family counseling

7. Individual counseling

8. Depression/mental health problem services

B. Programs/Training

1. Problem-solving skills training

2. Anger management training

3. Independent living class

4. Parenting class

5. "learning to have good relationships" class

6. Job/career skills

7. Sports/health/fitness training

8. Learning to be a better student

9. Sex education

10. General health education

In this entire sample 2.7 % identified as lesbian or gay and 10.6 % identified as bisexual. Girls (4.6 %) were almost three times as likely as boys (1.6 %) to identify as lesbian/gay, and girls (22.4 %) were more than six times as likely as boys (3.6 %) to identify as bisexual. When combining lesbian/gay with bisexual to create an SMS variable, 13.4 % of the entire sample was SMS (lesbian, gay, or bisexual). Girls (27.0 %) were over five times as likely as boys (5.2 %) to report an SMS (lesbian, gay, or bisexual). Notably, these incarcerated boys' self-report SMS rates (5.2 %) are similar to community (non-incarcerated) boys' self-reported SMS: In Himmelstein and Brückner's (2011) community sample, 5.6 % of boys reported an SMS and in

Table 11.1 Incarcerated youth's self-reported sexual identity by sex/gender and race[a]

	N	Lesbian/Gay		Bisexual		Non-SMS		χ^2
		%	(n)	%	(n)	%	(n)	
Total	404	2.7	(11)	10.6	(43)	86.6	(350)	
Girls		4.6	(7)	22.4	(34)	73.0	(111)	
Boys		1.6	(4)	3.6	(9)	94.8	(239)	39.85*

		Sexual minority status (Lesbian/Gay/Bisexual)		Non-SMS (Straight)		χ^2
	N	%	(n)	%	(n)	
Total	404	13.4	(54)	86.6	(350)	
Girls		27.0	(41)	73.0	(111)	
Boys		5.2	(13)	94.8	(239)	38.97*
Total	401					
Girls of color[b]		32.5	(25)	67.5	(52)	
White girls		21.3	(16)	78.7	(59)	
Boys of color[c]		4.3	(6)	95.7	(132)	
White boys		6.3	(7)	93.7	(104)	42.57*

[a] This table is reproduced verbatim from Belknap et al. (2012, p. 175)
[b] 51 of the girls were African American, 16 biracial, 2 Native American, 1 Latina, and 7 "other"
[c] 107 of the boys were African American, 15 biracial, 8 Native American, 5 Latino, and 3 "other"
* $p \leq .001$

Pathela and Schillinger's (2010) community sample, 6.9 % of boys reported SMS. However, the 27 % of girls in our incarcerated sample reporting an SMS is about twice what these same studies found for girls in the community, at 14.5 % in Himmelstein and Brückner's (2011) study and 11.9 % in Pathela and Schillinger's (2010) study. Thus, our findings indicate that SMS boys are similarly represented in juvenile incarceration facilities as they are in the community, but SMS girls are far more at risk than non-SMS girls of being offenders, consistent with *general strain theory*, or being labeled offenders, consistent with *labeling theory*. Of course, it is difficult for our data to answer which of these are at play or if both are, and if so, to what degree. Perhaps the sex differences in SMS identities in our study could be influenced by what was found in a prior study by Savin-Williams and Diamond (2000): compared to girls/young women, boys/young men tend to have an earlier onset of same-sex attraction, self-labeling and sexual behaviors, but a later onset of disclosure to others, although the gap between attraction and first disclosure averaged 10 years for both sexes. Moreover, the girls/young women were more likely to label themselves as sexual minorities prior to same-sex sexual contact, whereas the boys/young men were more likely to engage in sexual behavior prior to self-assigning a sexual minority label (Savin-Williams and Diamond 2000).

Our data also indicate significant sex and race/ethnicity intersections regarding incarcerated youths' SMS (see Table 11.1 and Fig. 11.3). Almost a third of the girls of color (32.5 %) report an SMS, while about a fifth (21.3 %) of the White girls do. About 6 % of White boys and 4 % of boys of color report an SMS. Again,

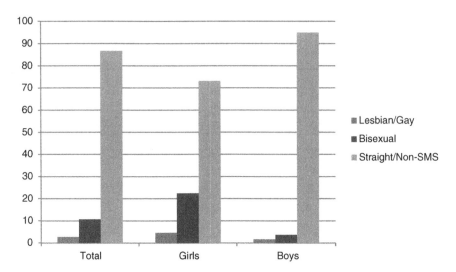

Fig. 11.2 Incarcerated youths' self-reported sexual identities

it is not clear if girls of color who are also SMS experience even more strain and/or even more offender labeling than White SMS girls, and far more than SMS White boys and SMS boys of color. However, these sex and race differences might be explained at least in part by some previous research. Specifically, one study found that while internalized homophobia and rates of same-sex involvement did not differ across racial groups for boys, Latinos reported earlier awareness of same-sex attraction than boys from other race/ethnic groups, and African Americans were more likely to engage in same-sex sex first, and later accept the label (Dubé and Savin-Williams 1999); as well, African American boys had lower rates of disclosure than boys of other race/ethnic backgrounds.

Although we do not reproduce here any of the data from our previous publication regarding incarcerated youth, SMS, and self-harming and abuse victimization, these findings are also worth summarizing. Given that so few boys in our incarcerated sample reported an SMS identity, our data on self-harming and victimization were restricted to the girls. Notably, in our data of incarcerated youth, unlike most of the previous research on community samples, self-esteem, substance abuse, antisocial attitudes, and educational experiences did not differ among the SMS and non-SMS youth (Belknap et al. 2012). Consistent with prior research, we found the SMS girls, relative to the non-SMS girls, reported more victimizations and self-harming (a scale made of summing suicide attempts, self-injury, etc.). However, to our knowledge we are the first researchers of community or incarcerated samples who examined whether the SMS youths' (girls in our study) increased self-harming was mediated by their elevated abuse victimization. Indeed, once we controlled for the girls' victimizations, there was no longer a relationship between SMS and self-harming. Stated alternatively, among this incarcerated sample, the SMS girls' (relative to non-SMS girls') self-harming is

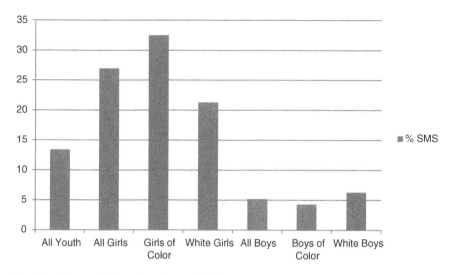

Fig. 11.3 Percent SMS × Sex × Race/Ethnicity

likely a result of their increased likelihood of abuse victimization (relative to the non-SMS girls) (see Belknap et al. 2012).

Current Analyses Regarding SMS Youth and Programming

For this chapter, we extend our previous analyses to examine programming desired and received by our incarcerated youth sample. Given the more problematic experiences reported by the SMS youth among our incarcerated sample, it was hypothesized that these experiences would lead to significant differences in programs received and requested. In particular, given SMS youths' increased risk of victimization, we expect a greater desire for more counseling and psychological treatment. For five of the of the eight treatment/counseling options, there were significant differences based on SMS (see Table 11.2), and as expected, in all cases the SMS youth were more likely to want these programs. The biggest differences were for sexual abuse and physical abuse treatment/counseling. Although SMS and non-SMS youth were equally likely to report having received these (5–7 %), SMS youth were more than twice as likely as non-SMS youth to report desiring these treatments/counseling. The next biggest difference in the treatment/counseling requests was family counseling, again with SMS more likely to want this type of counseling. Finally, regarding treatment/counseling, SMS youth were far more likely to want both individual and depression (or other mental health) counseling than their non-SMS counterparts, and far less likely to say they had not had these and did not want them (see Table 11.2). Surprisingly, there were no significant differences based on SMS regarding the youths' emotional abuse counseling requests. There were also no significant differences for either sex offender treatment or drug/alcohol treatment.

Table 11.3 reports the relationships between SMS and 10 programs (as opposed to treatment/counseling), and only three of these varied significantly by SMS. The largest difference among these was for parenting programs, with non-SMS youth far more likely to desire these programs than SMS youth, and non-SMS youth far less likely than SMS youth to report that they have not had and do not want parenting programs. The other two programs that reached significance were independent living and job/career skills training. Regarding the independent living program, the distinction between the SMS and non-SMS youth is explained by the fact that all 37 youth who received this program were non-SMS.[3] It is not clear why only non-SMS youth had participated in the independent living program. It appears that the non-SMS youth were more likely than the SMS youth to receive the job/career skills programs, and the SMS youth were more likely than the non-SMS youth to report that they had not had and did not want these programs (see Table 11.3). Notably, there were no significant differences in terms of SMS regarding these incarcerated youths' reports on wanting and having problem-solving skills, anger management, good relationships, sports/health/fitness, sex education, and general health education training or programs.

In our efforts to determine whether SMS differentiated incarcerated youths' reports on receiving/wanting versus not receiving/not wanting participation in the 18 treatment and program options, we ran logistic regression models controlling for SMS, sex, and race/ethnicity. Table 11.4 reports the programs where SMS remained significant while controlling for both sex and race/ethnicity. Again, the largest differences were for sexual abuse and physical abuse counseling. Notably, although SMS youth were more likely to report receiving or desiring these services than their non-SMS counterparts, sex had an even stronger impact than SMS (girls were more likely than boys to receive/desire sexual and physical abuse counseling), and race/ethnicity was not related to either sexual or physical abuse counseling requests. SMS remained a significant predictor when controlling for sex and race/ethnicity in two of the three programs that had significant differences based on SMS, as reported in Table 11.3. More specifically, as shown in Table 11.4, non-SMS youth were more likely than their SMS counterparts to want parenting skills programs and job/career skills programs. For both of these programs, neither sex nor race/ethnicity predicted the youths' requests.[4]

---

[3] When Chi square analysis combined "received and/or desired" versus "has not had and does not want" (making "Independent Living Program" a dichotomous variable, as was done for the multivariable analyses in Table 11.4), SMS no longer significantly distinguished the differences for having or desiring an independent living program (58.5 % of SMS youth and 67.8 % of non-SMS youth had or desired independent living, $X^2 = 1.76$, p = .12).

[4] As stated in footnote 3, the relationship between SMS and "Independent Living" disappeared when taking account for the fact that all 37 youth who received this program were non-SMS. Thus, as expected, SMS was not related to "Independent Living" received or desired in the logistic regression analysis conducted for Table 11.4.

Table 11.2 Incarcerated girls' and boys' reported received and desired treatment and counseling by sexual minority status (SMS) ($N = 404$)

Treatment or counseling options	N	Received		Desired		Has not had and does not want		X^2
		%	(n)	%	(n)	%	(n)	
Drug/alcohol treatment	388							1.63
SMS		26.4	(14)	41.5	(42)	32.1	(17)	
Non-SMS		27.2	(91)	33.1	(111)	39.7	(133)	
Sex offender treatment	385							1.52[a]
SMS		11.3	6	17.0	9	71.7	38	
Non-SMS		8.1	27	12.7	42	79.2	263	
Sexual abuse counseling	386							17.34***[a]
SMS		7.5	4	39.6	21	52.8	28	
Non-SMS		6.3	21	15.9	53	77.8	259	
Physical abuse counseling	386							16.03***[a]
SMS		5.7	17	41.5	22	52.8	28	
Non-SMS		5.1	17	17.7	59	77.2	257	
Emotional abuse counseling	386							1.98[a]
SMS		3.8	2	35.8	19	60.4	32	
Non-SMS		6.6	22	27.3	91	66.1	220	
Family counseling	388							9.43**
SMS		9.4	5	52.8	28	37.7	20	
Non-SMS		12.2	41	31.3	105	56.4	189	
Individual counseling	387							7.06*
SMS		15.1	8	54.7	29	30.2	16	
Non-SMS		21.0	70	35.6	119	43.4	145	
Depression/other psych.	385							6.07*
SMS		11.3	6	43.4	23	45.3	24	
Non-SMS		9.9	33	27.7	92	62.3	207	

[a] One cell had an expected frequency of <5
* $p \leq .05$
** $p \leq .01$
*** $p \leq .001$

Finally, on this largely quantitative survey, there were two brief open-ended questions allowing qualitative responses. One question was "What would you change about [the name of the facility where they were incarcerated]?" and the other was "Is there anything else you'd like to report?" Among these two open-ended items in the 404 surveys, six youth raised SMS issues: three comments were from SMS youth and three from non-SMS youth. More specifically, regarding the former question, one non-SMS, 15-year-old African American girl wrote "gay girls out of here," and one 18-year-old SMS White boy wrote "gay support group." In response to the "anything else?" question, two non-SMS 15-year-old White girls wrote "everyone's gay," and two SMS White boys (one 17 and one 18 years old) wrote that there was "discrimination against gays" in the institution. Notably, all of three of the SMS youth writing about the need for a support group/the problem of discrimination against gays in the institution were (White) boys; and all of the

Table 11.3 Incarcerated girls' and boys' reported received and desired programs by sexual minority status (SMS) ($N = 404$)

Program options	N	Received		Desired		Has not had and does not want		X^2
		%	(n)	%	(n)	%	(n)	
Problem-solving skills training	389							2.06
SMS		7.5	4	52.8	28	39.6	21	
Non-SMS		13.7	46	44.6	150	41.7	140	
Anger management training	388							1.04
SMS		13.2	7	52.8	28	34.0	18	
Non-SMS		16.1	54	45.4	152	38.5	129	
Independent living program	391							7.00*[a]
SMS		0.0	0	58.5	31	41.5	22	
Non-SMS		10.9	37	56.8	192	32.2	109	
Parenting program	391							10.76**[b]
SMS		3.8	2	30.2	16	66.0	35	
Non-SMS		6.5	22	51.5	174	42.0	142	
Good relationships program	390							2.01[b]
SMS		5.7	3	66.0	35	28.3	15	
Non-SMS		8.3	28	55.8	188	35.9	121	
Job/career skills training	390							6.68**[b]
SMS		1.9	1	62.3	33	35.8	19	
Non-SMS		10.4	35	66.5	224	23.1	78	
Sports, health, fitness	391							0.02[b]
SMS		7.5	4	62.3	33	30.2	16	
Non-SMS		7.7	26	63.0	213	29.3	99	
Better student training	393							1.68[b]
SMS		3.8	2	50.9	27	45.3	24	
Non-SMS		7.1	24	55.6	189	37.4	127	
Sex education	387							0.42
SMS		18.9	10	34.0	18	47.2	25	
Non-SMS		22.8	176	33.2	111	44.0	147	
General health education	383							0.28[b]
SMS		7.7	4	46.2	24	46.2	24	
Non-SMS		9.7	32	43.2	143	47.1	156	

[a] This finding should be interpreted with caution as the significance difference between SMS and non-SMS youth disappeared when combining the "received" and "desired" into one group. We have no explanation for why all of the youth who received the Independent Living program were non-SMS youth

[b] One cell had an expected frequency of < 5

* $p \leq .05$

** $p \leq .01$

*** $p \leq .001$

anti-gay responses were written by non-SMS girls (2 White and 1 Black), indicating non-SMS girls' fear/hatred of the prevalence of SMS girls in their institution. Although these qualitative responses are from a very small handful of the surveyed

Table 11.4 Logistic regressions: Incarcerated youths' received or desired treatment and programs related to SMS when controlling for sex and race/ethnicity[a] ($N = 404$)

	N	β	Wald	Odds Ratio	Model χ^{2a}	Nagelkerke R^2
Sexual abuse counseling	383				38.93	0.14
Sexual identity (LGB = 1)		0.700	4.574*	2.014		
Sex (Girl = 1)		1.209	22.237***	3.351		
Race/Ethnicity (White = 1)		0.397	2.561	1.487		
Physical abuse counseling	383				29.22	0.11
Sexual identity (LGB = 1)		0.743	5.248*	2.102		
Sex (Girl = 1)		0.957	14.488***	2.604		
Race/Ethnicity (White = 1)		0.333	1.866	1.395		
Depression/mental health counseling	343				19.25	0.08
Sexual identity (LGB = 1)		0.338	0.980	1.402		
Sex (Girl = 1)		0.916	13.459***	2.499		
Race/Ethnicity (White = 1)		−0.129	0.296	0.879		
Parenting skills	388				17.63	0.06
Sexual identity (LGB = 1)		−0.862	6.951**	0.422		
Sex (Girl = 1)		−0.376	2.833	0.687		
Race/Ethnicity (White = 1)		−0.396	3.583[b]	0.673		
Job/career skills	387				5.29	0.02
Sexual identity (LGB = 1)		−0.704	4.372*	0.494		
Sex (Girl = 1)		0.148	0.325	1.159		
Race/ethnicity (White = 1)		−0.266	1.254	0.766		

[a] Three binary independent variables were listed in each abuse model: sexual identity, sex, race/ethnicity. There were 3 degrees of freedom in each model. The individual treatment and program options were coded as 0 = "had not had and did not want" and 1 = "had received or wanted to receive (desired without receiving)"
[b] This relationship approached significance: $p = 0.058$
* $p \leq .05$
** $p \leq .01$
*** $p \leq .001$

youth, the patterns seem important. First, these data suggest an increased level of isolation experienced by incarcerated SMS boys relative to incarcerated SMS girls. Second, among these incarcerated youth, non-SMS girls were the only ones to raise homophobic concerns in the surveys. Our data cannot answer whether this second point is due to the sizable representation (27.0 %) of SMS youth among the incarcerated girls relative to the distinct scarce representation (5.2 %) of SMS youth among the incarcerated boys, and/or that the non-SMS girls simply felt more comfortable raising homophobic points than non-SMS boys in this survey of incarcerated youth. However, the latter seems less likely.

Policy Implications and Recommendations

This study on incarcerated youth found that lesbian, gay and bisexual (SMS) youth were more likely to report wanting more treatment/counseling programs than their heterosexual (non-SMS) counterparts; for five of the eight treatment/counseling options SMS was significantly related, and in every case SMS youth desired this counseling more than non-SMS youth. This was most pronounced for both sexual and physical abuse counseling. SMS youth were also more likely than the non-SMS youth to want family, individual, and additional depression/mental health counseling. The relationships between SMS and these latter three types of counseling were no longer significant when controlling for sex and race/ethnicity, but more research needs to address this with larger samples. Girls requested more of all types of counseling than boys, but this is not surprising given girls' higher rates of trauma than boys' (see Belknap and Holsinger 2006). Surprisingly, although previous research reviewed in this chapter indicated an elevated risk of substance use and abuse and depression among SMS youth compared to their non-SMS counterparts, in this study of incarcerated youth, SMS identity was unrelated to the youths' requests for drug/alcohol counseling or emotional counseling. As expected, however, there were also no differences between SMS and non-SMS youth regarding their request for sex offender counseling.

There were far fewer relationships for program requests than treatment/counseling requests based on SMS in this incarcerated sample. Of the 10 program options, only three were significantly related to SMS, and in all three cases the non-SMS youth requested or had received the programming more than the SMS youth: independent living, parenting, and job/career skills training programs. There were no differences based on SMS for these incarcerated youths' desires/receipt of the following programs: problem-solving, anger management, good relationships, sports/health/fitness, wanting to be a better student, sex education, and general health education.

As suggested previously in this chapter, it is likely that bigotry and discrimination against SMS youth, including rejection by parents, other family members, peers, teachers, neighbors and others has decreased in recent years as there is growing realization that an SMS identity is, indeed, normal (see Eccles et al. 2003). More recently, research has focused on highlighting protective factors that may advantageously shield SMS youth from the harmful responses and outcomes found in community samples and our study. *SMS identity integration* is defined as becoming accepting of one's SMS identity (e.g., lesbian, gay, bisexual, transgender, queer), resolving internalized homophobia (if it is there), adopting positive attitudes toward SMS, feeling comfortable with others knowing and disclosing to them, and involvement in SMS activities (see Rosario et al. 2001, p. 135). As expected, SMS identity integration is a strongly protective factor against developing a range of problems associated with SMS (e.g., suicide ideation and attempts, self-injury, depression, unprotected sex) (Rosario et al. 2001). Some research indicates that recognizing same-sex attraction at a younger age may allow for better SMS identity integration and that with positive changes in attitudes toward SMS individuals in recent decades, more youth are coming out earlier and finding more support and less isolation for their SMS identities (see Herdt and Boxer 1993; Savin-Williams 1990, 1995; Swann and Spivey 2004). Clearly, SMS identity integration is enhanced by having those around an SMS youth support and respect this identity. For example, one study found SMS youth who self-injured/cut themselves were less likely than SMS who did not to be able to name a "safe adult" in their lives (Walls et al. 2010). Alternatively, and as expected, parental (e.g., Savin-Williams 1989) and peer support (Diamond and Lucas 2004; Swann and Spivey 2004) of SMS youth provide protection against many of the negative outcomes that prior research associates with SMS youth.

These findings and patterns are encouraging, and they are relevant for those working in facilities housing incarcerated youth. Our findings document the relatively high prevalence of SMS girls in these facilities, stressing the importance of recognizing the existence of these youth and how staff and even peers within the facilities can be supportive in an incarcerated youth's SMS identity integration. Yet, it is also possible that such support might be just as or more necessary in facilities incarcerating boys, given the more marginalized and isolated status these boys may have due to their far smaller representation, and perhaps elevated homophobia by peers (and staff) relative to incarcerated girls (see Pharr 1988, 1997). Positive and supportive staff and peers could facilitate an SMS youth's identity integration by supporting this identity and working to have a more SMS-friendly climate. In turn, such advancements in youth facilities would likely improve the physical and mental health of the youth and result in a decrease in self-injury, suicide, depression, antisocial behavior, and aggression.

Although this study provides some important guidance for programming for incarcerated SMS youth, it is not without limitations. First, the data are relatively "old," collected in 1998 and 1999. Although it is hoped that these institutions and society are less bigoted against SMS youth now, recent (as yet unpublished) data collected by the second author from staff and incarcerated girls in Missouri suggests that incarcerated SMS youth continue to face significant bigotry. Second, our definition of SMS was somewhat narrow and did not allow for transgender or transsexual identities. This limitation is particularly important given Garofalo and his colleagues' (2006) research on the high rates of arrest and incarceration among transgender youth and the likelihood that inclusion of other sexual identities would likely yield important findings. Third, our measure for SMS does not capture changes in sexual identity over time (e.g., Cover 2005; Kitzinger and Wilkinson 1995), nor whether the study participant "came out" while incarcerated. If the youth came out in the institution, perhaps s/he was less likely to experience trauma and conduct self-harming behaviors prior to entering the facility.

The findings from this and other recent studies support further investigation into the Labeling and General Strain theoretical frameworks. Although our data cannot answer the question of whether SMS youth, particularly SMS girls, are more likely to be labeled and processed as delinquents than their non-SMS counterparts, this study contributes to the findings from a few other studies indicating the potentially dire consequences of the police, court, youth facility, and other legal system staff discriminating against and unnecessarily labeling these youth as offenders (e.g., Garofalo et al. 2006; Himmelstein and Brückner 2011). Turning to general strain theory, given that SMS identity integration is deterred by hostile people and climates, such hostile climates likely serve as a strain that could result in externalized (e.g., aggression, antisocial) and internalized (e.g., self-injury, suicide ideation, substance abuse) behaviors among SMS youth. Conversely, SMS identity is aided by supportive people and climates, which could feasibly deter these troubling externalized and internalized behaviors. In short, the theoretical applications of strain and labeling also have practical implications, whereby increasing awareness of (and avoiding) SMS-discriminatory labeling could potentially keep more youth out of incarceration facilities, and expediting more SMS-friendly environments, including in delinquent facilities, could decrease offending behaviors and assist SMS youths to view these identities more positively and engage in less self-harming behaviors as well. Clearly, more research needs to be done on SMS among young offenders, to better understand the strains associated with SMS prior to, during, and after incarceration, but also how SMS may serve as a profiling bias by parents and guardians, teachers, criminal legal system workers (e.g., police, judges, incarceration staff, parole boards), and others, resulting in more labeling. Our data indicate that this bias and labeling may be particularly harsh for SMS girls (compared to boys). Finally, research on SMS youth both in the community and in juvenile and adult facilities needs to more fully address the protective factors where they exist, to guide policy, and allow more support for and less bias against SMS youth and adults.

Acknowledgments The authors are indebted to all of the incarcerated youth who took the time and energy to complete our survey, and we are particularly grateful to the lesbian, gay, and bisexual youth for having the courage to claim this identity, even in this anonymous survey that was distributed in the late 1990s, a time when there was even more homophobia in delinquent institutions. We also thank the Office of Criminal Justice Services (OCJS) in Columbus, OH for partial funding of this study, although the findings may not reflect OCJS's beliefs. Clearly any shortcomings in this chapter are the authors' and not OCJS.

References

Agnew, R. (1985). A revised strain theory of delinquency. *Social Forces, 64*(1), 151–167.

Agnew, R. (1992). Foundation for a general strain theory of crime and delinquency. *Criminology, 30*(1), 47–87.

Alexander, N., & Clare, L. (2004). You still feel different: The experience and meaning of women's self-injury in the context of a lesbian or bisexual identity. *Journal of Community & Applied Social Psychology, 14*(2), 70–84. doi:10.1002/casp.764.

Anhalt, K., & Morris, T. L. (1998). Developmental and adjustment issues of gay, lesbian, and bisexual adolescents: A review of the empirical literature. *Clinical Child and Family Psychology Review, 1*(4), 215–230.

Anzaldúa, G. (2007). *Borderlands/La Frontera: The new Mestiza.* San Francisco, CA: Aunt Lute Books.

Arnold, R. A. (1990). Processes of victimization and criminalization of Black Women. *Social Justice, 17*(3), 153–166.

Balsam, K. F., Beauchaine, T. P., Mickey, R. M., & Rothblum, E. D. (2005). Mental health of lesbian, gay, bisexual, and heterosexual siblings: Effects of gender, sexual orientation, and family. *Journal of Abnormal Psychology, 114*(3), 471–476.

Becker, H. S. (1963). *Outsiders: Studies in the sociology of deviance.* London, UK: Free Press of Glencoe.

Belknap, J., Dunn, M. A., & Holsinger, K. (1997). *A report to the governor: Moving toward juvenile justice and youth-serving systems that address the distinct experience of the adolescent female.* Columbus, OH: Office of Criminal Justice Services.

Belknap, J., & Holsinger, K. (1997). Understanding delinquent girls: The results of a focus group study. *Prison Journal, 77*(4), 381–404.

Belknap, J., & Holsinger, K. (2006). The gendered nature of risk factors for delinquency. *Feminist Criminology, 1*(1), 48–71.

Belknap, J., Holsinger, K., & Little, J. (2012). Sexual minority status, abuse, and self-harming behaviors among incarcerated girls. *Journal of Child and Adolescent Trauma, 5*(2), 173–185.

Birkett, M., Espelage, D. L., & Koenig, B. (2009). LGB and questioning students in schools: The moderating effects of homophobic bullying and school climate on negative outcomes. *Journal of Youth and Adolescence, 38*(7), 989–1000. doi:10.1007/s10964-008-9389-1.

Bontempo, D. E., & D'Augelli, A. R. (2002). Effects of at-school victimization and sexual orientation on lesbian, gay, or bisexual youths' health risk behavior. *Journal of Adolescent Health, 30*(5), 364–374.

Broidy, L. M. (2001). A test of general strain theory. *Criminology, 39*(1), 9–36.

Broidy, L., & Agnew, R. (1997). Gender and crime: A general strain theory perspective. *Journal of Research in Crime and Delinquency, 34*(3), 275–306.

Chauhan, P., Reppucci, N. D., Burnette, M., & Reiner, S. (2010). Race, neighborhood disadvantage, and antisocial behavior among female juvenile offenders. *Journal of Community Psychology, 38*(4), 532–540. doi:10.1002/jcop.20377.

Corliss, H. L., Cochran, S. D., Mays, V. M., Greenland, S., & Seeman, T. E. (2009). Age of minority sexual orientation development and risk of childhood maltreatment and suicide attempts in women. *American Journal of Orthopsychiatry, 79*(4), 511–521. doi:10.1037/a0017163.

Cover, R. (2005). Queer subjects of suicide: Cultural studies, sexuality and youth suicide concepts in New Zealand. *New Zealand Sociology, 20*(1), 78–101.

D'Augelli, A. R. (2002). Mental health problems among lesbian, gay, and bisexual youths ages 14 to 21. *Clinical Child Psychology and Psychiatry, 7*(3), 433–456.

D'Augelli, A. R., & Patterson, C. J. (Eds.). (1995). *Lesbian, gay, and bisexual identities over the lifespan: Psychological perspectives.* New York, NY: Oxford University Press.

Dodge, K. A., Bates, J. E., & Pettit, G. S. (1990). Mechanisms in the cycle of violence. *Science, 250*(4988), 1678–1683.

Diamond, L. M., & Lucas, S. (2004). Sexual-minority and heterosexual youths' peer relationships: Experiences, expectations, and implications for well-being. *Journal of Research on Adolescence, 14*(3), 313–340.

Dubé, E. M., & Savin-Williams, R. C. (1999). Sexual identity development among ethnic sexual-minority male youths. *Developmental Psychology, 35*(6), 1389–1398.

DuRant, R. H., Krowchuk, D. P., & Sinal, S. H. (1998). Victimization, use of violence, and drug use at school among male adolescents who engage in same-sex sexual behavior. *Journal of Pediatrics, 133*(1), 113–118.

Eccles, T. A., Sayegh, M. A., Fortenberry, J. D., & Zimet, G. D. (2003). More normal than not: A qualitative assessment of the developmental experiences of gay youth. *Journal of Adolescent Health, 32*(2), 137–138.

Erikson, K. T. (1962). Notes on the sociology of deviance. *Social Problems, 9*, 309–315.

Faith, K. (1993). *Unruly women: The politics of confinement and resistance.* Vancouver, Canada: Press Gang Publishers.

Finlinson, H. A., Colon, H. M., Robles, R. R., & Soto, M. (2008). An exploratory study of Puerto Rican MSM drug users—The childhood and early teen years of gay males and transsexual females. *Youth & Society, 39*(3), 362–384. doi:10.1177/0044118x07305998.

Fishbein, D. (2000). Sexual preference, crime and punishment. *Women and Criminal Justice, 11*(2), 67–84.

Gaarder, E., & Belknap, J. (2002). Tenuous borders: Girls transferred to adult court. *Criminology, 40*(3), 481–517.

Garofalo, R., Deleon, J., Osmer, E., Doll, M., & Harper, G. W. (2006). Overlooked, misunderstood and at-risk: Exploring the lives and HIV risk of ethnic minority male-to-female transgender youth. *Journal of Adolescent Health, 38*(3), 230–236. doi:10.1016/j.jadohealth.2005.03.023.

Giallombardo, R. (1966). *Society of women: A study of a women's prison.* New York, NY: Wiley.

Gilfus, M. E. (1993). From victims to survivors to offenders: Women's routes of entry and immersion into street crime. *Women and Criminal Justice, 4*(1), 63–89. doi:10.1300/J012v04n01_04.

Grossman, A. H., D'Augelli, A. R., & Salter, N. P. (2006). Male-to-female transgender youth: Gender expression milestones, gender atypicality, victimization, and parents' responses. *Journal of GLBT Family Studies, 2*(1), 71–91.

Hensley, C., Tewksbury, R., & Koscheski, M. (2002). The characteristics and motivations behind female prison sex. *Women & Criminal Justice, 13*(2–3), 125–139.

Herdt, G. H., & Boxer, A. (1993). *Children of horizons: How gay and lesbian teens are leading a new way out of the closet.* Boston, MA: Beacon Press.

Himmelstein, K. E. W., & Brückner, H. (2011). Criminal-justice and school sanctions against nonheterosexual youth: A national longitudinal study. *Pediatrics, 127*(1), 49–57.

Holsinger, K. (2003). Programming for incarcerated girls: Comparing what they want with what they get. *Women, Girls and Criminal Justice*, June.

Holsinger, K., & Holsinger, A. (2005). Differential pathways to violence and self-injurious behavior: African–American and White girls in the juvenile justice system. *Journal of Research in Crime and Delinquency, 42*(2), 211–242.

Huebner, D. M., Rebchook, G. M., & Kegeles, S. M. (2004). Experiences of harassment, discrimination, and physical violence among young gay and bisexual men. *American Journal of Public Health, 94*(7), 1200–1203.

Hunter, J. (1990). Violence against lesbian and gay male youths. *Journal of Interpersonal Violence, 5*(3), 295–300.

Kitsuse, J. I. (1962). Societal reaction to deviant behavior: Problems of theory and method. *Social Problems, 9*, 247–256.

Kitzinger, C., & Wilkinson, S. (1995). Transitions from heterosexuality to lesbianism: The discursive production of lesbian identities. *Developmental Psychology, 31*(1), 95–104.

Leiber, M. J. (1994). Comparison of juvenile court outcomes for Native Americans, African Americans, and Whites. *Justice Quarterly, 11*(2), 257–279.

Lemert, E. M. (1951). *Social pathology: A systematic approach to the theory of sociopathic behavior.* New York, NY: McGraw Hill.

McDaniel, J. S., Purcell, D., & D'Augelli, A. R. (2001). The relationship between sexual orientation and risk for suicide: Research findings and future directions for research and prevention. *Suicide and Life-Threatening Behavior, 31*(1), 84–105. doi:10.1521/suli.31.1.5.84.24224.

McDaniels-Wilson, C., & Belknap, J. (2008). The extensive sexual violation and sexual abuse histories of incarcerated women. *Violence Against Women, 14*(10), 1090–1127. doi:10.1177/1077801208323160.

Nesmith, A. (2006). Predictors of running away from family foster care. *Child Welfare, 85*(3), 585–609.

Pathela, P., & Schillinger, J. A. (2010). Sexual behaviors and sexual violence: Adolescents with opposite-, same-, or both-sex partners. *Pediatrics, 126*(5), 879–886. doi:10.1542/peds.2010-0396.

Pharr, S. (1988). *Homophobia: A weapon of sexism*. Inverness, CA: Chardon Press.

Pharr, S. (1997). *Homophobia: A weapon of sexism* (2nd ed.). Berkeley, CA: Chardon Press.

Pilkington, N. W., & D'Augelli, A. R. (1995). Victimization of lesbian, gay, and bisexual youth in community settings. *Journal of Community Psychology, 23*(1), 34–56.

Rafter, N. H., & Stanko, E. A. (Eds.). (1982). *Judge, lawyer, victim, thief: Women, gender roles, and criminal justice*. Boston, MA: Northeastern University Press.

Robson, R. (1992). *Lesbian (out)law: Survival under the rule of law*. Ithaca, NY: Firebrand Books.

Rosario, M., Hunter, J., Maguen, S., Gwadz, M., & Smith, R. (2001). The coming-out process and its adaptational and health-related associations among gay, lesbian, and bisexual youths: Stipulation and exploration of a model. *American Journal of Community Psychology, 29*(1), 133–160.

Rostosky, S. S., Owens, G. P., Zimmerman, R. S., & Riggle, E. D. B. (2003). Associations among sexual attraction status, school belonging, and alcohol and marijuana use in rural high school students. *Journal of Adolescence, 26*(6), 741–751.

Russell, S. T. (2003). Sexual minority youth and suicide risk. *American Behavioral Scientist, 46*(9), 1241–1257.

Russell, S. T., Driscoll, A. K., & Truong, N. (2002). Adolescent same-sex romantic attractions and relationships: Implications for substance use and abuse. *American Journal of Public Health, 92*(2), 198–202.

Russell, S. T., & Joyner, K. (2001). Adolescent sexual orientation and suicide risk: Evidence from a national study. *American Journal of Public Health, 91*(8), 1276–1281.

Saewyc, E. M., Bearinger, L. H., Heinz, P. A., Blum, R. W., & Resnick, M. D. (1998). Gender differences in health and risk behaviors among bisexual and homosexual adolescents. *Journal of Adolescent Health, 23*(3), 181–188.

Salomonsen-Sautel, S., Van Leeuwen, J. M., Gilroy, C., Boyle, S., Malberg, D., & Hopfer, C. (2008). Correlates of substance use among homeless youths in eight cities. *American Journal on Addictions, 17*(3), 224–234. doi:10.1080/10550490802019964.

Savin-Williams, R. C. (1989). Parental influences on the self-esteem of gay and lesbian youths: A reflected appraisals model. *Journal of Homosexuality, 17*(1/2), 93–109.

Savin-Williams, R. C. (1990). *Gay and lesbian youth: Expressions of identity*. New York, NY: Hemisphere Publishing Corporation.

Savin-Williams, R. C. (1995). Lesbian, gay male, and bisexual adolescents. In A. R. D'Augelli & C. J. Patterson (Eds.), *Lesbian, gay, and bisexual identities over the lifespan: Psychological perspectives* (pp. 165–189). New York, NY: Oxford University Press.

Savin-Williams, R. C. (2001a). A critique of research on sexual-minority youths. *Journal of Adolescence, 24*(1), 5–13.

Savin-Williams, R. C. (2001b). Suicide attempts among sexual-minority youths: Population and measurement issues. *Journal of Consulting and Clinical Psychology, 69*(6), 983–991.

Savin-Williams, R. C., & Diamond, L. M. (2000). Sexual identity trajectories among sexual-minority youths: Gender comparisons. *Archives of Sexual Behavior, 29*(6), 607–627.

Schur, E. M. (1984). *Labeling women deviant: Gender, stigma, and social control* (1st ed.). New York, NY: Random House.

Scourfield, J., Roen, K., & McDermott, L. (2008). Lesbian, gay, bisexual and transgender young people's experiences of distress: Resilience, ambivalence and self-destructive behaviour. *Health and Social Care in the Community, 16*(3), 329–336. doi:10.1111/j.1365-2524.2008.00769.x.

Striepe, M. I., & Tolman, D. L. (2003). Mom, dad, I'm straight: The coming out of gender ideologies in adolescent sexual-identity development. *Journal of Clinical Child and Adolescent Psychology, 32*(4), 523–530.

Swann, S. K., & Spivey, C. A. (2004). The relationship between self-esteem and lesbian identity during adolescence. *Child and Adolescent Social Work Journal, 21*(6), 629–646.

Thompson, M. P., & Light, L. S. (2011). Examining gender differences in risk factors for suicide attempts made 1 and 7 years later in a nationally representative sample. *Journal of Adolescent Health, 48*(4), 391–397. doi:10.1016/j.jadohealth.2010.07.018.

Walls, N. E., Laser, J., Nickels, S. J., & Wisneski, H. (2010). Correlates of cutting behavior among sexual minority youths and young adults. *Social Work Research, 34*(4), 213–226.

Walls, N. E., Potter, C., & van Leeuwen, J. (2009). Where risks and protective factors operate differently: Homeless sexual minority youth and suicide attempts. *Child and Adolescent Social Work Journal, 26*(3), 235–257.

Ward, D. A., & Kassebaum, G. G. (1965). *Women's prison: Sex and social structure.* Chicago, IL: Aldine Publishing Company.

Widom, C. S. (1989). The cycle of violence. *Science, 244*(4901), 160–166.

Wilsnack, S. C., Hughes, T. L., Johnson, T. P., Bostwick, W. B., Szalacha, L. A., Benson, P., & Kinnison, K. E. (2008). Drinking and drinking-related problems among heterosexual and sexual minority women. *Journal of Studies on Alcohol and Drugs, 69*(1), 129–139.

Chapter 12
Gender Integration in Sex-Segregated U.S. Prisons: The Paradox of Transgender Correctional Policy

Jennifer Sumner and Valerie Jenness

Abstract In the latter part of the twentieth century, the development of correctional policies in the United States related to transgender prisoners has rendered visible *trans*gender prisoners, disrupted the taken-for-granted policies and practices related to the operation of sex-segregated prisons, and presented considerable challenges to those charged with running penal institutions. The courts and correctional administrators in particular have grappled with how best to adjudicate tensions born of the visible presence of transgender prisoners in prisons charged with housing men (and only men). We draw on multiple sources of data, including correctional policies, published surveys, court opinions, activist testimony, news documents, and legal discourse, to analyze the parameters of extant transgender correctional policy in the U.S. Our examination reveals that transgender correctional policy is: shaped by "safety and security" concerns, arguably the central institutional logic underlying the management of prisons; unsettled insofar as there is both convergence and divergence in the content of policy related to transgender inmates (e.g., there is almost complete agreement on the enforcement of anatomy-based housing policies and there is considerable disagreement over policies related to hormonal treatment); and attentive to the control of place for transgender prisoners, although not comparable control of "presentation and demeanor" for transgender prisoners. A collateral consequence of these features of correctional policy is that prisons for men in the U.S. are at once sex-segregated and multi-gendered.

J. Sumner (✉)
Department of Criminal Justice, Seattle University, Casey 329, 901 12th Ave., 222000, Seattle, WA 98122, USA
e-mail: sumnerje@seattleu.edu

V. Jenness
Department of Criminology, Law and Society, School of Social Ecology, University of California Irvine, 5300 Social and Behavioral Sciences Gateway, Irvine, CA 92697-7050, USA
e-mail: jenness@uci.edu

D. Peterson and V. R. Panfil (eds.), *Handbook of LGBT Communities, Crime, and Justice*, DOI: 10.1007/978-1-4614-9188-0_12, © Springer Science+Business Media New York 2014

Keywords Transgender inmate · Transgender prisoner · Correctional policy · Safety and security · Sex/gender

Introduction

In 2011, the Cook County jail in Chicago, Illinois adopted a policy that made national news. The policy establishes guidelines and procedures for managing the custody, safety, and security of transgender inmates (Hawkins 2011). Prior to the adoption of this new policy, transgender inmates in the Cook County jail were treated as members of the gender that aligned with their sex at birth. Inmates with male genitalia were treated as males. End of discussion. In sharp contrast, the new policy specifies that transgender inmates can be housed, dressed, and searched according to their gender identity rather than the sex/gender they were assigned at birth; a Gender Identity Committee is charged with considering the case of each inmate who self-identifies as transgender or who is clinically verified as being transgender, recommending appropriate housing accommodations for the inmate, and specifying what clothes and toiletries transgender inmates should have, as well as how officers can (and cannot) search transgender inmates. As a result of this new policy, both men's and women's facilities are now options for housing transgender inmates.

This historic shift in the policy is informed by, and reflects, a new era. It is an era in which *Newsweek* introduced "transgender America" in a cover story (Rosenberg 2007), researchers have directed scholarly attention to the plight of transgender prisoners (Jenness et al. 2010; Sexton et al. 2010), advocates have brought newfound attention to the problematic nature of being a transgender prisoner (Just Detention International 2009; Transgender Law Center n.d.; Transgender Law and Policy Institute 2009), and those charged with administering jails, prisons, and other detention facilities have been challenged to develop policies and procedures that are more attentive to transgender prisoners. It is an era in which law and policy that addresses the treatment of transgender prisoners is being designed, adopted, and institutionalized across the U.S.

The development and institutionalization of law and policy that addresses the management of transgender prisoners calls into question one of the most basic underlying assumptions of prison operations: segregation by sex, with sex meaning male and female and only male and female. Prison systems constitute one of—if not the—most sex-segregated institutions in the modern world. For well over a century in the U.S., there have generally been two types of prisons: men's prisons and women's prisons (Britton 2003; Rafter 1985).[1] Historically, early moves

---

[1] A co-corrections experiment in the U.S. in the 1970s and 1980s, however, led to sex-integration in some federal and state facilities (Herbert 1985; Johnson 1987; Mahan et al. 1989).

toward sex segregation were sought in order to increase the safety of female inmates and to provide opportunities for "gender-appropriate" punishment and rehabilitative programming (Britton 2003). Sex segregation presumed gender segregation. The same assumption is in place in the modern era: sex segregation in prison and other carceral environments is arguably the least contested prison policy/practice across geographical region, local government, and type of detention facility.

The visible presence of transgender prisoners has problematized the taken-for-granted status of sex-segregated prisons, jails, and other detention facilities as a routine policy commitment and operational practice. Their visibility presents operational challenges and raises human rights questions (Arkles 2009; Emmer et al. 2011; Mann 2006; Peek 2003–2004; Rosenblum 1999–2000; Sylvia Rivera Law Project 2007; Tarzwell 2006–2007). The political work sustained by transgender prisoners, former prisoners, and their advocates has provided a catalyst for newfound critiques of the prison as a "gendered organization" (Acker 1990; Britton 2003). As with other gendered organizations, prisons are predicated on a slew of assumptions about sex and gender as well as the essential features of both. This is perhaps most evident in prison operational policies that link legislative mandates to correctional obligations, reflect the institutional logic and values of corrections, and guide the daily operations of prisons.

Prison policies that address inmate management often appear on the surface to be "gender-neutral," but they nonetheless clearly reflect and inform the social organization of a binary sex/gender system. As we describe in this chapter, prison policies that instruct officials on the management of transgender prisoners make assumptions about the social organization of gender, determine how gender is (and is not) revealed in social life, identify categorical divides that are (and are not) recognized, and mandate how both sex assignment and gender displays are to be managed institutionally. For example, housing policies generally require that inmates fit into one of two sex categories; medical policies prohibit sex reassignment and hormonal treatment unless a prisoner is pathologized via psychiatric diagnosis (i.e., gender identity disorder or gender dysphoria); and policies on clothing, cosmetics, and hygiene delineate the acceptable "GP" (general presentation) of prisoners. These types of policies constitute an emergent policy domain worthy of empirical examination.

Our analysis of these policies is situated in the larger context in which they have emerged and in which they reveal a paradox. These policies have taken shape within a new penology and culture of control (Feeley and Simon 1992; Garland 2001), a judicial and political context of "deference" toward corrections administrators and operations (Feeley and Rubin 1998; Jenness and Smyth 2011), and a correctional context that prioritizes safety and security (Gaes et al. 2004). Shaped by this context, correctional policies related to the management of transgender inmates: both affirm and interrogate the taken-for-granted assumptions about the intersection between gender and penality; manifest considerable dissensus among existing policies regarding some issues (e.g., hormonal treatment) and near consensus regarding other policy issues (e.g., anatomy-based housing); and, as revealed in our analysis, structure prisons that are both sex-segregated and gender-integrated.

The remainder of this chapter is organized around four major sections. In the next section, we briefly describe the correctional climate in which policies related to transgender prisoners have emerged and taken form. Thereafter, we describe the methods and data used for our analysis of transgender correctional policies and legal and public discourse surrounding those policies. In the main section of this chapter, we present an analysis of transgender policies by focusing on the key elements of policy: defining transgender, accessing medical care, determining housing, and displaying gender. We conclude with a discussion of our key empirical findings and theoretical implications.

Setting the Stage for Transgender Policy

Policy does not emerge and take form in a vacuum; rather, it is contextualized by the environment in which it comes into being, including the institutional logics that characterize that environment. Accordingly, below we describe key features of the environment that shape transgender correctional policy.

The New Penology and a Culture of Control

The consideration of transgender inmates as a policy concern emerged in the later part of the twentieth century, at the time when the so-called "new penology" (Feeley and Simon 1992) and a "culture of control" (Garland 2001) began to characterize the correctional landscape. The new penology is characterized by changes in discourse, policy, and practice toward probability and risk in contrast to individual treatment, reform, and punishment; new system objectives toward efficient control; and a reliance on actuarial techniques that privilege the aggregate over the individual (Feeley and Simon 1992; c.f. Lynch 1998). This change was accompanied by decreased expectations for criminal justice agencies to engage in rehabilitation as they began to use internal system measures as evaluative performance indicators instead of relying on externally imposed social goals, such as public safety and community reintegration. The result limits the potential to achieve objectives beyond those associated with operations. As Moynihan (2005) and others have pointed out, this correctional climate is coupled with a larger move in government toward an emphasis on measurable results, often referred to as performance metrics.

In *The Culture of Control*, David Garland (2001) offers a historical account of the emergence of the contemporary field of crime control in the U.S. and the U.K. that focuses attention on central discourses, strategies, and policies of crime control. He develops a critical understanding of the practices and discourses of crime control—what he calls "the field of crime control and criminal justice" (p. 72)—that have come to characterize the U.S. and the U.K. by directing attention to a wider field that encompasses the practices of non-state as well as state actors and forms of crime control that are preventative as well as penal. This includes a shift from differentiated crime control systems monopolized by the state to a de-differentiated system involving state and non-state partnerships. As others have discussed, this, in turn, has opened institutional space for outside stake-holders—indeed, entire policy communities—to make claims about the legitimacy of operational aspects of law enforcement in general and corrections in particular (Ismaili 2006; Pratt et al. 1998).

Legitimacy and the Centrality of Safety and Security in Organizational Policy

The relationship between organizations, policies, and legitimacy has been revealed in a large body of scholarship spanning over three decades (Edelman 1992; Grattet and Jenness 2005; Jenness and Grattet 2005; Meyer and Rowan 1978). This work reveals the important role institutionalized values and "myths" play in an orga-nization's ability to achieve legitimacy quite apart from technical efficiency and that an organization's legitimacy derives from its ability to instill these myths into its formal organizational structure, policies, and technical activities (Meyer and Rowan 1977). Myths might appear incompatible with a correctional climate that privileges technical efficiency, but not if technical efficiency is the centerpiece of the institutionalized values.

As Pratt et al. (1998) reveal, there are various sovereigns that compete for ownership of the correctional "problem." Sovereigns are those who are most influential with regard to the allocation of organizational resources and whose decisions "formally or informally hold the organization to institutionalized stan-dards of policy and performance" (Jenness and Grattet 2005, p. 343). Sovereigns relevant to state prisons include legislators, the judiciary, taxpayers, external oversight organizations, and correctional employee labor unions. In the case of transgender policies, transgender advocates in particular, and LGBT advocates more generally, are also easily recognized as stakeholders.

Organizational legitimacy is a product of the relationship between the organi-zation and entities well positioned to judge the organization, including its policies as formal expressions of organizational values and intended practices. Framed in this way, the study of the development of a policy domain is imperative precisely because it speaks to the legitimation of some values over others. As others have shown, the adoption of policies is often a function of what Maxson and Klein (1997) refer to as "philosophic resonance." According to them, philosophic res-onance is "the degree to which legislation is in agreement with the underlying philosophies of those meant to carry out the legislation" (Maxson and Klein 1997, p. 23; see also, Jenness and Grattet 2005).[2]

Given this work, it is reasonable to understand prison policies as a reflection of organizational responses to externalities that align with organizational culture and mission. Organizational culture can be understood as a mediating variable that shapes the relationship between external stakeholders/sovereigns and the development and adoption of operational policies. As such, prison policies can be seen as codified value statements that reveal the underlying logics and attendant expressed commitments of correctional systems.

In simple terms, correctional mission statements "articulate the [public and formal] purpose of imprisonment within a jurisdiction" (Gaes et al. 2004, p. 8). In their survey of mission statements of state departments of corrections in the U.S., the Federal Bureau of Prisons, and the Correctional Service of Canada, Gaes et al. (2004, p. 9) identify themes found across department "missions, vision, or core value statements." "Guaranteeing the safety of the public, staff, and inmates" (96.2 % of the jurisdictions) emerges as *the* central organizational value. Rehabilitative and inmate treatment goals are evident in organizational philosophies, albeit to a lesser degree.

Findings by Moynihan (2005) reveal that, in practice, some departments of corrections may be unable to pursue multiple goals, effectively rendering the top priority an exclusive value and attendant objective. "[T]he critical logic that shaped their management activities was coping to maintain the simple warehousing goal of incarcerating many prisoners in a limited space for low costs, while maintaining reasonable safety and constitutionally acceptable conditions" (Moynihan 2005, pp. 23–24). In other words, safety and security can be seen as the central organizing principle of correctional systems in the U.S.

It is within this context that we now turn to an examination of policies related to transgender prisoners housed in U.S. prisons. We do so by examining a range of policies—from those that speak to how transgender is defined to those that address hair care—for what they can reveal about the social organization of gender in carceral spaces defined by the culture of control, the new penology, and a resulting core value of safety and security in correctional settings. As Jenness and Grattet (2005), as well as others, have persuasively argued, policies are important points of departure for empirical analysis because they link legislative and judicial mandates to organizational operations, shape the practices of organizational personnel, and provide a window through which the stated goals and practices of agencies and personnel can be empirically documented and assessed.

---

[2] Extending this argument, Jenness and Grattet (2005; see also Jenness and Smyth 2011) found that "organizational perviousness," which refers to "both the organization's susceptibility to environmental influence and the degree to which a particular innovation aligns with the local agency's existing culture and practices" (p. 355), predicts the adoption of law enforcement policies.

Data and Method of Analysis

We collected several forms of archival data in order to examine the broad terrain of transgender correctional policy development and discourse. Our primary focus is on policy documents and judicial decisions, with a secondary focus on materials from advocacy organizations (e.g., reports, newsletters, press releases) and news media. We supplemented these materials with published surveys of transgender correctional polices and legal scholarly discourse presented in published law review journal articles. These materials were retrieved through searching Lexis Nexis Academic, Sociological and Criminal Justice Abstracts, and other public internet search engines (e.g., Google). Search terms included all variations and combinations of the following: transgender, transsexual, corrections, inmate, policy, jail, and prison.

Our examination of these documents allowed us to identify broad themes that anchor transgender correctional policy as well as key stakeholders associated with transgender correctional policy discourse. Throughout our analysis, we examined the correctional policies of one state in depth—those of the California Department of Corrections and Rehabilitation (CDCR). We did so because California is home to over 300 transgender inmates in prisons for men (Jenness et al. 2011). Assuming Browne and McDuffie's (2009) recent estimate—that there are approximately 750 transgender prisoners in the U.S.—is correct, California is home to nearly half of all transgender prisoners in the U.S. With this in mind, we collected the two central CDCR policy manuals (i.e., Department Operations Manual and the Title XV) and conducted searches using the following terms: female, male, sex, gender, trans, feminine, effeminate, and masculine.

Transgender Correctional Policy in the United States

Over the last few decades there has been a proliferation of correctional policies that focus on the management of transgender prisoners. Brown and McDuffie (2009) recently requested all policies and directives related to the management and/or treatment of transgender inmates from U.S. state Departments of Corrections, the Federal Bureau of Prisons, and the District of Columbia. Of those who responded (46 out of 52 jurisdictions), 27 jurisdictions provided policies, directives, or memos. This is a significant increase both in the response rate and the number of existing policies from prior efforts to gauge the growth of transgender polices and the content of such policies. For example, after seeking to retrieve all formal and informal prison policies addressing the management of transgender inmates, Tarzwell (2006–2007) identified only eight states with written policies of some kind (although over half of the states were unresponsive). Prior to that, Petersen et al. (1996) found that 20 % of jurisdictions responding to their survey (including systems in North America, Australia, and Europe) had formal policies.

Consistent with this pattern, Brown and McDuffie (2009) report that the first policies were adopted in 1993, and 70 % of current policies and directives were developed (or at least revised) recently (between 2002 and 2007). The result is a body of policy that speaks to a host of issues, the most prominent of which are addressed below.

Defining Transgender

What *transgender* means and who counts as transgender varies immensely outside of prison. Broad definitions consider "transgender" an umbrella term for many variations of gender identity and expression. For example, a recently released report titled *Injustice at Every Turn: A Report of the National Transgender Discrimination Survey* defined transgender broadly to include "those who transition from one gender to another (transsexuals), *and* those who may not, including gender queer people, cross-dressers, the androgynous, and those whose gender non-conformity is part of their identity" (Grant et al. 2011, p. 12, emphasis in original). Activists attentive to law and policy also tend to err on the side of over-inclusion such that transgender people may be "pre-operative, post-operative, and non-operative transsexual people; cross-dressers; feminine men and masculine women; and more generally, anyone whose gender identity or expression differs from conventional expectations of masculinity or femininity" (Transgender Law and Policy Institute 2009). Likewise, researchers use transgender as an umbrella term for those "who live outside of normative sex/gender relations—that is, individuals whose gendered self-presentation (evidenced through dress, mannerisms, and even physiology) does not correspond to the behaviors habitually associated with members of their biological sex" (Namaste 2000, p. 1; see also Forbes, this volume, for a discussion of how "sex" has been legally defined).[3] Thus, depending on the perspective, transgender includes a variety of types of people, sensibilities, and ways of being in the world.[4]

Medical definitions, however, often narrow these broad understandings of "transgender." As the lead California medical doctor for transgender clients in California prisons stated in a presentation she gave to the medical community: "Transgender refers to a person who is born with the genetic traits of one gender but the internalized identity of another gender" (Kohler 2005, n.p.). And still more

---

[3] Putting forth one of the most expansive definitions of transgender, historian Susan Stryker (2008, p. 1, emphasis in original) uses the term transgender to refer to: "People who move away from the gender they were assigned at birth, people who cross over (*trans-*) the boundaries constructed by their culture to define and contain that gender…it is *the movement across a socially imposed boundary away from an unchosen starting* place—rather than any particular destination or mode of transition."

[4] For a discussion of variability along these lines among transgender prisoners in California prisons, see Jenness et al. (2014).

specific: until recently, transgender people were those diagnosed with gender identity disorder (GID) as it was written in the *Diagnostic and Statistical Manual of Mental Disorders, Fourth Edition* (2000) (DSM-IV-TR). The DSM-V, just released in 2013, however, includes a significant change in which *gender dysphoria* replaces *gender identity disorder* (Moran 2013). In this case, the change signals an effort to remove the stigma associated with the prior diagnosis while still providing an avenue for treatment. While debates continue regarding the costs and benefits of the current role of the medical field in transgender lives, currently in the United States a person is usually required to be diagnosed with GID (and, presumably soon, gender dysphoria) before he or she can begin hormonal treatments or pursue sex reassignment surgery (Stryker 2008; see also Alexander and Meshelemiah 2010; Brown and McDuffie 2009). Thus, perhaps it is not surprising that medical definitions prevail in arenas of correctional policy.

Corrections departments frequently rely on medical definitions to define who is and is not transgender in their formal policies. In general, among the policies that exist, clinical language is usually explicit in the criteria for determining who is (and is not) transgender. Most of these cover those who are diagnosed with gender identity disorder as specified by DSM-IV (Brown and McDuffie 2009; Tarzwell 2006–2007). The Illinois policy, unique among the group with a focus on an inmate's gender over a diagnosis of a disorder, specifies that it does not include "homosexuals, transvestites, and cross-dressers" (Tarzwell 2006–2007, p. 207). Even more telling, committees charged with this determination consist primarily of medical and mental health staff. Finally, almost three quarters (74 %) of the reporting jurisdictions in the most recent survey include formal policies that specify a "psychiatric evaluation of inmates who claim to have symptoms consistent with a GID" (Brown and McDuffie 2009, p. 286).

With regard to the use of medical definitions, case law and correctional policies align. For example, in the precedent setting case, *Farmer v. Brennan* (1994), the Supreme Court cited the American Medical Association's Encyclopedia of Medicine and the DSM-III in its statement of what it means to be a "transsexual." In the opinion for the case, Justice Souter accepted, without questioning, the BOP's diagnosis that Brennan fit this definition as someone who has a "rare psychiatric disorder in which a person feels persistently uncomfortable about his or her anatomical sex and who typically seeks medical treatment, including hormonal therapy and surgery, to bring about a permanent sex change" (*Farmer v. Brennan* 1994, p. 829).

A few years later, in *Maggert v. Hanks* (1997), Judge Posner of the U.S. Court of Appeals for the 7th Circuit, also relied upon medical definitions. He cites the *American Medical Association Encyclopedia of Medicine* as well as the *Lawyers' Medical Cyclopedia of Personal Injuries and Allied Specialties* to conclude that:

Gender dysphoria—the condition in which a person believes that he is imprisoned in a body of the wrong sex, that though biologically a male (the more common form of the condition) he is "really" a female—is a serious psychiatric disorder, as we know because the people afflicted by it will go to great lengths to cure it if they can afford the cure. The cure for the male transsexual consists not of psychiatric treatment designed to make the patient content with his biological sexual identity—that doesn't work—but of estrogen therapy designed to create the secondary sexual characteristics of a woman followed by the surgical removal of the genitals and the construction of a vagina-substitute out of penile tissue...Someone eager to undergo this mutilation is plainly suffering from a profound psychiatric disorder (*Maggert v. Hanks* 1997, p. 671).

Some have argued that the deployment of medical definitions narrows the "eligible" group of transgender inmates significantly, which results in a denial of a variety of treatment benefits (when they do exist) for a large group of gender variant inmates (Peek 2003–2004; Rosenblum 1999–2000). The case of *Long v. Nix* (1995) reveals how a reliance on medical terminology excludes particular groups of inmates in practice. In brief, plaintiff Long sought to wear women's clothing in a men's facility. However, Long refused psychiatric treatment for gender identity disorder. As a result, the court pointed to distinctions made during expert testimony between "transvestic fetishism" and "gender identity disorder" and concluded that the "extent of Long's gender identity disorder does not constitute a serious medical need" (*Long v. Nix* 1995, p. 1365). Other arguments against the medical model point to the idea that the medicalization of gender identity "pathologizes and thus stigmatizes trans people" and "reinforces the oppressive gender binary" (see Lee's 2008 review of these arguments, p. 457; Rosenblum 1999–2000). A recent exception to these critiques, however, is presented by Lee (2008) who argues that transgender inmates are often seeking medical care and "it is difficult to imagine how one could engage in effective advocacy for access to medicine without resorting to the use of some sort of medical evidence" (p. 469).

Despite the use of relatively clear-cut medical definitions, correctional policies often conflate sexuality and gender. For example, in the Department Operations Manual for the California Department of Corrections and Rehabilitation (CDCR), the policies relevant to transgender prisoners make reference to those who have "gender dysphoria" in the chapter on health care services *and* later include pre-operative transsexuals among a group classified as "effeminate homosexuals" in the chapter on classification. A selection from the California policies reads:

Medical Services: Gender Dysphoria Treatment

Genetically, male inmates who may have problems of gender dysphoria (an emotional state characterized by anxiety, depression, etc.) may be referred for evaluation and possible treatment to the gender identification unit at CMF.[5] Genetically, female inmates with analogous problems shall be referred to the CMO at CIW[6] (CDCR Operations Manual 2010, Section 91020.26, p. 774).

Although reportedly no longer in place in practice, historically the CDCR classified "effeminate homosexuals" as:

---

[5] CMF refers to California Medical Facility, a California state prison for men that historically housed inmates with unique medical needs.

[6] CMO refers to the Chief Medical Officer and CIW refers to California Institution for Women.

Male inmates who are preoperative transsexuals, or active effeminate homosexuals whose appearance and personality make them incompatible with general population housing shall be presented to a CSR[7] for placement in Category "B".... Inmates shall not be placed in Category "B" solely on the basis of sexual preference or feminine traits nor remain in Category "B" longer than their appearance and conduct makes necessary.

[T]his category is provided only at CMF and is intended to provide safe, supportive housing for those likely to be easy victims of sexual assault as well as to avoid the conflict and disruption their presence would create in a general population institution (CDCR Operations Manual 2010, Section 62080.14, p. 575).[8]

Interestingly, "Cat B" prisoners are described as "active effeminate homosexuals" even as the policy includes an instruction not to place inmates in this category based on "sexual preference or feminine traits." These policies suggest that when medical treatment is implicated, the CDCR considers the group of prisoners distinct from "homosexuals"; but when medical treatment is not implicated, this group of prisoners is included as part of the population of inmates seen as vulnerable, "effeminate homosexuals," and thus managed in comparable ways (see also Arkles 2009, footnote 13; Jenness 2011).

In sum, there is considerable convergence among policies with regard to the categorization of this group of prisoners. Correctional policies most often define "transgender" consistent with medical definitions, which presumably facilitates continued sorting and screening according to concrete terms. The courts have repeatedly adopted this approach.

Accessing Medical Care

Given the reliance on medical definitions for understandings of "transgender," it is not surprising that medical concerns dominate correctional policy considerations for this group of prisoners. In large part, medical concerns are expressed in the context of lawsuits in which plaintiffs have argued that lack of medical treatment related to transgender health care is a violation of Eighth Amendment protections against cruel and unusual punishment (Mann 2006; Rosenblum 1999–2000). Indeed, as mentioned earlier, some have argued that the outcomes of many of these cases reveal that transgender inmates have a vested interest in the perpetuation of transgenderism as a medical issue in a correctional setting (Lee 2008).

The courts generally use "serious medical need" (see *Meriwether v. Faulkner* 1987) as a standard for whether or not the GID requires treatment (see *Kosilek v. Maloney* 2002) and occasionally require that hormonal treatment be provided (see

---

[7] CSR refers to Classification Staff Representative.

[8] Although this policy is no longer in practice, this delineation itself is fairly recent. Archival documents in the form of administrator and manager meeting minutes reveal that, as in the larger medical world, homosexuals were "treated" as medical cases 60 years ago (California Department of Corrections 1948).

Phillips v. Michigan Department of Corrections 1990). Recently in Wisconsin, a U.S. District Court found state legislation against hormonal treatment for transgender inmates to be a violation of the Eighth and Fourteenth Amendments (*Fields v. Smith* 2010). These patterns are at least partly due to cases that point to severe withdrawal symptoms as a result of discontinuing hormone treatment already underway (*Meriwether v. Faulkner* 1987). The decision in *Meriwether v. Faulkner* (1987), however, did not specify what kind of treatment needed to be provided; rather, it simply specifies that "some kind of treatment" be available. The Wisconsin ruling can be interpreted similarly (*Fields v. Smith* 2010).

In general, when hormones are provided to transgender inmates in U.S. correctional facilities, treatment strategies follow a "continuation" program in which hormones can be prescribed (and either maintained or furthered) if the inmate can prove hormone treatment was underway prior to incarceration (Brown and McDuffie 2009). Over 80 % of the jurisdictions with formal policies include this approach as a possibility. For eight of those it is at least possible that the approach is a maintenance or "freeze-frame" treatment program. This means that hormones are maintained at the same level of treatment upon admission. Until recently, this was also the policy of the Federal Bureau of Prisons (BOP). In 2011, however, the federal system changed its policy on hormonal treatment to allow consideration on a case-by-case basis (National Center for Lesbian Rights 2011). This means that inmates who had not previously undergone hormonal treatment in the community could potentially initiate treatment while incarcerated in the BOP. States without written policies do not tend to provide hormone therapy (Tarzwell 2006–2007), and some states continue to debate the parameters of hormone delivery.

The continuation and maintenance/freeze-frame policies usually require that the inmates provide proof of prior hormone treatment via medical records prior to incarceration (Brown and McDuffie 2009). Many argue that this is not consistent with the lives of transgender inmates who move from the street to carceral settings and back to the street (see Sexton et al. 2010) and is, therefore, an inaccurate measure of who is undergoing hormonal treatment at the time of incarceration (Rosenblum 1999–2000; Sylvia Rivera Law Project 2007). A large number of transgender inmates obtain hormones on the "underground market" and cannot provide formal documentation; these policies, thus, arguably discriminate against low-income transgender people who are unable to obtain formal health care that would provide this level of documentation (see Lee's 2008 review of these arguments). Other challenges arise even when hormonal treatments are provided because correctional facilities often do not provide accompanying psychological and medical services.

The most consistent policy for transgender prisoners across the United States (both in terms of medical care and otherwise) has been that sex reassignment surgery is not permitted while the inmate is in prison, even if paid for personally by the inmate (Brown and McDuffie 2009). For example, in the CDCR's Department Operations Manual, the chapter on "Medical Services" indicates that "genetically male inmates who may have problems of gender dysphoria" should be evaluated for possible treatment while in prison, but that "[i]mplementation of surgical castration, vaginoplasty, or other such procedures shall be deferred beyond the period of incarceration. Surgical procedure shall not be the responsibility of the Department" (Section 91020.26, p. 719).

The Court of Appeals for the Seventh Circuit affirmed this approach to sex reassignment when it decided in *Maggert v. Hanks* (1997) that sex reassignment surgery is not a form of treatment covered by insurance for citizens in the community; thus, it is not a required medical service due to incarcerated persons. The same court expressed concern that providing sex reassignment surgery to inmates would motivate them to deliberately end up in prison in order to secure a free transformation. As Judge Posner wrote in the decision (*Maggert v. Hanks* 1997, p. 672):

> Withholding from a prisoner an esoteric medical treatment that only the wealthy can afford does not strike us as a form of cruel and unusual punishment. It is not unusual; and we cannot see what is cruel about refusing a benefit to a person who could not have obtained the benefit if he had refrained from committing crimes. We do not want transsexuals committing crimes because it is the only route to obtaining a cure....[M]aking the treatment [for Gender Dysphoria] a constitutional duty of prisons would give prisoners a degree of medical care that they could not obtain if they obeyed the law.

Later, the decision in *Brooks v. Berg* (2003) ran counter to this ruling. It referred to a "decided body of case law" establishing that: "Prison officials cannot deny transsexual inmates all medical treatment simply by referring to a prison policy which makes a seemingly arbitrary distinction between inmates who were and were not diagnosed with GID prior to incarceration" (*Brooks v. Berg* 2003, p. 312). In addition, the court referred to established case law requiring that a medical physician, not corrections staff, make the decision regarding adequate treatment for particular inmates (*Brooks v. Berg* 2003). More recently, Lyralisa Stevens, a California transgender prisoner, was unsuccessful in advancing the argument that denial of the sex reassignment surgery is evidence of "deliberate indifference" to her serious medical needs (*Stevens v. Knowles* 2011).

Most recently, however, a surprising federal court decision ruled in favor of Michelle Kosilek, a transgender prisoner housed in a Massachusetts state prison, ordering the state to provide for the surgery calling it the "only adequate treatment" for this "serious medical need" (*Kosilek v. Spencer* 2012, p. 240). The court does not, however, specify where Kosilek should be housed once this process is complete, leaving that decision to the Department of Corrections. Although court documents reveal that there continue to be delays in moving this forward (*Kosilek v. Spencer* 2013) in spite of the original order to proceed "as promptly as possible," the landmark case signals a judicial shift. In January 2013, a federal appeals court overturned a lower court's dismissal of Ophelia Azriel De'Lonta's case against Virginia corrections officials and held that De'Lonta stated a plausible Eighth Amendment claim when she complained that prison officials refused to allow her sex reassignment surgery (*De'Lonta v. Johnson* 2013).

Notwithstanding the policies and rulings cited above, formal policies related to transgender medical services remain the exception rather than the rule despite a notable increase in department policies on medical treatment for transgender inmates in the past decade. In addition, there is considerable variability among those policies related to medical care that do exist. In addition to department-specific policy development, in late 2009, the National Commission on Correctional Health Care adopted a statement that included specifications regarding transgender inmate health care urging an individualized approach to decision making related to medical provisions for transgender prisoners (National Commission on Correctional Health Care 2009). Indeed, the BOP has followed suit. Arguably, a policy approach based on individualized treatment could perpetuate divergence or variability of medical treatment care across departments of corrections, leaving it persistently highly negotiable and contestable. Providing hormonal care to inmates is, of course, accompanied by changes in physical characteristics that complicate operational efforts to sort and screen according to concrete biological factors, as is most common in U.S. correctional facilities.

Determining Housing

In U.S. prisons and other detention facilities, inmates are, in the first instance, housed according to their (presumed) biological sex. Although there is no clear and definitive legal standard for determining the placement of transgender prisoners in particular types of prisons or housing units within prisons, the way California addresses this ambiguity is typical and thus instructive as a first step in understanding policy directives along these lines. California's Administrative Procedure Act (Government Code §§ 11340–11359) and the Penal Code § 5058 provide the CDCR with broad discretion to create and implement rules and regulations for the administration of the prisons. In this context, the CDCR routinely assigns convicted felons to men's or women's prisons on the basis of their genitalia, which is the same method used in most states (Brown and McDuffie 2009; Mann 2006; Peek 2003–2004; Rosenblum 1999–2000; Tarzwell 2006–2007). Accordingly, when processing inmates through the corrections system, the first determination—whether to send the person to a men's or a women's prison—is made via a "genitalia-based" approach rather than an "identity-based" approach.

This "genitalia-based" approach to classification and attendant housing assignments is so deeply ingrained that it is not usually documented in prison operational policies in general and transgender-related correctional policies specifically (Brown and McDuffie 2009). Just under half of the jurisdictions reporting formal policies for transgender inmates in Brown and McDuffie's (2009) survey explicitly indicate "housing is addressed by external genitals" (p. 285); this constitutes 71 % of the policies that mention housing at all. Those that do not address this issue presumably take it for granted. This approach to housing in the United States—assignment according to anatomy—appears to be the least variable and most taken-for-granted policy.

Taken-for-granted housing assignments based on anatomy are often justified as a means to an end, with the end being safety and security. In *Stevens v. Williams*

(2008) an Oregon Magistrate Judge concluded that "prevention of heterosexual crime in prisons is a substantial government interest" (p. 13) and anatomical sex segregation "is substantially related to this interest" (p. 14). Furthermore:

> Requiring that segregation be made upon a person's self-professed gender identity, rather than their anatomical gender, would impose the onerous burden on prison officials of sorting out those with gender identity issues from those who would feign such a condition in order to be placed into an opposite sex facility for more nefarious reasons. This could result in increased risk of heterosexual crime (*Stevens v. Williams* 2008, p. 14).

Beyond sex, inmates are often classified by and housed based on other designations that implicate physical vulnerability (e.g., sexual identity or orientation, physical appearance as effeminate) or other characteristics that have implications for safety and security such as race/ethnicity, gang activity, commitment offense (e.g., sex offender), sentence length, and known enemies (see Berk et al. 2003; Dolovich 2011; Goodman 2008). Each of these factors creates a need for particular housing considerations.

Legal challenges to genitalia-based approaches to housing decisions for transgender inmates are primarily rooted in claims of cruel and unusual punishment and deliberate indifference by correctional staff to the physical protection of transgender prisoners (*Farmer v. Brennan* 1994; *Greene v. Bowles* 2004). For example, in *Farmer v. Brennan* (1994) Dee Farmer, a 22-year-old male-to-female preoperative transgender inmate sued prison officials for a violation of her Eighth Amendment right to protection against cruel and unusual punishment. Farmer was sexually assaulted in the male general population of a maximum-security penitentiary two weeks after she was placed there. While the U.S. Supreme Court found that an inmate could bring an Eighth Amendment claim if she could show that prison officials were deliberately indifferent to prison rape, it adopted a subjective standard for the showing of deliberate indifference, which Farmer was not able to prove.

More recently, in California, the CDCR was faced with similar allegations in a case in which a transgender inmate, Alexis Giraldo, sued the organization for failing to protect her from serial sexual assault in Folsom State Prison (*Giraldo v. California Department of Corrections and Rehabilitation* 2007). Giraldo argued her case on many grounds, but of importance to her initial argument was the issue of where she was housed—and with whom—and how various decisions by the CDCR about her housing may have failed to protect her from sexual victimization by other inmates.

The critique of the genitalia-based approach to classification and housing as it relates to transgender prisoners—namely, that individuals with feminine characteristics are more vulnerable to physical victimization when housed among male inmates in a hypermasculine inmate culture—often evokes counter critiques of an identity-based approach to placement that relies upon self-identified gender, quite apart from whether it aligns with one's anatomy (Mann 2006; Peek 2003–2004; Rosenblum 1999–2000). Critics of an identity-based approach to housing placement argue that this approach poses an increased risk for inmates in women's facilities. While male-to-female transgender inmates may experience less victimization housed in facilities designated for female inmates, other female inmates there might be exposed to greater physical risk. In addition, corrections officials express concern that placing a male-to-female transgender inmate in a women's facility could lead to sex with other female inmates (Rosenblum 1999–2000), which in turn can result in pregnancy (Sylvia Rivera Law Project 2007). Finally, there is the concern that inmates who are biologically female may experience being housed with male-to-female transgender inmates as a violation of their privacy. This was the argument in *Crosby v. Reynolds* (1991) when the plaintiff argued that her privacy had been violated because she was housed in a county jail with a transgender woman. In response, the court pointed to the correctional physicians' recommendation that the transgender woman should remain housed with female inmates as it was in her best psychological and physical interests.

The use of protective custody or administrative segregation presents yet another dilemma. Generally intended for disciplinary purposes, it is also frequently used as a protective measure (Arkles 2009; Sylvia Rivera Law Project 2007). It is employed as a housing tool for the incarceration of vulnerable inmates in general and transgender inmates in particular. A case brought forward by a transgender inmate housed in the Sacramento county jail reveals the challenges of simultaneously considering (and confusing) biological sex and gender in housing decisions as well as prioritizations of safety and security in doing so (*Tates v. Blanas* 2002). In that case the:

> Defendant first seeks to justify this decision on the ground that state law "requires that members of the opposite sex be separated from each other at the jail," but then concedes that pre-operative inmates "are housed according to the biological gender." Defendant further represents that: "The general policy is to place such an individual in the general population of members of the same gender, unless there is reason to believe that doing so will jeopardize the safety of the inmate. Factors include whether the individual exhibits mannerisms and physical characteristics of the opposite sex." Plaintiff desired to be placed in the men's general population. Because of his female appearance and mannerisms, the Main Jail and classification officers were concerned for his safety, as it is not unusual for such persons to be subject to physical assault and rape if housed in general population. Based on these and other factors, it was determined that plaintiff should be classified as a total separation inmate and housed on the protective custody floor (*Tates v. Blanas* 2002, pp. 4–5).

Segregating transgender inmates from the larger inmate population can significantly limit their movement throughout the facility, participation in facility activities, access to resources beyond what is minimally needed for basic hygiene needs, and communication with others. Therefore, it is experienced as differentially punitive (Arkles 2009; Mann 2006; Peek 2003–2004; Rosenblum 1999–2000; Sylvia Rivera Law Project 2007).

Plaintiff Meriwether argued (among other issues) that confinement in administrative segregation indefinitely was a violation of her Eighth Amendment rights (*Meriwether v. Faulkner* 1987). The district court dismissed this claim, indicating that protective custody is "a means of assuring the safe and efficient operation of a prison on a day-to-day basis" (p. 411, internal quotation omitted). Although the

U.S. Court of Appeals for the 7th Circuit reversed the dismissal on different grounds, it could not reconcile what it perceived as a conflict: Meriwether claimed she had experienced assaults when in general population, but she did not want to be segregated (see Arkles 2009). Similarly, activist organizations argue that these segregation practices result in both a "double victimization" for victims of violence as well as a form of punishment for one's nonconforming gender identity status (Daley 2005; DC Trans Coalition 2010; Just Detention International 2009).[9] Two recent court decisions support the argument that this kind of solitary confinement or "total separation" used in the Sacramento County Jail did just that and, thus, was not permissible (*Medina-Tejada v. Sacramento County* 2006; *Tates v. Blanas* 2003; see also the discussion by Arkles 2009), even if presumably in pursuit of goals of safety and security.

Only a few large jails currently screen for transgender status and house inmates in separate sections and, even then, this group is usually housed in separate "wards" or "pods" for gay inmates (Dolovich 2011; Mann 2006; Peek 2003–2004; Rosenblum 1999–2000; Tewksbury and Potter 2005). In 2012, the Los Angeles Police Department announced the opening of a special 24-bed pod in the downtown jail in which transgender arrestees will be housed. As the Jail Division Commander who announced this innovation said in a public forum, "This is a major change [that will form an] environment that's safe and secure, as there's been a history of violence against transgender people" (Los Angeles Times 2012; see also Jenness 2013). In a Los Angeles County Jail, gay men and transgender women are housed in a segregated unit—an approach designed to protect the group from sexual harassment and violence (Dolovich 2011). The San Francisco County Jail protocol is also unique in that it provides more specific directives calling for transgender inmates to be housed according to their identified gender even within the larger jail for men (Scheel and Eustace 2002). Rosenblum (1999–2000) explains that the New York City Department of Corrections used a separate ward for both gay and transgender inmates and officials did not make distinctions between the groups. The challenge is to ensure that separation by transgender (or any other) status does not result in diminished resources and differentially punitive conditions.

---

[9] Taking a different perspective, and based on experiences with transgender, intersex, and gender nonconforming incarcerated legal clients, Arkles (2009) argues that isolating this group of prisoners in correctional facilities actually prohibits relationship and community building that, "resist violence and help people who are targets of violence to survive" (p. 518). Arkles (2009) posits that there are benefits of friendships, consensual romantic and sexual relationships, and familial relationships built in prison. Although recent empirical research by Jenness et al. (2011) similarly indicates that transgender inmates report benefits from relationships among each other and with non-transgender inmates, it also suggests that Arkles (2009) may be overstating these benefits and underestimating the negative effects. In their work, Jenness et al. (2011) reveal that transgender inmates who reported sexual and "marriage-like" relationships with other inmates were also more likely to experience sexual assault. In addition, transgender inmate culture may also facilitate competition that leads to violence within the group often related to competition for, and attention from, potential partners (Sumner 2009).

In the past decade, several local correctional systems have enacted policies that challenge sex segregation as an entirely taken-for-granted and normative practice. First, in New York juvenile detention centers, a new policy emerged after a 2006 lawsuit brought by a 15-year-old male-to-female transgender youth (Kates 2008). Among many provisions, a committee now considers youths' requests for gender-identity transfers or private sleeping quarters and showers. Second, Washington State's King County Department of Adult and Juvenile Detention (2006) similarly put forth a policy that establishes protocols for transgender inmates, including consideration of gender identity in housing and ensuring similar access to services if/when housed in protective custody. Third, the D.C. Department of Corrections released a new policy that addresses the treatment of transgender inmates, including privacy for strip searches and the development of a transgender committee that will determine the placement of transgender inmates who may be considered for gender-based placement (District of Columbia Department of Corrections 2009; Najafi 2009). Fourth, as mentioned in the introduction of this chapter, Cook County Jail in Chicago adopted a policy that considers the housing (and other aspects of custody and care) of transgender inmates on an individual basis (Hawkins 2011). This includes the possibility of being placed in housing units according to gender identity rather than biological sex. Fifth, and most recently, the Denver Sheriff's department established a policy that includes attending to gender pronouns and the gender of staff conducting searches, and a transgender review board that will examine the appropriate housing conditions for each transgender prisoner in place of segregation in efforts to ensure continued access to programming (Garcia 2012).

Clearly, there appears to be a move toward innovative policies at the local level and less so at the state and federal levels.[10] Within this context, the final type of policy to be considered is policy that addresses appearance, demeanor, and gender displays.

Displaying Gender

Relatively few recent correctional policies addressing transgender inmates are attentive to what many consider the minutia of correctional operations and others consider central to the well-being of transgender inmates. Beyond the larger, more

---

[10] Most frequently, calls for improvement in housing procedures related to transgender inmates are for identity-based placement (Broadus 2009; Mann 2006; Peek 2003–2004; Rosenblum 1999–2000; Transgender Law Center, n.d.) or at least for housing this group in a separate wing or unit. The expectation is that this will lead to increased safety. Recent work, however, complicates this issue. Respondents in the studies conducted by the Sylvia Rivera Law Project (2007) and Emmer et al. (2011) were not in agreement regarding housing preferences. Some respondents felt it was better to manage prison life while in segregation most of the day, others prefer to be housed in the general population. Related, Jenness et al. (2011) found that the majority of male-to-female transgender inmates in California prisons for men would prefer to be housed in facilities for men (65 %). Reasons provided included an emphasis on the access to men in a male facility.

visible and constitutionally contestable policies that differentially affect transgender inmates (discussed in the previous sections), there are policies that enable and curtail gender displays in prison. Transgender prisoners and their advocates repeatedly point to rules and regulations, as well as daily practices, that contribute to and detract from the identity and well-being of transgender prisoners. With this in mind, this final subsection focuses on policies designed to address gender expression in general and pronoun use and other gender displays in the form of clothing and adornment in particular. These policies encourage correctional efforts to couple gender and sex segregation through an explicit commitment to traditional heteronormative gender norms.

Name and Pronoun Use

In general, policies in place today in U.S. correctional systems do not explicitly address the use of gendered pronouns in prisons. However, transgender prisoners have routinely called for policies that require correctional staff to refer to them by the name that reflects their gender identity and use the appropriate pronoun. As Scheel and Eustace (2002) write in their commentary in the *Model Protocols on the Treatment of Transgender Persons by the San Francisco County Jail*, "One of the most consistent complaints from transgender inmates is that they are referred to by pronouns associated with their birth-identified gender instead of those pronouns which respect their gender identity" (p. 8). Testimony before the National Prison Rape Elimination Commission in 2005 by the Director of the Transgender Law Center supports this point. For transgender prisoners, this is not mere "name calling," it is a matter of respect.

Framed as a matter of respect, some correctional policies indirectly address the issue of deference embodied in "name calling." For example, the California departmental policy on *Rights and Respect of Others* located within "Article 1: Behavior" within the section on Rules and Regulations of Adult Operations and Programs (CDCR Title 15 2009, Section 3004, p. 19) suggests some discretion along these lines:

> (a) Inmates and parolees have the right to be treated respectfully, impartially, and fairly by all employees. Inmates and parolees have the responsibility to treat others in the same manner. Employees and inmates may use first names in conversation with each other when it is mutually acceptable to both parties.

Another policy on *Employee Conduct* within Subchapter 5 on Personnel, "Article 2: Employees" is perhaps more specific as it cautions against using anything other than "proper" names (CDCR Title 15 2009, Section 3391, p. 210):

> (a) Employees shall be alert, courteous, and professional in their dealings with inmates, parolees, fellow employees, visitors and members of the public. Inmates and parolees shall be addressed by their proper names, and never by derogatory or slang reference.

Depending on how the above policies are interpreted, failure to call a transgender prisoner a name that is preferred by the prisoner may be perceived as a show of disrespect and, thus, a violation of departmental policy. Alternatively, using pronouns that align with gender identity rather than (assumed) sex category (if different) may be interpreted as use of "slang," thus a departure from the use of "proper names" and a violation of policy.

This issue was recently addressed in *Stevens v. Williams* (2008) when a U.S. Magistrate Judge in Oregon reasoned that correctional officials were not required to use female pronouns even though Stevens had obtained a formal (i.e., legally recognized) name change from the County. The court concluded that even if undesired pronoun use was perceived as verbal harassment, verbal harassment does not violate Eighth Amendment protections. From an operational standpoint, this is perhaps not surprising given that the use of male and female pronouns challenges efforts to sort and screen by sex. Use of male *and* female pronouns would necessarily indicate that a "male facility" also housed "female" or feminine inmates, violating a fundamental (even if unwritten) correctional policy that segregates by sex (and, presumably gender). This potential confusion is highlighted in a pretrial motion in *Giraldo v. California Department of Corrections and Rehabilitation* (2007). Defendants requested:

> …the Court issue an order preventing plaintiff's attorney from attiring plaintiff in woman's [sic] clothing. Argument. The Court should issue an order preventing plaintiff's attorneys from referring to plaintiff in the feminine or using feminine pronouns at trial because such practices raise a danger of prejudice and of misleading of the jury. (Evid. Code, § 352; *Garfield v. Russell* (1967) 251 Cal.App.2d 275, 279.) Specifically, the jury would be unduly prejudiced against defendants if the jury gets the impression that defendants housed a female individual in a male prison…(Defendants' Motion in Limine No. 4 in *Giraldo v. The California Department of Corrections and Rehabilitation et al.* CGC-07-461473, p. 2).

The judge ruled against this motion.

Clothing and Adornment

While Petersen et al.'s (1996) research is over 16 years old, their indication that only 3 % of correctional jurisdictions specified an option for inmates to choose gender-appropriate clothing remains consistent with current trends—trends that will become clearer as transgender correctional policy continues to become institutionalized. Few recently developed policies in local systems go beyond issues deemed legally "necessary" to embrace practices related to daily confinement, human dignity, and respect that expand the domain of allowable gender displays in carceral environments. For example, the New York policy for youth includes provisions that allow for considerations of requests for gender-identity transfers or private sleeping quarters and showers mentioned earlier. Youth are also permitted to wear gender-appropriate uniforms, including bras and female underwear for male-to-female transgender youth. Grooming standards are the same for males and females. Youth may also request to be called any name, and staff are required to use the pronoun requested by the youth both in person and on any facility documents. Likewise, according to news reports, the new Denver Sheriff's Department policy allows for specifying preferred name and pronoun (Garcia 2012). As another example, the Washington D.C. jail policy requires that inmates are identified by last name (without pronoun use) and allows for clothing consistent with the gender of their housing assignment. Notably, changes in policies that facilitate gender presentation quite apart from biological sex are often accompanied by gender-, rather than sex-, based housing placement in these local jurisdictions.[11]

Far more often, however, clothing and cosmetics beyond what is outlined in state corrections' policies are usually considered contraband. This includes bras for transgender inmates who have developed breasts as a result of hormonal treatment (even if provided by the department of corrections) or implants. Likewise, there are rules and regulations that specify the use of cosmetics, grooming standards, and other issues related to adornment and gender displays.

In California, home to the largest *known* transgender prison population in the U.S. (Jenness et al. 2011; Sexton et al. 2010; c.f., Brown and McDuffie 2009), policies that reveal gendered distinctions along these lines are found in the Department Operations Manual. A search of all chapters directly related to inmate management in the 2009 version of this manual revealed the largest number of delineations along gender lines in the chapter on Custody and Security Operations and often when clothing and hygiene regulations are outlined. Additional distinctions with regard to "personal cleanliness" are made in another operations manual called the Title 15, an expanded version of the Department Operations Manual.

For example, Chap. 5 : *Adult Custody and Security Operations, Article 43: Inmate Property* in the *Department Operations Manual* specifies that "**Male** inmates shall not receive or possess items of clothing designed and manufactured specifically for **women** unless authorized for medical reasons" (Section 54030.17.2, p. 443). *Title 15, Article 5: Personal Cleanliness (Section 3062)* elaborates grooming standards for males and females in sections h and j–l as follows:

> (h) Facial hair, including short beards, mustaches, and sideburns are permitted for **male** inmates and shall not extend more than one-half inch in length outward from the face.
>
> (k) An inmate may not pierce any part of his/her body for the purpose of wearing an earring or other jewelry. A **male** inmate may not possess or wear earrings. A **female** inmate may wear authorized earrings with only one matching earring worn in each ear.

---

[11] In addition, innovative policies have begun to develop in other arenas of the criminal justice system. For example, recently the Los Angeles Police Department formalized a policy on "police interactions with transgender individuals" (Los Angeles Police Department 2012) which includes guidelines regarding what language to use when addressing transgender individuals and how to conduct a field search.

An inmate shall not possess or wear any type of jewelry or other object intended to be worn as a body piercing adornment.

(j) An inmate's fingernails shall not extend more than ¼ inch beyond the tips of the fingers. Nails shall be neat and clean. **Female** inmates may be permitted to wear only clear nail polish.

(l) A **female** inmate may wear cosmetics that blend with or match the natural, non-ruddy skin tone. False eyelashes are not permitted (Section 3062, p. 45, emphasis added).

In addition, the *Department Operations Manual* specifies that female inmates are allowed an eyebrow pencil/eyeliner, as well as an eye shadow kit and face powder. Male inmates are not afforded the same personal care items. Related, male inmates may possess a wedding band ("one only") whereas female inmates may possess a wedding ring or wedding/engagement ring set. Importantly, and as discussed earlier, who is female and who is male correspond to who is in a men's prison and who is in a women's prison, not prisoners' gender identity. Furthermore, the *Title 15* indicates that failure to adhere to these guidelines can result in disciplinary action. Finally, these policies contrast to the small number of matches found in the chapter on Health Care Services where it was expected there would be significant biological distinctions made.

Institutional rationales for gendered distinctions along these lines are frequently based on cautionary concerns with regard to safety and security, a priority with which judicial actors tend to agree (see Arkles 2012).[12] In addition, some argue that maintaining uniformity through myriad disciplinary tactics (including uniformity in physical appearance) is conducive to facility operations, including maintaining order and thus increased safety (DiIulio 1987). As Harada (2006) explained:

> If the proffered reason given the prison system is safety, the courts will likely find that a compelling reason. However, if the proffered reason is something akin to administrative convenience, that will likely trigger higher scrutiny of the classification regime (p. 653).[13]

This rationale was contested by Plaintiff Star in the case *Star v. Gramley* (1993). Star claimed that the warden violated her First Amendment rights to freedom of expression in forbidding her to wear women's makeup and clothing. The warden argued that clothing restrictions are in place for the purpose of security and inmates wearing women's clothing and makeup "could provoke and/or promote homosexual activity or assault" (*Star v. Gramley* 1993, p. 278). In addition, the warden argued that inmates' ability to change their physical appearances creates an escape concern. The U.S. District Court ruled in favor of the warden/defendant, effectively showing judicial deference to corrections administrators (Feeley and Rubin 1998).

---

[12] However, see the recent U.S. Court of Appeals for the First Circuit decision in *Battista v. Clarke* (2011), in which the court upheld the district court decision challenging the defendants' claims that hormonal therapy would result in an increased safety risk.

[13] However, see *Tates v. Blanas* (2003).

In a subsequent case, the U.S. Court of Appeals for the 6th Circuit in *Murray v. United States Bureau of Prisons* (1997) agreed that "an inmate is not entitled to the clothing of his choice, and prison officials do not violate the constitution simply because the clothing may not be esthetically pleasing or may be ill fitting" (at 2, internal quotation and citation omitted). In its denial of the plaintiff's requested hair and skin products, the court reasoned that, "Because routine discomfort is part of the penalty that criminal offenders pay for their offenses against society, only those deprivations denying the minimal civilized measure of life's necessities are sufficiently grave to form the basis of an Eighth Amendment violation" (at 2, internal quotation and citation omitted).

Although not brought as a transgender issue specifically, a similar matter was addressed in the case *Deblasio v. Johnson* (2000). The court applied intermediate scrutiny to the challenge of hair length requirements for male and female inmates. The State's reasoning underlying different hair length requirements for male inmates was based on the argument that males are a greater security threat and, thus require more precautionary guidelines. The U.S. District Court found that security was both an important and compelling "governmental and penological objective" and that the State's methods were "substantially related" to this objective (p. 328).

Pointing out the artificiality of this reasoning, Harada (2006) argues that:

> Although *Deblasio* appears to be a frivolous lawsuit, the court's reasoning appears to rely upon sex and gender stereotypes. The court does not question the essential meaning of the terms male or female in its analysis and as a result does not interrogate the assumption that males are more violent than females (p. 656).

Using the court's reasoning, perhaps feminine inmates in male facilities are also significantly less "prone" to violence and escape and, conversely, masculine inmates in female facilities may be more prone. If the above reasoning stands, policies could presumably vary according to gender identification rather than biological sex. These policies detailing how "males" and "females" are required to present themselves expose the gendering of correctional policy at the level of gender displays (see also Arkles 2012). Prison policies that manage physical gender presentation in these ways reveal that while the organization formally manages according to distinctions made by sex/anatomy, this correctional control extends to gender/identity distinctions. As with the use of gender- (rather than sex-) based pronouns, formally allowing gendered presentation of self would require the institution to concede to a change in practice or policy with regard to gender segregation.

However, it is notable that rules do not fully specify, much less effectively control, what Goffman (1979) refers to as gender display and demeanor. "If gender be defined as the culturally established correlates of sex (whether in consequence of biology or learning), then gender display refers to the conventionalized portrayals of these correlates" (p. 69). Demeanor includes "behavior typically conveyed through deportment, dress, and bearing" (Goffman 1967, p. 77). It is also consequential that these policies cannot regulate others' interpretations of gendered conduct that also imbue gendered identities and interactions (Kessler and McKenna 2000).

Decades of research reveal that the prison remains a multi-gendered culture with gendered interactions within the group even as it is administratively controlled to be otherwise (Coggeshall 1988; Donaldson 2001; Fleisher and Krienert 2009; Keys 2002; Sykes 1958). Thus, an unwavering commitment to safety and security through sex segregation confronted by the reality of the incarceration of trans*gender* inmates results in a key paradox: gender integration in sex-segregated facilities.

Discussion and Conclusion

The routine and seemingly unproblematic practice of sex segregation in U.S. detention facilities has gained newfound visibility and become the focus of legal, correctional, and public debate as transgender prisoners and their advocates press for a reconsideration of prison policy in general and the development of correctional policies for transgender inmates in particular. The development of this body of policy is, at best, in the incipient stages. This is not surprising because it is only recently in the history of penology—in the latter decades of the twentieth century and the first decade of the twenty-first century—that transgender inmates have come to the fore in public, activist, and correctional consciousness and attendant debates.

Situated within this historical context, this chapter has examined published surveys of correctional policies, original policies, judicial rulings, and legal and advocate discourse related to the management of transgender inmates. Our focus on policies and rulings addresses how transgender people are delineated in carceral environments; unique medical concerns for transgender inmates, especially those related to initiating and sustaining hormone therapy; complicated questions about where best to house transgender inmates—in the general population or in segregated housing assignments—in light of their amplified vulnerability to assault; and an array of dilemmas related to the physical appearance and grooming standards for transgender inmates, including the wearing of female clothing, the use of cosmetics that accentuate femininity, and the ability to wear long hair and be respectfully referenced by female names and pronouns in men's correctional facilities.

Looking across these policy concerns, there is considerable asymmetry in the degree to which policy has emerged and become homogenized. Within the larger body of transgender corrections policy, some policies regarding some specific issues reveal considerable variability while other policies regarding specific issues reveal near-uniformity. Most notably, there is almost complete agreement on three types of policies. First, the almost universal practice of genitalia-based prison assignments privileges genitalia over other markers of sex and gender. Second, there is comparatively little variation in the use of medical terminology to identify inmates as transgender. Seen in these terms, transgender prisoners are marked by disorder and pathology effectively categorized as a departure from a "normal" or "healthy" gender type around which correctional policies and practices in prisons for *men* and prisons for *women* are organized. The institutional reliance on the DSM designations is constant—although this may change form as recent changes in the DSM signal a shift away from necessarily pathologizing transgender prisoners. Third, although there remain policies that speak to presentation of self in daily life in sex-segregated prisons, these presume that male/female sex segregation constitutes gender segregation. What is and is not allowed and tolerated in terms of *gender*-specific clothing, adornment, and the use of gendered pronouns is most often *not* addressed by transgender correctional policy. Nor does it provide for regulations on other forms of gender display—walk, talk, and social interaction.

In contrast, policies that address the conditions under which initial and continuing hormone treatment can and must be provided in prison reveal contested terrain. In addition, whether or not transgender prisoners are entitled to sex change operations while in prison constitutes the most recently visible contested domain with regard to transgender prisoners. Although prisoner litigation has resulted in a move toward increased access to hormonal treatment while incarcerated (O'Day-Senior 2008–2009), this practice remains far from agreed upon as a normative approach to the treatment of transgender persons in carceral settings. And, while most judicial rulings have denied access to sex change surgery for transgender prisoners, the most recent court ruling reverses this trend.

One way to make sense of this asymmetry in the degree to which transgender correctional policy is settled is to situate the emergence, formulation, and adoption of some policies (and not others) within a particular context defined by three features. These policies have emerged and taken form in a culture of control that provides the opportunity for external, non-state actors to influence correctional policies (Garland 2001); in which judicial deference toward corrections administrators and operations is consequential (Feeley and Rubin 1998; Jenness and Smyth 2011); and among correctional systems that privilege safety and security above other concerns (Gaes et al. 2004).

Taken as a whole, this body of policy reveals a paradox. On the one hand, the deep and abiding commitment to sex segregation as a defining characteristic of carceral environments affirms a binary gender system. That remains constant and uncontested. On the other hand, however, the policies examined in this chapter reveal a plethora of organizational accommodations promised to transgender prisoners by authority of policy; taken as a whole, the provisions acknowledge gender variant prisoners who do not conform to a dichotomous gender system and thus mark carceral environments as multi-gendered institutions.

The mosaic of judicial rulings and organizational policies discussed in this chapter reveal how the production of gender is facilitated and constrained in carceral settings. At the level of macrosorting, transgender policy maintains a correctional commitment to sex segregation, despite political and legal challenges as well as recent research that reveals that current policy and practice have not kept transgender inmates safe (Jenness et al. 2007; 2011; Jenness 2014). At the level of microgender displays, however, transgender policies—or the absence thereof—

enable the production of multigendered prison environments by only minimally controlling deference, demeanor, and adornment. At the end of the day, these polices recognize the presence of transgender prisoners, even as they inevitably reaffirm a binary understanding of gender.

At this point in the development of transgender correctional policy, much remains to be considered. First and foremost, the inventory presented in this chapter needs to be kept current. During the time of this writing, the rate of change in policy development has accelerated considerably. Second, and related, the next step is to begin to turn the focus from policy as "law-on-the-books" to implementation as "law-in-action" to fully grasp the extent to which these changes in formalized policy have led to on-the-ground changes in practice. Consistent with decades of research in the field of law and society that reveal deep and continuous gaps between the "law-on-the-books" and "law-in-action," legal scholar, transgender activist, and founder of the Sylvia Rivera Law Project, Dean Spade, has argued that law—often relied upon as a central institution to motor social change, especially in the arena of penal practice and civil rights—is not a viable pathway toward it (Winter 2011). Instead, he argues for more efforts to be put into broad social movements (see also Arkles 2012). Regardless, to increase policy effectiveness, practitioners, activists, and researchers alike would do well to turn efforts toward implementation with a single two-pronged goal in mind: to respect the dignity of transgender prisoners and to keep them keep them safe while locked up (for more along these lines, see Jenness 2014). This two-tiered criteria is a reasonable means by which to assess both new and old policies.

Acknowledgments The authors would like to thank the following CDCR personnel who contributed to this work in important ways by providing and interpreting CDCR policies for us as we produced this chapter: Nola Grannis, Suzan Hubbard, and Wendy Still. In addition, the chapter has benefitted from comments provided by our academic colleagues, including Kitty Calavita, Kristy Matsuda, Cheryl Maxson, Jodi O'Brien, Joan Petersilia, Lori Sexton, and Brian Williams. Alyse Bertenthal provided very helpful comments on an earlier version of this chapter, which helped us clarify the legal underpinnings that provide the foundation for many judicial decisions presented. Finally, the following experts helped clarify the arguments presented in this chapter: Dr. Lori Kohler, Alexander L. Lee, Linda McFarlane, Lovisa Stannow, and Dr. Denise Taylor.

References

Acker, J. (1990). Hierarchies, jobs, bodies: A theory of gendered organizations. *Gender and Society, 4*(2), 139–158.

Alexander, R., Jr, & Meshelemiah, J. C. A. (2010). Gender identity disorders in prisons: What are the legal implications for prison mental health professional and administrators? *The Prison Journal, 90*(3), 269–287.

American Psychiatric Association. (2000). *Diagnostic and statistical manual of mental disorders: DSM-IV-TR*. Washington, DC: American Psychiatric Association.

Arkles, G. (2009). Safety and solidarity across gender lines: Rethinking segregation of transgender people in detention. *Temple Political and Civil Rights Law Review, 18*(2), 515–560.

Arkles, G. (2012). Correcting race and gender: Prison regulation of social hierarchy through dress. *New York University Law Review, 87*(4), 859–959.

Berk, R. A., Ladd, H., Graziano, H., Baek, J. (2003). A randomized experiment testing inmate classification systems. *Criminology & Public Policy, 2*(2), 215–242.

Britton, D. M. (2003). *At work in the iron cage: The prison as gendered organization.* New York, NY: New York University Press.

Broadus, K. W. (2009). The criminal justice system and trans people. *Temple Political and Civil Rights Law Review, 18*(2), 561–572.

Brown, G. R., & McDuffie, E. (2009). Health care policies addressing transgender inmates in prison systems in the United States. *Journal of Correctional Health Care, 15*(4), 280–291.

California Department of Corrections. (1948). California State Archives. *Corrections. Adult authority and director, department of corrections, meetings, minutes,* Sacramento, CA, F3717:13.

California Department of Corrections and Rehabilitation. (2010). *Department operations manual.* Retrieved from http://www.cdcr.ca.gov/Regulations/Adult_Operations/DOM_TOC.html

California Department of Corrections and Rehabilitation. (2009). *California code of regulations. Title XV: Crime prevention and corrections.* Retrieved from http://www.cdcr.ca.gov/Regulations/Adult_Operations/docs/Title15-2012.pdf

Coggeshall, J. (1988). Ladies behind bars: A liminal gender as cultural mirror. *Anthropology Today, 4*(4), 6–8.

DC Trans Coalition. (2010, March 12). *Testimony before the DC council committee on public safety and the judiciary regarding department of corrections oversight.* Retrieved from http://dctranscoalition.files.wordpress.com/2010/03/dc-trans-coalition-testimony-regarding-department-of-corrections-03-12-10.pdf

Daley, C. (2005, August 15). *At risk: Sexual abuse and vulnerable groups behind bars: Second public hearing of the National Prison Rape Elimination Commission, Testimony before the Commission in San Francisco, CA.* Retrieved from http://www.nclrights.org/site/DocServer/prison_daley081905.pdf?docID=941

DiIulio, J. J. (1987). *Governing prisons: A comparative study of correctional management.* New York, NY: Free Press.

District of Columbia Department of Corrections. (2009). *Program statement: Gender classification and housing, No. 4020.3.* Retrieved from http://doc.dc.gov/doc/frames.asp?doc=/doc/lib/doc/program_statements/4000/PS020_3GenderClassificationandHousing022009.pdf

Dolovich, S. (2011). Strategic segregation in the modern prison. *American Criminal Law Review, 48*(1), 1–110.

Donaldson, S. (2001). A million jockers, punks, and queens. In D. F. Sabo, T. A. Kupers & W. J. London (Eds.), *Prison masculinities* (pp. 118–126). Philadelphia, PA: Temple University Press.

Edelman, L. (1992). Legal ambiguity and symbolic structures: Organizational mediation of civil rights law. *American Journal of Sociology, 97,* 1531–1576.

Emmer, P., Lowe A., & Marshall, R. B. (2011). This is a prison, glitter is not allowed: Experiences of trans and gender variant people in Pennsylvania's prison systems. *A report by the Hearts on a Wire Collective.* Retrieved from http://www.galaei.org/documents/thisisaprison.pdf

Feeley, M. M., & Rubin, E. L. (1998). *Judicial policy making and the modern state: How the courts reformed America's prisons.* Cambridge, MA: Cambridge University Press.

Feeley, M. M., & Simon, J. (1992). The new penology: Notes on the emerging strategy of corrections and its implications. *Criminology, 30*(4), 449–474.

Fleisher, M. S., Krienert, J. L., & Jacobs, J. B. (2009). *The myth of prison rape: Sexual culture in American prisons.* Lanham, MD: Rowman and Littlefield Publishers.

Gaes, G. G., Camp, S. D., Nelson, J. B., & Saylor, W. G. (2004). *Measuring prison performance: Government privatization and accountability.* Walnut Creek, CA: AltaMira Press.

Garcia, N. (2012, June 22). Denver Sheriff department to implement new trans policies. *Out Front*. Retrieved from http://outfrontonline.com/ofcnow/denver-sheriff-implement-newtrans-policies/

Garland, D. (2001). *Culture of control: Crime and social order in contemporary society*. Chicago, IL: University of Chicago Press.

Goffman, E. (1967). *Interaction ritual: Essays in face-to-face behavior*. Chicago, IL: Aldine Publishing Company.

Goffman, E. (1979). *Gender advertisements*. New York, NY: Harper and Row.

Goodman, P. (2008). It's just black, white, or Hispanic: An observational study of racializing moves in California's segregated prison reception centers. *Law & Society Review, 42*(4), 735–770.

Grant, J. M., Mottet, L. A., Tanis, J. D., Harrison, J., Herman, J. L., & Keisling, M. (2011). *Injustice at every turn: A report of the National Transgender Discrimination Survey*. Washington, DC: The National Center for Transgender Equality and The National Gay and Lesbian Task Force.

Grattet, R., & Jenness, V. (2005). The reconstitution of law in local settings: Agency discretion, ambiguity, and a surplus of law in the policing of hate crime. *Law & Society Review, 39*(4), 893–940.

Harada, N. (2006). Trans-literacy within Eighth Amendment jurisprudence: Defusing gender and sex. *New Mexico Law Review, 36*, 627–660.

Hawkins, K. (2011, April 9). Jail has new policy for transgender inmates. *NBC Chicago*. Retrieved from http://www.nbcchicago.com/news/local/cook-county-jail-transgender-inmates-119516094.html

Herbert, R. (1985). Women's prisons: An equal protection evaluation. *The Yale Law Journal, 94*(5), 1182–1206.

Ismaili, K. (2006). Contextualizing the criminal justice policy-making process. *Criminal Justice Policy Review, 17*(3), 255–269.

Jenness, V. (2011). Getting to know "the girls" in an "alpha-male" community: Notes on fieldwork on transgender inmates in California prisons. In S. Fenstermaker & N. Jones (Eds.), *Sociologists backstage: Answers to 10 questions about what they do* (pp. 139–161). New York, NY: Routledge.

Jenness, V. (2014). Pesticides, prisoners, and policy: Complexity and praxis in research on transgender prisoners and beyond. *Sociological Perspectives*.

Jenness, V., & Grattet, R. (2005). The law-in-between: The effects of organizational perviousness on the policing of hate crime. *Social Problems, 52*(3), 337–359.

Jenness, V., Maxson, C., Matsuda, K., & Sumner, J. (2007). Violence in California correctional facilities: An empirical examination of sexual assault. *Report submitted to the California Department of Corrections and Rehabilitation*. Sacramento, CA. Retrieved from http://ucicorrections.seweb.uci.edu/pdf/FINAL_PREA_REPORT.pdf

Jenness, V., Maxson, C., Sumner, J., & Matsuda, K. (2010). Accomplishing the difficult but not impossible: Collecting self-report data on inmate-on-inmate sexual assault in prison. *Criminal Justice Policy, 21*(1), 3–30.

Jenness, V., Sexton L., & Sumner, J. (2011). Transgender inmates in California prisons: An empirical study of a vulnerable population. *Report submitted to the California Department of Corrections and Rehabilitation*. Sacramento, CA.

Jenness, V., & Smyth, M. (2011). The passage and implementation of the Prison Rape Elimination Act: Legal endogeneity and the uncertain road from symbolic law to instrumental effects. *Stanford Law & Policy Review, 22*(2), 489–528.

Jenness, V., Sumner, J., Sexton, L., & Alamillo-Luchese, N. (2014). Cinderella, Wilma Flinstone, and Xena the Warrior Princess: Capturing diversity among transgender women in men's prisons. In C. Renzetti & K. Bergen (Eds.), *Understanding diversity: Celebrating difference, challenging inequality*. Upper Saddle River, NJ: Allyn & Bacon Press.

Johnson, D. (1987, June 1). Women blend in with men at Illinois prison. *The New York Times*. Retrieved from http://www.nytimes.com/1987/06/01/us/women-blend-in-with-men-at-illinois-prison.html

Just Detention International. (2009, February). *A call for change: Protecting the rights of LGBTQ detainees*. Retrieved from http://www.justdetention.org/pdf/CFCLGBTQJan09.pdf

Kates, W. (2008, June 20). Advocates hail new policy for transgender youth at New York's juvenile detention centers. *StarTribune.com*. Retrieved from http://www.startribune.com/templates/Print_This_Story?sid=20595989

Kessler, S. J., & McKenna, W. (2000). Gender construction in everyday life. *Feminism and Psychology, 10*(1), 11–29.

Keys, D. (2002). Instrumental sexual scripting: An examination of gender-role fluidity in the correctional institution. *Journal of Contemporary Criminal Justice, 18*(3), 258–278.

King County Department of Adult and Juvenile Detention. (2006, August 31). Chapter 6: Inmate classification and discipline. Adult Divisions. *General Policy Manual*. Retrieved from http://www.aclu.org/files/images/asset_upload_file70_27801.pdf

Kohler, L. (2005, February 7). *Primary care for transgender people*. Presentation to the Hawaii AIDS education and training center: AIDS education project. Retrieved from http://www.hawaii.edu/hivandaids/links_TransgenderLoriKohler.htm

Lee, A. (2008). Trans models in prison: The medicalization of gender identity and the Eighth Amendment right to sex reassignment therapy. *Harvard Journal of Law and Gender, 31*, 447–471.

Los Angeles Police Department. (2012, April 10). Police interactions with transgender individuals. *Memorandum from LAPD chief of police to all department personnel*. Retrieved from http://www.google.com/url?sa=t&rct=j&q=&esrc=s&source=web&cd=2&ved=0CDkQFjAB

Los Angeles Times. (2012, April 18). LAPD plans separate transgender area in jail. *SFGate*. Retrieved from http://www.sfgate.com/cgi-bin/article.cgi?f=/c/a/2012/04/18/BAR51O4IVU.DTL&type=printable

Lynch, M. (1998). Waste managers? The new penology, crime fighting, and parole agent identity. *Law & Society Review, 32*(4), 839–870.

Mahan, S., Mabli, J., Johnston, B., Trask, B., & Hilek, J. (1989). Sexually integrated prisons: Advantages, disadvantages and some recommendations. *Criminal Justice Policy Review, 3*(2), 149–158.

Mann, R. (2006). The treatment of transgender prisoners, not just an American problem: A comparative analysis of American, Australian, and Canadian prison policies concerning the treatment of transgender prisoners and a "universal" recommendation to improve treatment. *Law and Sexuality: Review of Lesbian, Gay, Bisexual, and Transgender Legal Issues, 15*, 91–133.

Maxson, C. L., & Klein, M. W. (1997). *Responding to troubled youth*. New York, NY: Oxford University Press.

Meyer, J. W., & Rowan, B. (1977). Institutionalized organizations: Formal structure as myth and ceremony. *The American Journal of Sociology, 83*(2), 340–363.

Meyer, J. W., & Rowan, B. (1978). The structure of educational organizations. In M. W. Meyer & Associates (Eds.), *Environments and organizations* (pp. 78–109). San Francisco, CA: Jossey-Bass, Inc.

Moran, M. (2013). New gender dysphoria criteria replace GID. *Psychiatric News, 48*(7), 9–14.

Moynihan, D. R. (2005). The impact of managing for results mandates in corrections: Lessons from three states. *Criminal Justice Policy Review, 16*(1), 18–37.

Najafi, Y. (2009, March 5). Prison progress: Activists offer measured praise for transgender plans. *Metroweekly*. Retrieved from http://www.metroweekly.com/news/?ak=4090

Namaste, V. K. (2000). *Invisible lives: The erasure of transsexual and transgendered people*. Chicago, IL: University of Chicago Press.

National Center for Lesbian Rights. (2011). *Federal bureau of prisons makes major change in transgender medical policy*. Retrieved from http://www.nclrights.org/site/PageServer?pagename=press_2011_Prisons_TransgenderPolicy_Change_093011

National Commission on Correctional Health Care. (2009). *Position statements: Transgender health care in correctional settings.* Retrieved from http://www.ncchc.org/transgender-health-care-in-correctional-settings

O'Day-Senior, D. (2008–2009). The forgotten frontier? Healthcare for transgender detainees in immigration and customs enforcement detention. *Hastings Law Journal, 60,* 453–476.

Peek, C. (2003–2004). Breaking out of the prison hierarchy: Transgender prisoners, rape, and the Eighth Amendment. *Santa Clara Law Review, 44,* 1211–1248.

Petersen, M., Stephens, J., Dickey, R., & Lewis, W. (1996). Transsexuals within the prison system: An international survey of correctional services policies. *Behavioral Sciences & the Law, 14*(2), 219–229. doi:10.1002/(sici)1099-0798(199621)14:2<219:aid-bsl234>3.0.co;2-n.

Pratt, T. C., Maahs, J., & Stehr, S. D. (1998). The symbolic ownership of the corrections "problem": A framework for understanding the development of corrections policy in the United States. *The Prison Journal, 78*(4), 451–464.

Rafter, N. H. (1985). *Partial justice: Women in state prisons, 1800–1935.* Boston, MA: Northeastern University Press.

Rosenblum, D. (1999-2000). "Trapped" in Sing Sing: Transgendered prisoners caught in the gender binarism. *Michigan Journal of Gender and Law, 6,* 499–571.

Rosenberg, D. (2007, May 21). The mystery of gender: Aside from the obvious, what makes us male or female? The new visibility of transgender America is shedding light on the ancient riddle of identity. *Newsweek, 50–51,* 53–57.

Scheel, M. D., & Eustace, C. (2002, July 25). Model protocols on the treatment of transgender persons by San Francisco County Jail. *National Lawyers Guild & City & County of San Francisco Human Rights Commission.* Retrieved from http://www.google.com/url?sa=t&rct=j&q=&esrc=s&source=web&cd=1&ved=0CC0QFjAA

Sexton, L., Jenness, V., & Sumner, J. (2010). Where the margins meet: A demographic assessment of transgender inmates in men's prisons. *Justice Quarterly.* doi:10.1080/07418820903419010.

Stryker, S. (2008). *Transgender history.* Berkeley, CA: Seal Studies.

Sumner, J. M. (2009). *Keeping house: Understanding the transgender inmate code of conduct through prison policies, environments, and culture.* (Unpublished doctoral dissertation) University of California, Irvine, CA.

Sykes, G. M. (1958). *The society of captives: A study of a maximum security prison.* Princeton, NJ: Princeton University Press.

Sylvia Rivera Law Project. (2007). *"It's war in here": A report on the treatment of transgender and intersex people in New York State men's prisons.* Retrieved from http://archive.srlp.org/resources/pubs/warinhere

Tarzwell, S. (2006–2007). The gender lines are marked with razor wire: Addressing state prison policies and practices for the management of transgender prisoners. *Columbia Human Rights Law Review, 38,* 167–219.

Tewksbury, R., & Potter, R. H. (2005). Transgender prisoners: A forgotten group. In S. Stojkovic (Ed.), *Managing special populations in jails and prisons* (pp. 15.1–15.14). Kingston, NJ: Civic Research Institute.

Transgender Law Center. (n.d). *Policy recommendations regarding LGBT people in California prisons.* Retrieved from http://transgenderlawcenter.org/issues/prisons/policy-recommendations-regarding-lgbt-people-in-california-prisons

Transgender Law and Policy Institute. (2009). *About us.* Retrieved from http://www.transgenderlaw.org/aboutTLPI.htm

Winter, M. (2011, March 1). Trans-formative change. *Guernica.* Retrieved from http://www.guernicamag.com/interviews/spade_3_1_11/

Cases Cited

Battista v. Clarke, 645 F.3d 449 (1st Cir. 2011).
Brooks v. Berg, 270 F. Supp. 2d 302 (N.D. NY 2003).
Crosby v. Reynolds, 763 F. Supp. 666 (D. ME. 1991).
DeBlasio v. Johnson, 128 F.Supp.2d 315 (E.D. VA. 2000).
De'Lonta v. Johnson, 708 F.3d 520 (4th Cir. 2013).
Farmer v. Brennan, 511 US 825 (1994).
Fields v. Smith, 712 F. Supp. 2d 830 (E.D.Wis. 2010).
Garfield v. Russell, 251 Cal.App.2d 275 (1967).
Giraldo v. California Department of Corrections and Rehabilitation, 2007 WL 4355775 (2007).
Greene v. Bowles, 361 F.3d 290 (6th Cir. 2004).
Kosilek v. Maloney, 221 F.Supp.2d 156 (D. MA. 2002).
Kosilek v. Spencer, 889 F.Supp.2d 190 (D. Mass. 2012).
Kosilek v. Spencer, F.Supp.2d, 2013 WL 204696 (D. Mass. 2013).
Long v. Nix, 877 F. Supp. 1358 (S.D. IA. 1995).
Maggert v. Hanks, 131 F.3d 670 (7th Cir. 1997).
Medina-Tejada v. Sacramento County, 2006 WL 463158 (E.D. Cal. 2006).
Meriwether v. Faulkner, 821 F.2d 408 (7th Cir. 1987).
Murray v. United States Bureau of Prisons, 1997 WL 34677 (6th Cir. 1997).
Phillips v. Michigan Department of Corrections, 731 F.Supp. 792 (W.D. M.I. 1990).
Star v. Gramley, 815 F. Supp. 276 (C.D. IL. 1993).
Stevens v. Knowles, 2011 WL 7430402 (C.D. Cal. 2011).
Stevens v. Williams, 2008 WL 916991 (D. Or. 2008).
Tates v. Blanas, 2003 WL 23864868 (E.D. Cal. 2002, 2003).

Statutes Cited

California Evidence Code § 352.
California's Administrative Procedure Act. Government Code §§ 11340–11359.
California Penal Code § 5058.

Chapter 13
LGBT Issues and Criminal Justice Education

Kevin Cannon, P. Ann Dirks-Linhorst, P. Denise Cobb,
Florence Maatita, Dawn Beichner and Robbin Ogle

Abstract This chapter reviews the state of the literature regarding college students' attitudes toward LGBT individuals, and then narrows that focus to discuss criminal justice majors in particular. The status of criminal justice education on LBGT issues is discussed, with particular attention to why such issues are important for undergraduate criminal justice education. The authors suggest a paradigm for inclusion of such issues in criminal justice curriculum globally, modeled after the decision to include race and gender issues in that same curriculum.

Keywords LGBT · Criminal justice · Education · Undergraduate curriculum

K. Cannon (✉) · P. A. Dirks-Linhorst · P. D. Cobb · F. Maatita
Department of Sociology and Criminal Justice Studies,
Southern Illinois University Edwardsville, P.O. Box 1455
Edwardsville, IL 62026, USA
e-mail: kcannon@siue.edu

P. A. Dirks-Linhorst
e-mail: pdirksl@siue.edu

P. D. Cobb
e-mail: pcobb@siue.edu

F. Maatita
e-mail: fmaatit@siue.edu

D. Beichner
Criminal Justice Studies and Women's and Gender Program, Illinois State University,
Campus Box 5250, Normal, IL 61790, USA
e-mail: dmbeich@ilstu.edu

R. Ogle
Criminology and Criminal Justice, University of Nebraska at Omaha,
Omaha, NE 68182, USA

D. Peterson and V. R. Panfil (eds.), *Handbook of LGBT Communities,
Crime, and Justice*, DOI: 10.1007/978-1-4614-9188-0_13,
© Springer Science+Business Media New York 2014

LGBT Issues and Criminal Justice Education

It can be safely presumed that most undergraduate criminal justice majors in the United States have a desire to work in some aspect of the criminal justice system upon completion of their education. As workers in the U.S. criminal justice system, they will have a responsibility to treat all citizens in an unbiased manner. Whether they become police officers, probation or parole officers, correctional workers, rehabilitative counselors, representatives of the court, or actors in any other capacity, it is a certainty that employees of the criminal justice system will have to interact with people who identify as Lesbian, Gay, Bisexual, or Transgender (LGBT). A central component of a properly working justice system is insuring that all people are treated fairly. As such, it is important to understand what types of attitudes and biases undergraduate criminal justice majors may hold toward LGBT citizens.

This chapter focuses on the attitudes toward LGBT people held by criminal justice undergraduate students in the U.S. There has been extensive research conducted on college students and their attitudes towards the LGBT communities. However, there has been relatively little research specifically assessing the attitudes of criminal justice majors toward LGBT communities. The fact that dozens of studies could be found on college students in general, but only four studies could be found that estimated attitudes of criminal justice students indicates a lack of adequate attention being paid to this issue. Couple that fact with the consistent findings that criminal justice students hold more negative attitudes toward LGBT people than do other students, this is clearly an area deserving of attention by the discipline of criminal justice.

College Students' Attitudes Toward LGBT People

Attitudes toward gay and lesbian victims held by undergraduate students are the subject of substantial academic research. There are several factors which are consistently identified as being related to attitudes toward gays and lesbians by college students. These variables include self-esteem, friendship, or acquaintances with openly gay or lesbian people, and political ideology, to name only a few. The primary factors consistently found to be related to attitudes toward LGBT people, and thus will be discussed in more detail here, include gender, religious affiliation, race, age, and the various roles played by educational factors. The literature is silent as to the perceptions of undergraduate student attitudes toward LGBT people specifically as offenders. As well, it should be noted that the majority of the literature assesses students' attitudes about sexual minority (i.e., LGB) people and less so their attitudes about people who are transgender. Nonetheless, we retain the use of the acronym "LGBT" to refer to the broader populations captured within this term and with whom criminal justice students, in particular, will interact in their chosen careers.

Studies show that male students are significantly more likely to hold negative attitudes toward homosexuals than females (Cullen et al. 2002; D'Augelli and Hershberger 1995; Ellis et al. 2002; Herek and Capitanio 1995; Kite and Whitley 1998; Kurdek 1988; Olivero and Murataya 2001; Seltzer 1992). This may be related to the concept of homosexuality in men as being closely aligned with characteristics of femininity. Greenberg and Bystryn (1982) suggest that disapproval of feminine characteristics exhibited by men has been one of the key factors related to the condemnation of male homosexuality throughout history (see, too, discussions in this volume by Dennis; Nichols). Upholding the expectations of masculinity tends to be very important for typical, college-age males. Herek (1986) suggests that the pressure to conform to social expectations of masculinity increases homophobic attitudes in men. This hypothesis has been supported by research finding that college males who believe that femininity is undesirable, and who feel they do not possess adequately masculine characteristics, are the most homophobic (Theodore and Basow 2002). Studies have also shown that males have a more negative attitude toward gay men than they hold toward lesbians (Herek 1988; Kite and Whitley 1998). This also supports the idea that it may be femininity stereotypically associated with gay males that influences negative attitudes.

Studies also suggest that those with a strong religious affiliation are more likely to hold negative attitudes toward gays and lesbians (Berkman and Zinberg 1997; Ellis et al. 2002; Herek 1988; Seltzer 1992). Although not universally condemned by religion, homosexuality is often viewed as a sin. Christianity, presumably the predominant religion represented in research, uses Biblical references to condemn homosexuality. Fulton, Gorsuch and Maynard (1999) find that fundamentalist religious beliefs are significantly correlated with anti-homosexual attitudes. This may be related to both the moral justifications offered by their religion and the greater likelihood of believing in traditional gender roles.

The connection between gender, religion, and negative attitudes toward gays and lesbians has been found not only in research conducted in the United States, but also in research conducted around the world. Studies conducted in Belgium (Hooghe and Meeusen 2012), Hong Kong (Winter et al. 2008), and Canada (Meaney and Rye 2010) have all found that college-age males and those with stronger religious affiliations are more likely to hold negative attitudes toward gays and lesbians.

Another predictor of negative attitudes that has consistently emerged in research is race. African–Americans are more likely to hold negative attitudes toward gays and lesbians (Ellis et al. 2002; Klamen et al. 1999). The increased anti-homosexual attitudes of African–American culture may be related to the "desperate need for a convenient Other *within* the community, yet not truly of the community-an Other on which blame for the chronic identity crises afflicting the Black male psyche can be readily displaced" (Riggs 1991, p. 390, emphasis in original). Increased negative attitudes toward homosexuals may strengthen the bond between heterosexual African–Americans.

Prior research consistently finds that the age of an individual is related to holding negative attitudes toward gays and lesbians; younger people hold more negative attitudes (Hudson and Ricketts 1980; Kurdek 1988; Oliver and Hyde 1995; Whitley and Kite 1995). Although age is consistently found to be related to anti-gay attitudes, there seems to be little theoretical explanation offered for this relationship. The expansion of social interactions is one possible explanation for this change in attitudes during the relatively short period of time in a person's college career. It is common to be exposed to gays or lesbians, at least through informal acquaintances if not friendships, during the college experience. Studies have also shown that students become more liberal during their college career (Lottes and Kuriloff 1994). This may be an explanation of the change in attitudes toward gays and lesbians.

The level of education achieved has been used in numerous studies as a predictor variable. This relationship indicates that those with more education, including those who are progressing toward the completion of a baccalaureate degree, hold more positive attitudes toward gays and lesbians (Herek and Capitanio 1995; Herek and Glunt 1993; Klassen et al. 1989; Lottes and Kuriloff 1994; Seltzer 1992). As college students progress through their education, they become exposed to a broad spectrum of ideas and knowledge which serve to dispel prejudices.

In examining what effect college curriculum has on attitudes, research finds that coursework addressing gay and lesbian issues is influential in improving a student's attitude. Patton and Morrison (1993, 1994) found that a student's attitude improved after completing a course on human sexuality in which homosexuality was explicitly addressed. Similarly, interactions which occur within the classroom, either between gay and straight students or involving guest speakers who identify as gay, improve attitudes toward gays and lesbians (Goldberg 1982; Green et al. 1993; Herek 1984; Lance 1987). This finding is promising because it implies that we, as professors, can alter negative opinions held by our students.

Previous studies indicate that there is variation in attitudes toward gays and lesbians among college majors. Specifically, psychology students hold more positive attitudes toward gays and lesbians than students in other majors (Matchinsky and Iverson 1996). This is related to the increased focus on human interaction in psychology courses. Art and social science majors, more generally, hold more positive attitudes when compared to science or business majors (Schellenberg et al. 1999). This may be related to the increased education regarding matters of the individual or the interactions of individuals which those in the arts and social sciences receive.

Given that most criminal justice programs are housed in Humanities and Social Science colleges, one could hypothesize that criminal justice majors should hold more positive attitudes toward gays and lesbians than business or science majors. Moreover, similarities in the emphasis on human interaction between psychology and criminal justice should lead to the hypothesis that criminal justice majors will hold attitudes toward gays and lesbians similar to those of psychology majors.

Criminal Justice Majors and Attitudes Towards LGBT People

There have only been a few studies directly examining the issue of criminal justice students and homophobia. Olivero and Murataya (2001) surveyed 254 students enrolled in law and justice classes, and other classes, at Central Washington University. At Central Washington University, law and justice majors have the choice of three emphasis areas: Law Enforcement, Corrections, and Paralegal studies. They found that law enforcement students held more homophobic attitudes than either students who were majoring in paralegal studies or other majors (Olivero and Murataya 2001). The reason for this finding was unclear, as the authors theorized that it may be related not to major selection, but rather to gender. The sample of law enforcement majors included 89.75 % male respondents. The authors state that they were "unsure whether this high level of homophobia is a product of homophobic persons finding law enforcement careers attractive or a high concentration of males among law enforcement students" (Olivero and Murataya 2001, p. 277).

Olivero and Murataya's (2001) study, although a good foundation, is limited in several ways. First, this study did not use multivariate analysis to determine if, after other factors related to attitudes toward gays and lesbians are held constant, being a criminal justice major is still related to holding more negative attitudes towards gays and lesbians. The research outlined above clearly indicates that a number of variables may be related to negative attitudes toward gays and lesbians. The failure to use multivariate analysis prohibits drawing valid conclusions regarding whether criminal justice students are significantly different from other students. Second, Olivero and Murataya (2001) selected a homophobia scale which treated attitudes toward both gay men and lesbians as a single concept. This may not be the best operationalization of the concept of homophobia. Third, Olivero and Murataya (2001) derived their sample from only one university and this sample consisted overwhelmingly of men. This causes potential problems of generalizability.

Olivero and Murataya's (2001) study served as a foundation for later researchers who sought to improve on the methodological concerns outlined above. Ventura, Lambert, Bryant and Pasupuleti (2004) conducted a study using multivariate analysis to determine if criminal justice students held more negative attitudes toward gays and lesbians. Ventura et al. surveyed a total of 484 undergraduate students at a Midwestern university. The authors selected 22 classes, including both criminal justice and non-criminal justice courses. The final sample obtained consisted of 46 % criminal justice majors and 54 % non-criminal justice majors. The sample also consisted of 54 % males and 46 % females, addressing the problem of the disproportionate number of male respondents in the Olivero and Murataya (2001) study (Ventura et al. 2004).

Ventura et al. also expanded on the previous research by examining not just attitudes toward gays and lesbians, but also the "willingness to extend rights to gay and lesbian people" and "willingness to socialize with gay and lesbian individuals" (2004, p. 165). The results of the OLS regression analysis indicated that criminal justice majors held more negative views toward gays and lesbians overall, but were not less likely to support rights for gays and lesbians and were not less willing to associate with gays and lesbians (Ventura et al. 2004).

In examining the sample results they found that criminal justice majors reported having fewer gay friends or family members and that less than half of criminal justice majors supported gay marriage or gay adoption. They also found that criminal justice majors were not overwhelmingly supportive of the idea of working with gay clients or co-workers, or having close friends who were gay or lesbian (Ventura et al. 2004). Although these differences were not statistically significant, they were concerning. In order to better understand these results Ventura et al. decided to test if education influenced the likelihood of holding negative views toward gays and lesbians (2004).

They conducted two t-tests, one for criminal justice majors only, one for non-CJ majors, comparing lower level (freshmen and sophomores) and upper level (juniors and seniors) students. For criminal justice majors there was no difference between lower level and upper level students in attitudes. For non-criminal justice students, upper level students held significantly better attitudes toward gays and lesbians (Ventura et al. 2004). The authors concluded that "it appeared that higher education had little impact on criminal justice majors" (Ventura et al. 2004, p. 173). This is an important finding since it may indicate a failing on the part of the discipline of criminal justice to provide a proper education to our students. If non-criminal justice majors are significantly improving their attitudes throughout their college education, it may be reasonable to conclude that the lack of attention paid to LGBT issues by the criminal justice discipline may be at fault (see Cannon and Dirks-Linhorst 2006; Olivero and Murataya 2001).

Cannon (2005) furthered the understanding of criminal justice majors' attitudes towards gays and lesbians. His study has been the largest, surveying 1,055 students, and the only to involve students from more than one university. His study also involved students in both the Midwest and Southern parts of the United States. Although hardly representative of the total criminal justice undergraduate population, the attempt to survey at more than one university is important. He surveyed students at different stages of their college careers as well, allowing for some comparisons similar to Ventura and colleagues' (2004) study with respect to differences in attitude as students progress through their undergraduate careers. Although he did not measure attitudes supporting gay rights or interaction with gay people, he did use a scale, Herek's (1984) "Attitudes Toward Lesbians and Gay Men Scale," which allowed for the analysis to focus not just on gay people as a whole, but also to differentiate between attitudes toward gay men and attitudes toward lesbians. Once again building on the recommendations of Olivero and Murataya (2001), multivariate analysis was the primary statistical method used, allowing for a better understanding of the role being a criminal justice major plays when other factors are taken into consideration.

Cannon's (2005) study found that when controlling for variables such as age, credit hours completed, gender, race, religiosity, gay friends or family members, affiliation with Greek organizations, self-esteem, taking a course with LGBT content, and taking a course from a professor believed to be gay, the effects of being a criminal justice major were still significantly related to holding more negative attitudes toward gay people. When using attitudes toward both gay men and lesbians as the dependent variable, Cannon (2005) found that being a criminal justice major was a significant predictor of holding more negative attitudes, along with religiosity and gender. When differentiating the attitudes held toward gay men only and attitudes toward lesbians, being a criminal justice major is also a significant negative predictor in both models. Cannon noted that other independent variables were not as consistent across the separate models for gay men and lesbians. When attitudes toward lesbians only were considered, gender was no longer a significant variable, indicating that males did not hold the same negative attitudes toward gay women as they did gay men. When examining attitudes only towards gay men, taking a class which addressed LGBT issues became a significant predictor of a more positive attitude (Cannon 2005). This finding is especially important since it indicates that criminal justice educators may be able to improve our students' attitudes if we make an effort to address the issue.

Due to the larger sample collected, Cannon was also able to make direct comparisons between criminal justice majors and students majoring in psychology, business, education, and political science. Overall, he found that psychology majors held significantly more positive attitudes on all three scales than criminal justice majors. This is important to note since there were no differences between criminal justice majors and business majors, the latter of whom prior research has shown to be more homophobic than social science majors in general (Schellenberg et al. 1999).

The most recent study of anti-gay attitudes and criminal justice education was conducted by Miller and Kim (2012). Their study followed a similar perspective to Olivero and Murataya's (2001), focusing on the attitudes of students desiring a career in law enforcement compared to other criminal justice majors. They surveyed a total of 354 criminal justice majors at a Southwestern university with a large, well-established criminal justice program. The majority of their sample, 56.2 %, expressed a desire to work in law enforcement after completing their education. They used the Modern Homophobia Scale developed by Raja and Stokes (1998) which measures attitudes toward all gay people, as well as differentiating attitudes toward gay men and lesbians. This scale also measures the belief that female/male homosexuality is deviant and changeable and support for equal rights for gays and lesbians.

Miller and Kim (2012) used multivariate analysis to generate their findings. They found that "law enforcement students were not significantly more homophobic toward gay men than criminal justice students with other desired careers" (Miller and Kim 2012, p. 160). Distinct from the previous studies mentioned above, they used the independent variables of patriarchal attitude and completion of a minor, in addition to the more established independent variables such as gender and religion. They found that criminal justice majors who had a minor in another social science held significantly more positive attitudes towards both gay men and lesbians than criminal justice majors who either had no minor or were minoring in a field outside of social science (Miller and Kim 2012). This supports the idea that curricular development may play an important role in changing the attitudes of criminal justice students, even when the discussion of LGBT issues is not occurring in criminal justice courses.

It is important to note that Miller and Kim's (2012) study focused only on criminal justice majors and compared students with a desire to work in law enforcement to those who desire a career in corrections, legal services, etc. Their finding that criminal justice majors with a minor in another social science hold more positive attitudes can be interpreted as illustrating just how poor of a job the discipline of criminal justice is doing at educating our students regarding issues of the LGBT community.

Status of Criminal Justice Education on LGBT Issues

The criminal justice system can often be summarized by the very motto which appears on the side of police vehicles, "to protect and serve." This public service function mandates that criminal justice professionals, whether law enforcement, courts personnel, or correctional staff, continually interact with the citizens in the communities in which they serve. It is well established that the criminal justice system, and by definition the members within it, hold a great deal of power and authority over those with whom they come into contact (Robinson 2010), and monitoring of the discretion with which they exercise that power and authority is important. The appropriate utilization of such discretion, power, and authority is already discussed in a variety of criminal justice courses (e.g., courses focusing on ethics, introductory courses on law enforcement and corrections, and justice studies courses, to name but a few examples). The fact that the discipline is titled criminal *justice* is no accident. Justice for the communities served is critical, and it is also incumbent upon the profession to provide an inclusive work environment for all individuals who choose criminal justice as their career path (see, e.g., Colvin's chapter in this volume for a discussion of gay and lesbian police officers). Therefore, any criminal justice programs should, as one goal, promote justice within and among those public and work interactions. Part of that justice definition should include interactions free from bias or discrimination, no matter the age, race, gender, or sexual orientation of the affected community members. Issues of race and gender, whether included in victimology courses or discussions of minority representation in the criminal justice system, are typically required course content in criminal justice curriculum. Certainly, these are not the only categories by which equity in treatment should occur since the conception of 'justice' rests on a bedrock of fairness to all. This concept of justice applies whether those inter-actions take place at the enforcement level, within prosecutorial decisions, or after incarceration in correctional institutions. The current work focuses on law enforcement interactions, as the bulk of the existing research also targets this arena.

Potential for Bias or Discriminatory Interactions

While it should not be generalized that all criminal justice professionals are intolerant, there are many examples where allegations of bias or discrimination unfortunately occur in either public or work community interactions. O.J. Simpson and Rodney King are probably two of the most publicly recognized interactions that led to a bitter divide regarding treatment of African–Americans by the criminal justice system (Enomoto 1999; Overby et al. 2004). Racial profiling, or the stop and/or arrest of an individual based upon her/his physical attributes alone, has resulted in a loss of confidence concerning the criminal justice system by some community members (Engel and Calnon 2004; Geiger-Oneto and Phillips 2003; Wood and May 2003), and among those who believe they have been the victim of employment discrimination (International Association of Chiefs of Police 1998; Pogrebin et al. 2000). Potential disparities in the effects of gender on treatment within the criminal justice system, including charging decisions, potential plea options, and disparate treatment by probation officers, is the focus of steadily increasing review (Ammar and Weaver 2005; Bui and Morash 2010; Covington and Bloom 2007; Gaarder et al. 2004).

Similar examples exist in the LGBT community. They include high profile crimes involving LGBT individuals as hate crime victims, even when those crimes were not regarded as hate crimes (e.g., Matthew Shepard and Brandon Teena), and investigations of police department interactions with the LGBT community. The United States Department of Justice released its report into the investigation of the New Orleans Police Department on March 16, 2011, finding discriminatory policing on the basis of LGBT status (U.S. Department of Justice 2011). Portland's gay pride festival was overshadowed by allegations that participants were not protected from physical attacks during the event by Portland law enforcement, an example of underpolicing in this arena (Dwyer 2011; Parks 2009; see also Dwyer, this volume, for examples of over-policing). Some correctional policy initiatives regarding segregation based on sexual orientation have been thought to be examples of institutional discrimination (Blackburn et al. 2011). Some international research suggests acceptance of a 'homosexual advance defense,' or a defense which allows a violent response where the claim is that the LGBT person initiated contact or a potential relationship, resulting in acquittals and/or lenient sentences for those accused of murder of LGBT individuals (Dwyer 2011).

Meanwhile, concerns about equitable treatment and the organizational climate for LGBT police officers have gained increasing attention. LGBT police officers in the Los Angeles Police Department have alleged that a hostile work environment exists, which denies promotional opportunities and increases the likelihood of disciplinary action because of the officers' sexuality (Zamichow 2004). There are numerous other instances of officers filing suits and alleging discrimination and disparate treatment because of their sexuality. Moreover, the hyper-masculine environment of policing, as evidenced in Prokos and Padavic's (2002) work, suggests that the kind of masculinity expressed in the "hidden curriculum" of law enforcement academies could also disadvantage LGBT members.

These negative events raise the issue, similar to race and gender issues, of how to improve the potential loss of trust experienced by all these communities. This loss of trust becomes particularly relevant as police officers routinely respond to calls involving reports of very personal crimes such as hate crimes, domestic violence situations, and calls involving juveniles (either as perpetrators or victims), including bullying and/or harassment complaints. According to procedural justice perspectives, public trust in law enforcement is critical to maintaining its social legitimacy (Hough et al. 2010). Thus, these interactions become a critical mechanism through which the public makes determinations about the fairness, transparency, and acceptability of policing. The volume of interactions in these areas supports the case for improved educational responses to those entering the criminal justice profession.

In 2012, the Federal Bureau of Investigation released results from the 2011 Uniform Crime Reports on hate crimes. With over 14,000 law enforcement agencies reporting, approximately 21 % of such crimes had a sexual orientation bias (see Stotzer, this volume, for further discussion of bias crimes based on sexual orientation and/or gender identity). The majority, 57.8 %, were classified as anti-male homosexual bias, 11 % as anti-female homosexual bias, and 1.5 % as anti-bisexual bias (U.S. Department of Justice 2012). The overall percentage of 21 % has increased from 13 % in the 1997–1999 timeframe (Strom 2001), and from 18 % in 2003 (Harlow 2005), representing a 61 % increase in reported incidents. It is important to note that the Bureau of Justice Statistics reports that all victims only reported approximately 50 % of violent acts in 2011 (Truman and Planty 2012). Studies, although limited, portray reluctance on the part of the LGBT communities to report potential bias or hate crimes to police (Dwyer 2011; Kuehnle and Sullivan 2003). When hate crime laws are present, law enforcement is required to enforce the law prohibiting attacks on an individual based upon sexual orientation or gender identity bias (Katz-Wise and Hyde 2012). Given these numbers, training curricula, law enforcement policies, and procedures should reflect increased sensitivity and a perspective that promotes equity among all groups should be present in all components of the criminal justice system. The findings also suggest that education of criminal justice professionals should be better suited to promoting a safe zone for incident reporting.

Police may also respond to calls involving domestic violence allegations between same-sex couples. The 2010 Census found 901,000 same-sex households, up from 594,000 such households in 2000 (U.S. Department of Commerce 2012). Same-sex couples have comparable rates of domestic violence with heterosexual couples, anywhere from 25 to 35 % (McClennen 2005; see also Messinger, this volume, for a discussion of same-sex intimate partner violence prevalence rates).

However, research indicates that same-sex couples are hesitant to report such complaints, and indeed only did so 48 % of the time (Kuehnle and Sullivan 2003). It may be that such couples do not trust the police, or they may feel they will be further victimized (Kuehnle and Sullivan 2003). While the body of research on whether these fears are justified is extremely limited, one study found no discernible difference in police response to domestic violence calls from same-sex couples (Younglove et al. 2002). However, that limited result may not positively affect the community perception or beliefs.

School settings are another area of potential police response to hate crimes or other potential LGBT victimization reports (see also Warbelow and Cobb, this volume, for a discussion of legislative and policy responses to bullying of LGBT youth). In 2011, 9.2 % of reported sexual orientation bias hate crimes took place at schools or colleges (U.S. Department of Justice 2012). In fact, 83 % of LGBT youth reported either being physically or verbally abused at school (Weiler 2004) and 64 % had the impression that they were unsafe at school (Birkett et al. 2009), including harassment while on university campuses (Katz-Wise and Hyde 2012). This renders schools as potentially hostile environments for LGBT youth (Kosciw et al. 2009).

Since the response to potential bullying or harassment may be in the form of an on-site school resource police officer, the need for additional education for criminal justice professionals is again warranted. This training is particularly important to assure that law enforcement is attune to the characteristics and needs of LGBT youth or, in other words, that a 'one size fits all' approach may be not be the best response (Kosciw et al. 2009). Moreover, recognizing the intersectional characteristics of students and considering how race, gender, and other factors may intersect with a student's sexuality can be critical to developing interventions. Additionally, the victimization experience may vary by geographic location, thus requiring different curriculum inclusion for criminal justice professionals (Kosciw et al. 2009). For example, Kosciw et al.'s (2009) work determined that living in largely rural areas, poor areas, and areas with lower overall educational attainment may result in less tolerance and increased victimization for LGBT individuals. For U.S. youth, interactions with the school resource officer may provide the initial perception of how law enforcement interacts with the LGBT populations, thus reinforcing the need for an inclusive, respectful, and safe environment. While the actual interactions between police and LGBT youth are only rarely studied, initial research appears to posit that such youth are less likely to report potential victimization to police, fearing discriminatory attitudes, or less-than-zealous complaint follow-up (Dwyer 2011).

Whether criminal justice professionals are inclusive in the work environment is another area that may support increased education. While overall studies are limited, some research considers the work environment for LGBT individuals in criminal justice, typically in law enforcement. Law enforcement agencies usually have a goal of a diverse workforce, or one that reflects the demographics of a specific community (Bernstein and Swartwout 2012; Sklansky 2006; see too, Colvin, this volume, for lesbian and gay police officers' perspectives about community policing in LGBT communities). In fact, law enforcement agencies have become more racially integrated in the last 50 years, more gender integrated in the past 40 years, and have experienced increased LGBT integration in the past 30 years (Sklansky 2006). Nevertheless, increasing demographic representation does not preclude discrimination.

Past research concludes that up to 66 % of LGBT participants surveyed reported discrimination at the work site (Katz-Wise and Hyde 2012). Specific to criminal justice, one study found that "...homosexuals are the social group most disliked by police" (Myers et al. 2008, p. 18, citing Burke 1994). The depiction of law enforcement as macho and conservative may create a culture that is neither welcoming nor inclusive for LGBT professionals (Myers et al. 2008). Organizationally, when groups are socially isolated, they may be reluctant to speak out or challenge law enforcement professionals, or co-workers. This "silence" and caution can have deleterious effects for organizations, such as low morale (Bowen and Blackmon 2003).

Homophobia, as discussed elsewhere in this chapter, may be present in such groups, leading to a negative opinion of both potential co-workers, as well as the community members law enforcement are designated to protect (Bernstein and Swartwout 2012; Myers et al. 2008). The loss of trust discussed earlier in the chapter can be applied to LGBT police officers and heterosexual police officers. It may be that both groups are hesitant to trust the other, or feel safe while working with the other (Bernstein and Swartwout 2012; Myers et al. 2008). This may have similarities to the potential for bias and discrimination encountered when considering race and gender issues within law enforcement (Bernstein and Swartwout 2012).

Race and Gender Education Initiatives as a Paradigm for LGBT Education Initiatives

Education, academy training, and personal beliefs all combine to determine the effectiveness of each criminal justice professional's community interactions. Since race and gender have been under scrutiny as areas ripe for potential discriminatory outcomes, how criminal justice programs include such issues in the education arena is the paradigm utilized to review the status of U.S. criminal justice education on LGBT issues. This is particularly important as existing research, albeit limited, finds that criminal justice undergraduates are more homophobic (Olivero and Murataya 2001), more disapproving of the gay community (Miller and Kim 2012; Ventura et al. 2004), and hold increased negative attitudes toward the LGBT community (Cannon 2005; Ventura et al. 2004). In addition, LGBT issues are only infrequently included as important subject matter in existing criminal justice undergraduate courses (Cannon and Dirks-Linhorst 2006) or textbooks (Olivero and Murataya 2001). Cannon and Dirks-Linhorst (2006) further found that when criminal justice studies were combined at the departmental level with other disciplines (such as sociology or social work), LGBT issues were more commonly incorporated. However, given the attitudinal findings regarding criminal justice majors, much work yet needs to be done for those standalone criminal justice departments.

Race and gender issues, and indeed entire courses devoted to them, have been incorporated and required as part of criminal justice undergraduate and graduate education. By incorporating such topics into the framework of a multicultural curriculum, the hoped-for outcome is to alleviate disparate experiences by community members (Barlow and Barlow 1995; Bass 2001; Tsoudis 2000) and alter prior negative attitudes or opinions (Miller 2001). This multicultural approach has been utilized with respect to other diverse groups served by other professions, evidenced by curriculum shifts for teachers (Capella-Santana 2003; Warring et al. 1998); nursing students (Sowers and Smith 2004; Valois et al. 2001); and social workers (Cramer 1997; Oles et al. 1999), all with positive outcomes.

A long-standing belief generally holds that any knowledge is useful in widening the scope of a person's opinions and ideas concerning society (Stalans and Lurigio 1990). As one example, Stake and Hoffmann (2001) found those completing women's studies courses were more focused on the potential of gender discrimination. Participating in multicultural educational opportunities yielded more positive attitudes for teachers (Capella-Santana 2003). Likewise, nurses educated on HIV/AIDS issues became more sensitive to the HIV-positive population (Valois et al. 2001). Furthermore, Grapes (2006) found that those in the general public who held post-high school degrees held more positive outlooks on issues concerning LGBT rights. Bernstein and Swartwout's (2012) work had similar findings, although it did not hold true for law enforcement officers.

Given the race and gender education construct, the question becomes whether LGBT content has been included in the criminal justice curricula. The focus is the U.S. undergraduate criminal justice major, which can prepare students for entry into all aspects of the criminal justice profession (Younglove et al. 2002). Queer Studies Programs, as listed at www.trans-academics.org, and the University LGBT/Queer Studies in the USA and Canada (www.people.ku.edu/~jyounger/lgbtqprogs.html) were reviewed to determine the extent of potential Queer Studies Programs, and then whether there were any affiliations of those programs with undergraduate criminal justice programs. Twenty-seven colleges or universities were listed as having an undergraduate major in Gender/Women's/Queer Studies, with an additional 17 offering an undergraduate minor (www.trans-academics.org), for a total of 44 such colleges or universities offering the major or the minor. An additional 11 offered a certificate or concentrations in this area of study (www.people.ku.edu/~jyounger/lgbtqprogs.html). None of those appeared to have an affiliation or relationship with criminal justice studies nor to offer criminology or criminal justice-related courses. Cannon and Dirks-Linhorst's (2006) study found that LGBT content was not typically included in existing criminal justice courses focusing on race or gender, nor was content related to hate crimes. Criminal justice, compared to other social science disciplines, significantly fails to include such content (Fradella et al. 2009; Miller and Kim 2012). Fradella et al.

(2009) suggest that it is unethical not to include some LGBT content when it is clear that criminal justice students may seek careers involving law enforcement, corrections, or within the court system. Given the previous discussion of discretion, power, and authority as applied to public interactions, or even co-worker interactions, the need for sensitivity is, indeed, highlighted.

Future Directions

While determining whether inclusion of LGBT issues occurs at the undergraduate criminal justice level appears to be an emergent area of research, the findings that criminal justice fails to include such content in existing programs in the U.S. are disturbing. Although the conceptualization of Criminal Justice curricula in the United States is different than in other countries, the inclusion of LGBT issues is something that should be considered in public service disciplines around the globe, whether they be called criminal justice or justice studies or by some other label. Factors as evidenced by an increase of bias or hate crimes based upon sexual orientation and/or gender identity, the apparent hostile environment LGBT youth face in school settings, the probability that the criminal justice system will need to respond to and work with same-sex couples for domestic violence allegations, and potential discriminatory issues in criminal justice workplace settings (to name just a few examples) all point to the need for incorporation of LGBT issues into educational offerings. The question then becomes why an opportunity to decrease such potential bias, whether by creating new courses, or adding content to existing courses, has not been undertaken (Miller 2001). Cannon and Dirks-Linhorst's (2006) work outlined the possibility that criminal justice programs consider exploring some level of affiliation with Queer Studies Programs, but the review of existing programs indicate no movement in that direction.

Miller and Kim (2012) make several curriculum recommendations for criminal justice programs. One interesting suggestion is that criminal justice majors who complete a minor in the social sciences have increased positive attitudes to the LGBT community. Since Miller and Kim's (2012) work finds more negative attitudes associated with gay males, content should also reflect that focus and acknowledge the importance of an intersectional approach. Negative perceptions were also decreased for those having gay friends. This finding may also inform potential curricular content. One potential content addition is to invite guest speakers from the criminal justice system who are also members of LGBT communities. Not only could such guest speakers spend time in the classroom, they could also present to a student organization in a more informal setting, allowing more opportunities for personal interactions. Finally, framing class discussion, perhaps around extending basic rights to LGBT communities by using the example of "what would you think if your friend could not...," and then providing specific examples (such as "visit a partner in the hospital"), may assist the students with conceptualizing these issues in a more personal context. Miller and Kim (2012) make a key point that research does not exist which has determined whether such content changes are successful. However, these could be future research directions.

Perhaps such content could reflect zero tolerance language for LGBT discrimination. This may be useful in improving attitudes when responding to crime allegations or within criminal justice workplace settings (Bernstein and Swartwout 2012). Miller and Kim (2012) suggest reviewing existing gender and ethics courses for treatment of patriarchic attitudes, as that was an important predictor of negative opinions toward LGBT individuals. Such content could also encourage promoting an atmosphere of safety for reporting alleged crimes, as the criminal justice system has a duty to enforce laws such as hate crime statutes. Emphasizing to criminal justice professionals that they will be in contact with LGBT individuals can assist with the concept that responding to LGBT communities is not the 'one size fits all' response, and that sensitivity to individualized situations and needs is important, as it is with responding to all inquiries.

Undergraduate education may not be the only learning environment to consider for providing information and increasing sensitivity. A limited number of police departments have partnered with, or at least accepted, local LGBT police association ideas for training content for their officers (Dwyer 2011). One example is the Lesbian Gay Police Association-Gay Officers Action League of Chicago (LGPA/GOAL Chicago), whose function is to provide encouragement and assistance to LGBT officers (www.goalchicago.info). These types of groups can assist individuals responding to calls from individuals who identify as LGBT, as well as negotiate a potentially difficult working environment. Requiring an undergraduate degree that includes such material can build a strong foundation to improve all these interactions.

It is promising that some research finds success in providing information and thereby effecting change, which will ostensibly carry over into students' professional lives. Therefore, information for those considering a criminal justice career, and for those already working in the field, can be useful tools to assist them in understanding "…the complex dynamics of race, gender and sexuality that shape and give meaning to policing" (Sklansky 2006, p. 1243), and to all of criminal justice. Either increasing, or in most cases actually developing, course content specifically incorporating the intersection of race, gender, sexuality, and gender identity moves the discipline closer to this goal. For example, helping students to understand that "female youth were less likely and transgender youth were more likely to report being victimized because of their gender expression than male youth" (Kosciw et al. 2009, p. 982), can assist them when they begin their professional career. These steps can assist criminal justice with truly providing justice to those they protect and serve.

References

Ammar, N. H., & Weaver, R. R. (2005). Restrained voices: Female inmates' views of health services in two Ohio prisons. *Women & Criminal Justice, 16*(3), 67–89.

Barlow, M. H., & Barlow, D. E. (1995). Confronting ideologies of race and crime in the classroom: The power of history. *Journal of Criminal Justice Education, 6*, 105–122.

Bass, S. (2001). Policing space, policing race: Social control imperatives and police discretionary decisions. *Social Justice, 28*, 156–176.

Bernstein, M., & Swartwout, P. (2012). Gay officers in their midst: Heterosexual police employees' anticipation of the consequences for coworkers who come out. *Journal of Homosexuality, 59*(8), 1145–1166.

Berkman, C. S., & Zinberg, G. (1997). Homophobia and heterosexism in social workers. *Social Work, 42*, 319–332.

Birkett, M., Espelage, D. L., & Koenig, B. (2009). LGB and questioning students in schools: The moderating effects of homophobic bullying and school climate on negative outcomes. *Journal of Youth and Adolescence, 38*, 989–1000.

Blackburn, A. G., Fowler, S. K., Mullings, J. L., & Marquart, J. W. (2011). Too close for comfort: Exploring gender differences in inmate attitudes toward homosexuality in prison. *American Journal of Criminal Justice, 36*, 58–72.

Bowen, F., & Blackmon, K. (2003). Spirals of silence: The dynamic effects of diversity on organizational voice. *Journal of Management Studies, 40*(6), 1393–1417.

Bui, H. N., & Morash, M. (2010). The impact of network relationships, prison experiences, and internal transformation on women's success after prison release. *Journal of Offender Rehabilitation, 49*(1), 1–22.

Cannon, K. (2005). Ain't no faggot gonna rob me! Anti-gay attitudes of criminal justice undergraduate majors. *Journal of Criminal Justice Education, 16*, 227–244.

Cannon, K., & Dirks-Linhorst, P. A. (2006). How will they understand if we don't teach them?: The status of criminal justice education on gay and lesbian issues. *Journal of Criminal Justice Education, 17*(2), 262–278.

Caapella-Santana, N. (2003). Voices of teacher candidates: Positive changes in multicultural attitudes and knowledge. *The Journal of Educational Research, 96*, 182–190.

Covington, S. S., & Bloon, B. E. (2007). Gender responsive treatment and services in correctional settings. *Women & Therapy, 29*(3), 9–33.

Cramer, E. P. (1997). Effects of an educational unit about lesbian identity development and disclosure in a social work methods course. *Journal of Social Work Education, 33*, 461–472.

Cullen, J. M., Wright, L. W., & Alessandri, M. (2002). The personality variable openness to experience as it relates to homophobia. *Journal of Homosexuality, 42*, 119–134.

D'Augelli, A. R. & Hershberger, S. L. (1995). A multiyear analysis of changes in AIDS concerns and homophobia on a university campus. *Journal of American College Health, 4*, 3–10.

Dwyer, A. E. (2011). Policing lesbian, gay, bisexual and transgender young people: A gap in the research literature. *Current Issues in Criminal Justice, 22*(3), 415–433.

Fradella, H. F., Owen, S. S., & Burke, T. W. (2009). Integrating gay, lesbian, bisexual, and transgender issues into the undergraduate criminal justice curriculum. *Journal of Criminal Justice Education, 20*(2), 127–156.

Fulton, A., Gorsuch, R., & Maynard, E. (1999). Religious orientation, antihomosexual sentiment, and fundamentalism among Christians. *Journal for the Scientific Study of Religion, 38*, 14–22.

Ellis, S., Kitzinger, C., & Wilkinson, S. (2002). Attitudes toward lesbians and gay men and support for lesbian and gay human rights among psychology students. *Journal of Homosexuality, 44*, 121–133.

Engel, R. S., & Calnon, J. M. (2004). Examining the influence of drivers' characteristics during traffic stops with police: Results from a national survey. *Justice Quarterly, 21*, 49–90.

Enomoto, C. E. (1999). Public sympathy for O. J. Simpson: The roles of race, age, gender, income, and education. *The American Journal of Economics and Sociology, 58*, 145–161.

Gaarder, E., Rodriguez, N., & Zatz, M. S. (2004). Criers, liars, and manipulators: Probation officers' views of girls. *Justice Quarterly, 21*, 547–578.

Geiger-Oneto, S., & Phillips, S. (2003). Driving while black: The role of race, sex, and social status. *Journal of Ethnicity in Criminal Justice, 1*, 1–25.

Goldberg, R. (1982). Attitude change among college students toward homosexuals. *Journal of American College Health, 30*, 260–268.

Grapers, E. (2006). Ignorant discrimination: How education levels affect attitudes toward homosexuality and gay rights. *Sociological Viewpoints, 22*, 51–59.

Green, S., Dixon, P., & Gold-Neil, D. (1993). The effects of a gay/lesbian panel discussion on college student attitudes toward gay men, lesbians and persons with AIDS (PWAs). *Journal of Sex Education and Therapy, 19*, 47–63.

Greenberg, D. F., & Bystryn, M. H. (1982). Christian intolerance of homosexuality. *The American Journal of Sociology, 88*, 515–548.

Harlow, C. W. (2005). Hate crime reported by victims and police. *U.S. Department of Justice, Office of Justice Programs, Bureau of Justice Statistics Special Report* (NCJ 209911).

Herek, G. M. (1984). Attitudes toward lesbians and gay men: A factor-analytic study. *Journal of Homosexuality, 10*, 39–51.

Herek, G. M. (1986). On heterosexual masculinity. *American Behavioral Scientist, 29*, 563–577.

Herek, G. M. (1988). Heterosexuals' attitudes towards lesbians and gay men: Correlates and gender differences. *Journal of Sex Research, 25*, 451–477.

Herek, G. M., & Capitanio, J. P. (1995). Black heterosexuals' attitudes toward lesbians and gay men in the United States. *Journal of Sex Research, 32*, 95–105.

Herek, G. M., & Glunt, E. K. (1993). Interpersonal contact and heterosexuals' attitudes toward gay men: Results from a national survey. *Journal of Sex Research, 30*, 239–244.

Hooghe, M., & Meeusen, C. (2012). Homophobia and the transition to adulthood: A three year panel study among Belgian late adolescents and young adults, 2008–2011. *Journal of Youth and Adolescence, 41*, 1197–1207.

Hough, M., Jackson, J., Bradford, B., Myhill, A., & Quinton, P. (2010). Procedural justice, trust, and institutional legitimacy. *Policing, 4*(3), 203–218.

Hudson, W. W., & Ricketts, W. A. (1980). A strategy for the measurement of homophobia. *Journal of Homosexuality, 5*, 357–371.

International Association of Chiefs of Police. (1998). *The future of women in policing: Mandates for action,* Alexandria.

Katz-Wise, S. L., & Hyde, J. S. (2012). Victimization experiences of lesbian, gay, and bisexual individuals: A meta-analysis. *Journal of Sex Research, 49*(2–3), 142–167.

Kite, M. E., & Whitley, B. E. (1998). Do heterosexual women and men differ in their attitudes toward homosexuality? A conceptual and methodological analysis. In G. M. Herek (Ed.), *Stigma and sexual orientation: Understanding prejudice against lesbians, gay men and bisexuals* (pp. 39–61). Thousand Oaks, CA: Sage.

Klamen, D., Grossman, L., & Kopacz, D. (1999). Medical student homophobia. *Journal of Homosexuality, 37*, 53–63.

Klassen, A. D., Williams, C. J., & Levitt, E. E. (1989). *Sex and morality in the U.S.: An empirical inquiry under the auspices of the Kinsey Institute.* Middletown, CT: Wesleyan University Press.

Kosciw, J. G., Greytak, E. A., & Diaz, E. M. (2009). Who, what, where, when, and why: Demographic and ecological factors contributing to hostile school climate for lesbian, gay, bisexual, and transgender youth. *Journal of Youth Adolescence, 38*, 976–988.

Kuehnle, K., & Sullivan, A. (2003). Gay and lesbian victimization: Reporting factors in domestic violence and bias incidents. *Criminal Justice and Behavior, 30*, 85–96.

Kurdek, L. A. (1988). Correlates of negative attitudes toward homosexuals in heterosexual college students. *Sex Roles, 18*, 727–737.

Lance, L. M. (1987). The effects of interactions with gay persons on attitudes toward homosexuality. *Human Relations, 40*, 329–335.

Lottes, I. L., & Kuriloff, P. J. (1994). The impact of college experience on political and sexual attitudes. *Sex Roles, 31*, 31–54.

Matchinsky, D. J., & Iverson, T. G. (1996). Homophobia in heterosexual female undergraduates. *Journal of Homosexuality, 31*, 123–128.

McClennen, J. C. (2005). Domestic violence between same-gender partners: Recent findings and future research. *Journal of Interpersonal Violence, 20*, 149–154.

Meaney, G. J., & Rye, B. J. (2010). Gendered egos: Attitudes functions and gender as predictors of homonegativity. *Journal of Homosexuality, 14*, 1274–1302.

Miller, A. J. (2001). Student perceptions of hate crimes. *American Journal of Criminal Justice, 25*, 293–307.

Miller, H. A., & Kim, B. (2012). Curriculum implications of anti-gay attitudes among undergraduate criminal justice majors. *Journal of Criminal Justice Education, 23*(2), 148–173.

Myers, K. A., Forest, K. B., & Miller, S. L. (2008). Officer friendly and the tough cop: Gays and lesbians navigate homophobia and policing. *Journal of Homosexuality, 47*(1), 17–37.

Oles, T. P., Black, B. M., & Cramer, E. P. (1999). From attitude change to effective practice: Exploring the relationship. *Journal of Social Work Education, 35*, 87–100.

Oliver, M. B., & Hyde, J. S. (1995). Gender differences in attitudes towards homosexuality: A reply to Whitley and Kite. *Psychological Bulletin, 117*, 155–158.

Olivero, J. M. & Murataya, R. (2001). Homophobia and university law enforcement students. *Journal of Criminal Justice Education, 12*, 271–281.

Overby, L. M., Brown, R. D., Bruce, J. M., Smith, Jr., C. E., & Winkle III, J.E. (2004). Justice in black and white: Race, perceptions of fairness, and diffuse support for the judicial system in a southern state. *The Justice System Journal, 25*, 159–182.

Parks, C. (2009, July 13). Gay community angry at police over problems during Pride festival. *OregonLive.com.* Retrieved from http://blog.oregonlive.com/portland_impact/print.html?entry=/2009/07/gay_community_angry.

Patton, W., & Morrison, M. (1993). Effects of a university subject on attitudes toward human sexuality. *Journal of Sex Education and Therapy, 19*, 93–107.

Patton, W., & Morrison, M. (1994). Investigating attitudes toward sexuality: Two methodologies. *Journal of Sex Education and Therapy, 20*, 185–197.

Pogrebin, M., Dodge, M., & Chatman, H. (2000). Reflections of African-American women on their careers in urban policing: Their experiences of racial and sexual discrimination. *International Journal of the Sociology of Law, 28*, 311–326.

Prokos, A., & Padavic, I. (2002). 'There oughtta be a law against bitches': Masculinity lessons in police academy training. *Gender, Work and Organization, 9*(4), 439–459.

Raja, S., & Stokes, J. P. (1998). Assessing attitudes toward lesbians and gay men: The Modern Homophobia Scale. *Journal of Gay, Lesbian, and Bisexual Identity, 3*(2), 113–134.

Riggs, M. T. (1991). Black macho revisited: Reflections of a snap! Queen. *Black American Literature Forum, 25*, 389–394.

Robinson, M. (2010). Assessing criminal justice practice using social justice theory. *Social Justice Research, 23*, 77–97.

Schellenberg, G. E., Hirt, J., & Sears, A. (1999). Attitudes toward homosexuals among students at a Canadian university. *Sex Roles, 40*, 139–152.

Seltzer, R. (1992). The social location of those holding antihomosexual attitudes. *Sex Roles, 26*, 391–398.

Sklansky, D. A. (2006). Not your father's police department: Making sense of the new demographics of law enforcement. *The Journal of Criminal Law and Criminology, 96*(3), 1209–1243.

Sowers, J., & Smith, M. R. (2004). Evaluation of the effects of an inservice training program on nursing faculty members' perceptions, knowledge, and concerns about students with disabilities. *Journal of Nursing Education, 43*, 248–252.

Stake, J. E., & Hoffmann, F. L. (2001). Changes in student social attitudes, activism, and personal confidence in higher education: The role of women's studies. *American Educational Research Journal, 38*, 411–436.

Stalans, L. J., & Lurigio, A. J. (1990). Lay and professionals' beliefs about crime and criminal sentencing. *Criminal Justice and Behavior, 17*, 333–349.

Strom, K. J. (2001). Hate crimes reported in NIBRS, 1997–99. *U.S. Department of Justice, Office of Justice Programs, Bureau of Justice Statistics Special Report.* (NCJ 186765).

Theodore, P. S., & Basow, S. A. (2002). Heterosexual masculinity and homophobia: A reaction to the self? *Journal of Homosexuality, 40*, 31–48.

Tsoudis, O. (2000). Does majoring in criminal justice affect perceptions of criminal justice? *Journal of Criminal Justice Education, 11*, 225–236.

Truman, J. L., & Planty, M. (2012). *Criminal victimization, 2011.* U.S. Department of Justice, Office of Justice Programs, Bureau of Justice Statistics (NCJ 239437).

U. S. Bureau of the Census. (2012). *Households and families: 2010.* U.S. Department of Commerce, Economics and Statistics Administration.

U. S. Department of Justice, Civil Rights Division. (2011). *Investigation of the New Orleans police department.* Retrieved from www.justice.gov/crt/about/spl/nopd_report.pdf.

U.S. Department of Justice, Federal Bureau of Investigation. (2012). Hate crime statistics, 2011: Uniform Crime Reports.

Ventura, L. A., Lambert, E. G., Bryant, M., & Pasupuleti, S. (2004). Differences in attitudes toward gays and lesbians among criminal justice and non-criminal justice majors. *American Journal of Criminal Justice, 28*, 165–180.

Valois, P., Turgeon, H., Godin, G., Blondeau, D., & Cote, F. (2001). Influence of a persuasive strategy on nursing students' beliefs and attitudes toward provision of care to people living with HIV/AIDS. *Journal of Nursing Education, 40*, 354–358.

Warring, D. F., Keim, J., & Rau, R. (1998). Multicultural training for students and its impact. *Action in Teaching Education, 20*, 56–63. www.goalchicago.info. Retrieved from http://www.goalchicago.info/?page_id=8.

Weiler, E. M. (2004). Legally and morally, What our gay students must be given. *Education Digest, 69*, 38–44.

Whitley, B. E., & Kite, M. E. (1995). Sex differences in attitudes toward homosexuality: A comment on Oliver and Hyde (1993). *Psychological Bulletin, 117*, 146–154.

Winter, S., Webster, B., & Cheung, P. K. E. (2008). Measuring Hong Kong undergraduate students' attitudes towards transpeople. *Sex Roles, 59*, 670–683.

Wood, P. B., & May, D. C. (2003). Racial differences in perceptions of the severity of sanctions: A comparison of prison with alternatives. *Justice Quarterly, 20*, 605–631.

Younglove, J. A., Kerr, M. G., & Vitello, C. J. (2002). Law enforcement officers' perceptions of same sex domestic violence. *Journal of Interpersonal Violence, 17*, 72–76.

Zamichow, N. (2004, November 25). LAPD still biased, gays allege. *Los Angeles Times*, p. 1.

Part IV
LGBT Communities, Law, and Justice

Chapter 14
Rethinking the "World Polity" Perspective on Global Sodomy Law Reform

Neil Cobb

Abstract Sociologist John W. Meyer's neo-institutionalist "world polity" perspective has had considerable influence on scholarly interrogations of globalization, international relations, and transnational governance. Put simply, Meyer and his collaborators argue that modern nation states are embedded increasingly within dense webs of shared cultural meaning, grounded predominantly in "Western" values, norms, and standards such as international human rights, which script their behavior and have led to striking levels of isomorphism or homogeneity across otherwise highly differentiated country contexts. Recently, the world polity perspective has been used by other sociologists to analyze why so many states across all regions of the world have apparently moved so swiftly since the Second World War to liberalize their criminal laws against same-sex genital relations (so-called "sodomy laws"). This chapter reappraises the world polity perspective on global sodomy law reform. In doing so, it draws attention to long-standing criticisms that Meyer's work, in its emphasis on convergence of global cultural values, underplays or ignores entirely the continuing role of conflict in world society, and the dynamics of power and resistance through which that conflict is resolved. In turn, the chapter uses four recent case studies to evaluate the relevance of world polity analysis to the social process of sodomy law reform given the particular regimes of conflict, power, and resistance, especially between global North and South, which it shows are also shaping this particular social process.

Keywords Sodomy laws · Sexuality · Uganda · United Nations · Organization of Islamic Cooperation · Africa · U.S. Christian Right · World polity · Meyer · Wallerstein · Global South · Aid conditionality · India · Naz Foundation · Queer

N. Cobb (✉)
School of Law, University of Manchester, Williamson Building Oxford Road, Manchester M13 9PL, UK
e-mail: neil.cobb@manchester.ac.uk

D. Peterson and V. R. Panfil (eds.), *Handbook of LGBT Communities, Crime, and Justice*, DOI: 10.1007/978-1-4614-9188-0_14,
© Springer Science+Business Media New York 2014

Introduction

This chapter's focus is the emerging global politics of sodomy law reform, involving on-going struggles over state-sponsored criminal prohibitions imposed by national legal systems to regulate same-sex genital relations.[1] Sodomy and its regulation have been shrouded historically in what Moran (1996) describes as "an economy of silence".[2] However, world society today is increasingly saturated in discourse and counter-discourse on sodomy and its criminalization, encouraged by a nascent but rapidly expanding transnational lesbian, gay, bisexual, and transgender (LGBT) rights movement and its focus on worldwide sodomy law repeal. This outpouring of speech about sodomy seems to stretch now across almost every continent, and to implicate a growing number of intergovernmental bodies, nation states, and global civil society organizations. How should we begin to make sense of these stories about sodomy law reform; what can they tell us about the changing relationship between domestic conflicts over marginalized sexualities, sexual rights and justice, and the dynamics of international relations and global governance; and how might these stories help to inform future strategizing by progressive movements working on behalf of marginalized sexualities, as they continue to work to challenge state sodomy laws in specific country contexts?

These questions are explored in more detail by building on a wealth of sociological research that explains the act of criminalization as a complex social process (see, generally, Jenness 2004). More specifically, this chapter takes as its starting point recent research that has sought to understand global sodomy law reform through the lens of sociologist John W. Meyer's neo-institutionalist "world polity" perspective on patterns of contemporary social change. Meyer and his many collaborators suggest that we are witnessing the expansion of a highly integrated world culture, grounded primarily in Western values, norms, and standards such as individualism, rationality, progress, and justice, which they see as diffusing rapidly around the world so that it now increasingly scripts the behavior of nation states (Driori and Krucken 2009; Meyer 2009a). In recent years, Meyer's world polity perspective has been applied by sociologists to explain patterns of global homogeneity in spheres as diverse as state educational policy, environmental planning, and women's rights regimes (Meyer et al. 1997b; Meyer and Ramirez 2000; Boyle 2002).

---

[1] The term "sodomy law" is used as shorthand in this chapter for the criminalization of adult same-sex sexual activity between men or between women in private. This avoids important questions, of course, about the implications of criminal regulations applied to public same-sex sexual activities, which are often aggressively policed even when private sexual behavior is legalized. It also leaves to one side other targets for criminalization to regulate same-sex desire, such as recent controversial legislation in Russia that extends liability for distributing "propaganda of non-traditional sexual relations" to minors.

[2] This "economy of silence," which reflects the shame and cultural suppression associated with homosexuality, especially in the West, is illustrated most clearly by English jurist Blackstone's description of buggery as "that horrible crime not to be named among Christians" (Moran 1996, p. 36).

The world polity perspective has also been applied to the social phenomenon of worldwide sodomy law reform by Frank et al. (2009, 2010), Frank and McEneaney (1999). In their ground-breaking empirical project, Frank and his colleagues reveal what appears to be an overwhelming global shift toward sodomy law liberalization in this period across almost all regions of the world. More importantly, the researchers also propose that this emerging worldwide convergence toward decriminalization demonstrates the development and expansion of a powerful and progressive world sexual culture, grounded in Western liberal conceptions of sexual freedom, rights, and justice, which has embedded sodomy law liberalization within "taken for granted" shared understandings of the properly-behaving nation state (see, e.g., Frank et al. 2009).

Undoubtedly, Frank and his colleagues' attentiveness to evidence of world-cultural convergence around sodomy law liberalization offers a useful, important, and thought-provoking contribution to recent critical scholarship on the relationship among globalization, modernity, and sexual rights claims (see, e.g., Altman 2001; Binnie 2004; Stychin 2003). This chapter argues, however, that the world polity perspective has significant limitations as a framework for explaining the scope, characteristics, and wider implications of this arena of global sexual justice. To do so, the chapter draws from the literature that considers how the world polity perspective, in its eagerness to uncover cultural convergence, tends to underestimate the significance of conflict in contemporary world society, and the role played by dynamics of power and resistance in resolving that conflict (Beckfield 2003; Buttel 2000; Finnemore 1996; Hirsch 1997; Koenig and Dierkes 2012). This literature informs later analysis of the chapter's four case studies, which each point to different aspects of the conflict, power, and resistance that arguably still define the global processes of contemporary sodomy law reform.

Global Sodomy Law Reform and the "World Polity" Perspective

Frank and his collaborators' longitudinal, cross-national study of sodomy law reform involved a wide-ranging analysis of legal materials drawn from a sample of 125 of the 196 recognized countries in the world. The researchers used this data set to trace expansions and contractions in the scope of national criminal laws regulating same-sex genital relations between 1945 and 2005, including ages of consent, as well as maximum punishments for each offense (Frank et al. 2009; Frank and McEneaney 1999). The study was completed as part of a broader project, also led by Frank, which set out to identify worldwide trends in the criminalization of four types of sexual behavior: sodomy, rape, adultery, and child sexual abuse (Frank et al. 2010). Their findings contribute to a relatively small but growing literature on the global reach, scope, and evolution of sodomy laws (c.f. Asal et al. 2013). Significantly, much of these data are being generated by international nongovernmental organizations (INGOs) such as the International Lesbian Gay, Bisexual, Trans, and Intersex Association (ILGA) and Amnesty International, as an evidence base designed to support their on-going work to secure the abolition of sodomy laws worldwide (Amnesty International 2013; Itaborahy and Zhu 2013).

Frank and his colleagues present their findings on sodomy law reform as significant primarily because of their consistency; between 1945 and 2005, reform in this sphere was "strikingly patterned, almost uniformly moving in a common, liberalizing direction" (2009, p. 129). The statistics reveal that more than 90 % of the changes to state sodomy laws in the 60 years following the Second World War involved reductions in scope or punishment; conversely, just eight countries took steps to expand their laws or increase the maximum sentence during that same period of time: "[d]ecriminalization was a seldom-broken rule" (ibid.). Nor—point out the researchers—was the shift toward sodomy law liberalization limited to particular regions of the world such as the global North; instead, the data show that though much of the Western world did indeed decriminalize rapidly in this era, so too did several non-Western states as diverse as Mongolia (in 1961), Panama (in 1982), Laos (in 1990), and Kazakhstan (in 1998). In turn, Frank and his colleagues offer a particular causal explanation for this apparently wide-ranging worldwide convergence over sodomy law liberalization since 1945; they propose that state sodomy law reform during this period was influenced in large part by emerging global cultural forces, using Meyer's world polity framework to explain the character of the transnational dynamics at play in this arena.

A Brief Introduction to Meyer's World Polity Perspective

Stanford sociologist John W. Meyer developed his world polity perspective on social change as part of his broader contributions to organizational studies from the late 1970s (Driori and Krucken 2009; Jepperson 2002; Meyer 2009a). It was conceived, significantly, as a corrective to the prevailing assumption of American "realist" sociology that organizations are constituted from the "bottom up" by the complex interactions of individual and collective actors, understood as motivated primarily by their own autonomous interests and functional needs. Given this conceptual starting-point, Meyer pointed out, realist sociologists might expect to find considerable divergence in the characteristics of specific organizations depending on their particular social, political, and economic environment. He argued instead, however, that empirical data he was gathering on organizational norms, values, and behavior often contradicted these predictions. He showed how organizations located within otherwise highly differentiated environments displayed levels of homogeneity or isomorphism that could not be explained simply by interest-driven or functional interactions between local actors.

Over time, Meyer would begin to explain this disjuncture between theory and practice using the world polity conceptual framework. Put simply, this framework proposes that since at least the end of the Second World War, social processes of globalization, transnationalism, and modernization have encouraged the rapid diffusion of an integrated, rationalized, and increasingly stable world society, made up of a highly dense web of meanings within which both individual and collective actors are embedded and through which their conduct is shaped by powerful cultural scripts. These scripts, Meyer argues, are absorbed by actors at the cognitive and normative level until they are presumed to be simply the inevitable way of doing things, acquiring a taken for granted quality. The result of this acculturative process is growing convergence across otherwise differently situated actors around certain prescribed norms and behavior, or what he describes as structural "isomorphism." In short, "for Meyer, macrostructures influence norms and behavior: It is not actors and their interests who constitute society ('bottom up'), but rather society, whose main cultural characteristics have become global over time, which constitutes actors in on-going processes of rationalization ('top down')" (Driori and Krucken 2009, pp. 21–22).

What makes Meyer's account of global integration perhaps most striking and controversial, however, is the detailed account he also offers of the specific content of this expanding and integrated world culture. For Meyer and his collaborators the emerging world culture is without doubt Western in origin, and remains firmly grounded in an ideal-type Weberian conception of occidental modernity, forged within Christian and then secular liberal thought, and marked by high levels of bureaucratic rationalization (Meyer et al. 1987). Meyer's world polity perspective draws attention to the worldwide diffusion of several specific Western-inspired cultural scripts, including: (1) the constitution of individuals and nation states as legitimate actors; (2) the emergence of progress and development as shared global objectives; and (3) the embedding of concepts like freedom, equality, and justice as guiding principles for achieving those shared ends. One example of world culture often cited by world polity scholars is the intensifying worldwide consensus over the legitimacy of international human rights frameworks, which reflect global cultural notions of progress and development as well as the constitution of individuals as legitimate actors who must be sufficiently empowered to hold states to account (Meyer 2009b; Ramirez et al. 2002).

The world polity perspective draws particular attention to the contradictory position of the sovereign nation state within this institutionalized world culture (McNeely 1995; Meyer et al. 1997a). On one hand, it is the global diffusion of world-cultural scripts that ensures the taken for granted sovereignty of nation states; on the other hand, that same world culture appears to undercut state sovereignty in practice by scripting the appropriate ways in which nation states can legitimately act. As Meyer and his collaborators put it, state actorhood is "infused with world-cultural conceptions of the properly behaving nation state" so that even what might at first appear to be endogenous or "'internally' generated changes" within particular nation states are actually pre-determined by exogenous cultural factors (Meyer et al. 1997a, p. 160). In short, while states are nominally at the heart of this expanding world polity, their actions are dictated to an ever greater extent by powerful global norms, including those espoused by human rights frameworks. These norms, suggest Meyer and his collaborators, are diffused to nation states primarily through the growing proliferation of intergovernmental organizations (IGOs) and INGOs as well as (most influentially) the epistemological authority of "putatively disinterested" scientists and other transnational experts (Koenig and Dierkes 2012, p. 8; Meyer et al. 1997a, pp. 164–166). The effect of this cross-national cultural influence is growing isomorphism across otherwise highly differentiated country contexts, which also extends, it seems, to an emerging homogeneity between national legal systems (Boyle and Meyer 1998).

The "World Polity" Perspective on Global Sodomy Law Reform

Frank and his colleagues' world polity perspective on global sodomy law reform leads them to several conclusions about the social processes at work in this arena. Firstly, the authors highlight what they consider to be the methodological limitations of recent research on sodomy law reform that typically focuses narrowly on struggles over liberalization within bounded country or regional contexts (see, e.g., Bernstein 2003; Currier 2011; de la Dehesa 2010; Moran 1996; Stychin 1998, 2003). In adopting this focus, they argue, such research reinforces the common assumption that the liberalization of sodomy laws is shaped predominantly by esoteric micro-dynamics specific to particular local geopolitical environments. Conversely, the world polity perspective usefully shifts attention, they suggest, *from the national or regional to the global* by foregrounding the particular influence of contemporary world culture.

In turn, the world polity perspective explicitly downplays the significance of local social factors in sodomy law liberalization, including domestic social movements. Frank and his colleagues note that sodomy law repeal in many countries between 1945 and 2005 occurred well before the emergence of meaningful grassroots activism on behalf of marginalized sexualities. This demonstrates, they suggest, that local social movements were neither necessary nor sufficient factors in the decision by nation states to reduce the scope of sodomy laws or their penalties, while strengthening the claim that exogenous world-cultural factors had a greater influence overall on patterns of sodomy law liberalization during this period (Frank et al. 2009).[3]

---

[3] Frank and his colleagues are careful to avoid emptying local social movement activity around sodomy law reform of any and all significance. The authors acknowledge, for instance, recent work that shows how sodomy law reform is motivated by goals of cultural transformation (especially group recognition) and social movement mobilization, as much as it is by political change to sodomy laws themselves, and that these equally significant aims are usually achieved most successfully by local social movements (Bernstein 2003). They also recognize that local social movements can have important implications for the relative speed with which sodomy law reform is achieved (Kane 2007).

Finally, Frank and his colleagues draw from Meyer's world polity approach to reach specific conclusions about the origins and nature of the cultural scripts that they suggest now structure global sodomy law liberalization. They see liberalization as the inevitable by-product of the "over-arching logic of individualization" that the world polity perspective positions at the very heart of Western-inspired world culture (Frank et al. 2010, p. 881; see also Frank and Meyer 1998). They suggest that global cultural conceptions of sexuality have been reworked by this social process of individualization, encouraging a shift from understandings of sexuality as a collective concern—tied to the demands of nation, religion, and family—to one shaped primarily by individual autonomy and consent. Over time, "[i]ndividualization gave rise to expressive and pleasure-orientated definitions of sex," with important implications for state sexual regulation: "increasingly, criminal regulations eschewed questions of collective order and public morality and aimed instead to restrict those sexual activities that threatened individual sovereignty" (Frank et al. 2009, p. 137). Significantly, Frank and his colleagues contend that this logic of sexual individualization applies not only to sodomy laws but laws against rape, adultery, and child sex abuse. Their broader empirical project, which considered reform to all four types of law, also demonstrates that while many nation states moved rapidly in this period to repeal their laws against both adultery and sodomy, on the basis that they infringed personal sexual liberty, many took steps simultaneously to ratchet up their laws against rape and child abuse to punish non-consensual sexual activity and protect individual sexual autonomy (Frank et al. 2010).

Conflict as the World Polity Perspective's "Blind Spot"

The world polity perspective on global sodomy law reform makes a significant contribution to recent explorations of the complex social dynamics that influence the reach, scope, and evolution of these laws. It shifts our attention to worldwide patterns of sodomy law liberalization while foregrounding the global cultural influences that have encouraged this cultural convergence, especially the purportedly rapid transnational diffusion of sexual individualization from the West. The problem, however, is that the explanation that Frank and his colleagues provide of the effects of globalization and modernization on the social process of sodomy law reform suffers from the same limitations as John Meyer's world polity perspective more generally.

The world polity perspective has been the subject of particularly significant, ongoing criticism by scholars who claim that it fails to account sufficiently for the continuing and profound conflict in world society (Buttel 2000; Finnemore 1996; Hirsch 1997; Koenig and Dierkes 2012). Meyer's conceptual framework draws our attention to the convergence of individual and collective actors around powerful Western-inspired taken for granted cultural scripts, diffused to local settings by decentralized institutions like IGOs, INGOs, and transnational experts. In doing so, it implies a primarily consensus-driven, non-hierarchical, and peaceable account of globalization. As Martha Finnemore notes, caustically, "the picture painted by institutionalist studies is one in which world culture marches effortlessly and facelessly across the globe" (1996, p. 327). The difficulty with this interpretation, critics argue, is that it downplays or ignores entirely the role of conflict, power, and resistance in the enactment and transmission of (Western) world-cultural scripts.

For this reason the presence, characteristics, and broader implications of conflict in world society have been described by some as the world polity perspective's "blind spot" (Koenig and Dierkes 2012, p. 8).[4] It has been pointed out, for instance, that "world polity theorists eliminate the struggles over power and meaning that … are central to normative change" (Keck and Sikkink 1998, p. 210). In doing so, others argue, the world polity perspective quite simply "marginalizes politics" (Finnemore 1996, p. 327). In reality, world polity analysis is often more attuned to conflict than its critics can sometimes assume (see, generally, Koenig and Dierkes 2012). Nevertheless, it is also clear that in its account of social change, the world polity framework tends to underestimate or ignore entirely the existence of conflict and the dynamics of power and resistance by which that conflict is then resolved.

In this respect, the first weakness of the world polity perspective is its limited capacity and willingness to interrogate meaningfully evidence of on-going resistance to the world culture it describes. There is some recognition that explicit rejection of world-cultural scripts occurs, especially by conservative religious or nationalist movements, but this resistance is assumed to be localized and relatively insignificant in the face of world culture's onward march (see, e.g., Meyer et al. 1997a).[5] Yet other scholars have set out rather different views. Perhaps most well-known and controversial is the position taken by Samuel Huntington, who first described globalization as bringing about a cultural "clash of civilizations," by which, "[s]purred by modernization, global politics is being reconfigured along

---

[4] Given its assumption that contemporary world society marks the ascendance of a Western world view, it also appears to echo the much discredited "end of history" thesis proposed by Francis Fukuyama in the 1990s (c.f. Fukuyama 1992; see also Koenig and Dierkes 2012, p. 8).

[5] Meyer does grapple briefly with the question of direct resistance to world culture in his work, with particular focus on religious and nationalist extremism. He notes: "[e]xplicit rejection of world-cultural principles sometimes occurs, particularly by nationalist or religious movements whose purported opposition to modernity is seen as a threat to geopolitical stability" (Meyer et al. 1997a, p. 187). However, his analysis of these oppositional forces then downplays the implications of this resistance, foregrounding instead how religious and nationalist movements are always already located within the same world culture they seek to reject. He suggests that that there is a tendency to "[underestimate] the extent to which such movements conform to rationalized models of societal order and purpose. These movements mobilize around principles inscribed in world-cultural scripts, derive their organizing capacity from the legitimacy of these scripts, and edit their supposedly primordial claims to maximize this legitimacy" (p. 187). From this perspective, Meyer and his collaborators conclude that: "[i]n general, nationalist and religious movements intensify isomorphism more than they resist it" (ibid). Similar arguments have been made by world polity theorists questioning the long term significance of the purported conflict between Islam and the West (see Lecher and Boli 2005, Chap. 9).

cultural lines. People and countries with similar cultures are coming together. People with different cultures are coming apart" (1996, p. 125). Huntington's thesis attracted immediate controversy, and remains subject to continued criticism, given its suggestion that there is a fundamental cultural conflict between coherent and essential "Islamic" and "Western" cultural traditions (see, e.g., Said 2001).[6] However, what the clash of civilizations thesis does foreground, contrary to the assumptions of the world polity perspective, is the existence of a fragmenting world culture of competing claims to truth, which has become more, not less, divergent as a consequence of globalization and modernization (see also Barber 1995; c.f. Fukuyama 1992). Similar recent perspectives include Eisenstadt's (2000, pp. 2–3) conception of "multiple modernities," or the view that "modernity and Westernization are not identical; Western patterns of modernity are not the only 'authentic' modernities, though they enjoy historical precedence and continue to be a basic reference point for others."

This recognition that world culture remains fragmented, divergent, and prone to contestation raises a second important question about conflict within world society, which relates to the processes by which world culture is transmitted. The world polity perspective tends to assume that global isomorphism is primarily the result of the diffusion of world-cultural scripts to nation states at the cognitive and normative level. However, where states explicitly resist these scripts it is clear that social change is unlikely to occur through these subtle and consensual accultur-ative mechanisms. Recalcitrant states must instead be actively persuaded to alter their normative positions or else, more significantly, coerced into compliance with world-cultural norms (Goodman and Jinks 2004; Powell and DiMaggio 1991; Scott 1995). Coercion here is defined broadly as a mechanism "whereby states and institutions influence the behavior of other states by escalating the benefits of conformity or the costs of nonconformity through material rewards or punish-ments" (Goodman and Jinks 2004, p. 633). The problem, once again, is that the world polity perspective tends to downplay the extent to which world level cultural compliance is achieved through coercive practices or, as Finnemore has put it, how sometimes "[c]ultural rules are often established not by persuasion or cognitive processes of institutionalization but by force and fiat" (1996, p. 340).

What makes coercive mechanisms especially significant is that they raise important and difficult issues about the global power inequalities that enable some actors—such as nation states—to successfully enforce cultural compliance over others. Given Meyer's over-arching assumption that world culture is diffused through decentralized, non-hierarchical flows, he offers no real insight into the dynamics of power and resistance that coercive change entails. The world polity perspective can be contrasted in this respect with other theoretical frameworks that present globalization, transnationalism, and modernization as always already

---

[6] See also the criticism that Huntington's clash of civilizations thesis "remains at best unproven, and at worst subject to the criticism that it oversimplifies and overgeneralizes the nature of contemporary cultural schisms" (Holton 1998, p. 184).

shaped by on-going conflict between differently situated actors with unequal access to material, political, and/or symbolic power. For instance, neo-Marxist Immanuel Wallerstein has traced the power inequalities between countries defined by their economic positioning as "core," "semi-peripheral," and "peripheral" within global capitalism, drawing attention to the greater potential for coercive cultural enforcement by the global North over the global South (Karatzogianni and Robinson 2010; Wallerstein 2004; cf. Hardt and Negri 2000).

However, it is not solely the dynamics of conflict, power, and resistance underlying coercive mechanisms of cultural compliance that the world polity perspective underestimates; arguably, even the non-coercive and apparently wholly consensual worldwide diffusion of culture through taken for granted scripts operating at the cognitive and normative level raise further important questions about cultural contestation and domination. This is the third problem with the perspective, which effectively side lines the wealth of scholarly interventions that have drawn attention to the power inequalities tied up with the constitution of individual subjectivities through culture; Foucault's (1991) study of governmentality, or the micro-physics of power, is perhaps the best known example of these approaches. Indeed, others have recently shown that while Meyer's world polity perspective shares many similarities with Foucault's work in its concern with cultural structuration, it is the former's inattention to power in the formation of subjectivity that most clearly differentiates the two (Driori and Krucken 2009, pp. 21–22). Considered in light of Wallerstein's work on structural inequalities in the world order, Foucault's engagement with power and subjectivity also draws attention to the domination that the diffusion of Western-inspired world culture might entail for nations in the global South, even where this diffusion operates at the non-coercive level of the cognitive and normative.

Conflict, Power, and Resistance in Global Sodomy Law Reform

To summarize: Meyer's world polity perspective provides an important but controversial framework for understanding the social processes of globalization, transnationalism, and modernization. The previous section considered in more detail the particular criticism that in its concern with cultural convergence, the perspective underestimates or ignores entirely the contemporary role of conflict in world society, and the dynamics of power and resistance through which conflict is resolved. In this respect, three particular weaknesses about the perspective were considered: that the perspective fails to recognize the extent of explicit resistance to the world culture it describes; that resistance may lead in turn to the use of coercive mechanisms for enforcing compliance with cultural norms, raising questions about the relative capacity of some nation states to enforce cultural compliance over others; and that even where worldwide cultural change might seem entirely consensual and non-coercive, it may well still entail its own regimes of power over individual subjectivities.

The remaining sections of this chapter suggest that these criticisms of the world polity perspective are also especially relevant to understanding the limitations of the perspective's application by Frank and his colleagues to the social processes of global sodomy law reform. Their work contends that the rapid worldwide liberalization of sodomy laws since the Second World War, across highly differentiated country contexts, and often in the absence of local social movements working toward reform, must be explained primarily by the existence of a Western-inspired progressive world sexual culture. This sexual culture has crystallized, they argue, around notions of sexual individualization, and has diffused rapidly around the world as an increasingly taken for granted norm tied to the legitimacy of the properly functioning nation states leading to structural isomorphism focused on sodomy law liberalization.

Like world polity theorists more generally, however, Frank and his colleagues fail to offer a sufficiently sophisticated account of the extent to which the global diffusion of this progressive world sexual culture has been shaped by on-going dynamics of conflict, power, and resistance. In some ways this is to be expected. Frank is one of the world polity perspective's long-standing proponents, who worked with Meyer in the late 1990s to refine a number of its basic tenets and methodologies (Meyer et al. 1997a). Frank's broader investment in the world polity perspective might suggest that his project on global sodomy law reform was aimed primarily at strengthening the case for Meyer's account of social change.

The following sections seek instead to reintroduce conflict dynamics back into an appraisal of the global social processes of sodomy law reform by adopting what Beckfield has described as a "conflict-centred model of the world polity" (2003, p. 401). To do so, four case studies are interrogated as to what each might reveal about the conflict, power, and resistance entailed by the influence of progressive world sexual culture on worldwide sodomy law reform.

Case Study One

Geneva, June 2011. The United Nations Human Rights Council (UN HRC) agrees for the first time to an historic resolution on the human rights of LGBT people. The resolution's scope is limited; it simply instructs the UN High Commissioner for Human Rights to produce a report on the abuses suffered by LGBT people worldwide. The report is released in December and describes serious violations relating to sexual orientation and gender identity across almost all regions of the world, including the continued prohibition of homosexuality by 76 countries. Soon after, the High Commissioner calls for the immediate repeal of these laws and equalization of the age of consent to gay sex. At the first UN HRC meeting to discuss the findings, however, members of the Organization of Islamic Cooperation (OIC) walk out in protest.

In recent years, the UN has emerged as a significant forum for emerging struggles over global sexual justice (Correa et al. 2008). It has become the new setting for an "explosion in discourse and normative acts on sexuality and rights" brought about by "the unprecedented elaboration and expansion of the formal international human rights system since 1989" (Roseman and Miller 2011, pp. 316–317). Sexual rights claims before the UN followed initially from feminist activism around women's reproductive autonomy and the human response to the global AIDS pandemic (Correa et al. 2008). These early successes have since driven at least two decades of incremental developments relating to the rights of marginalized sexualities within the UN's expert and political institutions (Cobb 2012; Roseman and Miller 2011; Saiz 2004; Waites 2009). The UN HRC's historic resolution on worldwide violations of the rights of LGBT people, and the subsequent report on sexual orientation and gender identity discrimination, reflect the most recent stage in these developments. The UN HRC's resolution and report have refocused attention in particular on the continuing prevalence of state sodomy laws worldwide.

Frank and his colleagues might well reasonably argue that these recent developments provide further support for the claim that we are witnessing the emergence of an expanding and increasingly integrated progressive world sexual culture. For world polity theorists, it is global institutions—IGOs, INGOs, and transnational experts and professionals—that remain the primary generators and carriers of world-cultural norms (Boli and Thomas 1999; Meyer et al. 1997a). The UN is especially significant in this respect; as Driori suggests, it has emerged since its foundation in 1945 as a primary "site for global cultural work" (2005, p. 189; see also Lechner and Boli 2005, Chap. 4).

That 23 members of the UN HRC voted in favor of the 2011 resolution on LGBT rights may reflect in turn what Finnemore and Sikkink describe as a "tipping point" in which agreement is reached "among a critical mass of actors on some emergent norm" leading to the elevation of that norm to the status of a world-cultural script (1998, pp. 252–53). In other words, the resolution seems to support Frank and his colleagues' suggestion that the logic of sexual individualization, rights, and justice have shifted now from the local to the global level and into world culture, so as to "become the business of the world [and] not just internal national issues" (Ramirez et al. 2002, p. 1).

The difficulty with this world polity analysis, of course, is that it has much more difficulty accounting for evidence of continuing and explicit resistance to this emerging progressive world culture demonstrated by the decision of the OIC to walk out of the first panel meeting held to discuss the High Commissioner's report on LGBT rights violations. The OIC, previously known as the Organization of the Islamic Conference, was established in 1969. It has permanent UN delegation status, and is made up at present of 59 member states from across the Muslim world, making it the second largest IGO after the UN (see Akbarzadeh and Connor 2005). The OIC's global significance makes its opposition to the resolution stance especially important.

The OIC preceded its staged walk out with an open letter submitted to the Human Rights Council by Zamir Akbam, Pakistan's representative to the UN. In it, he accuses the Council of attempting "to create controversial 'new notions' or 'new standards'" by "misinterpreting the Universal Declaration of Human Rights and international treaties to include such notions that were never articulated or agreed to by the U.N. membership" before describing homosexuality as simply "personal preferences and behavior" (Kirchick 2012).[7] On one hand, of course, the letter seems to reinforce the dynamics of Meyer's world society, by taking implicitly for granted the broad world-cultural legitimacy of the UN's international human rights framework. On the other hand, it then explicitly opposes the logic of sexual individualization in its description of the resolution as "misinterpreting" international human rights law.

This act of direct opposition by the OIC to progressive world sexual culture appears to lend some support to the argument posited by Inglehart and Norris (2003) that world culture is being defined less by the unstoppable march of sexual individualization, rights, and justice across the globe, as Frank and his colleagues' world polity perspective suggests, than it is by a "sexual clash of civilizations" in which the rapid globalization of sexual discourses, especially surrounding homosexuality, are the primary cause of worldwide cultural fragmentation between global actors (c.f. Fassin 2010). Like Huntington's original thesis, on which the authors build their claims, particular attention is drawn to the purportedly fundamental fault line over questions of sexuality between "the West" and "Islam." The co-ordinated resistance to the UN HRC's resolution by OIC member states challenges the view that progressive world sexual culture is diffusing uncontested around the world while also indicating that the recent strengthening of that culture—demonstrated by the UN HRC resolution itself—may be sharpening the fault lines between these competing claims to truth about sexuality. Instead, it seems to support the claim that "sexuality remains a battleground within the UN human rights system" (Saiz 2004, p. 50). The extent of this cultural fragmentation is reflected in the fact that the resolution was passed by only the narrowest margin, with 23 states voting in favor, 19 states voting against, and 3 states abstaining.

The OIC's act of resistance to the UN HRC resolution may also further complicate Frank and his colleagues' faith in worldwide progress toward sodomy law liberalization through the diffusion of progressive world sexual culture. In another more recent longitudinal, cross-national analysis of sodomy law reform between 1972 and 2002, Asal et al. (2013) foreground Islamic influence as a significant factor affecting the likelihood that a state will repeal existing sodomy laws, although the authors go on to note wide variation in outcome between different Islamic countries depending on types of legal system, state of development, democratic culture, and openness to globalization. The further question left

---

[7] The letter in full can be found at http://www.unwatch.org/atf/cf/%7B6deb65da-be5b-4cae-8056-8bf0bedf4d17%7D/OIC%20TO%20PRESIDENT.PDF.

unanswered by the study is whether Islam's apparent inertia over liberalization is set to become more, rather than less, pronounced and entrenched as progressive world sexual culture further embeds itself within the political institutions of intergovernmental organizations like the UN.

Of course, the variability of Islam's influence on sodomy law reform highlighted by Asal et al.'s study also demonstrates the intrinsic simplification involved in Inglehart and Norris's clash of civilizations thesis. The practical role of Islam in resisting progressive world sexual culture and sodomy law liberalization is inevitably complicated by other localized dynamics in particular nation states, which require further interrogation. Moreover, it would be highly misleading to assume that Islam is the only source of explicit resistance to progressive world sexual culture and sodomy law liberalization. Another inevitable focus for any analysis of the merits of the sexual clash of civilizations thesis must be sub-Saharan Africa where it is increasingly apparent that a new pattern is emerging, across some African countries, whereby sodomy laws are being strengthened in response to what seem to be new waves of virulent homophobia grounded in constructions of "traditional" African heterosexuality. Undoubtedly, the most well-known example of this shift is the Uganda Anti-Homosexuality Bill, which forms the focus of the second case study (see too, in this volume, DeJong and Long for additional analysis of this Bill).

Case Study Two

Kampala, October 2009. Ugandan Member of Parliament David Bahati introduces a legislative bill designed to strengthen existing laws against homosexuality. Bahati defends the Anti-Homosexuality Bill as necessary in the face of "internal and external threats to the heterosexual family." It includes a new crime of "aggravated homosexuality" attracting the death penalty, and would criminalize anyone failing to report violations of the Bill's provisions within 24 h. The Bill (commonly referred to as the 'Kill the Gays Bill' by Western media) is a global cause celebre, attracting worldwide media attention and condemnation. It is shelved temporarily in response to this outcry, only to be laid down again for debate two years later. As of 2013, the current legislative status of the Anti-Homosexuality Bill remains uncertain.

Just over half of the 76 remaining sodomy laws worldwide are found in sub-Saharan Africa; most such laws were introduced through colonial era penal codes, especially by the British (Amnesty International 2013; Human Rights Watch 2008). These sodomy laws, and the homophobia they have helped to ferment, belie the historic recognition of indigenous homosexualities across the African continent, though this history has often been denied or ignored in favor of explanations that treat African same-sex desire and practices as European in origin (Epprecht 2008; Hoad 2007; Murray and Roscoe 1998). The Uganda Anti-Homosexuality Bill reflects a more recent post-colonial development in the politics of sodomy law reform in Africa, however, in which domestic sodomy laws are being further strengthened by national governments, or even introduced for the first time. The Ugandan Bill has garnered particular global attention for the severity of its proposed new crime of "aggravated homosexuality," which would attract the death penalty if enacted.

The international outcry that followed the introduction of the Anti-Homosexuality Bill to the Uganda Parliament strengthens the world polity claim that the politics of sodomy law is being shaped increasingly by progressive world sexual culture. News about the Bill spread remarkably rapidly around the world, as did the mounting opposition, including protests outside the Ugandan embassy in London; a condemnatory resolution by the European Parliament; on-line petitions on social networking sites such as Facebook and Twitter; critical editorials in major world newspapers; briefings by Human Rights Watch, Amnesty International, and the ILGA; and objections by several spokespersons of national governments. The speed and readiness with which the Bill emerged in this way as a specifically *global* problem—of concern to IGOs, INGOs, governments, media outlets, experts, and individuals around the world—seems to demonstrate the extent to which progressive sexual cultures are now circulating at a truly worldwide level.

However, the world polity perspective offers rather less traction as an explanatory framework when it comes to locating the social processes behind the Bill itself. Recent scholarship on sodomy laws has often focused on dynamics of nationalism to explain the defense of sodomy law prohibitions. As Stychin (1998, p. 35) notes, sodomy laws are powerful symbolic tools, which continue to be deployed to constitute (or reconstitute) the state around constructed national heteronormativities. In a similar vein, Cheney (2012) has argued recently that the introduction of the Bill reflects various "cultural logics" within the country, tied to a constructed nationalism based on a traditional, heterosexual identity and concerns with the effect of homosexuality on social and sexual reproduction. What is less explicit in Cheney's analysis is the extent to which the Bill might also be seen as a direct reaction, in part at least, to the dynamics of progressive world sexual culture within which Uganda is increasingly immersed. In fact, Frank and his colleagues, though focusing primarily on explanations for convergence over sodomy law liberalization since 1945, do point in this direction when they suggest that a spate of sodomy law expansions in the 1970s—including the sub-Saharan African nations of Gabon and Cameroon—were a response to the perceived threat of sexual globalization emerging within world culture in that period. As they put it: "[b]y bucking the global trend and strengthening sanctions against sodomy, Gabonian and Cameroonian officials signaled their resolve to reclaim their countries, standing apart from the West and the world" (2009, p. 130). In much the same way, the Anti-Homosexuality Bill can be understood as an effort by Ugandan political actors to assert the country's sovereignty in the face of the rapidly expanding and integrated progressive world sexual culture exemplified by recent political developments at the UN.

Cheney's analysis also understates the extent to which the Anti-Homosexuality Bill seems to be located within broader regional dynamics. While the Bill is by far the most internationally well-known and most contested example of sodomy law expansions in Africa, it is certainly not exceptional. Since 2006, South Sudan, Nigeria, Burundi, and Malawi have each taken steps to strengthen criminal laws prohibiting same-sex genital relations, as well as other behaviors connected to homosexuality, while new legislation is being introduced in Liberia (Amnesty International 2013, pp. 18–19). There have been some changes in direction. For instance, in Malawi, sex between women was criminalized for the first time in 2011; however, soon after her election to office in 2012 President of Malawi, Joyce Banda, agreed to impose a moratorium on the prosecution of all same-sex sexual offenses (International Commission of Jurists 2011; Mapondera and Smith 2012). Nevertheless, a pattern of sodomy law expansion seems to be emerging once again across parts of sub-Saharan Africa. The rapidity with which dynamics of sodomy law expansion have spread between these states also provides evidence of transnational cultural diffusion across the continent.

It is now increasingly apparent that one such transnational force shaping sodomy law expansion in Africa has been the influence of U.S. Christian Evangelical movements (Koama 2009, 2012). The Anti-Homosexuality Bill was introduced to the Ugandan Parliament shortly after a conference organized in Kampala by three leading American evangelicals including U.S. pastor Scott Lively, in which the threat of homosexuality to Africans was shored up by Christian doctrine and support given to long-standing claims of Western neo-imperialism. U.S. Christian evangelism is now bound intimately to the explicit rejection of progressive world sexual culture in Africa, as these movements seek out new environments from which to resist that culture, especially given the growing tolerance of homosexualities in the U.S. itself (for further discussion of the U.S. Christian Right and homosexuality, see Herman 1998).

Importantly, this growing evidence of the extent of American evangelical influence in Africa also challenges certain assumptions underpinning both the world polity perspective and the "sexual clash of civilizations" thesis. The role played by the U.S. Christian Right on the continent reveals the incoherency of the implicit claim shared by both theories that the West is now fully integrated within progressive world sexual culture. More specifically, evidence of the circulation of homophobia from the U.S. to Africa complicates the otherwise easy assumption that the Anti-Homosexuality Bill and other sodomy law expansions reflect deepening divisions between the distinct sexual cultures of the global North and South; instead, it draws attention to the complex homophobias that remain embedded across Western nations as these states continue to come to terms only equivocally with the demands of progressive world sexual culture.

At present, the legislative status of the Anti-Homosexuality Bill remains uncertain. Ugandan President Yoweri Museveni, while initially supportive of the Bill, withdrew his support from the legislation after international outcry, leading to the Bill's withdrawal from Parliament in May 2010 (Seckinelgin 2012, p. 4). One element of this global reaction has been the threat by several Western countries to cut financial aid to Uganda unless the Bill was withdrawn. The question of aid conditionality connects to the second weakness of the world polity perspective as a framework for understanding the dynamics of conflict, power, and resistance at work in global sodomy law reform—its under-interrogation of the role played by coercive mechanisms in enforcing sodomy law liberalization and the structural power inequalities between nation states that use of coercive mechanisms entails. Aid conditionality forms the focus of the third case study.

Case Study Three

> Perth, October 2011. British Prime Minister David Cameron chooses the Commonwealth Heads of Government Meeting in Australia to announce plans to withdraw U.K. foreign development aid from countries with poor gay rights records, including those that refuse to repeal sodomy laws in line with their international human rights obligations. His statement receives a muted response from LGBT organizations in the global North but there is vocal opposition from African civil society organizations, many of which sign a public declaration denouncing Cameron's intervention for setting back local activism. Subsequently, Secretary of State Hillary Clinton delivers a speech indicating that the U.S. would also consider the case for aid conditionality to protect LGBT rights abroad.

The origins of aid conditionality can be traced back to the lending criteria imposed on developing countries by international financial institutions, especially the World Bank and the International Monetary Fund, in the wake of the 1980s worldwide debt crisis (Koeboele et al. 2005). Since then conditions tied to foreign assistance have also been acknowledged as a legitimate "material leverage" to encourage human rights compliance, though this application remains controversial (Keck and Sikkink 1998, p. 23; c.f. Alameny and Dede 2008). The threat of aid conditionality by the U.K. government in support of sodomy law liberalization in the last months of 2011 was a continuation of earlier condemnatory responses by predominantly Western states to the rapid escalation of sodomy law expansion across several African countries, including Uganda's Anti-Homosexuality Bill. Shortly after Cameron's statement, then-Secretary of State Clinton issued her own declaration, on behalf of the U.S. government, supporting the principle of aid conditionality to advance LGBT rights worldwide, although unlike the British Prime Minister, Clinton tied her own threat to a further promise of more U.S. funding to support local social movements working with marginalized sexualities abroad (Kretz 2013).

On one hand, the emerging threat of aid conditionality to enforce sodomy law liberalization provides additional support for Frank and his colleagues' evocation of an increasingly integrated and expanding progressive world sexual culture. As Goodman and Jinks note, coercive strategies by states to enforce cultural norms usually require those norms to be so embedded in world culture already that the coercion is generally accepted as legitimate by the global community: in this way, "socialization processes may direct influence over third parties (e.g., donor countries), who in turn use traditional coercive techniques to effect compliance in the target state" (2004, p. 631). It can be argued similarly that the U.K. and U.S.

governments' decisions to threaten aid conditionality against recalcitrant states is evidence that worldwide cultural opposition to sodomy laws has become sufficiently diffused across world society for both governments to feel sufficiently confident that their threats would be perceived by the international community as justifiable in the circumstances.

On the other hand, aid conditionality also creates further problems for the world polity perspective. Meyer focuses in his work on global isomorphism brought about by the diffusion of highly embedded cultural scripts to local settings cognitively and normatively or at the level of the taken for granted. As others have pointed out, however, this approach tends to underestimate the extent to which shared cultural values, norms, and standards are contested and, in doing so, how they are enforced in some circumstances through coercive means. There has been some recognition of the role of coercive mechanisms of cultural change in achieving isomorphism by proponents of sociological neo-institutionalism and the world polity perspective, including specific attention to the role of coercion in enforcing cultural compliance in international relations and human rights (Goodman and Jinks 2004; Powell and DiMaggio 1991; Scott 1995). However, engagement with coercion as a mechanism of cultural change tends to remain relatively superficial within the world polity approach.

For instance, Frank and his colleagues acknowledge that sodomy law liberalization between 1945 and 2005 was not in each and every case the result of the diffusion of progressive world sexual culture at the cognitive and normative level. They recognize instead that sometimes coercion was involved; in particular, they use the example of the on-going expectation that countries joining the European Union must first liberalize their sodomy laws, which led to the repeal of Romania's sodomy laws in 1996 in advance of the country's EU accession (Frank et al. 2009, citing Stychin 2003; see, too, Pearce and Cooper, this volume). However, what the co-authors fail to consider in turn is the extent to which the deployment of coercive mechanisms in such circumstances raises questions about the inequalities of power within world society that allow coercion to occur.

This is also a problem with recent criticism leveled specifically at the threat of aid conditionality by the U.S. and U.K. governments in support of LGBT rights. This writing has tended for the most part to take a functionalist approach to the question; in other words, it has focused on the extent to which the imposition of conditions on foreign assistance are effective in practice in bringing about adherence to prescribed cultural norms. Take for instance the open letter written by African NGOs soon after Cameron's statement following the Commonwealth Heads of Government Meeting in Perth. The concerns expressed in the letter are complex and multi-faceted, but all are limited to the claim that aid conditionality would do more harm than good to African sexual politics. The letter notes, among other things, the possible scapegoating of marginalized sexualities in targeted countries; the divisions it threatens between social movements working on behalf of marginalized sexualities and other civil society groups; and broader harm to development work in Africa.[8] Others have since raised similar concerns about aid conditionality (Abba 2012; Anguita 2012; Kretz 2013).

These criticisms are well-founded and important. However, they fail to attend also to the broader underlying geopolitical power dynamics that ultimately underpin the coercive enforcement of sexual rights and sodomy law liberalization. In this respect, the material inequalities and dependencies that enable Western nations like the U.K. and U.S. to impose (or at least threaten to impose) aid conditionality on countries in the global South might well raise questions about the extent to which the diffusion of progressive world sexual culture, and the sodomy law liberalization that it demands, is being dictated by what Wallerstein has conceptualized as the economic inequalities between core, semi-peripheral, and peripheral nations, as aid dependencies across the global South are manipulated by the West to effect changes to nation states' sodomy laws.

In addition, there are broader implications involved in the growing legitimacy with which Western states, acting ostensibly in the name of marginalized sexualities worldwide, are now engaging in coercive practices like aid conditionality to enforce LGBT rights and the repeal of sodomy laws. One significant note of caution might be drawn, for instance, from recent critical scholarship. Like world polity theorists, critical sexuality scholars (particularly "queer" scholars) have been tracing the rapid acculturation of the global North to the logic of sexual individualization, and especially to the discourse of LGBT rights. In doing so they have also identified what they see as evidence of the intertwining of racism and nationalism with notions of (global) sexual justice. While some marginalized sexualities in the West are now increasingly integrated into the national body politic (especially those who are white, middle class, and express 'normal' sexual desires), they have become implicated simultaneously in the on-going reconstruction of certain racialized populations as internal or external threats to the nation who are therefore legitimately subject to authoritarian forms of state control to protect all citizens, including LGBT people. Marginalized sexualities in the West are themselves complicit in this state co-option of sexual identity politics for racist, oppressive, and neo-imperialist ends by generating and adhering to complex "homonationalisms" in which their sexual identities are bound up increasingly with regimes of nationalistic and racist subjectivity. This is especially evident where particular racialized others (such as the paradigmatic Muslim immigrant or terrorist) are perceived by LGBT communities as direct threats to the gains of progressive Western sexual culture (Agathangelou et al. 2008; Haritaworn 2011; Puar 2007).

The emerging threat of aid conditionality draws attention once again to the growing cultural confidence with which Western nations seem willing to enforce the emerging world-cultural norm of sodomy law liberalization using coercive measures. This confidence in coercion points also to the concerns of some critical theorists that the global politics of sexual justice may be susceptible to co-option

---

[8] The statement can be found in full at http://www.amsher.net/news/ViewArticle.aspx?id=1200

by national governments in order to legitimate racist, oppressive, and neo-imperialist state aggression against other countries—especially in the global South—even where this aggression is only tangentially related (if at all) to furthering sexual rights abroad. Like the evocation of gendered violence by the Bush administration as part of the "war rhetoric" used to justify the U.S. invasion of Afghanistan, the perceived rejection of progressive world sexual culture and mistreatment of marginalized sexualities by nation states in the global South may be deployed by Western governments in the future in this way to denote those states as being appropriate targets for military action (Stables 2003, pp. 108–109; Stabile and Kumar 2005). In this respect, sodomy laws may well take on the role of (crude) markers by which countries falling short of world sexual standards can be identified as global problems or even "failed states," necessitating coercive interventions.

However, it is not merely explicitly coercive responses by the West to enforce sodomy law liberalization in the name of world sexual culture that should give pause for thought about the unequal power dynamics that may persist between differently situated nation states in the West and global South. The following, final case study considers a recent example of the apparently successful taken for granted, non-coercive world-cultural diffusion of the logic of sexual individualization, and especially the discourses of sexual rights, as the basis for the repeal of state sodomy laws by national courts. It is easy to view this diffusion of universal human rights standards to local settings at the cognitive and normative level (as world polity theorists do) as non-hierarchical and consensual, and so outside the power relations that more obviously appear to define the use of coercive strategies such as aid conditionality. Nevertheless, even in such circumstances there is a need to remain vigilant to the subtle global power dynamics that also inform these cognitive mechanisms of sodomy law reform.

Case Study Four

> New Delhi, July 2009. The Delhi High Court delivers its long-awaited judgment in *Naz Foundation v Union of India*, reading down section 377 of the Indian Penal Code prohibiting "unnatural sexual offences," to decriminalize private, consensual sexual activity between adults of the same sex. The Court's decision is the culmination of litigation lasting over fifteen years, brought by HIV/AIDS civil society organizations including Naz Foundation, which challenged section 377 as a violation of the rights to privacy, equality, and dignity enumerated in the Indian Constitution and for undermining effective HIV prevention work in India. While opposed by national religious leaders, the High Court's decision receives a rapturous reception from LGBT social movements in India and around the world.

The Delhi High Court's judgment in *Naz Foundation* seems to stand in stark contrast to the previous three case studies. The UN HRC's disputed resolution on LGBT rights, Uganda's Anti-Homosexuality Bill, and the threat of aid conditionality by the U.K. and U.S. governments, each point to the existence of on-going and explicit conflict and contestation over sodomy law liberalization, which seems to be becoming more rather than less entrenched in the face of an expanding and increasingly integrated progressive world sexual culture. *Naz Foundation* appears, conversely, to offer an important example of the worldwide convergence over sodomy law liberalization, grounded in the consensual and non-coercive diffusion of progressive world sexual culture to local country contexts, which lies at the heart of Frank and his colleagues' world polity perspective on the social process of global sodomy law reform.

Naz Foundation forms part of a wave of repeals of state sodomy laws by national courts in the last decade, which has stretched from South Africa, to the U.S., Fiji, and Nepal. What *Naz Foundation* shares with these other judicial decisions is its reliance on exogenous universalized human rights standards on sexuality and sodomy laws, drawn from international treaties and the domestic case law of other countries. Katyal (2010, p. 1441) describes this as the effect of a "constitutional diaspora," in which constitutional and human rights materials about sexuality, sexual rights, and sexual justice are borrowed from across jurisdictions (and often reworked in the new setting in which they are then applied and integrated). *Naz Foundation* relied in particular on two emerging global rights frameworks: (1) the civil and political rights of privacy, equality, and non-discrimination and (2) the associated discourses linking human rights and public health, by which demands for sexual rights and sodomy law liberalization are tied explicitly to the response to HIV/AIDS (Cobb 2012; Seckinelgin 2009).

In this way, *Naz Foundation* encapsulates the world-cultural processes that Frank and his colleagues suggest are primarily responsible for global sodomy law liberalization. The judges of the Delhi High Court amount to little more than the expert enactors of the powerful, pre-existing scripts of a progressive sexual world culture that now defines the legitimacy of the properly functioning modern nation state, in which India has become increasingly integrated. This is not to say, of course, that Indian society is entirely embedded in these world sexual scripts; the often extreme resistance by nationalist and religious leaders to the *Naz Foundation* decision echoes the opposition found within the Organization of Islamic Cooperation and segments of society in African nations like Uganda. However, India seems to have become sufficiently embedded in world sexual culture to support sodomy law repeal.

For world polity theorists, the diffusion of universalized human rights standards seems to operate largely outside the dynamics of conflict, power, and resistance. Meyer evokes a vision of world culture that focuses much more on non-hierarchical, decentralized, and egalitarian relations between global actors (Driori and Krucken 2009, p. 10). We have seen already how the coercive enforcement of progressive world sexual culture—illustrated by aid conditionality—is bound up inevitably with conflict, power, and resistance, especially between the global North and South. However, the non-coercive diffusion of universal human rights standards through judicial processes, in cases like *Naz Foundation*, might be said to be subject to similar global inequalities, given the fact that, as the world polity perspective readily acknowledges, these standards are derived predominantly from Western cultural norms. In this regard, critical scholars of sexuality, modernity, and globalization have been rather more attentive than world polity theorists to the subtle dynamics of power that continue to underpin even the successful cultural diffusion of sexual identities, values, and norms from the Western world to the global South (Altman 2001; Binnie 2004; Stychin 2003–2004).

These scholars have focused in particular on what they consider to be the displacement of localized understandings of sexuality resulting from the globalization of sexuality and, more specifically, the universalization of the notion of "LGBT human rights" and the rapid diffusion of concepts such as "sexual orientation" and "gender identity" (Massad 2007; Waites 2009). These discursive frameworks can be vital in strengthening local rights claims, such as calls for sodomy law liberalization, by embedding them within globally shared and recognized meanings (Altman 2001; Stychin 2003–2004). However, they may also threaten to displace indigenous conceptions of sexuality and gender variance within a Western-inspired one-size-fits-all global cultural regime, "imposing one socio-historically contingent understanding of homosexuality as the substance for subjectivity in diverse and multiple social contexts" (Seckinelgin 2012, p. 16). These processes of displacement have two main strategic implications for global sexual justice. On one hand, they may jeopardize locally generated understandings of sexuality that might well provide a more sustainable basis for rights claims including sodomy law reform; on the other hand, they may also serve to strengthen the claims of Western neo-colonialism that we have already seen continue to bedevil sexual rights strategies focused on sodomy law reform in countries such as Uganda.

More recently, critical scholars have pointed additionally to the power dynamics entailed by the worldwide cultural diffusion of transnational expertise in the wake of the human response to HIV/AIDS. In *Naz Foundation*, sodomy law repeal was achieved in part because the Delhi High Court was also embedded in the world-cultural scripting of transnational HIV/AIDS expertise that continues to argue for worldwide decriminalization of marginalized sexualities on public health grounds (Cobb 2012). This focus on sodomy law reform as a public health measure has been commended by some scholars for helping to neutralize long-standing religious and moral resistance to traditional LGBT rights discourse in countries like India by reconstituting sodomy law liberalization in the language of ostensibly neutral, biomedical expertise (Katyal 2002, 2010). Others have argued, however, that the global circulation of this biomedical expertise, while perhaps strategically useful in securing specific goals such as sodomy law repeal, may again be helping to displace simultaneously the complexity of the embodied lives of indigenous marginalized sexualities, only this time through discourses of risk, prevention, and securitization that seem to shore up their long-standing construction as threats to the well-being of the (heteronormative) state and in turn their position as "anti-citizens" in the era of HIV/AIDS (Cobb 2012; c.f. Seckinelgin 2009; see also Levy, this volume).

Concluding Thoughts

John W. Meyer's world polity perspective locates social processes of change within nation states firmly within the dynamics of contemporary globalization. Meyer's theoretical framework is of course just one of a wealth of competing conceptualizations of the meaning and impact of globalization on nation states (see generally Holton 1998). It can be differentiated from these other accounts, however, by its focus on the cultural (rather than economic) effects of globalization on states; its emphasis on the emergence of a shared world culture encouraging convergence, homogeneity, or "isomorphism" across otherwise highly differentiated geopolitical environments; and its assumption that this expanding world culture reflects the primarily consensual worldwide acceptance by nation states of the ascendance of a coherent Western view of modernity based on taken for granted values, norms, and standards such as individualism, rationality, progress, and justice.

The world polity framework offers a valuable and novel perspective on the social dynamics shaping the social processes of global sodomy law reform by nation states. As applied by Frank and his colleagues, it identifies apparently striking homogeneity around sodomy law liberalization in nation states across all parts of the world. Scholars working within the world polity tradition explain this purported isomorphism as the effect of rapidly expanding cultural scripts since the Second World War, grounded in Western-inspired values, norms, and standards, which have supported an emerging progressive world sexual culture, grounded in the interplay between sexual individualization, rights, and justice. The problem with this analysis of the social process of sodomy law reform, foregrounded in this chapter, is that it tends to underestimate or ignore entirely the role of conflict in the diffusion of these cultural scripts, and the role of power and resistance in the resolution of that conflict.

Recognizing the on-going existence of conflict in global sodomy law reform also suggests there is a need for closer scrutiny of the broader strategic implications of Frank and his colleagues' observations. These authors imply that much can be left to the diffusion of world culture through IGOs, INGOs, and other transnational professionals to effect change to sodomy laws while they downplay the role of local actors in particular country contexts. The continued conflict over the diffusion of progressive world sexual culture this chapter has identified suggests instead that the benefits of relying on the cultural globalization of sexual individualization, rights, and justice must be considered at all times against the inevitable costs that this can entail. The problem of backlash to perceived Western sexual imperialism, the questionable rise of coercive interventions by the West to enforce compliance with progressive world sexual culture, and the possible displacement of indigenous conceptions of marginalized sexualities by the imposition of universalized sexual rights, all suggest that more work must be done to refocus energies on supporting "bottom up" local cultural change as far as possible in struggles over sodomy law repeal, in an effort to avoid some of the dangers of over-reliance on world-cultural dynamics to effect change to domestic sodomy law regimes.

In this respect, this author shares Seckinelgin's (2009, 2012) concern that more attention should be paid to local voices when sexual rights claims are made including demands for sodomy law liberalization. Progressive world sexual culture—whether constituted through the universalized language of sexual rights or HIV prevention expertise—can be usefully drawn upon by local actors to support their demands for the repeal of domestic sodomy laws; it is also possible for productive hybridity to emerge between global and local sexual cultures; and in many cases, of course, especially where state sodomy laws are in place and actively enforced, there may be little scope for local activism to take root and for domestic social movements to effect change without the support of global IGOs, INGOs, and transnational experts. Nevertheless, there remains a need to ensure that—as far as is possible—sufficient space is opened up for local voices in ongoing struggles over sodomy law reform, rather than relying simply on the onward march of world sexual culture to effect that change, as Frank and his colleagues' world polity perspective might appear to encourage.

Acknowledgments A version of this chapter was first presented as a seminar paper at Kent Law School, England, in May 2013. My thanks go to all those who attended the seminar for their invaluable comments and criticisms on that earlier draft, and especially Emilie Cloatre for organizing the event. Thanks also to Dana Peterson and Vanessa Panfil for their patience throughout the writing process, as well as their helpful advice and support. As ever all errors remain my own.

References

Abba, H. (2012). Aid, resistance and queer power. In Sexual Policy Watch, *The Global Context: Sexuality and Geopolitics, Selected Texts*. SPW Working Paper (April), (7), 16–19. Retrieved from http://www.sxpolitics.org/wp-content/uploads/2012/04/spw-wp7-the-global-context-sexuality-and-politics.pdf

Agathangelou, A., Bassicis, M. D., & Spira, T. L. (2008). Intimate investments: Homonormativity, global lockdown, and the seductions of empire. *Radical History Review, 100*, 120–143.

Alemany, C., & Dede, G. (2008). *Conditionalities undermine the right to development: An analysis based on a women's and human rights perspective*. Cape Town, South Africa: Association for Women's Rights in Development (AWID). Retrieved from http://staging.awid.org/eng/About-AWID/AWID-Initiatives/IDeA/Resources-on-Aid-Effectiveness/Conditionalities-Undermine-the-Right-to-Development

Altman, D. (2001). *Global sex*. Chicago, IL: Chicago University Press.

Amnesty International. (2013). *Making love a crime: Criminalization of same-sex conduct in Sub-Saharan Africa*. London: Amnesty International. Retrieved from http://www.amnesty.org/en/library/asset/AFR01/001/2013/en/9f2d91b7-bc0e-4ea7-adae-7e51ae0ce36f/afr010012013en.pdf

Anguita, L. A. (2012). Aid conditionality and respect for LGBT people rights. In Sexual Policy Watch, *The Global Context: Sexuality and Geopolitics, Selected Texts*. SPW Working Paper (April), (7), 9–15. Retrieved from http://www.sxpolitics.org/wp-content/uploads/2012/04/spw-wp7-the-global-context-sexuality-and-politics.pdf

Akbarzadeh, S., & Connor, K. (2005). The Organization of the Islamic Conference: Sharing an illusion. *Middle East Policy, 12*(2), 79–92.

Asal, V., Sommer, U., & Harwood, P. G. (2013). Original sin: A cross-national study of the legality of homosexual acts. *Comparative Political Studies, 46*, 320–351.

Barber, B. (1995). *Jihad vs McWorld: How globalism and tribalism are reshaping the world.* New York, NY: Crown Press.

Boli, J., & Thomas, G. (1999). *Constructing world culture: International nongovernmental organizations since 1875.* Stanford, CA: Stanford University Press.

Boyle, E. H. (2002). *Female genital cutting: Cultural conflict in the global community.* Philadelphia, PA: John Hopkins University Press.

Boyle, E. H., & Meyer, J. W. (1998). Modern law as secularized and global model: Implications for the sociology of law. *Soziale Welt, 49*, 275–294.

Beckfield, J. (2003). Inequality in the world polity: The structure of international organization. *American Sociological Review, 68*, 401–424.

Bernstein, M. (2003). Nothing ventured, nothing gained? Conceptualizing social movement 'success' in the lesbian and gay movement. *Sociological Perspectives, 46*, 353–379.

Binnie, J. (2004). *The globalization of sexuality.* London: Sage.

Buttel, F. H. (2000). World society, the nation state, and environmental protection. *American Sociological Review, 65*(1), 117–121.

Cheney, K. (2012). Locating neocolonialism, "tradition", and human rights in Uganda's "gay death penalty." *African Studies Review, 55*(2), 77–95.

Cobb, N. (2012). Contagion politics: Queer rights claims, biopower, and the "public health" rationale for the repeal of sodomy laws. *Jindal Global Law Review, 4*(1), 60–88.

Correa, S., Petchesky, R., & Parker, R. (2008). *Sexuality, health and human rights.* London, UK: Routledge.

Currier, A. (2011). Decolonizing the law: LGBT organizing in Namibia and South Africa. In S. Sarat (Ed.), *Special issue: Social movements/legal possibilities, studies in law, politics, and society, 54,*17–44.

De la Dehesa, R. (2010). *Queering the public sphere in Mexico and Brazil: Sexual rights movements in emerging democracies.* Durham, NC: Duke University Press.

Driori, G. S. (2005). United Nations' dedications: A world culture in the making? *International Sociology, 20*(2), 175–199.

Driori, G. S., & Krucken, G. (2009). World society: A theory and a research program in context. In G. Krucken & G. S. Driori (Eds.), *World society: The writings of John W. Meyer.* Oxford, UK: Oxford University Press.

Eisenstadt, S. N. (2000). Multiple modernities. *Daedulus, 129*, 1–29.

Epprecht, M. (2008). *Heterosexual Africa?: The history of an idea from the age of exploration to the age of AIDS.* Athens, OH: Ohio University Press.

Fassin, E. (2010). National identities and transnational intimacies: Sexual democracy and the politics of immigration in Europe. *Public Culture, 22*(3), 507–529.

Finnemore, M. (1996). Norms, culture, and world politics: Insights from sociology's institutionalism. *International Organization, 50*(2), 325–347.

Foucault, M. (1991). Governmentality. In G. Burchell, C. Gordon, & P. Miller (Eds.), *The Foucault effect: Studies in governmentality* (pp. 87–104). Chicago, IL: Chicago University Press.

Frank, D. J., & McEneaney, E. H. (1999). The individualization of society and the liberalization of state policies on same-sex sexual relations, 1984–1995. *Social Forces, 77*, 911–944.

Frank, D. J., & Meyer, J. W. (1998). The profusion of individual roles and identities in the postwar period. *Sociological Theory, 20*, 86–105.

Frank, D. J., Boutcher, S. A., & Camp, B. (2009). The repeal of sodomy laws from a world-society perspective. In S. Barclay, M. Bernstein, & A.-M. Marshall (Eds.), *Queer mobilizations: LGBT activists confront the law* (pp. 123–141). New York, NY: New York University Press.

Frank, D. J., Bayliss J. Camp, B., & Boutcher, S. A. (2010). Worldwide trends in the criminal regulation of sex, 1945 to 2005. *American Sociological Review, 75,* 867–893.

Fukuyama, F. (1992). *The end of history and the last man.* New York, NY: Free Press.

Goodman, R., & Jinks, D. (2004). How to influence states: Socialization and international human rights law. *Duke Law Journal, 54*(3), 621–703.

Hardt, M., & Negri, A. (2000). *Empire.* Cambridge, MA: Harvard University Press.

Haritaworn, J. (2011). Queer injuries: The cultural politics of "hate crimes" in Germany. *Social Justice, 37*(1), 69–91.

Herman, D. (1998). *The anti-gay agenda: Orthodox vision and Christian Right.* Chicago, IL: University of Chicago Press.

Hirsch, P. M. (1997). Sociology without social structure: Neoinstitutional theory meets brave new world. *American Journal of Sociology, 102*(6), 1702–1723.

Hoad, N. (2007). *African intimacies: Race, homosexuality, and globalization.* Minneapolis, MN: Minnesota University Press.

Holton, R. J. (1998). *Globalization and the nation state.* London, UK: Macmillan.

Human Rights Watch. (2008). *This alien legacy: The origins of "sodomy" laws in British Colonialism.* New York: Human Rights Watch. Retrieved from http://www.hrw.org/reports/2008/12/17/alien-legacy-0

Huntington, S. (1996). *The clash of civilizations: Remaking of world order.* New York, NY: Simon & Schuster.

Inglehart, R., & Norris, P. (2003). The true clash of civilizations. *Foreign Policy, 135,* 62–70.

International Commission of Jurists. (2011). *Press release: Sex between women now a crime in Malawi: New law violates human rights obligations of Malawi.* Retrieved from http://globalequality.files.wordpress.com/2011/02/malawi-section-137a-press-release.pdf

Itaborahy, L. P., & Zhu, J. (2013). State-sponsored homophobia. *A world survey of laws: Criminalisation, protection and recognition of same-sex love.* Brussels, Belgium and Mexico City, MX: International Lesbian and Gay Association. Retrieved from http://old.ilga.org/Statehomophobia/ILGA_State_Sponsored_Homophobia_2013.pdf.

Jepperson, R. L. (2002). The development and application of sociological neoinstitutionalism. In J. Belger & M. Zeldich (Eds.), *New directions in contemporary sociological theory* (pp. 229–266). Oxford, UK: Rowman and Littlefield.

Jenness, V. (2004). Explaining criminalization: From demography and status politics to globalization and modernization. *Annual Review of Sociology, 30,* 147–171.

Karatzogianni, A., & Robinson, A. (2010). *Power, resistance and conflict in the contemporary world: Social movements, networks and hierarchies.* New York, NY and Abingdon, UK: Routledge.

Kaoma, K. J. (2009). *Globalizing the culture wars: UN conservative, African churches and homophobia.* Somerville, MA: Political Research Associates. Retrieved from http://www.publiceye.org/publications/globalizing-the-culture-wars/

Kaoma, K. J. (2012). *Colonizing African values: How the US Christian Right is transforming sexual politics in Africa.* Somerville, MA: Political Research Associates. Retrieved from http://www.politicalresearch.org/resources/reports/full-reports/colonizing-african-values/

Katyal, S. (2002). Exporting identity. *Yale Journal of Law and Feminism, 14,* 97–176.

Katyal, S. (2010). The dissident citizen. *UCLA Law Review, 57,* 1415–1476.

Kane, M. (2007). Timing matters: Shifts in the causal determinants of sodomy law decriminalization, 1961–1998. *Social Problems, 54*(2), 211–239.

Keck, M. E., & Sikkink, K. (1998). *Activists beyond borders: Advocacy networks in international politics.* Ithaca, NY and London, UK: Cornell University Press.

Kirchick, J. (2012, March 6). It's not about gay rights – it's about human rights. *The Washington Post.* Retrieved from http://articles.washingtonpost.com/2012-03-06/opinions/35450316_1_gay-rights-homosexuality-on-religious-grounds-gay-individuals

Koeboele, S., Beyoda, H., Silarszky, P., & Verheyen, G. (2005). *Conditionality revisited: Concepts, experiences and lessons.* Washington, DC: The World Bank. Retrieved from http://siteresources.worldbank.org/PROJECTS/Resources/40940-1114615847489/Conditionalityrevisedpublication.pdf

Koenig, M., & Dierkes, J. (2012). Conflict in the world polity—neo-institutional perspectives. *Acta Sociologica, 54*(1), 5–25.

Kretz, A. (2013). Is aid conditionality the answer to anti-gay legislation? An analysis of British and American aid policies designed to protect sexual minorities. *Vienna J of International Constitutional Law, 7,* forthcoming.

Lechner, F. J., & Boli, J. (2005). *World culture: Origins and consequences.* Oxford, UK: Blackwell Publishing.

Massad, J. (2007). *Desiring Arabs.* Chicago, IL: University of Chicago Press.

McNeely, C. L. (1995). *Constructing the nation-state: International organization and prescriptive action.* Westport, CT: Greenport Press.

Meyer, J. W., Boli, J., & Thomas, G. M. (1987). Ontology and rationalisation in the Western cultural account. In G. M. Thomas, J. W. Meyer, F. O. Ramirez, and J. Boli (Eds.), *Institutional structure: Constituting state, society and the individual* (pp. 12–37). London, UK and New Delhi, India: Sage.

Meyer, J. W. (2009a). Reflections: Institutional theory and world society. In G. Krucken & G. S. Driori (Eds.), *World society: The writings of John W. Meyer* (pp. 36–66). Oxford, UK: Oxford University Press.

Meyer, J. W. (2009b). World society, the welfare state, and the life course: An institutionalist perspective. In G. Krucken, & G. S. Driori (Eds.), *World society: The writings of John W. Meyer* (pp. 261–279). Oxford, UK: Oxford University Press.

Meyer, J. W., Boli, J., Thomas, G. M., & Ramirez, F., O. (1997a). World society and the nation state. *American Journal of Sociology, 103,* 144–181.

Meyer, J. W., Frank, D. J., Hironaka, A., Schofer, E., & Tuma, N. B. (1997b). The structuring of a world environmental regime, 1870–1990. *International Organization, 51,* 623–651.

Meyer, J. W., & Ramirez, F. O. (2000). The world institutionalization of education. In J. Schriewer (Ed.), *Discourse formation in comparative education* (pp. 111–132). Frankfurt, Germany: Peter Lang Publishers.

Moran, L. (1996). *The homosexual(ity) of law.* London, UK: Routledge.

Murray, S. O., & Roscoe, W. (Eds.) (1998). *Boy-wives and female husbands: Studies of African homosexualities.* New York, NY: St. Martin's Press.

Powell, W. W. & DiMaggio, P. J. (Eds.) (1991). *The new institutionalism in organizational analysis.* Chicago, IL: Chicago University Press.

Puar, J. K. (2007). *Terrorist assemblages: Homonationalism in queer times.* Durham, NC and London, UK: Duke University Press.

Ramirez, F. O., Meyer, J. W. Wotipka, C. M., & Driori. G. S. (2002). *Expansion and impact of the world human rights regime: Longitudinal and cross-national analyses over the twentieth century.* National Science Foundation grant proposal. Retrieved from http://www.stanford.edu/group/csw/hr_proposal2002.doc

Roseman, M. J., & Miller, A. M. (2011). Normalizing sex and its discontents: Establishing sexual rights in international law. *Harvard Journal of Law and Gender, 34,* 313–375.

Said, E. (2001, October 22). The clash of ignorance. *The Nation.* Retrieved from http://www.thenation.com/article/clash-ignorance

Saiz, I. (2004). Bracketing sexuality: Human rights and sexual orientation—A decade of development and denial at the UN. *Health and Human Rights, 7*(2), 49–80.

Scott, R. (1995). *Institutions and organizations.* Thousand Oaks, CA: Sage.

Seckinelgin, H. (2012). Global civil society as shepherd: Global sexualities and the limits of solidarity from a distance. *Critical Social Policy, 32*(4), 536–555.

Seckinelgin, H. (2009). Global activism and sexualities in the time of HIV/AIDS. *Contemporary Politics, 15*(1), 103–118.

Smith, D., & Mapondera, G. (2012, May 18). Malawi president vows to legalise homosexuality. *The Guardian (UK).* Retrieved from http://www.theguardian.com/world/2012/may/18/malawi-president-vows-legalise-homosexuality

Stabile, C., & Kumar, D. (2005). Unveiling imperialism: Media, gender and the war on Afghanistan. *Media, Culture and Society, 27*(5), 765–782.

Stables, G. (2003). Justifying Kosovo: Representations of gendered violence and U.S. military intervention. *Critical Studies in Media Communication, 20*(1), 92–115.

Stychin, C. F. (1998). *A nation by rights: National cultures, sexual identity politics and the discourse of rights*. Philadelphia, PA: Temple University Press.

Stychin, C. F. (2003). *Governing sexuality: The changing politics of citizenship and law reform*. Oxford, UK: Hart.

Stychin, C. F. (2003–2004). Same-sex sexualities and the globalization of human rights discourse. *McGill Law Journal, 49*, 951.

Waites, M. (2009). Critique of 'sexual orientation' and 'gender identity' in human rights discourse: Global queer politics beyond the Yogyakarta Principles. *Contemporary Politics, 15*(1), 137–156.

Wallerstein, I. (2004). *World-systems analysis: An introduction*. Durham, NC: Duke University Press.

Chapter 15
LGBT Movements in Southeast Europe: Violence, Justice, and International Intersections

Susan C. Pearce and Alex Cooper

Abstract The Southeast Europe region of the Western Balkans and Turkey has witnessed a burgeoning growth of LGBT organizing within and across countries. It also continues to experience patterns of homophobic violence, including attacks on public Pride events. This region has been coming under increasing scrutiny by the European Union and international bodies for rights protections for gender and sexual minorities. Scrutiny has been particularly intense as each of these countries moves toward European Union accession. This chapter comparatively chronicles the continued patterns of violence, the legal and social changes to address the violence, and the activists' use of external rights instruments as boomerangs or ricochets to advance their social inclusion and reverse the impunity for violence at the individual and systemic levels.

Keywords Albania · Asylum · Bisexual · Boomerang effect · Bosnia and Herzegovina · Croatia · European Union · FYR Macedonia · Gay · Gender · Gender-based violence · Gender identity · Honor crimes · Intersex · Kosovo · Lesbian · Montenegro · Serbia · Sexual orientation · Transgender · Transsexual · Turkey

S. C. Pearce (✉)
Department of Sociology, East Carolina University, E. Fifth Street, Greenville, NC 27858, USA
e-mail: pearces@ecu.edu

A. Cooper
Department of Gender Studies, Central European University, Nador u. 9, Budapest 1051, Hungary
e-mail: wgalexander.cooper@gmail.com

D. Peterson and V. R. Panfil (eds.), *Handbook of LGBT Communities,*
Crime, and Justice, DOI: 10.1007/978-1-4614-9188-0_15,
© Springer Science+Business Media New York 2014

Introduction

During the early to mid-2010s, eight Southeast European countries were undergoing a major shift that will hold consequences for their legal and judicial systems: entrance into the broader continental structure of the European Union (EU). Those countries, Albania, Bosnia and Herzegovina (BiH), Croatia, Kosovo, Former Yugoslav Republic of Macedonia (FYR), Montenegro, Serbia, and Turkey, are all at varying stages of the accession process, which are also proceeding at different levels of speed. Croatia joined on July 1, 2013. Upon eventual completion of these memberships, the European continent will be administratively united all the way to its southern border. This accession process, with its unevenness and stops and starts, holds particular consequences for sexual and gender minorities of those countries. One of the yardsticks for preparation for acceptance into the club is the level of legal protections for women and sexual/gender minorities as integral to the continent's human rights regime, as well as each country's record on implementing those protections.

Based on our interviews and news reports within the region, we have surmised that the LGBT issue is the most prominent "story of the hour" regarding citizen rights for this region during the accession talks in 2012 and 2013. In this chapter, we examine the current status of these countries' compliance with EU and international guidelines for LGBT rights, including, in particular, the institutionalization of legal, juridical, and other criminal justice measures for these countries. We give central attention to the perpetration of violence against individuals due to their membership in these groups and their activism in defense of their rights, as well as state protections and prosecutions regarding such violence. We compare and contrast the activities and reports of LGBT activists on the ground regarding their experiences and observations of the situation. The particular situation of the negotiation exercises between these countries and the EU offers a unique opportunity to study this issue, because, in contrast to other regional organizations such as NATO (North Atlantic Treaty Organization), the EU is stricter in applying democratic conditionality to new member states (Pridham 2005). Acceding countries must meet an entire range of criteria to be eligible to join, which can delay accession for years, if not decades.

We contextualize these reports in the broader cultural and structural climates in which these problems are manifest. For seven of the countries, the transitions from state communism have been rocky and incomplete, accompanied by tragic civil war and the dissolution of Yugoslavia.[1] Turkey has had its distinct historical trajectory from these countries, but has been undergoing its own political and economic transitions that define some of the tensions that the growing visibility of openly gay, lesbian, bisexual, transgender, and intersex individuals uncover. Further, due to the region's shared history, including that of the former Ottoman

---

[1] The one former Yugoslav country not included here is Slovenia, since it was already a member of the European Union when this research was conducted.

Empire, there are some common cultural and political patterns across these countries. Each of these nations (and one nation—Kosovo—currently carving itself out of Serbia) has seen the expansion, at various speeds, of a freer and comparatively more robust civil society sector including the growth of single-issue social movements such as LGBT activism. In all countries, there have been public attacks of individuals involved in "Pride" events, such as parades. The extent of police protection has ranged from place to place and event to event, but has not consistently been able to create a zone of safety.

The present time is a moment in history where several relatively independent social-cultural processes are undergoing dramatic change. One is the emergence, growth, and public presence of LGBT activism in this geographical region, in contrast to past eras of little or no widespread mobilization. Another is the political-economic transformations that all of these countries are undergoing, encompassing a blend of more global integration and Western investment, integration into the political union of the continent, and, simultaneously, political changes that shore up more autonomous national systems and political cultures. And at the macro intergovernmental and nongovernmental levels, a spurt of new initiatives is asserting the need or requirement for states to protect more formally the rights of gender and sexual minorities, signaling a change in the international normative climate. Like the major shift toward gender mainstreaming regarding women's issues, which moves such concerns more closely to the center of development policy and international relations, the international rights regime is also heralding new sexuality/gender-identity mainstreaming. All three of these domains (grassroots social movements, political-economic transitions, and the international rights regime) could be described as shifting ground, both independently from one another and in conversations over LGBT rights.

There is a complex geographical and historical context in which any discussion of homophobic violence in Southeast Europe and other non-"Western" countries must be couched. As we will discuss, there is a sensitivity toward the more powerful region(s) of the world that are the most resourced, generally set the prevailing global norms, and also hold the means to punish through either military, diplomatic, or economic action. Serbians, in particular, collectively remember the NATO invasions from less than 20 years ago. Both authors observed the obliterated buildings left standing in central Belgrade as monuments to those bombings, and heard about some Serbs' bitter memories of that time. Further, countries that grant fewer rights or criminalize gay, lesbian, bisexual, and/or transgender behaviors become subject to even stronger stereotyping or condescension from societies that consider themselves to be more enlightened. An irony may result: societies that profess an attitude of openness toward one group of minorities (sexual) might translate into attitudes of exclusion toward another group (national or ethnic). Thus, some of the backlash against the dominating "center" regarding gender rights that will be discussed here is related to a resistance to the condescension and stereotyping. If one were to look for some strict division between the West (or former colonists) and the "rest" of the world, a rainbow line is not fully evident. For example, as Lennox and Waites (2013) have discussed in their review of LGBT legislative history in the British Commonwealth, many countries' laws can be traced to imperial impositions of official Christian hostilities toward homosexuality that became codified into state law.

We now move to an overview of the experiences with homophobic violence across the region, particularly as they relate to the LGBT movement's growing societal visibility. We then discuss the current international instruments that address LGBT rights, and the "mainstreaming" of needs of sexual minorities into treaties and international bodies. Finally, we review report cards on these countries' progress on protecting LGBT rights. The authors collected this information through individual interviews, participant observation, and review of existing sources, during 2012 and 2013. The first author conducted interviews and reviewed literature in Washington, DC, and interviewed activists, nongovernmental organization (NGO) representatives, and government officials in Bosnia, Macedonia, and Turkey in 2012 and 2013. The second author worked for LGBT rights organizations in Serbia during the summer of 2012 and in Bosnia during the summer of 2013. Both have attended Pride events in the region during these years.

Grassroots Movements, Violence, and Public Actions

We begin with a review of the state of activist organizations and their experiences with public actions, including threatened or actual violence against their mobilizing efforts. Grassroots organizations are on the ground in each of these countries, with varying degrees of freedom to exist visibly in each society.

Each of these countries has seen the rise of LGBT support and activist organizing networks within their borders, springing from the grassroots, with particular intensity since the beginning of the twenty-first century. However, as one of these activists in Bosnia explained to the first author, LGBT community worries about the consequences of being publicly "out" were common, resulting in the community's decision to hold private social events before moving into political demands or major public events. This strategy of starting with safer or less controversial moves was evident in other countries as well. In Turkey, for example, one activist explained to the first author that they were tackling some basic problems of putting anti-discrimination laws on the books and making sure they were applied; they viewed goals such as legalizing gay marriage as far off the radar for Turkish society at the present day.

Among the organizations active in these countries are Aleanca LGBT in Albania, an NGO that resulted from the work of young volunteers within the past 3 years, offering networking, social support, advocacy, and lobbying (Aleanca LGBT 2013). We interviewed a number of members of two organizations in BiH, the former Organization Q and Sarejevo Open Centre. Organization Q (2013) forged more public awareness of LGBT issues and the community until an assault that will be described below; Sarajevo Open Centre began its work in 2007 and currently focuses on political participation and human rights, such as fighting discrimination (Sarajevo Open Centre 2013). Kosovo hosts the organization Libertas Kosova, which has a drop-in center, library, and weekly activities (Libertas Kosova 2013). The populous country of Turkey hosts a number of grassroots groups, such as Black Pink Triangle Izmir Association, the Gay & Lesbian to Socialize and Rehabilitation [sic], Kaos GL, Lambdaistanbul LGBT Solidarity Association, LİSTAG (Families of LGBTs in Istanbul), Pink Life Association LGBTT[2] Solidarity, and the Social Policies, Gender Identity, and Sexual Orientation Studies Association (ILGA-Europe 2013e, http:// www.spod.org.tr). A sign of the youthful nature and tech-savvy global connectedness of these movements is the prominence of social media and links on their websites, including Facebook, Twitter, and YouTube. Relating such public presence to the themes of violence and crime, this publicity makes it difficult for any country to hide such matters from international scrutiny.

This activism is characterized by cross-national and cross-ethnic networking and organizing. For example, one of the first transnational networks of its kind in the region, the Southeastern European Queer Network of LGBT activists from the former Yugoslavia (Organization Q 2013) consisted of approximately 20 LGBT organizations. Although the Q Network became inactive in 2007, it remains active as a list-serv to disseminate invitations for LGBT events and news updates about the LGBT movement from around the world. It is notable that in a region well known for ethnic conflict, this cross-border collaboration has been forged, and, according to reports that the authors received on the ground, those collaborations are going strong and are highly valued.

Other transnational networks that currently operate include ILGA-Europe, Kaos GL, IGLYO, and BABELNOR. ILGA-Europe, created in 1996 as a region of the NGO and network ILGA (International Lesbian and Gay Association), is the largest of these LGBT networks. ILGA works with over 400 organizations in 45 European countries (ILGA-Europe 2013g), possesses participative status at the Council of Europe (COE), and is heavily funded by the European Commission. The organization works with the UN to advocate for better human rights for LGBT people (ILGA-Europe 2013g). ILGA-Europe successfully lobbied for policies at the EU, the COE, and the Organization for Security and Co-operation in Europe (OSCE). The network also supports the LGBT movement across Europe, with an emphasis on Southeastern and Eastern Europe. Kaos GL (Kaos Gay and Lesbian Cultural Research and Solidarity Association) focuses its work on the Middle East, the Caucasus, and the Balkans. The network plans to hold meetings across the region for participating LGBT organizations and create an e-group to share information and promote communication (Kaos GL 2013a).

IGLYO (International Gay, Lesbian, Bisexual, Transgender, Queer Youth, and Student Organization) was founded in 1984 at the first International Gay Youth Congress and Festival in Amsterdam, the Netherlands and focuses on LGBT youth

---

[2] In this instance "LGBTT" stands for "Lesbian, Gay, Bisexual, Transvestite, and Transsexual."

in Europe (IGLYO 2013). Two years later, the third meeting of the Congress established the network to promote the rights of LGBT people. IGLYO now concentrates on capacity building for LGBT youth organizations through non-formal education programs and online portals and advocates for better representation of LGBT youth in policy making (IGLYO 2013). One of the newest LGBT networks in Southeast Europe is BABELNOR, consisting of 20 organizations across 15 countries in Southeast Europe, Eastern Europe, and Scandinavia with the goal to "share experiences and best practices" across borders for "a stronger voice." Like IGLYO, BABELNOR focuses on LGBT "mobilizing and empowering youth" to find solutions to pressing issues of LGBT people (BABELNOR 2013).

LGBT organizing is occurring along with, and helping to contribute to, these societies' more general cultural shifts. Many of the dynamics that are observable in the former state-communist countries (all in this study except Turkey) are appearing in countries with the same history: culture wars whose opposing groups include LGBT and feminist groups on the one hand, and groups, including political and religious authorities, on the other hand who attempt to block these movements' agendas. Both the women's and LGBT activists are perceived as threats to pro-natalist agendas behind the resurgence of nationalism, the former activists due to family planning agendas and the latter due to their perceived noncontributions to procreation, in addition to charges of immorality (for discussion of these issues in other countries, see in this volume Cobb; DeJong and Long). The backlash has appeared in the form of a recent anti-gay law in Russia and violent attacks on Pride participants in the Republic of Georgia, violence condoned by some Orthodox Church clergy (Dzhindzhikhashvili 2013). Ronald Holzhacker (2013) has labeled the patterns of denying LGBT groups the freedom to assemble in these countries, and throughout other Central and Eastern European locations, "state-sponsored homophobia" (p. 1).

Violence Against Organizing

As these domestic and transnational activist organizations have gotten their legs, they have become emboldened to go public: to come out of the closet collectively, so to speak. Often they have been strategic about doing this gradually, to introduce their presence to their societies through baby steps. Here, we narrate selected examples of the events and violent reactions.

Table 15.1 presents a historical timeline of Pride events across the countries of the region and reports of violence during the events. The first on this list, the 2001 parade in Belgrade, Serbia, was attacked by a number of groups. The deputy police chief reportedly responded to the violence by saying, "Our society is not environmentally mature for expressing that sort of sexuality" (Belgrade Pride Parade 2011). More broadly, the table maps out a progression toward larger and more peaceful gatherings. Particularly striking was the leap from 500 marchers in

Table 15.1 LGBT developments in Southeast Europe

Years	Country: Activity
2001	Serbia: Pride parade attempted in Belgrade. Violently attacked (Belgrade Pride Parade 2011)
2002	Croatia: First Pride parade. 200 marched. Heckling and jeering from some bystanders (Croatian gays join… 2002)
2003	Turkey: Istanbul: First legal Pride parade in Turkey (the *first* Muslim majority country to hold a gay *Pride march*) (All about Istanbul 2013)
2007	FYR Macedonia: Skopje authorities refused public space permits for closing party of a Queer Square festival (Global Rights 2008, p. 12)
2008	Bosnia and Herzegovenia: Q Festival met with violence (never held Pride parade) (Clashes at Bosnia's… 2008)
	Turkey: Ankara: First Pride parade (All about Istanbul 2013)
2010	Serbia: Belgrade: Pride parade backed by government and police, violently attacked (Belgrade Pride Parade 2011)
2011	Serbia: Belgrade: unauthorized Pride parade violently attacked (Belgrade Pride Parade 2011)
	Croatia: First Pride parade in Split. 200 marchers and 8,000 anti-gay protesters. Marchers were attacked with stones and bottles (Anti-gay protesters… 2011)
2012	Serbia: announced in news media as international hub for sex-change surgery (Bilefsky 2012)
	Serbia: Belgrade: government bans Pride parade scheduled for the fall, citing public safety concerns (LGBT activists hold mini-parades in June) (Human Rights Watch 2012)
	Kosovo: (December) Launch party of multimedia organization's publication on sexuality attacked by 20 people, resulting in one serious injury of a staff member (Russo 2012)
	Albania: (May) First Pride parade in Tirana. Anti-gay protesters threw tube bombs at them; no injuries (Garcia 2013)
2013	Croatia: (June) 10,000 march in Pride parade in Zagreb, Croatia without violence; government officials participate (Thousands march… 2013)
	Croatia: (June) Pride parade in Split, attended by 500, including city and national government officials. Violence-free; protected by several hundred riot police (Split's gay Pride… 2013)
	FYR Macedonia: (June) Pride events commenced in Skopje, Macedonia, but not a parade. Violent gang attack on LGBT Center, using stones, bottles, and bricks; 1 police injured attempting to protect them. (July) LGBT Center torched, fire spread throughout building (Human Rights Watch 2013)
	Montenegro: (July) First Pride parade. The 40 marchers were attacked violently by 200 protesters, including throwing objects at police guarding the parade (Vasiljevic 2013)
	Turkey: (June) LGBT activists are visible participants in the Gezi Park protests in Istanbul, Turkey, suffered police violence against them (Taksim stages… 2013)
	Turkey (June): Istanbul's Trans* parade occurs simultaneous with Gezi Park protests; attended by officials and deputies from the main opposition Republican People's Party (CHP), no violence (Potts 2013)
	Turkey: Istanbul's (larger) Pride parade is attended by tens of thousands (estimates range up to 100,000), including family members of marchers and Gezi Park protesters. It is the largest Pride parade in Eastern Europe. Also attended by deputies from the main opposition Republican People's Party (CHP), no violence (Taksim stages… 2013)
	Turkey (June): First Pride parades in the cities of Izmir and Antalya (After the protests 2013)

Zagreb, Croatia who were violently attacked in 2012, to the 10,000 who marched in 2013 without incident, and with government officials participating (Thousands march... 2013). This event took place on the eve of Croatia's July 1 entry into the EU.

Similarly, the Istanbul, Turkey parade has expanded over time, with decreasing incidents of violence, and is replicated in other Turkish cities; by 2013, at least four cities hosted parades. And, while officials participated in both the Trans* and LGB Pride parades in Istanbul, these were representatives of the opposition party (CHP), not the ruling party, AKP. In contrast, the Croatia parades included members of the ruling party. The Istanbul LGB Parade on June 30, 2013 set a record, drawing between 40,000 and 100,000 participants; many allies joined them, including parents of participants and co-protesters from Gezi Park (Browner 2013). The Gezi Park/Taksim Square grassroots protest to save a central Istanbul park in late May 2013 expanded into a general anti-government protest movement that is ongoing as of this writing. LGBT individuals joined these protests, as many of them live, work, organize, and socialize in the neighborhood. There were reports of gay-bashing by police as part of the general police crackdown on activists, with tear gas and water cannon attacks. The swelling of the Pride parade numbers was, to the activists, a happy accident of the timing during the Gezi Park protests. Strikingly, among the parade signs were many saying "My Child is Gay" in the Turkish, Arabic, and Kurdish languages (Browner 2013). The first author participated in the parade, which was positive and exuberant. With the exception of one small silent protest by a right-wing youth group, onlookers seemed mostly amused and curious, with many photographing the brightly attired transvestites.

In Sarajevo, BiH, organizers chose to bring an LGBT Pride festival ("Q Festival") to their city in 2008, with a focus on the arts, rather than a more risky Pride parade. Two of these organizers narrated for the first author their experience with this positive event that escalated into violence. Held at the Academy of Fine Arts and supported by allies, the opening of the exhibition was packed with visitors. Outside, however, several groups that opposed the festival gathered, including football hooligans and members of the Verhabis (or Wahhabi) Muslim sect. As the event ended, covered Muslim women and others spat on those leaving the festival. The hooligans blocked one exit. Some police tried to help the attendees but others were afraid, and did not. By the end of the night, at least one taxi had had its windows smashed, several activists suffered injuries by baseball bats, including one broken nose, and one hooligan pulled out a gun. Organizers felt little sympathy or protection from the police or many bystanders. By the time the dust settled, the activists' faces and names had become so recognizable through the unrelenting media coverage that their safety could no longer be assured. As a result, two of the activists now live safely and legally in the United States, but feel that they have left both a passion and an important mission behind. Since the violence that accompanied the Q Festival, no similar demonstrations have been organized in Sarajevo. However, activists in Sarajevo told the second author that they are planning a march with other human rights groups. This would not be a Pride parade, but something along the lines of a solidarity march. From there, the activists would like to build up to planning a Pride parade for Sarajevo, hopefully in 2014.

On June 27, 2012 in Belgrade, Serbia, the second author marched with a group of 50 lesbian-gay-bisexual-transgender-queer activists, with rainbow flags and banners waving in support of International Gay Pride Day in a small-scale Pride parade along the main pedestrian street of the city, Knez Mihailova. After the event, the second author sat with several parade organizers to discuss the event. The activists were shocked at the success of the march, and looked forward to the larger Pride event scheduled for later in the year. A few months later, in October 2012, a weeklong Pride celebration was supposed to end with a large-scale Pride parade around the city; however, in the middle of the week, the Serbian government canceled the Pride parade due to "security concerns." Inevitably, the size and scope of the parade impacted the state and public's reaction to Belgrade's Pride parades. This reaction underscores the depth and breadth of homophobia in Serbian society. Serbia possesses laws that protect the rights of LGBT citizens, but those laws go against many Serbians' belief that "homosexuality" is wrong and should not be legally recognized or protected. Those anti-discrimination policies that are in place exist largely due to pressure from the international community, including the EU and the COE. The first, smaller, event met with no violence or conflict; however, politicians and the Serbian media forced the second, larger event, to be canceled.

The 2012 banning of the Pride events in Belgrade drew international comment from watchdog groups and international governmental organizations. The Centre for Euro-Atlantic Studies (CEAS), for example, gave two reasons for the cancellation of the events: that Serbia's security sector is unable to protect its citizens, and that Serbian authorities use the "services" of anti-gay protesters from paramilitary groups to carry out what they cannot do officially. CAES (2012) wrote that if Serbia does not have control over its security sector, then it is a "regional security threat." In October 2012, Serbia was taken to task by the United Nations High Commissioner for Human Rights, Navi Pillay, who publicly stated that "Responding to violent attacks against a vulnerable community by banning them from peacefully gathering and expressing themselves further violates their fundamental human rights... States should confront prejudice, not submit to it" (UNHCR 2012b).

The EU also weighed in. In October of 2012, a spokesperson for the EU Enlargement commissioner responded that the EU "regrets" Serbia's decision and that "respect for sexual minorities is one of the 'core foundations of the European project'" (Rettman 2012). In September, just prior to this announcement, Serbian Prime Minister Ivica Dačić had announced to his own country, "Screw the kind of Union for which gay Pride marches are the entry ticket" (Rettman 2012). This issue had become a sensitive sticking point in the accession negotiations. Nevertheless, EU spokespeople indicated that the ban would not actually have the weight of delaying negotiations.

In December 2012, the multimedia website Kosovo 2.0 launched a publication event for the release of its fourth magazine issue, *Sex,* covering stories, among others, on "LGBT life in Kosovo and the Balkans,.. homophobic violence in the

Balkans,.. homosexuality and war,..." (Kosovo 2.0 2012). According to Priština police, an employee from Kosovo 2.0 was assaulted by a mob of between 20 and 30 people who attacked the launch party for the magazine (Demolli 2012; ILGA-Europe 2012). The mob that entered the building attacked the attendees, including a staff member, and broke furniture and decorations. Although two police officers did try to protect the participants, they too were attacked by the hooligans (ILGA-Europe 2012). Following this melee, members of the football fan group Pilsat posted the following message on Facebook: "Our past and culture do not allow these degenerate and anti-family 'cultures' to be promoted in our midst. Pilsat will take action against these degenerate characteristics in the future as well" (Demolli 2012).

The attack on Kosovo 2.0's launch party was largely condemned. Civil society organizations (CSOs) in Kosovo showed solidarity with Kosovo 2.0 by releasing a statement, writing, "We want to emphasize that these attacks… flagrantly violate our dignity, our right to think, to free speech and the right of assembly" (Demolli 2012). The police arrested one person after the attack, but the individual was released after being interviewed. The head of the OSCE Mission in Kosovo, Elaine Conkievich, released a statement saying, "This is an attack on freedom of expression, a basic human right, as well as an attempt to limit freedom of the media. I call on the law enforcement agencies to conduct a swift investigation, identify perpetrators and prevent violations of human rights and attacks on media freedom" (Demolli 2012).

Interviews with activists in the Former Yugoslav Republic of Macedonia unearthed reports of a series of public attacks over several years. Pride events were banned in 2007, and the country has yet to hold a Pride parade. Only recently have LGBT individuals begun to come out of the closet publicly; among those was a prominent Macedonian television actor who is on the executive board of the Macedonian Helsinki Committee of Human Rights (MHCHR). The Committee's office, which includes a center for individuals to gather and hold events, in a visible location at the center of the old Turkish bazaar in Skopje and clearly labeled in rainbow colors, has seen a series of violent attacks to the property since it opened. The first author sat in those offices in March of 2013 to interview staff and volunteers, and observed the regular daily comings-and-goings of LGBT community members and allies, on public view with a large plate-glass window facing the street. Until 2013, the attacks were not during daytime hours, so no personal injuries resulted.

In June 2013, rumors were spread in the media that Skopje would host a Pride parade. This was inaccurate; the events were to consist of a week of film screenings and similar gatherings. As the events commenced, however, a gang of 30 violently attacked the building, and participants inside feared for their safety. A police officer who attempted to protect the activists was hurt. In July 2013, the LGBT Center was torched, sending flames across all three floors and damaging equipment such as computers. Among the organizations that condemned the attacks and called for government investigation and action were Amnesty International, Human Rights Watch, and the Dutch embassy. Boris Dittrich, the LGBT rights advocacy director in Skopje, responded with the following condemnation of the attackers as well as officials:

> Anti-gay thugs are targeting people who support equal rights on the basis of sexual orientation and gender identity, and the Macedonian government seems to be turning a blind eye. Not a single government official has publicly spoken out against these blatant attacks, leaving LGBTI people even more vulnerable to violence and discrimination (Human Rights Watch 2013).

Montenegro's 2013 Pride parade met violence from anti-gay protesters. This was the country's first Pride parade. According to Reuters news, protesters called out "Kill the gays!" and "You're sick!" during the march. Human Rights Campaign reported that the LGBT activists responded by shouting, "Kiss the gays!" (Simon 2013). The protesters numbered about 200, and threw objects at the police guarding the parade of about 40 marchers. Out of the anti-gay protestors, approximately 10 were arrested. Before the parade, the anti-gay protesters placed flyers around Budva announcing the death of Zdravko Cimbaljević, "the first person to come out in Montenegro." This was a hoax, and Cimbaljević told reporters that he had not anticipated such violence (Vasiljevic 2013). He also said, "I expected opposition but this attack is actually the real image of Montenegro" (Predrag 2013). Montenegrin Prime Minister, Milo Đukanović, condemned the attack.

The successful Trans* and LGB parades in Istanbul in 2013, particularly the massive numbers that the latter attracted, point to potential gradual change in the region toward peace, stability, and police protection. This does not mean that Turkey has closed the door on homophobic violence. The same year, 2013, a 17-year-old Turkish youth was killed, allegedly as an honor crime by his family due to suspicions that he was gay. The court heard conflicting testimony, one by the deceased's uncle who quoted the boy's father as planning the murder because of his son's sexual orientation, and the other by the father who claimed that an argument with his son over his orientation turned aggressive and a gun accidentally went off. LGBT activists report that when individuals are killed in Turkey due to gender identity or sexual orientation, the defendant gets a very light punishment. The trial was ongoing at the time of this writing, and an LGBT activist lawyer was pushing for guilty verdicts from all family members involved in the killing (Father confesses to... 2013).

Scholars who have studied the role of Pride events point to their centrality in progress on societal change. Prides exist to allow LGBT persons to create "a space for vindication, [visibility], and commemoration" (Enguix 2009, p. 15). Pride parades push perceived social boundaries and contribute to participants' social power through mobilization. Further, the events push the limits of the society's perception of its norms. Cities act as a medium to create myriad sexual identities through public demonstration and celebrations like Pride (Aldrich 2004). The celebrations thus allow LGBT individuals to generate social power through this demonstration of presence and claim to physical space. These individuals turn the stigma of homosexuality on its head, embracing what societies perceive as deviance. Pride parades directly challenge the idea that these public spaces, like Knez Mihailova, are inherently heterosexual (Johnston 2005). In our research on the ground, we have also noted the passion with which Pride event organizers use the events to publicize their presence as integral to their respective countries. If a parade is canceled or attacked one year, planning continues for a subsequent year.

Global Gender/Sexuality Mainstreaming

The 2010s are a time of rapid cultural shifts regarding acceptance and promotion of LGBT rights internationally, including within national and global political culture(s). On the one hand, there has been an international gender/sexuality "mainstreaming" into international relations, human rights instruments, and development. The EU is one of those actors that has integrated this approach into its normative and legal codes (ILGA-Europe 2010). On the other hand, within the continent, there has been a rise of right-wing political parties, resurgent conservative religious and nationalist allegiances, and fringe extremist groups who are sometimes tolerated or courted by politicians as voting constituencies, all of which tend to oppose rights for gender and sexual minorities. These latter trends are evident in both existing and potential new member states, but have been especially hegemonic in the case of the candidate countries. The intersection of these two contrasting directions has resulted in culture clashes both within and between countries. Although the external bodies and instruments pose dilemmas for EU aspirants who are expected to codify rights for all groups, they present opportunities for activists who use such external pressures as "boomerangs." Social movement scholars Keck and Sikkink (1998) created the concept of "boomerang effect" to describe the tools that activist organizations use from outside their borders when they are powerless, including transnational networks, treaties, courts, and other pressures. Among those with the least power in these societies are LGBT-identified individuals, making these tools even more necessary and potent.

In his comparison of LGBT rights organizing in Eastern Europe, Holzhacker (2013) extends the boomerang metaphor to incorporate another dynamic that has proved useful to activists: the ricochet. He states that a rapid exchange of information and ideas results in a "ricochet process" which "is a powerful transborder, transinstitutional circulation of information and argumentation between institutions and civil society that may lead to concrete changes" (p. 2). This process has been visible in Southeast Europe; the growing number of actors propelling and receiving the ricochets include multiple domestic LGBT organizations and ally groups; the regional networks; ILGA; international NGOs and granting agencies such as Amnesty International and Helsinki Watch; academics; and a host of international governing bodies and their binding rights instruments. The latter are potentially backed by transnational courts such as the European Court of Human Rights. Holzhacker (2013) suggests that the ricochet creates synergies in words and actions among European organizations, the NGOs, and CSOs to counter the discriminatory actions of national governments that violate human rights by placing pressure on states to respect their international human rights commitments. By acting in this way, these institutions can achieve objectives that they could not achieve if acting separately (p. 3).

We review the current state of such instruments here. We gathered the information through interviews with NGO and government representatives and reviews of existing sources such as published reports. Table 15.2 presents the key instruments that are available to activist organizations and potential participants in the boomerang-ricochet dynamics. What is clear is that the gender/sexuality mainstreaming within these instruments is still historically relatively recent, but within the past several years, appears to be proliferating quite rapidly. This proliferation is paralleled and partially fed by some new developments in countries such as the U.S., which has begun to mainstream gay rights in such institutions as the military and marriage laws in several states and the federal government.

Among the new mainstreaming initiatives was the speech by then-U.S. Secretary of State Hilary Clinton in December 2011 to a United Nations (U.N.) body in Geneva, asserting that gay and lesbian rights are human rights. One of her statements was: "It is a violation of human rights when governments declare it illegal to be gay, or allow those who harm gay people to go unpunished" (Richard 2013, p. 4). The U.S. State Department's Bureau of Population, Refugees, and Migration (PRM) is responsible for implementing such policies; although the Bureau already offered assistance to gender and sexual minorities, Ms. Clinton's statement translated these efforts into a stronger mandate. Further, it advertised publicly the State Department's intention of inclusion of these minorities and made its stance clear in stark detail. U.S. embassies now explicitly provide support for Pride events and other needs of LGBT communities in the country where the embassy is located. The first author met with a U.S. State Department representative in Turkey who is responsible for encouraging Turkish support for the LGBT community and administering grants. She confirmed that these measures are being implemented, and expressed her strong commitment to doing so. The first author also learned from two State Department staff who work with the Balkans that they have unquestioningly integrated LGBT mainstreaming into their on-the-ground work in the region. In 2013, the websites of LGBT organizations in the region were beginning to list their country's U.S. Embassy as one of their sponsors (see Libertas Kosova 2013).

The year 2011 also saw the launch of a major new European instrument to address gender-based violence. Entitled "The Council of Europe Convention on Preventing and Combating Violence against Women and Domestic Violence" and labeled the "Istanbul Convention" due to the city where it was signed and launched, it incorporates inclusive language to apply the measures to all women and girls regardless of their sexual orientation or gender identity. By 2013, seven of the countries in this study were signatories. The exception was Kosovo. Turkey ratified the Convention in 2012, followed by Montenegro in April of 2013 (Council of Europe 2013a) and BiH in July of 2013 (Council of Europe 2013b). After a state

Table 15.2 Timeline international instruments addressing LGBT rights

Years	Instrument, directive, or report
1950	The Council of Europe's Convention for the Protection of Human Rights and Fundamental Freedoms opens for signature (Council of Europe 1950)
1981	The European Court of Human Rights first applies the Convention for the Protection of Human Rights and Fundamental Freedoms to the issue of sexual orientation, due to the right to privacy, in the Dudgeon case from Ireland (Lennox and Waites 2013, p. 18). Sets the stage for decriminalization of homosexual acts in EU member states
2007	A new rights framework created by human rights experts, academics, NGOs, and treaty bodies called the Yogyakarta Principles (from Yogyakarta, Indonesia, where the principles were written) to apply international human rights law to sexual orientation and gender identity. States that sign on are held accountable to protect such rights as human and personal security. This has been called "the most internationally important campaigning document related to sexual orientation and gender identity" (Lennox and Waites 2013, p. 9)
2008	The U.N. High Commissioner on Refugees announces that individuals who flee a country due to feared persecution for sexual orientation and gender identity should be granted asylum under the category of "membership in a particular social group" (Hansen 2010)
2010	The Council of Europe recommends guidelines for all 47 member countries to abide by international conventions to protect the rights of sexual and gender minorities, naming protections from hate crimes among other protections. The document stated that "Member States should ensure that national human rights structures are clearly mandated to address discrimination on grounds of sexual orientation and gender identity" (ILGA-Europe 2010)
2011	The U.N. High Commissioner on Refugees announces guidelines prohibiting countries from denying asylum to persecuted individuals based on sexual orientation or gender identity
	The Council of Europe Convention on Preventing and Combating Violence against Women and Domestic Violence ("Istanbul Convention") is launched: a sweeping, binding convention that includes sexual orientation and gender identity (Council of Europe 2013a)
	U.S. Secretary of State Clinton announces U.S. State Department support for LGBT activities globally, including gender-based asylum. This is backed by an Obama-administration directive for all federal U.S. agencies to institute supportive workplaces and policies for LGBT people (Richard 2013, p. 4)
2012	The American-based NGO, Human Rights First, publishes specific recommended guidelines for the U.S. and other international bodies to attend to needs of LGBT individuals in refugee situations (Human Rights First 2012a)
	(September) The U.N. publishes document, "Born Free and Equal," underscoring LGBT rights as basic human rights (UNHCR 2012a)
2013	The U.S. Agency for International Development (USAID) launches an LGBT Global Development Partnership, to give assistance to LGBT communities in developing countries (USAID 2013)
	The European Union sets out the first *binding* rules for LGBT rights in member countries (EU Foreign Affairs… 2013)

ratifies, this Convention will be legally binding, and states have to answer to the Council in reporting on the application of the measures. The Convention will not enter into force until 10 states have ratified, which had not happened as of this writing. Notably, of the five European states that had ratified, three are among these Southeast European countries. One of the Convention authors explained to the first author that countries need to translate the Convention into their own languages before ratification, which is one reason behind the differing speeds through which ratification happens. Further, the independence of Kosovo from Serbia was still in flux in 2013, but had passed a major hurdle in April of 2013 with the signing of a widely hailed historic agreement to normalize relations, and paving the way for Kosovo to begin EU accession negotiations (Smolar 2013). A European human rights convention of this magnitude and force that explicitly details gender-based violence in the form of homophobic crimes and calls for targeted remedies does not yet exist.

The U.N. has increasingly entered the dialog with its own bold statements. In 2012, the U.N. released a report entitled "Born Free and Equal" that made the following declaration: "The case for extending the same rights to LGBT persons as those enjoyed by everyone else is neither radical nor complicated. It rests on two fundamental principles that underpin international human rights law: equality and non-discrimination. The opening words of the Universal Declaration of Human Rights are unequivocal: 'All human beings are born free and equal in dignity and rights'" (UNHCR 2012a, p. 7). These words are notable for their adamant insistence that protection for sexual minorities rests firmly in widely-accepted human rights standards and needs no new legislation for particular protection. Nevertheless, the booklet was offered as a tool to help implement these rights on the ground, citing multiple articles from the Universal Declaration of Human Rights and applying them to the situations that LGBT individuals face, such as the right to assemble and freedom from torture. Among the demands that the authors make to states is: "Repeal laws criminalizing homosexuality, including all laws that prohibit private sexual conduct between consenting adults of the same sex" (p. 13).

One of the more recent international organizations to join the sexuality/gender mainstreaming bandwagon is The U.S. Agency for International Development (USAID). In April of 2013, it unveiled its new initiative that provides funding to assist organizations on the ground around the world to address the needs of LGBT communities. Labeling this one of the other programs of "inclusive development," the initiative will begin in Ecuador, Honduras, and Guatemala, and expand to other countries. Citing that "85 countries and territories criminalize LGBT behavior and seven countries have a death penalty for same-sex sexual activity," while "[f]ewer than 50 countries punish anti-gay discrimination in full or in part," the announcement follows the 2011 directive by President Obama (USAID 2013). The announcement predicts that there will be both economic and political impact from addressing these issues, including the full democratic participation of LGBT individuals in their societies.

Other remedies available to individuals who need to escape their countries due to violence or threats of violence based on sexuality and gender are refugee and asylum policies. Internationally recognized refugee and asylum law states that the remedy is available to: "… [A]ny person who… owing to well-founded fear of

being persecuted for reasons of race, religion, nationality, membership of a particular social group or political opinion, is outside the country of his [or her]
nationality and is unable or, owing to such fear, is unwilling to avail himself [or
herself] of the protection of that country..." (UNHCR 2012c). An increasing
number of countries do interpret the clause of "membership in a particular social
group" to include sexual orientation or gender identity, and a growing number of
individuals are taking advantage of this opening. Statistics are not available on the
number that have been granted worldwide to date. Despite the opening of this
remedy, claimants are highly dependent on the rulings of individual judges and
their interpretation. One study found that courts in Europe were not consistent in
their rulings, and that claimants confronted traditional stereotypes during their
hearings that sometimes determined the outcome. Lesbians, gays, and, with much
more frequency, Trans* individuals were returned to their countries; one rationale
that was given was that if the individuals returned to the "closet," they would be
safe back home (Jansen and Spijkerboer 2011, p. 8). Research has shown that
courts in the U.S., including the Board of Immigration Appeals, have also
reportedly been inconsistent in the granting of gender-based asylum to women and
LGBT people (Gomez 2004, p. 963).

In June of 2013, the EU Foreign Affairs ministers issued new binding rules on
LGBT rights in member countries. This announcement represented the first time
that none of the member ministers resisted the inclusion of LGBT language in such
guidelines. Further, the new rules carry more weight because they are now
binding, whereas the EU's 2010 toolkit on LGBT rights had not been binding (EU
foreign affairs... 2013). The new guidelines require the following: "(1) Eliminate
discriminatory laws and policies, including the death penalty; (2) Promote equality
and non-discrimination at work, in healthcare and in education; (3) Combat state
or individual violence against LGBTI persons; and (4) Support and protect human
rights defenders" (EU foreign affairs... 2013). In the fall of 2013, the EU will
begin to monitor compliance across the current member states (EU foreign
affairs... 2013).

How effective are such international boomerangs? Records are extremely
mixed. On the one hand, experience shows that some governments are able to
defy, ignore, or get around them. For example, the current government in power in
Turkey, the AKP, has ignored repeated rulings by the European Court of Human
Rights (ECHR) charging Turkish police and authorities with abuse of power,
including interfering with citizens' right to assemble. The Court issued a severe
ruling in December 2012, stating that the Turkish people's right to assembly was
violated during May Day protests in Istanbul on May 1, 2008, and that the police
must stop using brutal force on demonstrators (Sinclair-Webb 2013). (European
countries outside of the EU are still subject to cases in this Court, and citizens of
these countries have the right to take their cases before the court.) And yet, Turkey
has also witnessed a particular twist on the boomerang effect in a recent court case
regarding hate speech in Istanbul. LGBT activists had objected to a 2012 booklet
that referred to "homosexuals" as deviants. A local prosecutor had ruled that this
booklet's verbiage was protected under Article 10 of the European Convention on

Human Rights that guarantees free speech. The use of international human rights law *against* the LGBT community resembled a boomerang force from an unintended direction. However, the organization Kaos GL appealed to the Istanbul Criminal Court, which reversed the ruling in 2013, *not* by citing international instruments but using Turkey's own Penal Code that outlaws insulting social groups (Kaos GL 2013b). Although Turkey's Penal Code already reflected revisions required by the EU, it was nevertheless a domestic challenge to a domestic interpretation of international rights law.

A 2010 report by an independent scholar stated that the nation of BiH was complying with legal changes required by the EU to protect sexual and gender minorities, including the decriminalization of homosexual acts in 1998. This scholar did point out, however, that "[T]here appears to be no true and genuine interest or actions on the larger governmental front in improving human rights and equality for everyone, in the way of progressive achievement of realisation of human rights and equality long term" (Durkovic 2010, p. 8), hinting that officials are simply jumping through required hoops.

On the other hand, research has found naming-and-shaming by international watchdogs to be more effective at promoting human rights and democracy than other approaches, such as military aid or intervention, and general economic aid. Further, targeted economic aid (such as that provided through USAID) has a strong record in resulting in strengthening democracy and human rights (Peksen 2012).

Country Report Cards and Gay-Rights Diplomacy

We now move to a review of recent available data that on these eight countries' laws, and their application, related to violence against LGBT people, drawn from international organizations that are issuing report cards on LGBT rights. We begin with a report from 2011.

The Office for Democratic Institutions and Human Rights (ODIHR) of the OSCE gathers data on human rights across the OSCE region. The organization's 2011 Annual Report, "Hate Crimes in the OSCE Region: Incidents and Responses," is a compilation of data on crimes motivated by homophobia or bias against LGBT individuals from its participating states. This report indicates that the participating states have no clear consensus on the definition of a "hate crime." This lack of a solid definition is due to various opinions within the member states on topics like LGBT rights (OSCE 2012). Definitions of religion and ethnicity are consistent across borders; definitions of hate crimes are not. Because of this, the data provided by OSCE are gathered through various state and civil society channels. The report underscores the lack of information on the reporting of hate crimes against groups, including LGBT people, by states. In fact, none of the governments of the countries discussed in this chapter reported data of crimes against LGBT people (Kosovo was not listed in the report). This nonreporting on

LGBT hate crimes from OSCE participating states dates back to at least 2008, our review concluded, and most likely prior to 2008.

Albania did not send any official data on the subject to ODIHR. However, the NGO Pink Embassy reported two transphobic attacks to OSCE. These cases involved an arson attack on a house where transgender people lived and an attack on a transgender person. The NGO TGEU (Transgender Europe) also reported transgender violence in FYR Macedonia. Two transgender people were murdered in Turkey and 11 transgender people were physically assaulted. Two men were assaulted in BiH as reported by the OSCE Mission in the country. Further, ILGA-Europe reported violence at the Split, Croatia Pride parade. Montenegro's NGO Juventas reported several physical attacks on LGBT persons, including attacks on the International Day Against Homophobia. Several organizations in Serbia reported attacks on a lesbian woman and several gay men. These assaults occurred in front of clubs, near assault survivors' homes, and on public transport. A boy was also attacked in Serbia due to his perceived sexual orientation. Kaos GL reported that four gay men were murdered in Turkey, and another gay man was assaulted (OSCE 2012). In addition to these OSCE reports, local organizations also send known reports of violence to ILGA-Europe, and publicize them on their websites and through social media. The years 2012 and 2013 saw the release of several international watchdog reports that compared progress on gay rights in the countries across the region. ILGA-Europe, which participates in the COE and receives funding from the EU, released a ranking of European countries on gay rights in May of 2013 (ILGA-Europe 2013b). At that time, ILGA stated that the country in the Balkans ranking the highest on supportive laws for LGBT people was Croatia, and the worst was Macedonia. Among the changes that helped Croatia to receive that mark was higher police protection and official government support for a Pride parade in Split, which had been attacked in 2011. FYR Macedonia does not have hate crimes statutes on the books.

ILGA-Europe's report did indicate an uneven and incomplete process in codifying laws regarding sexual orientation and gender identity in this part of Southeast Europe. Macedonia, Montenegro, Serbia, and Turkey currently have no laws on the books governing hate speech and crimes toward individuals based on their gender identity or sexual orientation, or toward intersex people. Albania does have laws that cover hate speech and crime against people based on sexual orientation and gender identity, but no policies tackling hatred or laws that explicitly refer to intersex people. In Bosnia, hate crimes are recognized in criminal law only for sexual orientation (not gender identity or for intersex individuals) and only in the Republica Srpska and Brčko District, not in the third administrative district, the Federation of Bosnia and Herzegovina. These districts do not have hate speech legislation, or policies tackling hatred. The country in the region that can check all but one of these boxes is Croatia: it now has laws against hate speech and hate crime based on gender identity and sexual orientation; it has policies tackling hatred, but no laws specifically referring to hate crime or speech targeting intersex people.

Notably, similar gaps in records on these legal provisions, especially for intersex people, can be found in EU member states as well. In fact, Croatia now has laws covering more of these categories of hate speech and violence than some Western European countries, such as Germany (ILGA-Europe 2013f). ILGA reported on widespread continuation of hate speech across Europe, not confined to Southeast Europe, and from the top levels down: "Degrading, offensive, and defamatory language is being used by public officials at all levels—starting from heads of states to local councillors" (2013b, p. 12). In fact, migration to existing EU member countries is not necessarily a panacea. In the U.K., 98–99 % of all who seek asylum because of fear of persecution for gender identity or sexual orientation are dismissed at the initial interview phase, in contrast to a 73 % general rejection rate (Nguyen 2013). Among typical questions asked in the interview were "Can you prove you are a homosexual?" (Miles 2010). The Czech Republic had been imposing "phallometric" testing on male asylum seekers who sought asylum for this reason: the applicant had to have his penis connected to a machine that measured blood flow to it, while viewing a heterosexual porno-graphic film. If he was aroused, his application was denied (Schweiger 2011). Across the Central and Eastern European region, the trend is to allow applicants for asylum for LGBT individuals only if homosexual acts are criminalized in their home countries (Sexual orientation and... 2013). Kosovo is among the ten European countries with a constitutional ban on discrimination due to sexual orientation; its marriage clause also does not explicitly mention gender. However, many LGBT people routinely experience hostility in Kosovo, including aban-donment by their families and communities, and being married off to try to "cure" them. In fact, many parliamentary deputies angrily walked out when the consti-tutional language was passed. Like its neighboring countries, Kosovo is one of the source countries from which people migrate due to fears for their safety based on sexual orientation. And yet, because of this progressive legislation, asylum courts in destination countries have ruled that the asylum seeker could safely return to Kosovo without fear of persecution. The asylum seekers' claims are further delegitimized by the number of false claims made on this basis, due to the dire unemployment situation in the country, leading to desperate means to escape (Fauchier 2013, p. 37).

The majority of Southeast European countries discussed here have passed anti-discrimination laws protecting lesbian and gay individuals. Albania, BiH, Croatia, Kosovo, Montenegro, and Serbia passed legislation protecting against discrimi-nation based on sexual orientation across arenas that include employment, education, access to health care, and provision of state services. Macedonia and Turkey do not have such policies in place. Legislation has not been passed in many of these countries that criminalize discrimination based on gender identity (U.S. Department of State 2013a). In its April 2013 report on LGBT rights in the Western Balkans and Turkey, the European Parliament reported that Turkey has not moved forward in including sexual orientation and gender identity in the anti-discrimination legislation that was currently being drafted. The report also cited Turkey for the higher-than-average rate of violence and murder of transgender people (European Parliament 2013). Further, these policies still lack teeth when it comes to actual prosecution against discriminatory actions. However, in some countries, NGOs are taking it upon themselves to work on this issue. Representatives from the Sarajevo Open Centre told the second author that the Centre was working with police departments to ensure adequate reporting and investigations of possible hate crimes and discrimination cases, even holding seminars to sensitize police to LGBT rights.

Even with anti-discrimination laws on the books, state-sponsored homophobic statements and texts abound. For example, government officials in Turkey have publicly referred to "homosexuality" as a disease. This declaration was made by the former Minister of Family Affairs, Aliye Kavaf. Turkish LGB activists reacted strongly to this declaration, and publicized it during the June 2013 Pride parade (Taksim stages... 2013). In BiH, school textbooks still list "homosexuality" as one of a group of disorders that includes pedophilia and drug addiction (Barreiro and Vasić 2012). And, as recently as 2010, the vice chairman of the Parliamentary Commission for Social Issues and Health made the following declaration in a hearing: "homosexuality should be cured with hormonal treatment and psychological consultations" (U.S. Department of State 2013b).

Progressive Cultural Shifts

Recently, there have been noticeable shifts in the support of LGBT communities in the Southeast European region. The government of Montenegro, along with several organizations, organized the first Balkan governmental conference on the rights of the LGBT community on March 22, 2012. At the conference, Montenegro's Prime Minister Igo Lukšić, stated, "We want to ensure that the concrete actions that everybody expects from us will respond to real needs. The ultimate goal is the creation of a social environment in which people of different sexual orientation enjoy full legal protections and social inclusion" (Balkan states vow... 2012). The Deputy Prime Minister of Croatia also spoke at the event, telling reporters the idea that a society can be judged by the way it treats its weakest members still holds true today. A representative from Serbia also spoke on the need to fight discrimination because of sexual orientation or identity, and a representative from BiH was at the conference. Strikingly, in April 2013, Dr. Sali Berisha, the Albanian Prime Minister who represents the right-wing Democratic Party, met with LGBT representatives as he campaigned for re-election, appearing in a photograph with the two young leaders, marking a first for an Albanian Prime Minister. Dr. Berisha had been the first politician to express support for same-sex marriage in his 2009 campaign. He had also voiced his condemnation of the Vice-Minister of Defense Ekrem Spahiu's statement about members of the LGBT community: "What remains to be done is to beat them up with a stick. If you don't understand this, I can explain it: to beat them with a rubber stick" (ILGA-Europe 2013a).

Albania has reported progress. In May of 2013, Albanian activists reported success in holding a second annual Diversity Fair to mark International Day Against Homophobia, Biphobia and Transphobia (IDAHO). Scores of organizations contributed to the events such as roundtables, including several departments from the University of Tirana; representatives of the Ministry of Labour, Social Affairs and Equal Opportunities; the People's Advocate; and the Commissioner for Protection from Discrimination (ILGA-Europe 2013c).

The first author interviewed NGO representatives in the LGBT and refugee-settlement arenas to learn about migration into Turkey. This country represents a unique situation in the region due to its geographical location and its contribution to broader European gay culture. As a bridge between Asia, the Middle East, and Europe, and as a country with a relatively open visa policy, it is a common destination for individuals escaping countries where gay and lesbian activities are criminalized, including those where the death penalty is applied. Until April of 2013, Turkey's asylum policy did not allow for asylum for nonEuropeans, so these individuals were temporary dwellers in Turkey until they could gain entrance to other countries.[3] Most would eventually move to the U.S. The new Law on Foreigners and International Protection, which will not be fully implemented until 2015, liberalizes the visa policy and establishes structures to manage refugees and asylees (Soykan 2012).

According to interviews with activists and other observers, the first author learned about the extent to which the city of Istanbul represents a cosmopolitan urban culture with a thriving gay social scene, attracting Western European gay tourism. However, this report must be qualified: Activists and NGO representatives explained to the first author that contrasts between urban and certain areas of rural Turkey are stark, and that asylum seekers who are housed outside of the urban centers do not always find a welcoming environment, particularly if they are placed with co-ethnics who exhibit homophobic attitudes.

Other cultural shifts are also observable in the region. The realm of popular culture, which is near impossible to restrain in a mass-mediated, social networking, and Internet age, has moved forward with its own relative, though largely unselfconscious, autonomy. This has been one medium of cultural diffusion that has been noticed to have an impact on attitudes. For example, while the second author was in Serbia in 2012, he heard the buzz about the 2011 Serbian film called "The Parade." The film depicts an unlikely partnership between a gay male couple and a heterosexual couple in order to organize a Pride Parade. The film confronts the homophobia found in Serbia and the region, and it was even screened in Serbian schools to begin a dialog on sexuality. The film was hugely successful in Serbia and across the region.

Similarly, in Turkey, the year 2012 saw several bursts of LGBT visibility in the film world. The film "Zenne Dancer," for example, was inspired by the story of a

---

[3] The 2013 law is Turkey's first domestic law on asylum. Previously, asylum procedures fell under secondary legislation.

26-year-old university student named Ahmet Yildiz. His father allegedly killed him in Istanbul in 2008 for being gay, presumably to protect the family honor (Göksel 2013). A new documentary entitled "My Child" was released, based on interviews with LGBT people's family members, and Turkey held its first gay film festival. Further, journalists and other writers were doing more to expose homophobic and transphobic violence (Göksel 2013). And in July of 2013, popular Turkish singer Sezen Aksu ended a duet with a guest singer with the unfurling of a rainbow flag as she shouted to the audience, "Where are you, my dear?", which had been the June 2013 Istanbul Pride parade's slogan (Akpınar 2013). These productions and performances exemplify another aspect of the work of the LGBT movements in these countries that we witnessed first hand and learned from interviews: the growing integration of the arts and the use of the arts as vehicles to express themes of sexual orientations and gender identities.

Conclusions

This review has highlighted the issues that are shared across the Southeast European region regarding continued violence toward sexual and gender minorities, as well as the variations across countries. Despite the differences between these societies, all are participants in the shifting grounds that are moving in more than one direction: gender/sexuality mainstreaming of international instruments, negotiations toward continental inclusion, cultural openings, more visible social movements, and the backlashes of culture wars. These dynamics are interacting with each of these countries' own economic and democratic developments that are in various stages of stability. From our observations and interviews in the region, we found a simultaneous mix of hope, passionate commitment, frustration, and disappointment among LGBT community members.

The international instruments enumerated here were still relatively new at the time of this writing, and not yet implemented fully in any country, including this Southeast European region. The task ahead would involve the international dialogs on the meaning of compliance and sanctions for noncompliance. As this region participates more fully in global LGBT organizing and shifting its laws to comply with international instruments, it is participating in a more global shift that is in process, toward a model that some proponents label "global governance," counterbalancing those globalizing dynamics that are largely removing power and rights from the individual, such as the global economy.

Within this emerging model, we have seen the boomerang effects that these instruments can offer to grassroots movements. Transnational networks may become a more common tool for LGBT organizations to use because they allow resources to be shared, and create a "comfort zone." This transnational assistance potentially bolsters the influence that these groups can have on their domestic issues. And, as multiple international governmental and nongovernmental players mainstream LGBT issues, they undoubtedly resemble ricochets: witness the number of watchdog groups that commented publicly on the banning of the Belgrade Pride parade. LGBT movements may, in fact, be highly dependent on such players, even as some grassroots resistance movements around the world are vocally wary of some of these high-profile organizations.

In line with the concerns raised within postcolonial studies, political backlash and standoffs can be partly understood as resistance to condescending Western pressure that put these countries into defensive positions regarding their own norms and autonomy. However, as Lennox and Waites (2013) have observed, noting this dynamic in former British colonies, "it is also important to recognise how accusations of racism, as well as of neo-colonialism and cultural imperialism, may be strategically utilised by political leaders to justify continuing criminalisation, often to serve domestic political audiences and circumstances" (p. 29). The countries discussed here, however, are obligated to uphold these protections of LGBT persons through their agreements with various international treaties and conventions that their governments willingly accepted. Not all of these treaties were pushed by EU accession talks or ECHR rulings, but by the governments' own accord. Therefore, despite the growing power of transnational bodies, the impetus to end violence against LGBT people in Southeast Europe ultimately rests in the hands of the leadership on the ground in each of the region's constituent countries.

If these Southeastern European countries can be described as perched on the continent's administrative edges, they are simultaneously on one of the globe's front lines of LGBT organizing. Activists are working at an intersection of transnational or international rights regimes and these countries' transforming historical cultures. Working within the systems already in place due to these countries' agreements over human rights, including LGBT rights, these activists are attempting to enforce these protections while mainstreaming LGBT identity. If present trends continue, these groups can only expect further support and legitimation of their efforts by the EU and watchdog organizations, along with public shaming, when each state's governance does not comply. Turkey in particular represents a gateway not only into Europe, but as a door into the majority-Muslim nations of the Middle East and North Africa, a place that is largely new to LGBT organizing. This geographical position places the region's activists and governments in unique positions of leadership on these issues.

We close with this quote from a June 25, 2013 speech by Nevin Öztop, representing Kaos GL in Turkey, to the annual meeting of the EU Conference of Parliamentary Committees for Union Affairs, in the midst of violent police attacks on protesters in Taksim Square, Istanbul. Mr. Öztop is clearly inviting a boomerang effect:

> We, as lesbian, gay, bisexual, trans and intersex people, demand that you stand up for us, and stand against those who play with our lives. That you stand up with us against those who try to cover up discrimination in the name of morality, culture, and traditions and conceal hate crimes, hate speeches and even hate murders.... All member countries should carefully look at what they stand for, urge an end to discrimination in Europe, and never bargain or negotiate with member of associate member countries on the lives of LGBTI people during EU accession periods (ILGA-Europe 2013d).

Acknowledgments Susan Pearce would like to thank the Woodrow Wilson International Center for Scholars in Washington, DC for the Title VIII East European Studies research grant that funded this research and provided office space at the Center. She especially appreciates the support of Christian Ostermann, Nida Gelazis, Kristina Terzieva, Janet Spikes, Rebecca Akdeniz, and Elena Volkava. Alex Cooper would like to thank the faculty at The College of William and Mary for their support, which allowed him to conduct this research. He would also like to thank his mentors Leslie M. Waters, Monica D. Griffin, Paula M. Pickering, and Tomoko Hamada Connolly for their assistance and continued encouragement. Both authors would like to express their humble appreciation to the individuals who shared their stories and helped arrange for interviews during field research in the United States and Europe.

References

After the protests, Turkey's LGBT community gains sympathy but not of the gov't. (2013, July 4). Retrieved from http://akncl.wordpress.com/2013/07/04/after-the-protests-turkeys-lgbt-community-gains-sympathy-but-not-of-the-govt/

Akpınar, Ö. (2013). Turkish singer gave support to LGBTs during concert. Kaos GL. Retrieved from http://www.kaosgl.org/page.php?id=14555

Aldrich, R. (2004). Homosexuality and the city: An historical overview. *Urban Studies, 41*, 1719–1737.

Aleanca LGBT. (2013). *About.* Retrieved from http://www.aleancalgbt.org/en/about-us

All about Istanbul. (2013). Retrieved from http://istanbuldayandnight.wordpress.com/2013/06/28/11st-lgbt-pride-parade/

Anti-Gay protesters charged after Split parade violence. (2011, June 13). *BalkanInsight.* Retrieved from http://www.balkaninsight.com/en/article/anti-gay-protesters-charged-after-split-parade-violence

BABELNOR. (2013). *About.* Retrieved from http://babelnor.org/about.html

Balkan states vow to tackle gay discrimination. (2012, March 20). *BalkanInsight.* Retrieved from http://www.balkaninsight.com/en/article/balkans-vows-to-fight-discrimination-against-lgbt

Barreiro, M., & Vasić, V. (2012). Monitoring the implementation of the Council of Europe committee of ministers recommendation on combating sexual orientation or gender identity discrimination. Bosnia and Herzegovina: Sarajevo Open Centre.

Belgrade Pride Parade. (2011). History of prides. Retrieved from http://www.belgradepride.info/index.php/en/history

Bilefsky, D. (2012, July 23). Serbia becomes a hub for sex-change surgery. *The New York Times.* Retrieved from http://www.nytimes.com/2012/07/24/world/europe/serbia-becomes-a-hub-for-sex-change-surgery.html?pagewanted=all&_r=0

Browner, E. (2013, July 11). Istanbul protests help build unity for LGBT Pride. *Women's eNews.* Retrieved from http://womensenews.org/story/lesbian-and-transgender/130710/istanbul-protests-help-build-unity-lgbt-pride

CEAS [Center for Euro-Atlantic Studies]. (2012, October 3). On occasion of the ban of Belgrade pride parade. Retrieved from http://ceas-serbia.org/root/index.php/en/announcements/408-on-occasion-of-the-ban-of-belgrade-pride-parade

Clashes at Bosnia's gay festival. (2008). *BBC News.* Retrieved from http://news.bbc.co.uk/2/hi/7635197.stm

Council of Europe. (1950). Convention for the protection of human rights and fundamental freedoms as amended by protocols no. 11 and no. 14. Retrieved from http://conventions.coe.int/Treaty/en/Treaties/Html/005.htm

Council of Europe. (2013a). About the Convention. Strasbourg: Council of Europe. Retrieved from http://www.coe.int/t/dghl/standardsetting/convention-violence/about_en.asp

Council of Europe. (2013b). The parliament of Bosnia and Herzegovina ratified the Istanbul Convention. Strasbourg: The Council of Europe. Retrieved from http://www.coe.int/t/dghl/standardsetting/convention-violence/default_en.asp

Croatian gays join first "pride" march. (2002, June 29). *BBC News.* Retrieved from http://news.bbc.co.uk/2/hi/europe/2074653.stm

Demolli, D. (2012, December 17). Attack on Kosovo 2.0 widely condemned. *Balkan Insight.* Retrieved from http://www.balkaninsight.com/en/article/attack-on-kosovo-2-0-widely-condemned

Dzhindzhikhashvili, M. (2013, May 17). Georgia's gay pride rally derailed after protests. Retrieved from http://www.huffingtonpost.com/2013/05/17/georgia-gay-pride-rally-_n_3293652.html

Durkovic, S. (2010). Study on homophobia, transphobia and discrimination on grounds of sexual orientation and gender identity. *Legal Report: Bosnia and Herzegovina.* Kongens Lyngby, Denmark: COWI: The Danish Institute for Human Rights.

Enguix, B. (2009). Identities, sexualities and commemorations: Pride parades, public space and sexual dissidence. *Anthropological Notebooks, 15*, 15–33.

EU foreign affairs ministers adopt ground-breaking global LGBTI policy. (2013, June 24). Brussels: The European Parliament's Intergroup on LGBT Rights. Retrieved from http://www.lgbt-ep.eu/press-releases/eu-foreign-affairs-ministers-adopt-lgbti-guidelines/

European Parliament takes stock of LGBT rights in Western Balkans and Turkey. (2013, April 22). Retrieved from http://www.lgbt-ep.eu/press-releases/ep-takes-stock-of-lgbt-rights-in-western-balkans-and-turkey/

Father confesses to killing his own son in landmark homosexual murder case. (2013, May 24). Retrieved from http://www.hurriyetdailynews.com/father-confesses-to-killing-his-own-son-in-landmark-homosexual-murder-case.aspx?pageID=238&nid=47579

Fauchier, A. (2013). Kosovo: What does the future hold for LGBT people? *Forced Migration Review, 42*, 36–39.

Garcia, A. (2013, April 1). Albania is Europe's most homophobic country according to a new survey. *The Daily Grind.* Retrieved from http://www.thegailygrind.com/2013/04/01/albania-is-europes-most-homophobic-country-according-to-a-new-survey/

Global Rights. (2008, March). Violations of the rights of lesbian, gay, bisexual and transgender persons in the former Yugoslav Republic of MACEDONIA: A shadow report. Retrieved from http://www.globalrights.org/site/DocServer/Shadow_Report_Macedonia.pdf

Göksel, D. N. (2013, March 28). Gay rights: Where is Turkey heading? Washington, DC: German Marshall Fund. Retrieved from http://www.gmfus.org/archives/gay-rights-where-is-turkey-heading/

Gomez, D. (2004). Last in line: the United States trails behind in recognizing gender-based asylum claims. *Whittier Law Review, 25*, 959–987.

Hansen, P. (2010). UNHCR calls upon states to recognise the needs of people persecuted on grounds of sexual orientation or gender identity. London, UK: UNHCR United Kingdom. Retrieved from http://www.unhcr.org.uk/resources/monthly-updates/october-2010/lgbt.html

Holzhacker, R. (2013). State-sponsored homophobia and the denial of the right of assembly in Central and Eastern Europe: The 'boomerang' and the 'ricochet' between European organizations and civil society to uphold human rights. *Law & Policy*, 35, 1–2, January–April, 1–28.

Human Rights First. (2012, May). The road to safety: Executive summary. Retrieved from http://www.humanrightsfirst.org/our-work/refugee-protection/lgbti-refugees/key-documents/the-road-to-safety-executive-summary/

Human Rights Watch. (2012, October 5). Serbia: Revoke ban on Belgrade pride parade. Retrieved from http://www.hrw.org/news/2012/10/05/serbia-revoke-ban-belgrade-pride-parade

Human Rights Watch. (2013, July 10). Macedonia: Spate of anti-gay attacks. Retrieved from http://www.hrw.org/news/2013/07/10/macedonia-spate-anti-gay-attacks

IGLYO. (2013). Who we are. Retrieved from http://www.iglyo.com/about/

ILGA-Europe. (2010, March 31). 47 European countries unanimously agree on historic human rights recommendations for lesbian, gay, bisexual and transgender people. Brussels, Belgium: ILGA-Europe. Retrieved from http://www.ilga-europe.org/home/news/for_media/media_releases/

    47_european_countries_unanimously_agree_on_historic_human_rights_recommendations_for_
    lesbian_gay_bisexual_and_transgender_people
ILGA-Europe. (2012). Violence during the launch event of the magazine 2.0 dedicated to sexuality.
    Xheni Karaj and Krisi Pinderi. Retrieved from http://www.ilga-europe.org/home/guide_europe/
    country_by_country/albania/violence_during_the_aunch_event_of_the_magazine_kosovo_2_
    0_dedicated_to_sexuality
ILGA-Europe. (2013a). Albanian right-wing PM fully supports LGBT. Berisha, first PM officially
    to meet representatives. Retrieved from http://www.ilga-europe.org/home/guide_europe/
    country_by_country/albania/albanian_right_wing_pm_fully_supports_lgbt_berisha_first_pm_
    officially_to_meet_representatives2
ILGA-Europe. (2013b). Annual review of the human rights situation of lesbian, gay, bisexual,
    trans and intersex people in Europe. Retrieved from http://www.ilga-europe.org/home/
    publications/reports_and_other_materials/rainbow_europe
ILGA-Europe. (2013c). LGBT community in Albania takes over the center of the capital with
    IDAHO events. Retrieved from http://www.ilga-europe.org/home/guide_europe/country_by_
    country/albania/lgbt_community_in_albania_takes_over_the_center_of_the_capital_with_
    idaho_events
ILGA-Europe. (2013d). Score sheets per country. Retrieved from http://www.ilga-europe.org/
    home/publications/reports_and_other_materials/rainbow_europe/score_sheet
ILGA-Europe. (2013e). Turkey. Retrieved from http://www.ilga-europe.org/home/guide_europe/
    country_by_country/turkey
ILGA-Europe. (2013f). A Turkey and Europe with no LGBTIs. Till when exactly? Retrieved
    from http://www.ilga-europe.org/home/guide_europe/country_by_country/turkey/A-Turkey-
    and-Europe-with-no-LGBTIs.-Till-when-exactly
ILGA-Europe. (2013g). What is ILGA-Europe? Retrieved from http://www.ilga-europe.org/
    home/about_us/what_is_ilga_europe
Jansen, S., & Spijkerboer, T. (2011). *Fleeing homophobia: Asylum claims related to sexual
    orientation and gender identity in Europe.* A project of COC Netherlands and VU University
    Amsterdam. Retrieved from http://www.academia.edu/900410/Fleeing_Homophobia._
    Asylum_Claims_Related_to_Sexual_Orientation_and_Gender_Identity_in_Europe
Johnston, L. (2005). *Queering tourism: Paradoxical performances of gay pride parades.* London,
    UK: Routledge.
Kaos GL. (2013a). Retrieved from http://www.kaosgl.com/anasayfa.php
Kaos GL. (2013b). Istanbul Criminal Court: Insulting homosexuals is not freedom of expression.
    Retrieved from http://www.kaosgl.org/page.php?id=14501
Keck, M. E., & Sikkink, K. (1998). *Activists beyond borders.* Ithaca, NY: Cornell University
    Press.
Kosovo 2.0. (2012). *Kosovo 2.0 issue #4—Sex.* Retrieved from http://www.kosovotwopointzero.
    com/en/magazine
Lennox, C., & Waites, M. (2013). Human rights, sexual orientation and gender identity in the
    Commonwealth: From history and law to developing activism and transnational dialogues. In
    C. Lennox & M. Waites (Eds.), *Human rights, sexual orientation and gender identity in the
    Commonwealth: Struggles for decriminalisation and change* (pp. 1–59). London, UK:
    Institute of Commonwealth Studies, Institute of Historical Research, Human Rights
    Consortium, University of London.
Libertas Kosova. (2013). *About.* Retrieved from http://libertas-kos.org/about
Miles, N. (2010). *No going back: Lesbian and gay people in the asylum system. Stonewall UK.*
    Retrieved from http://www.stonewall.org.uk/at_home/immigration_asylum_and_international/
    2665.asp
Nguyen, K. (2013). *UK asylum process painful for lesbians fleeing death threats.* Thomson
    Reuters Foundation. Retrieved from http://www.trust.org/item/20130516115734-fuqwb/
Organization Q. (2013). *SEE Q network.* Retrieved from http://www.queer.ba/en/seeqnetwork
OSCE. (2012). *Hate crimes in the OSCE region—incidents and responses: Annual report for
    2011.* Retrieved from http://www.osce.org/odihr/97294

Peksen, D. (2012). *Liberal interventionism and democracy promotion*. Lanham, MD: Lexington Books.

Potts, A. (2013, June 24). *Istanbul Trans Pride parade turns into Gezi Park protest*. Retrieved from http://www.gaystarnews.com/article/istanbul-trans-pride-parade-turns-gezi-park-protest 240613

Predrag, M. (2013, July 24). Extremists attack Montenegro's first gay pride. *Associated Press*. Retrieved from http://www.google.com/hostednews/afp/article/ALeqM5jEyphfzqwn6d M1NDkjNE6Oyr12vw?docId=CNG.470e327ad52be090f21791c767e12d34.211

Pridham, G. (2005). *Designing democracy: EU enlargement and regime change in post-communist Europe*. Basingstoke, UK and New York, NY: Palgrave Macmillan.

Rettman, A. (2012, April 10). Gay rights not decisive for Serbia-EU talks. *EU Observer*. Retrieved from http://euobserver.com/enlargement/117756

Richard, A. C. (2013). LGBT: Equally entitled to human rights and dignity. *Forced Migration Review, 42*, 4. Retrieved from http://www.fmreview.org/sogi/richard

Russo, R. (2012, December 15). Thugs attack LGBT event in Pristina. *Kosovo News*. Retrieved from http://www.kosovo-news.com/2012/12/thugs-attack-lgbt-event-in-pristina-the-battle-for-everyones-personal-freedom/

Sarejevo Open Centre. (2013). *About us*. Retrieved from http://soc.ba/index.php/en/about-us

Schweiger, L. (2011, May 19). *EU asylum policy for gays and lesbians criticized by LGBT groups*. Retrieved from http://www.dw.de/eu-asylum-policy-for-gays-and-lesbians-criticized-by-lgbt-groups/a-15089739

Sexual orientation and gender identity and the protection of forced migrants. (2013, April). *Forced Migration Review 42*, 16–19. Retrieved from www.fmreview.org/sogi#sthash. oOLBhmRj.dpuf

Sinclair-Webb, E. (2013, June 5). *The voices from Taksim*. Open Democracy website, Retrieved from http://www.opendemocracy.net/emma-sinclair-webb/voices-from-taksim

Simon, C. (2013, July 24). *Violence, shouts of 'kill the gays' disrupt Montenegro's first pride parade*. [HRC Blog]. Retrieved from http://www.hrc.org/blog/entry/violence-shouts-of-kill-the-gays-disrupt-montenegros-first-pride-parade

Smolar, P. (2013). Serbia and Kosovo sign historic agreement. *Guardian Weekly*. Retrieved from http://www.guardian.co.uk/world/2013/apr/30/serbia-kosovo-historic-agreement-brussels

Soykan, C. (2012). The new draft law on foreigners and international protection in Turkey. *Oxford Monitor of Forced Migration, 2*(2), 38–47.

Split's Gay Pride parade passes without incident. (2013, June 8). *Croatia Herald*. Retrieved from http://www.croatiaherald.com/splits-gay-pride-parade-passes-without-incident/

Taksim stages exuberant gay pride march joined by Gezi protesters (2013, June 30). *Hürriyet Daily News*. Retrieved from http://www.hurriyetdailynews.com/taksim-stages-exuberant-gay-pride-march-joined-by-gezi-protesters.aspx?pageID=238&nID=49779&NewsCatID=339

Thousands march for gay rights in Croatia. (2013, June 17). *BalkanInsight*. Retrieved from http://www.balkaninsight.com/en/article/more-than-10-000-support-gay-rights

UNHCR [United Nations High Commissioner for Refugees]. (2012a). *Born free and equal: Sexual orientation and gender identity in international human rights law*. New York, NY and Geneva, Switzerland: UNHCR. Retrieved from http://www.ohchr.org/EN/NewsEvents/Pages/ BornFreeAndEqual.aspx

UNHCR [United Nations High Commissioner for Refugees]. (2012b). *Pillay urges Serbia to allow LGBT parade, confront prejudice against minorities*. Retrieved from http://www.ohchr. org/en/NewsEvents/Pages/DisplayNews.aspx?NewsID=12621&LangID=E

UNHCR [United Nations High Commissioner for Refugees]. (2012c). *Refugees: Flowing across borders*. Retrieved from http://www.unhcr.org/pages/49c3646c125.html

U.S. Department of State. (2013a). *Country reports on human rights practices for 2012*. Bureau of Democracy, Human Rights and Labor. Retrieved from http://www.state.gov/j/drl/rls/hrrpt/ 2011/eur/index.htm

U.S. Department of State. (2013b). *Country reports on human rights practices for 2012*. Albania: Bureau of Democracy, Human Rights and Labor. Retrieved from http://www.state.gov/j/drl/rls/hrrpt/2011/eur/index.htm

USAID. (2013, April 8). USAID announces new partnership to promote LGBT human rights abroad. Retrieved from http://www.usaid.gov/news-information/press-releases/usaid-announces-new-partnership-promote-lgbt-human-rights-abroad

Vasiljevic, S. (2013, July 24). Violent protests disrupt Montenegro's first gay pride parade. *Thomas Reuters*. Retrieved from http://www.reuters.com/article/2013/07/24/us-montenegro-gay-idUSBRE96N0V120130724

Chapter 16
The Death Penalty as Genocide: The Persecution of "Homosexuals" in Uganda

Christina DeJong and Eric Long

Abstract From 2009 to 2012, the Ugandan government attempted to pass legislation mandating the death penalty as punishment for "homosexuality." Typically, the wholesale execution of a group of people is considered to be genocide, but sexual orientation is not a protected group as specified in the *Convention on the Prevention and Punishment of the Crime of Genocide*, which was signed into law immediately following World War II. Increased violence against "homosexuals" and the murder of an outspoken gay activist in Uganda indicate a growing public hatred of gays and lesbians, which mirrors events from genocides. In this paper we review events in Uganda and relate them to other genocidal incidents to determine whether the treatment of gay, lesbian, and bisexual individuals constitutes genocide, based on findings from social science research, if not legally. Recommendations are made regarding the current definition of genocide used by the international community.

Keywords Homophobia · Genocide · Uganda · Death penalty for homosexuality · Capital punishment for homosexuality · Othering · Dehumanization · Anti-gay violence

Anti-gay hatred reached a peak in Uganda in 2009. In that year, the country's government proposed that individuals convicted of "aggravated homosexuality" receive the death penalty, and that any friends or family members who harbor such individuals be incarcerated (Houreld and Olukya 2009). While many considered these actions to be tantamount to the genocide of "homosexuals," sexual orientation is not one of the criteria used to define the groups protected by the *Convention on the Prevention and Punishment of the Crime of Genocide* (United Nations 1948).

C. DeJong (✉)
School of Criminal Justice, Michigan State University, 655 Auditorium Road, Room 560, East Lansing, MI 48824, USA
e-mail: dejongc@msu.edu

E. Long
School of Public Policy, University of Maryland, College Park, MD, USA
e-mail: longeric@umd.edu

D. Peterson and V. R. Panfil (eds.), *Handbook of LGBT Communities, Crime, and Justice*, DOI: 10.1007/978-1-4614-9188-0_16, © Springer Science+Business Media New York 2014

The *Convention* specifies that actions taken with intent to destroy a group based on race, ethnicity, nationality, or religion may be considered genocide. Thus, the actions against the ethnic Tutsi in Rwanda legally constituted genocide, as did the genocide of those who practiced the religion of Judaism in the Holocaust, or Islam in the former Yugoslavia. Genocide scholars have argued that specifying only four groups omits actions that might otherwise constitute genocide; for example, the mass murder in Sri Lanka of members of a Marxist political party was not legally recognized as genocide, yet victims were targeted due to their group identification (Harff 2003). In addition, the systematic rape and assault of women and girls is not generally considered to be genocide (MacKinnon 1994), and the Convention does not include gender as a defining characteristic of protected groups.

In this chapter, we argue that the legal definition of genocide does not reflect the reality of genocide as examined by scholars on this topic. Using findings from academic research, we identify factors related to genocide and determine whether they are relevant to the proposed use of capital punishment in Uganda against "homosexuals;" that is, people who engage in same-sex sexual relationships.

The 2009 "Anti-Homosexuality" Bill in Uganda

The draconian "anti-homosexuality" bill proposed in Uganda has been widely criticized since its introduction in Parliament by member David Bahati in October 2009 (Strand 2011; see also discussion by Cobb, this volume). Sexual activity between members of the same sex was (and is still) criminal in Uganda prior to the introduction of this legislation, with penalties as severe as life in prison. In addition, sodomy is defined as a felony criminal offense with a penalty of up to 7 years in prison. However, these laws have been rarely enforced since their inception in 1950 (Hollander 2009). In 2005, the Ugandan constitution was amended to include a clause prohibiting same-sex marriage (Mujuzi 2009).

The "anti-homosexuality" bill introduced in 2009, however, proposed making the crime of "homosexuality" punishable by life imprisonment, and the crime of "aggravated homosexuality" punishable by death (Law Library of Congress 2011). "Homosexuality" is defined as the commission of one of three acts: (1) when a male penetrates the mouth or anus *of another male* with his penis or any other sexual contraption (emphasis added), (2) when a male or female uses an object or sexual contraption to penetrate or stimulate the sexual organ of a person of the same sex, or (3) a male or female touches another person with the intention of committing the act of homosexuality (Bahati 2009). Part 1 implies that male-on-male oral sex is outlawed, but female-on-female oral sex is not—nor is oral sex between a man and a woman. Part 2 is clearly intended to outlaw same-sex activities involving use of objects, and Part 3 appears to be an attempt to cover any other activity not included in Part 1 or Part 2. Part 3 is so broadly defined, however, that it would seem nearly any kind of touching (with any parts of the body) between members of the same sex would be defined as criminal under the law. Therefore, oral sex between two women could be criminalized under Part 3, although it is not criminal under Part 1. Essentially, Part 3 allows a wide variety of behaviors occurring between two members of the same sex to be criminal—thus providing an extremely broad definition under which many activities could be included.

"Aggravated homosexuality" as defined in the Ugandan bill involves having sex with a member of the same sex who is (1) younger than 18 years old, (2) a child of the offender, and/or (3) disabled. In addition, "aggravated homosexuality" includes having sex with a member of the same sex when the offender is (1) HIV positive, (2) holds a position of authority over the victim, (3) has plied the victim with a drug in order to facilitate sex, or (4) is a serial offender (Bahati 2009). Several acts in this definition contain behaviors that are criminal in many countries and involve issues of consent. For example, it is generally criminal for an adult to have sex with a minor/child, as is having sex with one's own child. However, the penalty (i.e., capital punishment) proposed for members of the same sex is much greater than those proscribed for members of the opposite sex who engage in these same behaviors.

Current law in Uganda dictates severe punishment for several of these acts when the victim is female, but crimes against boys are (1) either ignored in the law, or (2) have less severe punishments. The Ugandan Penal Code Act (1990, Chap. 106) states that raping a girl or woman, and "non-forcible" sex with a girl under the age of 18 are both offenses punishable by death (Chap. XV, Sections 118 and 123, respectively). In addition, having sex with a known family member, including aunts, uncles, cousins, parents, and children, carries a penalty of 7 years with an additional 11 years if the victim is a child (Chap. XV, Section 144). It is important to note that the law does mention male victims—anyone, regardless of sex, found guilty of indecent assault against a boy younger than 18 years is liable for imprisonment up to 14 years. With the exception of non-forcible sex with under-age girls, none of these "comparable" crimes among opposite-sex persons would garner the death penalty.

With regard to disability, many countries have laws against sex with someone who is mentally disabled (and therefore not able to provide consent), but there are few restrictions against sex between people who are *physically* disabled. There are certainly exceptions, as when physical disability renders individuals incapable of providing consent, or of caring for themselves. Ugandan law currently dictates the penalty for a person (male or female) found guilty of having sex with a woman or girl who is known "to be an idiot or imbecile" at imprisonment for 14 years (Ugandan Penal Code Act 1990, Chap. 106, Chap. XV Section 124). Once again, there is no provision for punishment of offenders who victimize males with mental disability, and victimization of those with physical disability is not mentioned at all. In Uganda's "Anti-Homosexuality" bill, disability is defined as "a substantial limitation of daily life activities caused by physical, mental, or sensory impairment and environment barriers resulting in limited participation" (Bahati 2009). The definition of disability here is much broader than in other countries, and does not imply that the nature of the disability must affect consent. Thus, the law could be applied against people who engage in sexual activity with a member of the same sex who has a physical disability, such as a severe limp, thus expanding governmental control over the population and allowing greater ability to justify prosecution of gays and lesbians when no comparable prohibitions govern the same behavior by heterosexuals.

Knowingly spreading HIV is a criminal offense in several countries, and behaviors that can be punished include consensual sex, pregnancy, breastfeeding, and even *unknowingly* spreading the HIV virus (Bernard and Cameron 2013). Critics have argued that these laws stigmatize people with HIV/AIDS, lead to discrimination against HIV-positive persons, and distract from efforts to reduce transmission through medically proven methods (Bernard and Cameron 2013; see also Waldman, this volume). The Uganda Bill contains a provision allowing criminal prosecution of same-sex behavior when the "perpetrator" is HIV-positive, but does not specify that the perpetrator must be aware of his or her HIV status. Thus, an individual could be sentenced to death for having sex without being aware that he or she is HIV positive. Knowingly transmitting HIV/AIDS is currently not criminal in Uganda, but the government has been trying to criminalize HIV transmission for several years. Rather than requiring the death penalty, however, the current proposal recommends punishment up to 14 years for "willfully and intentionally transmit[ting] HIV to another person" (Human Rights Watch 2009).

Next, "aggravated homosexuality" includes having same-sex relations with a person under the perpetrator's "authority" (as defined in the bill, "having power and control over other people because of your knowledge and official position; and shall include a person who exercises religious, political, economic, or social authority" (Bahati 2009, p. 3). This definition incorporates a wide variety of relationships between individuals, and the bill does not clearly define what is meant by each of these terms. The intent, perhaps, might have been to imply coercion of one person over another into a same-sex sexual relationship, such as employer/employee, teacher/student, or pastor/parishioner. There are two major problems with this component of the bill: (1) it does not appear that these types of relationships are illegal for those engaging in opposite-sex relationships, and (2) because these terms are undefined, the government has the ability to prosecute individuals engaging in same-sex sexual relationships in a wide variety of situations. For example, does someone exercise "economic authority" over another if they have a higher income? How does one individual have political authority over another? The nebulous use of these terms would give the Ugandan government significant power in charging and prosecuting its citizens with "aggravated homosexuality" and sentencing them to death, yet these sexual relationships are not currently illegal in Uganda if they occur between a man and a woman.

The bill also includes a provision for prosecuting individuals for plying same-sex victims with drugs or alcohol to facilitate sex. "Date rape" laws exist in many countries, but most are relatively new and it is unclear how often they are used to prosecute offenders. In South Africa, for example, the issue of consent is addressed in their laws against rape, which were amended in 2007 to be gender-neutral. Victims who are asleep, unconscious, in an altered state of consciousness (via drugs, alcohol, or another substance that affects their judgment), younger than 12, or mentally disabled cannot form consent (Republic of South Africa 2007). The proscribed punishments for these offenses in South Africa vary depending on the severity of the offense and the offender's criminal record, but the death penalty is not indicated for these crimes in any situation. Current Ugandan law contains no specific avenue for punishing an offender for this type of sexual assault.

The final, and most problematic, component of the bill allows prosecution of "serial offenders" for "aggravated homosexuality." A serial offender is defined as "a person who has previous convictions of the offence of homosexuality or related offenses" (Bahati 2009). The bill defines a group (serial offenders) based on frequency of their behavior. Scholarship on human sexuality has differentiated sexual identity from sexual behavior—individuals may identify as gay, lesbian, bisexual, etc., which indicates a sexual attraction to someone of the same or a different sex. Sexual attraction, however, is not the same as sexual behavior. Individuals sexually attracted to members of the same sex may not actually act on that attraction (Ross et al. 2003). However, while sexual behavior does not define sexual identity, there is a strong correlation between the two (Chandra et al. 2011). The inclusion of "serial offender" in the portion of the bill carrying the death penalty would allow the government of Uganda to execute members of a group without defining it as such in the law.

As discussed above, several behaviors defined under "aggravated homosexuality" are not illegal when male–female couples engage in such acts and those that are do not always carry the penalty of death, especially if committed against a male. The vagaries in the bill allow for capricious and arbitrary prosecution of gays and lesbians, which can be used to inculcate fear in the LGBT population of Uganda. The bill effectively targets a group (LGBT individuals) for execution based on the behaviors most strongly correlated with membership in that group.

In addition to the proposed penalties for "homosexuality" and "aggravated homosexuality," the bill also would also have imposed criminal sanctions on anyone who withheld information regarding the location of anyone in violation of the bill, and proposed to criminalize any "promotion of homosexuality," a provision that would make it difficult for human rights advocates to work in Uganda (CNN 2011). The majority of the international community has condemned the bill (National Public Radio Staff 2011), several European governments have threatened to cut aid to countries that support the bill, and U.S. President Obama has called the bill "odious" (Associated Press 2012).

In May 2011, the bill expired without a vote in parliament, but was eligible for another vote after the start of the new legislative section that began in June 2011 (CNN 2011). In October 2011, debate of the bill was reopened, and by the end of 2012 the Ugandan government initially agreed to pass a revised bill that removed the death penalty clause (BBC News 2012). However, the possibility of its inclusion has not been completely abandoned by its proponents. The bill sets a precedent of premeditated, state-sanctioned killing of a targeted group based on a distinguishable characteristic—a characteristic that proponents (including Bahati) claim is immoral for Uganda, regardless of the status and acceptance of LGBT individuals worldwide (NPR 2011).

Public Attitudes on Same-Sex Relationships

Throughout Africa, a large number of clergy and political leaders have taken staunch anti-gay positions. These individuals identify "homosexuality" as the root cause of social problems, most notably increased HIV/AIDS prevalence rates. Anti-gay Bishops and other Christian leaders have attempted to mobilize a Christian universalism that focuses heavily on notions of the nation and family (from which homosexuals are excluded) by using the Bible to expound anti-gay sentiment (Hoad 2007). In Uganda, Bishop Eustace Kamanyire has stated that same-sex relationships are immoral in the eyes of the church and are condemned as immoral in both the Old and New Testaments (Hoad 2007, p. 54). Many Anglicans in Uganda have made a point to exclude gays and lesbians from the church, as Bishop Wilson Mutebi explains that scripture condemns same-sex relationships. He argues that although science and philosophy have different views on gay relationships, the Bible—and perhaps more accurately, the interpretation thereof by church leaders—has the final say in the region (Hoad 2007, p. 54).

American evangelical leaders have also played a key role in anti-gay sentiment in Uganda, including wielding indirect influence over the introduction of the anti-homosexuality bill in 2009. Bahati has stated that it was in the U.S. that he first became close with a group of influential social conservatives, including politicians, known as The Fellowship, which was influential in supporting the bill (Kron 2012). He said the idea for the bill began out of a conversation with members of The Fellowship in 2008, who claimed that it was "too late" in America to propose such legislation (Kron 2012).

Seven months before the introduction of the Ugandan anti-homosexuality bill, three American evangelical Christians spoke at an event in Uganda to pontificate on the "threat homosexuals posed to Bible-based values and the traditional African family" (Gettleman 2010, para. 2). At the event, the speakers explained how "gay men often sodomized teenage boys and how 'the gay movement is an evil institution' whose goal is 'to defeat the marriage-based society and replace it with a culture of sexual promiscuity'" (Gettleman 2010, para. 3). Although these men deny condoning the enactment of the death penalty for same-sex behavior, the use of such anti-gay rhetoric clearly influences public opinion on the issue. However, having public opinion lean heavily toward a general societal disapproval of gay and lesbian lifestyles could logically have influence over political discourse surrounding the issue.

"Homosexuality" and the Legacy of Colonization

Although the history of same-sex sexual behaviors in Uganda and in Africa pre-dates colonialism, it is the belief of many homophobic leaders that colonization is the reason why gays and lesbians exist in Africa, and that same-sex attraction is inherently contrary to African values and behavioral norms (Tamale 2007, pp. 18–19). In Uganda,[1] same-sex relationships predated colonialism and were at that time neither condoned nor suppressed; for example, the "mudoko dako" of the northern Ugandan Langi region were males who were treated like women and allowed to have relations with men (Tamale 2007, pp. 18–19). Same-sex relationships were also seen in various other tribes throughout Uganda, including the Iteso, Bahima, Banyoro, and the Baganda (Jjuuko 2013; Tamale 2007, p. 19). Same-sex sexual activities in precolonial Africa were often viewed as "play" or a means of socialization, and gender-role reversal was also common (Ward 2013).

African leaders, most notably Zimbabwe's president, Robert Mugabe, have ignored the history of same-sex relationships in precolonial Africa and classify them as "un-African" (Spurlin 2006; Tamale 2007). A popular anti-gay belief in Uganda is that white colonial discourse had emasculated Africa, and that supporting gay and lesbian lifestyles in black Africa is an ideological imposition by whites that emasculates the nation-state, undermining male power and conventional gender relations and hierarchies (Spurlin 2006; Tamale 2007, p. 19). This belief is common despite the fact that same-sex relationships in Uganda—and throughout Africa—predate European colonization. In addition, scholars now suggest that anti-sodomy laws were *imposed on* British colonies by the Commonwealth (Kirby 2013, p. 63), rather than Europeans introducing same-sex sexual behavior to Africa. Uganda is not alone in this rewriting of history—a similar situation exists in India, where anti-sodomy laws have been referred to as consistent with Indian values, unlike the values of the United Kingdom and United States where gay and lesbian relationships are "tolerated." Their lack of recognition that anti-sodomy laws were imposed under British colonial rule has been referred to as "sheer amnesia" (Human Rights Watch 2013, p. 84). The government of Nigeria has also referred to same-sex relationships as "un-African," in opposition to increasing support of such relationships in the West. Human Rights Watch (2013) describes the situation in Nigeria thusly:

> The paradox remains that a democratic government promoted this repressive legislation as part of indigenous values, although it actually extended old, undemocratic colonial statutes. (p. 114)

Some suggest that homophobia in Africa is the result of a perceived threat on national sovereignty by globalization and by the West (Hoad 2007, pp. xii–xiii; Jjuuko 2013; see also Cobb, this volume). In parts of Africa (including Uganda), the proper "modern" family structure takes the form of the Western 1950s ideal—the "nuclear family"—with the wife keeping house and the husband supporting the family financially. This may be a postcolonial response to the perceived tolerance of LGBT individuals that has resulted from modernity in the West (Hoad 2007, p. 57).

---

[1] It is important to note that the state currently known as "Uganda" did not exist prior to colonial rule by the British. Prior to colonization, this region contained several "kingdoms" and smaller communities not formally defined as a nation-state (Jjuuko 2013).

Public opinion surveys have indicated that the vast majority of Ugandans (96 %) believe that the gay and lesbian "lifestyle" should be rejected ("Homosexuality is a way of life that should not be accepted by society"), as do citizens of many countries in Africa (Pew Research Center 2013). Ugandans were surveyed by Pew in 2002, 2007, and 2012, and while specific questions about same-sex relationships were not asked in 2002, Ugandans reported they were greatly concerned about the spread of AIDS and disease at that time (91 % say it was a "very big" problem in their country), a consistent finding in most African countries. Other problems identified as "very big" by Ugandans include corrupt political leaders (81 %), crime (67 %), and moral decline (56 %) (Pew Research Center 2002).

Sexual relations between same-sex partners are illegal in many countries, with punishments ranging from fines, to corporal punishment, to death. Over 50 % of African governments have taken steps to formally criminalize same-sex sexual activity, with three currently implementing a death penalty for some offenses (Itaborahy and Zhu 2013). Capital punishment is typically reserved for "chronic offenders" in several African countries such as Sudan, Mauritania, and Nigeria, as well as several non-African states such as Saudi Arabia, the United Arab Emirates, Yemen, Afghanistan, and Iran. For example, Section 148 of the 1991 Penal Code in Sudan (Act No. 8 1991) states that acts of sodomy are punishable by flogging and imprisonment, with a third offense punishable by death. In Mauritania, male-to-male sex is punishable by death, as well as in parts of Nigeria and Somalia under Islamic law (Itaborahy and Zhu 2013); however, these laws may not apply to individuals who engage in female-to-female sex.

In many countries, criminalization of same-sex relationships tends to focus more on relations between gay men than those between lesbians. As an example, in Nazi Germany gay men were deemed a threat to the "masculine state" and, unwilling to reproduce with female partners, were deemed "parasites" and branded enemies of the state (United States Holocaust Memorial Museum, n.d.). Thousands of gay men were incarcerated, subjected to sterilization/castration, and murdered as part of the Nazis' attempt to build a "master race." Lesbian women were not a threat in the same sense—they still held the ability to procreate with men, even as a result of rape, and were not perceived as a threat to the masculinity of the Nazi party (U.S. Holocaust Memorial Museum, n.d.). In a patriarchal state, there may be a pervasive belief that lesbians need only be "cured" of their same-sex attraction through "corrective rape." This form of violence against women is particularly problematic in South Africa, where a history of apartheid and minimal efforts to prosecute rape have resulted in the highest rates of rape in the world (Brown 2012). It is ironic that South Africa is one of the most (legally) progressive African countries on LGBT rights–allowing same-sex marriage, protecting against LGBT discrimination, and allowing adoption by same-sex couples (Itaborahy and Zhu 2013)–but the low support for these measures in the population (32 % in 2012; Pew Research Center 2013) may help explain this type of violence against lesbian women.

African discourse on the HIV/AIDS crisis frequently blames gay men for the spread of the disease around Africa, and AIDS is often characterized as a "gay disease" (Hoad 2007, p. xiv). However, statistics collected by the World Health Organization (WHO) indicate that HIV/AIDS is not exclusively a "gay problem." WHO provides statistics for HIV prevalence in men who have sex with men (MSM) in countries where information is available, showing that MSM are 19.3 times more likely to be HIV-positive than the general population (WHO 2011). Despite the fact that HIV prevalence rates are higher among MSM, evidence overwhelmingly indicates that HIV transmission resulting in new infections is much higher among opposite-sex partners (Hoad 2007, p. xiv). Due to the large size of the population engaging in opposite-sex intercourse relative to that engaging in same-sex intercourse, it is likely that more HIV-positive individuals were infected while engaging in opposite-sex intercourse.

Homophobia in Uganda has actually harmed AIDS prevention there. Between 1991 and 2006, Uganda's track record on addressing the HIV/AIDS crisis was relatively good, with national prevalence in adults aged 15–49 dropping from 10.7 to 6.3 percent; however, the prevalence rate increased after 2006, correlating with a radical shift in AIDS policy (Schoepf 2010, p. 108). From that point on, Uganda shifted from a multi-sector and NGO-based initiative against HIV/AIDS toward a more religious-based approach, with half of the television stations in the country streaming religious programs, along with programs in favor of youth abstinence and against condom distribution (Schoepf 2010, p. 108). This shift was influenced by the U.S.—the largest single HIV/AIDS donor to Uganda—becoming more staunchly in favor of abstinence-only programs (Cohen and Tate 2006, p.177). Religious leaders, such as Pope Benedict XVI, stated publicly that condoms and "sexual immorality" were to blame for the spread of HIV/AIDS in Africa (suggesting that the use of condoms leads to immorality), and the only solution to the HIV/AIDS crisis was through "abstinence and fidelity" (BBC News 2005). This period also witnessed increasing stigmatization of HIV-positive people and the expansion of conservative evangelical churches in sub-Saharan Africa (Schoepf 2010, p. 111). Attempts to educate Ugandans on these issues may fall on deaf ears, however. Some scholars suggest that homophobia is so entrenched in Uganda that many citizens would rather remain uninformed about these issues (Jjuuko 2013).

In addition, the WHO indicates that criminalization of same-sex sexual behavior is a barrier for gay men to gain access to valuable health services as a result of their ability to be prosecuted (WHO 2011, p. 10; and see Waldman, this volume). A circular dilemma is thus created by anti-homosexuality laws such as the one proposed in Uganda, in which a group that is statistically at a higher risk of contracting HIV/AIDS is targeted through criminal prosecution, which makes it even more difficult for members of that group to receive proper treatment and counseling.

Genocidal Intention of the Ugandan "Kill the Gays" Bill[2]

Public opinion about homosexuality and HIV/AIDS in Uganda has led to an attempted genocide against homosexuals through use of the death penalty. While not legally defined as genocide according to the *Convention on the Prevention and Punishment of the Crime of Genocide*, findings from social science research on the nature and causes of genocide has identified several precursors and related social factors explaining how genocide occurs. According to the *Convention*, the crime of genocide encompasses one of several actions intended to eliminate or greatly reduce the numbers of a group defined by their race, ethnicity, religion, or nationality (United Nations 1948). Because the *Convention* does not include sexual orientation as a method for defining victimized groups, Uganda's attempt to pass the death penalty for homosexuality does not legally constitute genocide.

Sentencing gay and lesbian persons to death may not constitute genocide according to international law, but this is because the definition of genocide is narrow. Social groups are defined by—and discriminated against based on—more descriptors than race, ethnicity, religion, and nationality. Scholars in a range of disciplines (but primarily sociology and political science) have been analyzing data on genocides and other related actions against groups for the past 20 years. Gregory Stanton (1998) has suggested that genocides pass through several stages before mass killings result, which he terms "extermination." Other scholars have identified sociological, economic, and political factors that increase the likelihood of genocide. We will review these perspectives and relate them to the situation in Uganda.

Stanton's 'Eight Stages of Genocide'

Gregory Stanton of *Genocide Watch* has identified eight stages that help explain the evolution of genocidal events (1998). The process begins with identification of the "other" and, depending on structural forces, can escalate to extermination of the other group. Stanton explains that while earlier stages must precede later stages, the process does not necessarily proceed in a linear path—in some instances, aspects of later stages might appear sooner in the process and there may be overlap between them. In addition, the progression and timing of the stages is different in each genocide. During The Holocaust, for example, the stages unfolded over several years, starting with Hitler's appointment in 1933 and most of the mass killings taking place between 1941 and 1945 (U.S. Holocaust Memorial Museum 2013b). In Rwanda, however, the early stages of classification and symbolization occurred over decades but the latter stages developed quickly, with

---

[2] The official name of the Ugandan bill is the "Anti-Homosexuality Bill" (Bahati 2009), but the Western media has taken to calling it the "Kill The Gays" Bill.

over 800,000 Tutsi executed in a 3-month period (Mayerson 2010). In this section, we explain each stage of genocide and present evidence of how this process has developed in Uganda with regard to homosexuality.

Classification

Stanton (1998) indicates that all cultures have mechanisms by which to classify groups. Race, ethnicity, class, religion, gender, political party, sexual orientation, and many other factors can define the groups with which people identify. Negative classification can result in othering, in which groups defined as being "different from" the majority group are denigrated (Stokes and Gabriel 2010). In every genocide, othering has been used not only to define the victimized group, but also to distance the oppressors from the oppressed. Genocidaires have used nationality, race, ethnicity, and religion to define "the other": examples from modern genocides include Jews in the Holocaust, Tutsi in Rwanda, the "new people" in Cambodia, and Muslims in the Balkans.

Sexual orientation has been used to define groups in many cultures, typically using dichotomous categories of homosexual/heterosexual; however, categorizing sexual orientation is more complicated than using groups defined by gay/straight (Sell 1997; also see related discussions in this volume, by Frederick; Johnson; Messinger; Woods). For example, the Kinsey Scale is a continuum of sexual orientation, with categories of heterosexual/homosexual feelings and behavior defining the end points and a range of orientations in between (Kinsey et al. 1948). Current scholarship has suggested that even Kinsey's scale is limiting and that sexuality includes more than just behavior—sexual orientation, gender identity, and gender expression all serve to explain sexuality (Kosciw et al. 2012; Lennox and Waites 2013). Othering is difficult when continua are more descriptive than dichotomous categories, but binary categories are much more conducive to defining "us" and "them." As a result, binary categories such as "gay" or "straight" are used to denote classifications, while middle status categories such as "bisexual" or "transgender" are minimized in public debates. This method of classification is consistent with other genocides. Stanton (1998) indicates that "bipolar societies" (that is, societies where groups are clearly delineated) are most likely to experience genocide.

The othering of LGBT individuals has been studied extensively in Western cultures in the context of homophobia. Definitions of what constitutes "appropriate" masculinity are used to identify gay men as members of a marginalized out-group—one classified using a subordinate definition of masculinity (Perry 2001). Once an out-group has been identified, influential members of the in-group may work to distance themselves from the out-group. Western studies have demonstrated that "othering" is less likely when members of the majority are familiar with more members of the minority. For example, in a U.S. study, knowing someone who is gay or lesbian was the greatest (negative) predictor of homophobia (Walch et al. 2010).

In other countries, beliefs about the spread of disease (specifically, HIV and AIDS) are frequently rooted in homophobia and othering (Petros et al. 2006). This is facilitated by a climate of moral panic, which has emerged in Uganda over the so-called "gay agenda" (Ward 2013). As explained by Cohen (1980, p. 1), a moral panic occurs when "A condition, episode, person or group of persons emerges to become defined as a threat to societal values and interests…" Folk devils are then identified as the "evil" to blame for the issue that began the panic (Cohen 1980)—in the case of HIV/AIDS, the scapegoat becomes gay men.

The othering of homosexuals and other LGBT individuals has become common practice in Uganda. Speakers at workshops in Uganda have preached about "the gay agenda," which includes the sodomizing of teenage boys, and how the gay movement in general is an "evil institution" whose main purpose is to destroy the institution of marriage and replace it with a "culture of sexual promiscuity" (Dicklitch 2012). Leaders in Uganda have pinned homosexuality as inherently "un-African," a product of the West that has been a neo-colonial imposition, attempting to undermine "African values" (Dicklitch 2012). "Homosexuals" have been targeted as a group in Uganda that is inherently different than "normal" Ugandans; they have been classified as a foreign entity that is un-African. Negative connotations attributed to "homosexuals" in Uganda have led to a high level of animosity toward them, particularly by state and church leaders.

Anti-gay groups also inculcate fear of homosexuality (and subsequently, othering) through the mass media. *Rolling Stone*, a Ugandan tabloid publication, published the names of "known homosexuals," with a banner reading "Hang Them" on the front page of one issue (Olukya and Straziuso 2010), and later published a second issue with several more "known homosexuals" identified before the High Court of Uganda determined the publication of such information was unconstitutional (Jjuuko 2013). The tabloid published several other anti-LGBT issues, with titles such as "We Shall Recruit 1,000,000 Innocent Kids by 2012—Homos" (Rice 2011). These publications incite fear of homosexuality by implying that gay men and women prey on children, sexually victimizing them and "converting" them to a "homosexual lifestyle." Even a terrorist attack in Kampala was blamed on homosexuals in *Rolling Stone* (Melloy 2010).

In other contexts, this behavior could be considered incitement to genocide, as was the case in Rwanda. In 2003, the International Criminal Tribunal for Rwanda convicted three media executives on charges of "direct and public incitement to genocide," among other charges (International Criminal Tribunal for Rwanda 2003). Lacking inclusion of sexual orientation in the Convention, it is not possible to charge owners of the Ugandan tabloids with the same crime.

Symbolization

In this second stage of genocide, genocidaires use names and/or symbols to denote members of the targeted group. Symbols and group names are common methods of self-identification and a normal aspect of society, but genocidal states can use these negatively in order to marginalize victimized groups. Indeed, symbols used in genocides are frequently appropriated from the victimized groups, such as the Star of David being used to identify Jews during The Holocaust. Similarly, pink triangles were used to denote homosexual prisoners in Nazi prison camps (Plant 1988); but in the years since, the pink triangle has been reappropriated by the LGBT community as a symbol of gay pride.

Evidence of symbolization has occurred in Uganda and also in other countries where homosexuality is not tolerated. Othering is facilitated when the majority identifies symbols associated with the minority. For example, children's entertainment has been a frequent target of these accusations in the U.S., with anti-gay groups suggesting that some television characters in children's programming encourage a "gay lifestyle." The Reverend Jerry Falwell denounced the British television show "Teletubbies" for including an allegedly gay character named "Tinky Winky," who is purple (a color frequently denoting gay pride), carries a purse, and has a triangle-shaped antenna. The triangle—perhaps referring back to symbols in The Holocaust—has been used as another symbol of gay identity (Aderet 2013).

In Uganda, language has been more commonly used to encourage othering rather than pictorial symbols. Tabloid publications borrowing names from major American outlets (such as "Rolling Stone" and "The Onion") frequently publish headlines using this type of language to encourage othering. In these publications, gay and lesbian persons are referred to as "homos" and "lesbos." For example, the Ugandan tabloid *Rolling Stone* published an article with the headline "More Homos' Faces Exposed," using a degrading term to increase public shame of members of Uganda's LGBT community (Onziema 2013) and facilitate the next stage, dehumanization.

Dehumanization

The process of othering facilitates dehumanization, in which members of the "other" group are seen as less deserving of rights than the majority group, or even "less than human"—members of the target group(s) are equated with animals, vermin, insects, or diseases. Dehumanization can often overcome the normal human revulsion against murder (Stanton 1998), and propaganda can be used by the media to facilitate othering and dehumanize the victimized group.

LGBT people are denied equal rights in most countries. While not always criminal, discrimination against people who are openly LGBT occurs frequently and is legally sanctioned in many countries including much of the U.S. (Itaborahy and Zhu 2013). In the case of Uganda, propaganda is used to dehumanize and subjugate "homosexuals." At public service meetings (also recorded and broadcast on YouTube), government officials and religious leaders describe homosexuality as equivalent to pedophilia, and explain that homosexual men eat fecal matter as a regular part of their lifestyle. One of the most vocal proponents of the

"Kill the Gays" bill is Pastor Martin Ssemba, who has been chided for screening gay pornographic films in his church (with children present) and has supported publication of names of known gay men in the media (Agence France-Press 2010). Such propaganda encourages the dehumanization of people who are gay and lesbian and justifies restriction of equal rights and criminal penalties for same-sex sexual behavior.

Organization

In this phase of genocide, violence begins against the victimized group, either obviously perpetrated by the state or unofficially organized by the state through militia groups. In past genocides, government agencies have been able to deny their participation in genocide by working secretly through armed civilian groups. Militia groups were armed by the Rwandan military during that genocide, which was responsible for carrying out massacres of Tutsi (Dallaire 2004). Members of sporting clubs were recruited by the Serbs during the Bosnian Genocide to facilitate killings of Muslims and Croats; in fact, they proved to be some of the most violent actors against their victims (Alvarez 2001).

Unfortunately, it is difficult to assess the prevalence of anti-gay violence in Uganda, given the strong anti-gay sentiment by the government. Victims fear prosecution, and thus are unlikely to report assaults to the police. Just 2 months after the publication of the names of known gay men, LGBT activist David Kato was murdered. Gay Ugandans reported an upswing in violence and threats after that incident (Gatsiounis 2011). Increased levels of threat among the victimized group can cause them to retreat and be silenced, which eases transition to the next stage: polarization.

Polarization

During the polarization phase, extremists attempt to distance themselves (and the rest of the majority) from the minority group. This process begins during the "classification" phase, but is exacerbated during polarization. The use of propaganda typically continues during this stage, as the marginalized group is increasingly distanced from the majority. It is during this stage that the government begins to pass laws limiting the rights of the minority. Laws against intermarriage and social interaction between groups are frequently enacted in this stage, in order to further separate the groups (Stanton 1998). A genocidal government that reaches this stage may also expel the "voices of reason" that typically advocate against polarization—moderate politicians, academics, and human rights groups. Thus, polarization reinforces the binary definitions created in the 'othering' phase.

The most well-known example of polarization occurred with the passage of the "Nuremberg Race Laws"—laws against intermarriage and socialization with Jews—by the Nazi government in 1935. These laws served to effectively remove Jews (and many others, including the Roma) from German social and economic life (Friedlander 1994). In the Bosnian Genocide, Slobodan Milosevic conspired to remove political moderates from the governing Central Committee (Woolf and Hulsizer 2005).

In Uganda, the "Anti Homosexuality" bill contains a provision that punishes "aiding and abating [*sic*] homosexuality" as well as "promoting homosexuality." Anyone guilty of promoting homosexuality (through publishing, disseminating, or otherwise distributing "pornographic" materials), who funds or sponsors homosexuality, uses electronic devices for promoting homosexuality, or "abets homosexuality in any way" can be incarcerated for between 5 and 7 years (Bahati 2009). "Pornographic materials" are not defined in the bill, thus incorporating another vague term under which many different types of offenses could be charged. This serves to silence supporters of LGBT individuals in Uganda, who do not have to personally engage in same-sex sexual relations, but only publicly support the LGBT community in order to be arrested. Passing this law would serve to silence the moderates, and further polarize Ugandan society.

Preparation

Preparation involves the identification and separation of targeted groups, often because of their ethnic or religious identity. Death lists are drawn up and victimized groups are identified (through symbols) and separated from general society in ghettos or camps. Some genocidal actors engage in significant and organized preparation, as in The Holocaust. In others, this phase occurs very rapidly or is practically non-existent, as in the Rwandan Genocide. At the start of the Cambodian genocide, the cities themselves were evacuated, with most urban Cambodians marked for execution (Jones 2006). It is during this phase when refugees attempt to leave the country en masse, and bordering states must deal with the influx of foreigners.

In Uganda, gay and lesbian people fear living openly because of their sexual identities. The proposed capital punishment for homosexuality also contains a mechanism for punishing those who harbor homosexuals, thereby enticing the public to turn them in and help "round up" any lawbreakers. Although there have not been reports of gay men and lesbians fleeing Uganda in light of this attempted legislation, they may not fare well in neighboring countries. LGBT individuals feeling persecution in Uganda face violence in neighboring countries, and may have to deal with other issues, such as corrupt police officers (Human Rights First 2012).

Extermination

Extermination occurs during the mass killing legally called "genocide." It is "extermination" (rather than murder) to perpetrators, because they do not believe their victims to be fully human. When extermination is state sponsored, armed forces often work with militias to conduct the killing (Stanton 1998). The media can also be an important tool for facilitating the extermination stage in genocides. In Rwanda, radio stations encouraged the public to "exterminate the cockroaches" when the genocide escalated (Smith 2003).

Genocide in this context differs in one important way from genocides in the past. In the case of Uganda, those accused of "inappropriate" sexual activity would be charged and face trial for violation of the law. Prior genocides involved the mass killings of civilians by civilians and military, and did not require the use of the legal process. A notable exception to this practice occurred during the Holocaust, when gay men were arrested under Paragraph 175 for committing "lewd and lascivious acts" with other men (Johannson and Percy 1990). Given the police state that existed during Nazi rule, the court process was frequently subverted and gay men were held in "protective custody" in concentration camps rather than prisons after their arrests, where many were killed (U.S. Holocaust Memorial Museum 2013a). Thus, gay men during The Holocaust were subject to a *de facto* death penalty, even though official state penalties for their behavior were restricted to incarceration for no longer than 10 years (Johannson and Percy 1990).

Some may argue that Uganda's "Anti-homosexuality" bill cannot be considered to be an attempted genocide because it focuses on illegal *behavior* rather than on the persecution of a group. This could be a reflection of the simplistic nature in which same-sex relationships are perceived in homophobic countries. Rather than rely on a more sophisticated understanding of gays and lesbians that incorporates gender identity and sexual orientation, laws targeting LGBT individuals focus only on behavior. Of course, this is likely done intentionally—to recognize the issues surrounding LGBT identities requires an understanding that sexuality is more complicated than defining it by behaviors alone. Evidence of this intentionality can be found in the draft of Uganda's bill, which specifically states "definitions of 'sexual orientation', 'sexual rights', 'sexual minorities', 'gender identity' shall not be used in anyway [*sic*] to legitimize homosexuality, gender identity disorders and related practices in Uganda" (Bahati 2009).

Denial

Stanton indicates that the final stage of every genocide is denial—leaders deny they have perpetrated genocide, and deaths are typically blamed on "ethnic conflict" or on the victims themselves. In the case of Uganda, denial occurs in many forms—homophobic Ugandans deny the history of same-sex relationships in

Africa, the facts about HIV/AIDS spreading primarily through heterosexual contact, and the very nature of what it means to live as an LGBT individual. In the U.S., politicians who oppose same-sex marriage (such as Rick Santorum) explain that such opposition does not imply hatred of gays and lesbians, homophobia, or bigotry, but is instead devotion to the Christian religion (Killough 2011). Religion is used as a justification for genocide, as it has been to justify violence against others throughout history.

Harff's Political Model

In a study of 55 genocides and politicides, Barbara Harff (2003) found several factors significantly related to the likelihood of genocide. Not restricting her sample to incidents defined as genocide in the *Convention*, she includes actions against political groups (politicide) in her analysis. Her results indicate that there are several important predictors of genocide that are also apparent in Uganda.

Political Upheaval

Harff finds that greater political upheaval in the preceding 15 years is likely to result in genocide/politicide. Uganda has experienced significant upheaval since their independence from Britain in 1962 (Mutibwa 1992). After a period of political instability, Idi Amin Dada staged a coup and took over the government, installing himself as leader. A tyrannical leader, Amin's rule was characterized by violence against the population (Jackson and Rosberg 1982). After Amin was defeated and exiled by the Uganda National Liberation Front, the government experienced a series of forcible takeovers until 1986 (Kasozi 1994), when Yoweri Kaguta Museveni was installed as President and has served since (Oloka-Onyango 2004). Uganda has not experienced significant upheaval in the last 25 years; however, the political landscape prior to that time was characterized by constant upheaval, tyrannical dictators, and violence.

Prior Genocides

Harff indicates that countries with prior genocides are more likely to experience future genocides. These are sometimes referred to as bilateral genocides, which occur when genocides are retributive, in retaliation for a prior genocide (Stanton 1998). Some also argue that countries that have experienced genocide are habituated to killing as well as the general violence that goes along with genocide (Fein 1993). Genocidal action against groups has occurred several times in

Uganda. Amin expelled the Asian population in 1972, blaming them as a group for economic conditions in Uganda (Jamal 1976). This type of forced relocation has been identified as a form of genocide in other conflicts, in particular, the forced removal of Armenians from Turkey (Smith et al. 1995). Some have also accused Uganda's current President of attempting genocide against the Acholi people in Northern Uganda (Otunnu 1998). Based on these events, Uganda may be primed for another genocidal action.

Exclusionary Ideologies

Genocides are more likely to occur when rulers subscribe to exclusionary ideologies. Harff (2003, p. 63) defines these as belief systems that identify "some overriding purpose or principle that justifies efforts to restrict, persecute, or eliminate certain categories of people." Harff defines these predominately through political party and religion, and the overlap of the two. For example, governments operating under (extremist Muslim) Shari'a law are exclusionary—the law is defined by religious beliefs, and other religions are not allowed to exist. In Uganda, the extremist Christian majority supports the restriction, persecution, and execution of gay and lesbian people.

Autocratic Rule

Democratic systems of government are unlikely to result in genocide. The checks and balances inherent in these systems usually restrict executive power that can keep a leader from wielding genocidal power (Harff 2003, p. 63). Freedom House (2012) finds that Uganda is not an electoral democracy, and has an overall low freedom score. They cite flawed elections, corruption, crackdown on journalists, and lack of enforcement of human rights violations as contributing to limited freedom. Even though a multiparty system was introduced in 2005, it has not yet delivered a representative democracy. Partially to blame is the degree of power held by the current ruling party, which influences the media to report in their favor and spends significant monies on behalf of incumbents. The position of President in Uganda holds significant power and can run for an unlimited number of 5 year terms (the current President has been in power since 1986).

The ruling National Resistance Movement party (NRM) dominates the political arena, with other parties unable to exert enough political momentum to challenge them. This is due in large part to restrictive party registration requirements, voter and candidate eligibility rules, a lack of access to media coverage, voter intimidation by para-military groups, as well as NRM's use of government resources to support its candidates (Freedom House 2012).

Economic and Political Interdependence

The greater a country depends on other countries and international relationships, the less likely that country will experience a genocide. Countries not dependent on others are unlikely to succumb to international pressure. Harff's (2003, p. 69) analysis indicated that "trade openness" was an important variable for predicting genocides—countries with increased levels of trade openness are much less likely to succumb to genocide and state failures in general. For example, in both Rwanda and Yugoslavia, levels of trade openness decreased steadily leading up to their respective genocides (in 1994, and 1992–1995, respectively) (World Bank 2013).

Uganda's lowest level of trade openness was from 1984 to 1986—the period during which several violent overthrows of the government occurred, resulting in the presidency of Yoweri Museveni in 1986 (the current president). Trade openness was relatively stable from 1991 to 2006, but has increased significantly since then (World Bank 2013). This increased dependence on other countries may serve as a protective factor against genocide, and international pressure may result in a genocide avoided.

Conclusions and Recommendations

In this chapter, we have presented evidence that (1) the attempt to enact the death penalty against "homosexuals" has progressed through the stages of genocide in a similar fashion as other genocides, and (2) the social factors related to genocide are present in Uganda, indicating that the conditions for a genocidal state exist. Even if not recognized as genocide in international law, using capital punishment for homosexuality meets the criteria for genocide as defined by academic research.

According to the *Convention against Genocide*, the execution of homosexuals cannot be considered genocide. By specifying a limited number of groups in the *Convention*, the definition of genocide is narrow, but the range of discrimination that exists is broad. There are social groups in addition to race, ethnicity, religion, and nationality that are also discriminated against and are vulnerable to crimes on the level of genocide. Sexual orientation, political party, gender, and gender identity seem to be important additions to the *Convention*, but there are many other groups not included. While expanding the definition of victimized groups in the *Convention* might help to avoid future genocides, there is likely always a group missing from categories defined in international law. Scholars have suggested broader definitions of genocide that may be more descriptive than the strict legal definition in the *Convention*. Fein (1993) suggests the following definition, which has greater inclusivity:

> Genocide is one way that non-democratic ruling elites resolve real solidarity and legitimacy conflicts, or challenges to their interests against victims decreed outside their universe of obligation [by ideology, religion, nationalism, or group ethnocentrism]

in situations in which 1) a crisis or opportunity [most often associated with war] a) is caused by or blamed on the victim or b) leads people to view the victim as inhibiting national or economic development; and 2) they believe that they can get away with it (Fein 1993, p. 101).

If the "Anti-Homosexuality" bill is an indication that Uganda is headed toward genocide, it is vital that action be taken to halt this progress. Based on Stanton's "Eight Stages," Uganda is currently in the *polarization* stage and attempting to pass laws that have potential to incarcerate much of the LGBT population in that country. According to Stanton, a genocide at this stage can be halted by providing international support to moderate leaders and strengthening human rights groups. More severe measures might include denying international travel visas to extremist leaders, and if necessary, seizing their assets. If the bill is successfully passed, criminal trials and increased incarceration rates of LGBT Ugandans will mark the start of the *preparation* stage, and members of the group will be physically separated from the general population. According to Stanton (1998), armed intervention or heavy assistance from the United Nations is recommended at this stage, which is immediately followed by the *extermination* stage. In addition, the international community should prepare for refugees from Uganda. Given the homophobia in neighboring countries, however, the best strategy to handle people fleeing Uganda (both people of LGBT status as well as their supporters, who are also subject to incarceration) is unclear.

The implications for Uganda from Harff's (2003) work might include the maintaining of a stable political system in the future. The international community should be wary of revolution or government overthrow, as political instability can provide an opportunity for extremists on either side to take control. Encouraging Uganda to adopt a democratic system of government (or at least attempt to reduce corruption and election fraud in the country) could also minimize the chances of a genocide occurring against LGBT Ugandans. As mentioned previously, the increased trade openness demonstrated by Uganda in recent years may help protect the country from becoming a genocidal state.

Uganda is not the only country in which LGBT individuals are under attack. At the time this chapter was written, Russia passed a "Gay Propaganda" law outlawing the publication and distribution of materials that equate gay and straight relationships, as well as outlawing the distribution of gay rights materials (Elder 2013). Thus, Russia appears to be demonstrating evidence of negative classification and symbolization, thereby facilitating the "othering" of LGBT individuals in that country. Public outcry and international pressure may help to ameliorate the situation, but for now Russia's LGBT population is facing increasing marginalization.

Greater awareness of sexual orientation and sexual identity is an important factor in reducing violence against LGBT individuals. The "Kill the Gays" bill in Uganda punishes homosexuality as a behavior, not as an identity. This distinction, however, is not important considering that the behavior is a product of identity, and thus individuals are still being targeted by their identity as gays and lesbians. Since this identity is as inalterable as those that the Convention currently defines in their definition of genocide, it stands to reason that sexual identity should be included as well. Paper presented at the Annual Meeting of the Academy of Criminal Justice Sciences in Dallas, Texas in March 2013. The authors would like to thank Horia Dijmarescu, Vanessa Panfil, and Dana Peterson for their valuable suggestions and feedback.

References

Aderet, O. (2013, September 30). *Israel's monument to gays persecuted by Nazis planned for Tel Aviv Haaretz*. Retrieved from http://www.haaretz.com

Agence France-Presse. (2010, February 17). *Uganda pastor screens gay porn in church*. Retrieved from http://afp.com.

Alvarez, A. (2001). *Governments, citizens, and genocide: A comparative and interdisciplinary approach*. Bloomington, IN: University of Indiana Press.

Associated Press. (2012, November 12). Uganda to pass anti-gay law as 'Christmas gift'. *USA Today*. Retrieved from http://www.usatoday.com.

Bahati, D. (2009). *Bill No. 18: The Anti Homosexuality Bill*.

BBC News. (2005, June 10). Pope rejects condoms for Africa. *BBC News*. Retrieved from http://news.bbc.co.uk.

BBC News. (2012, November 13). Uganda to pass anti-gay law as 'Christmas gift'. *BBC News*, Retrieved from http://www.bbc.co.uk/news/world-africa-20318436.

Bernard, E. J., & Cameron, S. (2013). *Advancing HIV justice: A progress report on achievements and challenges in global advocacy against HIV criminalisation*. Amsterdam, The Netherlands: The Global Network of People Living with HIV (GNP +).

Brown, R. (2012). Corrective rape in South Africa: A continuing plight despite an international human rights response. *Annual Survey of International and Comparative Law, 18*, 45–66.

Chandra, A., Mosher, W. D., Copen, C., & Sionean, C. (2011). Sexual behavior, sexual attraction, and sexual identity in the United States: Data from the 2006–2008 National Survey of Family Growth. *National Health Statistics Reports* (No. 36). Hyattsville, MD: National Center for Health Statistics.

CNN Wire Staff. (2011, May 13). Uganda's parliament takes no action on anti-gay bill. *CNN*. Retrieved from http://edition.cnn.com/2011/WORLD/africa/05/13/uganda.gay/.

Cohen, J., & Tate, T. (2006). The less they know, the better: Abstinence-only HIV/AIDS programs in Uganda. *Reproductive Health Matters, 17*(4), 174–178.

Cohen, S. (1980). *Folk devils and moral panics: The creation of the Mods and Rockers*. Oxford, UK: Martin Robertson & Co.

Dallaire, R. (2004). *Shake hands with the devil: The failure of humanity in Rwanda*. New York, NY: Carroll & Graf.

Dicklitch, S., Yost, B., & Dougan, B. M. (2012). Building a barometer of gay rights (BGR): A case study of Uganda and the persecution of homosexuals. *Human Rights Quarterly, 34*(2), 448–471.

Elder, M. (2013, June 11). Russia passes law banning gay 'propaganda'. *The Guardian*. Retrieved from http://www.guardian.co.uk.

Fein, H. (1993). Accounting for genocide after 1945: Theories and some findings. *International Journal of Group Rights, 1*, 79–106.

Freedom House. (2012). *Freedom in the world: Uganda*. Retrieved from http://www.freedomhouse.org.

Friedlander, H. (1994). Step by step: The expansion of murder, 1939–1941. *German Studies Review, 17*(3), 495–507.

Gatsiounis, I. (2011, February 14). Killing of gay activist in Uganda triggers more threats of violence. *The Washington Times*. Retrieved from http://www.washingtontimes.com.

Gettleman, J. (2010, January 3). Americans' role seen in Uganda anti-gay push. *The New York Times*. Retrieved from http://www.nytimes.com/2010/01/04/world/africa/04uganda.html.

Harff, B. (2003). No lessons learned from The Holocaust? Assessing risks of genocide and political mass murder since 1955. *American Political Science Review, 97*(1), 57–73.

Hoad, N. (2007). *African intimacies: Race, homosexuality, and globalization*. Minneapolis, MN: University of Minnesota Press.

Hollander, M. (2009). Gay rights in Uganda: Seeking to overturn Uganda's anti-sodomy laws. *Virginia Journal of International Law, 50*(1), 220–221.

Houreld, K., & Olukya, G. (2009, December 8). Uganda considering death penalty for gays. *The Huffington Post*. Retrieved from http://www.huffingtonpost.com/2009/12/08/uganda-considering-death_n_384650.html.

Human Rights First. (2012). *The road to safety: Strengthening protection for LGBTI refugees in Uganda and Kenya*. New York, NY: Human Rights First.

Human Rights Watch. (2009). *Comments to Uganda's parliamentary committee on HIV/AIDS and related matters about the HIV/AIDS prevention and control bill*. Retrieved from http://www.hrw.org.

Human Rights Watch. (2013). This alien legacy: The origins of 'sodomy' laws in British colonialism. In C. Lennox & M. Waites (Eds.), *Human rights, sexual orientation and gender identity in The Commonwealth: Struggles for decriminalisation and change* (pp. 83–123). London, UK: Institute for Commonwealth Studies, Institute of Germanic & Romance Studies, Human Rights Consortium.

International Criminal Tribunal for Rwanda. (2003). *Summary: The Prosecutor v. Ferdinand Nahimana, Jean-Bosco Barayagwiza, and Hassan Ngeze* (Case No. ICTR-99-52-T).

Itaborahy, L. P., & Zhu, J. (2013). *State-sponsored homophobia: A world survey of laws: Criminalisation, protection, and recognition of same-sex love*. Brussels, Belgium: The International Lesbian, Gay, Bisexual, Trans and Intersex Association.

Jackson, R. H., & Rosberg, C. G. (1982). *Personal rule in Black Africa*. Berkeley, CA: University of California Press.

Jamal, V. (1976). Asians in Uganda, 1880–1972: Inequality and expulsion. *The Economic History Review, 29*(4), 602–616.

Johannson, W., & Percy, W. (1990). *Homosexuals in Nazi Germany*. Los Angeles, CA: Simon Wiesenthal Center Annual, Vol 7.

Jones, A. (2006). *Genocide: A comprehensive introduction*. New York, NY: Routledge.

Jjuuko, A. (2013). The incremental approach: Uganda's struggle for the decriminalisation of homosexuality. In C. Lennox & M. Waites (Eds.), *Human rights, sexual orientation and gender identity in The Commonwealth: Struggles for decriminalisation and change* (pp. 381–408). London, UK: Institute for Commonwealth Studies, Institute of Germanic & Romance Studies, Human Rights Consortium.

Kasozi, A. B. K. (1994). *The social origins of violence in Uganda: 1964-1985*. Quebec, ON: McGill-Queen's University Press.

Killough, A. (2011, August 31). Santorum decries charges of bigotry. *CNN*. Retrieved from http://www.cnn.com.

Kinsey, A. C., Pomeroy, W. B., & Martin, C. E. (1948). *Sexual behavior in the human male*. Philadelphia, PA: W.B. Saunders Co.

Kirby, M. (2013). The sodomy offence: England's least lovely criminal law export? In C. Lennox & M. Waites (Eds.), *Human rights, sexual orientation and gender identity in The Commonwealth: Struggles for decriminalisation and change* (pp. 61–82). London, UK: Institute for Commonwealth Studies, Institute of Germanic & Romance Studies, Human Rights Consortium.

Kosciw, J. G., Greytak, E. A., Bartkiewicz, M. J., Boesen, M. J., & Palmer, N. A. (2012). *The 2011 national school climate survey: The experiences of lesbian, gay, bisexual and transgender youth in our nation's schools*. New York, NY: Gay, Lesbian & Straight Education Network.

Kron, J. (2012, February 29). Resentment toward the West bolsters Uganda's new Anti-Gay Bill. *The New York Times*. Retrieved from http://www.nytimes.com/2012/02/29/world/africa/ugandan-lawmakers-push-anti-homosexuality-bill-again.html?pagewanted=all.

Law Library of Congress. (2011, January 4). *Uganda: Court rules leaking of homosexuals' identity by media unlawful*. Retrieved from http://www.loc.gov/lawweb/servlet/lloc_news?disp3_l205402456_text.

Lennox, C., & Waites, M. (2013). Human rights, sexual orientation and gender identity in the Commonwealth: From history and law to developing activism and transnational dialogues. In C. Lennox & M. Waites (Eds.), *Human rights, sexual orientation and gender identity in The Commonwealth: Struggles for decriminalisation and change* (pp. 1–59). London, UK: Institute for Commonwealth Studies, Institute of Germanic & Romance Studies, Human Rights Consortium.

MacKinnon, C. A. (1994). Rape, genocide, and women's human rights. *Harvard Women's Law Journal, 17*, 5–16.

Mayerson, D. (2010). Race relations in Rwanda: An historical perspective. Proceedings from *Challenging Politics: Critical Voices, Abstracts, and Papers*. Brisbane, Australia: University of Queensland Press.

Melloy, K. (2010, November 16). Uganda newspapers continue gay-hate campaign. *Edge Boston*. Retrieved from http://edgeboston.com.

Mujuzi, J. (2009). The absolute prohibition of same-sex marriages in Uganda. *International Journal of Law, Policy, and the Family, 23*(3), 277–288.

Mutibwa, P. (1992). *Uganda since independence: A story of unfulfilled hopes*. Trenton, NJ: Africa World Press.

National Public Radio Staff. (2011, May 12).The history of Uganda's anti-gay bill. *National Public Radio*. Retrieved from http://www.npr.org/2011/05/12/136241591/professor-traces-history-of-ugandas-anti-homosexuality-bill.

Olukya, G., & Straziuso, J. (2010, October 19). Gays in Uganda say they're living in fear. *NBC News*. Retrieved from http://www.nbcnews.com.

Oloka-Onyango, J. (2004). 'New breed' leadership, conflict, and reconstruction in the Great Lakes region of Africa: A sociopolitical biography of Uganda's Yoweri Kaguta Museveni. *Africa Today, 50*(3), 29–52.

Onziema, P.J. (2013, January 25). Living proudly in face of Uganda's anti-gay bill. *CNN*. Retrieved from http://www.cnn.com/2013/01/25/opinion/onziema-uganda-anti-gay.

Otunnu, O. 1998. The path to genocide in northern Uganda. *Refuge: Canada's Journal of Refugees, 17*(3), 4–13.

Petros, G., Airhihenbuwa, C. O., Simbayi, L., Ramlagan, S., & Brown, B. (2006). HIV/AIDS and 'othering' in South Africa: The blame goes on. *Culture, Health & Sexuality: An International Journal for Research, Intervention and Care, 8*(1), 67–77.

Perry, B. (2001). *In the name of hate: Understanding hate crimes*. New York, NY: Routledge.

Pew Research Center. (2002). *What the world thinks in 2002*. Washington, DC: The Pew Research Center.

Pew Research Center. (2013). *The global divide on homosexuality*. Washington, DC: The Pew Research Center.

Plant, R. (1988). *The pink triangle: The Nazi war against homosexuals*. New York, NY: Henry Holt and Company.

Republic of South Africa. (2007). *Criminal law (sexual offences and related matters) Amendment act (No. 32)*. Retrieved from http://www.info.gov.za.

Rice, X. (2011, April 26). Death by tabloid. *The Atlantic*. Retrieved from http://www.theatlantic.com/.

Ross, M. W., Essien, E. J., Williams, M. L., & Fernandez-Esquer, M. E. (2003). Concordance between sexual behavior and sexual identity in street outreach samples of four racial/ethnic groups. *Sexually Transmitted Diseases, 30*(2), 110–113.

Schoepf, B. G. (2010). Assessing AIDS research in Africa: Twenty-five years later. *African Studies Review, 53*(1), 105–142. World Health Organization, Global Health Observatory Health Repository. Available at: http://apps.who.int/ghodata/?theme=country.

Sell, R. L. (1997). Defining and measuring sexual orientation: A review. *Archives of Sexual Behavior, 26*(6), 643–658.

Smith, R. (2003, December 3). The Impact of Hate Media in Rwanda. *BBC News.* Retrieved from http://news.bbc.co.uk.

Smith, R. W., Markusen, E., & Lifton, R. J. (1995). Professional ethics and the denial of Armenian genocide. *Holocaust and Genocide Studies, 9*(1), 1–22.

Spurlin, W. J. (2006). *Imperialism within the margins: Queer representation and the politics of culture in Southern Africa.* New York, NY: Palgrave Macmillan.

Strand, C. (2011). Kill Bill! Ugandan human rights organizations' attempts to influence the media's coverage of the anti-homosexuality bill. *Culture, Health, and Sexuality, 13*(8), 917.

Stokes, P., & Gabriel, Y. (2010). Engaging with genocide: The challenge for organization and management studies. *Organization Studies, 17*(4), 461–480.

Stanton, G.H. (1998). *The 8 stages of genocide.* Washington, DC: Genocide Watch. Retrieved from http://www.genocidewatch.org/genocide/8stagesofgenocide.html.

Tamale, S. (2007). Out of the closet: Unveiling sexuality discourses in Uganda. In C. M. Cole, et al. (Eds.), *Africa after gender?* (pp. 18–19). Bloomington, IN: Indiana University Press.

Uganda Penal Code Act. (1990). *Chapter 106.* Kampala, Uganda: Universal House Law Reports.

United Nations. (1948). *Convention on the prevention and punishment of the crime of genocide.* Retrieved from http://treaties.un.org/.

United States Holocaust Memorial Museum. (n.d.). *Nazi persecution of homosexuals: 1933–1945.* Retrieved from http://www.ushmm.org.

United States Holocaust Memorial Museum. (2013a). Law and justice in the Third Reich. *Holocaust Encyclopedia.* Retrieved from http://www.ushmm.org.

United States Holocaust Memorial Museum. (2013b). The Holocaust and World War II: Timeline. Retrieved from http://www.ushmm.org.

Walch, S. E., Orlosky, M. A., Sinkkanen, K. A., & Stevens, H. R. (2010). Demographic and social factors associated with homophobia and fear of AIDS in a community sample. *Journal of Homosexuality, 57*(2), 310–324.

Ward, K. (2013). Religious institutions and actors and religious attitudes to homosexual rights: South Africa and Uganda. In C. Lennox & M. Waites (Eds.), *Human rights, sexual orientation and gender identity in The Commonwealth: Struggles for decriminalisation and change* (pp. 409–427). London, UK: Institute for Commonwealth Studies, Institute of Germanic & Romance Studies, Human Rights Consortium.

Woolf, L. M., & Hulzer, M. R. (2005). Psychosocial roots of genocide: Risk, prevention, and intervention. *Journal of Genocide Research, 7*(1), 101–128.

World Bank. (2013). World development indicators. Retrieved from http://data.worldbank.org/country/Uganda

World Health Organization. (2011). *Prevention and treatment of HIV and other sexually transmitted infections among men who have sex with men and transgender people.* Retrieved from http://whqlibdoc.who.int/publications/2011/9789241501750_eng.pdf.

Chapter 17
Presumptive Criminals: U.S. Criminal Law and HIV-Related Aggravated Assaults

Ari Ezra Waldman

Abstract In choosing to criminalize the attempted spread of the Human Immunodeficiency Virus (HIV), several United States jurisdictions not only ignore the public health harms associated with their draconian approach, but also commit logical and due process errors in their prosecutions, thus discriminating against the HIV-positive population. In this chapter, I consider a common case where jurisdictions use aggravated assault—an assault by means likely to produce grievous bodily harm or death. By looking at several cases in depth, I show that certain courts use a guilt-by-association rule, sweeping in all HIV-positive individuals under the criminal law regardless of the likelihood of transmission, which is a key element in any aggravated assault charge. Many courts do not distinguish between those who have high viral loads and those who virtually cannot transmit the disease at all—namely, those who are on highly active antiretroviral therapy, have an undetectable viral load, use condoms, and have no sexually transmitted infections. The chapter concludes by highlighting the discriminatory effect of criminalization.

Keywords HIV · AIDS · Criminal law · Gay · LGBT · HIV criminalization · HIV-positive · Aggravated assault · Due process · Public health

Ari Ezra Waldman, Associate Director, Institute for Information Law and Policy, New York Law School; Ph.D. Candidate, Columbia University; J.D., Harvard Law School; A.B., *magna cum laude*, Harvard College. A version of this chapter was originally published as an article at Ari Ezra Waldman, *Exceptions: The Criminal Law's Illogical Approach to HIV-Related Aggravated Assaults*, 18 VA. J. L. & SOC. POL'Y 552 (2011). It has been used with permission. It also includes excerpts from Ari Ezra Waldman, *Ask a Lawyer: The Injustice of HIV Criminalization*, BETA Blog, May 3, 2013, at http://betablog.org/ask-a-lawyer-the-injustice-of-hiv-criminalization.

A. E. Waldman (✉)
New York Law School, 185 West Broadway, New York, NY 10013, USA
e-mail: ari.waldman@nyls.edu

D. Peterson and V. R. Panfil (eds.), *Handbook of LGBT Communities, Crime, and Justice*, DOI: 10.1007/978-1-4614-9188-0_17, © Springer Science+Business Media New York 2014

Introduction

In the U.S. State of Georgia, a woman was sentenced to 8 years in jail for failing to disclose her HIV status to a male partner, despite witnesses' statements that he already knew she was HIV-positive. There is a man in Ohio who is serving 4 years for failing to tell his ex-girlfriend that he was HIV-positive, even though the case was motivated by the ex-lover's jealous rage. And an Iowa jury ignored two essential facts—an undetectable viral load and condom use—when it sentenced a young man to 25 years after a one-time sexual encounter with another man. These cases (*Ginn v. Georgia* 2008; *Ohio v. Roberts* 2004; *Rhoades v. Iowa* 2012; Schoettes 2011) are not aberrations. They are products of outdated laws and irrational legal standards that are ostensibly justified on the ground of preventing the spread of HIV, but bear little connection to that or any other legitimate public health goal.

Many U.S. jurisdictions use the traditional criminal law—specifically, the crime of aggravated assault—to criminalize HIV exposure. Some states have created a separate crime of intentional HIV exposure, passed statutes that enhance criminal penalties when someone who is HIV-positive commits a crime, or applied general sexually transmitted infection statutes to HIV exposure. Numerous scholars (e.g., McGuire 1999; Wolf and Vezina 2004) have traced the development of these criminal laws, analyzed their effectiveness, and detailed doctrinal issues plaguing these statutes, such as overbreadth, vagueness, and practical difficulties of proving intent. And yet, while this scholarship has ably criticized these various strategies from afar, it has failed to address certain details. In particular, I argue that HIV-positive defendants charged with aggravated assault for risking transmission of HIV are victims of rules of thumb: instead of requiring the State to prove that the defendant on trial acted in a manner "likely" to cause substantial harm or death—a necessary element of aggravated assault—some courts rely on the generalized rule of thumb that unprotected sex can transmit HIV. At issue in aggravated assault prosecutions is likelihood, and the likelihood of transmission varies from one HIV-positive individual to another. This chapter identifies how courts use rules of thumb in HIV-related aggravated assault cases and, as a result, run afoul of logic and violate the due process rights of most HIV-positive defendants.

The Science of the Likelihood of Transmitting HIV

The members of the HIV-positive community are fungible, or interchangeable, only as individuals distinct from members of the HIV-negative community. But once an individual is HIV-positive, his or her particular condition—its gestation, physical manifestation, susceptibility to infection, and risk of transmission, to name just a few factors—takes a unique track that requires more narrowly tailored classifications (Murphy 2009; The different stages of HIV infection 2011). Those narrow classifications can mean the difference between guilt and innocence on an aggravated assault charge because conviction of that crime requires proof of *likelihood* of harm. There are two major medical factors that speak directly to the likelihood that a given HIV-positive individual's actions could transmit the virus. First, the amount of virus in the individual's blood and his/her body's immunological response, and second, the nature and effectiveness of his particular therapy. In many cases, United States jurisdictions ignore both.

There are two commonly used tests that track HIV progression. The $CD4^+$ cell count, more commonly known as the T-cell count, has traditionally been the best marker. $CD4^+$ tests measure the number of T-cells containing the $CD4^+$ receptor. It is this $CD4^+$ cell, or lymphocyte, that HIV progressively destroys (Berkow 1997). Therefore, the lower the $CD4^+$ count, the further the disease has progressed and the worse the patient's symptoms are (http://TheBody.com 2010). By contrast, HIV-positive persons who are able to keep viral replication at low levels and maintain high $CD4^+$ T-cell counts over a prolonged period of time are considered long-term nonprogressors (Murphy 2009). Approximately 5 % of the HIV-positive population meets this definition and many more can become long-term nonprogressors by taking effective medication (Murphy 2009). Because they maintain high $CD4^+$ cell counts over many years, long-term nonprogressors deviate from the hypothetical average HIV-positive individual, whose $CD4^+$ cell count drops upon infection, increases shortly thereafter, and then begins a mostly gradual decline (Goicoechea 2009).

The other type of HIV marker tracks the virus's viral count. A viral load test measures the amount of a virus present in the blood by measuring the amount of HIV-specific RNA (Murphy 2009). This is a more accurate, direct way to measure the virus. Studies have shown that HIV viral RNA levels are highly correlated with response to therapy and can predict progression to AIDS (Murphy 2009). They also can assess the extent to which the HIV virus poses a risk to the patient and his or her sexual partners: the lower a patient's viral load, the healthier the patient, the lower the chance of progression from HIV to AIDS, and the lower the probability of transmission (Atia 2009).

Viral load tests can indicate "low" (between 40 and 500 copies/mL) and "undetectable" viral loads (lower than 40 copies/mL) (Wilson 2008). Long-term nonprogressors usually have undetectable levels of HIV RNA for much of their lives, but any HIV-positive individual's viral load can drop to undetectable levels for shorter periods (Murphy 2009). Although an undetectable viral load does not mean that the patient is cured, it may mean that either the HIV RNA is not present in his or her blood or that the level of HIV RNA is below the threshold needed for detection. Studies indicate that the risk of transmission varies directly with the viral load at all levels (Atia 2009). A recent study confirmed that those with undetectable viral loads who take Highly Active Antiretroviral Therapy (HAART), use a condom during sexual intercourse, and have no other infections or sexually transmitted diseases could not transmit HIV (HPTN 2011). The test can efficiently distinguish among HIV-positive individuals as to the likelihood that their actions could transmit the disease.

There are various drugs currently available that tend to impede the progression of HIV, reduce and ameliorate symptoms, and improve a patient's immunoresponse (U.S. Department of Health and Human Services 2012), with the most effective treatment being HAART. HAART is the combination of at least three antiretroviral drugs that attack different parts of HIV or stop the virus from entering blood cells, and it has been shown to modulate an HIV-positive patient's immune system and even reduce his/her viral load to undetectable levels (Montaner 2010). HAART is not a cure (DeNoon 2010), but studies have shown that the combination of effective HAART and low viral loads have effectively neutralized HIV's ability both to replicate inside the patient's blood and to be transmitted through his/her bodily fluids to another (Atia 2009).

The HIV-positive population, then, is varied with respect to each individual's risk of transmission. For example, there are those who remain asymptomatic and whose conditions never progress, those who experience symptoms for 5 years and then none for 50, and those whose only symptom is fatigue. It is rare that these HIV-positive individuals can transmit the virus, even with unprotected sex. And the scientific and medical tools to identify this heterogeneity or, more specifically, to identify deviations from the average, are readily available.

The risk of transmission is of paramount legal significance. HIV status often becomes an issue at trial specifically because an HIV-positive defendant committed an act that risked the transmission of the virus (e.g., McGuire 1999; Wolf and Vezina 2004). The elements of the crime of aggravated assault, for example, make this clear. The crime is incumbent upon the *likelihood* of harm through a particular means, not the harm itself. The victim's HIV status after the interaction should be irrelevant to the prosecution's case. Rather, the likelihood that the defendant could have caused harm is pertinent, and this likelihood varies with a defendant's viral load. Since a viral load test is readily available, there is no need to rely on a general rule of thumb about transmission through bodily fluids. The viral load test, as well as the T-cell count before it, not to mention an effective HAART regimen, can distinguish among the heterogeneous HIV population and find the exceptional cases to which the general rule does not apply.

Despite the ability to single out those with exceedingly low risk of transmission, U.S. jurisdictions that use the traditional criminal law to criminalize the possible transmission of HIV tend to rely on generalized evidence that refers to the average HIV-positive individual. Some simply rely upon a general rule of thumb that all the State needs to do to satisfy the likelihood of transmission prong of aggravated assault is to introduce into evidence the Centers for Disease Control and Prevention's (CDC) fact sheet that states that "HIV is spread by sexual contact" (CDC 1999). Even where the rule of thumb happens to apply to the particular defendant on trial, principles of due process suggest that such generalized information should not fulfill the State's obligation to prove that the defendant on trial, as opposed to the HIV-positive population as a whole, committed the charged crime. Other courts will even apply the rule of thumb to a case *they know* is unique—one in which the defendant is a long-term nonprogressor. In these jurisdictions, it does not matter that the likelihood of transmission was infinitesimally small because "likelihood" has been interpreted to mean mere "possibility." This makes the unique circumstances of the defendant's situation irrelevant. In other words, these courts commit the Fallacy of Accident.

The Accident Fallacy

The Fallacy Explained

The Accident Fallacy occurs when a general rule is applied to a specific situation in which the rule—because of unique individual facts, or "accidents"—is inapplicable. The mistake occurs when the general rule is applied inappropriately so it misses salient differences in a heterogeneous population and fails to recognize exceptions where they should exist or when a rule of thumb is used to come to over-inclusive conclusions. It has two steps: (1) generalize about a population, and (2) incorrectly use that generalization to describe a unique subset of that population (Engel 1999). For example, the statement "birds can fly" may be true, but it is not always true. There are exceptions: flightless birds, injured birds, or birds whose feet are stuck in gum (De Lollis 2007). Because of these observable exceptions, flight is not the determinative factor for classifying animals as birds. Rules of thumb, then, can be useful shorthand descriptors only when ignoring distinctions or denying heterogeneity in a population is acceptable. The Fallacy, then, is a problematic tool for legal reasoning.

It should already be evident how this Fallacy applies to certain defendants in HIV-positive aggravated assaults. The general rule that HIV is spread through sexual contact with an infected person may be true, but it fails to account for infected persons who, by virtue of their low viral loads, highly effective HAART regimes, use of condoms, and lack of sexually transmitted infections have been found to be virtually unable to transmit HIV during sexual contact. Admittedly, "virtually unable" and "unable" are two different things. To be absolutely certain that someone cannot transmit the disease would require a cure, without which, there is always some possibility of transmission. However, that something is medically *possible* is not sufficient to prove criminality. Aggravated assault requires a means *likely* to cause substantial harm or death. A prosecutor should not be able to use evidence of a statistically insignificant possibility in order to prove likelihood.

Logical "Accident" as a Due Process Problem

The Accident Fallacy raises due process concerns. Implicit in the concept of due process is the requirement that the State prove beyond a reasonable doubt that the particular defendant on trial committed the charged crime (*In re* Winship 1970).

To do so, prosecutors must prove every element of the crime beyond a reasonable doubt (*In re* Winship 1970). To illustrate this, consider two hypothetical proffers of proof for two different crimes: It would be sufficient to prove intent to cause serious bodily injury if a defendant slashed at his victim with a pocket knife and repeatedly punched his victim's head. However, recourse to the dubious assumption that all socialists want to overthrow the government would be insufficient to prove that a defendant who attended a Socialist Party-sponsored pro-labor rally was guilty of plotting to overthrow the government. This is true for two reasons. First, some socialists may want to overthrow the government, but many would prefer to work within the system and change our social priorities to meet their preferences (Sanders 2011). So to convict a defendant of plotting to overthrow the government based on a general (and ill-informed) rule would ignore those exceptions. Second, the generalized assumption does not prove that the particular defendant's conduct met any element of the crime of plotting to overthrow the government, thus relieving the State of its burden of proving that the defendant is actually guilty of the crime with which he is charged.

There are, then, two due process problems in many HIV-related aggravated assault cases. One concerns *what* the State must prove and the other concerns *how* the state must prove it. The first problem occurs when courts allow the State to prove "likelihood" with evidence of mere "possibility." This "Anything is Possible" standard raises due process concerns: to permit conviction under a theory of mere possibility is to redefine the likelihood requirement.

The second due process error is in the manner in which the State proves likelihood. *In re Winship* (1970) requires the State to prove that the defendant's conduct meets each element of the crime beyond a reasonable doubt. This necessarily forces the State to distinguish between the defendant and any class of persons to which he belongs because generalizations as to the behavior of that class cannot logically speak to the allegedly culpable behavior of one of its members. This "Impersonal Guilt" theory stereotypes an entire class and, therefore, cannot establish criminal culpability.

"Anything is possible" as a legal standard. The principle that one can only be convicted of a crime if every element of that crime is proven "beyond a reasonable doubt" has always been a part of the bedrock of the criminal law, which, as Justice Brennan explained, was likely why the Court had never been so explicit before *In re Winship*. The Court explicitly laid out this principle in *Winship* and emphasized various rationales, including the need to balance the gravity of a criminal conviction against the possibility of fact-finding error. Justice Brennan noted that what is at stake in any criminal trial is the defendant's "transcend[ent]" interest in his liberty, and, given the nature of that interest, the reasonable doubt standard ensures that his liberty is not taken away because of a mere mistake (*In re Winship* 1970). But when the burden of persuasion is lowered to the point where a scintilla of evidence would be sufficient, a court would allow convictions despite errors of fact and logic. It would obviate the need for a reasonable doubt standard: there can be no reasonable doubt of anything since anything is possible.

Consider the opposite context—namely, what constitutes reasonable doubt. It seems clear that "anything is possible" has never been a *reasonable* doubt. Judge Posner, in affirming a conviction for an accountant who thought that embezzled funds were tax exempt, found that while it is possible for an experienced accountant to be so willfully obtuse, the possibility was too remote and implausible (*United States v. Ytem* 2001). After all, "*[a]nything* is possible; there are no metaphysical certainties accessible to human reason; but a merely metaphysical doubt... is not a reasonable doubt for the purposes of the criminal law" (*United States v. Ytem* 2001, pp. 395, 397). This principle does not only exclude the fanciful ("it is possible that I will burst into flames"), but also the realistic, yet remote: "It is possible to have doubts that are not reasonable" (*United States v. Delpit* 1996).

If mere possibility cannot survive as a reasonable doubt, it cannot survive as proof beyond a reasonable doubt. After all, there can be no reasonable doubt that anything is possible. And "anything is possible" cannot survive constitutional scrutiny as a basis for criminal conviction. This makes logical sense. The statement that "anyone could have grabbed the gun from me in the dark" is neither a reason to exclude anyone as a suspect nor a reason to charge everyone else with the crime (Lynn 1985). If it were, everyone would be charged with everything, no one would be convicted of anything, and the reasonable doubt standard would have no meaning.

That something may be possible, however, is exactly what certain U.S. states and the U.S. military courts have accepted as proof beyond a reasonable doubt in cases involving HIV-related aggravated assault. By lowering the burden on the government to prove only that HIV could possibly be transmitted, these jurisdictions have obviated the need for a reasonable doubt standard. There can be no scintilla of doubt, let alone a reasonable one, that HIV *can* theoretically be transmitted through sexual intercourse. For that matter, oral sex, spitting, biting, or getting scratched by a monkey can theoretically transmit HIV, but all are quite unlikely means of transmission (Avert 2011a, b).

Guilt is personal. The possibility of conviction pursuant to a mistake is overshadowed by the "certainty that [the defendant] would be stigmatized by the conviction" (*In re Winship* 1970). This is another possible rationale for the *Winship* decision. The reasonable doubt standard reduces the margin for fact-finding error and places the burden of persuasion on the government in order to protect the defendant from two independent errors—mistake and stigmatization—both of which are anathematic to due process (*In re Winship* 1970).

Stigmatization in the HIV context is evident in two ways. First, by making it easier to convict HIV-positive defendants on aggravated assault charges, conviction pursuant to nonspecific proof devalues *Winship*'s due process concern for the gravity of a criminal conviction. Second, permitting this factual mistake necessarily stigmatizes HIV-positive individuals as presumptive criminals. If one HIV-positive individual is considered to be just as infectious as another, all are subsumed under the average transmission rate and that rate is sufficient to prove likelihood of transmission for the purposes of aggravated assault, then merely being HIV-positive fulfills an element of the crime. This stigmatization is not only a product of assigning criminal culpability to the status of being HIV-positive, but it speaks to a salient rationale of the *Winship* Court: inherent in due process is that guilt must be "personal" (*Pinkerton v. United States* 1946).

The reasonable doubt standard "provides concrete substance for the presumption of innocence" (*In re Winship* 1970, p. 363) and animates the correlative moral assumption of the criminal law that conviction cannot be based on being a bad guy (Lynch 1987) or being a member of a certain group. Defendants are guilty not because they know, or are related to, known criminals or because they share a common identity with disfavored groups (*Templeton v. United States* 1945). In *Bridges v. Wixon* (1945) the Court faced a challenge to a statute that ordered deportation of all aliens affiliated with groups that advocated the violent overthrow of the government. The Court stopped Bridges's deportation but declined to address the constitutional issues in the case. Justice Murphy would have declared the statute unconstitutional: "The deportation statute completely ignores the traditional American doctrine requiring personal guilt rather than guilt by association.... The doctrine of personal guilt is one of the most fundamental principles of our jurisprudence" (*Bridges v. Wixon* 1945, p. 163). Similarly, in *Scales v. United States* (1961), though it upheld a statute criminalizing membership in the Communist Party, the Court saw personal guilt as a mandate of due process. Guilt is personal, the Court held, and the only way vicarious conspiracy liability could meet the requirements of due process was if the *mens rea* of a particular defendant could be implied from the extent of his participation in the Party's criminal activity (*Scales v. United States* 1961).

The personal guilt doctrine embodied in the reasonable doubt standard recognizes that culpability cannot be based on status, identity, or association, but must be based on action. HIV-positive individuals charged with aggravated assault for risking transmission of HIV face the risks of both factual mistake and stigmatization when the elements of the crime can be proven with nonspecific proof. The *average* risk of transmission posed by the average HIV-positive man who has a sexual encounter with the average HIV-negative woman does not speak to the particular risk posed by a particular defendant's sexual encounter. The defendant may have an exceedingly low viral load, which would place him far afield from the hypothetical average. He also may not have had any of the risk factors for making transmission more likely. To ignore these circumstances and convict based on averages is logical and constitutional error.

Nevertheless, defendants charged with aggravated assault for having unprotected sex while HIV-positive are confronted with this precise due process error. To allow the likelihood element of aggravated assault to be proven without reference to a defendant's specific risk of transmission, but instead by the medical possibility that, as a member of the HIV-positive community, he could transmit the virus, is to subject a defendant to guilt by association. If such so-called evidence can prove an element of a crime, then mere membership in that class—regardless of any unique facts that could distinguish a particular individual from the crowd—becomes part of the crime.

Logical "Accident" and Errors in the Criminalization of Transmission Through the Traditional Criminal Law

Different U.S. jurisdictions have chosen different ways to use the criminal law as a sword against HIV. Some state legislatures have created the crime of "criminal transmission of HIV" while other jurisdictions have taken recourse to common law crimes, such as aggravated assault. In the latter case, the specific elements of the crime vary across jurisdictions, but they usually involve some combination of the (1) use of a dangerous weapon (2) in a physical attack (3) in a manner that is likely (4) to cause serious harm or death. It is when considering the likelihood element of the crime that certain courts may commit the Accident Fallacy.

This chapter studies proof of the likelihood element in HIV-related aggravated assaults in two radically different contexts. The first series of cases involves biting, where a belligerent HIV-positive individual bites another person. The second series of cases involves consensual sex between an HIV-positive individual and an HIV-negative individual who is unaware of his or her partner's HIV status. In some of these cases, courts commit only the first step toward the Accident Fallacy, i.e., using general rules of thumb as evidence. This occurs when the likelihood element is satisfied by recourse to general data about HIV infections without determining if the defendant differs from the norm in some way. In other cases, courts commit the Accident Fallacy by taking a general rule of thumb and inappropriately applying it to a unique situation. This occurs when the defendant proves he deviates from the norm and yet the court still applies the general rule to his case. In both scenarios, due process errors accompany the logical errors.

The Biting Cases

Brock v. State (1989) is one in a series of "biting" cases, in which an HIV-positive individual bit his victim (Avert 2011). It is also a case where a court sought generalized proof of the likelihood prong, potentially misapplying a rule of thumb to a particular case in the process. While only potential Accident Fallacies, these cases represent real violations of due process.

Brock was a prisoner confined to the AIDS unit of an Alabama correctional facility where, during a routine search for contraband, he bit a prison guard on the arm (*Brock v. State* 1989). He was found guilty of first-degree assault, a conviction ultimately overturned on appeal. In Alabama at the time, the first-degree assault statute required proof, in relevant part, that the defendant "cause[d] serious physical injury to any person by means of a deadly weapon or a dangerous instrument" (*Brock v. State* 1989, p. 287). In dispute in this case was the "dangerous instrument" prong, which was defined as anything that "under the circumstances in which it is used… is highly capable of causing death or serious physical injury" (p. 287).

This language is common to many aggravated assault statutes. In Alabama, the "capability" of the weapon to cause great harm is modified or delimited both by "highly" and by "the circumstances in which it is used" in the particular case at hand. Therefore, in order to prove this element of the crime beyond a reasonable doubt, the government must put forth specific evidence that whatever weapon was used in this case was actually used in a way that was highly capable of causing serious harm or death (*Medford v. State* 1919). If the legislature had intended otherwise, it could have crafted a first-degree assault statute that omitted the modifier "highly." In such a statute, the word "weapon" would modify the word "capable," implying that the proof of capability must be about the weapon itself. In the Alabama statute at issue in *Brock*, the "circumstances in which [the weapon] was used" modified the phrase "highly capable," suggesting a qualitatively different source of proof.

Even the *Brock* Court recognized this distinction when it noted that Alabama follows the minority view that "depending upon the circumstances of their use," fists could constitute "deadly weapons" or "dangerous instruments" for the purposes of first-degree assault (*Brock v. State* 1989; *Stewart v. State* 1981). Therefore, the specific circumstances that gave rise to the indictment are salient. To the court's credit, it found that the State failed to prove that Brock used his bite in a way that was highly capable of causing serious physical injury (*Brock v. State* 1989). In stating what evidence would have sufficed, however, the court ignored the language of the statute and, if not for the State's ineptitude, would have allowed the State to commit the Accident Fallacy. In *Brock* (1989), the State failed to present any evidence about HIV or AIDS in the form of expert testimony or scientific evidence. Therefore, the court concluded that "[w]hile AIDS may very well be transmitted through *a* human bite, there was no evidence to that effect at trial…." (*Brock v. State* 1989, p. 288). But if evidence that a hypothetical human bite could transmit HIV or AIDS would have sufficed for the purposes of meeting the "highly capable" prong of first-degree assault, "the circumstances in which it is used" prong and the individual characteristics of the bite are neglected entirely. The court would have accepted generalized proof, if any existed, of the rule of thumb that HIV can be transmitted through a human bite. Had it applied that general rule, the court might have committed the Fallacy of Accident and lessened the prosecution's burden by broadening an essential element of the crime.

A similar error occurred in the Georgia case of *Scroggins v. State* (1990). During a violent fracas involving officers, a belligerent Scroggins brought up saliva into his mouth and bit an officer on the forearm, tearing through the officer's shirt, and leaving distinct bite marks (*Scroggins v. State* 1990). A jury convicted him of aggravated assault with intent to murder, and Scroggins appealed, claiming that "there was no evidence the HIV virus can be transmitted by human saliva,… [and] there is at best only a 'theoretical possibility' the virus can be transmitted" this way (*Scroggins v. State* 1990, p. 16).

Scroggins identified the potential for two logical fallacies. At trial, a medical expert testified that while theoretically possible, there had been no documented cases and only two reports of HIV transmission through saliva (*Scroggins v. State* 1990).

Scroggins argued, therefore, that he was the victim of an illogical double whammy where a hasty generalization, creating a general rule from insufficient facts, was erroneously applied to the unique circumstances, or "accidents," of his case. Even if it were possible to transmit the disease through a bite, he argued that his particular bite could not (*Scroggins v. State* 1990).

Responding to the merits of Scroggins' argument in dicta, the court concluded as Scroggins feared. The expert had testified that even though there were only two unconfirmed reports of transmission through biting, he would not French kiss an HIV-positive woman and that standard medical procedure required physicians to wear protective gloves when dealing with any bodily fluids (*Scroggins v. State* 1990). After this and other testimony from the expert, the court concluded that "hardly anything [could be] ruled out as 'impossible'" and, therefore, the jury could rationally "consider the human bite of *a person* infected with the AIDS virus" to be deadly (*Scroggins v. State* 1990, p. 20). That recourse to a hypothetical person was not a linguistic oversight. The court made clear its willingness to accept generalized proof of likelihood of infection from the bite of some hypothetical person, rather than from Scroggins, when it used risk assessments in evidence to define the word "deadly" in the aggravated assault statute:

> The expert testified that the "risk" of transmitting the virus via saliva was somewhat less than the documented risk of transmitting the virus into the blood stream via a needle prick, which was one in 250. From this, we think a reasonable juror could conclude, in common wisdom, that the statistical "risk" of contracting AIDS from an infected person via a needle prick is in actuality a random risk, which alike applies to each and every one of the 250 persons, or to all of them if a large enough theory group is considered, i.e., the total population; and that therefore every needle prick introducing the blood of an infected person is as potentially deadly as the next, and therefore, in the most reasonable common sense of the word, every one is deadly. The same may be said of the supposed much-reduced "risk" of transmitting the virus through saliva (*Scroggins v. State* 1990).

Every needle prick, like every sample of saliva, the argument goes, carries the same risk across all HIV-positive needles and saliva, respectively. That may indeed suffice as a neat heuristic or rule of thumb to discourage needle sharing or spitting on people, but it cannot survive as a logical rule of law for two reasons, both of which were also true in *Brock*. First, it assumes homogeneity in the HIV-positive population. If the blood of one HIV-positive person is "as potentially deadly" as the blood of any other HIV-positive person, HIV-positive persons become fungible. If that were true, recourse to the general assumption that saliva can transmit HIV in some hypothetical case would have merit; just as generalized proof of a hypothetical bite in *Brock* would suffice to prove the elements of first-degree assault. But, of course, that has never been true. Even as early as 1990, when Scroggins stood trial, immunologists could determine the relative infectiousness of HIV-positive patients (Murphy 2009). Variety comes from the stage of infection, $CD4^+$ T-cell count, viral load, symptom manifestation, aggravating infections, and other factors (Murphy 2009). To consider one HIV-positive individual to be the same as any other is to ignore science and common sense.

The second logical fallacy is created by the alleviation of the State's burden of persuasion on the likelihood prong. Like the Alabama statute at issue in *Brock*, the Georgia aggravated assault statute includes a circumstances-contingent element that states that the object, device, or instrument used must be used "offensively against a person." If statistical analysis from a hypothetical bite or saliva is sufficient for determining likelihood, then the particular manner in which either was used becomes irrelevant. Allowing this type of proof to satisfy the State's evidentiary burden, therefore, would be tantamount to ignore the words of the legislature (*Duncan v. Walker* 2001). *Scroggins* also illustrates the second due process error common to many HIV-related aggravated assault cases. The statute requires "an instrument which, when used offensively against a person, is likely to... result in serious bodily injury." As evidence of likelihood, the court noted that it would have accepted the medical conclusion that "hardly anything [is] impossible" (*Scroggins v. State* 1990). In doing so, the court lowered the State's burden from proving that something is likely to prove that it is possible. It is difficult to imagine what proof would not be sufficient under an "anything is possible" standard.

Weeks v. State (1992) further illustrates the defects in *Brock* (1989) and *Scroggins* (1990). In *Weeks*, the defendant spit in a prison officer's face during a belligerent tantrum. The saliva covered the guard's glasses, lips, and nose (*Weeks v. State* 1992). Weeks was convicted of attempted murder, which in Texas, requires the specific intent to commit murder as well as an overt act that "tends but fails to effect the commission" of the murder (*Weeks v. State* 1992, p. 561). On appeal and in his habeas proceeding, Weeks argued that the State failed to prove an element of the offense because it offered insufficient evidence to prove that his spit "tend[ed] to" cause death (*Weeks v. State* 1992; *Weeks v. Scott* 1995). On direct appeal, the Texas Court of Criminal Appeals equated "tends to" with "can," (*Weeks v. State* 1992) significantly easing the State's burden, and found the evidence sufficient to convict where medical experts testified that the possibility of transmission was low, "but certainly not zero" (*Weeks v. State* 1992). Like the court in *Scroggins*, the *Weeks* court accepted the "any possibility" standard.

Lowering the State's burden to require proof of possibility rather than some level of probability certainly doomed Weeks's case. However, *Weeks* does represent an improvement over *Brock* and *Scroggins* because the medical testimony in *Weeks* included specific testimony as to the capacity of Weeks's saliva to transmit the disease. In fact, one expert discussed a study showing that HIV developed in saliva in 3 out of 55 instances and that the chances of HIV being in saliva increased if there was blood present (*Weeks v. State* 1992). Another expert examined Weeks and found evidence of gingivitis and tartar on his gums (*Weeks v. State* 1992). Gingivitis and the irritation caused by tartar, the expert noted, can result in blood in the saliva (*Weeks v. State* 1992). In addition, Weeks's medical records showed that his HIV was moderately advanced and that he experienced nausea, vomiting, and diarrhea near the time of the incident, increasing the likelihood that *Weeks* had lesions in his mouth or blood in his saliva (*Weeks v. State* 1992). Three experts agreed that the degree of probability of infection through saliva depended upon where the spit landed with one stating that the eyes and nasal cavity were "exceptionally" bad places for contact (*Weeks v. State* 1992). Additionally, an expert explained that the chances of transmitting the virus increase as the stage of the infection progresses (*Weeks v. State* 1992). Another expert testified that Weeks's medical records showed that he was HIV-4, one week before he spit on the prison officer (*Weeks v. State* 1992), thus distinguishing the risk of contagion from Weeks's blood from that of another HIV-positive individual whose condition had not progressed as far. Under the low standard set by the Texas courts, this testimony sufficiently proved that HIV was likely to—or could—be transmitted through Weeks's saliva as opposed to that of a hypothetical HIV-positive individual.

The salient difference between *Weeks* (1992), on the one hand, and *Brock* (1989) and *Scroggins* (1990), on the other hand, is the specificity of proof. In *Weeks* (1992), expert testimony on the risk of HIV transmission directly related to the likelihood that Weeks's particular actions could have transmitted HIV. In *Brock* (1989) and *Scroggins* (1990), the expert testimony spoke only to a hypothetical risk of transmission that could apply to any case involving any HIV-positive defendant, regardless of his or her unique "accidents" or circumstances. Reasoning from such generality is not only illogical and contrary to due process, but it is also unnecessary.

The Sex Cases

Aggravated assault charges against HIV-positive individuals who have unprotected sex without informing their partners of their HIV status have been more common than similar charges for biting. Whether these acts occur more often or simply are charged more often is unclear. What is clear is that certain jurisdictions tackling this behavior through aggravated assault continue to alleviate the State's logical and constitutional burden of proving that a given defendant's particular behavior satisfied the likelihood prong of the crime.

There are several cases out of the U.S. military's criminal justice system that are emblematic of the kind of generalized proof some jurisdictions use to convict HIV-positive individuals of aggravated assault., Aggravated assault in the military is governed by Article 128 of the Uniform Code of Military Justice (UCMJ) (2011), which states that anyone under UCMJ jurisdiction who "commits an assault with a dangerous weapon or other means… likely to produce death or grievous bodily harm" is guilty of aggravated assault. This language is similar to the language at issue in *Brock* (1989) and *Weeks* (1992) in that each clearly uses likelihood as a way to describe how the weapon or other instrument is used in the assault. In the ordinary aggravated assault case, then, satisfying this formulation beyond a reasonable doubt requires answering four questions: First, what weapon or means of force did the defendant use? Second, how was that instrument of harm used? Third, does that mode of use make serious harm likely? And, fourth, what level of probability qualifies as "likely"? The Manual for Courts-Martial (MCM) sheds some light on these issues:

> [A] bottle, beer glass, a rock, a bunk adaptor, a piece of pipe, a piece of wood, boiling water, drugs, or a rifle butt may be used in a manner likely to inflict death or grievous bodily harm. On the other hand, an unloaded pistol, when presented as a firearm and not as a bludgeon, is not a dangerous weapon or a means of force likely to produce grievous bodily harm, whether or not the assailant knew it was unloaded (2008, pp. IV–101).

Therefore, consideration of the particular manner in which the defendant uses his or her weapon is essential for proving aggravated assault, as is the likelihood that that particular use could cause harm. For the purposes of aggravated assault, the MCM defines "likely" as when "the *natural and probable consequence of a particular use* of any means or force would be death or grievous bodily harm" (2008, pp. IV–101). This language is notable for two reasons. First, it appears to set the military apart from courts in Texas and Georgia, which, as discussed in *Weeks* (1992) and *Scroggins* (1990), accept mere possibility as sufficient evidence of likelihood without direction from the legislature. The military requires a higher threshold of likelihood. Second, it makes the need for specific proof clear. Likelihood can only be determined from a defendant's "particular use" of whatever means he has employed. The Court of Appeals for the Armed Forces (C.A.A.F.) made this clear in *United States v. Outhier* (1996). Distinguishing between circumstances that could make a weapon qualify as a "means likely" to cause harm and those circumstances that could not, the court noted that there is always a

> lynch-pin between a means that is used in a manner "likely" to produce death or grievous bodily harm and one that is not.... [Some] "means"... [a]re unique for an aggravated assault case, i.e., a fist.... The question is whether the means were "used *in a manner likely* to produce death or grievous bodily harm." Thus, in this instance, the circumstances define whether the means used were employed in a manner likely to cause grievous bodily harm or whether appellant's actions were performed in such a manner that the natural and probable consequences were necessarily death or grievous bodily harm (*United States v. Outhier* 1996, p. 329).

In the standard aggravated assault case involving deadly weapons, therefore, the court took the MCM's explanation to heart. Circumstances matter, and likelihood is contingent upon the natural and probable consequences of using a weapon under those circumstances. This would appear to disqualify the kind of generalized evidence in *Brock* (1989) and *Scroggins* (1990).

The UCMJ, MCM, and C.A.A.F.'s precedents thus offer military prosecutors clear instructions on how to indict and prove the elements of aggravated assault for an HIV-positive service member who has sex without informing his partner of his HIV-positive status. The particular nature of the defendant's condition and its correlative risk of transmission are essential elements of that calculus because both factor into determining the consequences of the sexual act and whether those consequences were "natural and probable." But, as the cases suggest, these instructions were ignored in two distinct ways.

First, the military courts, like the state courts in *Brock* (1989) and *Scroggins* (1990), have ignored the particular circumstances of the HIV-positive defendant on trial. In *United States v. Johnson* (1990), for example, a general court-martial convicted the appellant, in relevant part, of aggravated assault for engaging in oral sodomy while HIV-positive and attempted aggravated assault for attempting to engage in anal sodomy with another man (*United States v. Johnson* 1990). A physician with the Air Force Medical Corps testified that there was a 35 % chance that an HIV-positive individual will develop AIDS and that mortality rates were 50 % (*United States v. Johnson* 1990). Notably, the court felt compelled to cite other evidence stating that nearly 99 % of those infected with HIV will develop AIDS (*United States v. Johnson* 1990). The physician also testified that intravenous drug use and unprotected sex represented the greatest risks for transmission and that the risk increased with anal intercourse or if either partner has "genital ulcers" or other abrasions (*United States v. Johnson* 1990). He admitted that fellatio is an "unlikely" means of transmission of HIV (*United States v. Johnson* 1990). And yet, the only evidence of Sergeant Johnson's conduct was that he performed oral sex on another man and intended to engage in anal sodomy before his partner objected. There was no indication that Johnson had any genital ulcers or exhibited any risk enhancement factors, nor was intravenous drug use at issue. Still, the court found the physician's testimony sufficient to prove the likelihood prong of aggravated assault (*United States v. Johnson* 1990).

The court made its decision without considering whether Johnson conformed to a rule of thumb—that HIV can be transmitted through sexual intercourse—or was unique in some way. After all, the Accident Fallacy only occurs when a general rule of thumb is applied to a particular case that is somehow unique, different, or outside the general rule. In *Johnson* (1990) and a series of similar cases, the court must have assumed that differentiation among HIV-positive individuals was impossible. In *United States v. Klauck* (1997), the court believed that an aggravated assault may occur "any time" one person exposes another to a deadly disease, as if there were no differences between diseases, patients, or circumstances. But, as early at 1991, when the Department of Defense issued Directive 6485.1 governing the military's policy toward HIV and AIDS, it was clear that the military could distinguish between types of HIV-positive individuals. It is also clear that at the time of Johnson's case, $CD4^+$ cell testing could quickly and easily distinguish between types of HIV infections and how they manifested in a particular individual (Murphy 2009). Why such distinctions could not be used to classify HIV-positive criminal defendants is unclear.

Johnson (1990), therefore, is a pure example of the Accident Fallacy and its correlative due process violation. The unique activity that gave rise to the assault charge should have distinguished Johnson from the average case. The court in *Johnson* (1990) operated under the general rule that unprotected sex, in whatever form, could transmit a deadly disease. Blind to any unique "accidents" in Sergeant Johnson's case and relying on medical testimony that only tended to validate a general rule of thumb rather than its particular applicability to this case, the court erroneously used a broad generalization as proof of criminal activity. What made that due process violation possible, however, was a second parallel due process error that lowered the government's burden of proof as to likelihood from the MCM's "natural and probable consequences" standard to the simple and clearly lower requirement of "more than merely a fanciful, speculative, or remote possibility" (*United States v. Johnson* 1990). In doing so, C.A.A.F. transformed the MCM's meaningful definition of "likelihood" into an "anything is possible" standard similar to the one used in *Scroggins* (1990) and *Weeks* (1990).

Lowering the government's burden is the second way in which the military courts have ignored the plain language of the UCMJ and MCM and, in so doing, violated the due process rights of HIV-positive criminal defendants. To see the contours and gravity of both of these errors, consider the case of *United States v. Dacus* (2008), and the jurisprudential history on which it stands. Dacus was HIV-positive and had known about his condition since 1996. In July 2004, Dacus had sex with two female staff sergeants—once with one and eleven times with the other. He failed to inform either woman of his HIV-positive status, and though he allegedly wore a condom when having sex on one occasion, he admitted that he did not wear one on several other occasions (Transcript of Record, *United States v. Dacus* 2008). During his providence inquiry, which is similar to a plea hearing, Dacus admitted that he knew he should have discussed his HIV status before engaging in sexual activity, that he knew wearing a condom could not always prevent transmission, and that he understood he could transmit the virus through pre-ejaculate fluid (Transcript of Record, *United States v. Dacus* 2008).

During his sentencing hearing, Dacus presented the testimony of Dr. Mark Wallace, an expert in AIDS and infectious disease (Transcript of Record, *United States v. Dacus* 2008). Dr. Wallace testified that the likelihood of transmission of HIV from one person to another is a direct function of the viral load (Transcript of Record, *United States v. Dacus* 2008). He further noted that, according to a recent study out of Rakai, Uganda, a person with a viral load of 38,000 would have a 1 in 450 chance of transmitting the HIV virus for every heterosexual act of sexual intercourse, whereas a person with a viral load under 1,700 would have a 1 in 10,000 chance of doing so (Transcript of Record, *United States v. Dacus* 2008). When a person uses a condom, the risk of transmitting the HIV virus falls by an additional 80–90 % (Transcript of Record, *United States v. Dacus* 2008). After examining Dacus, Dr. Wallace also noted that Dacus's viral load was so low as to be undetectable by existing technology, estimating that it was somewhere between 1 and 50 (Transcript of Record, *United States v. Dacus* 2008). As such, using the Rakai numbers, Dacus had a maximum 1 in 612,000 chance of transmitting the HIV virus to the first staff sergeant if there was any pre-ejaculate fluid present and a maximum 1 in 440,000 chance of transmitting HIV to the second. Dacus was in fact a "very, very rare" HIV-positive individual whose immune system could suppress replication of HIV without medication (Transcript of Record, *United States v. Dacus* 2008). While Dacus could still transmit the HIV virus despite his low viral load, his likelihood of doing so was "[e]xtremely low" or "very, very unlikely" (Transcript of Record, *United States v. Dacus* 2008, pp. 101–102).

This case had one promising feature: the evidence at trial as to Dacus's viral load and the particular type and frequency of sexual contact with two staff sergeants went directly to the unique "accidents" of Dacus's case. His single sexual act with one of his sexual partners made transmission less likely and his exceedingly low viral load put him on the fringe of transmission risk in all cases. However, even though Dacus was able to offer specific evidence of his unique situation, the Air Force Court of Criminal Appeal (AFCCA) found the evidence consistent with a plea of guilty to aggravated assault because, according to C.A.A.F. precedents, the risk of transmission need only be "more than merely a fanciful, speculative, or remote possibility" (*United States v. Dacus* 2008, p. 238). The court committed two errors in one. By virtue of his undetectable viral load and the infrequency of sexual contact, Dacus's case was indeed unique. Yet, the "anything is possible" standard allowed the court to ignore these "accidents."

There are three possible reasons for this result, each of which fails to justify the lower standard. First, the military seems to have confused risk of transmission with risk of harm. If aggravated assault under the UCMJ requires a means likely to cause grievous bodily harm or death, a judge could interpret "likely" as modifying only "cause." This suggests that given an attack by the particular weapon or means used, what is important for the likelihood prong is the probability of death or serious injury once the weapon is used. And since HIV causes AIDS and AIDS is incurable and leads to death, death is the natural and probable consequence of contracting HIV. There is some indication that C.A.A.F. has adopted this interpretation. For example, in *United States v. Joseph* (1993, p. 396), another aggravated assault case involving HIV, the court analogized HIV to a rifle bullet, stating that "the question would be whether the bullet is likely to inflict death or serious bodily harm *if* it hits the victim, not the statistical probability of the bullet hitting the victim." That interpretation is misleading, however. It is beyond cavil that great harm or death must be a likely consequence. *Joseph* ignores the fact that it is not the weapon that must likely cause great harm, but rather the manner in which it is used must be likely to cause the resulting harm. As C.A.A.F. explained in *Outhier* (1996), "likely" modifies "means." The question in *Outhier* (1996) was whether "the means were 'used *in a manner likely*'" to cause harm. Fists could cause sufficient harm if used a certain way, whereas a gun, if an attacker loads it with bubblegum and pulls the trigger, could not. To narrow the likelihood prong to the consequential harm, therefore, ignores the saliency of a particular weapon's use. What is more, since there can be no harm without a risk of transmission of HIV, any aggravated assault conviction must assess whether the particular means employed—unprotected sex by an HIV-positive man with an undetectable viral load—would naturally and probably transmit HIV.

Second, C.A.A.F. might have justified its low risk of transmission standard on its assumption that an HIV infection is an unquestioned death sentence. In other words, if the gravity of the harm is so great, the risk of transmission of HIV need not be. Indeed, that is what *United States v. Weatherspoon* (1998) appears to suggest. *Weatherspoon* (1998) was a traditional aggravated assault case involving choking and repeated kicks to the head. C.A.A.F. cited LeFave for the proposition that the

> concept of likelihood... has two prongs: (1) the risk of harm and (2) the magnitude of the harm.... [L]ikelihood... is determined by measuring both prongs, not just the statistical risk of harm. Where the magnitude of the harm is great, there may be an aggravated assault, even though the risk of harm is statistically low (*United States v. Weatherspoon* 1998, p. 211).

Not only is this theory not universally applied (*United States v. Corralez* 2005), it is also nothing more than a *post hoc* justification for the military courts' unequal treatment of HIV-positive criminal defendants charged with aggravated assault. *Weatherspoon* (1998) accepts the "more than merely a fanciful, speculative, or remote" standard as given, relying on various C.A.A.F. precedents that neither discussed LeFave nor indicated a reliance on an inverse variation to determine likelihood. In those cases, the magnitude of harm was assumed to be great because HIV/AIDS is incurable. Yet C.A.A.F. uses the MCM's "natural and probable consequence" standard for typical aggravated assaults and LeFave's inverse variation for HIV-related assaults.

Since C.A.A.F. created its "more than merely a fanciful, speculative, or remote" standard long before *Weatherspoon*'s use of LeFave's inverse variation to justify it, it would seem that there is a third possibility: the military courts have continued to perpetuate a mistake made long ago, when judges were scared and ignorant of HIV. The precedents upon which the "more than merely a fanciful, speculate, or remote possibility" standard is based are unsubstantiated and *Weatherspoon's post hoc* justification for it does not suggest otherwise. The cases bear this out. In *Dacus* (2008), C.A.A.F. cites its previous decisions in *Klauk* (1997), *Joseph* (1993), and *Johnson* (1990) for support (*United States v. Dacus* 2008; *United States v. Johnson* 1990; *United States v. Joseph* 1993). *Klauk* (1997) cites *Joseph* (1993), which in turn relied on *Johnson* (1990). *Johnson* (1990) relied on *United States v. Stewart* (1989) and *United States v. Womack* (1989), but that is where the precedents end. Moreover, neither *Stewart* nor *Womack* provides any reason for lowering the MCM's natural and probable consequences standard other than judicial fiat. *Stewart* (1989) employed the MCM's standard without mentioning the words fanciful, speculative, or remote. And *Womack* (1989), a case challenging the validity of a safe sex order, is even less helpful and more far afield, as it never even addressed the natural and probable consequences standard. To say that *Womack* (1989) and *Stewart* (1989) required *Johnson* (1990) to adopt the low "more than merely a fanciful, speculative, or remote possibility" standard is to read into the cases something that is simply not there.

This jurisprudential quicksand doomed Sergeant Dacus's appeal. Even though his undetectable viral load made him significantly less likely than a hypothetical HIV-positive individual to transmit HIV, the fact that anything is possible satisfied the "more than merely a fanciful, speculative, or remote possibility" standard (*United States v. Dacus* 2008). There are two major problems with the decision in *Dacus* (2008). First, specific proof was available and before the military judge, yet the general rule of thumb was still applied despite unique circumstances: another Accident Fallacy. This occurred because of the second error, that the bar for proving likelihood had been previously set well below the instructions of the MCM to the lowest "mere possibility" standard. Therefore, even specific proof as to the qualitative and quantitative unlikelihood that Dacus could transmit HIV was insufficient to rebut the government's case. If all the government had to prove was a mere possibility that was more than "fanciful, speculative, or remote," even the medical reality that "anything is possible" would suffice. After all, the testifying physicians in *Dacus* (2008), *Johnson* (1990), *Klauck* (1997), and *Joseph* (1993) all stated that the likelihood of transmission was relatively low, albeit possible. But proof of possibility is not proof of likelihood beyond a reasonable doubt.

Conclusions and Implications

Problematic cases like *Brock* (1989), *Scroggins* (1990), *Weeks* (1995), *Johnson* (1990), and *Dacus* (2008) suggest that the traditional criminal law is a legally flawed tool for addressing the spread of HIV. The spread of HIV constitutes a public health concern, but the aggravated assault approach has proven over-inclusive by reaching HIV-positive individuals who could rarely, if ever, transmit the virus. At a minimum, then, jurisdictions that continue to use the traditional criminal law in this context should recognize the potential logical fallacies and due process errors that can occur and guard against them. When likelihood of harm is at issue, prosecutors should introduce evidence of the defendant's viral load or some measure of the status of the defendant's HIV as a means of proving likelihood. Defendants likewise should introduce evidence of their low viral load to raise doubts about whether they could have likely transmitted the disease. And judges should pay attention.

Even if the logical and due process errors discussed above were resolved, there are three reasons why the criminal law would still be an inappropriate tool to stem the spread of HIV. First, these laws make the dubious assumption that the criminal law can effectively deter behavior that risks spreading HIV (Posner 1985; Shavell 1985). There is no evidence that making HIV exposure a crime actually deters anyone from having sex with the intent of spreading HIV and, in fact, it may encourage nondisclosure. There is not a single study showing any correlation between the implementation of harsh criminal penalties or increases in prosecutions with reductions in the HIV infection rate. There are also myriad reasons why someone might not disclose his or her HIV status in the anticipatory heat of a sexual encounter. Once nondisclosure "happens," these laws discourage subsequent honesty; therefore, the fear of prosecution incentivizes concealment at all stages even though we know that honesty about HIV status is an important tool in preventing the spread of the virus. HIV criminalization doubles down on its perverse incentives by discouraging testing in addition to discouraging disclosure: You cannot be guilty of knowingly failing to disclose your status as an HIV-positive person, for example, if you do not know you are HIV-positive. The CDC estimates that of the 1.1 million Americans with HIV, nearly 20 % do not know it (CDC 2010; Knox 2008). Blindness to your status carries personal risks and can cause social harm, especially if you engage in risky behaviors. Laws that perpetuate this ignorance by making it an absolute defense to a criminal conviction serve no legitimate purpose.

Second, by disincentivizing testing and elevating ignorance, HIV criminalization also impedes effective communication between HIV-positive individuals and their health care providers. Unique among us, individuals with all manner of chronic conditions require close relationships with doctors they can trust. But when laws discourage us from getting tested, physicians are denied access to crucial diagnostic information and could, as a result, fail to catch important symptoms, misdiagnose, or do more harm than good. What's more, even those who do get tested may decline to disclose their status to their physicians out of fear, embarrassment, or shame, further alienating a key ally in the HIV-positive journey.

Third, the implications of a criminal conviction do not end with jail; the resulting stigmatization of an already marginalized population may be the most troubling. Stigma, as United Nations Secretary-General Ban Ki-moon has said, is "the single most important barrier to public action" on seeking treatment and stemming the spread of HIV. As a result, stigma "helps make AIDS the silent killer because people fear the social disgrace of speaking about it, or taking easily available precautions" (UNAIDS 2008). San Francisco AIDS Foundation (SFAF) Chief Executive Officer Neil Giuliano has called stigma "a lethal wingman" that allows HIV to thrive on the margins (SFAF 2011). Turning HIV into the tool of a crime makes those margins wider and provides tacit endorsement to stigma's attendant discrimination. According to surveys conducted between 2005 and 2010, an estimated 27 % of Americans would prefer not to work closely with a woman living with HIV. The number is even higher for men. More than 17 % of respondents living with HIV in the United Kingdom had been denied health care, and 21 % report experiencing verbal and physical assaults. In the United States, nearly 25 % of HIV-positive survey respondents have reported some discrimination at work or in the provision of health care, with employers and physicians justifying their behavior on the stigmas associated with being HIV-positive (Center for HIV Law and Policy 2010, 2012).

And by any good measure stigma is actually worse today than it was 20 years ago. This might sound counterintuitive to some: when we think of stigmatization, we think of "fear of casual contagion" through touching toilet seats or drinking glasses, as Sean Strub, HIV/AIDS activist and Executive Director of the Sero Project, noted to me in an e-mail on April 8, 2012. Although that fear is still remarkably high (11 % for toilet seats and 20 % for drinking glasses), this is a fraction of the whole story, as he states: "Stigma is pre-judgment, marginalization, 'othering' and ways of diminishing the humanity, voice and importance of a section of society." Criminalization helps make Mr. Strub's case that this kind of stigma is indeed worse today.

Stigma and criminalization are partners in a devastating reinforcing matrix: HIV-positive individuals are stigmatized as promiscuous and immoral carriers of a public health nightmare. Those erroneous perceptions ostensibly justify criminalizing and regulating the sexual conduct of HIV-positive individuals. By making the intimate behavior of an entire community subject to decades of imprisonment, criminalization codifies the dangerous and offensive notion that being HIV-positive is just like being a criminal, which gives credence to discrimination and reinforces the stigma that justified criminalization in the first place. This straightjacket is that much worse because HIV has long been associated with the gay community, a paradigmatic marginalized population that has spent decades at the fringes of a systemically hostile society.

At best, the problem of criminalization is one of over-inclusiveness—using general rules of thumb to describe too many peculiar and unique cases. At worst, it is one of stereotyping, which is itself a product of ignorance. The average voter, prosecutor, or judge may think that sex transmits HIV, that HIV leads to AIDS and that HIV kills, but those "rules-of-thumb" are not universally applicable. Sexual intercourse can transmit HIV, but when an undetectable viral load is combined with antiretroviral treatment, condom use, and no attendant sexually transmitted infections, the statistical probability of transmission is basically nil. Such conduct should rarely, if ever, create a likelihood of transmission sufficient for conviction under an aggravated assault statute.

Acknowledgments The author would like to thank The Honorable Scott W. Stucky, Associate Judge of the Court of Appeals for the Armed Forces, and James A. Young, Chief Commissioner in Judge Stucky's chambers, for advice and support in writing the original article. Special thanks to the faculty at California Western School of Law and the Faculty Development Committee for providing essential feedback and an opportunity to workshop the arguments contained herein.

References

Atia, S., Egger, M., Müller, M., Zwahlen, M., & Low, N. (2009). Sexual transmission of HIV according to viral load and antiretroviral therapy: Systematic review and meta-analysis. *AIDS, 23*(11), 1397–1404. Retrieved from http://www.who.int/hiv/events/artprevention/attia_sexual.pdf

Avert. (2011a, March 21). *The different stages of HIV infection*. Retrieved from http://www.avert.org/stages-hiv-aids.htm

Avert. (2011b, March 21). *HIV transmission—frequently asked questions*. Retrieved from http://www.avert.org/hiv-aids-transmission.htm

Berkow, R., Beers, M. H., & Fletcher, A. (Eds.). (1997). *The merck manual of medical information*. New York, NY: Pocket Books.

Bridges v. Wixon. (1945). 326 U.S. 135.

TheBody.com. (2010, October 4). *CD4 cell tests*. Retrieved from http://www.thebody.com/content/art6110.html

Brock v. State. (1989). 555 So. 2d 285 (Ala. Crim App.).

Centers for Disease Control and Prevention. (1999, July). *HIV and transmission 1*. Retrieved from http://img.thebody.com/cdc/pdfs/transmission.pdf

Centers for Disease Control and Prevention. (2010, September 24). Prevalence and awareness of HIV infection among men who have sex with men–21 cities, United States. *CDC Morbidity and Mortality Weekly Reporter, 59*(37), 1201–1207. Retrieved from http://www.cdc.gov/mmwr/preview/mmwrhtml/mm5937a2.htm

Center for HIV Law and Policy. Fall 2010 (2012). *Ending and defending against HIV criminalization: A manual for advocates* (Vol. 1). Retrieved from www.hivlawandpolicy.org/resources/download/564

De Lollis, B. (2007, March 8). Some hotels don't skip the 13th floor anymore. *USA Today.* Retrieved from http://www.usatoday.com/money/biztravel/2007-03-08-13th-floor-usat_N.htm

DeNoon, D. (2010, July 9). Discovery may pave way to AIDS vaccine. *WebMD.* Retrieved from http://www.webmd.com/hiv-aids/news/20100709/antibodies-discovery-may-pave-way-to-aids-vaccine

Duncan v. Walker. (2001). 533 U.S. 167.

Engel, S. M. (1999). *With good reason: An introduction to informal fallacies* (6th ed., pp. 104–111). New York, NY: Bedford/St. Martin's.

Ginn v. State. (2008). 667 S.E.2d 712, 713 (Ga. Ct. App.).

Goicoechea, M. (2009, January). *Presentation at University of California.* San Diego, CA: Antivirals for Starters.

Grant, I. (2008). The boundaries of the criminal law: The criminalization of the non-disclosure of HIV. *Dalhousie Law Journal, 31,* 123–180.

HIV Prevention Trials Network (HPTN). (2011). A randomized trial to evaluate the effectiveness of antiretroviral therapy plus HIV primary care versus HIV primary care alone to prevent the sexual transmission of HIV-1 in serodiscordant couples. Retrieved from www.hptn.org/research_studies/hptn052.asp.

The Harvard Law Review Association (1992–1993). Note, Winship on rough waters: The erosion of the reasonable doubt standard. *Harvard Law Review, 106,* 1093–1095.

Hunter v. State. (1990). 799 S.W.2d 356 (Tex. Ct. App.).

In re Winship. (1970). 397 U.S. 358.

Jennings, D. (2009, May 30). Man who spread HIV gets 45 years. *Dallas Morning News,* 1B.

Lynn, J. (1985). *Clue [Motion Picture].* United States: Paramount Pictures. (Screenwriter/Director).

Knox, R. (2008, November 24). Many Americans with HIV don't know they have it. *NPR.* Retrieved from http://www.npr.org/templates/story/story.php?storyId=97315837

LabTestsOnline. (2012, November). *HIV viral load.* Retrieved from http://www.labtestsonline.org/understanding/analytes/viral_load/test.html

Lynch, G. E. (1987). RICO: The crime of being a criminal. *Columbia Law Review, 87,* 920–984.

Manual for Courts-Martial. (2008). *United States (MCM),* Part IV, 54.c(4)(a)(ii).

McGuire, A. (1999). Comment, AIDS as a weapon: Criminal prosecution of HIV exposure. *Houston Law Review, 36,* 1787–1817.

Medford v. State. (1919). 216 S.W. 175 (Tex.).

Montaner, J. S., Hogg, R., Wood, E., Kerr, T., Tyndall, M., Levy, A. R., et al. (2006). The case for expanding access to highly active antiretroviral therapy to curb the growth of the HIV epidemic. *Lancet, 368,* 531–536.

Montaner, J. S., Lima, V. D., Barrios, R., Yip, B., Wood, E., & Kendall, P. (2010, August). Association of highly active antiretroviral therapy coverage, population viral load, and yearly new HIV diagnoses in British Columbia, Canada: A population-based study. *Lancet, 376,* 532–539.

Murphy, R. L. Flaherty, J. P., & Taiwo, B. O. (2009). *Contemporary diagnosis and management of HIV/AIDS infections* (3rd ed., pp. 14–17). New York, NY: Handbooks in Health Care Co.

Ohio v. Roberts. (2004). 805 N.E.2d 594 (Ohio Ct. App.).

Pinkerton v. United States. (1946). 328 U.S. 640.

Posner, R. A. (1985). An economic theory of the criminal law. *Columbia Law Review, 85,* 1193–1231.

Rhoades v. Iowa. (2012). No.12-0180 (Iowa).

Rosenberg, I. M. (1970). Winship redux: 1970 to 1990. *Texas Law Review, 69*, 114–117.

Royce, R. A., Seña, A., Cates, W, Jr., & Cohen, M. S. (1997). Sexual transmission of HIV. *New England Journal of Medicine 336*, 1072–1078.

Rubin, A. (1996). Comment, HIV positive, employment negative? HIV discrimination among health care workers in the United States and France. *Comparative Labor Law Journal, 17*, 404–443.

San Francisco AIDS Foundation (2011, January 20). The view from here: CEO Neil Giuliano. *Status.* Retrieved from http://www.thebody.com/content/art60323.html

Sanders, S. B. (2011, March 1). *Sanders socialist success.* United States Senate: Bernie Sanders. Retrieved from http://sanders.senate.gov/newsroom/news/?id=7b6eba9b-67f5-4d8f-bc75-ce63a07035d2

Scales v. United States. (1961). 367 U.S. 203.

Schoettes, S. (2011, October 19). *When sex is a crime and spit is a dangerous weapon.* Presentation to the Chicago Bar Association LGBT Committee.

Scroggins v. State. (1990). 401 S.E.2d 13 (Ga. Ct. App.).

Shavell, S. (1985). Criminal law and the optimal use of nonmonetary sanctions as a deterrent. *Columbia Law Review, 85*, 1247–1259.

State v. Musser. (2006). 721 N.W.2d 734 (Iowa).

Stewart v. State. (1981). 405 So. 2d 402 (Ala. Crim. App.).

Templeton v. United States. (1945). 151 F.2d 706 (6th Cir.).

Transcript of Record, United States v. Dacus. (2008). 66 M.J. 235 (C.A.A.F.) (No. 20050404).

UNAIDS (2008, July). *Report on the global AIDS epidemic.* Retrieved from http://www.unaids.org/en/dataanalysis/knowyourepidemic/epidemiologypublications/2008reportontheglobalaidsepidemic/

Uniform Code of Military Justice. (2011). 10 U.S.C. § 928.

United States v. Corralez. (2005). 61 M.J.737 (A.F.Ct.Chm.App).

United States v. Dacus. (2008). 66 M.J. 235 (C.A.A.F.).

United States v. Delpit. (1996). 94 F.3d 1134 (8th Cir.).

United States v. Johnson. (1988). 27 M.J. 798 (A.F.C.M.R.).

United States v. Johnson. (1990). 30 M.J. 53 (C.M.A.).

United States v. Joseph. (1993). 37 M.J. 392 (C.M.A.).

United States v. Klauck. (1997). 47 M.J. 24 (C.A.A.F.).

United States v. Outhier. (1996). 45 M.J. 326 (C.A.A.F.).

United States v. Stewart. (1989). 29 M.J. 92 (C.M.A.).

United States v. Weatherspoon. (1998). 49 M.J. 209 (C.A.A.F.).

United States v. Womack. (1989). 29 M.J. 88 (C.M.A.).

United States v. Ytem. (2001). 255 F.3d 394 (7th Cir.).

U.S. Department of Health and Human Services (2012). *HIV and its treatment—Approved medications to treat HIV.* Retrieved from http://www.aidsinfo.nih.gov/ContentFiles/ApprovedMedstoTreatHIV_FS_en.pdf

Weeks v. State. (1992). 834 S.W.2d 559 (Tex. Ct. App.).

Weeks v. Scott. (1995). 55 F.3d 1059, 1062 (5th Cir.).

Wilson, D., Law, M. G., Grulich, A. E., Cooper, D. A., & Kaldor, J. M. (2008). Relation between HIV viral load and infectiousness: A model-based analysis. *Lancet, 372*, 314–320.

Wolf, L. E., & Vezina, R. (2004). Crime and punishment: Is there a role for criminal law in HIV prevention policy? *Whittier Law Review, 25*, 821–885.

Chapter 18
Define "Sex": Legal Outcomes for Transgender Individuals in the United States

Alexis Forbes

Abstract Transgender individuals have unique experiences with the law. Legal protections against pervasive discrimination have come slowly and, in some cases, not at all. Through litigation, attorneys in the United States have challenged the law's conceptualization of gender and its definition of sex. Some of these cases have served to fortify protections against discrimination and victimization for transgender individuals. Despite this progress, transgender individuals continue to experience discrimination that affects their physical, psychological, and socioeconomic health. The following chapter discusses a few of the landmark U.S. cases and changes in legislative policy that have been crucial in determining the rights of transgender and gender nonconforming individuals.

Keywords Transgender · Law · Gender nonconformity · Discrimination · Justice

Define "Sex": Legal Outcomes for Transgender Individuals

In the United States, branches of government are in place to keep citizens safe, maintain the protection of civil rights, and punish the people who deprive citizens of those rights. The judicial system affords citizens adjudication and, optimally, justice for their grievances. Unfortunately, the laws that protect civil rights are not equally effective or applicable to all members of society. Transgender individuals experience discrimination based on their gender identity and gender nonconformity or presentation (Friedman and Leaper 2010; Grant et al. 2011; Taylor 2007; Weinberg 2009). Justice for trans-identified persons who experience discrimination and victimization in the realm of their occupation, their personal relationships,

A. Forbes (✉)
Psychology Department, John Jay College of Criminal Justice,
524 West 59th Street, New York, NY 10019, USA
e-mail: amurray-forbes@jjay.cuny.edu

D. Peterson and V. R. Panfil (eds.), *Handbook of LGBT Communities,*
Crime, and Justice, DOI: 10.1007/978-1-4614-9188-0_18,
© Springer Science+Business Media New York 2014

or within their familial relationships is not as accessible as it is for non-LGBTQ individuals who experience discrimination or victimization in similar contexts (Martin and Meezan 2003). The definition of "sex" or "gender," as it applies to the law, has been used to include and, in many cases, exclude transgender individuals from utilizing legal protections on which many victims of discrimination rely. This chapter provides a review of transgender individuals' interactions with the legal system; including the systematic and institutionalized discrimination, court experiences, and the landmark rulings in four specific areas of the law. First, there is a complicated history of employment discrimination for transgender individuals and a recent employment discrimination case that has resulted in changes for how private and public employers must treat their transgender employees. Second, housing discrimination against transgender and gender non-conforming individuals has prompted concerns about the financial and physical health of the transgender community. Third, trans-identified and gender noncon-forming youth are a particularly vulnerable population in their homes, their schools, and on the streets. Finally, losses in family court have led to disparities in rights for transgender individuals, their partners, and their children. Some of these cases indicate setbacks in the pursuit of equality for transgender individuals. However, many of the following cases describe victories that indicate positive momentum in the fight for legal protections for this disadvantaged group.

The Transgender Experience

The transgender experience is included by LGBQ (lesbian, gay, bisexual, and queer) researchers and advocacy groups because transgender people experience similar stigmas and discrimination due to their gender nonconformity and gender presentation (Gerhardstein and Anderson 2010; Grant et al. 2011). However, it is important to note, a transgender identity does not imply a specific sexual orientation. Transgender individuals can identify as lesbian, gay, bisexual, asexual, pansexual, or heterosexual. Transgender people live as the gender that is not associated with their birth sex. For example, a transgender woman, also known as MTF (male to female), is a woman who was born with male sex characteristics, but identifies and lives as a woman. Likewise, a transgender man (female to male (FTM)) is a man who was born with female sex characteristics, but lives and identifies as a man. As the transgender experience has become more prominent in the United States, so too have the terms with which transgender individuals identify. Some transgender individuals choose to label their identity as gender variant or, more simply, gender nonconforming.

Throughout their lifetime, transgender individuals may feel discord between their gendered appearance or their gender presentation and their birth sex (Gagné and Tewksbury 1998; Grant et al. 2011). This discord often produces an emotional conflict because trans-identified individuals are born with physical characteristics of the sex with which they do not identify (Grant et al. 2011). Some transgender individuals opt to take hormones to enhance or suppress secondary sex characteristics such as facial hair or their voice octave. Other trans-identified individuals may decide to undergo surgery for sexual reassignment, facial feminization or masculinization, breast reduction, or breast augmentation. In addition to biological methods of gender reconciliation, transgender individuals can also take "lessons" to change their speech, posture, cadence, and other gender norms that help them present as the gender with which they identify (Grant et al. 2011). Within the transgender community, individuals and their allies understand that gender nonconformity is the common, defining characteristic of transgender individuals. However, transgender individuals' experiences with discrimination differ on a diverse array of issues that depend on myriad factors including age, familial ties, status of gender transition, and lifestyle factors.

A wealth of psychological, medical, and sociological research indicates that being transgender is linked to an increased likelihood of experiencing discrimination (Friedman and Leaper 2010; Himmelstein and Bruckner 2010), economic hardship (see Quintana 2009, for a review; Quintana et al. 2010), mental (Almeida et al. 2009; Herek and Garnets 2007) and physical (Harcourt 2006) health disparities, victimization (Tomsen and Mason 2001), academic sanctions (Himmelstein and Bruckner 2010), physical and sexual assault (Grant et al. 2011), as well as an increased risk of suicide (Herek and Garnets 2007; Suicide Prevention Resource Center (SPRC) 2008) as compared to cisgender (i.e., non-transgender, gender conforming) individuals. Researchers, clinicians, and advocates that work with the transgender population have articulated the need for policies and laws that can reduce transgender discrimination, increase therapeutic jurisprudence, and, consequently, reduce the economic and health disparities between transgender and non-transgender populations (Badgett 2007; Badgett et al. 2007; Balsam et al. 2011; Meyer 2003; Sullivan 1996; Taylor 2007).

Typically, stigmatized groups have access to policies and laws that prevent or punish discrimination that they endure based on their minority-group membership. Antidiscrimination policies and the enforcement of those policies help women and people of color (POC) to retain or regain rights to employment, equality in pay, housing, medical care, and other services that have, at some point in history, been threatened or revoked because of those individuals' membership in one or multiple minority groups. These policies also provide minorities a promise of procedural justice in that there are explicit recourses for protecting their rights and restoring their lives. Unfortunately, some of those policies have not been extended to prevent discrimination against people who are or are perceived to be transgender, gender variant, or of a minority sexual orientation (Herek 2004, 2007).

Defining Employment Discrimination

Transgender individuals experience economic hardship through increased unemployment, wage gaps, housing discrimination, and higher rates of poverty than heterosexual cisgender individuals do (Albelda et al. 2009; Badgett 2001). Transgender individuals are especially at risk for high rates of homelessness and unemployment, as well as earning lower wages. In a sample of 6,450 transgender individuals in the United States and Puerto Rico, 19 % of the sample reported having experienced homelessness at least once in their lives, and 15 % of the sample, compared with only 4 % of the general population, lived on $10,000 or less per year. Data from that same survey indicated that, during the six-month period between September 2008 and February 2009, 11 % of transgender individuals were unemployed compared to only 7 % of the general population (Grant et al. 2011; U.S. Department of Labor 2008). Within that same sample of 6,450 participants, an overwhelming 97 % reported experiencing discriminatory encounters at their job, including harassment and mistreatment (Grant et al. 2011). Almost half (47 %) of the sample reported that their employer had denied them a promotion or fired them because of their transgender identity. Job loss due to transphobic discrimination was associated with high rates of subsequent unemployment. Twenty-six percent of the respondents who experienced transphobic discrimination were still unemployed at the time of the survey. For transgender individuals, employment discrimination appears to translate into negative financial outcomes and forces them to pursue illegal sources of income such as sex work and drug dealing (Grant et al. 2011).

By providing legal protections from employment discrimination, the U.S. court system could serve to insulate transgender individuals from the negative consequences associated with unemployment. The fight against transgender employment discrimination has drawn most of its support from the legal precedent set in 1989 by the United States Supreme Court. The victim of the discrimination, Ann Hopkins, did not identify as transgender; however, her employers discriminated against her because they believed her appearance and behaviors were not feminine enough. In *Price Waterhouse v. Hopkins*, 490 U.S. 228 (1989), the Supreme Court upheld the lower court's decision that it is illegal for a company to discriminate against an employee because of that employee's nonconformity to stereotypes about sex or gender. Before the *Price Waterhouse* ruling, the Title VII employment discrimination law (Civil Rights Act of 1964) protected citizens from receiving disparate treatment based on age, race, and sex, but the *Price Waterhouse* ruling indicated that the courts were willing to broaden the definition of "sex" as it pertained to Title VII litigation.

After the *Price Waterhouse* case, many LGBTQ individuals began to file charges against their employers for sexual orientation-based discrimination. LGBTQ individuals hoped that judges would interpret the *Price Waterhouse* ruling to mean that discrimination based on gender nonconformity or sexual orientation was impermissible according to the law. Unfortunately, LGBTQ citizens rarely win employment discrimination lawsuits that are associated with their gender presentation, sexual identity, or sexual preference (Gulati 2003; Weinberg 2009). Judges' decisions often focus on how the *Price Waterhouse* ruling and the original Title VII law define sex. Reviews of court decisions indicate that employers that have been accused of GNC-based discrimination against a heterosexual, non-transgender employee are more likely to receive sanctions from the courts than are employers in cases where the employee is lesbian, gay, bisexual, or transgender (Weinberg 2009). The transgender litigants argue that the employment discrimination they encountered was based on their gender or gender identity and therefore qualifies as sex discrimination. Unfortunately, judges across the country define "sex" in many different ways and the lack of a uniform federal ruling that explicitly includes the terms "transgender" and "gender identity" complicates justice in employment discrimination for transgender individuals.

After the *Price Waterhouse* ruling, LGBTQ individuals continued to lose Title VII discrimination cases against their employers. Judges in these cases often acknowledged that employers had discriminated against the employee but that the reason for that discrimination was not included in the broadened definition of sex. For instance, some transgender employees have alleged Title VII sex discrimination after being fired during or after their transition to the gender with which they identify. Transitioning refers to the process through which a transgender individual incorporates identity and lifestyle changes that correspond to their gender identity while also eliminating customs, behaviors, and physical characteristics that are associated with the gender with which they do not identify. Transitioning is an important aspect of a transgender person's life. It is a time when they begin to reconcile their gender identity with their outward appearance, including dealing with the changes in how others interact with them. In 1975, prior to the *Price Waterhouse v. Hopkins* ruling, one of the earliest transgender employment discrimination court cases involved a tenured elementary school teacher who was fired after her MTF transition. The judge denied the plaintiff, Ms. Grossman's, claim of Title VII discrimination and stated that Ms. Grossman was not fired because of her "sex," but because of her "change in sex" (*Grossman v. Bernards Township Board of Education*, No. 74-1904 (D.N.J. Sept. 10, 1975)).

Fortunately, some transgender individuals have successfully argued their case for "sex" discrimination since the Price Waterhouse case. In another MTF transgender woman's case, *Doe v. United Consumer Financial Services (UCFS)* (N. D. Ohio 2001), the court decided that the employer fired Ms. Doe because her appearance did not meet the standards of dress that the company set for male employees. Judges also cited UCFS's statement that they did not approve of Ms. Doe's appearance because they could not discern which gender she was by the way that she presented herself at work. The judge believed that the way that UCFS used sex or gender stereotypes to evaluate Ms. Doe constituted sex discrimination and ruled in favor of Ms. Doe.

Public sector employees such as firefighters and police officers have also brought suit against their employer through Title VII sex discrimination claims. After working as a firefighter in Salem, Ohio for 7 years, Lieutenant Smith received a diagnosis of gender identity disorder. Smith began to experience discrimination and harassment at her fire company after the department found out about her transgender identity (*Smith v. City of Salem, Ohio* 378 F.3d 566 (6th Cir. 2004)). In 2004, a judge ruled that the discrimination that Smith experienced qualified as sex discrimination because the judge believed that the fire company would not have harassed Ms. Smith if she had been born female. If Ms. Smith was not born male, it would be appropriate for her to wear dresses; thus, the discrimination was based on Ms. Smith's birth sex and therefore qualified as "sex" discrimination. In 2005, another transgender woman, Philecia Barnes, obtained a financial judgment against the City of Cincinnati Police Department in a Title VII sex discrimination victory. Barnes, who was born male, wore the male uniform and did not behave femininely while on duty as a police officer (*Barnes v. City of Cincinnati,* 401 F.3d 729 (6th Cir. 2005)). However, Barnes dressed and behaved as a woman when she was not on duty. The City of Cincinnati Police Department stated that it was Barnes's failure in an important evaluation, and not her transgender identity, that led to the denial of a promotion. However, the court determined that the police department denied Barnes's promotion because Barnes did not conform to the masculine stereotypes associated with "his" birth sex.

Prior to 2012, judges denied many Title VII claims brought by transgender individuals who believed that their employer discriminated against them because of their transgender identity. Fortunately, a 2012 employment discrimination case, *Macy v. Holder* (EEOC April 20, 2012), resulted in a ruling that specifically prohibits discrimination against transgender employees. Mia Macy was tentatively offered a position with the Bureau of Alcohol, Tobacco, Firearms, and Explosives (ATFE) but after Macy, an MTF transgender woman, informed an ATFE administrator of her intent to transition from male to female, the job offer was rescinded. The ATEF lied to Macy and told her that the position no longer existed, but Macy later learned that another candidate was hired for the same position. Macy filed a Title VII complaint and asked that the Equal Employment Opportunity Commission (EEOC) classify her claim as a case of sex discrimination. The EEOC reviewed Macy's complaint and ruled that the transgender woman could file a sex discrimination case against the ATFE. This case has the potential to curb and, eventually, eliminate the type of discrimination that is common for many transgender individuals. As a result, all federal agencies can be investigated for claims of discrimination against a federal employee on the basis of that employee's transgender identity or presentation. Transgender complainants can also bring charges against their employers in private companies. The EEOC released a statement with advice for public and private employers to ensure that they are not violating the rights of their transgender employees. These recommendations include educating staff and implementing changes in employee dress code, the type of restrooms available (i.e., unisex), personnel records, the use of appropriate pronouns, and the types of health insurance benefits available to its employees. Transgender employees across the country can now bring cases against companies for discriminatory hiring, promotion, and termination policies, harassment, and other forms of transphobic employment discrimination.

Some employers may not fire a transgender employee because of their transition or because of their transgender identity, but the employers might engage in another form of transphobic discrimination by not including transgender-related medical treatment in the employee insurance benefits. Marc Mario, a transgender man, began his transition after working for a grocery food chain for a few years. Mr. Mario's employer was supportive of his transition but they refused to reimburse Marc for his transition-related medical treatment. P&C Food Markets told Marc that the costs related to his hormone therapy and sexual reassignment surgery were not eligible for reimbursement because they were not "medically necessary." Marc sued his employers in federal court to get reimbursement for the treatment that his doctors had recommended. Unfortunately, the court sided with P&C Food, and Marc did not receive any reimbursement from the insurance company (*Mario v. P&C Food Mkts.* 2000). Mr. Mario pursued a course of treatment that was standard for his medical condition but could not afford it. He is not alone. Many transgender individuals who wish to transition have difficulty finding access to affordable hormone replacement therapy, hair removal, mastectomies, prostheses, and genital surgery that is crucial to the transition process. Insurance companies and health care providers often use the terms "medically necessary" or "medical necessity" to decide which treatments and procedures should be covered by the insurer. By 2009, the American Medical Association (AMA HOD Resolution 122 2008), the American Psychological Association (APA Policy Statement 2008), and the National Association of Social Workers (NASW Policy on Transgender and Gender Identity, in Social Work Speaks 2009) had each released a statement about the importance of transgender-related physical and mental health care coverage. Despite endorsements from respected national agencies, transition-related care is still inaccessible to many transgender people who are in need of treatment. Fortunately, because of the endorsements from those agencies, transgender individuals and their advocates now have grounds to appeal any denied insurance claims related to their treatment.

Defining Housing Discrimination

In the absence of employment discrimination, LGBTQ-identified individuals who are gainfully employed may still experience negative consequences in their quality of life. Lesbian, gay, bisexual, and transgender individuals are often victims of housing discrimination (Grant et al. 2011). These individuals report being denied housing or being evicted because of perceived sexual orientation or transgender identity. In the same previously mentioned survey of 6,450 transgender and gender nonconforming individuals, 19 % reported being discriminated against and denied housing because of their gender identity or gender presentation. Being denied an apartment or a home can cause an individual to seek housing alternatives, including services for the homeless. Unfortunately, 55 % of transgender and gender nonconforming (GNC) individuals who seek homeless services report being harassed by residents of the shelter or by shelter employees. In addition to the likelihood of harassment, 22 % of respondents reported being sexually assaulted by shelter staff or other residents. In many places, housing discrimination against transgender individuals is not explicitly prohibited. Without housing policies that explicitly prohibit discrimination against GNC and transgender people, those citizens are unable to take legal action against landlords and housing agencies to prevent living on the street or residing in a homeless shelter where experiencing mental, physical, and sexual abuse are valid concerns (Grant et al. 2011).

In 2012, LGBTQ and gender nonconforming individuals acquired the support of the federal government in preventing housing discrimination based on sexual orientation or gender identity. The United States Department of Housing and Urban Development (HUD) is responsible for enforcing fair housing policies that prohibit discrimination based on an individual's sex, race, age, national origin, and disability. In 2012, HUD amended the Fair Housing/Equal Opportunity Policy so that housing agencies that receive funding for special HUD projects (i.e., public housing) cannot discriminate against someone based on that person's gender identity, marital status, or sexual orientation (Department of Housing and Urban Development 2012). The amendment allows lesbian, gay, bisexual, and transgender individuals to file charges against those HUD-funded property owners who deny them housing based on actual or perceived sexual orientation or gender nonconformity. The policy also serves as a model for property owners who do not participate in the HUD-funded projects. Despite this noteworthy example set by HUD, as of 2012, only 16 states and Washington, D.C. include gender identity as part of their housing discrimination laws (HRC 2013).

Unfortunately, there are not many resolved cases of housing discrimination that involve transphobic acts by landlords against their transgender residents. Title VII of the Civil Rights Act of 1968, also known as the Fair Housing Act (FHA), protects citizens from being denied housing because of "race, color, religion, sex, or national origin." The way in which the FHA protects from sex discrimination has typically applied to cisgender individuals being prevented from obtaining or retaining housing because of their sex (i.e., male or female). Title VII is different from the FHA in that Title VII discrimination has expanded to include cases that include sexual harassment while the FHA remains nondescript in its definition of sex discrimination. However, Esses (2009) notes that some judges have "transported" the arguments made in Title VII cases to apply to FHA cases brought by cisgender individuals (see *Shellhammer v. Lewallen* 1985; *Honce v. Vigil* 1993). In these cases, litigants have received judgments against their landlords for the landlord making repeated sexual advances or threatening to evict the tenant if the landlord's sexual or romantic demands are not met. Interestingly, in *Honce v. Vigil* (1993) the judge explicitly included the disparate treatment of one gender compared to another as FHA discrimination. Tenants' success in translating Title VII standards into favorable FHA judgments indicate that judges are continuing to expand the definition of "sex" as it relates to housing discrimination. Judges have yet to apply these standards in a FHA case involving a transgender litigant.

However, Esses (2009) suggests that the expansion of "sex" discrimination in FHA cases bodes well for transgender litigants. Just as litigation in employment discrimination has worked to expand the groups and circumstances to which sex discrimination applies, it is likely that this same process will catalyze protections for transgender and gender nonconforming individuals under the Fair Housing Act.

Defining Protections for Transgender and GNC Youth

Unlike transgender adults, transgender youth are unable to cite discrimination policies or civil court decisions to ensure safe housing. The home environment for some transgender youth may become unsafe after they have disclosed their gender identity to their parents or guardians. Some parents have responded to their child's GNC behavior so adversely they forced the child to leave home and they relinquished custody and parental rights to the State. Trans-identified youth may run away from home because their parents have invalidated their gender identity by refusing to call them by the proper gendered pronouns or by not allowing them to dress in a manner that is consistent with their gender identity. Typically, these displaced teens will have immediate or subsequent contact with the foster care or child welfare system and with the juvenile justice system.

Unfortunately, trans-identified youth that have been placed in the custody of the state will encounter invalidating statements or rules that prevent them from expressing their gender identity while living in a group home or with foster parent. *Doe v. Bell* (754 N.Y.S.2d 846, N.Y. Sup. Ct. 2003) involved the rights of gender expression for a 17-year-old transgender female who lived in an all-boys group home. Ms. Doe, who had been diagnosed with gender dysphoria, testified that she experienced significant psychological distress when her group home caregivers prevented her from dressing according to her gender identity (i.e., wearing skirts). The court ruled that part of the "treatment" of Ms. Doe's gender dysphoria was allowing her to wear the clothing that corresponded to her gender identity. The ruling stated that preventing Ms. Doe from having this "treatment" of wearing girls' clothing amounted to discrimination based on Ms. Doe's established "disability" of gender dysphoria. It is unfortunate that the legal argument requires the court to use terms like disability, illness, and treatment to refer to Ms. Doe's identity. Nevertheless, the ruling was a victory for the rights of transgender youth in the child welfare system. As a result of this litigation and similar movements around the country, trans-identified youth in foster care and juvenile detention facilities in New York, Illinois, California, and Hawaii are allowed to wear clothing that reflects their gender identity.

Transgender youth can experience invalidation and other types of hostility while living in a group home, with a foster parent, or with a biological parent. These hostile housing situations can increase depression symptomology and suicidality in transgender youth. It can also lead trans-identified and GNC youth to leave home even if they have no other place to go. Homeless transgender youth often encounter police officers and enter the juvenile justice system because of factors that are associated with living on the streets (see, too, Frederick, this volume). Homeless transgender youth do not continue to attend school and they may sell drugs or engage in sex work in order to pay for food, shelter, and safety. These "survival crimes" result in police officers charging the youth with truancy, selling illegal substances, prostitution, theft, trespassing, and public health violations. The circumstances under which transgender youth come into contact with police officers and the courts suggests that it is important that the juvenile justice system is acquainted with, sensitive to, and responsive to the needs of trans-identified and gender variant youth (Sullivan 1996).

Fortunately, organizations like the American Bar Association are informing attorneys of some resources that can help transgender youth gain legal protection from bullying, discrimination, and criminal charges. Bevel (2012) suggests that attorneys assist their transgender youth clients by using the provisions outlined by the Fostering Connections to Success and Increasing Adoptions Act of 2008 (Public Law (P.L.) 110–351). Fostering Connections provides financial support and other adoption incentives to guardians who are related to the child who they are interested in adopting (U. S. Department of Health and Human Services 2008). More specifically, some children have relatives that are willing to apply for custody but may not be able to afford care for the child. One of the project's goals is to allow families to reestablish connections and to keep children with a family member as opposed to going into foster care with a family to whom they are not related. The Fostering Connections Act is especially helpful for transgender youth because it affords training and mental health counseling, which can help potential guardians understand the special needs of trans-identified or gender nonconforming youth and provide access to the support services that will prevent the child from reentering the foster care system.

Unfortunately, transphobic and gender identity-related bullying continues to affect schoolchildren (Kosciw et al. 2012). The most recent statistics from a national sample of transgender youth ($N = 705$) indicated that almost 80 % of transgender youth did not feel safe while at school because of discrimination or victimization that was related to their gender identity. The survey revealed that between 12 and 56 % of the verbal and physical bullying targeted the youths' nonconforming gender expression. Approximately 59 % of the gender nonconforming students reported some form of verbal harassment that was related to their gender presentation while only 29 % of the gender conforming students reported experiencing verbal harassment associated with their gender presentation (Kosciw et al. 2012). Transphobic bullying is an overwhelming source of distress and victimization for trans-identified and GNC youth and is associated with an increased risk of negative emotional outcomes, including self-harm and suicide (SPRC 2008). Youth who identify as either transgender or GNC suffer significantly poorer mental health outcomes compared to youth who do not identify as LGBTQ or GNC (Birkett et al. 2009; Grossman and D'Augelli 2006; Kosciw et al. 2012).

Some school districts in Colorado, Florida, Maine, Massachusetts, New Hampshire, Kansas, and other states are beginning to implement nondiscrimination policies in order to protect their transgender and gender nonconforming students (and, see Warbelow & Cobb, this volume, for a review of U.S. state and federal anti-bullying legislation and policies). In New Jersey, a gender nonconforming male eighth grader, identified in the litigation as P.S., encountered teasing and bullying associated with his feminine gender presentation at school. The abuse became so severe that P.S. became extremely depressed. After P.S. attempted suicide, his mother placed him in another school that was outside of the school district. She then sued her local school district, Shore County, for the costs associated with sending P.S. to another school district. The mother won the case and was awarded tuition costs as well as attorney's fees, as the judge ruled that the Shore Regional High School Board of Education failed to provide P.S. with a safe school environment (*Shore Regional High School Board of Education v. P.S* 2004).

Transgender plaintiffs' legal victories do not always come with a financial settlement but with policy changes that should have a lasting impact on the culture of discrimination that originated the legal action. Katrina Harrington's school principal requested that Katrina, an MTF teenager, report to his office every morning before school so that he could approve Katrina's attire. Katrina was sent home on the days that the principal did not approve of her gender nonconforming attire. The LGBTQ legal advocacy group, GLAAD, helped Ms. Harrington bring a suit against the school for the transphobic dress code policies. The courts ruled that the school had violated Katrina's rights and that the middle school was not allowed to prevent their students from dressing and behaving according to their gender identity (*Doe v. Yunits* 2000). Nikki Youngblood, a gender nonconforming teen, sued her county's school board after the school removed Nikki's senior photo from her high school's yearbook. Instead of the feminine attire that the school required all of the female students to wear, Nikki wore a tuxedo. The county's school board decided to settle the case and amended their policies to allow students to decide not to wear "sex-differentiated" attire (*Youngblood v. School Bd. of Hillsborough Cty.* 2002 Florida, No. 02-15924-CC (11th Cir.)). Each of these legal victories for gender nonconforming youth help to increase school diversity and GNC-supportive climates.

Defining Family

Transgender and GNC individuals have expressed apprehension about relying on police officers and the courts for protection from discrimination and victimization (Almeida et al. 2009; Goldblum et al. 2012; Stoudt et al. 2012). Unfortunately, some family matters such as marriage, divorce, adoption, and custody proceedings require LGBTQ citizens to interact with family courts. Subsequently, transgender persons endure negative experiences with the family court system solely because some rights are explicitly or implicitly restricted to persons who identify and live as the biological gender that they were assigned at birth (i.e., cisgender). A transgender individual in a heterosexual relationship (i.e., MTF in a relationship with a cisgender male) will encounter the same restrictions on marriage and child custody as a same-sex (homosexual) couple. If a legal sex change reflected in identification documents is not recognized in their state of residence, transgender individuals may have to fight in the courts to obtain the civil rights and benefits of legal marriage (i.e., tax benefits, insurance benefits, and end-of-life care) that are provided to cisgender heterosexual couples.

Marriage inequality complicates the division of assets subsequent to a partner's death or the dissolution of a relationship. In lieu of marriage equality, some same-sex couples have used contracts and contract law to provide and protect privileges that are inherent in marriage (Christensen 1997). When legal marriage is not available for a same-sex couple, they may use legal contracts affording power of attorney to the opposite partner. A legal contract, in lieu of a legally recognized "marriage," can provide some financial relief to surviving partners and divorcees when one partner is transgender. Some "same-sex" (by way of transgender identity) couples get married in an area that legally recognizes their marriage but that couple may reside, and begin divorce proceedings, in a state that does not recognize their marriage and, therefore, does not accommodate their divorce. Transgender couples, who are seen as same-sex couples in the eyes of the law, that want to end their marriages are turning to mediators, as opposed to the courts, to resolve issues that deal with distributing property, spousal support, and child support or custody (Chambers and Polikoff 2000).

Typically, judges assess parental fitness by evaluating the type of home life that each parent is able to provide and other environmental influences relevant to the child's wellbeing. Unfortunately, some judges believe that transgender identity, alone, is indicative of parental unfitness. In some cases, transgender parents consult and pay expert witnesses to testify that the transgender parent's sexual orientation or gender identity is not harmful to the children. The appeals process can be discouraging and costly for a transgender-identified parent. Some transgender parents have reported taking out loans or filing for bankruptcy in order to continue the expensive process of ongoing litigation (Doskow 1999). Additionally, transgender individuals must often receive a stigmatizing, mental illness diagnosis of gender dysphoria (previously labeled gender identity disorder (GID)) before a doctor will prescribe hormone therapy or gender reassignment surgery that is crucial to their transition. Some non-transgender parents have used this mental illness diagnosis to discredit the transgender parent or to use as proof of the transgender parent's unfitness. The non-transgender parent has also used the courts' incomplete, and often disputed, definition of sex to invalidate their marriage so that the non-biological, transgender parent has no legal right to custody over the children raised during the marriage.

In *Kantaras v. Kantaras* (2004), the wife of a transgender man wanted to terminate her husband's parental rights and have the court invalidate the marriage. Mrs. Kantaras gave birth to the children but both she and Mr. Kantaras acted as the children's parents. When the couple decided to separate, Mrs. Kantaras sought to have the marriage invalidated and, therefore, eliminate Mr. Kantaras's parental rights over the children he had cared for during the marriage. The trial judge denied Mrs. Kantaras's request to invalidate the marriage because Mr. Kantaras had received hormone therapy, sexual reassignment surgery, and according to legal documents (i.e., amended birth certificate and driver's license), Michael Kantaras was male at the time of the marriage. The judge also granted custody of the children to Mr. Kantaras. However, an appeals court later overturned the trial court's ruling about the marriage and stated that the marriage was invalid because Mr. Kantaras was not "male" at the time of the marriage and same-sex marriage is prohibited in Florida. The ruling that invalidated the marriage also invalidated Mr. Kantaras's parental rights as he was not the biological father of either of his children, nor was he married to the children's mother. Mr. and Mrs. Kantaras settled on joint custody without returning to court. Mr. Kantaras was able to retain access to his children but the Appeals Court's ruling damaged the movement for transgender equality in the law. The most important aspect of this landmark case was that the courts allowed the attorneys to present witnesses and make legal arguments about how the law defines "sex." The court concluded that the law intended the word "sex" to mean biological sex at birth and that individuals who are born female cannot legally marry a woman in Florida.

Another interesting instance of the court's definition of sex in the realm of marriage and divorce involves Mr. and Mrs. Beatie. Thomas Beatie, a transgender man, transitioned using hormone therapy and was able to amend his identity documents so that his birth certificate and driver's license indicated that he was male. After his legal identification was amended to reflect his male gender identity, Mr. Beatie got married in his home state of Hawaii. While living in Hawaii, shortly after his marriage, Thomas and his wife Nancy discovered that Nancy was not able to bear children and they decided that Thomas, who had a double-mastectomy but had not undergone genital surgery or a hysterectomy, would carry their children. The media labeled Thomas Beatie, "The Pregnant Man" and the Beaties received a lot of public attention and interest during his pregnancy. The couple moved to Arizona with their children in 2010. When the couple decided to divorce in 2012, the presiding judge stated that their marriage was not recognized according to Arizona law because Thomas Beatie was born female and because Arizona prohibits same-sex marriage. However, the Beaties's marriage, as granted by the state of Hawaii, was a legally valid opposite-sex marriage. The Arizona judge stated that because Thomas had given birth to the couple's three children, Thomas was legally female. More specifically, the judge used Thomas' pregnancies to define Thomas's sex as female. That judge's definition of Mr. Beatie's gender as female meant that the couple was in a same-sex marriage, which is not recognized by Arizona law. In the beginning of 2013, the couple began the process of challenging the judge's ruling so that their marriage will be recognized by the law and so that they may obtain a legal divorce (*In re the Marriage of Beatie* 2012).

Other transgender individuals whose marriages ended with the death of their partner have also encountered problems related to the law's invalidation of their marriage. Christie Lee Littleton, a transgender woman, filed a wrongful death lawsuit against the hospital that cared for her husband when he died (*Littleton v. Prange* 1999). The court ruled that Littleton was legally male and that the same-sex marriage ban in her state (Texas) prevented the law from recognizing Littleton as the decedent's wife for the lawsuit. Another transgender wife, Mrs. Gardiner was prevented from inheriting her husband's estate when her husband's surviving son petitioned the court to invalidate his father's marriage to his stepmother (*In re Estate of Gardiner* 2002). As a result of her stepson's petition, Mrs. Gardiner was unable to obtain any proceeds from her husband's estate or other death benefits that are typically provided to a cisgender widow or widower. As explained above, legal definitions of marriage embroil legal battles when both spouses are living; but these definitions continue to obscure spousal rights after one spouse has passed away.

The complications in legal recognition of marriages for transgender individuals may be helped by a recent Supreme Court ruling related to legally granted same-sex marriages. On June 26, 2013, the United States Supreme Court (*United States v. Windsor*, 570 U.S. (2013)) found that Section 3 of the Defense of Marriage Act (DOMA) was unconstitutional under the right to due process and the Fifth Amendment. Section 3 of DOMA states that access to federal benefits (e.g., tax exemptions) and marriage recognition under federal law are restricted to spouses who are in opposite-sex marriages. The Supreme Court decision was interpreted as a groundbreaking win for the LGBTQ community. On a federal level, it eliminated one of the barriers to marriage equality, "redefined" marriage to include spouses who are of the same-sex, and made available many benefits that were previously reserved only for individuals in opposite-sex marriages. The *U.S. v. Windsor* helps transgender individuals by allowing them to enter a federally recognized marriage before they have had their "legal" sex changed on identity documents. For instance, a transgender man who has not changed his legal sex to male, can marry his female partner without concern that the marriage will be subject to federal restrictions related to his legally female sex status at the time of his marriage to a female. Individual states' laws continue to govern whether same-sex marriage can be granted or recognized in each state, but there is consensus among the LGBTQ advocates that the ruling changes the social and legal climate, which will help bring marriage equality one step closer than ever before.

Conclusion

Transgender individuals' experiences with discrimination have devastating emotional, physical, and financial consequences from childhood through adulthood. The legal system has, in some respects, reinforced a climate of discrimination against transgender individuals by restricting civil rights and failing to uphold the rights and protections that have been made available to non-LGBTQ populations. Experiences with verbal or physical harassment, employment and housing discrimination, police misconduct, and custody revocations and restrictions may have led many transgender individuals to mistrust the court system on which other people rely. This lack of trust can lead to transgender individuals reporting fewer incidents of discrimination or victimization because they believe that the court will not help them. It is important for the courts to accommodate and assist transgender individuals in order to restore a sense of trust and possibly increase the utility of a relationship with the courts for individuals who identify as transgender. The studies and statistics discussed above highlight that discrimination and harassment have real, negative consequences for transgender persons. Antitherapeutic jurisprudence and low procedural justice are common themes in transgender individuals' experiences with the courts. Adverse interactions with the agents of the law are harmful, not only to LGBTQ youth and adults themselves, but also to LGBTQ communities' trust in or reliance on police support or the judicial processes that are set in place to protect all citizens. Landmark transgender discrimination decisions allow for the enforcement of antidiscrimination laws but the policies do not, immediately, prevent discriminatory behavior in social, employment, or housing situations. LGBTQ individuals who feel that they were treated unfairly according to the law must first file a case against the offending party. However, many transgender victims of discrimination may not be aware of the legal protections that they have recently been afforded. Additionally, beginning litigation related to discrimination can be time-consuming and costly for trans-identified discrimination victims. Legal victories may help to ensure that LGBTQ individuals have support for fighting discrimination but the acceptance of landmark rulings and the implementation of fair treatment may not be immediate.

References

Albelda, R., Badgett, M. V. L., Schneebaum, A., & Gates, G. J. (2009). *Poverty in the lesbian, gay, and bisexual community*. Los Angeles, CA: The Williams Institute, Retrieved December 1, 2012 from http://escholarship.org/uc/item/2509p8r5

Almeida, J., Johnson, R. M., Corliss, H. L., Molnar, B. E., & Azrael, D. (2009). Emotional distress among LGBT youth: The influence of perceived discrimination based on sexual orientation. *Journal of Youth Adolescence, 38*, 1001–1014. doi:10.1007/s10964-009-9397-9.

American Medical Association (AMA). (2008). House of delegates (HOD) Resolution 122 (2008).

APA Policy Statement (2008). Retrieved from http://www.apa.org/about/policy/transgender.aspx

Badgett, M. V. L. (2001). *Money, myths, and change: The economic lives of lesbians and gay men*. Chicago, IL: University of Chicago Press.

Badgett, M.V., Lau, H., Sears, B., & Ho, D. (2007). *Bias in the workplace: consistent evidence of sexual orientation and gender identity discrimination*. Los Angeles, CA: The Williams Institute, Retrieved December 1, 2012 from http://www.law.ucla.edu/williamsinstitute/publications/Bias%20in%20the%20Workplace.pdf

Balsam, K. F., Molina, Y., Beadnell, B., Simoni, J., & Walters, K. (2011). Measuring multiple minority stress: The LGBT People of Color Microaggressions Scale. *Cultural Diversity and Ethnic Minority Psychology, 17*, 163–174. doi:10.1037/a0023244.

Barnes v. City of Cincinnati. (2005) 401 F.3d 729 (6th Cir. 2005).

Bevel, G. (2012). Representing transgender youth: Learning from Mae's journey. *ABA Child Law Practice, 29*, 169–174.

Birkett, M., Espelage, D. L., & Koenig, B. (2009). LGB and questioning students in schools: The moderating effects of homophobic bullying and school climate on negative outcomes. *Journal of Youth and Adolescence, 38*, 989–1000. doi:10.1007/s10964-008-938s1.

Chambers, D. L., & Polikoff, N. D. (2000). Family law and gay and lesbian family issues in the twentieth century. *Family Law Quarterly, 33*, 523–542.

Christensen, C. W. (1997). Legal ordering of family values: The case of gay and lesbian families. *Cardozo Law Review, 18*, 1299–1416.

Civil Rights Act of 1964. (1964). Pub.L. 88–352, 78 Stat. 241.

Department of Housing and Urban Development. (2012). 24 CFR Parts 5, 200, 203, 236, 400, 570, 574, 882, 891, and 982. Retrieved from http://portal.hud.gov/hudportal/documents/huddoc?id=12lgbtfinalrule.pdf

Doe v. United Consumer Financial Services. (2001). Case No. 1:01 CV 1112 (N.D. Ohio 2001).

Doe v. Yunits. (2000). 15 Mass. L. Rptr. 278, 2000 WL 33162199 (Mass. Super. Ct.).

Doskow, E. (1999). The second parent trap: Parenting for same-sex couples in a brave new world. *The Journal of Juvenile Law, 20*, 1–22.

Esses, D. L. (2009). Afraid to be myself, even at home: A transgender cause of action under the Fair Housing Act. *Columbia Journal of Law and Social Problems, 42*, 465–501.

Freidman, C., & Leaper, C. (2010). Sexual-minority college women's experiences with discrimination: Relations with identity and collective action. *Psychology of Women Quarterly, 34*, 152–164.

Gagné, P., & Tewksbury, R. (1998). Conformity pressures and gender resistance among transgendered individuals. *Social Problems, 45*, 81–101.

Gerhardstein, K. R., & Anderson, V. N. (2010). There's more than meets the eye: Facial appearance and evaluations of transsexual people. *Sex Roles, 62*, 361–373. doi:10.1007/s11199-010-9746x.

Goldblum, P., Testa, R. J., Pflum, S., Hendricks, M. L., Bradford, J., & Bognar, B. (2012). The relationship between gender-based victimization and suicide attempts in transgender people. *Professional Psychology: Research and Practice, 43*, 468–475. doi:10.1037/a0029605.

Grant, J. M., Mottet, L. A., Tanis, J., Harrison, J., Herman, J. L., & Keisling, M. (2011). *Injustice at every turn: A report of the National Transgender Discrimination Survey.* Washington, DC: National Center for Transgender Equality and National Gay and Lesbian Task Force.

Grossman, A. H., & D'Augelli, A. R. (2006). Transgender youth. *Journal of Homosexuality, 51*, 111–128. doi:10.1300/J082v51n01-06.

Gulati, S. (2003). The use of gender-loaded identities in sex-stereotyping jurisprudence. *New York University Law Review, 78*, 2177–2203.

Harcourt, J. (2006). Current issues in lesbian, gay, bisexual, and transgender (LGBT) health. *Journal of Homosexuality, 51*, 1–11. doi:10.1300/J082v51n01_01.

Herek, G. M. (2004). Beyond "homophobia": Thinking about sexual prejudice and stigma in the twenty-first century. *Sexuality Research & Social Policy, 1*, 6–24.

Herek, G. M. (2007). Confronting sexual stigma and prejudice: Theory and practice. *Journal of Social Issues, 63*, 905–925. doi:10.1111/j.1540-4560.2007.00544.x.

Herek, G. M., & Garnets, L. D. (2007). Sexual orientation and mental health. *Annual Review of Clinical Psychology, 3*, 353–375. doi:10.1146/annurev.clinpsy.3.022806.091510.

Himmelstein, K. E. W., & Bruckner, H. (2010). Criminal justice and school sanctions against non-heterosexual youth: A national longitudinal study. *Pediatrics, 127*, 49–58. doi:10.1542/peds.2009-2306.

Human Rights Coalition. (2013). Retrieved from http://www.hrc.org/files/assets/resources/Housing_Laws_and_Policies.pdf

Honce v. Vigil. (1993) 1 F.3d 1085, 1088 (10th Cir. 1993).

In re the Marriage of Beatie. (2012). Retrieved from http://transgenderlawcenter.org/wp-content/uploads/2013/01/amicusbeatie.pdf

In re Estate of Gardiner. (2002) 42 P.3d 120 (Kan. 2002).

Kantaras v. Kantaras. (2004) 884 So.2d 155 (2004).

Kosciw, J. G., Greytak, E. A., Bartkiewicz, M. J., Boesen, M. J., & Palmer, N. A. (2012). *The 2011 National School Climate Survey: The experiences of lesbian, gay, bisexual and transgender youth in our nation's schools.* New York: GLSEN.

Littleton v. Prange. (1999) 9 S.W.3d 223.

Macy v. Holder, Appeal No. 0120120821 (April 20, 2012).

Mario v. P&C Food Mkts. (2000). 313 F.3d 758 (2nd Cir. 2000).

Martin, J. I., & Meezan, W. (2003). Applying ethical standards to research and evaluations involving lesbian, gay, bisexual, and transgender populations. *Journal of Gay and Lesbian Social Services, 15,* 181–201. doi:10.1300/J041v15n01_12.

Meyer, I. H. (2003). Prejudice, social stress, and mental health in lesbian, gay, and bisexual populations: Conceptual issues and research evidence. *Psychological Bulletin, 129,* 674–697. doi:10.1037/0033-2909.129.5.674.

National Association of Social Workers. (2009). *Social work speaks. Transgender and gender identity issues.* Washington DC: NASW Press.

Price Waterhouse v. Hopkins. (1989). 490 U.S. 228 (1989).

Quintana, N. S. (2009). Poverty in the LGBT community. Retrieved from http://www.americanprogress.org/wp-content/uploads/issues/2009/07/pdf/lgbt_poverty.pdf

Quintana, N. S., Rosenthal, J., & Krehely, J. (2010). *On the streets: The federal response to gay and transgender homeless youth.* Retrieved from http://www.americanprogress.org/wpcontent/uploads/issues/2010/06/pdf/lgbtyouthhomelessness.pdf.

Shellhammer v. Lewallen (1985) No. 84-3573, 1985 WL 13505 (6th Cir. 1985).

Shore Regional High School Board of Education v. P.S. (2004).

Smith v. City of Salem, Ohio. (2004) 378 F.3d 566 (6th Cir. 2004).

Stoudt, B. G., Fine, M., & Fox, M. (2012). Growing up policed in the age of aggressive policing policies. *New York Law School Review, 56,* 1331–1370.

Suicide Prevention Resource Center. (2008). *Suicide risk and prevention for lesbian, gay, bisexual, and transgender youth.* Newton, MA: Education Development Center, Inc.

Sullivan, C. A. (1996). Kids, courts, and queers: Lesbian and gay youth in the juvenile justice and foster care systems. *Law & Sexuality: A Review of Lesbian, Gay, Bisexual, and Transgender Legal Issues, 6,* 31–62.

Taylor, J. K. (2007). Transgender identities and public policy in the United States: The relevance for public administration. *Administration & Society, 39,* 833–856. doi:10.177/0095399707305548.

Tomsen, S. & Mason, G. (2001). Engendering homophobia:Violence, sexuality, and gender conformity. *Journal of Sociology, 37,* 257–273.

United States v. Windsor. (2013) 570 U.S._(2013).

U.S. Department of Health and Human Services, Administration for Children and Families, (2008). *Fostering Connections to Success and Increasing Adoptions Act of 2008* (P. L. 110–351) (2008) Retrieved from http://www.childwelfare.gov/fosteringconnections

U.S. Department of Labor, Bureau of Labor Statistics. (2008). *The employment situation: September 2008.* Retrieved from http://www.bls.gov/news.release/archives/empsit_10032008.htm

Weinberg, J. D. (2009). Gender nonconformity: An analysis of perceived sexual orientation and gender identity protection under the Employment Non-Discrimination Act. *University of San Francisco Law Review, 44*(1), 1–31.

Youngblood v. School Bd. of Hillsborough Cty. (2002). Florida, No. 02-15924-CC (11th Cir.).

Chapter 19
Bullying of LGBT Youth in America: Prevalence, Effects, and Government Responses

Sarah Warbelow and Ty Cobb

Abstract Bullying in schools affects many students in harmful ways. The injurious effects that bullying can have on students cannot be understated, ranging from poor academic performance and anxiety, to depression and suicide. National statistics reflect that those students who are or who are perceived to be lesbian, gay, bisexual, or transgender (LGBT) experience substantially higher rates of bullying than their peers. Because of growing information on this topic, bullying has been elevated from a playground incident to a topic of public policy debated in the U.S. Congress as well as in state legislatures across the country. However, passage of state-level laws has created a patchwork of protections for LGBT students. At the federal level, the only protections available have come from executive action and application of Title IX's prohibition on schools engaging in discrimination against students on the basis of sex. Congress, despite widespread recognition of the need for further protections, has yet to move forward with legislation that would make schools a safer place for LGBT students. An analysis of U.S. state and federal bullying protections indicates that while some schools are becoming safer environments for LGBT students, there is much more progress to be made.

Keywords Lesbian · Gay · Bisexual · Transgender · LGBT · Human Rights Campaign · Cyberbullying · GLSEN · Youth · Bullying · Harassment · Schools · Educational · Discrimination · Title IX · Sexual harassment · Suicide · Opposite-sex harassment · Same-sex harassment · Gender stereotyping · Safe Schools Improvement Act · Student Non-Discrimination Act · Tyler Clementi Higher Education Anti-Harassment Act · Law · Policy

S. Warbelow (✉) · T. Cobb
Human Rights Campaign, 1640Rhode Island Avenue NW, Washington, DC 20036, USA
e-mail: Sarah.Warbelow@hrc.org

T. Cobb
e-mail: Ty.Cobb@hrc.org

D. Peterson and V. R. Panfil (eds.), *Handbook of LGBT Communities,*
Crime, and Justice, DOI: 10.1007/978-1-4614-9188-0_19,
© Springer Science+Business Media New York 2014

Introduction

The deck is stacked against young people growing up lesbian, gay, bisexual, or transgender (LGBT) in America. Official government discrimination or indifference, family rejection, and social ostracism leave many teens disaffected and disconnected in their own homes and communities. Moreover, when LGBT youth go to school, where they spend a large portion of their day, they often face harsh bullying by peers which disrupts their education and can leave them with physical and mental scars.

The prevalence of bullying of LGBT youth and its consequences are alarming. Our nation's laws and policies are responding, albeit slowly. This chapter focuses on U.S. federal and state responses to the bullying of LGBT young people, showing that there is a new commitment by federal elected officials to respond to the issue and that states are experimenting with anti-bullying laws, which are growing in scope and strength.

Prevalence and Consequences of Bullying

According to a 2012 report by the Centers for Disease Control and Prevention (CDC 2012), 20.1 % of students surveyed nationally reported being bullied at school in the past year, and 16.2 % reported being "cyberbullied." The numbers for LGBT youth are dramatically higher. The Human Rights Campaign (HRC) recently reported (2012) that LGBT students were twice as likely as non-LGBT students to be verbally harassed (51 vs. 25 %) or physically attacked (17 vs. 10 %). The Gay, Lesbian, and Straight Education Network (GLSEN) recently reported additional findings (Kosciw et al. 2012):

- Within the past year, 81.9 % of LGBT students reported being verbally harassed, 38.3 % reported being physically harassed, and 18.3 % reported being physically assaulted because of their sexual orientation.
- Within the past year, 63.9 % of LGBT students reported being verbally harassed, 27.1 % reported being physically harassed, and 12.4 % reported being physically assaulted because of their gender expression.[1]
- 55.2 % of LGBT students reported experiencing "cyberbullying."

Despite such persistent harassment, GLSEN reported that 60.4 % of LGBT students who were harassed or assaulted in school did not report the incident to

---

[1] Gender expression refers to all of the external characteristics and behaviors that are socially defined as either masculine or feminine, such as dress, grooming, mannerisms, speech patterns and social interactions. Social or cultural norms can vary widely and some characteristics that may be accepted as masculine, feminine or neutral in one culture may not be assessed similarly in another.

staff, believing little to no action would be taken or the situation could worsen (Kosciw et al. 2012). Further, 36.7 % of students who did report an incident said that school staff did nothing in response (HRC 2013). LGBT students are almost twice as likely to hear negative messages at school about being LGBT as they are to hear positive messages (HRC 2012). More than half reported hearing negative remarks from faculty and staff, and more than half reported feeling unsafe at school (Kosciw et al. 2012).

Research shows that there is an increased risk of suicidal thoughts or suicide attempts by victims of bullying (Brunstein 2012). LGBT youth are five times as likely to attempt suicide (Hatzebuehler 2011) and 3–4 times as likely to commit suicide as non-LGBT youth (Biegel and Kuehl 2010). While suicide prevention is a key aspect of the effort to address bullying, it is only the most visible aspect of the ramifications of bullying. Bullied students have lower self-esteem and higher levels of anxiety, depression, and loneliness [American Psychological Association (APA) 2012]. They are also more likely to skip school, to drop out of school, and correspondingly have lower academic achievement and lower reading and math skills (APA 2012). The APA (2011) also reported that bullying appears to contribute to lower test scores.

For LGBT students, these issues are acute, as demonstrated by Kosciw and colleagues (2012). LGBT students who experience higher levels of victimization have higher levels of depression and lower self-esteem than those who experience lower levels. Academic performance is also acutely affected. Thirty percent of LGBT students reported skipping a class, or an entire day of school, in the month prior to the survey, because they felt unsafe or uncomfortable at school. Those students who experience higher levels of victimization were more than twice as likely to miss class or school as those who experience lower levels. Overall, LGBT students who experience higher levels of victimization have lower GPAs and are twice as likely to report that they do not plan to pursue postsecondary education as those students who experience lower levels (Kosciw et al. 2012).

While the consequences of bullying are significant, research also shows that creation of supportive academic environments can significantly improve matters for LGBT students, even in the absence of formal legal protections.

- The suicide risk for LGBT students was 20 % lower in schools with an LGBT "supportive environment," meaning schools with a gay-straight alliance and non-discrimination or anti-bullying policies which include specific protections for lesbian, gay, and bisexual students (Hatzebuehler 2011, pp. 896–898).
- Among LGBT students who have been harassed or assaulted at school, those in schools with non-discrimination or anti-bullying policies that specifically protect sexual orientation and gender identity characteristics were more likely to tell school personnel about the events than LGBT students in schools with a generic policy or no policy at all (GLSEN 2005).
- Teachers are more likely to intervene to address and prevent incidents of bullying in schools with enumerated policies (GLSEN 2005).

- Students in schools with comprehensive bullying and harassment policies felt a greater sense of connectedness and belonging to their school communities (Diaz et al. 2010).

The need for comprehensive legislation and policies is clear. In states with comprehensive laws and schools with enumerated policies, including those that acknowledge sexual orientation and/or gender identity or expression, LGBT students experience less bullying, feel safer overall, and are less likely to skip classes because they feel uncomfortable or unsafe (Kosciw et al. 2012).

Defining Bullying Behavior

The "Severe, Pervasive, and Objectively Offensive" Legal Standard

Title IX of the U.S. Civil Rights Act (20 U.S.C. §§ 1681-88) is the federal law most applicable to bullying in the educational environment. This section provides some background on Title IX generally, and on how courts analyze complaints alleging violations. Later sections of this chapter discuss how Title IX and other federal laws and regulations apply specifically to addressing bullying of LGBT students. There are also state laws and regulations, some providing broader coverage than their federal equivalents; these are also discussed in later sections of the chapter.

Most people are familiar with Title IX for its impact on girls' and women's sports programs (Atal 2012). But Title IX is about much more than sports—Title IX broadly addresses sex-based discrimination in educational opportunities. The U.S. Department of Education (USDOE) oversees compliance with Title IX, which applies to all schools that receive federal funding (USDOE 2012). Title IX was enacted almost a decade after Title VII of the Civil Rights Act (42 U.S.C. § 2000e-2000e17), which addresses employment discrimination, overseen by the federal Equal Employment Opportunity Commission (EEOC). For this reason, many legal principles associated with Title IX discrimination derive from principles developed in earlier Title VII discrimination cases. It is important to note that both laws expressly cover "sex" but do not, by their language, address either sexual orientation or gender identity.[2] However, federal courts, the DOE, and the EEOC have interpreted the relevant statutes and regulations in ways that sometimes allow them to cover sexual orientation and gender identity.

---

[2] See, e.g., 20 U.S.C. § 1681(a) (2006) (applying Title IX to discrimination "on the basis of sex"); 42 U.S.C. § 2000e-2(a) (2006) (defining "unlawful employment practices" in terms of "race, color, religion, sex, or national origin").

When Title VII and Title IX were originally enacted, the focus was to address explicit discrimination, such as refusing to hire persons of a protected class, or by providing unequal educational opportunities on the basis of sex. Later, courts began to recognize that harassment in the work place was also a form of discrimination. In a 1986 decision, *Meritor Savings Bank v. Vinson*, the Supreme Court held that a "hostile workplace environment" could be, in and of itself, unlawful discrimination in violation of Title VII for which an employer is liable [477 U.S. 57 (1986)].

While on its face Title IX prohibits discrimination, case law has made it clear that a certain level of harassment reaches the threshold of discrimination. In 1989, in *Price Waterhouse v. Hopkins,* the Supreme Court held that discrimination based on gender stereotyping was actionable under Title VII, finding in favor of a woman who was denied a promotion on the basis that she did not act feminine enough [490 U.S. 228 (1989)]. And in 1998, the Supreme Court held in *Oncale v. Sundowner Offshore Services* that same-sex sexual harassment was discrimination based on sex [523 U.S. 75 (1998)]. These decisions (on opposite-sex harassment, gender stereotyping, and same-sex harassment) have been used, with varying degrees of success, to argue complaints of discrimination on the basis of sexual orientation and/or gender identity.

In 1998, the Supreme Court held in *Gebser v. Lago Vista Independent School District* that teacher-on-student sexual harassment could be actionable under Title IX [524 U.S. 274 (1998)]. The following year, in *Davis v. Monroe County Board of Education*, the Supreme Court held the same for student-on-student sexual harassment [526 U.S. 629 (1999)]. For a plaintiff to succeed in holding a school district liable for a complaint of student-on-student sexual harassment, the plaintiff must show that:

1. The harassment was severe, pervasive, and objectively offensive;
2. The school district had actual knowledge of the harassment; and
3. The school district acted with deliberate indifference to the harassment.

The plaintiff is not required to show that they were actually excluded from school or school activities. Rather, the plaintiff must show that the harassment undermined and detracted from the plaintiff's academic experience to the extent that the plaintiff was effectively denied access to the school's resources and opportunities.

The Supreme Court has not yet had an opportunity to hear a case specifically addressing student-on-student LGBT bullying, but the issue has arisen in lower federal courts, which have applied the principles from these cases. In 2000, federal district courts in California and Minnesota each applied *Davis* and *Oncale* to hold that a claim of student-on-student anti-gay bullying could be actionable under Title IX.[3] A number of federal district courts have followed the rationale of *Hopkins* to

---

[3] See *Ray v. Antioch Unified Sch. Dist.*, 107 F. Supp. 2d 1165 (N.D. Cal 2000); See *Montgomery v. Indep. Sch. Dist. No. 709*, 109 F. Supp. 2d 1081 (D. Minn. 2000).

find that LGBT bullying based on gender stereotyping was actionable under Title IX.[4] And one federal district court, in *Miles v. New York University*, found that teacher-on-student harassment of a male-to-female transsexual student was sex-based discrimination, and actionable under Title IX [F. Supp. 248 (S.D.N.Y. 1997)].

Not all of these cases were won by the plaintiffs. The test defined by *Davis* presents a high threshold for a plaintiff to meet. But a number of these cases were settled after the court ruled that Title IX applied to the plaintiffs' allegations. Although Title IX's text refers only to sex-based discrimination, the precedents in the federal courts, applying Title IX to sexual orientation and gender identity, render Title IX a powerful tool in the fight against harassment of LGBT youth.

Free Speech

Opponents of anti-bullying laws have attempted to oppose legislative protections by arguing that such policies infringe upon an individual's freedom of speech, protected by the First Amendment to the U.S. Constitution. Although the Supreme Court has not reached the issue of free speech in the context of anti-bullying policies, in 1969, in *Tinker v. Des Moines Independent Community School District*, the Supreme Court held that "conduct by the student, in class or out of it, which for any reason—whether it stems from time, place, or type of behavior—materially disrupts classwork or involves substantial disorder or invasion of the rights of others is... not immunized by the constitutional guarantee of freedom of speech." However, though the U.S. Supreme Court has not spoken directly to the dispute, in 2011 a federal circuit court flatly rejected the premise that anti-bullying laws violate the First Amendment. In *Kowalski v. Berkeley County School District*, the U.S. Court of Appeals for the 4th Circuit held that, "[f]ar from being a situation where school authorities 'suppress speech on political and social issues based on disagreement with the viewpoint expressed,' school administrators must be able to prevent and punish harassment and bullying in order to provide a safe school environment conducive to learning" [652 F.3d 565, 572 (4th Cir. 2011)].

Enumeration

Why Unenumerated Laws are Insufficient

The listing of specific characteristics for which students are frequently targeted through bullying, harassment, and intimidation, is called "enumeration." Research has shown that enumeration in anti-bullying laws and policies is critical to ensure

---

[4] See, e.g., *Theno v. Tonganoxie Unified Sch. Dist. No. 464*, 377 F. Supp. 2d 952 (D. Kan 2005); *Snelling v. Fall Mountain Regional Sch. Dist.*, 2001 WL 276975 (D.N.H. 2001).

that all students are protected. Compared to states without enumerated laws, students who attend schools in states with laws that enumerate categories report less bullying (Kosciw et al. 2012). Marginalized students, such as LGBT students in states without enumerated anti-bullying laws, have the same experience of bullying as students who live in states without any anti-bullying laws at all (Kosciw et al. 2012). Students who attend schools with enumerated policies are harassed far less often for reasons such as their physical appearance, their sexual orientation, or their gender expression; are less likely than other students to report a serious harassment problem at their school; and are 50 % more likely to feel very safe at school (GLSEN 2005). LGBT students who attend schools without an enumerated policy are three times more likely to skip a class because they feel uncomfortable or unsafe (Kosciw et al. 2012).

Enumeration also provides teachers and other educators the tools they need to implement anti-bullying policies, which makes it easier for them to prevent bullying and intervene when incidents occur. School staff often fear that they will themselves be targeted for intervening on behalf of LGBT students. When they can point to language that provides clear protection for LGBT students, they feel more comfortable enforcing the policy. Enumeration helps to increase educator awareness that anti-LGBT bullying is unacceptable behavior that warrants intervention, and students report that teachers were significantly more likely to intervene in states with enumerated laws, as compared to states with either unenumerated laws or no laws at all (GLSEN 2005).

Addressing Accusations of Exclusion

Several organizations and many legislators have pushed back against enumerated anti-bullying laws by raising the concern that enumerated laws exclude students who need protection. In essence, they argue that there should be no distinction drawn between students when anti-bullying laws and policies are written. Often cited are students bullied on the basis of weight or an inability to afford designer clothes.

Well-written anti-bullying laws and policies address this concern by including language such as:

> … which is based on any actual or perceived characteristic, including, but not limited to, race, color, religion, ancestry, national origin, sex, socioeconomic status, academic status, gender identity or expression, physical appearance, sexual orientation, or disability, or by association with a person who has or is perceived to have one or more characteristics…

The phrase "including, but not limited to" makes clear that the subsequent enumeration is only a subset of characteristics upon which students may face bullying. Enumeration is necessary to ensure that bullying and discrimination against vulnerable students cannot be ignored. Of equal import, inclusion of the phrase "based on any actual or perceived characteristic" highlights the necessity of protecting students who are bullied when others believe that they fall into a vulnerable category, even if the belief is inaccurate. States, municipalities, and even school districts can often tailor enumerated language by adding additional protected categories based on local needs. For example, a school district that serves large numbers of Native American students from different tribes might choose to include tribal affiliation as an enumerated category.

Federal Responses to Bullying of LGBT Youth

The federal response to bullying of LGBT youth has grown over the past several years. However, the fact remains that federal law fails to explicitly protect LGBT youth from bullying, harassment, or discrimination based on their sexual orientation or gender identity. As a result, three legislative proposals protecting LGBT students from bullying, harassment, and discrimination are gaining traction on Capitol Hill. And, President Barack Obama has made it a priority of the Administration to use the powers of the Executive Branch—to the greatest extent possible—to deter and address bullying of LGBT youth. This growing federal response to the bullying of LGBT youth began with the introduction of the Safe Schools Improvement Act (H.R. 1199) in 2009 and gained new focus after a tragic string of youth suicides in 2010.

Tragedy Followed by a Visible Federal Response

Recently, we've all been shocked and heartbroken by the deaths of several young people who had been harassed and bullied for being openly gay—or because people thought they were gay. It's a terrible tragedy. And it has turned a harsh spotlight on an issue that often doesn't get the public attention it deserves. The struggles of LGBT youth. The enormous pain that too many experience as a result of bullying. And the desperate, tragic decision by some young people who feel that their only recourse is to take their own lives.

I say this not only as an advisor to the President. I say this from my heart, as a mother. I cannot begin to fathom the pain—the terrible grief—of losing a child. There is no greater loss—and we have lost too many in just the past few months. (Valerie Jarrett, Speech at HRC National Dinner, Oct. 9, 2010).

On October 3rd, 2010, the *New York Times* published an article entitled "Suicides Put Light on Pressures Faced by Gay Teenagers" (McKinley 2010). The article details a string of youth suicides that occurred within several weeks of each other during the late summer and early fall of 2010. The four youths profiled in the article had all experienced bullying because they were gay or perceived to be gay. One of those teenagers, Seth Walsh, was found hanging from a tree in the backyard by his mom. Seth was openly gay; he came out to his mom in sixth grade and came out to several friends in seventh grade. He had been a target for bullying ever since fourth grade when it was first rumored that he might be gay. Seth lived in fear of walking home alone and was homeschooled on two separate occasions. He committed suicide at the beginning of his eighth grade year. Seth was only 13. Another chilling example—this time caused by cyberbullying—is of Tyler Clementi, who was a freshman at Rutgers University. Tyler jumped from the George Washington Bridge after a sexual encounter with another man was broadcast online by his roommate.

Following this string of youth suicides, LGBT rights organizations amplified their calls for immediate enactment of laws and policies that address bullying of LGBT youth. Openly gay writer and activist Dan Savage created the "It Gets Better Project" to tell LGBT youth via YouTube that despite what bullying they are currently facing, it gets better. Members of Congress spoke about the need to pass recently introduced legislation aimed at curbing bullying of LGBT youth. And, the Obama Administration began to highlight the work of its recently formed anti-bullying task force. As such, a coordinated federal response to bullying of LGBT youth reached a new level of visibility in 2010.

Leveraging Existing Legislation

Title IX. Only weeks after the string of youth suicides in 2010, the U.S. DOE issued a letter to schools that clarified how Title IX applies to bullying and harassment of LGBT youth (USDOE Office for Civil Rights 2010). As mentioned earlier in this chapter, Title IX is the primary federal law available for protecting LGBT youth from certain bullying behavior. It prohibits schools from discriminating against persons on the basis of sex, but it does not explicitly protect LGBT students from discrimination based on sexual orientation or gender identity.

The U.S. DOE's letter presents a series of hypothetical examples of how a school's failure to recognize student misconduct as discriminatory harassment violates students' civil rights. The following portion of the letter describes a hypothetical situation involving an LGBT youth and the applicability of Title IX.

> Over the course of a school year, a gay high school student was called names (including anti-gay slurs and sexual comments) both to his face and on social networking sites, physically assaulted, threatened, and ridiculed because he did not conform to stereotypical notions of how teenage boys are expected to act and appear (e.g., effeminate mannerisms, nontraditional choice of extracurricular activities, apparel, and personal grooming choices). As a result, the student dropped out of the drama club to avoid further harassment. Based on the student's self-identification as gay and the homophobic nature of some of the harassment, the school did not recognize that the misconduct included discrimination covered by Title IX (USDOE Office for Civil Rights 2010).

As the above example demonstrates, schools are often unaware of their obligations to protect LGBT youth from bullying behavior because Title IX does not explicitly prohibit discrimination based on sexual orientation and gender identity. The DOE letter, however, states that:

> Although Title IX does not prohibit discrimination based solely on sexual orientation, Title IX does protect all students, including lesbian, gay, bisexual, and transgender (LGBT) students, from sex discrimination. When students are subjected to harassment on the basis of their LGBT status, they may also, as this example illustrates, be subjected to forms of sex discrimination prohibited under Title IX. The fact that the harassment includes anti-LGBT comments or is partly based on the target's actual or perceived sexual orientation does not relieve a school of its obligation under Title IX to investigate and remedy overlapping sexual harassment or gender-based harassment. In this example, the harassing conduct was based in part on the student's failure to act as some of his peers believed a boy should act. The harassment created a hostile environment that limited the student's ability to participate in the school's education program (e.g., access to the drama club). Finally, even though the student did not identify the harassment as sex discrimination, the school should have recognized that the student had been subjected to gender-based harassment covered by Title IX.

> In this example, the school had an obligation to take immediate and effective action to eliminate the hostile environment. By responding to individual incidents of misconduct on an ad hoc basis only, the school failed to confront and prevent a hostile environment from continuing. Had the school recognized the conduct as a form of sex discrimination, it could have employed the full range of sanctions (including progressive discipline) and remedies designed to eliminate the hostile environment. For example, this approach would have included a more comprehensive response to the situation that involved notice to the student's teachers so that they could ensure the student was not subjected to any further harassment, more aggressive monitoring by staff of the places where harassment occurred, increased training on the scope of the school's harassment and discrimination policies, notice to the target and harassers of available counseling services and resources, and educating the entire school community on civil rights and expectations of tolerance, specifically as they apply to gender stereotypes. The school also should have taken steps to clearly communicate the message that the school does not tolerate harassment and will be responsive to any information about such conduct (USDOE Office for Civil Rights 2010).

As this excerpt from the DOE's letter shows, Title IX prohibits a school from overlooking sexual harassment between students, regardless of the sex of the harasser and the victim. In addition, Title IX prevents schools from overlooking gender based harassment, which often overlaps with the harassment experienced by LGBT youth because of their sexual orientation or gender identity. However, while Title IX can be helpful for some LGBT youth, it is not a silver bullet. Title IX does not explicitly prohibit discrimination based on sexual orientation or gender identity. Accordingly, school districts are often unaware of their obligations toward protecting LGBT youth. And, the extent of Title IX's protections for LGBT youth may not reach students who are—aside from their sexual orientation or gender identity—otherwise gender conforming.

Enforcement of Title IX. The U.S. DOE and Department of Justice (DOJ) are jointly responsible for enforcement of Title IX. In recent years the departments have utilized their enforcement authority to ensure that school districts are meeting their obligations under Title IX to protect LGBT youth from sex discrimination. They have done this by investigating school districts where they receive complaints, participating in lawsuits filed by private parties, filing legal briefs to assist the courts with interpreting Title IX, and negotiating settlement agreements requiring schools to remedy Title IX violations.

At the end of President Bill Clinton's second term as president, the DOJ weighed in on two cases involving Title IX and LGBT youth. In one case, *Putnam v. Board of Education of Somerset Independent Schools*, a male student alleged his rights were violated under Title IX when his school district failed to take adequate steps to protect him from an ongoing campaign of sexual harassment by male peers (E.D. Ky. 2000). The student alleged he was subject to repeated, unwanted sexual contact, including one male student grabbing his groin area and making other offensive sexual suggestive gestures, and another male student wrapping his arms around the student to see if he would hug back. The DOJ advised the court that a school district's failure to address same-sex sexual harassment is actionable under Title IX. Shortly after the DOJ inserted itself into the case, the student and school district settled their dispute. In addition to monetary relief for the sexually harassed student, the school district modified its sexual harassment policies to include same-sex sexual harassment. The other case, *Lovins v. Pleasant Hill Public School District*, involved a student subjected to harassment on the basis of sex "ostensibly because other students believed he was gay" (W.D. Mo. 2000). Like the previously mentioned case, this case settled after the DOJ intervened. Among other things, the settlement required the school district to conduct a climate assessment; develop a comprehensive plan to identify, prevent, and remedy harassment based on sex and sexual orientation; train teachers, staff, and students on the policy; and maintain written records of complaints and investigations.

While these two cases set precedent for protecting LGBT youth from sex discrimination under Title IX, a change in presidential administrations in 2001 led to an 8-year absence of additional action in this area. This changed with the election of President Obama in 2008. President Obama's DOJ and DOE picked up where the Clinton Administration left off. Below are four examples of how the federal government has been able to utilize Title IX to protect LGBT Youth.

- In March, 2010, the DOJ intervened in a Title IX case, *J.L. v. Mohawk Central School District*, brought by ACLU on behalf of J.L., a male student in Mohawk Central School District. J.L. did not conform to gender stereotypes in either behavior or appearance and as a result was subject to severe and pervasive verbal harassment, as well as physical threats and violence. Prior to the court ruling on the motion to intervene, the school district entered into an out-of-court settlement with the student and DOJ which required the district to take comprehensive measures to prevent this behavior in the future, as well as compensate J.L. for their failure to protect him (N.D.N.Y. 2010).
- In August, 2010, the DOJ filed a motion seeking to leave to participate as amicus curia in order to provide the court with the proper legal standards governing harassment on the basis of sex in Charles Patrick Pratt's complaint in the U.S. District Court for the Northern District of New York. In *Pratt v. Indian River Central School District*, Charles' complaint alleges that he faced years of

targeting and emotional and physical harassment by both peers and the staff of his school district because of his sexual orientation and failure to conform with masculine stereotypes (N.D.N.Y. 2010).

- In August, 2011, the U.S. District Court for the District of Minnesota asked the DOJ to join in the mediation of a lawsuit, *Doe, and U.S v. Anoka Hennepin School District*, brought by six students against the Anoka Hennepin School District. These students alleged that they were being harassed by other students because their clothing or behavior did not conform with gender stereotypes. In March, 2012, the school district filed a consent decree with the DOJ and the six students in court. This 5-year decree requires the school to take extensive proactive measures to prevent this harassment in the future as well as submit annual compliance reports (D. Minn. 2012).

- In 2010, middle school student Seth Walsh committed suicide at the age of 13. Following his death, the DOE's Office for Civil Rights (OCR) launched an investigation of the school district and found that Walsh faced more than 2 years of sexual and gender based harassment by his peers at school because of his gender stereotype nonconformity (See Tehachapi Unified School District, DOJ Case Number DJ 169-11E-38 E.D. Cal. 2011). After this investigation, the DOJ joined the OCR to help bring justice. In June, 2011, DOJ and OCR reached a resolution agreement with the school district to resolve the complaint. This resolution included comprehensive preventative measures, including revising policies, facilitating trainings, and reporting data to OCR and DOJ for 5 years.

Other Executive Branch Action

Using the bully pulpit. Aside from enforcing Title IX, the Executive Branch has addressed bullying of LGBT youth by using the ironically named "bully pulpit" and providing resources, research, and guidance to schools, parents, and youth. These actions, while not statutorily required of the president or his administration, are critical to a robust federal response to expose, prevent, and combat bullying of LGBT youth.

The term "bully pulpit" was coined by President Theodore Roosevelt to describe the ability of the president to highlight an issue, influence a national debate, and have impact beyond enforcement of the laws. For the first time in our nation's history, President Obama and members of his Cabinet have used the "bully pulpit" to focus national attention on addressing the problem of bullying of LGBT youth.

In the wake of the string of youth suicides in 2010, President Obama, along with members of his Cabinet, created "It Gets Better" videos telling LGBT youth that they are not alone and encouraging them to tell someone they trust about being victimized. President Obama's video, as of March 2013, had received nearly half a million hits on YouTube—displaying its relevance to parents and youth across the country. In addition, the President and his administration carried this message from venue-to-venue, articulating this message online and before audiences of students, parents, teachers, and advocates.

The President called attention to the issue by hosting the first-ever White House Conference on Bullying Prevention in 2011. The conference brought together students, teachers, advocates, the private sector, foundations, and policymakers to share best practices to make our schools safer. The conference was followed by a White House LGBT Conference on Safe Schools and Communities in Arlington, Virginia, and another Bullying Prevention Conference in Washington, DC in 2012.

Agencies have partnered with the White House on events such as a screening of the Lee Hirsch documentary *Bully*, hosted by the President's Senior Advisor, Valerie Jarrett and DOE Secretary, Arne Duncan. In addition, agencies such as the U.S. Commission on Civil Rights (USCCR) and the General Accounting Office (GAO) have released reports related to bullying. The USCCR report (2011) examined the federal response to peer-to-peer bullying, which found the following:

1. Bullying and harassment, including bullying and harassment based on sex, race, national origin, disability, sexual orientation, or religion, are harmful to American youth.
2. Current federal civil rights laws do not provide the U.S. Department of Education with jurisdiction to protect students from peer-to-peer harassment that is solely on the basis of religion.
3. The current federal civil right laws do not protect students from peer-to-peer harassment that is solely on the basis of sexual orientation.

The GAO report on school bullying looked at the prevalence of school bullying, methods of addressing school bullying, and the existing laws regulating school bullying. The report concluded that federal law does not do enough to protect students from bullying based on sexual orientation and that the federal response to bullying, while growing, could still be stronger.

The Administration has also engaged in key public–private partnerships aimed at reducing bullying behavior. SurveyMonkey has teamed up with the White House to promote a dedicated website for bullying detection which includes a 10-question survey that students can distribute via email. In addition, the White House has promoted Facebook's "Social Reporting" system, meant to enable people to report harassing behavior to Facebook staff, parents, and teachers. Moreover, the White House endorses LGBT-inclusive anti-bullying efforts by the National Education Association, American Federation of Teachers, and the National Parent-Teacher Association.

Providing resources. The Administration re-launched StopBullying.gov, a website that describes the federal government's anti-bullying initiatives and provides resources for young people, parents, educators, and advocates. The website includes pointers on creating a safe environment for LGBT youth and provides resources detailing what schools and communities can do to address bullying of LGBT youth. One such program highlighted on the website is the Human Rights Campaign's *Welcoming Schools*. *Welcoming Schools* is an LGBT-inclusive approach to addressing family diversity, gender stereotyping, and bullying and name-calling in K-5 learning environments. The program provides administrators, educators, and parents/guardians with the resources necessary to create learning environments in which all learners are welcomed and respected.

Issuing guidance. The U.S. DOE has produced guidance for school districts working to combat bullying of LGBT youth. The DOE issued guidance in 2010 that illustrated how some states have tried to prevent and reduce bullying through legislation. The guidance provides states and local school districts with key components of anti-bullying laws and policies. For example, the guidance shows that states and school districts should enumerate characteristics, such as sexual orientation and gender identity, in their anti-bullying laws and policies. In addition, the DOE issued legal guidance in 2011 to school districts across the country making clear that gay-straight alliances (GSAs) must be allowed to form on an equal basis with other student groups. GSAs can play an important role in promoting safer schools and creating more welcoming learning environments. Nationwide, students form these groups to combat bullying and harassment of LGBT students and to promote understanding and respect in the school community.

Legislative Proposals

Three legislative proposals that address bullying of LGBT youth have gained traction in Congress over the past several years.

The Student Non-Discrimination Act. The Student Non-Discrimination Act (SNDA, H.R. 1652), first introduced in 2011 and endorsed by President Obama, is modeled after Title IX. It prohibits federally funded primary and secondary schools from discriminating against any student on the basis of his or her actual or perceived sexual orientation or gender identity. It would impact student-on-student bullying by making a school legally responsible for responding to the bullying of LGBT youth.

The SNDA, unlike Title IX, also prohibits discrimination against any student because of the actual or perceived sexual orientation or gender identity of a person with whom a student associates or has associated. This would make schools legally responsible for intervening when a student is being bullied for having an LGBT parent or friend. Recent data shows that LGBT parents are raising approximately two-million children (Movement Advancement Project, Family Equality Council, and Center for American Progress 2011).

The SNDA would allow an aggrieved party—for purposes of our discussion, a bullied LGBT student (or the student's guardian)—to initiate a legal proceeding against a school for violating the SNDA. Aside from allowing a student to initiate a legal proceeding, the bill would also allow federal authorities to initiate an investigation into a school's potentially discriminatory conduct. If federal investigators find evidence of discriminatory conduct, the school must be given the chance to remedy this conduct. If the school does not remedy the conduct, the school could lose federal funding. Despite a similar provision in Title IX, and over four decades of Title IX enforcement, all schools have taken steps to remedy discrimination to avoid losing federal funding.

Schools do not want to be caught up in lawsuits over violating the SNDA and be under investigation by the DOJ and DOE for civil rights; as such, schools are likely to take proactive measures to decrease bullying of LGBT youth in their schools if the SNDA were to become law. After passage of the SNDA, schools would be more likely to include LGBT youth in their bullying and non-discrimination policies. In addition, schools would be more likely to train all school personnel on how to identify and respond to bullying of LGBT youth.

Safe Schools Improvement Act. The Safe Schools Improvement Act (SSIA, H.R. 1199), first introduced in 2009 and also endorsed by the President, addresses bullying in a different, yet complementary, manner. The SSIA would require schools receiving certain federal funds to adopt codes of conduct specifically prohibiting bully and harassment. It would require those policies to prohibit bullying based on race, color, national origin, sex, disability, sexual orientation, gender identity, or religion, as well as broader policies that address all forms of bullying related to other characteristics. Like the SNDA, the bill would require a school to prohibit bullying of a student based on the actual or perceived characteristics of a family member or friend. In addition, the SSIA would require the DOE to provide Congress with a report every 2 years on state data related to bullying and harassment.

Unlike the SNDA, the SSIA does not create a new mechanism for bullied students to seek redress in the court system. In addition, the SSIA does not provide the federal government new means to investigate or remedy discrimination. However, by requiring schools to adopt bullying policies that include LGBT youth, the SSIA would encourage schools to identify and respond to bullying of LGBT youth.

Tyler Clementi Higher Education Anti-Harassment Act. As mentioned earlier in this chapter, Tyler Clementi was an 18-year-old freshman at Rutgers University in the fall of 2010. Without Tyler's knowledge, his roommate streamed video footage on the Internet of Tyler in his dorm room with another male. After his roommate attempted to stream another such interaction a few days later, Tyler ended his life.

Lesbian and gay college students are nearly twice as likely to experience harassment when compared with their heterosexual peers, and were seven times more likely to indicate the harassment was based on their sexual orientation, according to a 2010 study by Campus Pride (Rankin et al. 2010). Additionally, transgender students are nearly twice as likely as their cisgender peers to experience harassment, and were four times more likely to indicate their harassment was based on their gender identity. Despite such statistics, there is no federal requirement that colleges and universities have policies to protect their students from harassment.

The Tyler Clementi Higher Education Anti-Harassment Act (H.R. 482) requires colleges and universities receiving federal student aid funding to enact an enumerated anti-harassment policy. Specifically, the legislation requires policies that prohibit harassment of enrolled students by other students, faculty, and staff based

on actual or perceived race, color, national origin, sex, disability, sexual orientation, gender identity, or religion and requires colleges to distribute their anti-
harassment policy to all students and employees, including prospective students
and employees upon request. It explicitly prohibits behavior often referred to as
cyberbullying.

The bill also creates a competitive grant program at the Department of
Education in which institutions can apply for funding to initiate, expand, or
improve programs that prevent the harassment of students; provide counseling to
victims or perpetrators; or educate or train students, faculty, and staff about ways
to prevent or address harassment.

Other Congressional Responses

The SNDA and SSIA have not received a committee or chamber vote in the U.S.
House of Representatives. That said, a committee of the U.S. Senate approved both
bills as part of a larger education bill in 2013. Despite minimal movement on both
bills, Congress has held several LGBT-inclusive hearings related to bullying. In
addition, Congressman Mike Honda (D-CA) recently formed the Congressional
Anti-Bullying Caucus, a bipartisan caucus comprised of Members of Congress
committed to anti-bullying efforts. Moreover, like the President and his administration, Members of Congress, from former Speaker of the House Nancy Pelosi (D-CA)
to New Jersey Republican Representatives Leonard Lance, Frank LoBiondo, and Jon
Runyan, have recorded "It Gets Better" videos supporting LGBT youth.

State Initiatives

State Safe School Legal Landscape

Absent a federal response to bullying, states have taken a variety of steps to
address the growing concern over student bullying safety. In the wake of the
Columbine school shooting and the bullying-related death of a Georgia student, in
1999 Georgia became the first state in the nation to pass a law explicitly addressing
bullying prevention. Between 2000 and 2010, an average of 12 safe schools laws
was passed each year (Stuart-Cassel et al. 2011). By 2013, 49 states had laws
addressing bullying, with Montana being the lone holdout. The laws vary drastically from one another in areas such as policy elements, reporting requirements,
mandatory training, and inclusion of harassment, intimidation, discrimination, and/
or cyberbullying.

For LGBT youth, laws requiring safe schools policies to have enumerated
categories, including explicit references to sexual orientation and gender identity,

☰ STATEWIDE SCHOOL
HUMAN
RIGHTS
CAMPAIGN。
ANTI-BULLYING LAWS & POLICIES

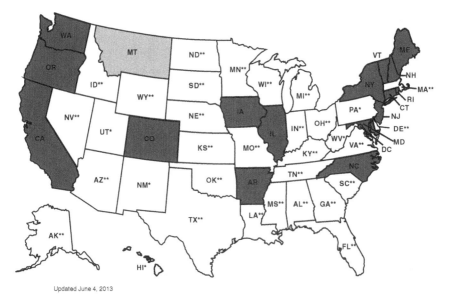

Updated June 4, 2013

Many states explicitly address harassment and/or bullying of elementary and high school students, though not all are LGBT inclusive. These protections can be in the form of statutory law, regulation or ethical codes of conduct for teachers. The states that explicitly address these issues for LGBT students are as follows.

■ **States with law that addresses harassment and/or bullying of students based on sexual orientation and gender identity** (16 states and D.C.): Arkansas (2011), California (2002), Colorado (2008), Connecticut (2001/2011), District of Columbia (2001), Illinois (2010), Iowa (2007), Maine (2005), Maryland (2008), New Hampshire (2010), New Jersey (2002), New York (2010), North Carolina (2009), Rhode Island (2012), Vermont (2001/2007), Washington (2002/2009) and Oregon (2007).

□ **States without statutory prohibition on bullying** (1 state): Montana.

* **Regulations and Ethical Codes of Conduct:** States with school regulation or ethical code for teachers that addresses harassment and/or bullying of students based on sexual orientation (3 states): New Mexico (regulation), Pennsylvania (regulation) and Utah (code of ethics). States with school regulation or ethical code for teachers that addresses discrimination, harassment and/or bullying of students based on both sexual orientation and gender identity (2 states): Hawaii (regulation) and West Virginia (regulation).

** **Policies/No Categories:** States that prohibit bullying in schools but list no categories of protection (26 states): Alabama, Alaska, Arizona, Delaware, Florida, Georgia, Idaho, Indiana, Kansas, Kentucky, Louisiana, Massachusetts, Michigan, Minnesota, Mississippi, Missouri, Nebraska, Nevada, North Dakota, Ohio, Oklahoma, South Carolina, South Dakota, Tennessee, Texas, Virginia, Wisconsin and Wyoming.

Please note that the quality of anti-bullying laws varies drastically from state to state. This map is only a reflection of the existence of such laws and policies.

Human Rights Campaign I 1640 Rhode Island Ave., N.W, Washington, D.C. 20036 I www.hrc.org/statelaws

Fig. 19.1 Statewide school non-discrimination laws and policies

are critical. Currently, 16 states and the District of Columbia have laws that prohibit bullying, harassment, and/or intimidation including on the basis of sexual orientation and gender identity (see Fig. 19.1). These states are distributed throughout the country and include states that lack other legal protections for LGBT people such as Arkansas and North Carolina. In contrast, some states that offer robust protections for LGBT people, such as Massachusetts and Nevada, lack enumerated safe schools laws.[5]

In lieu of enumerated safe school laws, several state boards of education have mandated enumerated policies. Both Hawaii and West Virginia have regulations protecting students on the basis of sexual orientation and gender identity. New Mexico, Pennsylvania, and Utah—under a code of ethics—cover sexual orientation only.

States prohibiting discrimination on the basis of sexual orientation and gender identity in education share significant overlap with states enumerating safe schools laws to include sexual orientation and gender identity. However, fewer states address discrimination against LGBT students than bullying of LGBT students. To date, 12 states plus the District of Columbia prohibit discrimination in education on the basis of sexual orientation and gender identity (see Fig. 19.2). In addition, Wisconsin prohibits discrimination in education only on the basis of sexual orientation.

"Don't Say Gay" Laws and "License to Bully" Provisions

Opponents of explicit legal protections for LGBT people have advocated for laws that would interfere with safe schools protections for LGBT students regardless of whether the safe schools laws are enumerated. These efforts are often framed as protections for religious students' freedom of expression or religious parents' freedom to protect their children from controversial topics; however, in practice the provisions permit the bullying of LGBT students to go unchecked so long as the bullying does not include physical violence.

It is important to note that, despite rhetoric to the contrary, people of faith overwhelmingly support anti-bullying protections for LGBT students. In a May 2011 poll conducted by Greenburg Quinlan Rosner Research for the Human Rights Campaign, the results showed 72 % of respondents who attend religious services weekly support safe schools laws that protect LGBT students (Greenburg Quinlan Rosner Research 2011). There was no statistically significant difference in support between people of faith and the public as a whole.

These laws and proposed legislation tend to take one of two forms: independent "Don't Say Gay" laws or "License to Bully" provisions—names given to such laws by advocates of LGBT equality.[6] "Don't Say Gay" laws and legislation vary

---

[5] As of publication, Massachusetts issues marriage licenses to same-sex couples, includes sexual orientation and gender identity in state hate crimes law, and prohibits discrimination in education, employment, and housing on the basis of sexual orientation and gender identity. Nevada provides same-sex couples civil unions and prohibits discrimination in employment, housing, and public accommodations on the basis of sexual orientation and gender identity.

[6] Earlier versions of these laws and bills were often referred to as "No Promo Homo" laws as in "no promotion of homosexuality." The first such proposed language was introduced by Senator Jesse Helms in 1987 as part of a federal spending bill.

STATEWIDE SCHOOL NON-DISCRIMINATION LAWS & POLICIES

Updated June 4, 2013

Increasingly, states are explicitly addressing discrimination against LGBT elementary and high school students. These protections can be in the form of statutory law, regulation or ethical codes of conduct for teachers. The states that explicitly address discrimination against LGBT students are as follows.

States with law that addresses discrimination against students based on sexual orientation and gender identity (12 states and D.C.): California (2002), Colorado (2008), Connecticut (2001/2011), District of Columbia (2001), Illinois (2010), Iowa (2007), Maine (2005), Massachusetts (2002/2012), Minnesota (1993), New Jersey (2002), Vermont (2001/2007), Washington (2002/2009) and Oregon (2007).

States with law that addresses discrimination against students based on sexual orientation only (1 state): Wisconsin (2001).

* **Regulations and Ethical Codes of Conduct:** States with school regulation or ethical code for teachers that addresses discrimination against students based on sexual orientation (3 states): New Mexico (regulation), Pennsylvania (regulation) and Utah (code of ethics). States with school regulation or ethical code for teachers that addresses discrimination against students based on both sexual orientation and gender identity (1 state): Hawaii (regulation).

Human Rights Campaign I 1640 Rhode Island Ave., N.W., Washington, D.C. 20036 I www.hrc.org/statelaws

Fig. 19.2 Statewide school anti-bullying laws and policies

from state to state, but at their core prohibit teachers and other school employees from mentioning sexual orientation in a positive light. "License to Bully" provisions provide a carve out to safe schools laws that prohibit schools from addressing bullying, provided students claim a sincerely held religious belief as the motivation for the bullying.

The bill introduced in Tennessee in 2009 (and every year since) is a classic example of the first category. Tennessee House Bill 821 (2009) read:

(c)(1) The general assembly recognizes the sensitivity of certain subjects that are best explained and discussed in the home. Human sexuality is an immensely complex subject with enormous societal, scientific, psychiatric and historical implications that are best understood by children with sufficient maturity to grasp such issues.

(2) Notwithstanding any law to the contrary, no public elementary or middle school shall provide any instruction or materials discussing sexual orientation other than heterosexuality.

The language of the bill was sufficiently vague as to allow an interpretation that would have prohibited teachers from explicitly addressing bullying based on sexual orientation. It clearly would have prohibited teachers and school administrators from proactively addressing the bullying of LGBT students through school assemblies or classroom discussions. To date, seven states have laws or policies that prohibit discussions of sexual orientation (see Fig. 19.3) (Kosciw et al. 2012).

The second category is typified by Michigan legislation from 2011 which provided an exemption for faculty, staff, and students who engage in bullying behavior based on moral grounds. The relevant provision in the original version of Michigan Senate Bill 137 (2011) as passed by the Senate read:

(8) This section does not abridge the rights under the First Amendment of the constitution of the United States or under article I of the state constitution of 1963 of a school employee, school volunteer, pupil, or a pupil's parent or guardian. This section does not prohibit a statement of a sincerely held religious belief or moral conviction of a school employee, school volunteer, pupil, or a pupil's parent or guardian.

While seemingly innocuous, the second sentence of the provision would have allowed both students and teachers to bully LGBT students, provided the verbal harassment was couched in religious or moral terms. The First Amendment clearly protects—and should protect—a student who wished to state that marriage for same-sex couples should be prohibited under law because it "violates biblical principles" or because "homosexuality is an abomination." However, schools, generally, can intervene in circumstances in which statements are targeting a particular individual as opposed to advancing an intellectual argument. Thus, a school could sanction a student who repeatedly approached a gay student to tell him that, because he is gay, he is "an abomination" or that he will "burn in hell." The "License to Bully" provision in the proposed Michigan law would have prohibited the school from intervening even when an individual was being targeted so long as the offending student made clear that his or her morality or religion inspired the behavior. Ultimately, the provision was removed from the final version of the bill that was signed into law.

As the Supreme Court of the United States so famously opined in *Tinker v. Des Moines Independent County School District*, "it can hardly be argued that either students or teachers shed their constitutional rights to freedom of speech or expression at the schoolhouse gate" [393 U.S. 503 (1969)]. Simultaneously, the

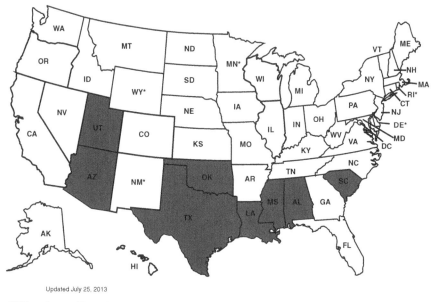

Updated July 25, 2013

States with "No Promo Homo" & "Don't Say Gay" Laws(8 states):
Alabama, Arizona, Louisiana, Mississippi, Oklahoma, South Carolina, Texas, and Utah.

Human Rights Campaign I 1640 Rhode Island Ave., N.W, Washington, D.C. 20036 I www.hrc.org/statelaws

Fig. 19.3 "No promo homo" and "don't say gay" laws

Supreme Court has repeatedly allowed sanctions to stand against students who verbally harass another with the effect of interfering with that student's ability to fully participate in school. A robust body of case law has developed on this issue stemming from the sexual harassment protections derived from Title IX.

Conclusion

Heartbreaking headlines from and around the U.S. demonstrate that bullying is a persistent issue with real life implications. These stories underscore the importance of making LGBT bullying both culturally unacceptable and the legal responsibility of school districts everywhere. Efforts to combat bullying continue to advance at every echelon of U.S. government. At the federal level, the Obama Administration has leveraged the existing Title IX framework to make schools take LGBT bullying seriously. And the Administration has spoken openly—from the very highest levels—of the need to combat this disturbing trend. Members of Congress have introduced the SNDA, SSIA, and the Tyler Clementi Higher Education Anti-Harassment Act. While each would further important policy goals, they face the same obstacles as any bill in traversing the legislative process.

As with most LGBT-friendly initiatives, progress in combating LGBT bullying differs from state-to-state. In many, advocates have realized important achievements, including strong, enumerated safe schools laws that require protective action at the school district level. In other states, efforts are more defensive, centered on stopping "Don't Say Gay" and "License to Bully" bills from becoming law. These bills constitute the latest trend in anti-LGBT legislation; they attempt to couch aversion to LGBT individuals as constitutionally protected religious and expressive rights.

While protection for all LGBT youth is still years away, the needle is moving in the right direction. This is an important trend for the LGBT movement and the country as a whole. All children deserve a safe and inclusive learning environment, no matter how they identify.

Acknowledgment A warm thank you to many individuals who contributed by providing assistance in research, writing, editing, feedback, and other support, including: Brian Moulton, Whitney Lovell, Nick Martin, David Wexelblat, Brendan Corrigan, Jillian Lenson, Hal Brewster, and Wyatt Fore.

References

American Psychological Association. (2011). *Bullying may contribute to lower test scores*. Retrieved from http://www.apa.org/news/press/releases/2011/08/bullying-test.aspx
American Psychological Association. (2012). *Bullying and school climate*. Retrieved from http://www.apa.org/about/gr/issues/cyf/bullying-fact-sheet.pdf
Atal, M. (2012). *Happy 40th anniversary Title IX: From girls' sports to women's wages*. *FORBES*. Retrieved from http://www.forbes.com/sites/mahaatal/2012/06/22/happy-40th-anniversary-title-ix-from-girls-sports-to-womens-wages/
Brunstein, K. A., Sourander, A., & Gould, M. (2012). The association of suicide and bullying in childhood to young adulthood: A review of cross-sectional and longitudinal research findings. *Canadian Journal of Psychiatry, 55*(5), 282–288.

Biegel, S. & James Kuehl, S. (2010). *Safe at school: Addressing the school environment and LGBT safety through policy and legislation.* Retrieved from http://williamsinstitute. law.ucla.edu/wp-content/uploads/Biegel-Kuehl-Safe-At-School-Oct-2011.pdf

Centers For Disease Control. (2012). *Youth Risk Behavior Surveillance System: 2011 national overview.* Retrieved from http://www.cdc.gov/healthyyouth/yrbs/pdf/us_overview_yrbs.pdf

Diaz, E. M., Kosciw, J. G., & Greytak, E. A. (2010). School connectedness for lesbian, gay, bisexual, and transgender youth: In-school victimization and institutional supports. *The Prevention Researcher, 17*(3), 15–17.

GLSEN. (2005). *From teasing to torment: School climate in America.* Retrieved from http://www.glsen.org/binary-data/GLSEN_ATTACHMENTS/file/499-1.pdf

Greenburg Quinlan Rosner Research. (2011). *Faith and fairness: Survey results show Christians support equality.* Retrieved from http://www.hrc.org/files/assets/resources/ReligionPolling 2011Memo.pdf

Hatzenbuehler, M. (2011). The social environment and suicide attempts in lesbian, gay, and bisexual youth. *Pediatrics, 127,* 896–898. Retrieved from http://pediatrics. aappublications.org/content/early/2011/04/18/peds.2010-3020.full.pdf

Human Rights Campaign. (2012). *Growing up LGBT in America.* Retrieved from http://www. hrc.org/files/assets/resources/Growing-Up-LGBT-in-America_Report.pdf

Human Rights Campaign. (2013). *Sexual orientation and gender identity: Terminology and definitions.* Retrieved from http://www.hrc.org/resources/entry/sexual-orientation-and-gender-identity-terminology-and-definitions

Kosciw, J. G., Greytak, E. A., Bartkiewicz, M. J., Boesen, M. J., & Palmer, N. A. (2012). *The 2011 National School Climate Survey: The experiences of lesbian, gay, bisexual and transgender youth in our nation's schools GLSEN.* Retrieved from http://www.glsen.org/ binary-data/GLSEN_%20ATTACHMENTS/file/000/002/2105-1.pdf

McKinley, J. (2010). Suicides put light on pressures faced by gay teenagers. *New York Times,* October 3. Retrieved from www.nytimes.com/2010/10/04/us/04suicide.html?_r=0

Movement Advancement Project, Family Equality Council, & Center for American Progress. (2011). *All children matter: How legal and social inequities hurt LGBT families.* Retrieved from http://lgbtmap.org/file/all-children-matter-condensed-report.pdf

Rankin, S., Blumenfeld, W. J., Weber, G. N., & Frazer, S. (2010). *The state of higher education for LGBT people.* Charlotte, NC: Campus Pride.

Stuart-Cassel, V., Bell, A., & Springer, J.F. (2011). *Analysis of state bullying laws and policies.* U.S. Department of Education. Retrieved from http://www2.ed.gov/rschstat/eval/bullying/ state-bullying-laws/state-bullying-laws.pdf

U.S. Commission on Civil Rights. (2011). *Peer to peer violence and bullying examining the federal response.* Retrieved from http://www.usccr.gov/pubs/2011statutory.pdf

U.S. Department of Education Office for Civil Rights. (2010). *Dear colleague letter.* Retrieved from http://www2.ed.gov/about/offices/list/ocr/letters/colleague-201010.html

U.S. Department of Education. (2012). *Sex discrimination: Overview of the law.* Retrieved from http://www2.ed.gov/policy/rights/guid/ocr/sexoverview.html

Part V
LGBT Communities, Crime, and Public Health

Chapter 20
Examining Dating Violence and Its Mental Health Consequences Among Sexual Minority Youth

Tameka L. Gillum and Gloria T. DiFulvio

Abstract Prior research has revealed a disturbingly high prevalence of dating violence among American youth. However, this research has not tended to focus on sexual minority youth. This is of concern as numerous studies have shown that individuals who experience such violence are at increased risk for adverse mental and physical health outcomes, including increased risk of HIV infection among LGBT populations. Research findings also indicate that individuals who are victimized as adolescents are at increased risk for victimization during their college years. This study assessed past and current dating violence (physical, sexual, and psychological aggression—perpetration and victimization) and its relationship to mental health outcomes among a sample of 109 college-enrolled sexual minority youth. Results indicate high rates of all forms of violence among this population during both adolescence and their college years. Physical and psychological perpetration and victimization were found to be associated with negative mental health outcomes including depression and PTSD. Sexual minority youth experience unique stressors that must be considered for appropriate interpretation of these findings and intervention. Implications for future research and practice with this population are presented.

Keywords Dating violence · Sexual minority youth · LGBT · Depression · PTSD

T. L. Gillum (✉)
Department of Public Health, University of Massachusetts Amherst, 715 N. Pleasant St.
302 Arnold House, Amherst, MA 01003, USA
e-mail: tgillum@schoolph.umass.edu

G. T. DiFulvio
Department of Public Health, University of Massachusetts Amherst, 715 N. Pleasant St.
302 Arnold House, Amherst, MA 01003, USA
e-mail: Gloria@schoolph.umass.edu

D. Peterson and V. R. Panfil (eds.), *Handbook of LGBT Communities,*
Crime, and Justice, DOI: 10.1007/978-1-4614-9188-0_20,
© Springer Science+Business Media New York 2014

Introduction

There exists a high prevalence of dating violence among our nation's youth (Eaton et al. 2007, 2012; Howard et al. 2007; Rothman et al. 2010, 2011; Sears et al. 2007; West and Rose 2000). National prevalence rates of victimization assessed from Youth Risk Behavior Surveillance (YRBS) data estimate 10 % (Eaton et al. 2007, 2012; Howard et al. 2007), while community-based assessments, including those sampling urban adolescents, have found prevalence rates for perpetration and victimization as high as 14–67 % (Rothman et al. 2010, 2011; Sears et al. 2007; West and Rose 2000).

The Centers for Disease Control and Prevention (CDC) define dating violence as a form of Intimate Partner Violence (IPV) that occurs between two people in a close relationship (CDC 2012a). The term is frequently used to describe partner violence (physical, emotional, and/or sexual) among adolescents and college student populations (Amar and Gennaro 2005). Physical forms include hitting, pinching, shoving, and kicking while sexual forms include forced nonconsensual sex acts. Emotional forms of this violence include behaviors such as stalking, threatening, intimidation, name calling, shaming, bullying, and/or keeping the victim from family and friends (CDC 2012a, b).

Of the available dating violence research and literature, relatively little has highlighted the voices and experiences of sexual minority youth. Efforts to assess dating violence among sexual minority youth have been minimal but reveal prevalence rates that exceed national estimates of youth in general and exceed most prevalence estimates from community-based assessments (Freedner et al. 2002; Halpern et al. 2004; Letellier and Holt 2000; Massachusetts Department of Education 2006; Pathela and Schillinger 2010). Massachusetts Youth Risk Behavior Survey (Massachusetts Department of Education 2006) results documented that sexual minority youth were significantly more likely than heterosexual youth to experience dating violence (35 % vs. 8 %). A study assessing prevalence of partner violence in same-sex adolescent relationships by Halpern and colleagues (2004) revealed a nearly 25 % prevalence rate of any form of violence. A survey conducted by a sexual minority youth-serving organization revealed that 49 % of youth participants reported "feeling abused" and 25 % reported having been abusive in their intimate relationships (Letellier and Holt 2000). In addition, results of a community-based assessment of sexual minority youth ($n = 521$) aged 13–22 indicated that 45 % of the gay male youth, 57 % of bisexual male youth, 44 % of lesbian youth, and 38 % of bisexual female youth surveyed had experienced such abuse (Freedner et al. 2002). Data from the New York City YRBS revealed that youth (grades 9–12) who identified as having both same and opposite sex partners were more likely to have experienced past year dating violence and forced sex than those reporting only opposite sex partners (Pathela and Schillinger 2010). A recent qualitative study by Gillum and DiFulvio (2012) indicted sexual minority youth perceptions that dating violence occurs at least as much but likely more than among their heterosexual peers. The youth also identified four contributing factors to dating violence in same-sex dating relationships: homophobia (both societal and internalized); negotiating socially prescribed gender roles; assumed female connection (assumption of a shared understanding between two females in relationship); and, other relationship issues.

Studies have shown that individuals who experience IPV are at increased risk for adverse mental and physical health outcomes (Banyard and Cross 2008; Belshaw et al. 2012; Bonami et al. 2009; Campbell 2002; CDC 2012b; Ely et al. 2011; Hedtke et al. 2008; Heintz and Melendez 2006; Howard et al. 2007; Ismail et al. 2007; Kramer et al. 2004; Naumann et al. 1999; Plichta 2004; West et al. 2010). This is of even greater concern with a population already at increased risk for negative mental and physical health outcomes as a result of being victims of hate crimes and the negative impacts of societal homophobia and systemic heterosexism (Follins 2011; Meyer 2003; Ryan and Futterman 1997; Sandfort et al. 2007). Such experience is compounded even more for LGBT persons of color who also experience the negative effects of racism and deal with the additional challenges of accepting and integrating their sexual, racial, ethnic, gender, religious, and spiritual identities and finding acceptance in their families and communities (Carballo-Dieguez et al. 2005; Follins 2011; Miller 2007, 2011; Ryan and Futterman 1997; Ryan et al. 2009).

Documented physical and mental health consequences of IPV include increased rates of depression, PTSD, sleep disturbances, chronic pain, fatigue, injury, gastrointestinal problems, gynecological problems, sexually transmitted infections (including HIV/AIDS), mortality, disability, poor pregnancy outcomes, substance abuse, and worse overall general health (Barnyard and Cross 2008; Bonami et al. 2009; Campbell 2002; CDC 2012b; Hedtke et al. 2008; Heintz and Melendez 2006; Kramer et al. 2004; Naumann et al. 1999; Plichta 2004). The effects of emotional abuse have been found to be just as detrimental as physical violence (Kramer et al. 2004). Recent research has linked teen dating violence to suicidal ideation and attempts, higher levels of depression and poor educational outcomes (Belshaw et al. 2012; Ely et al. 2011; West et al. 2010). For adolescent girls, experiencing youth dating violence has been linked to eating disorders, sleep disturbances, substance abuse, sexually transmitted infections, unplanned pregnancy, emotional distress, feelings of hopelessness, and thoughts of suicide (Howard et al. 2007; Ismail et al. 2007). Similar research is warranted that investigates the health effects among samples of adolescent boys. One may conclude from the above that sexual minority youth experiencing dating violence also experience these detrimental mental and physical health consequences.

Another cause for concern is that teen dating violence has been linked with increased engagement in risk behaviors such as early sexual activity, unprotected sex, alcohol and drug use, and greater number of lifetime sex partners (Alleyne-Green et al. 2012; Eaton et al. 2007; Howard et al. 2007; Ismail et al. 2007). In addition, two studies found increased risk of HIV infection among LGBT populations experiencing intimate partner violence (Heintz and Melendez 2006; Stall et al. 2003). Finally, research findings indicate that individuals who are victimized as adolescents are at increased risk for victimization during young adulthood (Smith et al. 2003).

Taken together, these findings demonstrate the importance of documenting experiences of dating violence among sexual minority youth and its relationship to mental health outcomes and future experiences of dating violence among this population. Such an assessment is essential for determining the need for dating violence services, including education, safety planning and referrals for mental and physical health services, and prevention for sexual minority youth starting in adolescence.

As part of a larger mixed-methods study designed to explore dating violence (past and current) and its health implications in a sample of college-aged sexual minority youth, we assessed whether experiences of Dating Violence (DV) were associated with poor mental health outcomes. For the purposes of this research, sexual minority youth were defined as individuals between the ages of 18–24 who identify as lesbian, gay, bisexual, transgender, queer, or questioning or who indicate dating or being sexually intimate with a member of the same sex.

Methods

Recruitment

Participants were recruited via flyers posted in strategic places at a large rural New England university campus and via active recruiting at campus-based queer groups and activities and community events. A research assistant attended these events, distributed flyers, and answered questions regarding the research. The study was explained as one exploring dating experiences among sexual minority youth. Interested participants contacted the project office and made an appointment to complete the questionnaire. Participants completed the questionnaire in the on-campus project office. Before completing the questionnaire, participants were read and signed informed consent. Questionnaires took on average 45 min to complete and participants were paid a stipend of $15 upon completion. University IRB approval was obtained prior to the commencement of the study.

Measures

Data were collected through the use of a structured, close-ended questionnaire. Depending on participant choice, questionnaires were either self-completed or administered orally by a member of the research team. The questionnaire contained measures of demographic characteristics, experiences with dating violence (victimization and perpetration; physical, psychological, sexual) and assessments of mental health sequelae, including depression and PTSD.

Demographic questionnaire. A questionnaire was designed by the authors to assess demographic characteristics including age, racial/ethnic identity, sexual orientation, gender identification, level of schooling, and relationship status. For sexual orientation and gender identification, participants had the option of selecting a pre-listed category or writing in their own preferred identification.

Victimization in Dating Relationships. This 18-item categorical scale was used to assess frequency of youth's current (during their college years) and adolescent (before entering college) physical dating violence victimization (e.g., slapped me, slammed me or held me against a wall, forced me to have sex) (Foshee et al. 1996). Participants were asked specifically to indicate if a dating partner did any of these things to them first, not if the dating partner engaged in these behaviors in self-defense. Categories for each item include never, 1–3, 4–9, and 10 or more times. Items were summed to create a composite score with a possible score range of 0–54. Cronbach's alphas for this study were 0.83 and 0.89 for current and adolescence, respectively.

Perpetration in Dating Relationships. This 18-item scale was used to assess frequency of youth's current (during their college years) and adolescent physical dating violence perpetration (e.g., slapped them, slammed them or held them against a wall, forced them to have sex) (Foshee et al. 1996). Participants were asked specifically to indicate if they did any of these things to a dating partner first, not if they engaged in these behaviors in self-defense. Items were summed to create a composite score with a possible score range of 0–54. Cronbach's alphas for this study were 0.74 and 0.86 for current and adolescence, respectively.

Revised Conflict Tactics Scale (CTS2). This widely used 39-item scale is designed to measure physical and psychological aggression between partners in a marital, cohabiting, or dating relationship. The measure consists of five sub-scales, including physical assault, psychological aggression, negotiation, injury, and sexual coercion. Only the psychological aggression sub-scale (8 items) was used in this study to assess this specific dimension of abuse. Participants responded to questions that assessed their experience of a particular action (victimization) or their perpetration of a particular action. For example, questions included 'I called my dating partner fat or ugly,' 'My dating partner called me fat or ugly,' 'I accused my dating partner of being a lousy lover,' 'My dating partner accused me of being a lousy lover,' 'I threatened to hit or throw something at my dating partner,' 'My dating partner threatened to hit or throw something at me.' Response options for each question included the following: Once in the past year; twice in the past year; 3–5 times in the past year; 6–10 times in the past year; 11–20 times in the past year; More than 20 times in the past year; Not in the past year, but it did happen before; and this never happened to me. This sub-scale has a demonstrated internal consistency of 0.79 (Straus et al. 1996, 2003). Psychological aggression was measured for both victimization and perpetration for both current (past year) and adolescent abusive experience. Items were summed as instructed in the CTS Handbook to create composites scores (Straus et al. 2003). Cronbach's alphas for this sample were 0.80 and 0.77 for current psychological aggression victimization and perpetration, respectively. They were 0.85 and 0.80 for adolescent psycho-logical aggression victimization and perpetration, respectively.

Center for Epidemiologic Studies-Depression Scale. Past 2-week depressive symptoms were assessed with the 20-item Revised Center for Epidemiologic Studies—Depression Scale (CES-D) (Hedtke et al. 2008; Radloff 1977, 1991). This DSM-IV-TR (APA 2000) concordant instrument measures symptoms of depressed mood, guilt/worthlessness, helplessness/hopelessness, psychomotor retardation, loss of appetite, sleep disturbance, agitation, and suicidal ideation. Responses to these questions included: None (<1 day), A little (1–2 days), Moderate (3–4 days), A lot (5–7 days), Nearly every day for 2 weeks. Scores are summed for a possible range of 0–80, with scores of 16 or higher being the standard indication of depression. The Revised CES-D is highly correlated to the original 20-item version (0.89), with demonstrated reliability (Cronbach's $\alpha = 0.86$–0.88) (Carpenter et al. 1998). Cronbach's alpha for this measure in the current study was 0.92.

Davidson Trauma Scale (DTS). Post-traumatic stress disorder (PTSD) was identified as a cluster of symptoms in concordance with the DSM-IV as measured by the Davidson Trauma Scale (Davidson 1996; Davidson et al. 1997). The 17-items assess the PTSD clusters of intrusion, avoidance and numbness, and hyperarousal for the past week in frequency and severity on a 0–4 Likert-type scale. Scores ranging from 0 to 4 are summed for each item. Overall PTSD symptoms were assessed as a continuous variable (0–136). A score of 40 or greater is defined as positive for a level of PTSD symptoms that is most clinically accurate. This instrument has demonstrated test–retest reliability ($r = 0.86$) (Davidson 1996; Davidson et al. 1997). Cronbach's alpha for the current study was 0.96 for the total scale.

Analysis

Questionnaire data were analyzed descriptively, to assess demographic characteristics of the sample and the prevalence of different types of dating violence, both current and adolescent. Mental health outcomes were also assessed. Composite scores were calculated for all measures. Then, Analysis of Variance (ANOVA) was performed to examine relationships between all forms of current violence (i.e., physical abuse and psychological aggression perpetration and victimization during college years) and mental health outcomes (depression and PTSD). Two way ANOVA was used when two factors were assessed; three way ANOVA was used when three factors were analyzed.

Results

Sample

A total of 109 youth completed the study questionnaire. Participants were between the ages of 18–24 with a mean age of 20 years, and all participants were enrolled in a 4-year college or university at the time of participation. Gender identification, sexual orientation, racial/ethnic background, and relationship status are presented in Table 20.1. The sample was comprised of a majority (58 %) of self-identified females, 34 % males, 4 % female-to-male transgendered, 3 % gender queer, and 1 % each "other" and "non-gender conforming." One-third (32 %) identified as gay, one-quarter each as bisexual and lesbian, 13 % as "other" (including those who identified as queer, pansexual, and non-orientation conforming), and 4 % as questioning. The sample was 76 % White, 6 % African American, 6 % Asian American, 4 % Latino, and 8 % "other" (including Cape Verdean, Middle Eastern, Armenian, Israeli, and mixed-race individuals). Nearly half (48 %) identified as single, 38 % as dating/in a relationship with a member of the same gender, 12 % dating/in a relationship with a member of the opposite gender (including those involved with transgender individuals), and 2 % identified as dating/in a relationship with a member of each gender.

Table 20.1 Sample demographics

	N (109)	% (100)
Gender identification		
Female	63	57.8
Male	37	33.9
Female-to-male transgendered	4	3.7
Gender queer	3	2.7
Non-gender conforming	1	0.9
Other	1	0.9
Sexual orientation		
Gay	35	32
Bisexual	28	26
Lesbian	27	25
Questioning	5	4
Other[a]	14	13
Race/ethnicity		
White	83	76
African–American	6	6
Asian–American	6	6
Latino	4	4
Other[b]	10	8
Relationship status		
Single	52	48
Dating/in a relationship with same gender	41	38
Dating/in a relationship with opposite gender	14	12
Dating/in a relationship with each gender	2	2

[a] Queer, Pansexual, and Non-conforming orientation
[b] Cape Verdean, Middle Eastern, Armenian, Israeli, Mixed-race

Table 20.2 Dating violence prevalence

	Adolescence (%)	College (%)
Psychological victimization	86	81
Physical victimization	58	60
Psychological perpetration	88	83
Physical perpetration	41	50
No physical perpetration or victimization	36	35
Both physical perpetration and victimization	40	46
No psychological perpetration or victimization	9	13
Both psychological perpetration and victimization	86	78

Adolescent Dating Violence

Fifty-eight percent (58 %) of participants indicated experiencing some form of physical victimization within the context of their adolescent dating relationships (see Table 20.2) with 12 years old being the youngest reported age for this experience. There were no differences in prevalence of adolescent dating violence within any of the demographic categories (not shown in table format). Forty-one percent (41 %) of participants acknowledged perpetrating some form of physical violence within the context of their adolescent dating relationships, with 13 years old being the youngest reported age for this experience. Thirty-six percent (36 %) of the sample reported neither victimization nor perpetration, while 40 % reported both. Regarding psychological aggression, 86 % of participants indicated experiencing psychological aggression within the context of their adolescent dating relationships, and 88 % acknowledged perpetrating psychological aggression. Twelve years old was the youngest reported age for both being the target of and perpetrating psychological aggression. Further, 9 % of the sample reported experiencing neither psychological aggression victimization nor perpetration during adolescence, while 86 % reported the co-occurrence of both.

Current Dating Violence

Sixty percent (60 %) of participants reported experiencing some form of physical victimization from a dating partner during their college years (see Table 20.2). Fifty percent (50 %) of participants acknowledged perpetrating some form of physical violence on a dating partner during their college years. Thirty-five percent (35 %) of the sample reported experiencing neither victimization nor perpetration, while 46 % reported both. Eighty-one percent (81 %) of participants indicated experiencing psychological aggression from a dating partner within the past year, and 83 % acknowledged perpetrating psychological aggression against a dating partner within the past year. Further, 13 % of the sample reported experiencing neither psychological aggression victimization nor perpetration, while 78 %

reported the co-occurrence of both. There were no differences in prevalence of current dating violence within any of the demographic categories (not shown in table format).

Mental Health Outcomes

Fifty percent (50 %) of participants met or exceeded the criteria score for depression, and 40 % met or exceeded the criteria score for post-traumatic stress (results not shown in table format). Rates were high across genders as well. Fifty-four percent (54 %) of females met or exceeded the criteria score for depression as did 43 % of males. Similarly, 43 % of females met or exceeded the criteria score for post-traumatic stress as did 34 % of male participants.

Univariate Analyses of Current (College-aged) Dating Violence

Due to incomplete responses of some participants on related measures, these analyses are for 104 of the 109 participants. Given that the current physical and psychological perpetration and victimization variables were not normally distributed, the scales were converted to categorical variables. For physical perpetration or victimization, scores were converted to 0/1 dichotomies. For psychological perpetration or victimization, scales were converted to three categories: 0, >0 to <7, >=7. Seven was the median score for these variables and was therefore used as the cutoff score.

The effect of violent experiences (physical perpetration, physical victimization, psychological perpetration, psychological victimization during college years) on recent depression and PTSD was analyzed using Univariate ANOVA. Results of the ANOVAs are presented in Tables 20.3 and 20.4. Given that with a sample size of 104, ANOVAs could be run with a maximum of two factors, one demographic variable at a time was added for each ANOVA. When two factors were considered, no statistically significant interaction effects were found. The one exception to this is that when relationship status (categorized as 1 = single, 2 = dating same gender, 3 = dating opposite gender; individuals dating both genders, $n = 2$, were excluded from these analyses) was entered as the second factor, relationship status was found to be associated with mental health outcomes (see Table 20.3). Those who reported being in a relationship with a member of the opposite gender were more likely to experience depression and PTSD. These individuals were also much more likely to experience a higher level of physical violence (both perpetration and victimization) than those in same gender relationships (not shown in table).

Table 20.3 Mental health outcomes, violence experience and relationship status

	Depression ($n = 104$)			PTSD ($n = 100$)		
	F	df	p	F	df	p
Physical victimization	1.538	1, 99	0.218	0.949	1, 95	0.333
Relationship status	2.981	2, 99	0.055	4.102	2, 95	0.020
Physical perpetration	4.302	1, 99	0.041	2.510	1, 95	0.116
Relationship status	3.507	2, 99	0.034	5.334	2, 95	0.006
Psychological victimization	1.883	2, 96	0.158	2.660	2, 92	0.075
Relationship status	5.487	2, 96	0.006	5.722	2, 92	0.005
Psychological perpetration	1.614	2, 96	0.204	3.476	2, 92	0.035
Relationship status	6.633	2, 96	0.002	5.559	2, 92	0.005

Table 20.4 Mental health outcomes, violence experience

	Depression ($n = 90$)			PTSD ($n = 86$)		
	F	df	p	F	df	p
Physical victimization	4.448	1, 89	0.038	3.038	1, 85	0.085
Physical perpetration	10.275	1, 89	0.002	7.825	1, 85	0.006
Psychological victimization	3.875	2, 88	0.024	4.254	2, 84	0.017
Psychological perpetration	2.601	2, 88	0.080	4.048	2, 84	0.021

Given there were only 14 people who reported their current relationship status as being with a member of the opposite gender, we removed them from the sample so that we could see the relationship of violence to mental health outcomes without the confounding factor of type of relationship. These analyses revealed psychological victimization was related to depression, psychological perpetration was related to PTSD, and physical perpetration and psychological victimization were related to both depression and PTSD (see Table 20.4). The association between physical victimization and PTSD and psychological perpetration and depression both trended toward, but not reach, the 0.05 level of significance.

Discussion

This study makes a significant contribution to the literature as it provides enhanced understanding of dating violence in an understudied population. To date, the literature is sparse in relation to dating violence among sexual minority youth. Though previous studies have made this connection for heterosexual youth (Amar and Gennaro 2005; Belshaw et al. 2012; Ely et al. 2011; Howard et al. 2007; Ismail et al. 2007; West et al. 2010), it appears that no studies have investigated the relationship between dating violence experience and adverse mental health outcomes among this particular population.

Results of this study are consistent with other literature that reveals a disturbingly high prevalence of dating violence among U.S. youth, both adolescent and college-age (CDC 2012b; Eaton et al. 2007, 2012; Freedner et al. 2002; Howard et al. 2007; Rothman et al. 2010, 2011; Sears et al. 2007; West and Rose 2000). It is also consistent with the limited body of literature that indicates an even higher prevalence of dating violence among sexual minority youth than their heterosexual peers (Freedner et al. 2002; Halpern et al. 2004; Massachusetts Department of Education 2006). However, prevalence rates of all forms in this study exceed dating violence prevalence rates documented in other studies of sexual minority youth. The likely reason for this is that these previous studies all assessed dating violence via the use of five questions or fewer. The current study utilized more complete instruments that assessed multiple forms of both physical and psychological aggression. The physical dating violence measure included 18 items, while 8 items assessed psychological aggression, thus conducting a more thorough assessment of the types of aggressive acts participants may have perpetrated or experienced. These results point to an even greater rate of dating violence among this population and thus a more pressing need for services addressing this issue. High prevalence of adolescent victimization and perpetration is indicative of the need for dating violence prevention programs at younger ages for all adolescents with an acknowledgement of the reality of same-sex dating among adolescents and a need to be inclusive of these relationships in such programs.

Another issue that warrants attention is evidence of the co-occurrence of both dating violence victimization and perpetration among this sample. There are a number of possible explanations for this. As indicted above, sexual minorities experience a significant number of stressors (Carballo-Dieguez et al. 2005; Follins 2011; Meyer 2003; Miller 2007, 2011; Ryan and Futterman 1997; Ryan et al. 2009; Sandfort et al. 2007). In addition, the period of adolescence is a time in which individuals are engaged in the process of forming their unique identities, transitioning from childhood into adulthood. Part of this identity is developing and coming to terms with one's sexual identity and the experience and negotiation of dating relationships. Research with young women has indicated this as a time in which peers and media exert pressure on female youth to develop committed relationships and have boyfriends (Ismail et al. 2007). The social pressure to fit in with peers is heightened during this period of development. For sexual minority youth, developing a positive sexual identity, often in the context of a homophobic/heterosexist environment, adds an additional challenge to this already fragile period of development. Not conforming to socially sanctioned dating practices may lead to teasing, ostracism, and violence for LGBT youth (Marrow 2004). Consequently, such an experience may lead to the development of internalized homophobia in sexual minority youth (Marrow 2004). Internalized homophobia is defined as the internalization of society's negative ideology of sexual minorities (Herek et al. 2007). This may have a direct impact on the ability of these youth to develop healthy relationships and the quality of their dating relationships, as internalized homophobia has been linked to both victimization and perpetration of same-sex intimate violence and less favorable perceptions of relationship quality

(Balsam and Szymanski 2005; Otis et al. 2006; Tigert 2001). This dynamic may also be attributed to a lack of positive lesbian and gay role models and models of healthy lesbian and gay relationships represented in communities and in the media for youth to look to for guidance and failure of school-based sex-education classes to address LGBT sexuality (Marrow 2004).

Of additional significance is the fact that dating violence experiences, both perpetration and victimization, were correlated with negative mental health outcomes. This is consistent with other research that has identified significant relationships between experiencing dating violence and psychological distress, including among college samples (Amar and Gennaro 2005; Belshaw et al. 2012; Ely et al. 2011; Howard et al. 2007; Ismail et al. 2007; West et al. 2010). Related to this is the fact that depression and PTSD rates were disturbingly high among this population. Other studies using the CES-D to assess depression among general college student samples of similar demographics have identified rates of about 33 % (Armstrong and Oomen-Early 2009; Fortson et al. 2007), while this sample revealed a rate of over 50 %. This is consistent with other research that has found high rates of depression among sexual minorities (Haas et al. 2011; King et al. 2008; Meyer 2003). Research has identified that sexual minorities experience multiple stressors, including stigma, prejudice, and discrimination, which increase their risk for neg-ative mental health outcomes (Balsam and Szymanski 2005; Marrow 2004; Meyer 2003). Considering the combination of these factors, it is not surprising that a sample of sexual minority youth, many experiencing dating violence, would identify a large prevalence of these disorders. While we cannot definitively determine the direction of this relationship, the association warrants further attention. Given that victim-ization and perpetration are both associated with poor mental health outcomes, regardless of the direction of association, it is imperative that interventions with sexual minority youth address mental health issues as well as dating violence.

Lastly, one significant finding warrants mentioning. For the small subset of individuals ($N = 14$) who identified as being involved in a relationship with a member of the opposite gender, this status was a stronger predictor of depression than was relationship violence. We may speculate that some of these individuals may be acting on social and/or societal pressure to engage in dating relationships with a member of the opposite gender when their true desire is to be in rela-tionships with members of the same gender. This circumstance may lead to increased feeling of depression and anxiety for not being able to be true to themselves. As indicated earlier, research suggests that adolescence is a time in which adolescent girls feel pressured to have boyfriends (Ismail et al. 2007) and adolescent boys experience pressure to have sexual intercourse with girls as a sign of hetero-normative masculinity (Forrest 2000). This is further evidenced in research by the authors where one youth expresses her frustrations around being in relationships with a male when her desire was to be with a female. She states:

> I think [dating violence] has lots to do with the internalization of how you feel about being in that relationship… I think people can have a lot of resentment towards themselves, towards their bodies, and towards their identities and especially like for me, being in a lot of straight relationships…in [those] relationships, any violence that I exhibited towards the

guy has always been my resentment towards him for not being able to express like a huge part of myself, which is like having feelings for girls. There's always having feelings for girls and the part of me that can't express [that] and that's definitely led to violence in [those relationships]. Like not knowing what you think or not always being okay with the relationship that you're having (Gillum and DiFulvio 2012, pp. 733–734).

While this is one plausible explanation, further research is needed to understand the complex relationship among relationships status, victimization/perpetration, and mental health outcomes.

Limitations

As with all research, this study has its limitations. First, this study was retrospective and not prospective. Therefore, participants were asked to recall experiences that happened years ago. Thus, faulty memory may have caused participants to forget past experiences or confuse current experiences with past experiences. Procedures were in place to reduce the possibility of this risk. Participants were asked to think about recent (college-age) experiences first, then asked to think back to their adolescent dating, including the youngest age at which they had a dating violence experience. This allowed for students to identify those most recent experiences first, as recent memories are likely to be most salient. Then, having already identified those experiences, they were asked to think back to adolescent years. In addition, participants were questioned about dating violence experiences that are likely to be quite salient to those who have perpetrated and experienced this victimization. Thus, it is likely that the recollections of participants are fairly accurate.

Social desirability may have been a factor as well, which could have prevented some students from revealing their experiences of perpetrating or being victimized, as neither is considered socially acceptable. However, given the high rates of reported victimization and perpetration, it is likely that this did not inhibit reporting for most participants.

This study included youth who identified with minority sexual identities and gender identities. It did not, however, explore the differences in dating violence between these groups. Gender identity and sexual identity are different constructs. In other words, youth who identify as transgender or gender non-conforming may have different experiences than youth who identify as lesbian, gay, or bisexual. Both groups were included in this exploratory study because each is underrepresented in the literature. However, to gain a deeper understanding of the unique aspects of dating violence for each group, further research is warranted.

This is a relatively small sample ($N = 109$), self-selected on the basis of self-identification as a sexual minority (defined above). Similar studies should be conducted with larger, population-based samples to get a better picture of this issue in the larger population of sexual minority adolescents and college age individuals.

Implications for Future Research

This research makes an important contribution to a limited body of the literature. It helps us to further understand the extent of dating violence experienced by sexual minority youth both during adolescence and during their young adulthood. Further research is needed with community-based samples to identify the extent of violence experienced by youth who may not go on to higher education. It would be particularly informative to conduct such research in urban areas where violence in general tends to be high. In addition, research that includes a more racially/ ethnically diverse sample is warranted.

This field would also benefit from research that further explores, both qualitatively and quantitatively, those factors that contribute to dating violence among this underrepresented population. Given the unique, multiple stressors that youth who identify as sexual minorities or are questioning their sexuality often encounter, it is likely that there are unique factors that contribute to violence within this population. Research similar to that of Gillum and DiFulvio (2012) that facilitates our understanding of some of these unique dynamics (discussed above) may help to inform services for this population.

This study found that relationship status was a confounding factor when examining the relationship between current physical or psychological victimization or perpetration and mental health outcomes. The number of individuals in this study who reported current involvement in an opposite sex relationship was small and therefore future research should be directed toward understanding the relationship between relationship status and mental health outcomes for sexual minority youth.

Implications for Service

This research supports other studies that highlight the problem of dating violence among sexual minority youth and demonstrates the need for services targeting this uniquely vulnerable population. Of particular interest are efforts that middle and high schools could engage in to address this issue. Middle and high school curricula that address relationships and/or dating violence should acknowledge same-sex dating among this population and address how to identify unhealthy relationships, whether the dating partner is the same or opposite sex. Dating violence awareness materials (posters, pamphlets) may also be placed within schools, including those that depict sexual minority youth. Increasing the number and quality of gay-straight alliances established at middle and high schools across the country would also contribute to these efforts.

In addition, youth need educational programs that teach them how to have healthy relationships and how to identify unhealthy ones. This is something most youth are missing in the formal education they receive. This is especially true for sexual minority youth whose relationships are often unacknowledged or ridiculed. As a result of continuing heterosexism and homophobia in our society, sexual minority youth often do not receive the benefit of having sexual minority role models to identify with and models of healthy same-sex relationships. Thus, such programming would be especially beneficial to this population, particularly given these findings that unhealthy relationship dynamics are prevalent and carry into adulthood with detrimental health consequences.

Lastly, community-based agencies that work with sexual minority youth should include dating violence awareness efforts within their agencies. They may inform youth about the existence of such violence, warning signs of abuse, and where/how they may seek assistance. These can include having a staff person receive training on dating violence. This person could hold dating violence workshops or programs at the agency and serve as a resource for youth who have experienced dating violence. Dating violence awareness materials (posters, pamphlets) may also be placed within the agency, especially those that depict sexual minorities. These agencies may also collaborate with local domestic violence agencies for programming if these agencies are willing to be sensitive to the unique challenges of this population (see Messinger, this volume, for additional discussion). Community-based domestic and sexual violence agencies should also begin to make their services more inclusive of sexual minority populations and their needs.

Acknowledgement The authors wish to thank those who participated in this study, sharing their voices and experiences with us, the research assistant who recruited diligently, and the editors for their invitation to contribute and their helpful feedback.

References

Alleyne-Green, B., Coleman-Cowger, V. H., & Henry, D. B. (2012). Dating violence perpetration and/or victimization and associated sexual risk behaviors among a sample of inner-city African-American and Hispanic adolescent females. *Journal of Interpersonal Violence, 27*(8), 1457–1473.

Amar, A. F., & Gennaro, S. (2005). Dating violence in college women: Associated physical injury, healthcare usage, and mental health symptoms. *Nursing Research, 54*(4), 235–242.

American Psychological Association (2000). *Diagnostic and statistical manual of mental disorders* (4th ed., text rev.). Washington, DC: Author.

Armstrong, S., & Oomen-Early, J. (2009). Social connectedness, self-esteem, and depression symptomatology among collegiate athletes versus non-athletes. *Journal of American College Health, 57*(5), 521–526.

Balsam, K. F., & Szymanski, D. M. (2005). Relationship quality and domestic violence in women's same-sex relationships: The role of minority stress. *Psychology of Women Quarterly, 29*(3), 258–269.

Banyard, V. L., & Cross, C. (2008). Consequences of teen dating violence: Understanding and intervening variables in ecological context. *Violence Against Women, 14*(9), 998–1013.

Belshaw, S. H., Siddique, J. A., Tanner, J., & Osho, G. S. (2012). The relationship between dating violence and suicidal behaviors in a national sample of adolescents. *Violence and Victims, 27*(4), 580–591.

Bonami, A. E., Anderson, M. L., Reid, R. J., Rivara, F. P., Carrell, D., & Thompson, R. S. (2009). Medical and psychosocial diagnoses in women with a history of intimate partner violence. *Archives Internal Medicine, 169*(18), 1692–1697.

Campbell, J. C. (2002). Health consequences of intimate partner violence. *Lancet, 359*(9314), 1331–1336.

Carballo-Dieguez, A., Dolezal, C., Leu, C. S., Nieves, L., Diaz, F., Decena, C., & Balan, I. (2005). A randomized controlled trial to test an HIV-prevention intervention for Latino gay and bisexual men: Lessons learned. *AIDS Care, 17*(3), 314–328.

Carpenter, J. S., Andrykowski, M. A., Wilson, J., Hall, L. A., Rayens, M. K., Sachs, B., et al. (1998). Psychometrics for two short forms of the CES-D scale. *Issues in Mental Health Nursing, 19*(5), 481–494.

Centers for Disease Control and Prevention (CDC). (2012a). *Understanding teen dating violence fact sheet*. Atlanta, GA: CDC.

Centers for Disease Control and Prevention (CDC). (2012b). *Understanding intimate partner violence fact sheet*. Atlanta, GA: CDC.

Davidson, J. R. (1996). *Davidson trauma scale*. North Tonawanda, NY: Multi Health Systems, Inc.

Davidson, J. R., Book, S. W., Colket, J. T., Tupier, L. A., Roth, S., David, D., et al. (1997). Assessment of a new self-rating scale for post-traumatic stress disorder. *Psychological Medicine, 27*(1), 153–160.

Eaton, D. K., Davis, K. S., & Barrios, L. (2007). Associations of dating violence victimization with lifetime participation, co-occurrence, and early initiation of risk behaviors among U.S. high school adolescents. *Journal of Interpersonal Violence, 22*(5), 585–602.

Eaton, D. K., Kann, L., Kinchen, S., Shanklin, S., Flint, K. H., Hawkins, J., et al. (2012). Youth Risk Behavior Surveillance—United States, 2011. *Morbidity and Mortality Weekly Report (MMWR), 61*(SS-4), 1–162.

Ely, G. E., Nugent, W. R., Cerel, J., & Vimbba, M. (2011). The relationship between suicidal thinking and dating violence in a sample of adolescent abortion patients. *Crisis, 32*(5), 246–253.

Follins, L. D. (2011). Identity development of young black lesbians in New York City: An exploratory study. *Journal of Gay Lesbian Mental Health, 15*(4), 368–381.

Forrest, S. (2000). Big and tough: Boys learning about sexuality and manhood. *Sexual and Relationship Therapy, 15*(3), 247–261.

Fortson, B. L., Scotti, J. R., Chen, Y., Malone, J., & del Ben, K. S. (2007). Internet use, abuse, and dependency among students at a southeastern regional university. *American Journal of College Health, 56*(6), 137–144.

Foshee, V. A., Linder, F., Bauman, K. E. Langwick, S. A., Arriaga, X. B., Heath, J. L., & Bangdiwala, S. (1996). The Safe Dates Project: Theoretical basis, evaluation design, and selected baseline findings. *American Journal of Preventive Medicine, 12*(5), 39–47.

Freedner, N., Freed, L. H., Yang, W., & Austin, S. B. (2002). Dating violence among gay, lesbian, and bisexual adolescents: Results from a community survey. *Journal of Adolescent Health, 31*(6), 469–474.

Gillum, T. L., & DiFulvio, G. T. (2012). "There's so much at stake": Sexual minority youth discuss dating violence. *Violence Against Women, 18*(7), 725–745.

Haas, A. P., Eliason, M., Mays, V. M., Mathy, R. M., Cochran, S. D., & D'Augelli, A. R. (2011). Suicide and suicide risk in lesbian, gay, bisexual, and transgender populations: Review and recommendations. *Journal of Homosexuality, 58*(1), 10–51.

Halpern, C. T., Young, M. L., Waller, M. W., Martin, S. L., & Kupper, L. L. (2004). Prevalence of partner violence in same-sex romantic and sexual relationships in a national sample of adolescents. *Journal of Adolescent Health, 35*(2), 124–131.

Hedtke, K. A., Ruggiero, K. J., Fitzgerald, M. M., Zinzow, H. M., Saunders, B. E., Resnick, H. S., et al. (2008). A longitudinal investigation of interpersonal violence in relation to mental health and substance use. *Journal of Consulting and Clinical Psychology, 76*(4), 633–647.

Heintz, A. J., & Melendez, R. M. (2006). Intimate partner violence and HIV/STD risk among lesbian, gay, bisexual and transgender individuals. *Journal of Interpersonal Violence, 21*(2), 193–208.

Herek, G. M., Chopp, R., & Strohl, D. (2007). Putting minority health issues in context. In I. Meyer & M. Northridge (Eds.), *The health of sexual minorities: Public health perspectives on lesbian, gay, bisexual, and transgender populations* (pp. 171–208). New York, NY: Springer.

Howard, D. E., Wang, M. Q., & Yan, F. (2007). Psychosocial factors associated with reports of dating violence among U.S. adolescent females. *Adolescence, 42*(166), 311–324.

Ismail, F., Berman, H., & Ward-Griffin, C. (2007). Dating violence and the health of young women: A feminist narrative study. *Health Care Women International, 28*(5), 453–477.

King, M., Semlyen, J., Tai, S. S., Killaspy, H., Osborn, D., Popelyuk, D., et al. (2008). A systemic review of mental disorder, suicide, and deliberate self-harm in lesbian, gay and bisexual people. *BMC Psychiatry, 8*(70), 1–17.

Kramer, A., Lorenzon, D., & Mueller, G. (2004). Prevalence of intimate partner violence and health implications for women using emergency departments and primary care clinics. *Women's Health Issues, 14*(1), 19–29.

Letellier, P., & Holt, S. (2000). *The California report on lesbian, gay, bisexual, and transgender domestic violence.* Los Angeles, CA: L.A. Gay and Lesbian Center.

Marrow, D. F. (2004). Social work practice with gay, lesbian, bisexual and transgender adolescents. *Families in Society, 85*(1), 91–99.

Massachusetts Department of Education. (2006). *2005 Massachusetts Youth Risk Behavior Survey results.* Boston, MA: Author.

Meyer, I. H. (2003). Prejudice, social stress, and mental health in lesbian, gay, and bisexual populations: Conceptual issues and research evidence. *Psychological Bulletin, 129*(5), 674–697.

Miller, R. L., Jr. (2007). Legacy denied: African American gay men, AIDS, and the Black Church. *Social Work, 52*(1), 51–61.

Miller, S. (2011). African American lesbian identity management and identity development in the context of family and community. *Journal of Homosexuality, 58*(4), 547–563.

Naumann, P., Langford, D., Torres, S., Campbell, J., & Glass, N. (1999). Women battering in primary care practice. *Family Practice, 16*(4), 343–352.

Otis, M. D., Rostosky, S. S., Riggle, E. D. B., & Hamrin, R. (2006). Stress and relationship quality in same-sex couples. *Journal of Social and Personal Relationships, 23*(1), 81–99.

Pathela, P., & Schillinger, J. A. (2010). Sexual behaviors and sexual violence: Adolescents with opposite-, same-, or both-sex partners. *Pediatrics, 126*(5), 879–886.

Plichta, S. B. (2004). Intimate partner violence and physical health consequences: Policy and practice implications. *Journal of Interpersonal Violence, 19*(11), 1296–1323.

Radloff, L. S. (1977). The CES-D scale: A self-report depression scale for research in the general population. *Applied Psychological Measurement, 1*(3), 385–401.

Radloff, L. S. (1991). The use of the Center for Epidemiological Studies depression scale in adolescents and young adults. *Journal of Youth and Adolescents, 20*(2), 149–165.

Rothman, E. F., Johnson, R. M., Azrael, D., Hall, D. M., & Weinberg, J. (2010). Perpetration of physical assault against dating partners, peers, and siblings among a locally representative sample of high school students in Boston, Massachusetts. *Archives of Pediatrics and Adolescent Medicine, 164*(12), 1118–1124.

Rothman, E. F., Johnson, R. M., Young, R., Weinberg, J., Azrael, D., & Molnar, B. E. (2011). Neighborhood-level factors associated with physical dating violence perpetration: Results of a representative survey conducted in Boston, MA. *Journal of Urban Health, 88*(2), 201–213.

Ryan, C., & Futterman, D. (1997). Lesbian and gay youth: Care and counseling. *Adolescent Medicine, 8*(2), 207–374.

Ryan, C., Huebner, D., Diaz, R. M., & Sanchez, J. (2009). Family rejection as a predictor of negative health outcomes in White and Latino lesbian, gay, and bisexual young adults. *Pediatrics, 123*(1), 346–352.

Sandfort, T. G. M., Melendez, R. M., & Diaz, R. M. (2007). Gender nonconformity, homophobia, and mental distress in Latino gay and bisexual men. *Journal of Sex Research, 44*(2), 181–189.

Sears, H. A., Byers, E. S., & Price, L. (2007). The co-occurrence of adolescent boys' and girls' use of psychological, physical, and sexually abusive behaviors in their dating relationships. *Journal of Adolescence, 30*(3), 487–504.

Smith, P. H., White, J. W., & Holland, L. J. (2003). A longitudinal perspective on dating violence among adolescents and college age women. *American Journal of Public Health, 93*(7), 1104–1109.

Stall, R., Mills, T. C., Williamson, J., Hart, T., Greenwood, G., Paul, J., & Catania, J. A. (2003). Association of co-occurring psychosocial health problems and increased vulnerability to HIV/AIDS among urban men who have sex with men. *American Journal of Public Health, 93*(6), 939–942.

Straus, M. A., Hambly, S. L., Boney-McCoy, S., & Sugarman, D. B. (1996). The revised Conflict Tactics Scales (CTS2): Development and preliminary psychometric data. *Journal of Family Issue, 17*(3), 283–316.

Straus, M. A., Hambly, S. L., & Warren, W. L. (2003). *The conflict tactics scale handbook*. Los Angeles, CA: Western Psychological Services.

Tigert, L. M. (2001). The power of shame: Lesbian battering as a manifestation of homophobia. *Women & Therapy, 23*(3), 73–85.

West, C. M., & Rose, S. (2000). Dating aggression among low-income African American youth. *Violence Against Women, 6*(5), 470–494.

West, B. A., Swahn, M. H., & McCarthy, F. (2010). Children at risk for suicide attempt and attempt-related injuries: Findings from the 2007 Youth Risk Behavior Survey. *Western Journal of Emergency Medicine, 11*(3), 257–263.

Chapter 21
The Queer Delinquent: Impacts of Risk and Protective Factors on Sexual Minority Juvenile Offending in the U.S.

Meredith Conover-Williams

Abstract The study of gender and crime has followed a trajectory, from finding that women offend differently, to exploring how gendered lives impact the nature and extent of offending. This has shown criminologists that our theories must account for the variance in gendered lives. With this chapter, I propose a similar trajectory for understanding the role of sexual orientation and offending, beginning with youth. Using The National Longitudinal Study of Adolescent Health (Add Health, n = 14,290), I provide a baseline, national examination of the nature and extent of juvenile delinquency in the United States, when sexual minority status is considered. I begin to show how the differential life experiences of sexual minority youth impact offending by exploring how various risk and protective factors related to social institutions influence juvenile offending, comparing sexual minority youth to their majority peers. I find that sexual minority youth, relative to their sexual majority peers, report more prevalence and frequency of several (mostly non-violent) criminal behaviors. I show that a variety of protective factors (such as school and family attachments) and risk factors (such as alcohol use, victimization, and housing instability) can account for much of that difference. I demonstrate that sexual orientation is indeed another crucial attribute for understanding the relationship between social inequality and delinquency, and discuss possible points of intervention with youth, based on these findings. I also show that current theories are insufficient to fully explain the offending of sexual minority youth.

Keywords Juvenile delinquency Delinquency Sex work · Drugs · Alcohol · Drug use · Violence · School · Education · Family · Parent-child relationships · Mentors · Religion · Work · Abuse · Sexual assault · Running away · Kicked out · Gender · Race · Graffiti · Life course · Risk factors · Protective factors

M. Conover-Williams (✉)
Department of Sociology, Humboldt State University, BSS 506, 1 Harpst Street,
Arcata, CA 95521, USA
e-mail: Meredith.Williams@humboldt.edu

D. Peterson and V. R. Panfil (eds.), *Handbook of LGBT Communities,*   449
Crime, and Justice, DOI: 10.1007/978-1-4614-9188-0_21,
© Springer Science+Business Media New York 2014

Introduction

Feminist criminologists, and other scholars, have well established that institutionalized sexism impacts the extent and nature of offending, with women offending less than, and differently from, men. This has shown criminology that exploring individual attributes, such as gender, is crucial to understanding how and why different people offend. From this, criminology has expanded our theoretical explanations for crime beyond "add women and stir" (Chesney-Lind 1986) to more nuanced understandings of the impacts of social inequality on crime. This chapter offers an examination of how sexual orientation may also be another important attribute for understanding the extent and nature of offending. It provides a baseline examination into the delinquency of sexual minority youth in the U.S., relative to their sexual majority peers. It explores how sexual minority youth may be experiencing different pushes and pulls toward and away from crime than other youth. With this, I explore how current theories may not be sufficient for understanding sexual minority offending.

Gender, Social Inequality, and Crime

Feminist criminologists have shown the discipline that gender is one of the most powerful correlates of crime, and crucial for understanding the impact of social inequality on offending. This research has followed a trajectory. First, it was established that women offend less, and that they offend differently, specializing in and being funneled to different types of crimes (Steffensmeier and Allan 1996). Next, deeper explorations found that these differences were largely due to the different pushes and pulls toward and away from crime that women experienced, given their status in their society, and gendered socialization (Steffensmeier and Allan 1996; Steffensmeier and Terry 1986). The pathways perspective emerged from feminist criminological examinations of women's lives and how they came to be involved in offending. This perspective posits that people's life experiences, whether normative or exceptional, can lead them in and out of antisocial activities. This gives researchers sites for intervention or prevention by studying common patterns. As pathways research has found, women experience different pushes and pulls toward and away from criminality, compared to men; they have different levels of exposure to factors that may increase their risk of offending, or act as protective factors from offending.

These deeper explorations into the lives of women, and the gendered nature of offending, showed the broader field of criminology both that the consideration of gender is crucial for understanding crime, and that established criminological theories were not sufficient to explain the extent and nature of female offending. Acknowledging the "add women and stir" approach to explaining female offending was not enough, feminist scholars expanded criminological theory to incorporate the unique life experiences of women. These differences in female and male life experiences, and subsequent offending, are a result of a patriarchal social structure that favors men over women, and demonstrate that the lives of women are framed by sexism within the social structure.

Sexuality and Crime

Another important point of stratification is sexual orientation. It is well established that our heteronormative social structure favors heterosexual individuals over members of LGBTQ communities, and that heterosexism shapes the lives of sexual minority people. The broader discipline of sociology has increasingly recognized the importance of studying sexuality as part of a robust understanding of social inequality (for a review, see Andersen 2005; Bernstein 2013), but this has only been minimally integrated into criminology. While there are studies about members of the Lesbian, Gay, Bisexual, Transgender, and Queer (LGBTQ) communities as *victims* of crimes, there has been little attention given to sexual minority individuals as *offenders* of crimes (but see, e.g., in this volume, Dennis; Panfil). This has left a substantial gap in the criminological literature that examines the effect of social inequality on offending.

This gap has recently been recognized, and scholars have begun to explore sexual orientation as a correlate of crime, much like gender. For example, Belknap, Holsinger and Little (2012) recently studied incarcerated girls, including sexual minority young women. Himmelstein and Brückner (2010) examined the delinquent behaviors and subsequent sanctions for heterosexual versus non-heterosexual youth. These recent studies on sexual orientation as a correlate of delinquency provide evidence that it is time to solidify the study of sexuality and crime, following a similar research trajectory as research on gender and crime. Criminology is due for a baseline exploration of sexual minority offending: are sexual minority individuals offending more or less than their majority peers? Are they committing similar crimes, or are they participating in other types of offending? What are the pushes and pulls toward and away from offending for sexual minority individuals, and do these differ due to different life experiences? To what extent can current criminological theories explain sexual minority offending? Can we "just add queers and stir" or do we need a more robust exploration of queer lives to understand sexual minority offending?

Currently, one of the most powerful paradigms in criminology for understanding the nature and extent of offending is Developmental and Life Course Criminology (DLC). This paradigm examines pushes and pulls toward/from offending across the life course to understand the propensity to offend or desist. DLC weaves together several established criminological theories that incorporate risk and protective factors across the life course, acknowledging that it is not one factor that leads a person to offend, but myriad influences from the individual, their family, their peers, school, neighborhood, community, and so forth (Cullen et al. 2012;

Farrington 2005). DLC perhaps offers the most nuanced paradigm for under-standing sexual minority offending, acknowledging (as the pathways perspective did for women) that differential life experiences shape the extent and nature of individual offending. Like the pathways perspective, it posits that people's life experiences, whether normative or exceptional, can lead them in and out of anti-social activities. This gives researchers sites for intervention or prevention by studying common patterns.

Risk and Protective Factors

As pathways research and DLC have both found, risk and protective factors, interacting with personal attributes such as gender, are a powerful avenue for understanding social inequality and criminal trajectories. The pathways perspec-tive and DLC together offer a way to connect sexual minority status and delinquent behaviors by exploring the similarities and differences in experiences between marginalized and privileged groups when it comes to risk and protective factors. Risk factors are aspects of an individual's life that predict higher probabilities of offending (Farrington et al. 2012). Protective factors are aspects of one's life that act as insulation from negative outcomes, or buffer the impacts of risk factors. I look at both to speak to prevention, looking for sites of protection and/or inter-vention. In this study, I use many established individual risk/protective factors from DLC and the pathways perspective. In addition, I consider other factors to accommodate the potential unique life experiences of sexual minority individuals, such as friendships and adult mentors.

For this study, I grouped protective factors into school, family, peers and mentors, religion, and work. I grouped risk factors into drug and alcohol use, victimization, and housing instability. For any factor, presence or absence could be important for criminality, but it could also be that the impacts (positive or nega-tive) are weaker or stronger, based on sexual minority status, and other risk/protective factors at play.

Protective Factors

School: Scholars have found that both school connectedness (Resnick et al. 1997) and commitment to school act as social controls for adolescents (Agnew 1992; Cernkovich and Giordano 1992; Krohn and Massey 1980). Schools may offer protective benefits from offending for some students, but may not have that effect for sexual minority youth. As a site of exclusion, harassment, and bullying for many sexual minority youth (Greytak, Kosciw, and Diaz 2009; see too Warbelow and Cobb, this volume), they may not feel as connected with the institution, eliminating or limiting its protective benefits.

Family: Attachments to parents (Hirschi 1969), parenting style (Farrington and Welsh 2007), and monitoring and supervision (Gorman-Smith, Tolan, Zelli, and Huesmann 1996) have all been shown to be protective from offending. The institution of family, though, may also be a site of exclusion (Ryan, Huebner, Diaz, and Sanchez 2009) and/or victimization (Savin-Williams 1994) for some sexual minority youth, due to their minority status.

Peers and Mentors: Much of the research on peers has focused on them as a risk factor for adolescents (Keenan, Leober, Zhang, Stouthamer-Loeber, and van Kammen 1995; Thornberry and Krohn 1997). Friends could, however, act as a makeshift "chosen family" (Weeks, Heaphy, and Donovan 2001; Weston 1997) providing family-like support for those who do not have access to a family of origin, such as sexual minority youth. Because of this, I treat attachment to friends as a protective factor. Adult mentors have been shown to act as a protective factor from crime (DuBois and Silverthorn 2005). They have also been shown to be beneficial to sexual minority youth, promoting resiliency in education (Gastic and Johnson 2009). They may, then, provide protection from delinquency for sexual minority youth.

Religion: The effects of religion on crime have long been debated (for a review, see Baier and Wright 2001). It could be that the preventative effects of religion, if any, may depend on the individual, based on personal attributes such as sexual orientation (see, for example, Rotosky, Danner, and Riggle 2007). It could be that participation in a religion does not provide protection for some sexual minority youth, as many major U.S. religions formally speak out against sexual minority rights, and many have restrictions on participation in their services (Garrigan 2009).

Work: Work has been considered both a risk and a protective factor for adolescents. While much of the research has consistently shown that employment during the high school years is correlated with more antisocial behavior (for a review, see Staff, Osgood, Schulenberg, Bachman, and Messersmith 2010), it has also been shown to be a "turning point" (Elder 1985) toward desistance (Sampson and Laub 1993). Work may act as protective from criminality, by having a job, or by the quality of the job (Uggen and Staff 2001), especially for youth lacking other connections. The positive impact of work may be diminished for some sexual minority workers, by pervasive workplace discrimination (Badgett, Lau, Sears, and Ho 2007) and heterosexism (Waldo 1999).

Risk Factors

Alcohol and Substance Use: There is a strong connection between drug/alcohol use and criminality and/or high-risk behaviors (Gilfus 1992; Laub and Sampson 1993; van Kammen and Loeber 1994). Sexual minority youth and adults have been found, repeatedly, to have higher rates of drug and/or alcohol use (for a review, see Marshal et al. 2008).

Victimization: The connection between victimization and offending has been well established in the criminological literature, across gender and race (Widom, Schuck, and White 2006). As has been explored above, sexual minority youth face high victimization levels at school (Greytak et al. 2009) and in families (for a review, see Savin-Williams 1994).

Housing Stability: Running away from home, as well as being kicked out, have strong connections to offending, especially survival offending, and may also play a part in the strong connection between victimization and offending (Kaufman and Widom 1999; also Frederick, this volume). Sexual minority youth often run away and/or are expelled from their households based on their sexuality. The National Network for Youth (2008) has estimated that 20–40 % of youths who become homeless each year are lesbian, gay, or bisexual, though individuals who are LGBTQ make up an estimated 3.5 % of the adult population (Gates 2011).

Hypotheses

Based on prior literature on risk and protective factors, with sexual minority youth seemingly experiencing much higher levels of risk factors and lower levels of protective factors, I hypothesize the following:

In comparison to their sexual majority peers:

H1   Sexual minority individuals will have a higher rate of offending
H2   Sexual minority individuals will participate in different crimes
H3   Sexual minority individuals will have lower levels of protective factors from offending
H4   Sexual minority respondents will have higher levels of risk factors for offending
H5   The levels of risk/protective factors for sexual minority youth will account for a proportion of their higher offending rates.

Just as the study of gender has helped criminologists to understand the role of social inequality in offending, the current study argues that sexual orientation matters. The social position that comes from being a sexual minority structures one's life experiences, shaping exposure to risk and protective factors. Navigating life through a series of social institutions where one's sexual minority status is perhaps correlated to higher levels of risk factors, and/or lower levels of protective factors, compared to one's heterosexual peers, could manifest in higher levels of antisocial behavior. A national study that asks questions both about delinquency and sexual minority status is needed to provide a baseline examination of the extent of offending among sexual minority youth, and the relevant risk/protective factors associated with such delinquency.

Data

The National Longitudinal Study of Adolescent Health (Add Health) is a longitudinal study of adolescents who were in grades 7 through 12 when sampled from a stratified sample of 80 U.S. high schools and 32 feeder middle schools during the 1994–1995 school year. Researchers used personal interviews, as well as Audio-CASI (audio computer-aided self interview) for sensitive topics. I used Wave I independent and dependent measures to study adolescents, who were a mean age of 16 at the time of the study, as well as some retrospective questions to measure independent variables that may have impacted the respondents during their youth, from Waves III (mentors and being kicked out of their homes) and IV (childhood victimization and sexual assault). It should be noted that since dependent variables and most independent variables were measured at the same wave, conclusions about causality should be interpreted with caution.

I chose Add Health for this study for four reasons. First, it is a national, random sample with enough respondents to do quantitative analysis on a relatively small population. Second, it asks questions about respondents' same- and opposite-sex attractions, allowing researchers to look at the experiences of sexual minority youth, whether or not they have self-identified as gay, lesbian, or bisexual. Third, Add Health asks questions about a range of delinquent behaviors, allowing me to capture differences in types and seriousness of offending. Fourth, it contains both offenders and non-offenders in the sample. Many prior studies have relied on institutionalized samples, limiting the ability to look at resistance and protective factors. Add Health allows us to look at both positive and negative predictors to identify preventative measures.

I performed these analyses using Stata Version 11. In order to account for the weighting, and nesting of respondents within schools and geographic regions, I used survey commands (svy: in stata) on all descriptive and logistic regression analyses.

Basic descriptive statistics of respondents' demographic characteristics, including sexual minority status, can be seen in Table 21.1. Respondents who are considered sexual minority youth for the sake of this study are those that expressed both-sex or same-sex attractions; this is about 6 % of the adolescents.

Dependent Variables

Respondents answered questions about a variety of crimes and violent behaviors; I separated these into *Non-Violent* and *Violent* indices (both frequency and a dichotomous prevalence measure), as well as created a variable for *Sex For Money* and a variable for *Selling Drugs*. See Table 21.2 for questions used in each measure.

Table 21.1 Descriptive statistics on basic demographics for all respondents, comparing sexual minority to sexual majority respondents

Variables mean (SD) or % (SE)	All respondents (n = 14,290)	Sexual minority (n = 903)	Sexual majority (n = 13,387)	Test of differences
Demographics				
Age (Mean)	15.9 (0.12)	16.4 (1.75)	15.9 (1.77)	t 5.74[***]
Race (Proportion)				
White	78.4 % (0.02)	71.5 % (0.03)	75.3 % (0.02)	z 0.48
Nonwhite	21.6 % (0.02)	28.5 % (0.03)	24.7 % (0.02)	z 0.48
Ethnicity (Proportion)				
Hispanic/Latino	11.5 % (0.02)	14.4 % (0.03)	11.3 % (0.02)	z 2.01[*]
Sex (Proportion)				
Female	50.7 % (0.01)	57.1 % (0.02)	48.5 % (0.01)	z 5.34[***]
Male	49.3 % (0.01)	42.9 % (0.02)	51.5 % (0.01)	z 5.34[***]

[*] $p < 0.05$
[**] $p < 0.01$
[***] $p < 0.001$

Table 21.2 Dependent variables (dichotomized for logistic regression analyses)

Non-violent crimes (In the past 12 months, how often did you...)[a]
- Vandalism: deliberately damage property that didn't belong to you?
- Steal < $50: steal something worth less than $50?
- Steal > $50: steal something worth more than $50?
- Break In: go into a house or building to steal something?
- Joyriding: drive a car without the owner's position?
- Graffiti: paint graffiti or signs on someone else's property or in a public place?
- Shoplifting: take something from a store without paying?

Violent crimes (In the past 12 months, how often did you...)
- Hurt Someone: hurt someone badly enough to need bandages or care?
- Fighting: participated in a serious physical fight?
- Group Fight: taken part in a fight with one group of friends against another?

Sex for money
- Have you ever given someone sex in exchange for drugs or money?

Selling drugs (In the past 12 months, how often did you...)
- Sell marijuana or other drugs?

[a] 0 = never; 1 = 1 or 2 times; 2 = 3 or 4 times; 3 = 5 or more times

Independent Variables

All independent variables were recoded to align with the convention of having a higher number correspond to a higher level of that risk or protective factor. Questions used for each measure are listed in Table 21.3. The key variable of interest, *Sexual Minority Status,* was created by using the respondent's sex as reported by the interviewer (verified at the interviewer's discretion) in combination with the questions, "Have you ever had a romantic attraction to a female?" and the

Table 21.3 Independent variable measures, with answer range and wave measured

Independent variable	Range	Wave measured
Sexual minority status[1]	0–1	I
• Have you ever had a romantic attraction to a female?		
• Have you ever had a romantic attraction to a male?		
Educational attachment (How much do you agree or disagree with the following:)	0–25	I
• You feel close to the people at your school		
• You feel like you are part of your school		
• You are happy to be at your school		
• Teachers at your school treat students fairly		
• You feel safe in your school		
Educational aspiration	1–5	I
• On a scale of 1–5, where 1 is low and 5 is high, how much do you want to go to college?		
Family attachments (How much do you feel…)	0–15	I
• the people in your family understand you?		
• that you and your family have fun together?		
• that your family pays attention to you?		
Parental attachment (Please tell me whether you agree or disagree with each of the following statements:)	0–15	I
• Most of the time, [parent] is warm and loving toward you		
• You are satisfied with the way [parent] and you communicate with each other		
• Overall, you are satisfied with your relationship with [parent]		
Adults care	1–5	I
• How much do you feel that adults care about you?		
Friends care	1–5	I
• How much do you feel that your friends care about you?		
Adult mentor	0–1	III
• Other than your parents or step-parents, has an adult made an important positive difference in your life at any time since you were 14 years old?		
Religiosity	1–4	I
• How important is religion to you?		
Current job	0–1	I
• In the last 4 weeks, did you work—for pay—for anyone outside your home?		
Alcohol Use	0–6	I
• During the past 12 months, on how many days did you drink alcohol?		
Substance use	0–903	I
• During the past 30 days, how many times did you use cocaine?		
• During the past 30 days, how many times did you use any of these types of illegal drugs? [LSD, PCP, ecstasy, mushrooms, speed, ice, heroin, or pills, without a doctor's prescription]		

(continued)

Table 21.3 (continued)

Independent variable	Range	Wave measured
Childhood abuse (Before your 18th birthday…) • how often did a parent or other adult caregiver say things that really hurt your feelings or made you feel like you were not wanted or loved? • how often did a parent or adult caregiver hit you with a fist, kick you, or throw you down on the floor, into a wall, or down stairs? • how often did a parent or other adult caregiver touch you in a sexual way, force you to touch him or her in a sexual way, or force you to have sexual relations?	0–15	IV
Sexual assault (Have you ever been…) • forced in a non-physical way, to have any type of sexual activity against your will? For example, through verbal pressure, threats of harm, or by being given alcohol or drugs? • physically forced to have any type of sexual activity against your will?	0–1	IV
Kicked out • Have your [did your] parents ever ordered you to move out of their house?	0–1	III
Running away (In the past 12 months, how often did you…) • run away from home?	0–3	I
Nonwhite • What is your race?	0–1	I
Latino • Are you of Hispanic or Latin origin?	0–1	I
Male • Determined by the interviewer (instructed to ask for clarification, if needed)	0–1	I
Parent education • How far in school did your [parent] go?	1–5	I

[1] Savin-Williams (2006) theorized that measures of attraction should be used over behavior or identity questions. Using attraction aligns with most other current research on sexual minority youth, including studies using Add Health (see for example Battle and Linville 2006; Teasdale and Bradley-Engen 2010)

same for attraction to male. To explore protective factors, the social institution of school was measured with both *Educational Attachment* and *Educational Aspiration*. Attachment to the institution of family was measured with *Family Attachment* generally, and a maximum score for one parent with *Parent Attachment*. To attempt to capture "chosen families" my measures for friends and mentors included a variable on whether or not the respondents felt *Adults Care* about them, whether or not they thought their *Friends Care*, and the presence or absence of an *Adult Mentor*. I also included a measure of *Religiosity,* and whether or not the respondents had a *Current Job*. To capture potential risk factors, I included measures of *Alcohol Use, Substance Use,* an index of *Childhood Abuse,* a measure for the presence or absence of *Sexual Assault* and two measures of housing stability: having ever been *Kicked Out*, and how often they had *Run Away* in the past year.

Control Variables

I used several demographic details about the respondents as control variables: *Nonwhite, Latino,* and *Male.* I also included two additional controls for levels of parent education (using the maximum score for any one residential parent), and family structure (with a series of questions used to develop a household roster). For *Parent Education,* I recoded responses to make a higher score correlate with a higher level of education, ranging from never attending school (= 0) to professional training beyond a 4-year college or university (= 5). If the respondent was not sure about any parent's level of education, the respondent was marked as missing for that parent; if s/he did not know the level of education for both parents, or for a single parent, the respondent was marked with a zero, to correspond with not having the protective impact of parent education. *Family structure* was determined using a series of questions about biological and/or residential parents, coded to a dichotomous variable (0 = other family type, 1 = two biological parents).

As seen in Table 21.1, the sexual minority respondents were slightly older (16.35 vs. 15.87), relative to their sexual majority peers. The sexual minority group also had more females (57 %), compared to the sexual majority respondents (48 %). Because the two comparison groups have a small difference in the sex composition, there may be some systematic differences between the groups. For example, beyond sex differences in offending, young men may overestimate their offending, or young women might underestimate theirs. If that is the case, if there seems to be a difference in offending rates between sexual minority youth and their majority peers, it may actually be somewhat larger than it seems in this study. The multivariate analysis helps to determine the role of sex, when risk and protective factors are also considered.

Results

To examine the first hypothesis, that sexual minority individuals would have a higher rate of offending than their majority peers, I looked at both prevalence and frequency for all types of offending considered in this study. As seen in Table 21.4, sexual minority youth have a higher prevalence and frequency for each of the crimes examined. In all comparisons, the differences were statistically significant, using a two-tailed t test. Respondents who were sexual minority youth had a substantially higher prevalence of participation in non-violent crime (more than half, in comparison to 38 %), and somewhat higher prevalence in violent crime (46 vs. 41 %), than their sexual majority peers. Though the numbers of participants are small, far more sexual minority youth reported having traded sex for money, and did so more often, on average, than sexual majority youth. More than twice as many sexual minority youth as majority youth reported selling drugs,

Table 21.4 Prevalence and mean (SE) frequency of offending, by sexual minority status

Variables mean or % (specified)	Sexual minority (n = 903)	Sexual majority (n = 13,897)	Test for statistical significance
Non-violent index (Prevalence)	53.2 % (0.03)	38.1 % (0.01)	z 7.03[***]
Non-violent index (Frequency 0–21)	2.24 (0.19)	1.26 (0.04)	t 5.20[***]
Violent index (Prevalence)	45.3 % (0.03)	40.2 % (0.00)	z 3.48[**]
Violent index (Frequency 0–9)	1.23 (0.11)	0.92 (0.03)	t 2.95[**]
Sex for money (Prevalence)	4.6 % (0.01)	1.1 % (0.00)	z 9.86[***]
Sex for money (Frequency 0–20)	0.45 (0.15)	0.04 (0.01)	t 2.64[**]
Selling Drugs (Prevalence)	15.6 % (0.02)	7.0 % (0.00)	z 6.91[***]
Selling Drugs (Frequency 0–3)	0.30 (0.04)	0.13 (0.01)	t 4.26[***]

[*] $p < 0.05$
[**] $p < 0.01$
[***] $p < 0.001$

with more than twice the frequency. This shows strong support for the first hypothesis; sexual minority youth report more delinquent behaviors than their sexual majority peers.

To examine the second hypothesis, that sexual minority individuals would participate in different crimes than sexual majority individuals, I compared the top five crimes each group reported, again by both frequency and prevalence (see Table 21.5). The differences between the two groups were that sexual minority youth reported hurting someone enough to need medical attention as their fifth most prevalent offense, and sexual majority youth reported group fighting as their third most prevalent offense. Sexual minority youth reported trading sex for money and graffiti among their most frequent offenses, while their majority peers reported group fighting and hurting someone. The biggest differences, then, might be that sexual minority youth are more likely to specialize in property and sex-related offenses, where sexual majority youth were more likely to be involved in violence. Again, across the top five, sexual minority respondents reported higher rates of offending than sexual majorities. These results demonstrate some support for the

Table 21.5 Top five crimes (in order of prevalence and frequency), by sexual minority status

	Prevalence		Frequency	
	Sexual minority %	Sexual majority %	Sexual minority	Sexual majority
1	Fighting (36.84)	Fighting (31.47)	Shoplifting (0.58)	Fighting (0.44)
2	Shoplifting (33.82)	Shoplifting (22.39)	Fighting (0.57)	Shoplifting (0.35)
3	Graffiti (26.68)	Group Fight (19.19)	Steal < $50 (0.48)	Steal < $50 (0.30)
4	Steal < $50 (26.32)	Steal < $50 (19.08)	Sex For Money (0.45)	Group Fight (0.25)
5	Hurt someone (22.64)	Graffiti (17.98)	Graffiti (0.40)	Hurt Someone (0.23)

Table 21.6 Mean or proportion (SD) score for protective and risk factors, by sexual minority status

Protective or risk factor	Sexual minority (n = 903)	Sexual majority (n = 13,897)	Test for statistical significance
Protective factors			
School			
School attachment (0–20)	12.64 (4.03)	13.58 (3.77)	t 5.16***
Educational aspirations (1–5)	4.36 (1.09)	4.42 (1.04)	t 1.12
Family			
Parental attachment (0–15)	12.63 (2.43)	13.10 (2.10)	t 4.24***
Family attachment (0–15)	10.59 (2.61)	11.28 (2.45)	t 5.84***
Peers and mentors			
Friends care (1–5)	4.19 (0.87)	4.26 (0.77)	t 1.75
Adult mentor (s.e.)	74.2 % (0.02)	77.2 % (0.01)	z 0.49
Adults care (1–5)	4.15 (0.95)	4.40 (0.80)	t 5.97***
Religion			
Religiosity (1–4)	2.85 (1.12)	3.00 (1.08)	t 2.97**
Work			
Current job (s.e.)	62.4 % (0.03)	60.3 % (0.01)	z 0.28
Risk factors			
Alcohol			
Alcohol prevalence (s.e.)	63.3 % (0.02)	46.2 % (0.01)	z 7.35***
Alcohol frequency (0–6)	1.33 (1.29)	0.95 (1.25)	t 6.62***
Substance Use			
SU prevalence (s.e.)	12.9 % (0.01)	4.2 % (0.00)	z 8.99***
SU frequency (0–900)	3.15 (1.66)	0.47 (0.08)	t 1.60
Victimization			
Childhood abuse (0–15)	4.10 (0.19)	3.30 (0.06)	t 3.95***
Sexual assault (%) (s.e.)	19.4 % (0.02)	14.3 % (0.00)	z 5.04***
Housing Stability			
Running away (%)	17.1 % (0.02)	7.4 % (0.00)	z 7.54***
Kicked out (%) (s.e.)	15.2 % (0.02)	10.6 % (0.00)	z 2.54**

* $p < 0.05$
** $p < 0.01$
*** $p < 0.001$

second hypothesis, that sexual minority and majority respondents participate in different crimes, but not enough to confirm the hypothesis, so it was rejected.

In my third hypothesis I stated that sexual minority respondents would have lower levels of protective factors, relative to the sexual majority respondents. To test this, I compared mean scores for sexual minority and sexual majority respondents. As seen in Table 21.6, sexual minority respondents report lower levels of all protective factors, to varying degrees, with several being statistically significant differences, compared to sexual majority youth. Sexual minority adolescents, then, are slightly less attached to school, slightly less attached to parents and family, and feel less that adults care about them. These differences, though, are small. These results show little support for the third hypothesis; the hypothesis was rejected.

My fourth hypothesis was that sexual minority youth would have higher levels of the risk factors being studied at each wave, relative to the sexual majority respondents. To test this, I compared means for sexual minority and majority respondents. As seen in Table 21.6, sexual minority youth, on average, report higher levels of all measured risk factors, and almost all of those differences are statistically significant. Sexual minority youth reported more frequent drinking, and 3 times the number of sexual minority youth reported use of an illegal substance (nearly 13 vs. 4 %), compared to their sexual majority peers. Sexual minority respondents reported a higher frequency of abuse prior to the age of 18, and a substantially higher rate of having been the victim of sexual assault (nearly 20 compared to 14 %). The differences in exposure to risk factors for these two groups are both substantially and significantly different, confirming the fourth hypothesis.

My final hypothesis was that those protective and risk factors would explain much of the sexual minority-majority gap in offending; if there was any difference in likelihood of offending, the variable levels of risk and protective factors would account for that difference. To test this, I used nested logistic regression models to predict odds of participation in four types of delinquency: non-violent, violent, sex work, and selling drugs. For each model, the cluster of variables added at each model was tested using an adjusted Wald test, to see if the addition of the new variables was statistically significant (multicollinearity was not a problem in the models). The number reported in the final row of each table signifies the strength of the additional clusters (as seen in a higher number), as well as the statistical significance of the additions, using the same significance indicators. Results for non-violent offending are shown in Table 21.7, and violent offending in Table 21.8. Trading sex for money is explored in Table 21.9, and selling drugs is in Table 21.10.

With just the baseline controls in the model (All Tables, Model 1), the effect of being a sexual minority was statistically significant for three of the four types of offending (excluding violent offending). This means that sexual minority adolescents are more likely to participate in many types of delinquency, relative to their sexual majority peers. The effect was not statistically significant for violent offending, though it did become significant with the addition of protective and risk factors, explored below. The effect of sexual minority status, given the baseline controls, was biggest for trading sex for money, with sexual minority youth nearly 4 times (3.65) more likely to participate. However, this effect of sexual minority status was largely accounted for, with all types of crimes, once controls for various protective and risk factors were entered into the models. Entering protective factors into the models for non-violent offending (Table 21.7, Model 3) decreased the effect of sexual minority status by 14 %. Entering those same protective factors

Table 21.7 Odds ratios for nested models of non-violent offending by sexual minority status, protective and risk factors and control variables

Variables	Model 1	Model 2	Model 3	Model 4	Model 5
Sexual minority status	1.71 (0.21)***	1.44 (0.18)**	1.47 (0.20)**	1.41 (0.19)*	1.26 (0.19)
Protective factors					
School attachment		0.94 (0.01)***	0.95 (0.01)***	0.96 (0.01)***	0.97 (0.01)***
Educ. aspirations		0.91 (0.06)	0.87 (0.05)*	0.89 (0.05)*	0.90 (0.05)
Parental attachment		0.98 (0.02)	1.00 (0.02)	1.01 (0.03)	1.03 (0.02)
Family attachment		0.85 (0.01)***	0.84 (0.02)***	0.86 (0.02)***	0.87 (0.02)***
Friends care			1.09 (0.06)	1.02 (0.05)	1.02 (0.06)
Adult mentor			1.08 (0.08)	1.05 (0.08)	1.03 (0.08)
Adults care			0.99 (0.04)	1.02 (0.04)	1.04 (0.04)
Religiosity			0.88 (0.03)**	0.91 (0.03)*	0.92 (0.03)*
Current job			0.98 (0.07)	0.91 (0.06)	0.91 (0.06)
Risk factors					
Alcohol frequency				1.45 (0.04)***	1.43 (0.04)***
SU frequency				1.03 (0.03)	1.02 (0.02)
Childhood abuse					1.01 (0.01)
Sexual assault					1.19 (0.11)
Running away					2.78 (0.32)***
Kicked out					1.33 (0.15)*
Control variables					
Parent education	1.01 (0.03)	1.06 (0.04)	1.07 (0.03)*	1.07 (0.03)*	1.08 (0.03)**
Family structure	0.79 (0.06)**	0.90 (0.07)	0.91 (0.06)	0.96 (0.07)	1.03 (0.08)
Nonwhite	1.11 (0.14)	1.15 (0.13)	1.20 (0.13)	1.27 (0.14)*	1.32 (0.14)*
Latino	1.23 (0.18)	1.35 (0.16)**	1.49 (0.18)**	1.46 (0.17)**	1.46 (0.16)**
Male	1.43 (0.09)	1.59 (0.11)***	1.70 (0.10)***	1.67 (0.10)***	1.65 (0.11)***
Adjusted Wald test		68.95***	2.56*	86.74***	25.08***

* $p < 0.05$
** $p < 0.01$
*** $p < 0.001$

into the models for trading sex for money (Table 21.9, Model 3) decreased the sexual minority effect by more than one-fifth (21.1 %). Those protective factors had a similar impact on selling drugs (Table 21.10, Model 3), with a 20.2 % drop in the effect of being a sexual minority. The effect again dropped with the addition of controls for various risk factors. Their addition to non-violent offending (Table 21.7, Model 5) decreased the effect of sexual minority status by another 14.3 %. The decreases were smaller with trading sex for money and selling drugs, with a decrease of 2.8 and 3.8 %, respectively. Cumulatively, the effect of controlling for all of the protective and risk factors decreased the effect of sexual minority status by 26 % for non-violent offending, 23.3 % for trading sex for money, and 23.2 % for selling drugs.

Given the full set of protective and risk factors (All tables, Model 5), the effect of sexual minority status was no longer statistically significant for non-violent offending, but it remained both strong and significant for trading sex for money,

Table 21.8 Odds ratios for nested models of violent offending by sexual minority status, protective and risk factors and control variables

Variables	Model 1	Model 2	Model 3	Model 4	Model 5
Sexual minority status	0.96 (0.12)	0.86 (0.11)	0.80 (0.11)	0.76 (0.10)*	0.72 (0.10)*
Protective factors					
School attachment		0.95 (0.01)***	0.95 (0.01)***	0.96 (0.01)***	0.97 (0.01)**
Educ. aspirations		0.84 (0.05)**	0.85 (0.05)*	0.86 (0.05)*	0.87 (0.05)*
Parental attachment		1.01 (0.03)	1.01 (0.03)	1.02 (0.03)	1.02 (0.03)
Family attachment		0.91 (0.12)***	0.92 (0.02)***	0.93 (0.02)**	0.94 (0.02)*
Friends care			1.04 (0.05)	0.98 (0.05)	1.00 (0.05)
Adult mentor			1.18 (0.09)*	1.16 (0.09)	1.12 (0.10)
Adults care			0.97 (0.05)	1.00 (0.06)	1.03 (0.06)
Religiosity			0.96 (0.05)	0.99 (0.05)	1.00 (0.05)
Current job			0.93 (0.09)	0.89 (0.09)	0.87 (0.09)
Risk factors					
Alcohol frequency				1.28 (0.04)***	1.26 (0.04)***
SU frequency				1.03 (0.01)*	1.02 (0.01)*
Childhood abuse					1.00 (0.01)
Sexual assault					1.16 (0.13)
Running away					2.35 (0.27)***
Kicked out					1.19 (0.12)
Control variables					
Parent education	0.87 (0.04)**	0.90 (0.05)	0.85 (0.03)***	0.84 (0.03)***	0.85 (0.02)***
Family structure	0.69 (0.07)***	0.76 (0.08)*	0.88 (0.07)	0.90 (0.07)	0.96 (0.07)
Nonwhite	1.31 (0.19)	1.34 (0.18)*	1.44 (0.20)*	1.50 (0.22)**	1.54 (0.23)**
Latino	1.12 (0.17)	1.21 (0.21)	1.23 (0.25)	1.19 (0.27)	1.27 (0.31)
Male	2.06 (0.18)***	2.16 (0.18)***	2.09 (0.16)***	2.06 (0.16)***	1.96 (0.19)***
Adjusted Wald test		21.03***	0.98	43.85***	24.17***

* $p < 0.05$
** $p < 0.01$
*** $p < 0.001$

and for selling drugs. For the latter two types of offending, the effect remained larger than that of race or ethnicity. Throughout the analyses, the effect of sexual minority status rivaled that of race, ethnicity, and sex, pointing to the need to consider sexual minority status as crucial of a correlate as other personal attributes that determine youths' placement in the unequal social structure. The effect of sexual minority status became statistically significant for violent offending at the full model (Table 21.7, Model 5), with an odds ratio of 0.72. This means that once all of the protective and risk factors are accounted for, sexual minority youth are 28 % *less* likely than their majority counterparts to violently offend. As seen in Table 21.4, more sexual minority youth reported violent offending, and at a higher frequency, than their majority peers. Multivariate analysis shows that this higher

Table 21.9 Odds ratios for nested models of sex for money by sexual minority status, protective and risk factors and control variables

Variables	Model 1	Model 2	Model 3	Model 4	Model 5
Sexual minority status	3.65 (1.13)***	3.68 (1.13)***	2.88 (0.98)**	2.86 (0.98)**	2.80 (0.98)**
Protective factors					
School attachment		0.98 (0.04)	0.97 (0.04)	1.02 (0.04)	1.02 (0.04)
Educ. aspirations		0.71 (0.11)*	0.84 (0.10)	0.82 (0.09)	0.83 (0.10)
Parental attachment		1.00 (0.07)	1.07 (0.09)	1.07 (0.09)	1.09 (0.09)
Family attachment		0.86 (0.05)*	0.86 (0.06)*	0.85 (0.07)*	0.85 (0.07)*
Friends care			0.86 (0.14)	0.85 (0.15)	0.95 (0.17)
Adult mentor			0.90 (0.25)	0.78 (0.20)	0.78 (0.20)
Adults care			0.74 (0.12)	0.76 (0.14)	0.78 (0.15)
Religiosity			0.80 (0.11)	0.86 (0.12)	0.82 (0.12)
Current job			2.11 (0.64)*	2.02 (0.68)*	2.28 (0.84)*
Risk factors					
Alcohol frequency				1.43 (0.13)***	1.40 (0.12)***
SU frequency				1.03 (0.01)**	1.03 (0.01)**
Childhood abuse					0.98 (0.03)
Sexual assault					1.69 (0.54)
Running away					1.67 (0.59)
Kicked out					1.34 (0.46)
Control variables					
Parent education	0.82 (0.08)*	0.90 (0.11)	0.83 (0.11)	0.86 90.10)	0.89 (0.11)
Family structure	0.54 (0.17)	0.65 (0.20)	0.88 (0.24)	0.78 (0.21)	0.85 (0.24)
Nonwhite	0.73 (0.21)	0.73 (0.23)	1.05 (0.32)	1.03 (0.34)	1.16 (0.38)
Latino	0.77 (0.32)	0.87 (0.36)	0.88 (0.46)	0.91 (0.49)	0.81 (0.48)
Male	2.88 (0.84)***	3.08 (0.97)***	1.83 (0.66)	1.50 (0.55)	1.83 (0.63)
Adjusted Wald test		8.37***	3.29***	13.63***	2.27*

* $p < 0.05$
** $p < 0.01$
*** $p < 0.001$

level of offending can be explained by considering protective and risk factors. Drinking and running away were both positively associated with violent offending, controlling for the other protective and risk factors, and educational aspirations had the largest negative association on violent offending (Table 21.8, Model 5). It seems the effects of protective and risk factors buffer the impact of being a sexual minority, when it comes to violent delinquency.

Throughout the analyses, the important protective factors were most often school and family attachment. School attachment, controlling for all other protective and risk factors, decreased the likelihood of non-violent and violent delinquency by only 3 % (Tables 21.7 and 21.8, Model 5), but decreased the likelihood of selling drugs by 10 % (Table 21.10, Model 5). Family attachment decreased the likelihood of non-violent offending by 13 % (Table 21.7, Model 5), and trading sex for money by 15 % (Table 21.9, Model 5). The strongest risk factors were drinking and running away. Controlling for all other protective and risk factors, drinking increased the likelihood of non-violent offending by 43 %

Table 21.10 Odds ratios for nested models of selling drugs by sexual minority status, protective and risk factors and control variables

Variables	Model 1	Model 2	Model 3	Model 4	Model 5
Sexual minority status	$2.28 (0.39)^{***}$	$1.91 (0.36)^{**}$	$1.82 (0.38)^{**}$	$1.75 (0.41)^{*}$	$1.75 (0.40)^{*}$
Protective factors					
School attachment		$0.89 (0.02)^{***}$	$0.88 (0.02)^{***}$	$0.90 (0.02)^{***}$	$0.90 (0.02)^{***}$
Educ. aspirations		$0.88 (0.06)$	$0.94 (0.06)$	$0.99 (0.07)$	$0.98 (0.06)$
Parental attachment		$0.91 (0.03)^{**}$	$0.93 (0.03)^{*}$	$0.94 (0.03)$	$0.96 (0.03)$
Family attachment		$0.92 (0.02)^{**}$	$0.92 (0.03)^{**}$	$0.94 (0.03)$	$0.95 (0.03)$
Friends care			$1.04 (0.10)$	$0.88 (0.07)$	$0.90 (0.08)$
Adult mentor			$1.04 (0.14)$	$0.97 (0.16)$	$1.02 (0.18)$
Adults care			$0.91 (0.07)$	$1.03 (0.09)$	$1.01 (0.09)$
Religiosity			$0.84 (0.05)^{**}$	$0.90 (0.06)$	$0.91 (0.06)$
Current job			$1.26 (0.19)$	$1.08 (0.17)$	$1.06 (0.16)$
Risk factors					
Alcohol frequency				$1.89 (0.09)^{***}$	$1.87 (0.09)^{***}$
SU frequency				$1.10 (0.03)^{***}$	$1.08 (0.02)^{**}$
Childhood abuse					$0.98 (0.01)$
Sexual assault					$1.37 (0.24)$
Running away					$3.23 (0.59)^{***}$
Kicked out					$1.44 (0.25)$
Control variables					
Parent education	$0.92 (0.04)$	$0.97 (0.05)$	$0.96 (0.07)$	$0.97 (0.06)$	$0.98 (0.06)$
Family structure	$0.50 (0.06)^{***}$	$0.61 (0.07)^{***}$	$0.69 (0.07)^{**}$	$0.68 (0.08)^{**}$	$0.73 (0.09)^{*}$
Nonwhite	$0.93 (0.14)$	$1.00 (0.17)$	$1.15 (0.23)$	$1.27 (0.24)$	$1.20 (0.21)$
Latino	$1.17 (0.23)$	$1.32 (0.26)$	$1.49 (0.36)$	$1.50 (0.33)$	$1.53 (0.32)^{*}$
Male	$2.19 (0.32)^{***}$	$2.76 (0.43)^{***}$	$2.68 (0.49)^{***}$	$2.53 (0.40)^{***}$	$2.84 (0.48)^{***}$
Adjusted Wald test		28.86^{***}	3.17^{***}	103.08^{***}	11.33^{***}

$^{*} p < 0.05$
$^{**} p < 0.01$
$^{***} p < 0.001$

(Table 21.7, Model 5) and selling drugs by 87 % (Table 21.10, Model 5). Net the effect of the other protective and risk factors, running away increased the likelihood of non-violent offending and violent offending by more than 2 times (2.78 and 2.35, respectively) (Tables 21.7 and 21.8, Model 5). The largest effect (3.23 times) was on selling drugs (Table 21.10, Model 5). Though prior research has connected running away to sex work (e.g., Browne and Minichiello 1996; see also Frederick, this volume), this was not found in the present study. Currently having a job, which was theorized to be a protective factor, increased the likelihood of trading sex for money by more than 2 times (2.28) (Table 21.9, Model 5), but was not statistically significant for the other crimes. It could be that respondents participating in trading sex for money were reporting this as a job.

To determine if the risk and protective factors have differential impacts on sexual minority individuals (i.e., it could be that it is not the *level* of a risk/ protective factor, but that it has a different *effect* on sexual minority youth), I also ran a series of models including interactions (not shown). I looked at sexual minority status as it interacted with each of the protective and risk factors that were statistically significant at the full model (All Tables, Model 5). None of the interactions was statistically significant.

My fifth hypothesis was that protective and risk factors would account for the higher offending rates of sexual minority youth. I predicted that sexual minority respondents would offend more than their majority peers, but that the differential rates of risk and protective factors would account for those variations. This was confirmed for all four types of delinquency, in that controlling for those protective and risk factors decreased the effect of being a sexual minority for all four delinquency types. Though more sexual minority youth had across the board reported offending in all four types, around one-quarter of that difference was explained by controlling for the protective and risk factors available for analysis in this study.

Discussion and Conclusion

When feminist criminologists brought the study of gender into the discipline, the research followed a trajectory; scholars provided baseline evidence, first qualitative then quantitative, that women offend less, and differently. Further research found that women experienced different pushes and pulls from offending due to their differential life experiences. This showed criminology, which had drawn general conclusions based largely on male offending, both that the study of gender was valid as a crucial correlate to understanding crime, and that their theories at the time were insufficient to explain all offending. This chapter is an attempt to set the study of sexuality and crime on the same trajectory, starting with an exploration of juvenile delinquency and sexual minority status.

In this study, I found that sexual minority youth do indeed offend differently from their sexual majority peers, in terms of higher levels (prevalence and frequency) of offending than sexual majority youth; but, they largely participate in the same offenses as their peers, with a few exceptions. To explore the pushes and pulls that impact sexual minority offending, I measured several risk and protective factors addressed in Developmental and Life Course Criminology (DLC) (Farrington et al. 2012). Sexual minority respondents have similar levels of protective factors than their peers, but higher levels of many established risk factors for offending. This leads to the final question in the trajectory: can current theories explain sexual minority offending? The risk and protective factors considered in this study did explain a proportion of the effect of being a sexual minority, but being a sexual minority was still associated with a greater likelihood of participating in several types of offending, especially trading sex for money. It seems that taking into consideration various established risk and protective factors was powerful for explaining some amount of sexual minority offending, but that the unique lives of sexual minority individuals could use further examination, to identify other risk and protective factors that may also be important. We may not be able to "just add queers and stir" with our current theoretical explorations.

It could be that current definitions of risk and protective factors are heteronormative, in that they have not considered the differential experiences of sexual minority youth. Additional, or different, risk or protective factors could be relevant to this group, and those may vary across the heterogeneity of the group. Much focus has been given to family structure, and attachments to parents. As expressed above, the family can be the site of victimization and exclusion for sexual minority youth. Many sexual minority individuals find alternative kinships systems, or "chosen families", through LGBTQ community centers, support groups, GSA (Gay Straight Alliance) and similar clubs in schools, and gay businesses and bars, for those of age. The results of this study do not show strong support for this, but it is likely that the measures used here were inadequate to capture this phenomenon, so it remains unknown if these "chosen families" can act as protections from offending, or mediators of risk factors. Future research should expand the definition of family for the risk and protective prevention paradigm, and perhaps consider both the quality of those alternative kinships, as well as the types of resources they provide.

This chapter points to not only the importance of considering sexual orientation, but also the need for understanding risk and protective factors for how they can offer sites of prevention and/or intervention. In all cases, taking into consideration risk and protective factors diminished the effect of being a sexual minority by about a quarter. This means that the effect of sexual minority status is being inflated if we do not examine how the differential experiences in social institutions like school and family impact sexual minority youths' lives, and how the varying experiences with risk factors like consuming drugs and alcohol may impact sexual minority youth. Based on this first set of models, for adolescence, it seems that several social institutions may offer a point of intervention before offending occurs, or mediation for the severity/longevity of a criminal career. For example, schools could provide emotional and homework support and mentorship for sexual minority students who may be struggling with grades, due to missing classes or feelings of fear and/or detachment due to victimization. There is some evidence that the presence of Gay Straight Alliances, or similar clubs in schools, helps students to feel more safe and included (GLSEN 2007). Schools could also improve the school climate to feel safe and inclusive, and work to reduce heteronormativity in both policies and class dynamics. The institution of family could be another site for intervention. Law enforcement and child protection agencies can ensure sexual minority youth will be safe before returning them to families of origin. Family therapists and school counselors can provide heterosexual parents support and education regarding issues their sexual minority children are facing. Additionally, the foster system could ensure safe housing is available for sexual minorities who have problems at home. Importantly, however, there are likely many other risk and/or protective factors outside of traditional social institutions not considered in the present study that can further explain the higher propensity to offend; these may be worth future examination.

By looking at specific social institutions, such as family and school, this study offered several sites for prevention or intervention, to keep sexual minority youth from getting involved with delinquency. These may also give insight into sites of prevention and intervention for other marginalized groups, and contribute to the conversation on more intersectional work, taking into consideration how sexual minority status interacts with race, class, age and gender. As seen in the results of this study, working with families, or in schools, may offer opportunities for prevention. Alcohol and substance use issues in mid-adolescence could be treated as a symptom, rather than a problem, and as an opportunity for prevention or intervention, especially when consumption is leaking over into problems at work or school and in relationships. Running away could be treated similarly; instead of criminalizing youth for running away, or sending sexual minority youth back to abusive homes, housing options could be explored for the sizable percentage of queer homeless youth (Durso and Gates 2012). This could prevent criminal survival strategies such as selling drugs, and offer greater life chances to sexual minority youth. It could be that there are opportunities to intervene, interrupt, and prevent criminality by acknowledging systemic inequalities (especially multiple marginalities from intersecting identities among race, class, gender, sexual orientation, ability, and so forth) and reacting accordingly.

This study faced several limitations. First, I was limited by the questions asked by Add Health researchers. This gave me imperfect measures of important components of the research, such as being able to measure the concept of a "chosen family." Future research could, possibly qualitatively, explore the relationship between having a group of peers that acts as a replacement for family, and various offending behaviors. Second, the answers to some questions could have been biased, based on placement within the survey. For example, the questions on attraction were asked with a series of questions on sexual assault, risky sexual behaviors, and sexually transmitted diseases. This may have potentially placed a negative light on already sensitive questions, subtly pressing respondents who may have been reluctant to be honest in their answer to deny same-sex attractions. In future waves, the questions could be placed in a section on relationships, demographics, or more positive sexual interactions, to see if the response rates differ. Third, questions regarding victimization were all asked retrospectively, potentially distorting some of the responses, due to memory issues. Fourth, the respondents were sampled in schools, which would exclude youth with the highest rates of offending. Still, a nationally representative sample of youth allowed for a powerful and unique baseline examination of sexual minority adolescents' offending. Last, both the dependent and most of the independent variables were measured at the same wave. This limits the ability to interpret these findings as causal; longitudinal analysis may help overcome this limitation, by examining time order across multiple waves.

Because this dataset offers unique advantages, there is much room for future research on the longitudinal aspects of sexual minority offending. Identical analyses could be conducted over several stages of the life course, to see if different, age-graded risk and protective factors became more or less salient over time. From this, research could determine if sexual minority respondents perhaps had a different age-crime curve, due to differential access to milestones, or had similar/different factors that promoted desistance from criminal careers. Future research could also further develop the ideas around the interactions between sexual minority status and the various risk and protective factors. It could be that it is not just the levels of various protective and risk factors that matter, but that some matter more or less based on sexual orientation. Based on this baseline examination, it seems that much is still unknown—there are likely many risk and protective factors not measured in this study that could be salient, at any stage of the life course.

References

Agnew, R. (1992). Foundation for a general strain theory of crime and delinquency. *Criminology, 30*, 47–88.

Andersen, M. L. (2005). Thinking about women: A quarter century's view. *Gender and Society, 19*, 437–455.

Badgett, M. V. L., Lau, H., Sears, B., & Ho, D. (2007). *Bias in the workplace: Consistent evidence of sexual orientation and gender identity discrimination.* Los Angeles, CA: The Williams Institute.

Baier, C. J., & Wright, B. R. E. (2001). "If you love me, keep my commandments": A meta-analysis of the effect of religion on crime. *Journal of Research in Crime and Delinquency, 38*, 3–21.

Battle, J., & Linville, D. (2006). Race, sexuality and schools: A quantitative assessment of intersectionality. *Race, Gender, & Class, 13*(3–4), 180–199.

Belknap, J., Holsinger, K., & Little, J. (2012). Sexual minority status, abuse, and self-harming behaviors among incarcerated girls. *Journal of Child and Adolescent Trauma, 5*, 173–185.

Bernstein, M. (2013). The sociology of sexualities: Taking stock of the field. *Contemporary Sociology: A Journal of Reviews, 42*, 22–31.

Browne, J., & Minichiello, V. (1996). Research directions in male sex work. *Journal of Homosexuality, 31*(4), 29–56.

Chesney-Lind, M. (1986). "Women and crime": The female offender. *Signs: Journal of Women in Culture and Society, 12*, 78–96.

Cernkovich, S. A., & Giordano, P. C. (1992). School bonding, race, and delinquency. *Criminology, 30*, 261–291.

Cullen, F. T., Benson, M. L., & Makarios, M. (2012). Developmental and life-course theories of offending. In B. C. Welsh & D. P. Farrington (Eds.), *The Oxford handbook of crime prevention* (pp. 23–45). Oxford, UK: Oxford University Press.

DuBois, D. L., & Silverthorn, N. (2005). Natural mentoring relationships and adolescent health: Evidence from a national study. *American Journal of Public Health, 95*, 518–524.

Durso, L. E., & Gates, G. J. (2012). *Serving our youth: Findings from a national survey of services providers working with lesbian, gay, bisexual and transgender youth who are homeless or at risk of becoming homeless.* Los Angeles, CA: The Williams Institute with True Colors Fund and The Palette Fund.

Elder, G. H. (1985). *Life course dynamics: Trajectories and transitions, 1968–1980.* Ithaca, NY: Cornell University Press.

Farrington, D. (2005). *Integrated developmental and life-course theories of offending.* New Brunswick, NJ: Transaction Publishers.

Farrington, D. P., Loeber, R., & Ttofi, M. M. (2012). Risk and protective factors for offending. In B. C. Welsh & D. P. Farrington (Eds.), *The Oxford handbook of crime prevention* (pp. 46–69). Oxford, UK: Oxford University Press.

Farrington, D. P., & Welsh, B. C. (2007). *Saving children from a life of crime: Early risk factors and effective interventions*. New York, NY: Oxford University Press.

Garrigan, S. (2009). Queer worship. *Theology and Sexuality, 15*, 211–230.

Gastic, B., & Johnson, D. (2009). Teacher-mentors and the educational resilience of sexual minority youth. *Journal of Gay and Lesbian Social Services, 21*, 219–231.

Gates, G. J. (2011). *How many people are lesbian, gay, bisexual and transgender?* Los Angeles, CA: The Williams Institute.

Gilfus, M. E. (1992). From victims to survivors to offenders: Women's routes of entry and immersion into street crime. *Women and Criminal Justice, 4*, 63–89.

GLSEN. (2007). *Gay-straight alliances: Creating safer schools for LGBT students and their allies*. New York, NY: Gay, Lesbian and Straight Education Network (GLSEN Research Brief).

Gorman-Smith, D., Tolan, P. H., Zelli, A., & Huesmann, L. R. (1996). The relation of family functioning to violence among inner-city minority youths. *Journal of Family Psychology, 10*, 115–129.

Greytak, E. A., Kosciw, J. G., & Diaz, E. M. (2009). *Harsh realities: The experiences of transgender youth in our nation's schools* (No. ISBN-978-1-934092-06-4). New York, NY: Gay, Lesbian and Straight Education Network (GLSEN).

Himmelstein, K. E. W., & Brückner, H. (2010). Criminal-justice and school sanctions against nonheterosexual youth: A national longitudinal study. *Pediatrics, 127*, 49–57.

Hirschi, T. (1969). *Causes of delinquency*. Berkeley, CA: University of California Press.

Kaufman, J. G., & Widom, C. S. (1999). Childhood victimization, running away, and delinquency. *Journal of Research in Crime and Delinquency, 36*, 347–370.

Keenan, K., Loeber, R., Zhang, Q., Stouthamer-Loeber, M., & van Kammen, W. B. (1995). The influence of deviant peers on the development of boys' disruptive and delinquent behavior: A temporal analysis. *Development and Psychopathology, 7*, 715–726.

Krohn, M. D., & Massey, J. L. (1980). Social control and delinquent behavior: An examination of the elements of the social bond. *Sociological Quarterly, 21*, 529–543.

Laub, J. H., & Sampson, R. J. (1993). Turning points in the life course: Why change matters to the study of crime. *Criminology, 31*, 301–325.

Marshal, M. P., Friedman, M. S., Stall, R., King, K. M., Miles, J., Gold, M. A., et al. (2008). Sexual orientation and adolescent substance use: A meta-analysis and methodological review. *Addiction, 103*, 546–556.

National Network for Youth. (2008). *National recommended best practices for serving LGBT homeless youth*. Washington, DC: National Network for Youth.

Resnick, M. D., Bearman, P. S., Blum, R. B., Bauman, K. E., Harris, K. M., Jones, J., et al. (1997). Protecting adolescents from harm: Findings from the national longitudinal study on adolescent health. *JAMA, 278*, 823–832.

Rotosky, S. S., Danner, F., & Riggle, E. D. B. (2007). Is religiosity a protective factor against substance abuse in young adulthood? Only if you're straight! *Journal of Adolescent Health, 40*, 440–447.

Ryan, C., Huebner, D., Diaz, R. M., & Sanchez, J. (2009). Family rejection as a predictor of negative health outcomes in white and Latino lesbian, gay, and bisexual young adults. *Pediatrics, 123*, 346–352.

Sampson, R. J., & Laub, J. H. (1993). *Crime in the making: Pathways and turning points through life*. Cambridge, MA: Harvard University Press.

Savin-Williams, R. C. (1994). Verbal and physical abuse as stressors in the lives of lesbian, gay male, and bisexual youths: Associations with school problems, running away, substance abuse, prostitution, and suicide. *Journal of Consulting and Clinical Psychology, 62*, 261–269.

Savin-Williams, R. C. (2006). Who's gay? Does it matter? *Current Directions in Psychological Science, 15*, 40–44.

Staff, J., Osgood, D. W., Schulenberg, J. E., Bachman, J. G., & Messersmith, E. E. (2010). Explaining the relationship between employment and juvenile delinquency. *Criminology, 48,* 1101–1131.

Steffensmeier, D., & Allan, E. (1996). Gender and crime: Toward a gendered theory of female offending. *Annual Review of Sociology, 22,* 459–487.

Steffensmeier, D. J., & Terry, R. M. (1986). Institutional sexism in the underworld: A view from the inside. *Sociological Inquiry, 56,* 304–323.

Teasdale, B., & Bradley-Engen, M. S. (2010). Adolescent same-sex attraction and mental health: The role of stress and support. *Journal of Homosexuality, 57,* 287–309.

Thornberry, T. P., & Krohn, M. D. (1997). Peers, drug use, and delinquency. In D. M. Stoff, J. Breiling, & J. D. Maser (Eds.), *Handbook of antisocial behavior* (pp. 218–233). Hoboken, NJ: John Wiley & Sons Inc.

Uggen, C., & Staff, J. (2001). Work as a turning point for criminal offenders. *Corrections Management Quarterly, 5,* 1–15.

Van Kammen, W. B., & Loeber, R. (1994). Are fluctuations in delinquent activities related to the onset and offset in juvenile illegal drug use and drug dealing? *Journal of Drug Issues, 24,* 9–24.

Waldo, C. (1999). Working in a majority context: A structural model of heterosexism as minority stress in the workplace. *Journal of Counseling Psychology, 46,* 218–232.

Weeks, J., Heaphy, B., & Donovan, C. (2001). *Same sex intimacies: Families of choice and other life experiments.* London, UK: Routledge.

Weston, K. (1997). *Families we choose: Lesbians, gays, kinship.* New York, NY: Columbia University Press.

Widom, C. S., Schuck, A. M., & White, H. R. (2006). An examination of pathways from childhood victimization to violence: The role of early aggression and problematic alcohol use. *Violence and Victims, 21,* 675–690.

Chapter 22
Diversity at the Margins: The Interconnections Between Homelessness, Sex Work, Mental Health, and Substance Use in the Lives of Sexual Minority Homeless Young People

Tyler Frederick

Abstract The unique challenges facing homeless sexual minority young people have received increasing attention in recent years. This chapter reviews the research surrounding LGBTQ young people on the street with a particular focus on the interconnections between homelessness, sex work, drug use, and mental health problems. Homeless sexual minority young people are consistently found to have higher rates of mental health problems, drug use, sexual health risk, and victimization than their heterosexual counterparts—findings that highlight the particular vulnerability of this group of young people. However, there is research that cautions against focusing on a single story by underscoring the resilience and creativity of homeless LGBTQ young people, the diversity of experience, and the opportunities that street life holds for finding acceptance and belonging. This chapter aims to capture the complexity of street life for homeless sexual minority young people and concludes with suggestions for avenues of future research and policy.

Keywords Homelessness · Sex work · Mental health · Addictions · Drug use · Youth

Introduction

Since the 1990s, attention has begun to focus on homeless and street-involved LGBTQ young people as a particularly vulnerable group within the already vulnerable population of homeless youth. Although estimates are difficult to make, approximately 45 % of the U.S. homeless population is under the age of 30 (U.S.

T. Frederick (✉)
Toronto Centre for Addiction and Mental Health, 455 Spadina Ave,
Suite 300, Toronto, ON M5S 2G8, Canada
e-mail: tyler.frederick@camh.ca

D. Peterson and V. R. Panfil (eds.), *Handbook of LGBT Communities,*   473
Crime, and Justice, DOI: 10.1007/978-1-4614-9188-0_22,
© Springer Science+Business Media New York 2014

Department of Housing and Urban Development 2010). This population includes an estimated 500,000 unaccompanied young people under the age of 25, of which 81,000 experience long-term homelessness (National Alliance to End Homelessness 2013). Estimates in Canada and the UK put the number of homeless young people at 65,000 and 75,000, respectively (Quilgars et al. 2008; Raising the Roof 2009). Within the homeless youth population, 15–40 % are transgender or identify their sexuality as something other than heterosexual (Cochran et al. 2002; Gangamma et al. 2008; Whitbeck et al. 2004). Homeless sexual minority young people are overrepresented among the homeless when this statistic is compared to estimates of 3–5 % in the general population (Ray 2006). Based on U.S. figures, we can estimate that there are between 75,000 and 200,000 unaccompanied, homeless, and sexual minority young people under the age of 25 living in the United States. This group will include a diversity of identifications outside the traditional gender and sexual binaries, such as, lesbian, gay, bisexual, queer, transgender, intersex, two-spirited, asexual, and pansexual.[1]

The following discussion reviews the research on homeless sexual minority young people, exploring the interconnections between homelessness, drug use, mental health problems, and sex work.[2] The chapter begins with a discussion of factors that push sexual minority young people from their homes and their heightened vulnerability on the street. The second half of the chapter explores the forces and factors that shape, contextualize, and complicate this experience, in particular: the variation that characterizes homeless sexual minority young people; the influence of social spaces, relationships, and belonging; and criminalization and social control.

Leaving Home

Sexual minority young people are overrepresented among the homeless population because being LGBTQ is associated with many of the risk factors for homelessness, such as family conflict, bullying, mental health problems, drug and alcohol use, and physical and sexual abuse (Rew et al. 2005; Savin-Williams 1994; Whitbeck et al. 2004). The most common reasons that sexual minority young people give for leaving home are family conflict, abuse, parental substance use, own substance use, and a desire for freedom (Cochran et al. 2002; Gangamma et al. 2008). Sexuality is often a contributing factor to these issues. Rew et al. (2005)

---

[1] In addition to problems of estimating homeless populations in general, estimating the number of sexual minority young people is complicated by the complexity of identity, including same-sex sexual behavior among individuals who might identify as heterosexual on surveys. Although there are a diversity of identities on the street, the research tends to focus on the more general categories of lesbian, gay, bisexual, and transgender.

[2] The discussion primarily focuses on the U.S. and Canada, but also includes research from Western Europe.

found that 73 % of homosexual and 25 % of bisexual homeless young people left home because of their parent's disapproval of their sexuality. Sexuality is most explicitly a factor when youth are kicked or forced out of the home because of their sexuality, but it also present in the messier tensions that often push young people on to the street—often a complex mix of issues such as problems with school, peers, drug and alcohol use, and disapproval over sexuality. For example, homophobic bullying may lead to poor grades or truancy (Kosciw 2004; van Wormer and McKinney 2003; see too Warbelow and Cobb, this volume). Problems at school may dovetail or exacerbate tensions at home creating a difficult situation for sexual minority young people. In their study, Kosciw et al. (2008) report that close to 40 % of students reported experiencing physical harassment at school because of their sexual orientation, and over 25 % because of their gender expression.

Furthermore, faced with bullying and nonacceptance, supportive peers take on a particular importance for sexual minority young people and play an important role in buffering against the psychological distress associated with the "coming out" process (Ueno 2005; Wright and Perry 2006). However, these peer relationships are also associated with increased drug and alcohol use and risky behavior (Wright and Perry 2006)—factors that may increase tensions at home or lead youth to lose their housing if they are living independently. Moreover, through peer relationships, youth may meet other LGBTQ youth who have already left home and are living on the streets. Research finds that relationships with street-involved peers can pull youth to the street, and that such peers play an important role in introducing youth to street life and street-based social networks (Karabanow 2004; McCarthy 1996). In this way, home leaving can happen suddenly in the case of youth being kicked out when tensions boil over, or it can happen more gradually as youth drift away from family conflict and bullying toward peers and acceptance on the street.

Homophobia can also lead to early home leaving through its relationship with psychological distress (Rosario et al. 1997; Savin-Williams 1994). Homophobia and nonacceptance are consistently found to have a significant psychological impact on young people and are strongly believed to be a significant cause of the particularly high rates of mental health problems and substance use among LGBTQ young people (Coker et al. 2010; Garofalo et al. 1999; Marshal et al. 2008; Russell 2006; Ziyadeh et al. 2007). For example, D'Augelli et al. (2005) found that parental psychological abuse and parental pressure to curb gender atypical behavior are associated with attempted suicide. Moreover, homophobia can create significant psychological distress through the internalization of negative attitudes toward homosexuality and gender atypical behavior (Rotheram-Borus and Fernandez 1995; Savin-Williams 1994; Szymanski et al. 2008). Youth, particularly in the early stages of the "coming out" process, are prone to internalizing the negative views of homosexuality and gender nonconformity they are exposed to at home, school, and in the wider culture. This leads to feelings of shame, self-loathing, low self-esteem, and anxiety. Wright and Perry (2006) find that youth reporting higher levels of sexual identity distress (internalized homophobia) experience more psychological distress (but that sexual identity distress decreases when youth are "out" to their social networks). The psychological distress from homophobia may lead to homelessness if it exacerbates family conflict or impairs a youth's ability to maintain an independent apartment (e.g., depression may make it difficult for youth to hold a job or to meet parental expectations about house work). Psychological distress may also lead to drug and alcohol use. However, evidence about the direct link between internalized homophobia and substance use is mixed—some research finds a connection (DiPlacido 1998), while other research finds no relationship or that homophobia decreases substance use (Amadio and Chung 2004; Wright and Perry 2006). These mixed findings lend support to the argument, introduced above, that homophobia may work indirectly by pushing youth toward alternative social spaces where drug use may be more prevalent. In the search for acceptance, LGBTQ youth may also come in contact with adults who provide an early introduction to drugs and alcohol.

Abuse is a particularly complex risk factor for early home leaving, in that the relationship between physical and sexual abuse and sexual minority status is complicated. Research consistently finds that sexual minority individuals are more likely to experience abuse and maltreatment than their heterosexual peers (Balsam et al. 2005; Corliss et al. 2002). There are a number of explanations for this relationship: caregivers may abuse or neglect the individuals in their disapproval over their sexual identity or gender atypical self-presentation; sexual minority young people may be targeted because they are vulnerable and isolated; sexual minority individuals may be more likely to adopt a stigmatized sexual identity because they already feel themselves to be outsiders because of their abuse; running away from home, and drug and alcohol use, may make them vulnerable to sexual exploitation at a young age; and some young people may look to explore their sexuality with adults fearing discovery by their peers (Austin et al. 2008; Robohm et al. 2003; Saewyc et al. 2006). Histories of abuse also link with homelessness through involvement with child protection services, another common pathway to the street (Courtney and Dworsky 2006). Reasons for leaving child protection services include conflicts with staff or foster parents, bullying, a desire for independence, abuse, and conflicts with peers in the home (Woronoff et al. 2006). Sexual abuse and early sexual involvement are also associated with involvement in sex work while on the street and will be discussed in more detail in a later section.

Not all sexual minority young people end up on the street because of factors related to their sexuality. In their work, Prendergast, Dunne, and Telford identify three groups of sexual minority young people on the streets: young people whose sexuality is a major factor in their homelessness, young people who are homeless and happen to be LGBTQ, and young people for whom homelessness brings about a shift in sexual identity (Dunne et al. 2002; Prendergast et al. 2001). The latter two groups of youth are often pushed out by the same factors (abuse, family conflict, drug use, or a search for freedom) as other sexual minority youth—they are just not specifically related to their sexuality (or are less clearly so). Less is known about youth who experience a change in their sexuality during their time on the street. The potential mechanisms at play beg larger questions about the roots of sexuality and sexual identification (Rosario et al. 2008; Savin-Williams 2001). Some youth will see the shift as a recognition of or identification with a sexual preference that predates their homelessness. Others may perceive it as experiences or relationships on the street bringing hidden or emerging feelings more clearly into focus. Still others might attribute their shift in sexual or gender identification specifically to their experiences on the street (e.g., a relationship sparking new romantic feelings). There are also other pathways to the street such as extreme poverty in the home and the death of a parent or caregiver (Martijn and Sharpe 2006).

On the Streets: Subsistence and Sex Work

Based on their backgrounds alone, homeless sexual minority young people are an exceptionally vulnerable population, often coming to the streets with histories of trauma, mental health problems, and substance use issues. These vulnerabilities are exacerbated by the stress, stigma, and conditions of homelessness (Baron 2006; Hagan and McCarthy 1997; Whitbeck and Hoyt 1999). This compounding vulnerability is supported by research that finds that homeless sexual minority young people have higher rates of suicidal ideation and attempts, drug and alcohol use, victimization, risky sexual behavior, and mental health problems (such as PTSD and depression) than their heterosexual counterparts (Clatts and Davis 1999; Cochran et al. 2002; Frederick et al. 2011; Gangamma et al. 2008; Gattis 2011; Kipke et al. 1997a; Leslie et al. 2002; Rew et al. 2005; Tyler 2008; Van Leeuwen et al. 2006; Walls et al. 2009; Whitbeck et al. 2004). Consistent with the notion of cumulative vulnerability, homeless sexual minority young people also report more sexual abuse before leaving home, as well as more discrimination and sexual and physical victimization on the street than their heterosexual peers (Cochran et al. 2002; Milburn et al. 2006; Whitbeck et al. 2004).

Once on the street, homeless young people must provide for themselves. Homeless youth can meet some of their basic needs through services, such as shelters and drop-ins (De Rosa et al. 1999), but the availability, quality, and safety of services are highly variable. Homeless individuals often do not have adequate public access to what they need and must find ways to provide for themselves. Providing for oneself is a serious challenge for homeless young people, and can be particularly challenging for sexual minority youth. Homelessness on its own creates significant barriers to securing employment in the mainstream labor market (Gaetz and O'Grady 2002). Homeless youth often have less than a high school education and limited work experience—two factors that greatly limit their chances to secure employment, particularly given the current economic times (Karabanow et al. 2010). Other barriers include no home address for job applications, limited work-appropriate clothing, and no government identification. Furthermore, the conditions of homelessness, such as inadequate nutrition, lack of sleep, and extreme stress, make it difficult to adequately reproduce one's labor power from day to day.

Securing employment in the mainstream labor market can be even more difficult for sexual minority young people because of discrimination. Current research shows that despite substantial gains in protections for LGBTQ individuals in the workplace, discrimination is still common (Herek 2009; Lambda Legal and Deloitte 2006; see too Forbes, this volume). Transgender young people are particularly vulnerable to employment discrimination, as few jurisdictions have protections against gender identity discrimination (Vitulli 2010). Homeless transgender young people report workplace discrimination and often feel that they have very few employment options (Frederick 2012; Gibson 1995; Laurindo da Saliva 1999).

Given their limited mainstream employment prospects, homeless youth typically rely on a range of subsistence strategies to meet their needs, including employment (both formal and informal), crime, minor hustles and scams, panhandling, squeegeeing, and social assistance (Clatts and Davis 1999; Gwadz et al. 2009; Hagan and McCarthy 1997; O'Grady and Gaetz 2004; Whitbeck and Hoyt 1999). Sex work or survival sex is another common subsistence strategy used by heterosexual and sexual minority young people alike, and it is often done in conjunction with other strategies (Davies and Feldman 1999). The term "sex work" usually refers to activities like prostitution, escorting, stripping, and pornography when they are in done in a somewhat professional manner and in exchange for money (Walls and Bell 2011). "Survival sex" is a broader term that generally refers to the exchange of sex for resources other than money like food, shelter, or drugs. It also tends to denote sexual exchange on a less formalized and professional basis (Greene et al. 1999).[3] Homeless young people engage in both types of practices. There is also a large degree of overlap between these terms, and there are plenty of activities that fall in the gray area between commercial sex work and sex for survival.[4] When it comes to the exchange of sex for resources, there is also a gray area between survival sex and sexual relationships. Watson (2011), in her research with homeless young women, discusses how they use relationships with men to secure more than just material resources, including physical protection, emotional security, and support; and that these partnerships often happen within the context of love relationships. In these relationships, young women may stay with a partner past the emotional end of the relationship because they rely on his practical support. Watson (2011) also reports that young women on the street may "consent" to sex in these relationships in response to the implicit

---

[3] For clarity, the remainder of the discussion will generally use the term "sex work" to capture the full range of activities denoted by the terms "survival sex," "prostitution," and "sex work." I prefer this term because it avoids connotations of desperation and coercion, it can be inclusive of formal and informal types of sexual exchange, and it highlights its connection to subsistence.

[4] Sexual exchange is a political topic and there are commentators who would challenge the distinction between these terms at both ends of the debate; arguing on one side that all sex work is usefully classified as for the purposes of survival, and on the other that what is typically labeled as survival sex should be redefined as sex work in order to give it legitimacy and make visible the economics of sexual exchange (see Simmons 1999).

threat of rape if they say no. We can expect some sexual minority young people to experience intimate relationships in a similar way. The strategic use of relationships with older men has been documented among gay and bisexual homeless young men (Browne and Minichiello 1995), but future research should explore these dynamics in intimate relationships with peers and among the full diversity of sexual minority identities.

Research on the prevalence of sex work and survival sex varies. A good estimate is that around 20 % of homeless young people exchange sex for money, shelter, food, or drugs, but rates vary from 10 % to 50 % (Tyler and Johnson 2006). There is evidence that sexual minority young people have higher participation rates than their heterosexual counterparts (Feinstein et al. 2001; Kipke et al. 1997a; Marshall et al. 2010; Tyler 2009; Whitbeck et al. 2004). For example, Walls and Bell (2011) find that lesbian, gay, and bisexual homeless young people are almost twice as likely to have engaged in survival sex as their heterosexual peers even when controlling for other factors. This finding, however, is not unanimous. Tyler (2009) finds that initial differences between GLB and heterosexual youth disappear when controlling for factors such as race/ethnicity, employment, peer involvement, and depression. Other research finds that survival sex is particularly common among young gay men and homeless young women regardless of their sexuality (Gangamma et al. 2008), or that participation is highest among young gay men and heterosexual young women (Whitbeck et al. 2004). Walls and Bell (2011) find that transgender young people are also more likely to engage in survival sex than their cisgender counterparts, but this gap is largely accounted for by differences between the two groups in terms of other correlates. Despite the mixed findings regarding who is most likely to participate in survival sex, there is indication that survival sex is particularly common among homeless young gay men (Gangamma et al. 2008; Whitbeck et al. 2004). There is also indication that the clients of homeless lesbian and bisexual young women involved in survival sex are most typically men (Arend 2005).

The research on prevalence raises an important question: why are homeless sexual minority young people disproportionately involved in sex work? Their increased involvement is explained, in part, by high rates of abuse, drug involvement, and previous street experience (Cochran et al. 2002; Gattis 2011; Whitbeck et al. 2004)—all factors that are linked with involvement in sex work among this population (Greene et al. 1999; Stoltz et al. 2007; Walls and Bell 2011; Wilson et al. 2009).[5, 6] In terms of abuse, the precise mechanisms linking these vulnerabilities

---

[5] There appear to be racial and ethnic differences in participation rates, but the findings are inconclusive and lack important detail. Greene et al. (1999), in their multicity study, find higher rates among whites and young people in the "other" racial/ethnic category. In comparison, Walls and Bell (2011), in another large multicity study, find that African-American and young people in the "other" category are more likely to participate in survival sex than whites.

[6] Earls and David (1989), in their matched comparison, find that men involved in sex work were no more likely to report abuse, but they did have earlier sexual experiences and were more likely to have sexual contact with a family member.

with involvement in sex work are unclear. Psychosocial explanations focus on the impact that abusive backgrounds can have on self-concept or behavior patterns (Coleman 1989; Coombs 1974). The risk with such explanations is they have the potential to reduce involvement in sex work to the expression of personal psychological "dysfunction," ignoring its more structural dimensions (West and de Villiers 1992). Further, abuse does not predetermine involvement in sex work (Holmes and Slap 1998; Robinson and Davies 1991), and there is evidence that gay male sex workers are no more psychologically dysfunctional than their noninvolved counterparts (Earls and David 1989).

An alternative mechanism is that abusive and neglectful home environments push sexual minority young people on to the street more frequently and at younger ages (Hagan and McCarthy 1997; Whitbeck and Simons 1991). Time on the street increases the exposure young people have to "foreground" factors such as financial need, hunger, and a lack of shelter. Younger youth can be particularly disadvantaged because social services (shelters and drop-ins) and financial assistance are often only available to those over a certain age (usually 16 or 18)—the preferred strategy being to return those who are under-age back home or to place them in some kind of supervised care. For this reason, younger youth may avoid social services for fear of being returned to a negative home environment, foster care placement, or group home (Kaye 2007).

The impact of foreground factors is supported by Greene et al.'s (1999) findings that survival sex is more common among youth living on the street than in shelters, that involvement increases with time on the street, that shelter youth who have lived on the street are more likely to be involved than those who have not, and that survival sex is associated with other deviant subsistence strategies (also see Gangamma et al. 2008; Walls and Bell 2011). Hagan and McCarthy (1997) have also linked involvement in prostitution to hunger and a lack of housing (also see McCabe et al. 2011; Rice et al. 2007). This argument is supported by findings from research with nonhomeless populations that involvement in sex work is linked to unemployment and that money is a frequent motivation (Allen 1980; Earls and David 1989; Jeffery and MacDonald 2006; Smith and Grov 2011). Marginalization can shape involvement in sex work in subtle ways as well. Sex work can provide opportunities for marginalized individuals to acquire benefits such as social status, agency, autonomy, and self-esteem—resources that are often in short supply at society's economic and social margins. These subtler dynamics will be discussed in a later section.

Other prominent factors identified in the research on sex work (among men) are contact with sex work-involved peers and the search for sexual experience or adventure (Allen 1980; Davies and Feldman 1999; Gibson 1995; Kaye 2007; Perkins and Bennett 1985). Peers introduce newcomers to the possibility of sex work as a job or subsistence strategy; as well provide tutelage in how it is done (e.g., where to go, how much to charge, how to interact, safe sex practices, etc.). The search for sexual experience, if it is a relevant factor, is most likely to be part of young person's initial introduction to sexual exchange. In the case of homeless young people, it is likely to operate alongside need, and be more salient for youth whose involvement in sex work predates their homelessness.

Although some researchers have devised typologies that imply distinct rationales (e.g., economic need vs. adventure) (Luckenbill 1985), the qualitative research in this area finds that entry into sex work is a complex process that happens as youth navigate challenging situations, including homelessness and poverty (Calhoun and Weaver 1996; Frederick 2012; Gibson 1995; Kaye 2007; Visano 1987; West and de Villiers 1992). Further, the reasons and rationales for involvement change over time as circumstances, experiences, and attitudes change.

Drug Use, Mental Health, and Victimization

There are important interconnections between homelessness, sex work, mental health problems, drug use, and victimization (McCabe et al. 2011). Homelessness increases involvement in sex work, and increases mental health problems and drug use (Frederick et al. 2012; Hagan and McCarthy 1997; Kidd 2004; Whitbeck and Hoyt 1999). There is also a large amount of concurrent mental health and substance abuse problems, which has to do with common etiology (e.g., homelessness as a common predictor) as well as a reciprocal relationship in that drug use exacerbates mental health problems and vice versa (Kirst et al. 2011).

There are also interrelationships between sex work, mental health problems, and drug use that intensify impacts and that lead to a further entrenchment in homelessness. For example, drug use, whether it predates homelessness, or develops or intensifies after arriving on the street, can lead to sex work by creating additional financial demands over and beyond those of meeting daily subsistence needs (Thukral and Ditmore 2003). Further, heavy drug use can make it even more difficult to obtain or hold employment, thereby directing young people toward deviant or illegal subsistence strategies. These demands can motivate homeless young people toward subsistence strategies that they might not otherwise consider, like sex work (including the exchange of sex for drugs or alcohol). The connection between street-based sexual markets and illicit drug markets also facilitates involvement in sex work through drug-using peers who are already involved, as well as pimps and facilitators who might force, encourage, or broker involvement (see Maher 1997 for a discussion regarding female sex workers).

Involvement in sex work can feed back into drug use by involving youth in drug-using milieus, as well as through the use of drugs to cope with the stress and trauma of sex work. Sex work is associated with a range of negative emotions including shame, fear, and disgust, and it is linked to psychological problems such as suicide, depression, and PTSD (Kidd and Kral 2002; McCabe et al. 2011; Sanders 2005).[7] Drugs can be a way of coping with negative emotions and psychological trauma.

---

[7] There are critics who point out that sex work is not inherently traumatizing and that much of its negative psychological consequences have to do with the current social attitude and response toward it (Sanders 2004).

For some homeless young people, herein lies a dangerous cycle: drug abuse and dependence encourages involvement in sex work, which in turn encourages mental health problems and further drug use, and so on (Kaye 2007; Visano 1987).

Drug use can also shape the nature and experience of sex work, in particular its safety. It is well established that sex workers are at risk of contracting HIV and STIs (sexually-transmitted infections).[8] The use of drugs or alcohol can heighten a worker's risk of HIV or STI because they can impair judgement and reduce an individual's ability to negotiate safe sex (Robinson and Davies 1991). Drug and alcohol dependence can also encourage individuals to engage in riskier behaviors, such as penetration or intercourse without a condom in order to attract clients (Venema and Visser 1990). However, drugs do not necessarily increase risk; for example, paranoia from cocaine use and impotence from alcohol have been linked to increased safety (Pleak and Mayer-Bahlburg 1990; Simon et al. 1993). Homeless sexual minority young people are particularly vulnerable to these interconnections in that they tend to be on the streets earlier, experience more psychological distress, engage in more substance use, and participate in more sex work than their heterosexual counterparts.

Homeless youth are at high risk of experiencing physical victimization (Kipke et al. 1997b), and there is some evidence that sexual minority young people are a particularly vulnerable group within this population (Whitbeck et al. 2004); although the results are mixed (Frederick et al. 2011). Homeless sexuality minority youth are vulnerable to homophobic bullying and violence from peers, adults, the police, and the public (Milburn et al. 2006)—a continuation of the victimization many experience at school and in the home. Furthermore, sexual minority youth are at particular risk because of their heightened involvement with sex work and drugs and alcohol. Sex work, especially street-based prostitution, is linked to physical and sexual victimization (Nixon et al. 2002; Tyler 2008; Whitbeck et al. 2001; Whitbeck et al. 2004). Further, drug use increases the risk of violence in sex work by making the individual a more vulnerable target and by increasing the likelihood of a confrontation with a client (who may also be using drugs or alcohol) (Selby and Canter 2009).

Complicating the Picture

The connections outlined so far represent only one way of understanding the relationship between homelessness, sex work, mental health, and drugs. The discussion has focused primarily on how sexual minority young people are forced on

---

[8] However, critics point out that risk posed by sex workers can sometimes be overblown in that the most common sexual services are low-risk, and that there is evidence that safe sex is a primary concern of many sex workers (Browne and Minichiello 1995, 1996). Further, there is evidence to suggest that sex with nonpaying partners may actually be riskier because individuals feel like they do not need to be as diligent with someone they know or who will perceive protection as a barrier to intimacy (Pleak and Meyer-Bahlburg 1990).

to the street where they must engage in sex work in order to meet their needs, and where they get caught up in cycles of drug abuse and mental health problems. Missing from this discussion are the numerous factors that contextualize and complicate this picture. Kaye (2007) cautions against falling into a narrow script for thinking about sexual minority sex workers (also see Browne and Minichiello 1996). The risk of a story that focuses on risk and vulnerability is that it can portray homeless sexual minority youth as desperate and without agency— implying simply that they are at the mercy of the streets and that they play no active role in their own experience. It also tends to downplay the range of factors that shape the nature and experience of homelessness and, relatedly, the inter-connections between homelessness, mental health problems, sex work, and drug use. The following section will focus on these complicating factors, including the diversity of sexual minority young people; peers, street culture, and belonging; and criminalization and social control.

The Diversity of Experience

Sexual minority homeless young people are a tremendously diverse group. They are diverse across a number of dimensions, including sexual and gender identity, race and ethnicity, family background, and relationship to street life and subsis-tence. One central source of variation is sexual and gender identity. The term "sexual minority" hides a large number of different gender and sexual identities, each with their own unique relationship to the social world (Savin-Williams 2001; Weinberg et al. 1999). Furthermore, gender and sexuality condition one another. Frederick et al. (2011), for example, find among a sample of young homeless people in Toronto, Canada that differences between sexual minority and hetero-sexual young people are largely driven by young sexual minority women, and that gender and sexuality intersect in complicated ways to direct young people toward or away from health risks. Of the four groups that were compared (sexual minority women, sexual minority men, heterosexual women, and heterosexual men), the sexual minority young women had the greatest odds of daily drug use and a self-reported mental illness. The heterosexual young men were particularly at risk of delinquent involvement and of being assaulted with a weapon, and the hetero-sexual young women of experiencing anxiety (along with sexual minority young women). Surprisingly, sexual minority young men were the least likely to report delinquency, anxiety, daily drug use, and a self-reported mental illness. Noting similar gender differences, Whitbeck et al. (2004) find that homeless lesbian young women are the most likely to report mental health and drug problems, and that heterosexual young men are the most likely to report conduct disorder (which is strongly related with delinquency).

These findings raise some interesting questions about the different ways that sexual minority young people experience street life.[9] Unfortunately, large gaps in the research make answering these questions difficult. Epidemiological and survey data tend to focus on broad categories of identity such as gay, lesbian, and bisexual—or collapse those categories into a single sexual minority reference group. The qualitative and ethnographic research tends to focus primarily on cisgender sexual minority young men. Further, transgender individuals tend to be missing from both types of research—particularly male transgender individuals. There is also a significant lack of research on homeless sexual minority young people of color. Research on ethnic minority LGBTQ youth in the general population suggests that these young people will have different experiences across a variety of dimensions of life, but to date little is known about the relationships between race, homelessness, and sexuality (see Arend 2005; Pettiway 1996 for exceptions; also see *Paris is Burning*, Livingston and Swimar 1990).

There is also significant diversity in the type of sex work that those involved in sexual exchange might participate in. The focus in the homelessness literature is on "survival sex," which lumps together a complex range of activities—from hook-ups, to pornography, to high-end escorting. A basic division in formal sex work is between "indoor" and "outdoor." Indoor includes escorting, pornography, massage parlors, and brothels. This type of work tends to have better working conditions and to be safer, although there is still significant exploitation and risk (Connell 2009; Ditmore 2011; Koken et al. 2009). Outdoor refers primarily to street prostitution. Street prostitution is considered to be the most dangerous in terms of sexual health risks and physical violence (Parsons et al. 2001; Thukral and Ditmore 2003). Street prostitution is also the type of sex work associated with homelessness and is the most implicated in the drug and mental health linkages discussed above. It is also the main focus of research on same-sex and opposite-sex sex work, despite being estimated to only account for one-fifth of sex work activity (Porter and Bonilla 2009; Weitzer 2009a).

Even within street prostitution, there can be important differences in the nature of the work (Porter and Bonilla 2009). For example, in Toronto, the two most prominent street prostitution areas frequented by sexual minority homeless youth are the "boys stroll" and the transgender or "tranny" stroll. The cisgender, or "boys stroll," is characterized by a preference for a masculine or "school boy" self-presentation and the sexual interactions tend to be rougher and more forceful. In contrast, the area for transgender female prostitution tends to be based around erotic scripts that emphasize the femininity of the workers. In this context, clients tend to affect a certain level of chivalry and so interactions are gentler and the going rate higher. For this reason, it is not uncommon for cisgender youth to dress up and work that area in order to take advantage of the improved working conditions.

---

[9] Caution should be used when interpreting these findings because this research was conducted with a relatively small sample (N = 147). The other research on the interaction between gender and sexual identity is mixed (Cochran et al. 2002; Gangamma et al. 2008; Leslie et al. 2002; Noell and Ochs 2001; Walls and Bell 2011; Whitbeck et al. 2004).

Although homelessness is most commonly associated with street prostitution, homeless sexual minority young people are involved in the full range of sexual exchange activities. Furthermore, the nature of involvement can shift over time as housing situations and needs change. The Internet is also drastically altering how sex work is being done by making it easier to work indoors and by reducing the need for a pimp, facilitator, or agency (Morrison and Whitehead 2007). In my recent research with homeless gay and transgender sexual minority young people, although many had experience "walking the stroll," it was common to work as an independent escort—soliciting dates through the Internet from online classified websites or from dating/hook-up websites that cater to gay men (Frederick 2012). During the research period, one of Toronto's most prominent outreach organizations for youth had to close its doors because, among other reasons, their traditional street outreach approach was struggling with the Internet age. Rather than being concentrated in a few key stroll areas, young people now were geographically dispersed and more hidden. This organization had begun to include Internet cafes on its designated outreach route to accommodate these changes, but was still finding it difficult to access potential clients.

In their ethnography of a male escort service in a small mid-Atlantic U.S. city, Smith and Grov (2011) contrast the image of the desperate, drug-addicted street hustler with the strategic and empowered young people whom they interviewed. Economic need was a defining factor for most of the young men they spoke with, but these men also felt like their involvement was the product of a conscious choice. Escorting provided practical benefits that employment in the service economy, or similar low-status work, could not provide, including flexibility, autonomy, and a higher per hour wage (also see Jeffery and MacDonald 2006). A similar rationale is echoed by some homeless young people (Calhoun and Weaver 1996; Frederick 2012; Visano 1987), suggesting that the image of the desperate street-kid willing to do whatever it takes to survive misrepresents the diversity of experience among homeless young people. The extent to which young people feel they have choice will depend heavily on their circumstances. For example, a 15-year old, new to the street, who is trying to avoid services because they do not want to be sent back home and who is offered a place for the night may perceive very little choice (the pronoun they is being used intentionally). In contrast, a 25-year old with work experience, who has been on and off the street, and who is aware of available services and subsistence options may feel that they are able to make more of an informed decision about involvement in sex work (see Kaye 2007).

A related source of diversity is how homeless young people are stratified within these activities. Factors like age, body type, demeanor, and appearance all shape the available sex work options and the money that can be charged. Young people with high levels of sexual capital[10] tend to have the greatest amount of choice and to charge the highest rates. Markets exist for all types of niche body types, ages,

---

[10] Those characteristics deemed physically attractive and that elicit an erotic response in others (Green 2008).

fetishes, and erotic fantasy. These more "exotic" sexual services tend to earn less money, but can entail less legal and sexual health risk because they do not involve contact with genitals or bodily fluids (Koken et al. 2009). Importantly, how young people are stratified within sexual markets shapes the extent to which they can negotiate safe sex practices. Young people with less erotic capital may have to offer risky sexual services in order to attract clients (Frederick 2012; Green 2008).

Social Relationships, Street Culture, and Belonging

A second set of factors that shape the nature and experience of street life are social relationships, street cultures, and belonging. Peers are an important aspect of homelessness and street life for all homeless young people. Peers provide practical assistance and information about how to meet basic needs on the street, but they also provide emotional support and acceptance (Hagan and McCarthy 1997). Peers may play a special role in the lives of sexual minority young people owing to the stigma and discrimination that they often face at home, school, and the street (Milburn et al. 2006). The search for acceptance raises questions about a narrative of street life that focuses only on exclusion and marginalization. Homelessness for many sexual minority young people is defined by a complex mix of inclusion and exclusion that shapes and complicates trajectories through homelessness (Browne and Minichiello 1995; Leary and Minichiello 2007). For example, it is not uncommon for some sexual minority youth to leave home expressly in search of acceptance and exploration in the gay enclaves of urban centers—particularly young people from smaller cities and towns (Dunne et al. 2002; Prendergast et al. 2001). In these spaces, young people make friends and often find levels of social support and understanding that they have never experienced before. Youth also comment on the self-esteem that comes from being desired—a feeling that would have been in short supply for youth who were hiding their sexuality or where growing up in a space without much social acceptance.

Group membership and belonging can also shape participation in sex work through involvement in a social world that is structured in such a way as to orient youth toward these kinds of activities (Frederick 2012; Gibson 1995). In my research, I find that particular types of social space shape street life and involvement in sex work by defining the types of economic, social, and status resources that are available and by providing cultural discourses that frame experience and involvement. For example, a group of gay men and transgender women found that their involvement in a social scene within Toronto's Village neighborhood provided access to status resources, such as popularity. In the context of this social world, homeless young people can use sex work to acquire status symbols such as nice clothes, or to participate in the scene by frequenting popular bars and clubs. These status resources are valuable sources of self-esteem (particularly for a group that has limited access to valued social roles), but can also be converted into valuable social capital (social ties and support). Further, status can be converted back into erotic capital and increase one's sex work and dating prospects.

The social space in which these young people are embedded also provides discursive frames through which they can make sense of their experience. Some young people talked about a desire to participate in the "glamorous life" and of sex work as a means through which to do that (also see Gibson 1995). Markers of this kind of life were having nice clothes, participating in the city's gay party scene, going out for dinner, and getting the attention of high-status partners (clients and potential romantic partners). The availability of these frames, tolerant attitudes toward sex work within gay enclaves, and the normalizing influence of having peers involved in sex work helps to explain the less negative (and sometimes positive) ways that some homeless young gay men describe their experiences (Calhoun and Weaver 1996; Visano 1987; Walls et al. 2009; West and de Villiers 1992). For some of the youth I interviewed, these discursive frames also shaped the perception of drug use by redefining it as part of living a "glamorous" life. Within these discourses, some young people even redefine their rapid weight loss from drugs as positive side-effect that increases their erotic capital and can improve their social standing within the scene. Importantly, employing discursive frames about a glamorous life did not preclude youth from also experiencing stress and shame about their involvement in sex work, but it did facilitate their participation by helping to neutralize those feelings—particularly in the context of limited alternatives. Moreover, these assessments coexist alongside ambivalent or outright negative attitudes, as these are also common. What it does highlight is the different ways that social space can structure the nature and experience of homelessness and sex work. The discursive frames available within some spaces of street life may neutralize the stigma of homelessness and may protect young people from some of the emotional harm associated with sex work, but it can be at the risk of minimizing the potential harms of sex work and drug and alcohol use.

Relationships with adults and clients are also complex for sexual minority young people involved in sex work (Leary and Minichiello 2007). Clients can provide economic, social, and emotional support beyond a strict sex for money (or shelter or food) exchange (Frederick 2012; Visano 1987). Young people may develop relationships with their regulars that involve some level of mutual support and companionship. It is also not uncommon for gay homeless youth involved in sex work to participate in quasi-dating relationships with older or more established men who may take them for dinner or buy them gifts in exchange for their company, which may or may not include sexual contact. However, even if sex is not explicitly requested, young people may feel pressured to accept sexual advances because of the gifts and attention (West and de Villiers 1992). This includes relationships with "sugar daddies" who may provide long-term support in exchange for routine social and physical contact, but for which the power structure often leaves young people vulnerable to exploitation and manipulation.

So far the discussion on belonging and peers has primarily addressed the experience of gay and bisexual young men, and to a lesser extent transgender women, because it is these groups who have been most studied. Noticeably absent from the discussion are homeless sexual minority young women and transgender men because research on these populations is woefully underdeveloped. There is indication that homeless sexual minority young women and transgender men lack access to the social inclusion and belonging that some gay and bisexual young men find on the street (Frederick et al. 2011). Gay enclaves tend to cater more to gay cisgender men than they do bisexuals, lesbians, and transgender individuals (Ochs 1996; Valentine and Skelton 2003). Lesbian, bisexual, and transgender communities are smaller and more circumscribed and so homeless young people in these groups are less likely to find a community of peers (Frederick 2012; also see Arend 2005). Moreover, this lack of social space has been linked to negative health outcomes among transgender individuals and bisexual and lesbian women (Mercer et al. 2007; Spicer 2010; Steele et al. 2009).

Criminalization and Social Control

The social control of homelessness, drug use, and sex work also shape and contextualize the experience of homeless sexual minority young people. Control is enacted through various institutions, including the legal system, the medical system, and social services. The legal control of homelessness began in Europe with the enactment of vagrancy laws intended to control the massive influx of the poor and unemployed into newly forming industrial cities (Adler 1989). In colonial North America, laws were enacted over fear of the moral and economic impact of wandering beggars and criminals. Over centuries, the vagueness of vagrancy statues have made them ideal tools for policing social order and of controlling social undesirables including, but not limited to, the homeless. In the 1970s, vagrancy laws in the U.S., Canada, and Europe began to be challenged on the grounds of being overly vague. In their place emerged a new set of "decency laws" that targeted the homeless more directly by criminalizing survival activities such as sleeping, soliciting donations, urinating, and washing in public (Aguirre and Brooks 2001; Amster 2003; Mitchell 1997). These decency laws have in turn been augmented with modern forms of banishment that more directly control space through "no go" orders, bans, and extension of trespassing laws (Beckett and Herbert 2011).

These laws limit the access that the homeless have to public space—arguably the only space they have legal access to—and shape their survival strategies. In a study of homeless young people after the implementation of anti-squeegeeing laws in Toronto, O'Grady and Greene (2003) found that young people were living in more dangerous places and engaging in riskier subsistence strategies than before the law. Laws criminalizing homelessness also effectively widen the criminal justice net by bringing more individuals into contact with the law. The impacts of these laws have unique implications for homeless sexual minority young people who already experience barriers to accessing social and physical space due to homophobia, but also because of the risk of mistreatment and homophobia on behalf of the police and the courts (see too, in this volume, related discussions by Dwyer; Johnson; Nichols; Pearce and Cooper). The criminalization of homelessness also limits the extent to which the homeless enjoy the full protection of the law. Young people may be reluctant to report victimization to the police for fear of harassment or disregard (Gaetz 2004). The criminalization of drug use also invites negative contact with the police and brings homeless young people into the criminal justice net. The current approach to drug control in most of North America and Europe has been questioned based on evidence that it is largely ineffective and has negative impacts on individuals and communities, including homeless and economically marginalized drug users who are often the primary targets of control efforts (Benavie 2009; Wacquant 2009).

Beyond the physical control of certain populations made possible by these laws, the discursive rhetoric which accompanies them in political debate and the media shapes the image and attitude toward the poor more generally. Wacquant (2009) makes the argument that these types of laws work to criminalize the poor—a strategy that culturally underwrites the political and economic status quo and justifies rising income inequality by framing anyone that fails in the current climate of social spending cutbacks as a criminal. Decency, prostitution, vagrancy, and drug laws have a long history of being used to label and control members of the "dangerous classes" including racial and ethnic minorities, sexual minorities, and the poor (Edelman 2011; Gordon 1994; Shelden 2001). In a current example, Edelman (2011) discusses how the police enforcement of "prostitution free zones" in Washington, D.C. works to displace and control transgender women of color.

Homeless sexual minority young people are also controlled and policed through social services, as well as through the medical and mental health care systems. Social services operate within discourses that construct the problem of homelessness and drug use in particular ways (Dordick 1997; Gowan 2010; Marvasti 2003). These discourses shape access to service by defining who is worthy of service and who is not. Marvasti (2003) describes how staff within the shelter he studied tended to construct the homeless in terms of their individual failings. This definition meant that staff were more receptive and engaged with individuals who presented their story in a way that was consistent with that prevailing discourse. Similarly, Gowan (2010) found that agencies subscribing to the view that addictions are at the root of homelessness put pressure on clients to present themselves and their problems in a similar way.

Accessing services can be particularly challenging for sexual minority young people because of discrimination or due to a lack of services that meet the unique needs of LGBTQ youth (Abramovich 2012; Coker et al. 2010; Spicer 2010; Welle et al. 2006). These challenges are particularly acute for transgender young people (Yu 2010). For example, many emergency shelters only have men's and women's dorms (or cater to one gender only) and have no specific policies for accommodating transgender individuals (see, in this volume, Sumner and Jenness for an in-depth review of this issue in U.S. correctional facilities). Lack of appropriate services may lead a transgender young person to avoid social services altogether.

The mental health care system is also a source of control in the lives of homeless sexual minority young people. At a broad level, homosexuality was only fully removed from the *Diagnostic and Statistical Manual* in 1987 and gender identity disorder/gender dysphoria (a strong discontent with the gender assigned at birth) is still included as a medical disorder despite widespread criticism (Psychiatric News 2003). These classifications reflect and shape societal attitudes toward LGBTQ people and can be highly stigmatizing. More specifically, many homeless young people experience contact with the mental health system prior to leaving home and throughout their time on the street. This contact may be welcomed but it can also generate stigmatizing labels and be experienced as controlling and oppressive (O'Reilly et al. 2009).

The social control of sex work also has important implications for sexual minority young people who are involved in the sex trade. There are various types of legal sex work (e.g., stripping, pornography), but prostitution is illegal in most jurisdictions in Europe, Canada, and the United States (Betteridge 2005; O'Neill and Pitcher 2010; Weitzer 2009b). Prostitution is controlled primarily through the criminalization of related activities such as solicitation, living off the avails of prostitution, or operating a brothel. In this way, although the act of engaging in sexual relations for money may be legal in some jurisdictions, it is very difficult to do so without breaking the law[11] (Weitzer 2009b). Current prostitution laws have been widely criticized for being ineffective and for having a range of negative consequences (Daly 1988; Lowman 2009; Lutnick and Cohan 2009; O'Neill and Pitcher 2010; Weitzer 2010). A central critique is that prostitution laws do very little to protect sex workers from violence and that they simply force prostitution into the shadows where sex workers are even more at risk (Connell 2009; Hubbard and Scoular 2009; Weitzer 2009b). Prostitution laws have also been critiqued for turning child sexual abuse on the part of johns into a public order offense, and increasing marginalization through criminal records that limit employability, increase the risk of eviction and homelessness, disrupt family relationships, and limit the autonomy of sex workers (Lowman 2009; O'Neill and Pitcher 2010; Sanders 2005; Weitzer 2009b). The criminalization of sex work has unique impacts on LGBTQ individuals. As chapters in this book discuss in detail, the police, courts, and prison system are playing catch up when it comes to addressing the unique needs of sexual minority offenders.[12]

---

[11] There are a few countries or jurisdictions where prostitution is legalized, such as the Netherlands and particular counties in Nevada. Although preferred to criminalization, some sex work advocates reject the regulation that accompanies legalization as unfair when compared with the limited regulation of other types of businesses (Lutnick and Cohan 2009; Stella 2012).

[12] The movement of sex work online also has implications for safety and social control. Although the Internet can bring workers indoors, increase autonomy, and facilitate political organizing, it can also break down some of the traditional protections that a community of workers can provide for each other, as well as isolate and separate sex workers from social services.

Conclusion

An effort has been made in this chapter to highlight the barriers and hard edges that structure the lives of sexual minority young people, but also to complicate this story by focusing on the factors that pull young people into street life and sex work. Sexual minority youth are often forced from their homes because of abuse and intolerance, but they also may drift out of the home as they search for acceptance and belonging. Further, these two trajectories are not mutually exclusive in that tensions in the home may encourage drift, and drift may exacerbate tensions in the home. Once on the street, youth are often driven into sex work by extreme need, and their involvement can feed into a complicated cycle of psychological distress and drug use. However, simultaneously, sex work can be a source of sought-after economic, social, and cultural resources and be part of a young person's involvement in an exciting and accepting social scene. There are also numerous forces that condition the nature and experience of street life for these young people such as diversity within the population, laws that control homelessness and sex work, service availability, and social service policies.

This more complicated picture of street life for sexual minority young people begs some larger questions about agency and constraint in the lives of homeless sexual minority young people; questions that are reflected in emerging literature around homelessness, sex work, and LGBTQ youth. Much of current ethnographic work on homelessness seeks to underscore the resilience and agency of the homeless, highlighting them as complex and diverse people caught in difficult circumstances who are making do the best they can (Bourgois and Schonberg 2009; Dordick 1997; Gowan 2010; Wasserman and Clair 2010). This is a move away from the pathologizing and patronizing image of the homeless as homogenously "needy" and "sick." Work in this area complicates simplistic agency versus structure debates by highlighting the dynamic interplay between choice and constraint in the lives of the homeless. It also highlights the humor, curiosity, wit, intelligence, and passion of the many people who find themselves without a home—characteristics that tend to get obscured by the label of "homeless" and the implicit meanings it carries.

The research on sex work has moved in a similar direction. This work comes from two main sources: work that is driven by activists to replace the image of sex workers as desperate and morally corrupt with an image of sex workers as empowered service workers (Lopez-Embury and Sanders 2009); and research that strives to highlight the humanity of even the most marginalized sex workers—to focus on their efforts to engage and cope with their difficult histories and circumstances as best they can (Harding and Hamilton 2009). In the former category of research, there is an effort to emphasize that sex work can be a legitimate service done by people who have chosen the work for its practical benefits and because it brings meaning and satisfaction to their lives (Bernstein 2007; Collins 2007; Escoffier 2007; Lantz 2005; Lucas 2005; Rickard 2001; Smith 2012). The latter collection of work aims to document the coexistence of coercion and choice in the lives of marginalized sex workers (Rosen and Venkatesh 2008; Thukral and Ditmore 2003). In their nuanced work with homeless women, Harding and Hamilton (2009) find that women see themselves as simultaneously being pushed into sex work and making a free choice about their own involvement. Phoenix and Oerton (2005) make a similar point in noting how financial need and difficult circumstances work to *funnel* choice for street-based sex workers. Both literatures capture dimensions of sex work in the lives of homeless sexual minority young people. For some individuals and at some moments in time, sex work might appear as a clear choice among other subsistence options—chosen for its perceived benefits, including the autonomy and independence that its income can provide, or the personal satisfaction that comes from providing a needed service. For others or at different times, the choice to engage in sex work will feel more constrained.

Themes of agency and complexity are also echoed in the literature on youth and sexuality. Here, the effort is to get beyond homogenizing stereotypes and confining categories to highlight the diversity of sexuality, as well as the complexity of human action across intersecting social categories (Hammack et al. 2009; Hwahng and Nuttbrock 2007; Saewyc 2011; Savin-Williams 2001; Smith et al. 2005; Vrangalova and Savin-Williams 2012). In this literature, young people are positioned as actors in their own lives, engaging with identity categories and negotiating the diverse factors that shape their lives at the intersection of social differentiations such as gender, race, and class.

These literatures provide important context for the discussion here—they remind us to be cautious about discussions of "homeless sexual minority young people" as a category because such terms flatten diversity and freeze youth in time—losing perspective on the process and complexity of youth transitions, as well as the people behind those transitions. Behind such terms are individuals who are living, changing, and making choices in a soup of micro-, meso-, and macro-level forces. Future research directions need to better reflect the diversity of sexual minority young people, as well as the complexity of their transitions. As noted, transgender youth (primarily transgender men) are largely absent from the research, as are sexual minority young people of color. Similarly, lesbian and bisexual young women are missing from the research, despite indications that they might be some of the most marginalized sexual minority young people. Further, the focus on homeless youth specifically misses the large number of youth who straddle mainstream and street spaces as they drift between home and the street. Relatedly, more longitudinal research is needed to understand trajectories over time and the interplay between background factors, identities, street experience, and pathways on and off the street.

Nuanced considerations of agency also remind us that even though sexual minority young people face significant barriers and challenges in making the transition to adulthood, it is important that we do not see them only as victims. Doing so minimizes the role they play in their own lives and the resilience they demonstrate in the face of often profound hardship. Homeless sexual minority young people are not waiting to be saved but are finding their own way. However, their ability to make the best of bad situations and to find moments of excitement and belonging should not blind us to the steps we can take as a society to make their way a little bit easier and to minimize the suffering that comes with having to make hard choices. Policy in this area needs to address the central issues at the heart of these young people's struggles: homophobia and discrimination, affordable housing, the criminalization of sex work and homelessness, and access to a diverse range of substance abuse services and options. The key is to undertake policies aimed at prevention and at maximizing life choices. This means challenging discrimination and increasing positive space across all facets of society so that homeless young people can feel confident to pursue a broad range of goals; it means making housing more affordable and addressing the systemic roots of poverty; and it means developing criminal justice strategies that respect diversity and the choices of consenting adults, and that minimize the long-term impacts of contact with the criminal justice system. Central to supporting these changes is the need for sustained government funding for organizations that create safe and welcoming spaces for all young people, that foster accepting families and schools, and that support diverse and creative strategies for skill development and youth employment.

References

Abramovich, I. A. (2012). No safe place to go: LGBTQ youth homelessness in Canada-Reviewing the literature. *Canadian Journal of Family and Youth, 4*(1), 29–51.

Adler, J. S. (1989). The historical analysis of the law of vagrancy. *Criminology, 27*(2), 209–230.

Aguirre, A., & Brooks, J. (2001). City redevelopment policies and the criminalization of homelessness: A narrative case study. *Research in Urban Sociology, 6*, 75–105.

Allen, D. M. (1980). Young male prostitutes: A psychosocial study. *Archives of Sexual Behavior, 9*(5), 399–426.

Amadio, D. M., & Chung, Y. B. (2004). Internalized homophobia and substance use among lesbian, gay, and bisexual persons. *Journal of Gay and Lesbian Social Services, 17*, 83–101.

Amster, R. (2003). Patterns of exclusion: Sanitizing space, criminalizing homelessness. *Social Justice, 30*(1), 195.

Arend, E. D. (2005). The politics of invisibility: Homophobia and low-income HIV-positive women who have sex with women. *Journal of Homosexuality, 49*(1), 97–122. doi:10.1300/J082v49n01_05.

Austin, S. B., Jun, H., Jackson, B., Spiegelman, D., Rich-Edwards, J., Corliss, H. L., et al. (2008). Disparities in child abuse victimization in lesbian, bisexual, and heterosexual women in the Nurses' Health Study II. *Journal of Women's Health, 17*(4), 597–606.

Balsam, K. F., Rothblum, E. D., & Beauchaine, T. P. (2005). Victimization over the life span: A comparison of lesbian, gay, bisexual, and heterosexual siblings. *Journal of Consulting and Clinical Psychology, 73*(3), 477–487.

Baron, S. W. (2006). Street youth, strain theory, and crime. *Journal of Criminal Justice, 34*, 209–223.

Beckett, K., & Herbert, S. K. (2011). *Banished: The new social control in urban America*. New York, NY: Oxford University Press.

Benavie, A. (2009). *Drugs: America's holy war*. New York, NY: Routledge.

Bernstein, E. (2007). Sex work for the middle classes. *Sexualities, 10*(4), 473–488. doi:10.1177/1363460707080984.

Betteridge, G. (2005). *Sex, work, rights: Reforming Canadian criminal laws on prostitution.* Toronto, CAN: Canadian HIV/AIDS Legal Network.

Bourgois, P., & Schonberg, J. (2009). *Righteous dopefiend.* Los Angeles, CA: University of California Press.

Browne, J., & Minichiello, V. (1995). The social meanings behind male sex work: Implications for sexual interactions. *British Journal of Sociology, 46*(4), 598–622.

Browne, J., & Minichiello, V. (1996). Research directions in male sex work. *Journal of Homosexuality, 31*(4), 29–56.

Calhoun, T. C., & Weaver, G. (1996). Rational decision-making among male street prostitutes. *Deviant Behavior, 17*(2), 209–227. doi:10.1080/01639625.1996.9968023.

Clatts, M. C., & Davis, W. R. (1999). A demographic and behavioral profile of homeless youth in New York City: Implications for AIDS and outreach and prevention. *Medical Anthropology Quarterly, 13*(3), 365–374.

Cochran, B. N., Stewart, A. J., Ginzler, J. A., & Cauce, A. M. (2002). Challenges faced by homeless sexual minorities: Comparison of gay, lesbian, bisexual, and transgender homeless adolescents with their heterosexual counterparts. *American Journal of Public Health, 92*(5), 773–777.

Coker, T. R., Austin, B., & Schuster, M. A. (2010). The health and health care of lesbian, gay, and bisexual adolescents. *Annual Review of Public Health, 31*, 457–477.

Coleman, E. (1989). The development of male prostitution activity among gay and bisexual adolescents. *Journal of Homosexuality, 17*(1–2), 131–150.

Collins, D. (2007). When sex work isn't 'work'. *Tourist Studies, 7*(2), 115–139. doi:10.1177/1468797607083498.

Connell, J. (2009). The personal safety of male prostitutes. In D. Canter, M. Ioannou, & D. Youngs (Eds.), *Safer sex in the city: The experience and management of street prostitution* (pp. 79–98). Burlington, VT: Ashgate.

Coombs, N. R. (1974). Male prostitution: A psychosocial view of behavior. *American Journal of Orthopsychiatry, 44*, 782.

Corliss, H. L., Cochran, S. D., & Mays, V. M. (2002). Reports of parental maltreatment during childhood in a United States population-based survey of homosexual, bisexual, and heterosexual adults. *Child Abuse and Neglect, 26*, 1165–1178.

Courtney, M. E., & Dworsky, A. (2006). Early outcomes for young adults transitioning from out-of-home care in the USA. *Child and Family Social Work, 11*, 209–219.

Daly, K. (1988). The social control of sexuality: A case study of the criminalization of prostitution in the progressive era. *Research in Law, Deviance and Social Control, 9*, 171–206.

D'Augelli, A. R., Grossman, A. H., Salter, N. P., Vasey, J. J., Starks, M. T., & Sinclair, K. O. (2005). Predicting the suicide attempts of lesbian, gay, and bisexual youth. *Suicide and Life-Threatening Behavior, 35*(6), 646–660.

Davies, P., & Feldman, R. (1999). Selling sex in Cardiff and London. In P. Aggleton (Ed.), *Men who sell sex: International perspectives on male prostitution and HIV/AIDS* (pp. 1–22). London, UK: UCL Press.

De Rosa, C. J., Montgomery, S. B., Kipke, M. D., Iverson, E., Ma, J. L., & Unger, J. B. (1999). Service utilization among homeless and runaway youth in Los Angeles, California: Rates and reasons. *Journal of Adolescent Health, 24*(3), 190–200. doi:10.1016/S1054-139X(98)00081-0

DiPlacido, J. (1998). Minority stress among lesbians, gay men, and bisexuals: A consequence of homophobia, heterosexism, and stigmatization. In G. M. Herek (Ed.), *Stigma and sexual orientation: Understanding prejudice against lesbians, gay men, and bisexuals* (pp. 138–159). Thousand Oaks, CA: Sage.

Ditmore, M. H. (2011). *Prostitution and sex work.* Santa Barbara, CA: Greenwood.

Dordick, G. A. (1997). *Something left to lose: Personal relations and survival among New York's homeless.* Philadelphia, PA: Temple University Press.

Dunne, G., Prendergast, S., & Telford, D. (2002). Young, gay, homeless, and invisible: A growing population. *Culture, Health and Sexuality, 4*(1), 103–115.

Earls, C. M., & David, H. (1989). A psychosocial study of male prostitution. *Archives of Sexual Behavior, 18*(5), 401–419.

Edelman, E. A. (2011). "This area has been declared a prostitution free zone": Discursive formations of space, the state, and trans "sex worker" bodies. *Journal of Homosexuality, 58*(6–7), 848–864. doi:10.1080/00918369.2011.581928.

Escoffier, J. (2007). Porn star/stripper/escort: Economic and sexual dynamics in a sex work career. *Journal of Homosexuality, 53*(1–2), 173–200. doi:10.1300/J082v53n01_08.

Feinstein, R., Greenblatt, A., Hass, L., Kohn, S., & Rana, J. (2001). *Justice for all? A report on lesbian, gay, bisexual and transgendered youth in the New York juvenile justice system.* New York, NY: Urban Justice Center.

Frederick, T. J. (2012). *Deciding how to get by: Subsistence choices among homeless youth in Toronto.* (Doctoral Dissertation, University of Toronto).

Frederick, T. J., Kirst, M., & Erickson, P. G. (2012). Suicide attempts and suicidal ideation among street-involved youth in Toronto. *Advances in Mental Health, 11*(1), 8–17.

Frederick, T. J., Ross, L. E., Bruno, T., & Erickson, P. G. (2011). Exploring gender and sexual minority status among street involved youth. *Vulnerable Children & Youth Studies, 6*(2), 166–183.

Gaetz, S., & O'Grady, B. (2002). Making money: Exploring the economy of young homeless workers. *Work, Employment & Society, 16*(3), 433–456.

Gaetz, S. (2004). Safe streets for whom? Homeless youth, social exclusion, and criminal victimization. *Canadian Journal of Criminology and Criminal Justice, 46*(4), 423–456.

Gangamma, R., Slesnick, N., Toviessi, P., & Serovich, J. (2008). Comparison of HIV risks among gay, lesbian, bisexual and heterosexual homeless youth. *Journal of Youth and Adolescence, 37*(4), 456–464.

Garofalo, R., Wolf, R. C., Wissow, L. S., Woods, E. R., & Goodman, E. (1999). Sexual orientation and risk of suicide attempts among a representative sample of youth. *Archives of Pediatrics and Adolescent Medicine, 153*(5), 487–493. doi:10.1001/archpedi.153.5.487.

Gattis, M. N. (2011). An ecological systems comparison between homeless sexual minority youths and homeless heterosexual youths. *Journal of Social Service Research, 39,* 1–12. doi: 10.1080/01488376.2011.633814.

Gibson, B. (1995). *Male order: Life stories from boys who sell sex.* London, UK: Cassell.

Gordon, D. R. (1994). *The return of the dangerous classes: Drug prohibition and policy politics* (1st ed.). New York, NY: W.W. Norton.

Gowan, T. (2010). *Hobos, hustlers, and backsliders: Homeless in San Francisco.* Minneapolis, MN: University of Minnesota Press.

Green, A. I. (2008). The social organization of desire: The sexual fields approach. *Sociological Theory, 26*(1), 25–60.

Greene, J. M., Ennett, S. T., & Ringwalt, C. L. (1999). Prevalence and correlates of survival sex among runaway and homeless youth. *American Journal of Public Health, 89*(9), 1406–1409.

Gwadz, M. V., Gostnell, K., Smolenski, C., Willis, B., Nish, D., Nolan, T. C.,... Ritchie, A. (2009). The initiation of homeless youth into the street economy. *Journal of Adolescence, 32,* 357–377.

Hagan, J., & McCarthy, B. (1997). *Mean streets: Youth crime and homelessness.* Cambridge, MA: Cambridge University Press.

Hammack, P. L., Thompson, E. M., & Pilecki, A. (2009). Configurations of identity among sexual minority youth: Context, desire, and narrative. *Journal of Youth and Adolescence, 38*(7), 867–883.

Harding, R., & Hamilton, P. (2009). Working girls: Abuse or choice in street-level sex work? A study of homeless women in Nottingham. *British Journal of Social Work, 39*(6), 1118–1137. doi:10.1093/bjsw/bcm157.

Herek, G. M. (2009). Hate crimes and stigma-related experiences among sexual minority adults in the United States: Prevalence estimates from a national probability sample. *Journal of Interpersonal Violence, 24,* 54–74. doi:10.1177/0886260508316477.

Holmes, W. C., & Slap, G. B. (1998). Sexual abuse of boys: Definition, prevalence, correlates, sequlae, and management. *Journal of the American Medical Association, 280*(21), 1855–1862.

Hubbard, P., & Scoular, J. (2009). Making the vulnerable more vulnerable? The contradictions of British street prostitution policy. In D. Canter, M. Ioannou, & D. Youngs (Eds.), *Safer sex in the city: The experience and management of street prostitution* (pp. 135–154). Burlington, VT: Ashgate.

Hwahng, S. J., & Nuttbrock, L. (2007). Sex workers, fem queens, and cross-dressers: Differential marginalizations and HIV vulnerabilities among three ethnocultural male-to-female transgender communities in New York City. *Sexuality Research and Social Policy: Journal of NSRC, 4*(4), 36–59. doi:10.1525/srsp.2007.4.4.36.

Jeffery, L. A., & MacDonald, G. (2006). "It's the money, honey": The economy of sex work in the Maritimes. *Canadian Review of Sociology/Revue Canadienne De Sociologie, 43*(3), 313–327.

Karabanow, J. (2004). *Being young and homeless: Understanding how youth enter and exit street life.* New York, NY: Peter Lang.

Karabanow, J., Hughes, J., Ticknor, J., Kidd, S., & Patterson, D. (2010). The economics of being young and poor: How homeless youth survive in neo-liberal times. *Journal of Sociology and Social Welfare, XXXVII*(4), 39–63.

Kaye, K. (2007). Sex and the unspoken in male street prostitution. *Journal of Homosexuality, 53*(1), 37–73.

Kidd, S. A. (2004). "The walls were closing in and we were trapped": A qualitative analysis of street youth suicide. *Youth and Society, 36*(1), 30–55.

Kidd, S. A., & Kral, M. J. (2002). Suicide and prostitution among street youth: A qualitative analysis. *Adolescence, 37*(146), 411–430.

Kipke, M. D., Montgomery, S. B., Simon, T. R., Unger, J. B., & Johnson, C. J. (1997a). Homeless youth: Drug use patterns and HIV risk profiles according to peer group affiliation. *AIDS and Behavior, 1*(4), 247.

Kipke, M., Simon, T., Montgomery, S., Unger, J., & Iversen, E. (1997b). Homeless youth and their exposure to and involvement in violence while living on the street. *Journal of Adolescent Health, 20*, 360–367.

Kirst, M., Frederick, T., & Erickson, P. G. (2011). Concurrent mental health and substance use problems among street-involved youth. *International Journal of Mental Health and Addiction, 9*, 543–553.

Koken, J., Bimbi, D. S., & Parsons, J. T. (2009). Male and female escorts: A comparative analysis. In R. Weitzer (Ed.), *Sex for sale: Prostitution, pornography, and the sex industry* (2nd ed., pp. 205–232). New York, NY: Routledge.

Kosciw, J. G. (2004). *The 2003 National School Climate Survey: The school-related experiences of our nation's lesbian, gay, bisexual and transgender youth.* New York, NY: Gay, Lesbian and Straight Education Network.

Kosciw, J. G., Diaz, E. M., & Greytak, E. A. (2008). *2007 National School Climate Survey: The experiences of lesbian, gay, bisexual and transgender youth in our nation's schools.* New York, NY: GLSEN.

Lambda Legal, & Deloitte Financial Advisory Services LLP. (2006). *2005 workplace fairness survey.* New York, NY: Lambda Legal.

Lantz, S. (2005). Students working in the Melbourne sex industry: Education, human capital and the changing patterns of the youth labour market. *Journal of Youth Studies, 8*(4), 385–401. doi:10.1080/13676260500431669.

Laurindo da Silva, L. (1999). Travestis and gigolos: Male sex work and HIV prevention in France. In P. Aggleton (Ed.), *Men who sell sex: International perspectives on male prostitution and AIDS* (pp. 41–60). London, UK: UCL Press.

Leary, D., & Minichiello, V. (2007). Exploring the interpersonal relationships in street-based male sex work: Results from an Australian qualitative study. *Journal of Homosexuality, 53*(1), 75–110.

Leslie, M. B., Stein, J. A., & Rotheram-Borus, M. J. (2002). Sex specific predictors of suicidality among runaway youth. *Journal of Clinical Child and Adolescent Psychology, 31*(1), 27–40.

Livingston, J., & Swimar, B. (Producers), & Livingston, J. (Director). (1990). *Paris is Burning* [Motion picture]. United States: Off White Productions.

Lopez-Embury, S., & Sanders, T. (2009). Sex workers, labour rights and unionization. In T. Sanders, M. O'Neill, & J. Pitcher (Eds.), *Prostitution: Sex work, policy, and politics* (pp. 94–110). London, UK: Sage.

Lowman, J. (2009). Violence and the outlaw status of (street) prostitution in Canada. In D. Canter, M. Ioannou, & D. Youngs (Eds.), *Safer sex in the city: The experience and management of street prostitution* (pp. 169–189). Burlington, VT: Ashgate.

Lucas, A. M. (2005). The work of sex work: Elite prostitutes' vocational orientations and experiences. *Deviant Behavior, 26*(6), 513–546. doi:10.1080/01639620500218252.

Luckenbill, D. F. (1985). Entering male prostitution. *Urban Life, 14*(2), 131–153.

Lutnick, A., & Cohan, D. (2009). Criminalization, legalization or decriminalization of sex work: What female sex workers say in San Francisco, USA. *Reproductive Health Matters, 17*(34), 38–46. doi:10.1016/S0968-8080(09)34469-9.

Maher, L. (1997). *Sexed work: Gender, race, and resistance in a Brooklyn drug market.* New York, NY: Clarendon Press.

Marshal, M. P., Friedman, M. S., Stall, R., King, K. M., Miles, J., Gold, M. A., Morse, J. Q. (2008). Sexual orientation and adolescent substance use: A meta-analysis and methodological review. *Addiction, 103*(4), 546–556.

Marshall, B. D., Shannon, K., Kerr, T., Zhang, R., & Wood, E. (2010). Survival sex work and increased HIV risk among sexual minority street-involved youth. *Journal of Acquired Immune Deficiency Syndrome, 53*(5), 661–664.

Martijn, C., & Sharpe, L. (2006). Pathways to youth homelessness. *Social Science and Medicine, 62*, 1–12.

Marvasti, A. B. (2003). *Being homeless: Textual and narrative constructions.* Lanham, MD: Lexington Books.

McCabe, I., Acree, M., O'Mahony, F., McCabe, J., Kenny, J., Twyford, J.,… McGlanaghy, E. (2011). Male street prostitution in Dublin: A psychological analysis. *Journal of Homosexuality, 58*(8), 998–1021. doi: 10.1080/00918369.2011.598394.

McCarthy, B. (1996). The attitudes and actions of others: Tutelage and Sutherland's theory of differential association. *British Journal of Criminology, 36*(1), 135–147.

Mercer, C. H., Bailey, J. V., Johnson, A. M., Erens, B., Wellings, K., Fenton, K. A., et al. (2007). Women who report having sex with women: British national probability data on prevalence, sexual behaviors, and health outcomes. *American Journal of Public Health, 97*(6), 1126–1133.

Milburn, N. G., Ayala, G., Rice, E., Batterham, P., & Rotheram-Borus, M. J. (2006). Discrimination and exiting homelessness among homeless adolescents. *Cultural Diversity and Ethnic Minority Psychology, 12*(4), 658–672.

Mitchell, D. (1997). The annihilation of space by law: The roots and implications of anti-homeless laws in the United States. *Antipode, 29*(3), 303–335.

Morrison, T. G., & Whitehead, B. W. (2007). *Male sex work: A business doing pleasure.* Binghamton, NY: Harrington Park Press.

National Alliance to End Homelessness. (2013). *The state of homelessness in America 2013.* Washington, D.C: NAEH.

Nixon, K., Tutty, L., Downe, P., Gorkoff, K., & Ursel, J. (2002). The everyday occurrence: Violence in the lives of girls exploited through prostitution. *Violence Against Women, 8*, 1016–1043.

Noell, J. W., & Ochs, L. (2001). Relationship of sexual orientation to substance use, suicidal ideation, suicide attempts, and other factors in a population of homeless adolescents. *Journal of Adolescent Health, 29*, 31–36.

Ochs, R. (1996). Biphobia: It goes more than two ways. In B. A. Firestein (Ed.), *Bisexuality: The psychology and politics of an invisible minority* (pp. 217–239). Thousand Oaks, CA: Sage.

O'Grady, B., & Gaetz, S. (2004). Homelessness, gender, and subsistence: The case of Toronto street youth. *Journal of Youth Studies, 7*(4), 397–416.

O'Grady, B., & Greene, C. (2003). A social and economic impact study of the Ontario safe streets act on Toronto squeegee workers. *Online Journal of Justice Studies, 1*(1).

O'Neill, M., & Pitcher, J. (2010). Sex work, communities, and public policy in the UK. In M. H. Ditmore, A. Levy, & A. Willman (Eds.), *Sex work matters* (pp. 217–239). New York, NY: Zed Books.

O'Reilly, M., Taylor, H. C., & Vostanis, P. (2009). "Nuts, schiz, psycho": An exploration of young homeless people's perceptions and dilemmas of defining mental health. *Social Science and Medicine, 68*(9), 1737–1744. doi:10.1016/j.socscimed.2009.02.033.

Parsons, J. T., Bimbi, D. S., & Halkitis, P. N. (2001). Sexual compulsivity among gay/bisexual male escorts who advertise on the internet. *Sexual Addiction & Compulsivity, 8*, 101–112.

Perkins, R., & Bennett, G. (1985). *Being a prostitute: Prostitute women and prostitute men.* Sydney, New South Wales: Allen & Unwin.

Pettiway, L. E. (1996). *Honey, honey, miss thang: Being black, gay, and on the streets.* Philadelphia, PA: Temple University Press.

Phoenix, J., & Oerton, S. (2005). *Illicit and illegal: Sex, regulation and social control.* Devon, UK: Willan Publishing.

Pleak, R. R., & Meyer-Bahlburg, H. F. L. (1990). Sexual behavior and AIDS knowledge of young male prostitutes in Manhattan. *Journal of Sex Research, 27*(4), 557–587.

Porter, J., & Bonilla, L. (2009). The ecology of street prostitution. In R. Weitzer (Ed.), *Sex for sale: Prostitution, pornography, and the sex industry* (2nd ed., pp. 163–186). New York, NY: Routledge.

Prendergast, S., Dunne, G., & Telford, D. (2001). A story of "difference", A different story: Young homeless lesbian, gay and bisexual people. *International Journal of Sociology and Social Policy, 21*(4–6), 64–91.

Psychiatric News (2003). Controversy continues to grow over *DSM's* GID diagnosis. *Psychiatric News, 38*(14), 25–32.

Quilgars, D., Johnsen, S., & Pleace, N. (2008). *Youth homelessness in the UK.* York, UK: Joseph Rowntree Foundation.

Raising the Roof. (2009). *Youth homelessness in Canada: The road to solutions.* Toronto, CAN: Raising the Roof.

Ray, N. (2006). *Lesbian, gay, bisexual and transgender youth: An epidemic of homelessness.* New York, NY: National Gay and Lesbian Task Force Policy Institute and the National Coalition for the Homeless.

Rew, L., Whittaker, T. A., Taylor-Seehafer, M. A., & Smith, L. R. (2005). Sexual health risks and protective resources in gay, lesbian, bisexual, and heterosexual homeless youth. *Journal for Specialists in Pediatric Nursing, 10*(1), 11–19.

Rice, E., Milburn, N. G., & Rotheram-Borus, M. (2007). Pro-social and problematic social network influences on HIV/AIDS risk behaviors among newly homeless youth in Los Angeles. *AIDS Care, 19*(5), 697–704. doi:10.1080/09540120601087038.

Rickard, W. (2001). 'Been there, seen it, done it, I've got the T-shirt': British sex workers reflect on jobs, hopes, the future and retirement. *Feminist Review, 67*, 111–132.

Robinson, T., & Davies, P. (1991). London's homosexual male prostitutes: Power, peer groups and HIV. In P. Aggleton, G. Hart, & P. Davies (Eds.), *AIDS: Responses, interventions, and care* (pp. 95–110). London, UK: Falmer Press.

Robohm, J. S., Litzenberger, B. W., & Pearlman, L. A. (2003). Sexual abuse in lesbian and bisexual young women: Associations with emotional/behavioral difficulties, feelings about sexuality, and the "coming out" process. *Journal of Lesbian Studies, 7*(4), 31–47.

Rosario, M., Hunter, J., & Gwadz, M. (1997). Exploration of substance use among lesbian, gay, and bisexual youth. *Journal of Adolescent Research, 12*(4), 454–476. doi:10.1177/0743554897124003

Rosario, M., Schrimshaw, E. W., & Hunter, J. (2008). Predicting different patterns of sexual identity development over time among lesbian, gay, and bisexual youths: A cluster analytic approach. *American Journal of Community Psychology, 42*(3–4), 266–282.

Rosen, E., & Venkatesh, S. A. (2008). A 'perversion' of choice: Sex work offers just enough in Chicago's urban ghetto. *Journal of Contemporary Ethnography, 37*(4), 417–441. doi:10.1177/0891241607309879.

Rotheram-Borus, M. J., & Fernandez, M. I. (1995). Sexual orientation and developmental challenges experienced by gay and lesbian youths. *Suicide and Life-Threatening Behavior, 25*, 26–34.

Russell, S. T. (2006). Substance use and abuse and mental health among sexual-minority youths: Evidence from Add Health. *Sexual orientation and mental health: Examining identity and development in lesbian, gay, and bisexual people* (pp. 13–35). Washington, DC: American Psychological Association. doi: 10.1037/11261-001.

Saewyc, E. M., Skay, C. L., Pettingell, S. L., Reis, E. A., Bearinger, L., Resnick, M., et al. (2006). Hazards of stigma: The sexual and physical abuse of gay, lesbian, bisexual adolescents in the United States and Canada. *Child Welfare, 85*(2), 195–213.

Saewyc, E. M. (2011). Research on adolescent sexual orientation: Development, health disparities, stigma, and resilience. *Journal of Research on Adolescence, 21*(1), 256–272. doi:10.1111/j.1532-7795.2010.00727.x.

Sanders, T. (2004). The risks of street prostitution: Punters, policy and protesters. *Urban Studies, 41*(9), 1703–1717. doi:10.1080/0042098042000243110.

Sanders, T. (2005). *Sex work: A risky business*. Portland, OR: Willan.

Savin-Williams, R. (1994). Verbal and physical abuse as stressors in the lives of lesbian, gay male, and bisexual youths: Associations with school problems, running away, substance abuse, prostitution, and suicide. *Journal of Consulting and Clinical Psychology, 62*(2), 261–269. doi:10.1037/0022-006X.62.2.261.

Savin-Williams, R. C. (2001). A critique of research on sexual-minority youths. *Journal of Adolescence, 24*, 5–13.

Selby, H., & Canter, D. (2009). The relationship between control strategies employed by street prostitutes and levels and varieties of client violence. In D. Canter, M. Ioannou, & D. Youngs (Eds.), *Safer sex in the city* (pp. 13–29). Burlington, VT: Ashgate.

Shelden, R. G. (2001). *Controlling the dangerous classes: A critical introduction to the history of criminal justice*. Boston, MA: Allyn and Bacon.

Simmons, M. (1999). Theorizing prostitution: The question of agency. *Sexwork and sex workers* (pp. 125–148) New Brunswick, NJ: Transaction.

Simon, P. M., Morse, E. V., Balson, P. M., Osofsky, H. J., & Gaumer, H. R. (1993). Barriers to human immunodeficiency virus related to risk reduction among male street prostitutes. *Health Education Quarterly, 20*(2), 261–273.

Smith, N. J. (2012). Body issues: The political economy of male sex work. *Sexualities, 15*(5–6), 586–603. doi:10.1177/1363460712445983.

Smith, M. D., & Grov, C. (2011). *In the company of men: Inside the lives of male prostitutes*. Santa Barbara, CA: Praeger.

Smith, L. H., Guthrie, B. J., & Oakley, D. J. (2005). Studying adolescent male sexuality: Where are we? *Journal of Youth and Adolescence, 34*(4), 361–377. doi:10.1007/s10964-005-5762-5.

Spicer, S. S. (2010). Healthcare needs of the transgender homeless population. *Journal of Gay & Lesbian Mental Health, 14*, 320–339.

Steele, L. S., Ross, L. E., Dobinson, C., Veldhuizen, S., & Tinmouth, J. M. (2009). Women's sexual orientation and health: Results from a Canadian population-based survey. *Women and Health, 49*(5), 353–367.

Stella. Legalization vs. decriminalization. Retrieved, 2012, from http://www.chezstella.org/stella/?q=en/debate

Stoltz, J. M., Shannon, K., Kerr, T., Zhang, R., Montaner, J. S., & Wood, E. (2007). Associations between childhood maltreatment and sex work in a cohort of drug-using youth. *Social Science and Medicine, 65*(6), 1214–1221. doi:10.1016/j.socscimed.2007.05.005.

Szymanski, D. M., Kashubeck-West, S., & Meyer, J. (2008). Internalized heterosexism. *The Counseling Psychologist, 36*(4), 525–574.

Thukral, J., & Ditmore, M. (2003). *Revolving door: An analysis of street based prostitution in New York City.* New York, NY: Sex Workers' Project Urban Justice Center.

Tyler, K. A. (2009). Risk factors for trading sex among homeless young adults. *Archives of Sexual Behavior, 38*(2), 290–297. doi:10.1007/s10508-007-9201-4.

Tyler, K. A. (2008). A comparison of risk factors for sexual victimization among gay, lesbian, bisexual, and heterosexual homeless young adults. *Violence and Victims, 23*(5), 586–602.

Tyler, K. A., & Johnson, K. A. (2006). Trading sex: Voluntary or coerced? The experiences of homeless youth. *The Journal of Sex Research, 43*(3), 208–216.

Ueno, K. (2005). Sexual orientation and psychological distress in adolescence: Examining interpersonal stressors and social support processes. *Social Psychology Quarterly, 68*(3), 258–277.

U.S. Department of Housing and Urban Development. (2010). *The 2009 annual homeless assessment report.* Washington, D.C.: Office of Community Development and Planning.

Valentine, G., & Skelton, T. (2003). Finding oneself, losing oneself: The lesbian and gay 'scene' as a paradoxical space. *International Journal of Urban and Regional Research, 274*, 849–866.

Van Leeuwen, J. M., Boyle, S., Salomonsen-Sautel, S., Baker, N. D., Garcia, J. T., Hoffman, A., et al. (2006). Lesbian, gay, and bisexual youth: An eight-city public health perspective. *Child Welfare, 85*(2), 151.

van Wormer, K., & McKinney, R. (2003). What schools can do to help gay/lesbian/bisexual youth: A harm reduction approach. *Adolescence, 38*(151), 409–420.

Venema, P. U., & Visser, J. (1990). Safer prostitution: A new approach in Holland. In M. Plant (Ed.), *AIDS, drugs, and prostitution* (pp. 41–60). London, UK: Tavistock/Routledge.

Visano, L. A. (1987). *This idle trade: The occupational patterns of male prostitution.* Concord: VitaSana Books.

Vitulli, E. (2010). A defining moment in civil rights history? The employment non-discrimination act, trans-inclusion, and homonormativity. *Sexuality Research and Social Policy, 7*(3), 155–167. doi:10.1007/s13178-010-0015-0.

Vrangalova, Z., & Savin-Williams, R. C. (2012). Mostly heterosexual and mostly gay/lesbian: Evidence for new sexual orientation identities. *Archives of Sexual Behavior, 41*(1), 85–101. doi:10.1007/s10508-012-9921-y.

Wacquant, L. J. D. (2009). *Punishing the poor: The neoliberal government of social insecurity.* Durham, NC: Duke University Press.

Walls, N. E., & Bell, S. (2011). Correlates of engaging in survival sex among homeless youth and young adults. *Journal of Sex Research, 48*, 423–436. doi:10.1080/00224499.2010.501916.

Walls, N. E., Potter, C., & Van Leeuwen, J. (2009). Where risk and protective factors operate differently: Homeless sexual minority youth and suicide attempts. *Child and Adolescent Social Work Journal, 26*(3), 235–257.

Wasserman, J. A., & Clair, J. M. (2010). *At home on the street: People, poverty, and a hidden culture of homelessness.* Boulder, CO: Lynne Rienner Publishers.

Watson, J. (2011). Understanding survival sex: Young women, homelessness and intimate relationships. *Journal of Youth Studies, 14*(6), 639–655.

Weinberg, M. S., Shaver, F. M., & Williams, C. J. (1999). Gendered sex work in the San Francisco tenderloin. *Archives of Sexual Behavior, 28*(6), 503–521.

Weitzer, R. (2009a). Sociology of sex work. *Annual Review of Sociology, 35*, 213–234. doi:10.1146/annurev-soc-070308-120025.

Weitzer, R. (2009b). Prostitution control in America: Rethinking public policy. In D. Canter, M. Ioannou, & D. Youngs (Eds.), *Safer sex in the city: The experience and management of street prostitution* (pp. 191–209). Burlington, VT: Ashgate.

Weitzer, R. (2010). The movement to criminalize sex work in the United States. *Journal of Law and Society, 37*(1), 61–84. doi:10.1111/j.1467-6478.2010.00495.x.

Welle, D. L., Fuller, S. S., Mauk, D., & Clatts, M. C. (2006). The invisible body of queer youth: Identity and health in the margins of lesbian and trans communities. *Journal of Lesbian Studies, 10*(1–2), 43–71. doi:10.1300/J155v10n01_03.

West, D. J., & deVilliers, B. (1992). *Male prostitution: Gay sex services in London.* London, UK: Duckworth.

Whitbeck, L. B., Chen, X., Hoyt, D. R., Tyler, K. A., & Johnson, K. D. (2004). Mental disorder, subsistence strategies, and victimization among gay, lesbian, and bisexual homeless and runaway adolescents. *The Journal of Sex Research, 41*(4), 329.

Whitbeck, L. B., & Hoyt, D. R. (1999). *Nowhere to grow: Homeless and runaway adolescents and their families.* New York, NY: Aldine de Gruyer.

Whitbeck, L. B., Hoyt, D. R., Yoder, K. A., Cauce, A. M., & Paradise, M. (2001). Deviant behavior and victimization among homeless and runaway adolescents. *Journal of Interpersonal Violence, 16*(11), 1175–1204.

Whitbeck, L. B., & Simons, R. L. (1991). Sexual abuse as a precursor to prostitution and victimization among adolescent and adult homeless women. *Journal of Family Issues, 12*(3), 361–379.

Wilson, E. C., Garofalo, R., Harris, R. D., Herrick, A., Martinez, M., Martinez, J., et al. (2009). Transgender female youth and sex work: HIV risk and a comparison of life factors related to engagement in sex work. *AIDS and Behavior, 13*(5), 902–913. doi:10.1007/s10461-008-9508-8.

Woronoff, R., Estrada, R., & Sommer, S. (2006). *Out of the margins: A report on regional listening forums highlighting the experiences of lesbian, gay, bisexual, transgender, and questioning youth in care.* New York, NY: Child Welfare League of America/Lambda Legal Defense and Education Fund.

Wright, E. R., & Perry, B. L. (2006). Sexual identity distress, social support, and the health of gay, lesbian, and bisexual youth. *Journal of Homosexuality, 51*(1), 81–110. doi:10.1300/J082v51n01_05.

Yu, V. (2010). Shelter and transitional housing for transgender youth. *Journal of Gay & Lesbian Mental Health, 14*(4), 340–345. doi:10.1080/19359705.2010.504476.

Ziyadeh, N. J., Prokop, L. A., Fisher, L. B., Rosario, M., Field, A. E., Camargo, C. A., Jr, & Austin, S. B. (2007). Sexual orientation, gender, and alcohol use in a cohort study of U.S. adolescent girls and boys. *Drug and Alcohol Dependence, 87*, 119–130.

Chapter 23
A State of Exception: Intersectionality, Health, and Social Exemption

Ryan A. Levy

Abstract Using an intersectionality framework for understanding the exception of certain bodies from processes of healthcare and justice, this chapter provides a theoretical basis for considering "minority" health issues, especially as they relate to sexuality and sexual behavior. For the purposes of this chapter, "minority" is meant to encompass those who practice same-sex sexual behavior, people of color, and the intersection of these two groups. This chapter seeks to explore various "states of exception" through a critical analysis of common processes of social (b)ordering and propose ethnographic methods as a potential solution to the negative effects of social assumptions on some public outreach and risk-based intervention programs.

Keywords Health inequality · MSM · MSM of color · Intersectionality · HIV/AIDS · Sexuality · Symbolic toxicity · Social border(s) · Symbolic violence · Social exemption · "State of Exception" · Critical analysis · Ethnography · (critical) Ethnography of sexuality · "Health as a human right" · (b)ordering · "Others"/"othering" · "Homosexual"

R. A. Levy (✉)
Department of Anthropology, University at Albany, 1400 Washington Ave.,
AS 237, Albany NY 12222, USA
e-mail: rlevy@albany.edu

D. Peterson and V. R. Panfil (eds.), *Handbook of LGBT Communities,*
Crime, and Justice, DOI: 10.1007/978-1-4614-9188-0_23,
© Springer Science+Business Media New York 2014

Introduction

"The state of exception…is…[a] no-man's land between public law and political fact, and between juridical order and life …this is an ambiguous zone…a zone of decidability…" (Agamben 2005, pp. 1–2).

In this chapter, I will explore several avenues of social exception and difference that condition diminished access to sexual health knowledge and care among "minority" men who have sex with men (MSM) in the United States. The use of "minority" is meant in the most general sense of the word. By adding this term I plan to draw connections between the experiences of MSM in general, people of color in general, and MSM of color in specific. All of these communities face similar effects of the processes of (b)ordering and methods of regulation and discrimination; although, arguably MSM of color encounter a double, "intersected" discrimination. Underscoring the ways in which the categorization of sex(uality) fits into a larger matrix of social othering, the organizing of people according to both their sexuality and sexual behaviors is subsumed within the domain of "(b)ordering" (from Van Houtum and Van Naerssen 2002). This theory of bordering as ordering allows for a more general theoretical understanding of the social processes by which individuals become lesser "others" and exposes how/ why sexually deviant people (those who fall outside conventional (b)orders) fall victim to such processes.

To adequately discuss the issues faced by MSM of color, it is important to explore and define social exemption and how it conditions the instability of the "health as a human right" framework. Briefly, this framework suggests that human rights should include access to equitable health knowledge and care, and that health may be one of the least contested human rights (Farmer 2005). As certain bodies are considered "exceptions" and thus "exempt" from normal social rules, human rights policies like these may not necessarily be applied to them. As a foundation for exploring social exception, I will explore the ways in which it is established, and discuss some of the inner workings of logics of exclusion. Central to these logics of exclusion are processes of categorizing and (b)ordering people, while determining the definitions of order and disorder.

Sexual health and the medicalization of sexual behavior are two avenues by which hegemonic processes work to define and exclude people largely according to their "risk." Complicating medical notions of sexual behavior, investigations of cultural difference will add complexity to simplified definitions of sexual preference and behavioral risk. Specifically, exploring the social stigma of HIV/AIDS shows how moral assignments are made to blame victims and paint certain individuals as inevitably sick. Also, this process of moral assignment is complicated by nationality, race, and/or ethnicity.

Additionally, a critique of state sponsored regulatory mechanisms is employed to show how official policies and practices use certain cultural assumptions (including the solidity of borders) as their foundation. Because of this, despite the well-intended motives of public health projects, many fail to reach the hardest hit groups for some of the reasons outlined in this chapter. In order to broaden the application of state critiques to an international stage, a transnational/transborder perspective is used. This school of thought aims to paint a more practical picture of different marked aspects of identity as conditional and constantly fluctuating. The transborder ideology also combats the common cultural assumptions of (b)ordering.

Applying perspectives gained from ethnographic techniques, critical ethnography is proposed as a tentative solution to the gaps in understanding that fail to inform current sexual health promotion policies and projects. This approach investigates how various axes of social difference converge to form individual subjectivities. It also allows for a detailed look at the many factors that condition the health inequities and other social injustices for MSM of color.

Social Exceptions, Abject Exemptions

Decades of rights movements show us that we often fail at being inclusive in our provision of social "privileges" and access to "rights." Thus, despite a discourse of inclusion and equal footing, the limiting of human potential has become an implicit societal characteristic. This restricting of capability is often referred to in terms of symbolic, structural, and political violence (Bourdieu 1977; Farmer 2004). Large- and small-scale limitations are informed by culturally and socially conditioned forms of prejudice and ideas of value and morality, inspiring what Bourdieu (1977) refers to as "violence…everywhere in social practice" (Scheper-Hughes and Bourgois 2004, p. 21). Through processes motivated by particular social stresses and historically conditioned cultural (in)sensitivities, the law itself becomes something that functions only for particular people. In other words, mundane characteristics become indicative of individuals lacking full human value, perpetuating a degree of impunity on the part of the justice system.

Scholars have argued that the causes of discrimination and exclusion are rooted in a certain "marked toxicity" (Douglas 1966; Goffman 1963). Specifically, Agamben (2005) discusses the ways in which bodies that are marked may be determined to be outside the "protected" social body. He constructs this condition as "a state of exception." In this space, marked bodies are characterized as "sacred humans" that can be killed without being "sacrificed" (i.e., they are disposable, and their "rights" are less significant) (Agamben 1998). A state of exception is a slippery and fluid place, one in which borders are established and reaffirmed at the "threshold of indeterminacy between democracy and absolutism" (Agamben 2005, p. 3).

Those characteristics, social or biological, that are deemed "toxic" are arbitrarily designated (Farmer 2005, p. 46; also see Wolf 1982). In an attempt to expose one such characteristic (or set of characteristics) a critical investigation of the symbolic toxicity of "homosexual (men)" moves to follow Farmer's (2005, p. 47) call for "more systemic analyses of power and privilege in discussions about who is likely to have their rights violated and in what ways." Although it does not reflect critical interpretations, "homosexual" is used here because all those who practice same-sex sexual behavior are subsumed into this marginalized category of people. This chapter focuses on men who engage in same-sex sexual behavior, not exclusively "homosexual" men. However, in order to explore the social marginalization that these men face, using the term "homosexual" is unavoidable.

Social Exceptions and Ephemeral Rights

Following developing theoretical orientations around human rights concerns, a rights agenda should be engaged in any critical analysis of social justice issues. At their most basic definition, human rights abuses involve a range of "limitations" on human potential and "capabilities" (opportunities "to achieve valuable combinations of human functionings") (Goodale 2010, p. 88; Sen 2005). This forges a furtively perpetual "lack of freedom to escape destitution" (Goodale 2010, p. 89). Additionally, access to rights and the ability to protest their violation is situated and contextual (Burrell 2010; Goldstein 2007).

Since dominant discourse considers "homosexuality" deviant and abnormal, we may theoretically conceive of sexual deviance as a *constant* "state of exception" (Agamben 2005): one that is essentialized into one's being through one's sexual desire. This "exception" involves a certain level of daily clandestine discrimination, marginalization, and human rights transgressions. Regarding global rights concerns in this vein, there has been international de-emphasis on/"bracketing" of discrimination related to sexual orientation (Saiz 2004). For instance, sexual orientation was removed from the Platform for Action at the Beijing Fourth World Conference on Women in 1995, as it was dubbed a "'non-subject' that would open the floodgates to many unacceptable behaviors" (Saiz 2004, p. 58).

Discursive silence regarding violence against "homosexuals"—much like gendered violence (Sanford 2008, and others)—allows for its hidden perpetuation. In addition to de-emphasizing certain issues, minority voices are generally left out of dominant discourse and political understanding (Appadurai 1996). This is because these categorized "others" are painted as immoral and dangerous. For example, much of the discourses involving minorities and men who have sex with men (MSM) underscore the risk and danger present as a result of their behaviors. "Ordinary people are transformed into killers, torturers, and rapists. Friends, neighbors, and coworkers are 're-presented' as 'objects of the deepest hatred'" (Appadurai 1996, p. 155).

Categorizing People, (B)ordering Lives

Categories of gender and sex(uality) are key aspects of social categorization; the appearances and behaviors associated with these categories are primary in the definition of individual identity and, thus, the distinction of "others" as well. Arguably, the act of categorizing promotes covert violences in attempts to establish uniform borders around the idiosyncratic lives of individual people.

For decades, feminist anthropologists have battled the naturalization of dichotomous gender categories (e.g., Collier and Yanagisako 1987, 1989; Reiter 1975). Scholars called attention to the way that culture is created and defined by men; they underscored how this trend leaves out many, if not most, features of women (Ardener 2006). The scientific value of alternative perspectives has been wielded to argue for more equitable understandings of the human experience. More recently, theorists suggest a logical connection between combating gender discrimination and critiquing stereotypical understandings of sex and sexuality (e.g., Manalansan 2003; Rubin 1984; Valentine 2007). The "question" of the geneses of gender and sexual oppression and subordination helps to determine our "visions of the future, and our evaluation of whether or not it is realistic to hope for a sexually egalitarian society" (Rubin 2006, p. 87).

Many aspects of social "othering" become naturalized and are considered acultural. Butler (1990) famously interrogates the ways in which gender and sex(uality) have become mistakenly characterized as such. She states, "gender is not to culture as sex is to nature; gender is also the discursive/cultural means by which 'sexed nature' or 'a natural sex' is produced and established as 'prediscursive,' prior to culture, a politically neutral surface *on which* culture acts" (p. 10). Also, the body is seen as a "passive" entity upon which culture acts and "inscribes" itself. Differential genders, sexes, and sexualities are perceived as indelible "marks" inscribed upon bodies. Thus, these labels become ascribed within a matrix of multiple under-recognized cultural constructions. Importantly, since identity is "assured" and "stabilized" by the concepts of gender, sex, and sexuality, the "very notion of 'the person' is called into question by the cultural emergence of those 'incoherent' or 'discontinuous' gendered beings who appear to be persons who fail to conform to...norms of cultural intelligibility" (Butler 1990, p. 23). Thus, not only are simplistic, dichotomous identities ascribed to all individuals, but the traversing or blurring of categorical lines will draw one's personhood into question (see related discussions in this volume by Ball; Johnson). Writing against this essentialized form of sex/gender, simplified understandings of sexual behavior are complicated by exploring "'ethnographies of the particular' as instruments of tactical humanism" (Abu-Lughod 2006, p. 153). In short, this is the work of recognizing the oppression of the other (Strathern 1987).

A key component of understanding how social labeling is performed is appreciating the social categories themselves. While discursive explanations of social categories may seem trivial, these discourses very much produce and buttress ways of knowing oneself and understanding others (Valentine 2007).

Specifically, scholars have levied important critiques that examine the falsities that buttress psychological categories used to "govern" popular and theoretical thinkings of gender and sex (e.g., Butler 1990; Haar 1977). For example, the illusion of a "substantial," categorical identity supports a misguided, simplistic view of human (sexual) experience. Instead, in the anthropological tradition, culture (and its resulting images of personhood, gender, and sex) is viewed as a shifting sense of meaning that is wielded in different ways depending on the context of social interaction (e.g., Valentine 2007). These contingent cultural understandings are infused with certain "moral intuitions" that influence the marking of behavioral "choices" (Verweij 1999). As discussed, certain images and understandings of self, society, and sexuality are privileged over others. Alternative voices are silenced and made less visible. This diminishing and devaluing of voices and ways of living represent acts of social and symbolic violence (see DeJong & Long, this volume, for an example of this process in Uganda). In order to adequately understand the gendered, sexual experiences of various human beings, it becomes crucial to see forms of desire (and the bordered subject positions associated with them) as conditioned by social relations and understandings (e.g., Corrêa et al. 2008; Deleuze and Guattari 1977; Foucault 1995[1977]; Lacan 1968).

Building upon Rubin's (1973) conception of a sex hierarchy developed to regulate sex(uality), Butler (1990) discusses how reified categories of gender and sex(uality) can be conceptualized as a (legal) self-regulation of social spaces. This regulation becomes necessary to avoid the deterioration of civilization into the imaginary "before." Despite the hegemonic preoccupation of cultural norms with stability and regulation, Butler and Foucault have both focused upon the inconsistencies and instabilities of gender/sexual identities. These inconsistencies motivate considerations of merging sexual and cultural differences in terms of social deviance and "polluted" "risk" behavior. Seeing sexuality as part of culture and culture as an informant of sexual behavior paints a more complete picture of how sexual deviance is conceived, understood, and policed.

Disordered Bodies, Disbordered Lives

A particularly productive way in which the social "other" may be conceptualized is in respect to its "disorder." Social "disorder" emerges, in part, from an inability to adequately border/categorize someone or something. Marked by an anxiety toward complexity, conditions that threaten known borders are cast in a destructive light and persecuted as disorderly and threatening (see, e.g., Dennis, this volume, for discussion of historical depictions and treatment of gay men). That body which does not follow social conventions is both disorderly and dangerous; it breaks social convention and destabilizes the borders through which society functions.

The paradigm of the disordered individual/body is especially relevant because it bridges the gap between otherification and disease; it creates a productive metaphor that considers the social "other" as a contagion, a disorder. This metaphor serves useful in problematizing current conceptions of medicalized versus unmedicalized disorder. Concerning sexual behavior, medicalized understandings have been especially prevalent. Despite their claims to being devoid of social stigma, medical discussions of sexual risk behavior operate within the same paradigm of border policing and otherification. For example, in regulating the spread of HIV/AIDS, many medical professionals tend to strictly survey and judge particular behaviors (such as anal intercourse and other same-sex sexual behaviors) over others. Additionally, stereotypes about who is most likely to practice such behaviors figure into the treatment of particular individuals (e.g., MSM) (Holmes 2012; Jenks 2011; Kleinman and Benson 2006).

Also, within the context of disorder and deviance, border crossing remains an overarching theme. Figuratively speaking, disordered bodies cross borders of social normativity, and enter into an ambiguous, liminal social space. According to Goffman (1963), stigmatized persons often find themselves unaware of how "normals" will view them and unable to influence these prevailing understandings of their identity. This process of stigmatization simultaneously strips them of the agency to find out. Throughout their life, stigmatized people are instilled with social norms through which their place as inferior is reinforced, because they do not correspond to these norms. The result is a set of values that naturalizes poor treatment and substantiates life-long shame (i.e., symbolic violence). Thus, some populations are disproportionately devalued, while others are unduly favored.

Douglas (1966) notably claims that the "border" is particularly important social construction; a site of ambivalence and social control. She (among others) considers crossing borders and fluid identity definitions as part of everyday human existence. However, certain border crossings may be made highly visible and fiercely contested. A primary aspect of (b)ordering is the creation of social roles that exist to categorize individuals within a heterogeneous group. For example, Turner (1967) shows that rites of passage (or the transcending of one bordered role into another) are particularly contentious social events. At these events, as individuals change their social categorization, they are more loosely defined, culturally and, thus, difficult to understand, manage, and control. Social processes of (b)ordering are metaphorically similar to physical borders, but they are more than spatial demarcations. They are symbolic methods of differentiating people, roles, and behaviors (Van Houtum and Van Naerssen 2002, p. 126).

Borders of social normativity are especially prevalent and particularly controversial in relation to sexual behavior, but they are not new. There are a series of processes and logics of exclusion that have made sexual borders so provocative. In modern times, human sexuality should be viewed as something that has been a victim of (sexual) repression as produced by particular Western traditions (Foucault 1984). Foucault (1984) famously discusses the ways in which the historical production of a discourse of sex has been "governed by the endeavor to expel from reality the forms of sexuality that…[are] not amenable to the strict economy of production…" (Foucault 1984, p. 316). In other words, "deviant" sexuality has been conditioned this way in part as a result of its non-productive nature: it arguably threatens the reproduction of necessary labor power (Seidman 2003).

As we consider Foucault's work, the long historical trajectory of the construction of the threatening sexual individual must be briefly addressed. In addition to the exoticizing and sexualizing images of indigenous populations, colonial "civilizing" also produced strict regulations of sexual behavior. As part of the civilizing mission of the seventeenth century, natural bodily functions became taboo, and "the body's sexual needs and other appetites were denied" (Hatty and Hatty 1999, p. 19). The body that violated this model (often indigenous, or "other") was viewed as socially inappropriate. Thus, the deviant sexualized individual is characterized as ugly and incongruent with social visibility.

As patriarchy has forged a society that seeks to preserve male bodies from the "physical dangers of...women" (Hatty and Hatty 1999, p. 37), this idea of the dangerous polluting body has come to characterize those who practice same-sex sexual behavior as well. The relatively recent abundance and political visibility of these "sexually disordered" bodies in the United States has helped to reinforce a state of moral panic that elicits and permits violence within certain communities. For example, in 2013 there has been a marked increase in the incidence of violent hate crimes against gay men in New York City, including historically accepting neighborhoods like Greenwich Village (Goodman 2013). Arguably, the escalation of the gay rights movement in the face of marriage equality laws has brought "alternative" and "deviant" family images to the forefront of national public consciousness. The resulting "moral panic" among certain (very vocal) communities involves an escalating essentialization of an "'uncontrolled' family form" that is emblematized by "an increasingly visible 'homosexual minority'" (Jakobsen 2002, p. 61). According to Jakobsen (2002), this perpetuates an understanding of the "apocalyptic homosexual" that threatens a continually reinforced normative family. While many in the U.S. may not subscribe to this idea, and legal and social structures are certainly changing to be more inclusive, this moral panic regarding "homosexuality" continues to inform a contentious view of "gay" people in America. This belief is stronger among some than others, but as the New York City incidences evidence, the very strong opinions of few can have very real effects on the lives of "homosexuals."

Further engaging neoliberal definitions of personhood, the responsible modern citizen is seen as self-regulating and rational. Similar to the behaviors illustrated by Martin (2007) in her description of manic-depressives, sexual deviants are perceived as failing at "monitoring" their desires and "harnessing" their emotions. Their behavior is not seen as "adaptive," and it degrades their value as a rational human individual. Foucault (1984, p. 317) argues that there is a "garrulous attention" to "multiple implantation[s] of 'perversions'" that "has us in a stew over sexuality." Ideally, sexuality should be both economically productive and politically conservative. As a result, revitalized tropes of safe sex ethics and moral citizenship have been reinforced in opposition to stigmatized sexual subjectivities. This certainly corresponds well with the current authority of neoliberal discourse and action (e.g., Fadlalla 2008; Gledhill 2007).

In addition to noting how deviance is considered "inefficient," scholars underscore the various other ways that deviant sexual cultures are portrayed as degenerate, dangerous, and contaminating. Regardless of the distance of posited unethical sexual engagement from the daily lives of most, specified acts are cast as denigrating one's moral self and denying the attendant benefits of "citizenship." Although the foundational ideologies of safe sex practices are pure, the ways in which their inverses are used to characterize "others" serve to make a "risky" person's life as futilely disease-ridden. The efforts of "risky" individuals to prove they are not passive receivers of this morally laden knowledge have resulted in various challengings of safe sex education (Davis 2009). For example, the rejection of the "spectacularized risk" of same-sex sexual behavior among men has sometimes amounted to a downplaying of sexual risk altogether (Davis 2009). As a counter-reaction to revitalized "moral panic" (Cohen 1972), a broader contestation of HIV prevention has emerged, which may be reflected in the increase in "barebacking stories" among men who have sex with men (Davis 2009).

Showing how rigid categorizations have been historically produced, Foucault's interrogations demystify and reinforce the existence of a "continuum" of sexuality. Also, Rubin's (1984) critical examination of a "sex hierarchy" evidences how sexual identities are laden with power differentials. She states that, according to the current system, "'good,' 'normal,' and 'natural' [sexuality] that should ideally be heterosexual, marital, monogamous, reproductive, and non-commercial is raised above those sexualities that…are understood as work of the devil, dangerous, psychopathological, infantile, or politically reprehensible" (Rubin 1984, pp. 280–282). The borders established here are meant to maintain order and, arguably, sexual repression. Additionally, the associated system bases its classification system on a specific portion of the population, disregarding "minority" sexualities.

Sexual Disorder and HIV/AIDS: The Perils of Medicalization

"HIV/AIDS stigmatization…is expressed [even within the gay population] as a set of beliefs that portray HIV-positive men as sexually promiscuous and uncaring, as ultimately responsible (paradoxically) both for their own infections and for infecting others" (Díaz 2007, p. 62).

A key aspect of the imaginary of "deviance" involves medicalizing individuals and populations. Medicalization is generally defined as the process that analyzes social phenomena in light of medically based knowledge (sometimes at the expense of socially and culturally based information). For example, medicalization has sponsored a re-evaluation of behavioral deviance as disease. In doing so, this process puts various bodies under the purview of medical professionals, and imbues these professionals with a special power in determining the course of peoples' lives. With the proliferation of advanced medical technologies, together with associated biomedical ideologies, medicalization has become a particularly prominent trend.

Coupled with logics of neoliberal subjecthood, trends of medicalization involve a dangerous reification of ("homosexual") identity and risk (for HIV/AIDS) despite evidence that risk behavior is much more complex than any particular bordered identity (Farmer 1992, 2005; Fassin 2007; Lock 2001; Padilla 2009). The concept of "risk" is deeply entrenched in social perceptions of marginalized people, as well as in the medicalization of subjectivities. As mentioned, medicalization has been identified as a major strategy of the state regulation used to ensure "security" (Wacquant 2009). Scholars have theorized the panoptic imposition of medical establishments upon "deviants" as a "clinical gaze" that seeks to identify, categorize, and rectify risky bodies (Foucault 1994[1963]; Holmes 2012).

Since the 1980s HIV/AIDS epidemic, same-sex sexual behavior has come into focus primarily as a dangerous (dirty) "risk" behavior. This has fostered further discrimination of "homosexual bodies" as "toxic" and threatening, as well as constructing the disease as a punishment of sorts. Fear of Lakoff's (2010) "health [in]security" has forged an environment of exception in which bodies can be further excluded, oppressed, and marginalized. As Farmer (1992) and others (e.g., Tan 1995; Vance 1991) evidence, a strict epidemiological approach to the spread of HIV/AIDS is wholly inadequate. Discussing the tendency for medical literature to remain falsely apolitical, Vance (1991, p. 47) addresses the propensity "to count acts rather than explore meaning." This individualizing medical narrative functions as "an ideological foundation" for avoiding the provision of quality health care information and services (Quam 1990, p. 42). Social scientists researching HIV/AIDS must be more critically engaged with questions of the conceiving of particular statuses, intentions, relationships, and social scripts regarding the modern "gay" "intersubjectivity" (Tan 1995, p. 96) through exploring the social construction of the sexual experience.

Same-sex sexual behavior has fallen victim to a great deal of social criticism. This has had the effect of painting individuals who practice these behaviors in a particular (negative) light. Additionally, those individuals who practice same-sex sexual behavior become subsumed into the cultural categories of "gay" and/or "homosexual." These processes involve moral arguments against same-sex behavior, as well as medicalized tropes of problematic riskiness. For example, gay-identified individuals have long been blamed for their own "riskiness" associated with HIV/AIDS transmission. However, their heterosexual counterparts are painted as innocent bystanders in regard to this disease. Early on in the HIV/AIDS epidemic, Morse and colleagues (Morse et al. 1991) referred to gay sex workers as vectors of HIV transmission into the heterosexual community. HIV/AIDS has been, and continues to be, referred to as a "gay disease." However, many scholars have recognized the incongruencies between the label "gay" and same-sex sexual behavior among men. For example, in Humphreys's (1970) ethnographic study of men who have sex with men (MSM), more than 50 % were married (to women), and "only 14 % of the individuals were primarily interested in homosexual relationships" (Loue 2008, p. 9). Furthermore, in 2005, a Swedish study by Ross and others determined that, of 244 men "of varying nationalities who had engaged in cybersex," 8.2 % "were self-identified heterosexuals who *reported* sex with other men" (Loue 2008, p. 9, emphasis added). Finally, in a study by Absalon and colleagues (2006), 50 % of MSM in a sample of 590 men in New York City (mostly black and Latino) reported sex with both men *and* women.

The identity of "homosexuality" and risk for HIV/AIDS should not be unified, reified, or objectified. Risk behavior is much more complex than sexual orientation. As Fassin (2007) evidences in South Africa, HIV/AIDS morbidity is linked to many socio-political factors. President Mbeki's radical claims that poverty and social inequity, rather than the HIV virus, lead to AIDS directly challenge biomedical explanations for AIDS. While his suggestions were viewed negatively by many in the international community, his explanations reflect a reality in South Africa and around the world: the social patterning of disease. Mbeki's assertions underscore the salience of experiences of poverty, malnutrition, and risk for other illnesses as conditioning vulnerability to all disease, but particularly HIV/AIDS. More deeply, Mbeki represents an important backlash in response to the insurgence of Western ideals in South Africa. While global public health initiatives strive to make modern medical advances available around the world, they also bring with them culturally laden foundations of the Western biomedical framework. HIV/AIDS and (homo)sexuality are increasingly medicalized even though "access to treatment is contingent on social relations and the ability to capitalize on social networks" (Ong and Collier 2005, p. 133). Mbeki's reactions and other social analyses of HIV/AIDS challenge strict medical perspectives and call attention to sociopolitical inequality as a driving force in HIV/AIDS morbidity and mortality. Although biomedically based perspectives are increasingly exploring social and political and even psychological influences on health risk, there is still a privileging of the knowledge produced by biological explanations.

Endeavoring to account for and understand the myriad forms of inequality that intersect as part of the lives of MSM of color, it is productive to see how ideologies and identities circulate globally. For example, Ong and Collier (2005) consider the tenuous nature of our current global climate: a "global assemblage" is created from a composite of forces that form a "broadly encompassing, seamless, and mobile" condition that remains "heterogeneous, contingent, unstable, partial, and situated" (Ong and Collier 2005, p. 12). Within this climate, complex "global forms" materialize as phenomena that exist "across diverse social and cultural situations" but are "only [completely] intelligible in relation to a common set of meanings, understandings, or societal structures" (Ong and Collier 2005, p. 11). These "global forms" are decontextualized and recontextualized in disparate global contexts by "specific technical infrastructures, administrative apparatuses, or value regimes" (Ong and Collier 2005, p. 11; also see Merry 2006). The importance of the global assemblage framework lies in its ability to assist us in making sense of a global world in which generalities and particularities interact to forge the lived experiences of individuals. Ideas of "biological life" (e.g., health and disease), and "access to goods and services" are tied up within these global forms (Ong and Collier 2005, p. 11). Concepts of HIV/AIDS prevention and treatment are no exception. Certain cultural variations, including Mbeki's school of thought and other "native" ways of understanding how and why people get HIV/AIDS, dictate alternative views of HIV/AIDS etiology and methodologies for prevention and treatment. However, the hegemonic forces of biomedical "technoscience" (Nguyen 2005) and politico-financial neoliberalism have extensive effects upon the structure and arrangement of global forms and tend to devalue alternative interpretations. Perspectives on HIV/AIDS presentation and treatment are greatly influenced by biomedical views of subjects as patients, and patients as a series of functioning parts to be approached in a clinical setting. A "medicalized body" is viewed through a Cartesian lens as a machine rather than a social entity (Hatty and Hatty 1999). An "invaded" or "infected" machine is faulty and, thus, less valuable. This defective and disordered body is both polluted and polluting, these bodies come to be conceptualized as "dangerous" (Douglas 1966, and others). Stigma associated with medicalized sexual risk exists *within* the body: race, "unbridled sexuality, disease, and other physical dangers" (Quam 1990, p. 41). Thus, all or many of these characteristics become synonymous with particular "dangerous" bodies.

HIV and AIDS are considered especially dirty and endangering because the orifices of the body where the HIV virus enters are symbolically dirty. HIV is painted as a disease that is received in polluted ways that are abnormal and repulsive. For instance, as Quam (1990) states, "within American culture and society, gays and intravenous drug users are anomalous, they do not fit 'normal' social categories. Such persons have [already] crossed some line, some boundary of nature that makes them less than human and essentially dangerous" (Quam 1990, p. 38). Because the cultural line between sickness and crime is "blurred" (Quam 1990, p. 34), risky individuals are assigned personal responsibility for their sickness and even the sickness of other "innocent" bystanders (e.g., heterosexuals). This process functions to take the responsibility of suffering away from society at large. Despite health "risk's" historical association with the individual's behaviors, individual behavior and psychology have been repeatedly found to be an insufficient method of intervention and prevention in terms of HIV/AIDS and other STIs (e.g., CDC 2010a). It has since been proven, instead, that health "risk" is constructed from a far more complex interaction of social, cultural, political, and economic forces.

The overemphasis on biomedical explanations for specific bodily conditions creates a picture of human experience that is wholly inadequate (e.g., Nguyen 2005). However, individuals are still increasingly motivated to couch the explanation of their conditions in biomedical terminology in order to gain access to advanced medical technologies. Also, despite great improvements in HIV treatments, access to treatment is still somewhat contingent on social relations, and "the ability of individuals to leverage social relations to obtain treatments…is constrained by the political economy of the transnational pharmaceutical…industry and, behind it, the global organization of capitalist production" (Nguyen 2005, p. 142). Finally, in the U.S., the escalating economic crisis has motivated a re-evaluation of the subsidization of AIDS treatment programs, which could threaten the health of many people (Chan 2006; Kane 2013).

"HIV Has Touched Them All"

Level of medical risk has become closely associated with the public and private definitions of identity. Valentine (2007) draws upon a deep scholarly tradition (Boellstorff 2005; Foucault 1983; Kulick 2003; West and Zimmerman 1987) as he shows how one's identity is forged based on a "complexly intertwined" relationship between self-identity and other identification as shaped by social power. He foregrounds the tensions and politics of self as they interact with various social definitions of personhood. The same argument can be applied to the technocratics of medicalization. In this vein then, technologies of medicine become technologies of the self.

As discussed, the medical establishment has become a powerful social force, and the associated "technomedical" perspective "objectifies the patient, mechanizes the body, and exalts practitioner over patient in how to manipulate the technology and decode the information it provides" (Davis-Floyd and Sargent 1997, p. 8). Discourses of "responsibility" and "discipline" often serve to advocate obedience to the authority of medical knowledge and health care personnel. Failure in one's capacity to follow certain behavioral prescriptions casts one as an "undesirable" patient and ("non-compliant") citizen. This is a project of panoptic surveillance and subject-making.

Additionally, the use of numbers and statistics creates a false objectivity that obscures subjective experiences of disease. A primary reason for the insufficiency of many current risk-based understandings of sexual behavior can be found in the disconnect between statistical explanations and lived realties. The use of statistical methods are not only scientific procedures for exposing "veiled implications of numbers; they are a language of…'numerical subjectivity,' where numerical considerations play a critical role in how life is both imagined and lived" (Sangaramoorthy 2012, p. 293). In addition to being incredibly flexible for experts (and not so for others), statistical categorizations and calculations maintain a monopoly on "truth" production. If the group to which one belongs appears to be statistically "at risk," this marks one as a "risky" individual, and this marking may paradoxically increase the chances of a "risky" life experience. Thus, co-occurring discourses of technocratics and risk management often breed feelings of internal and external mistrust and buttress moral discourses of self-governing more than they shape healthier lives (Foucault 1986; Gálvez 2011). HIV/AIDS is a clear example where medical technocratic knowledge, particularly that gleaned from statistical surveillance procedures, supports a simplified view of who is at risk and what it means to acquire and live with HIV (see also in this volume, Waldman's critique of the use of generalized knowledge in criminal prosecutions for HIV transmission). This employment of "objective methods and the logic of standardization…are ill-equipped to capture the local context that affects the way in which health is understood and acted upon" (Lock and Nguyen 2010, p. 53). However, this is not to say that quantitative data has no place; it simply is not the whole story. A valuing of both types of analysis is incredibly important, and something that is necessarily emerging as a standard in health research. In addition to broad understandings of disease patterning, ethnographically minded critiques of the violent normalcies that become intertwined with these perceptions can assist health promotion projects in being more effective.

If one is considered to be "risky" or "at risk," one must learn to adequately manage this risk. These ideas of self-regulation of risk correspond to Foucault's interpretations of sexual discipline and ethical mandate to control one's sensual desires (Foucault 1986). A failure here marks a failed personhood. In order to show inconsistencies in the self-regulatory model, Farmer (2005) critically identifies its patterned nature in terms of poverty. Adding to this discussion, this chapter focuses on the significance of multiple discriminations associated with HIV/AIDS, sexual behavior, and ethnicity. The stigma of "homosexuality" is often "enmeshed" with that of HIV/AIDS (Manalansan 2003, and others). While strides have been made in organizing for HIV/AIDS education and outreach, this should not downplay the significance of homophobia in producing the marginalization of "homosexuals" and buttressing their risks for suffering and disease. Furthermore, social marginalization on the basis of this "toxic" sexuality complicates socio-economic status and may add another dimension of marginalization to those struggling to make ends meet (particularly ethnic minorities). Differential assessments of worth and layered marginalization regarding sexual toxicity and disease suffering produce a space in which those who practice same-sex sexual behavior exist at the margins of society inscribed with particular effects on their bodies. For all three "discriminations" examined in this chapter, a congregation of social, symbolic, and ideological forces coerces individuals into an ideological margin that creates and perpetuates negative physical/health effects (Nelson 2009). Exploring aspects of these immaterial processes paint a fuller picture of how individuals become disadvantaged.

It is apparent that sexuality is a fundamental part of human experience with transnational application. Sexuality, while linked to biological processes, is yet another aspect of human identity, featuring continuous processes of performance, reconciliation, and negotiation. However, theorists of sexuality must grapple with an important paradox: the discrimination of the private and intimate act of sexuality through the corpus of a discourse that is fundamentally public. In support of this, the International Council on Human Rights Policy (2009) recognizes that sexual rights fundamentally exist at the intersection of the private body and the body politic. Thus, a private–public methodology that examines public discourse and its interpolation into private life "is essential for [an adequate] defense" of (sexual) inequality (Sen 2005, p. 94). Furthermore, a critical investigation of the construction of a multi-faceted identity may assist in the prevention of what Farmer (2004, p. 287) terms the "conflation" of structural violence with cultural difference and/or "otherness." An inadequate consideration of idiosyncratic differentiations in identity, generally, and the naturalization of sexual difference with disease, specifically, allows one to distance oneself from marginal segments of society and perpetuate generalizing assumptions. This then permits the targeting of such marginalized identities as dangerous and morally reprehensible, or targets for violence.

The development of biosocial communities that are intimately connected with the biomedical community and its definitions of risk have simplified the experiences of diseases like HIV/AIDS. For example, regardless of individual desire and sexual practices, same-sex sex (especially anal intercourse) has come to define individuals more than personal activities or "rationally based desire" (Lang 1990). Bad sex and dirty bodies are attached to medical risk, and are used to define the lives of men who have sex with other men. Although "there are substantial numbers of [men] for whom sex is but one entry among many on the social menu...AIDS has touched, influenced and marked them all" (Lang 1990, p. 176). Thus, popular thought views these men as tainted and polluted for life.

The State and State Interventions

Every state is ethical in as much as one of its most important functions is to raise the great mass of the population to a particular cultural and moral level; a level...which corresponds...to the interests of the ruling classes (Gramsci 1971, p. 258).

In the modern world, the state has various functions. A primary venture of the state apparatus is the maintenance of a healthy population. Healthy subjects not only provide a more successful labor force (Lock and Nguyen 2010), but the cultivation of adequate healthcare preserves state privileges in the moral politics of health ideologies (Andaya, forthcoming). In other words, promoting and preserving healthy subjects (or, at least, promulgating a convincing picture of this) affords state organizations more legitimacy in determining the structure of health care access. In cultivating and preserving a "healthy" society, state policies, and activities target "risky" individuals as threats to state security. Medical deviance and disease are cast as crimes against the general populace. In preventing these "crimes," "unprecedented priority" is contracted to the police and other "justice" making arms of the state "to bend indocile categories and territories to the common norm" (Wacquant 2009, p. 8). One of Weber's "basic functions of the state," security making involves a strict punitive approach to broadly defined "criminal" offenses. Included in the strategies employed for this security making is medicalization and penalization (Wacquant 2009). According to the "global obsession with security" (Goldstein 2010, p. 490), the perception of omnipresent criminality incites a constant "feeling of insecurity" upon which the state must fiercely enact its strategies.

In order to fulfill its "promise" to ensure "security" and to promote "efficiency," the state must maintain a vigilant monitoring of its population. As Foucault (Foucault 1995[1977]) famously discussed, the panoptic power of the state makes efficient use of resources to create an impression of ever-present supervision that shapes daily lives. For instance, in the United States, a logic of "punitive panopticism" has increasingly ordered the "management" of "dispossessed, deviant, and dangerous categories" of people (Wacquant 2009, p. 225). In so doing, peoples labeled as "deviant" have been vilified and criminalized to various degrees. While many scholars (Gledhill 2007; Lock and Nguyen 2010; Martin 2007; Wacquant 2009) have linked this process to the insurgence of neoliberal ideologies of efficiency and self-regulation into modern state policies, ideologies of responsibility beyond "technologies of the self" also serve as regulatory forces (Andaya, forthcoming).

The most obvious example of (punitive) state regulation penetrating people's sexual lives is the "hypercriminalization" of sex offenders in the United States. Sexual criminality has long been feared as a corrupting social force. However, "sexual predators" have been increasingly portrayed as a threat to society's children and, consequently, one that must be kept behind bars, or under very strict supervision. The system of "blacklisting" that has been put in place has ensured that these "perverts" remain vilified wherever they go. A "panic over the 'sexual psychopath'" (Wacquant 2009, p. 226) has, in a very real way, stripped the humanity of these sexual deviants. Without arguing that sex offenders do not deserve punishment, Wacquant (2009) discusses how the essentialization and vilification of sex offenders misleads communities into a false sense of security while simultaneously dispossessing and permanently criminalizing large numbers of people.

Same-sex sexual behavior is yet another type of essentialized sexual deviance. In fact, same-sex acts are still criminalized in various locations around the world (ILGA 2011, p. 9; UN HRC 2011; see too, in this volume, Cobb; DeJong and Long; Dwyer; Nichols; Pearce and Cooper). Similar to sex offenders, "homosexual" populations in the U.S. are "branded" with certain essentialized characteristics: they too are seen to threaten the sacred institution of the American family, act without sexual restraint, and exploit children as sexual predators. The "canonization" of the "working family" in the face of changing gender relations and the general deterioration of the domestic sphere plays a strong role in both the demonization of the "sexual predator" (Wacquant 2009, p. 214) and the social contention regarding same-sex sexual behaviors. In other words, a state of "sexual panic" motivates a vilification of most—if not all—sexual deviants (Lancaster 2011).

The American punitive state may not overtly criminalize "homosexual" behavior today, but many of the same principles of ambivalence, and even "panic," are associated with same-sex sexual behavior and its consequent "deviant" sexual "risk." A history of police surveillance and invasions of gay baths and bars in the New York and San Francisco evidences public anxiety toward gay culture, particularly gay men (Bérubé 1996). Although this regulation may no longer be as overtly anti-gay as past "anti-bath" and "anti-bar" campaigns, the foundational ideology remains the same. The growing powers of medical theories and knowledge have served as a continuing rationale to monitor gay establishments (e.g., Colfax et al. 2011; Elford et al. 2011). While these intervention techniques may be honorably motivated and successful (i.e., they attempt to increase the effectiveness of public health outreach programs by targeting places where "at risk" populations congregate), they are built upon historical feelings of distress regarding "homosexual" behavior. Despite the proliferation of "impartial" medical endeavors, a masked social and political "concern" about gay life remains.

Transnationalism and Crossing Borders

As we become an increasingly globalized society, it is imperative that we consider the ways in which types of social discrimination interact with one another. For example, while analyzing and critiquing the demonization of same-sex sexual behavior is incredibly beneficial, it is also necessary to consider the different forms this behavior takes as it interacts with different social/cultural characteristics and conditions. Not only does this diversify our perspectives on sexual behavior, but it also helps us to better understand various subjectivities. In order to better understand how borders and boundaries are expressed and policed across various social settings, anthropological analysis has targeted a transnational approach as a way of reflecting ideas of inherent border permeability. Beyond a simple critical perspective, post-national theories allow scholars to deconstruct (b)ordering techniques that tend to disregard and devalue large numbers of "deviant" individuals. The transnational perspective works to critique the foundational assumptions of those logics of exclusion that have been discussed thus far in this chapter.

The paradigm of transnational or, more appropriately, transborder (Stephen 2007) studies sets forth to consider the artificial construction of borders (in their physical *and* social dimensions). Resisting the confines of national boundaries and other socially delineated borders, the framework of transnationalism opens new and important avenues for scholarly inquiry. Transnationalism brings focus to the ways in which individual and collective identities are constructed, challenged, and reinforced within transnational social fields and "meshworks" (Escobar 2003 *in* Stephen 2007). More broadly, transnational analysis also questions our theoretical bounding of peoples and topics. In relation to Stephen's (2007) transbordered fields, the more general study of border crossers endeavors to broaden our conceptions of social boundaries to include variously constructed social categories as they attempt to rigidly categorize a much more fluid human experience. For example, since "hetero" and "homo" are "assumed to index [heteronormative] gender" categories, these distinctions themselves must be called into question (Boellstorff 2005, p. 92). The destabilizing of heteronormative (b)ordering may be aided by viewing "homosexual" behavior through the lens of cultural difference and multilayered understandings. Seeing homosexual and heterosexual as falsely bordered identities with sets of assumed behavioral characteristics and social implications makes the transnational/transborder framework incredibly instructive for MSM public health outreach projects. Injecting conceptions of sex and sexuality into this post-modern, post-national paradigm, this chapter seeks to diversify understandings of transbordered lives and build upon other anthropological accounts of social "othering" resulting from the traversing of certain boundaries. Individuals who cross such taboo boundaries may be considered hybrid and, thus, difficult to categorize. In this sense, they are especially vulnerable to discrimination and abuse. Interrogating hybrid and layered identities as part of the experience of the marginalized "other" and "outsider" (Baker-Cristales 2008) exposes the complexity behind processes of social marginalization.

In order to adequately advocate for modern subjects of scientific inquiry, scholars are concerned with forms of "transnational governmentality" that subject hybrid populations to "tactics of containment and control" (Baker-Cristales 2008, p. 351). Originally explored at length by Foucault (1991), governmentality is defined as that regulation which is wielded through disciplinary discourse, using knowledge and power to define what is normal/natural and what is toxic/unacceptable to the state and its populace. The application of such processes to a global stage expands governmentality beyond individual nation states and their regulatory apparatuses (discussed earlier). Transnational governmentality is especially concerned with regulating subjects that cross national borders. Problematically, the ideological underpinnings of this regulation are often based in ideas of cultural and ethnic difference. Therefore, many ethnic minorities are assumed to be border crossers, and descendants of immigrants may still be treated as foreigners depending on their ability to assimilate.

Connecting AIDS to Sontag's (1979) discussion of cancer as a pollutant, parallels can be drawn to HIV/AIDS: "alien cells" performing a "ruthless, [yet] secret invasion" (Quam 1990, p. 39). Cancer and AIDS are two major modern plagues that remain incurable and are at the center of social consciousness. While cancer is largely painted as more 'honorable' and its victims less culpable, HIV/AIDS is dirtier and more heavily stigmatized (though, smokers who acquire lung cancer are similarly blamed for their disease). Both afflictions are perverse invaders that are particularly devious as they alter the body's natural mechanisms of healing. Cultural "aliens" are similarly conceptualized as invading germs that threaten the unified fabric of society.

The migration of individuals who practice same-sex sexual behavior have forged a layering of seemingly disparate marked identities (gendered, ethnic, sexual, migratory, etc.). Importantly, these identities have differential salience depending on situational and social conditions. While exploring the layering of these toxicities and investigating the ways in which ethnic identity, cultural knowledge, and sexuality interact with each other, a more nuanced investigation of discrimination is established. The possession of multiple marked identities can often contribute to increased marginalization (e.g., as one is ostracized from both mainstream ethnic groups and mainstream LGBT organizations). To better understand this condition, scholars use the framework of intersectionality (see Crenshaw 1994; and earlier works).

Scholars of intersectionality avoid essentializing any particular characteristic (see, e.g., in this volume, Ball; Johnson; Woods). Instead, identity is understood as a complex interaction of many contextual characteristics. For instance, social context related to ethnicity, class, and access to resources differentiates the experiences of sexual identities. Making use of this conceptual model makes our understanding of human thought and behavior more comprehensive and practical. Specifically, intersectionality brings into better relief categories of behavior conditioned by flexible and multifaceted subjective identities. The imperative to investigate these categories may be associated with the exacerbated health risks of intersectional populations.

Valentine (2007, p. 63) evidences the ways in which certain (re)presentations of those who practice same-sex sexual behavior have forged a sense of mainstream "sameness" that forefronts "sober, respectable" images. This concept of "sameness" is also prevalent in medical ideologies of risk (e.g., Lock 2001). As a result, elements of social difference (e.g., class, race, and culture/ethnicity) "are made invisible" (Valentine 2007, p. 63). An intersectional analysis is one productive way of recognizing the interplay between social definitions of identity and everyday lived experiences and making these interactions more visible.

In the vein of fluid and varied experience, Valentine (2007) elegantly points out important differences in the uses of categories like gay, transgender, drag queen, etc. Although some service providers and activists affiliate this variation to a Marxian "false consciousness" (Abu-Lughod 1990), Valentine claims that the fluidity of identity shown at Clubhouse balls is more congruent with lived realities than the institutionalized meanings of gay and transgender. For instance, characteristics of age, race, and class greatly affect the "practices and understandings" of gender and sexuality (Valentine 2007, p. 100). Thus, these categories "don't merely inflect or intersect with those experiences we call gender and sexuality, but rather *shift the very boundaries of what 'gender' and 'sexuality' can mean* in particular contexts" (Valentine 2007, p. 100, emphasis in original). Just as the gendered selves of those within the conceptualized transgender community are "fluid or androgynous," those lumped into the category of "homosexual," or even "at risk" for HIV/AIDS, have much more variable experiences than those "captured by the firm categories of identity politics" (Valentine 2007, p. 101).

Intersections in identity have significant ramifications in terms of understanding the variation in health outcomes. For example, the construction of HIV/AIDS as congruent with "gay identity" adds to existent social othering to procure violent outcomes. The significant social ramifications of HIV/AIDS are exacerbated by certain ethnic (or other) "minority" statuses (Díaz 2007). For instance, the CDC reports that Latino Americans are the second most likely group to develop HIV/AIDS following African Americans (CDC 2010b). Racial discrimination, low socioeconomic status, and distrust of authority have been shown to contribute to these higher incidence rates (CDC 2010b; Lemelle 2003). Many outreach programs attempting to curb the HIV/AIDS epidemic fail to adequately explore the various other social processes at work that affect the health and wellbeing of those who have or are at risk for HIV/AIDS.

Toward a Critical Ethnography of Sexuality

Acting as proper advocates for health and human rights, the social-structural and symbolic characteristics of perpetual, everyday violence must be taken into account (especially their implications on health). Following Beasley (2005), Halberstam (1998), and others, I advocate a nuanced (*queer*) critical ethnography of sexuality that merges critical medical anthropology, a critical anthropology of human rights (including engagement and compassionate solidarity), and an assessment of the interaction of these discourses and disciplines with sexuality and sexual rights. This perspective is queer oriented not only because it grapples with issues of deviant sexuality, but because it is oriented toward viewing boundaries of (sexual) expression as fluid and mutable instead of absolute (see too, Ball, this volume). Linking sexual health promotion to human rights approaches may offer particular benefits in terms of gaining social support (Parker 2007). In accordance with Merry's (2006) understanding of the significance of ethnographic accounts and the pursuance of ethnography through a human rights framework, a critical ethnography of sexuality considers ethnographic methods as important avenues for chronicling and understanding "grievances" and approaching their solutions in a holistic and socially engaged manner. This engagement also involves a sense of compassionate involvement that personalizes violence and inequality.

As a result of cultural trepidations, sex and sexuality are underexplored fundamental characteristics of human identity. As we attempt to construct freedom of sexuality as a "human right," it is important to recognize that (at least contemporarily) discrimination on the basis of sexual identity occurs cross culturally (albeit in disparate contexts, for different reasons, and to differing degrees). Methodologically, Kendall (1995) states human sexuality fundamentally complicates "scientific research" because it is simultaneously "biological, psychological, physiological, social, cultural and economic" (Kendall 1995, p. 249). The holistic approach of anthropological ethnographic inquiry certainly aids in demystifying this conundrum.

Anthropological analyses are especially useful in their consideration of both macro and micro levels (Erickson 2011). Although ethnographic studies are often situated in particular communities and based on what individual people say, the discipline's holistic perspective affords anthropologists a more culturally, historically, and politically situated evaluation of social issues (Burrell and Shuford 2011). In addition to hallmark methods like participant observation requiring significant in-depth understandings of local conditions (and the ways they are influenced by global forces), anthropologists tend to build more long-standing and intimate relationships with their informants. "Subjects" become humanized in a unique way, and the day-to-day effects of social issues are foregrounded.

Contemporary anthropology's use of multivocal dialog to enhance scientific rigor supports a passion for public engagement and social critique. We should reject the individualization of shame that is prevalent in systems of symbolic and structural violence. A certain "state of hypervigilance" and "steadfast refusal" of naturalized social inequalities must be incorporated into any powerful analysis of violence (Scheper-Hughes and Bourgois 2004, p. 27). Intimate dialogic engagement with informants assists researchers in better encapsulating the daily interactions of individuals, and their underlying social conventions and assumptions. Studying the ways in which people perceive and categorize their world is not a novel concept. Importantly, however, knowledge of these categorizations can be (mis)used as ways of denying people access to resources. Thus, anthropological investigations of categorizing processes expose an essential part of human existence, while evidencing important discrepancies in peoples' material lives. Performing analyses on how individuals become placed in these social categories can assist in better identifying "vulnerable" populations, and responding to human rights abuses (e.g., Messer 2009).

Broadly, critical ethnographers of sexuality draw particular "attention to the diversity of social arrangements for sexual expression, the existence of sexual subcultures that may have different health risks from other groups, and the extent to which political-economic factors" limit the potential for people to pursue their desires (Erickson 2011, p. 283). Additionally, these ethnographers provide "thick description" (Geertz 1973) of the personal experiences of gender, sex, love, and reproduction. This "meaning-centered understanding" of sexual health can contribute to the development of "interventions that speak to the real needs and concerns that people have" (Erickson 2011, p. 283). Thus, ethnographic insights are increasingly called upon to add to public health initiatives. Corresponding to a long anthropological tradition of exploring human diversity, it is imperative to pay careful attention to various social and cultural constitutions across the globe, and the way they may be merged into a "radically new understanding of the full range of human sexual experience" focusing on the importance of "detailed interpretation" of diversity (Corrêa et al. 2008, p. 120).

Conclusion

Through exploring the various ways in which MSM and MSM of color are marginalized, this chapter underscores the complexity of sexual discrimination. Initial discussions regarding processes of producing and understanding discriminatory social categories focus upon the maintenance and reinforcement of social borders. In doing so, I attempt to generalize my discussion of a particular case study to apply to "minorities" more broadly. Additionally, implicating cultural processes and state apparatuses highlights the naturalization of social suffering and its effects on the health of MSM of color, among others. Specifically, risk-based interventions are critiqued for their contribution to substantiating cultural assumptions. In order to combat naturalizations of symbolic dirtiness and riskiness, anthropology's traditions on "listening" and critically engaging are promoted to better support our discourses of inclusion and equality, specifically those related to health (e.g., "health as a human right"). Although many health promotion projects are dominated by a desire for objective scientific truth, we know that ideas of healthy behavior and intervention solutions are couched in cultural assumptions and misguided reductions (e.g., Hahn and Inhorn 2009; Singer and Erickson 2011). While understandings of medical risk are not useless, they are only one feature of a much more complex picture.

In an increasingly globalized and transnational world, it is imperative to be concerned with how various social conditions and assumptions interact to inhibit equal agency, justice, and access to (health) "rights." Studying this very interaction exposes a great deal about each individual deleterious social category as well as the procedures by which they interact and hybridize. Engaged in a tradition of listening to unheard and underheard voices, anthropologists are decisively considerate of how these voices can be used to combat biases and inequities inherent in social programs. Over 100 years of modern anthropological theory and practice suggests that ethnographers may be particularly well suited to contribute to a cultural self-reflexivity that may increase the effectiveness and expediency of movements for social justice and projects pursuing health equity.

References

Absalon, J., Fuller, C. M., Ompad, D. C., Blaney, S., Koblin, B., Galea, S., et al. (2006). Gender differences in sexual behaviors, sexual partnerships and HIV drug users in New York City. *AIDS Behavior, 10*, 707–7015.
Abu-Lughod, L. (1990). The romance of resistance: Tracing transformations of power through Bedouin women. *American Ethnologist, 17*(1), 41–55.
Abu-Lughod, L. (2006). Writing against culture. In E. Lewin (Ed.), *Feminist anthropology: A reader* (pp. 153–169). Malden, MA: Blackwell Publishing.
Agamben, G. (1998). *Homo sacer: Sovereign power and bare life*. Stanford University Press.
Agamben, G. (2005). *State of exception*. Chicago, IL: The University of Chicago Press.
Andaya, E. (Forthcoming) Conceiving statistics: The local practice and global politics of reproductive health care in Havana. In N. Burke (Ed.), *Health travels: Cuban health(care) on and off the Island*. Berkeley, CA: University of California Press.
Appadurai, A. (1996). *Modernity at large: Cultural dimensions of globalization*. Minneapolis, MN: University of Minnesota Press.
Ardener, E. (2006). Belief and the problem of women and the 'problem' revisited. In E. Lewin (Ed.), *Feminist anthropology: A reader* (pp. 47–65). Malden, MA: Blackwell Publishing.
Baker-Cristales, B. (2008). Magical pursuits: Legitimacy and representation in a transnational political field. *American Anthropology, 110*(3), 349–359.
Beasley, C. (2005). *Gender and sexuality: Critical theories, critical thinkers*. London, UK: Sage Publications.
Bérubé, A. (1996). The history of gay bathhouses. In E. G. Colter, W. Hoffman, E. Pendleton, A. Redick, & D. Serlin (Eds.), *Policing public sex* (pp. 187–220). Boston, MA: South End Press.
Boellstorff, T. (2005). *The gay archipelago: Sexuality and nation in Indonesia*. Princeton, NJ: Princeton University Press.
Bourdieu, P. (1977). *Outline of a theory of practice*. New York, NY: Cambridge University Press.
Brodkin, K. (2006). Toward a unified theory of class, race, and gender. In E. Lewin (Ed.), *Feminist anthropology: A reader* (pp. 129–146). Malden, MA: Blackwell Publishing.

Burrell, J. (2010). In and out of rights: Security, migration, and human rights talk in postwar Guatemala. *Journal of Latin American and Caribbean Anthropology, 15*(1), 90–115.

Burrell, J. & Shuford J. (2011). Ethnography. In *Encyclopedia of immigrant health* (pp. 65–660). New York, NY: Springer.

Butler, J. (1990). *Gender trouble*. New York, NY: Routledge.

Centers for Disease Control and Prevention (CDC) (2010a). *Establishing a holistic framework to reduce inequities in HIV, viral hepatitis, STDs, and tuberculosis in the United States*. Retrieved from www.cdc.gov/socialdeterminants

Centers for Disease Control and Prevention (CDC) (2010b). *HIV among gay, bisexual and other men who have sex with men (MSM)*. Retrieved from http://www.cdc.gov/hiv/topics/msm/pdf/msm.pdf

Chan, S. (2006). Adults on welfare with H.I.V. or AIDS hit with rent increase. *The New York Times*, October 5. Retrieved from http://www.nytimes.com/2006/10/05/nyregion/05aids.html

Cohen, S. (1972). *Folk devils and moral panics*. New York, NY: Routledge.

Colfax, G. N., Mansergh, G., Guzman, R., Vittinghoff, E., Marks, G., Rader, M., et al. (2011). Drug use and sexual risk behavior among gay and bisexual men who attend circuit parties: A venue-based comparison. *Journal of Acquired Immune Deficiency Syndromes (JAIDS), 28*, 373–379.

Collier, J. F., & Yanagisako, S. J. (Eds.). (1987). *Gender and kinship: Essays toward a unified analysis*. Stanford, CA: Stanford University Press.

Collier, J. F., & Yanagisako, S. J. (1989). Theory in anthropology since feminist practice. *Critique of Anthropology, 9*(2), 27–37.

Corrêa, S., Petchesky, R., & Parker, R. (2008). *Sexuality, health, and human rights*. London, UK: Routledge.

Crenshaw, K. W. (1994). Mapping the margins: Intersectionality, identity politics, and violence against women of color. In M.A. Fineman & R. Mykitiuk (Eds.), *The public nature of private violence* (pp. 93–118). New York, NY: Routledge.

Davis, M. (2009). Spectacular risk, public health and the technological mediation of the sexual practices of gay men. In A. Brook & P. Tovey (Eds.), *Men's health: Body, identity and social context*, pp. 107–125. Oxford, UK: Wiley-Blackwell.

Davis-Floyd, R., & Sargent, C. F. (1997). *Childbirth and authoritative knowledge: Cross-cultural perspectives*. Berkeley, CA: University of California Press.

Deleuze, G., & Guattari, F. (1977). *Capitalism and schizophrenia: Anti-Oedipus*. New York, NY: The Viking Press.

Díaz, R. M. (2007). In our own backyard: HIV/AIDS stigmatization in the Latino gay community. In N. Teunis & G. H. Herdt (Eds.), *Sexual inequalities and social justice* (pp. 50–65). Berkeley, CA: University of California Press.

Douglas, M. (1966). *Purity and danger: An analysis of concepts of pollution and taboo*. New York, NY: Routledge.

Elford, J., G. Bolding, & Sherr, L. (2011). Peer education has no significant impact on HIV behaviors among gay men in London. *AIDS, 15*(4), pp. 535–538.

Erickson, P. I. (2011). Sexuality, medical anthropology, and public health. In M. Singer & P. I. Erickson (Eds.), *A companion to medical anthropology* (pp. 271–288). Malden, MA: Blackwell Publishing.

Fadlalla, A. H. (2008). The neoliberalization of compassion. In J. L Collins, B. Williams, & M. di Leonardo (Eds.), *New landscapes of inequality: Neoliberalism and erosion of democracy in America* (pp. 209–228). Santa Fe, NM: School of Advanced Research Press.

Farmer, P. (1992). *AIDS and accusation: Haiti and the geography of blame*. Berkeley, CA: University of California Press.

Farmer, P. (2004). On suffering and structural violence: A view from below. In N. Scheper-Hughes & P. Bourgois (Eds.). *Violence in war and peace* (pp. 281–289). Malden, MA: Blackwell Publishing.

Farmer, P. (2005). *Pathologies of power: Health, human rights, and the new war on the poor*. Berkeley, CA: University of California Press.

Fassin, D. (2007). *When bodies remember: Experiences and politics of AIDS in South Africa.* Berkeley, CA: University of California Press.

Foucault, M. (1983). The subject and power. In H. L. Dreyfus & P. Rabinow (Eds.), *Michel Foucault: Beyond structuralism and hermeneutics* (pp. 208–226). New York, NY: Pantheon Books.

Foucault, M. (1984). Sex and truth: The repressive hypothesis. In P. Rabinow (Ed.), *The Foucault reader* (pp. 301–330). New York, NY: Pantheon Books.

Foucault, M. (1986). *The care of the self: Volume 3 of the history of sexuality.* New York, NY: Pantheon Books.

Foucault, M. (1991). Governmentality. In G. Burchell, C. Gordon & P. Miller (Eds.), *The Foucault effect: Studies in governmentality* (pp. 87–104). Chicago, IL: University of Chicago Press.

Foucault, M. (1994[1963]). *The birth of the clinic.* New York, NY: Vintage Press.

Foucault, M. (1995[1977]). *Discipline and punish: The birth of the prison.* New York, NY: Vintage Press.

Gálvez, A. (2011). *Patient citizens, immigrant mothers: Mexican women, public prenatal care, and the birth-weight paradox.* New Brunswick, NJ: Rutgers University Press.

Geertz, C. (1973). *The interpretation of cultures.* New York: Basic Books.

Gledhill, J. (2007). Neoliberalism. In D. Nugent & J. Vincent (Eds.), *A companion to the anthropology of politics* (pp. 332–348). Malden, MA: Blackwell Publishing.

Goffman, E. (1963). *Stigma: Notes on the management of spoiled identity.* Englewood Cliffs, NJ: Prentice-Hall, Inc.

Goldstein, D. (2007). Human rights as culprit, human rights as victim: Rights and security in the state of exception. In M. Goodale & S. E. Merry (Eds.), *The practice of human rights: Tracking law between the local and the global* (pp. 49–77). Cambridge, UK: Cambridge University Press.

Goldstein, D. (2010). Toward a critical anthropology of security. *Current anthropology* 51(4), 487–527. Retrieved from http://www.jstor.org

Goodale, M. (Ed.). (2010). *Human rights: An anthropological reader.* Malden, MA: Blackwell Publishing.

Goodman, J. D. (2013). 2 more antigay attacks are reported in Manhattan. *The New York Times,* May 21. Retrieved from http://www.nytimes.com/2013/05/22/nyregion/2-more-antigay-attacks-are-reported-in-manhattan.html

Gramsci, A. (1971). *Selections from the prison notebooks.* New York, NY: International Publishers.

Hahn, R. A., & Inhorn, M. C. (Eds.). (2009). *Anthropology and public health: Bridging differences in culture and society.* Oxford, UK: Oxford University Press.

Halberstam, J. (1998). *Female masculinities.* Durham, NC: Duke University Press.

Hatty, S. E., & Hatty, J. (1999). *The disordered body: Epidemic disease and cultural transformation.* Albany, NY: State University of New York Press.

Holmes, S. (2012). The clinical gaze in the practice of migrant health: Mexican migrants in the United States. *Social Science and Medicine, 74,* 873–881.

Humphreys, L. (1970). *Tearoom trade: Impersonal sex in public places.* Chicago, IL: Aldine.

International Council on Human Rights Policy (2009). Sexuality and human rights: A discussion paper. Versoix, Switzerland: International Council on Human Rights Policy.

International Lesbian, Gay, Bisexual, Transgender and Intersex Association (ILGA) (2011). *State-sponsored homophobia: A world survey of laws criminalising same-sex sexual acts between consenting adults.* Retrieved from http://www.ilga.org

Jakobsen, J. (2002) Can homosexuals end western civilization as we know it? Family values in a global economy. In A. Cruz-Malave & M. F. Manalansan (Eds.), *Queer globalizations: Citizenship and the afterlife of colonialism* (pp. 49–70). New York, NY: NYU Press.

Jenks, A. C. (2011). From "lists of traits" to "open-mindedness": Emerging issues in cultural competence education. *Culture, Medicine and Psychiatry, 35*(2), 209–235.

Kane, J. (2013). Health reform's uncertain impact on HIV patients. *PBS NewsHour*, June 3. Retrieved from http://www.pbs.org/newshour/rundown/2013/06/health-reforms-impact-on-hiv-groups.html.

Kendall, C. (1995). The construction of risk in AIDS control programs. In R. G. Parker & J. H. Cagnon (Eds.), *Conceiving sexuality: Approaches to sex research in a postmodern world* (pp. 249–258). New York, NY: Routledge.

Kleinman, A. & Benson, P. (2006). Anthropology in the clinic: The problem of cultural competency and how to fix it. *PLoS Medicine, 3*(10). Retrieved from http://www.plosmedicine.org

Kulick, D. (2003). No. *Language and Communication, 23*(2), 139–151.

Lacan, J. (1968). *The language of the self: The function of language in psychoanalysis.* Baltimore, MD: Johns Hopkins University Press.

Lakoff, A. (2010). Two regimes of global health. *Humanity, 24,* 60–80.

Lancaster, R. N. (2011). *Sex panic and the punitive state.* Berkeley, CA: University of California Press.

Lang, N. G. (1990). Sex, politics, and guilt: A study of homophobia and the AIDS phenomenon. In D. A. Feldman (Ed.), *Culture and AIDS* (pp. 169–182). New York, NY: Praeger.

Lemelle, A. J., Jr. (2003). Linking the structure of African American criminalization to the spread of HIV/AIDS. *Journal of Contemporary Criminal Justice, 19*(3), 270–292.

Lock, M. (2001). The tempering of medical anthropology: The troubling of natural categories. *Medical Anthropology Quarterly, 15*(4), 478–492.

Lock, M., & Nguyen, V. (2010). *An anthropology of biomedicine.* Malden, MA: Wiley-Blackwell.

Loue, S. (2008). Defining men who have sex with men (MSM). In S. Loue (Ed.), *Health issues confronting minority men who have sex with men* (pp. 3–23). New York, NY: Springer.

Manalansan, M. F. (2003). *Global divas: Filipino gay men in the diaspora.* Durham, NC: Duke University Press.

Martin, E. (2007). *Bipolar expeditions: Mania and depression in American culture.* Princeton, NJ: Princeton University Press.

Merry, S. E. (2006). Human rights and gender violence: Translating international law into local justice. Chicago: University of Chicago Press.

Messer, E. (2009). Anthropology, human rights, and social transformation. In M. Goodale (Ed.), *Human rights: An anthropological reader* (pp. 103–134). Oxford, UK:John Wiley & Sons.

Morse, E. V., Simon, P. M., Osofsky, H. J., Balson, P. M., & Gaumer, R. H. (1991). The male street prostitute: A vector for transmission of HIV infection into the heterosexual world. *Social Science and Medicine, 32*(5), 535–539.

Nguyen, V. (2005). Antiretroviral globalism, biopolitics and therapeutic citizenship. In A. Ong & S. J. Collier (Eds.), *Global assemblages: Technology, politics and ethics as anthropological problems* (pp. 124–144). Malden, MA: Blackwell Publishing.

Nelson, D. M. (2009). *Reckoning: The ends of war in Guatemala.* Durham, NC: Duke University Press.

Ong, A., & Collier, S. J. (2005). *Global assemblages: Technology, politics, and ethics as anthropological problems.* Malden, MA: Blackwell Publishing.

Padilla, M. B. (2009). The limits of "heterosexual AIDS": Ethnographic research on tourism and male sexual labor in the Dominican Republic. In R. A. Hahn & M. C. Inhorn (Eds.), *Anthropology and public health: Bridging differences in culture and society* (pp. 142–164). Oxford, UK: Oxford University Press.

Parker, R. G. (2007). Sexuality, health and human rights. *American Journal of Public Health, 97*(6), 972–973.

Quam, D. (1990). The sick role, stigma and pollution: The case of AIDS. In D. A. Feldman (Ed.), *Culture and AIDS* (pp. 29–44). New York, NY: Praeger Publishers.

Reiter, R. (1975). *Toward an anthropology of women.* New York, NY: New York University Press.

Ross, M. W., Månsson, S-A., Daneback, K. & Tikkanen, R. (2005). Characteristics of men who have sex with men on the internet but identify as heterosexual, compared with heterosexually identified men who have sex with women. *Cyberpsychology & Behavior, 8*(2), 131–139.

Rubin, G. (1984). Thinking sex: Notes for a radical theory of the politics of sexuality. In C. Vance (Ed.), Pleasure and danger: Exploring female sexuality (pp. 143–179). New York, NY: Routledge.

Rubin, G. (2006). Traffic in women: Notes on the "political economy" of sex. In E. Lewin (Ed.), *Feminist anthropology: A reader* (pp. 87–106). Malden, MA: Blackwell Publishing.

Saiz, I. (2004). Bracketing sexuality: Human rights and sexual orientation: A decade of development and denial at the UN. *Health and Human Rights, 7*(2), 48–80.

Sanford, V. (2008). From genocide to feminicide: Impunity and human rights in twenty-first century Guatemala. *Journal of Human Rights, 7*(2), 104–122.

Sangaramoorthy, T. (2012). Treating the numbers: HIV/AIDS surveillance, subjectivity, and risk. *Medical Anthropology, 31*(4), 292–309. doi:10.1080/01459740.2011.622322

Scheper-Hughes, N., & Bourgois, P. (Eds.). (2004). *Violence in war and peace: An anthology.* Malden, MA: Blackwell Publishing.

Seidman, S. (2003). *The social construction of sexuality.* New York, NY: W. W. Norton & Co.

Sen, A. (2005). Human rights and capabilities. In M. Goodale (Ed.), *Human rights: An anthropological reader* (pp. 86–98). Malden, MA: Blackwell Publishing.

Singer, M. & Erickson, P. I. (2011). *A companion to medical anthropology.* Malden, MA: Wiley-Blackwell.

Stephen, L. (2007). *Transborder lives: Indigenous Oaxacans in Mexico, California, and Oregon.* Durham, NC: Duke University Press.

Strathern, M. (1987). An awkward relationship: The case of feminism and anthropology. *Signs, 12*, 276–292.

Tan, M. L. (1995). From bakla to gay: Shifting gender identities and sexual behaviors in the Philippines. In R. G. Parker & J. H. Gagnon (Eds.) *Conceiving sexuality: Approaches to sex research in a postmodern world* (pp. 85–96). New York, NY: Routledge.

Turner, V. (1967). *The forest of symbols: Aspects of Ndembu ritual.* Ithaca, NY: Cornell University Press.

United Nations Human Rights Council (UN HRC) (2011). *Discriminatory laws and practices and acts of violence against individuals based on their sexual orientation and gender identity: Report of the United Nations high commissioner for human rights.* Retrieved from http://www.ohchr.org

Valentine, D. (2007). *Imagining transgender: An ethnography of a category.* Durham, NC: Duke University Press.

Van Houtum, H., & Van Naerssen, T. (2002). Bordering, ordering and othering. *Tijdschrift voor Economische en Sociale Geografie, 93*(2), 125–136.

Vance, C. E. (1991). Anthropology rediscovers sexuality: A theoretical comment. In R. G. Parker & P. Aggleton (Eds.) *Culture, society and sexuality: A reader* (pp. 41-57). London, UK: University College London.

Verweij, M. (1999). Medicalization as a moral problem for preventative medicine. *Bioethics, 13*(2), 89–113.

Wacquant, L. (2009). *Punishing the poor: The neoliberal government of social insecurity.* Durham, NC: Duke University Press.

West, C., & Zimmerman, D. H. (1987). Doing gender. *Gender & Society, 1*(2), 125–151.

Wolf, E. (1982). *Europe and the people without history.* Berkeley, CA: University of California Press.

Part VI
Future Directions and Concluding Thoughts

Chapter 24
What's Queer About Queer Criminology?

Matthew Ball

Abstract The term "queer criminology" is increasingly being used in criminological discussions, though there remains little consistency with regard to how it is used and to what it refers. It has been used broadly to describe criminological research on LGBTQ people and their interactions with the justice system, more specifically to describe those analyses that identify and critique the heteronormative knowledges or binarized understandings of gender and sexuality within criminal justice research, and also to label theoretical and conceptual pieces that argue for a greater connection between queer theory and criminology. However, there are some important distinctions between "queer criminology" and "queer theory" more widely, particularly the deconstructive approaches of the latter. This chapter explores the engagements between queer theory and "queer criminology," specifically focusing on whether "queer criminology" adopts an understanding of "queer" as an *attitude*, and as signifying a deconstructive project—a position that features in many strands of queer theoretical work. It will argue that while there are different ways of engaging with "queer" as a concept, and that each of these engagements produces different kinds of "queer" projects, "queer criminology" does not always engage with the deconstructive approaches drawn from queer theory. Ultimately, this can limit the ways that "queer criminologists" are able to address injustice.

Keywords Queer theory · Queer · Criminology · Crime and justice · LGBT people · Critique · Poststructural theory

M. Ball (✉)
Center for Sex, Gender, and Sexualities, Durham University, Durham, UK

School of Justice, Queensland University of Technology, PO Box 2434,
Brisbane, QLD 4001, Australia
e-mail: mj.ball@qut.edu.au

D. Peterson and V. R. Panfil (eds.), *Handbook of LGBT Communities,
Crime, and Justice*, DOI: 10.1007/978-1-4614-9188-0_24,
© Springer Science+Business Media New York 2014

Introduction

Asking what is "queer" about "queer criminology" might seem a simple question—one that can be answered in a straightforward way. It could be argued that "queer criminology" is "queer" because, as a criminological project, it is devoted to including lesbian, gay, bisexual, and trans* (LGBT) people in the knowledge produced about crime, accounting for their experiences of justice and injustice when interacting with justice institutions, and recommending reforms to those practices that might be considered unjust. Thus, it might be assumed that "queer criminology" is "queer" because of what it often takes as its object: queer people and communities.

However, "queer" is a very slippery and elusive term, and "queer criminology" can be just as elusive. "Queer criminology" is a term that is slowly being used with greater frequency in academic work, yet there remains little consistency as to the work that is collected by scholars within its ambit. Even those authors that make explicit calls for the forging of greater connections between queer theory and criminology do not often use the term "queer criminology." Some of the work using this term explores criminal justice issues and is "queer" by virtue of the fact that it concerns queer (read LGBT) communities—in these works, "queer" is used as a noun or a label with which to categorize a group of people and to refer to a similar set of experiences or political interests. Other works of "queer criminology" might be considered "queer" because they bring to bear some of the theoretical and conceptual insights of queer theory on issues relating to criminology. Rarely, though, has the term "queer criminology" been used to signify an *attitude*—a broader project of deconstruction moving beyond a focus on gender and sexuality.

While there are many productive examples of queer theory being used to explore criminal justice issues, and diversity in these projects is important for the development of this body of thought, this chapter will argue that as long as this work does not engage with the broader projects of deconstruction that are an identifying feature of much queer theoretical work, and as long as it avoids adopting the idea that queer can signify an attitude, "queer criminology" will continue to involve only a partial engagement with the notion of "queer." Additionally, this chapter will argue that maintaining this partial engagement can potentially perpetuate some of the problems that those working in these areas seek to address through their very attempts to forge greater connections between queer theory and criminology.

Importantly, the critique provided here is not intended to suggest that the work that has gone before is not "queer," or that there are not or should not be other ways of doing "queer" work. In fact, "queer" is a term that can be productively utilized to signify a wide variety of approaches and ideas (Ball 2013b). Rather, this discussion responds in part to Jordan Blair Woods's suggestion that "queer criminology" can be an open discursive space for a variety of different paradigms (Woods, this volume). It suggests that, while "queer criminology" can feasibly develop along a variety of lines, there are ongoing costs and unintended consequences of maintaining such an open stance. It is important to critically reflect on the work that is undertaken under the sign of "queer criminology" and open a space for new ways of thinking in order to contribute to the development of this body of work.

This chapter will explore what is "queer" about "queer criminology" in two ways. It will first identify the ways in which the notion of "queer" features within criminological discussions at present—asking what *is* (currently) queer about it— and then critically analyze these uses of "queer" in criminology—asking what is *queer* about it. While this constitutes a reflexive critique of a criminological position that is often thought to have more urgent tasks (such as identifying the silences and filling the gaps in conventional criminological knowledges, or responding to material injustices), such reflection is nevertheless an important contribution to the development of these studies. This is particularly the case if forging greater connections between queer theory and criminology is to make a substantial contribution to criminological discourses and not simply become another "nominalist rebranding" of the critical enterprise (Carlen 2011, p. 98).

"Queer"

Before exploring the way in which the notion of "queer" has been employed in criminological discourse, it is important to explore the term more generally, particularly as it has been developed in queer theory.[1] Queer theory is an academic field of study and also a political intervention focused on charting the various forms of regulation through which we are shaped as subjects, particularly with regard to sexuality and gender. It excavates the forms of (usually hetero-) normativity that are embedded in social institutions and relations, and, drawing from poststructural thought, challenges essentialized notions of identity and identity politics (including traditional forms of gay and lesbian politics). In the modern period, the term has an interesting trajectory—it has moved from traditionally meaning "strange" or "odd," to being a term of homophobic abuse, and more recently to being reclaimed and embraced by a range of (often, but not restricted to, LGBT) activists in order to signify a more positive embrace of non-normativity (Jagose 1996, p. 74).

While the term "queer" is often used as an umbrella term with which to refer to lesbian, gay, bisexual, and trans* communities as a whole when the initialism

---

[1] "Queer theory" is a contested term, particularly as "queer theory" does not offer a theory of anything in particular, nor does such research have a stable referent. "Queer studies" and "queer commentary" have been suggested as more effective terms to use when referring to the studies discussed here. (See, for example, Berlant and Warner 1995, pp. 344, 348; Wiegman 2012, p. 305.) Notwithstanding those debates, the term "queer theory" is used throughout this discussion because it is that which most often features in the criminological discussions canvassed.

LGBT becomes unwieldy (Duggan 2001, p. 224), queer theorists generally do not use the term solely (if at all) as a label or category. This is for much the same reason that they avoid putting too much faith in *any* such category—identity categories can be homogenizing, overlook differences between those so categorized, lead to essentialized understandings about people, and, by extension, lead to problematic forms of politics (Anzaldúa in Sullivan 2003, p. 44; Giffney 2009, p. 2; Sedgwick 2011, p. 200).

As a result, a substantial amount of queer theoretical work takes the view that "queer" denotes an attitude or a position, especially in relation to what is taken to be "normal." To "queer" something is therefore to *do* something (Sullivan 2003, p. 50). As Sullivan highlights, dictionary definitions of "queer" often define it as "to quiz or ridicule, to spoil, to put out of order" (Sullivan 2003, p. 52). While many authors focus on deconstructing or "queering" norms of sexuality and gender (Doty in Jagose 1996, p. 97; Duggan 2001, p. 223; Smith in Sullivan 2003, p. 43), others suggest that the constituency of "queer" is open-ended, and thus what connects those working in this area is their shared position *vis-à-vis* norms and normativity, not just sexuality and gender (Giffney 2004, pp. 73–74; Jagose 1996, p. 98; Sullivan 2003, p. 43).

David Halperin has articulated this view of "queer" quite clearly. He suggests that "queer" "...acquires its meaning from its oppositional relation to the norm. 'Queer' is by definition *whatever* is at odds with the normal, the legitimate, the dominant. *There is nothing in particular to which it necessarily refers*" (Halperin 1995, p. 62, emphases in original). This means that "queer" is a *position* in relation to the norm, rather than a positivity (Halperin 1995, p. 62). The deconstruction undertaken by those drawing from this position entails pulling apart ideas of essences and understanding how phenomena and bodies of knowledge have been constructed and divided in specific ways (Sullivan 2003, p. 51). It advocates for a denaturalizing and confounding of the categories that we use to think about the world (Jagose 1996, p. 98). Thus, in this sense, many argue that "queer" might best be understood as "...an ongoing and necessarily unfixed site of engagement and contestation" (Berry and Jagose in Sullivan 2003, p. 43). While certainly not all of those who engage with queer theory do so in this way, as this chapter will come to show, it can be a productive approach and ought to be further explored in the context of "queer criminology."

Engagements Between "Queer" and Criminology

While the above discussion offers only a brief survey of the concerns of queer theorists, it provides the basis for an analysis of the multiple engagements between "queer" and criminology offered in this chapter. Three such engagements dominate: first, those that explore criminological and criminal justice issues of relevance to queer communities (where "queer" is used as an identity category); second, those that use some of the *concepts* of queer theory to explore and critique criminal justice institutions and practices, or to understand and represent the lives of sexuality- and gender-diverse people; and third, those explicit calls for a "queer criminology" or for greater connections between queer theory and criminology, which offer a vision of how future work in the area might proceed. While there is always some movement between these categories, the aforementioned themes tend to dominate in discussions on this issue.[2] Furthermore, while this chapter is ultimately seeking to critically reflect on these different kinds of "queer criminology," it is not arguing that these approaches have failed to engage with queer theory, are doing so incorrectly, or are inherently problematic. It is simply exploring *how* they have done so, and the potential *effects* of this engagement.

"Queer" as Identity Category

"Queer" is used in many criminological studies as an identity category. Often, research of this kind identifies a criminological problem of relevance to gay, lesbian, bisexual, trans*, or queer identified people (among others)—whether this is a unique crime that is experienced by them (homophobic or transphobic hate crime, for example); a crime conventionally studied by criminologists but where queer people have been overlooked or are largely invisible (such as intimate partner violence); or a particular (usually negative) experience of one or another aspect of the criminal justice system (such as the impacts of policing or prison). These approaches largely involve gaining knowledge of the experiences of those subject to such injustices and forms of victimization. This research is often geared toward offering some recommendations about how this particular injustice might be resolved. Suggestions about how one ought to improve or reform the justice system, policing practices, or criminological research more broadly in order to foster greater inclusion of queer communities also tend to be made.

Some recent examples of work of this kind include Marian Duggan's (2012) *Queering Conflict: Examining Lesbian and Gay Experiences of Homophobia in Northern Ireland*, Mogul et al.'s (2011) *Queer (In)justice: The Criminalization of LGBT People in the United States*, and Janice Ristock's (2011) edited volume *Intimate Partner Violence in LGBTQ Lives*. Each of these utilizes "queer" largely to refer to a group of people. For example, while "queering" is used in the title of Duggan's (2012) work to imply that something is done to our understanding of conflict, "queering" here involves collecting the voices of gay men, lesbians, and some trans-people and their experiences of discrimination and policing against the backdrop of the "Troubles" in Northern Ireland, and making recommendations for

---

[2] The following analysis (drawing on and developing Ball, 2013b) provides an in-depth discussion of key works in this area, and, importantly, does not engage with all works that explore sexuality and criminology. While those works are often focused on LGBT people, they do not engage with the notion of "queer." It is the *engagement* with "queer" (and the way the term is mobilized, and their effects) that is of interest here.

change. To "queer," here, is to add the voices of LGBT people to a conversation. Additionally, the works collected in Ristock's (2011) volume address gaps in our knowledge about intimate partner violence and how this might be responded to, the lives of victims improved, and perpetrators engaged with appropriately. Here, "queer" is largely another identity category that people can take up in this context, and its inclusion allows for these discussions to canvass a wide range of experiences. Finally, Mogul et al.'s (2011) *Queer (In)justice* provides an important and comprehensive discussion of the experiences that LGBT people have in the criminal justice system in America, and systematically catalogs the specific problems, discrimination, and inequalities that LGBT people face at all stages of their interactions with the justice system—from policing, to the courtroom, to the prison. Each of these works provides knowledge about a particular social or criminal justice problem, experienced by "queer" people; highlights injustices encountered by these groups; and poses suggestions or recommendations in order to produce change.

Queer Theory as a Set of Theoretical Tools

Many of the works that incorporate an engagement between queer theory and criminology utilize queer theoretical insights in a variety of ways in order to explore many of the issues that concern criminologists. This might not come as a surprise, as queer theoretical work offers many conceptual tools that can help explore new questions about particular forms of regulation, or ways of understanding sexuality and gender, for example. In this way, one could argue that queer theory provides some "sensitizing concepts" for researchers to use when designing and undertaking their research, so that LGBT people might be more accurately or appropriately represented in that research.[3] While these approaches largely anchor "queer" to sexuality and/or gender—an approach that is being problematized here—this is again not to suggest that such approaches have not been (and will not continue to be) productive.

Queer theoretical discussions about the government of sexuality through norms embedded in a variety of social sites have been used to explore the regulation and often criminalization of those that live non-heteronormative lives, particularly as this occurs through the law and the justice system (Dalton 2006, 2007; Duggan 1993, p. 75; Moran et al. 1998; Mason 2001a; Narrain 2008, p. 51; Robson 2011;

---

[3] It ought to be noted that many of the following issues or approaches are not unique to "queer criminology," nor have they originated in queer theoretical work. For example, the examination of essentialized identities and a concern with their regulation has been central to a variety of feminist criminologies (Carrington 2002, pp. 119–120, 130), as well as other critical perspectives including post- or counter-colonial criminologies (Cunneen 2011, pp. 261–262), and work on victims of crime (Walklate 2011, pp. 54–58). This should not cause us to question whether "queer criminology" can make a contribution at all, but rather reiterates the importance of identifying precisely the original contribution that "queer criminology" might make.

Stychin 1995, p. 7; Umphrey 1995, p. 26; see, too, in this volume, Cobb; DeJong and Long; Waldman).[4] For example, Mogul et al. (2011, p. 23) and Dwyer (2011, 2012, p. 18) detail the way that those living outside "appropriately gendered" heterosexual norms, or performing kinds of queer embodiment, are made to appear "out of place" in public space, thought of as contributing to disorder and deviance, and thereby become the focus of differential policing (also see Nichols, this volume). Other works look at how forms of surveillance regulate "normal" moral progression through, and use of, public space, including the government of public sex (Conrad 2009; see also Johnson and Dalton 2012). And still others look at the regulation of other forms of sexual activity or sexual performativities and visibilities (Dalton 2006, 2007; Lamble 2009; Mason 2001a) and explore how criminology might engage with these concerns, and how criminal justice might be improved. For example, Backus has explored the issue of child sexual abuse and used queer theory to point to the issues of desire, pleasure, consent, and power in this context. She suggests that a queer theory of sexual violence needs to be developed in order to fully grapple with the boundaries between queer sexuality, children's desires, and abuse (Backus 2009, pp. 237–238).

One of the core aspects of queer theory is the critique of essentialized identities—particularly essentialized sexual identities—and these insights have been used to explore criminal justice issues. This has largely occurred in the context of investigations into hate crime, homophobic violence, and murder. Stephen Tomsen and Sarah Lamble have both utilized such a critique of essentialized understandings of victims and perpetrators of hate crimes in their research, and used these understandings to examine current approaches to addressing hate crimes (Lamble 2008, p. 29; Tomsen 1997, 2006, 2009, pp. 10–13, 15).

Tomsen is critical of hate crime paradigms that take an individualized approach and suggest that such crimes are the result of homophobia, heterosexism, or a pathology (Tomsen 2006, pp. 391–392; 2009). He problematizes these approaches partly because they often require victims to engage in forms of self-government that might reduce "queer" expressions, and thus produce distinctions between "legitimate" citizenship and "irresponsible" citizenship (Tomsen 2006, pp. 393–394). These dynamics not only reproduce forms of mainstream gay and lesbian respectability, but, in essentializing the ideas of victims and offenders, they also maintain divisions between heterosexuality and homosexuality (Tomsen 1997, pp. 39, 40, 42; 2006, p. 394; 2009).

Additionally, Lamble notes that campaigns that seek the discussion and memorializing of hate crimes, such as the Transgender Day of Remembrance, often work to obscure the multiple ways that race, class, and sexuality impact on and allow hate crime to be made intelligible. These campaigns, Lamble argues, often reduce the violence to one dynamic and then use this single dynamic to

---

[4] There are also many works of this kind within social and legal studies, which touch on criminal law and connect very closely to the concerns of criminological investigations (see, for example, Carline 2006; Lamble 2009; Mason 2001b).

provide a lens with which to understand the violence. In transphobic hate crimes, race, class, and sexuality are obscured and "...transgender bodies are universalized along a singular plain of victimhood and rendered visible primarily through the violence that is acted upon them" (Lamble 2008, p. 25). Both Tomsen and Lamble here are attuned to queer theory and its critiques of essentialized and binarized identities, as well as its explorations of intersections of injustice.[5]

As mentioned above, some researchers use queer theory in order to more effectively understand sexuality- and gender-diverse people, and how these factors play out in criminal justice contexts. For example, in *Hate Crime: Impact, Causes and Responses* (2009), Neil Chakraborti and Jon Garland bring together a whole range of discussions on hate crime in different contexts, including homophobic and transphobic hate crimes. In the chapter on transphobic hate crime, they discuss queer theory and say that such work "...is important for developing a framework that can include some of those who are the victims of homophobic and transphobic violence... [because s]uch a framework challenges commonly-held societal assumptions about the demarcation of gender, sexual desire and identity" (p. 75). This is an example of the use of queer theory as a set of tools with which to understand and accurately represent the lives of sexuality- and gender-diverse people.

There are also some researchers who have used queer theoretical critiques of heteronormativity to not only identify such norms operating within criminal justice institutions, but also to question whether the injustice experienced by LGBT people can be addressed through the reform of such institutions. These scholars question the investment of queer people and political campaigns in the criminal justice system and in achieving change within these institutions. They point out that hate crime legislation and campaigns that seek to address hate crimes, for example, often adopt an individualized focus and do not dismantle the systemic forces that produce hate crimes in the first place (Mogul et al. 2011, pp. 123–127; Narrain 2008, p. 50; Tomsen 2006, 2009). In addition, Conrad critiques the investment that gay men can make in the state when they request that police protect them from homophobic violence, especially around beats. This is particularly a problem, Conrad suggests, because the very same police figure in the policing of public sex (Conrad 2009, pp. 339, 341–342). These investments in the state are troubling, these authors argue, because they can exclude many within queer communities, and create divisions between "respectable" and "non-respectable" members of these communities, and, by extension, those worthy of state protection and those not worthy of the same privileges (Mogul et al. 2011, p. 145).

These works point to the diversity of ways that queer theoretical concepts—particularly those concerned with deconstruction, regulation, and normalization in the context of sexuality and gender diversity—have been engaged with within criminological discussions. Not all of the works that have done this have been canvassed here, and not all discussed here are necessarily considered criminological,

---

[5] The recognition that injustices are intersectional is explored in much feminist research (Crenshaw 2000), including within criminology, and also other queer theoretical work.

but those that have been discussed are indicative of the various forms of such engagement. Each of these works engages with queer theory and offers new ways of understanding and representing queer people, becoming attuned to the complexities of sexuality and gender diversity, and appreciating the impact of forms of heteronormativity within the criminal justice system. And each of these works demonstrates the productive uses to which queer theory and the concepts utilized within or derived from it (such as heteronormativity) can be put, and the diversity of issues that can be explored with these tools. And while these studies overwhelmingly anchor "queer" to sexuality and gender and largely do not draw from the notion of queer as an attitude, they have pushed criminological research in this area in important directions and opened up a space for these kinds of debates.

Calls for a "Queer Criminology"

There have been a number of explicit calls for a "queer criminology," for the "queering" of criminology, or reflections on how to forge stronger connections between queer theory and criminology. Stephen Tomsen (1997), Nic Groombridge (1999), Arvind Narrain (2008), and most recently, Jordan Blair Woods (this volume) have offered the most thorough suggestions in this regard, and the directions that they propose for criminology offer another context in which to explore the engagements between "queer" and criminology.[6]

Stephen Tomsen made one of the earliest calls for criminology to engage with queer theory. In "Was Lombroso a Queer? Criminology, Criminal Justice, and the Heterosexual Imaginary," Tomsen argues that the "critical eye" of queer theory "…has not yet been fully turned on the more conventional output of the social sciences," and that "[t]he role of criminology and crime researchers in defining the boundaries of this homo/hetero divide in modern culture and academic discourse, and their relationship to homophobic oppression in the twentieth century, has not yet been explored" (1997, p. 34). Nic Groombridge echoes these arguments in "Perverse Criminologies: The Closet of Doctor Lombroso" (1999; also see Groombridge 1998), where he suggests that in much criminological work, sexuality is understood as "…normatively heterosexual and often explicitly possessed by the young or black" (1999, p. 543), thereby necessitating a greater focus on exploring the question: "[w]hat explanations might a queer criminology offer?" (p. 539).

Both Tomsen and Groombridge offer histories of the various engagements that criminology has had with sexuality. They note the various (missed) opportunities that criminologists have had to consider sexuality and develop a queered criminology—from the origins of criminology in the regulatory projects initiated by

---

[6] There have been other calls for a "queer criminology", or for the "queering" of criminology (Ferrell and Sanders 1995, pp. 318–319; Sorainen 2003), however the authors discussed here offer the most extensive and detailed articulation of how this might proceed and thus constitute the focus of discussion.

sexologists and those following Lombroso's work (Groombridge 1999, pp. 534, 543; Tomsen 1997, pp. 33–36), through the sociological study of delinquency and deviance in subcultures (Groombridge 1999, p. 536), and the gendered approaches to criminology that Groombridge suggests open a space to draw queer theory and criminology closer together (1999, p. 538). (Woods also offers a more extensive discussion and thorough critique of this engagement in his contribution to this volume.) These historical explorations are provided as a prelude to the suggestions that these authors make about how a "queer criminology" ought to proceed.

For Tomsen, one of the major aims of any intersection between queer theory and criminology ought to be deconstructing the primacy attached to the division between homosexual and heterosexual, as this binary has important implications and its deconstruction "is imperative in any sexually emancipatory politics" (1997, p. 34; see the way this is taken up in later work, such as Tomsen 2006, 2009). In a later article he adds that his view of a "queered understanding of crime" would include an "ongoing emphasis on the performativity of criminalized masculine identities and a progressive psychoanalytic stress on the tense proximity of homo and hetero desire that feeds much male aggression, misogyny and risk taking" (2006, p. 403). Tomsen's "queered understanding of crime" is clearly framed in some ways as an explanatory project, seeking to understand crime, how engagement with notions of identity feed into the commission of crime, and how this links to gender performance as well as the state of mind of perpetrators.

Groombridge (1998, p. 119) develops a more detailed argument about how a "queered criminology" might proceed. He suggests that such an approach would be connected to a sociological enterprise within criminology, where, following Seidman's definition, it would not just study a minority but also incorporate "...the study of those knowledges and social practices that organize 'society' as a whole by sexualizing—heterosexualizing and homosexualizing—bodies, desires, acts, identities, social relations, knowledges, culture and social institutions" (Seidman in Groombridge 1999, p. 533). An example of such work, Groombridge (1999, p. 542) suggests, is that which points to the invention of the category of the "homosexual" and how this category is taken up in various projects of regulation. Ultimately, he suggests that such queer criminological work "...belong[s] squarely within mainstream criminological concerns, not on the criminological margins" (1999, p. 543), working alongside, contributing to, and being part of, mainstream criminology.

Arvind Narrain makes a similar point about a criminology attuned to queer theory needing to move away from the "homosexual" as an object of study and toward the knowledges and social practices that regulate sexuality instead.[7] This is

---

[7] Feminist research (including feminist criminologies) have also engaged with such questions, when seeking to move away from the category of "woman" as the object of study and towards exploring the ways that knowledges and social institutions privilege masculinity and reinforce patriarchal power (Carrington 2002). This is also present in feminist challenges to the heteronormativity of liberal feminism, which was central to the development of queer theory (Jagose 1996, p. 44).

difficult in criminology, though, because he argues that criminology "…returns to the task of identifying the homosexual" and "who the criminal/homosexual is," as well as seeking to explain the causes of crime (2008, p. 48). As such, "[t]he distance between queer theory and criminology appears to be an unbridgeable chasm based upon the very different starting points of the two disciplines" (p. 48). The kind of work that Narrain seeks to produce here is that which focuses on the regulation of sexualities through the law, medicine, the media, and the family, and how such regulation produces particular bodies and specific effects.

Most recently, Jordan Blair Woods (this volume) has made an argument for a "queered criminology." In "'Queering Criminology': Overview of the State of the Field," Woods undertakes an extensive analysis of the ways that major criminological schools of thought have remained silent about, or misrepresented, "LGBTQ populations," and how these schools have understood sexuality and sexual deviance. He suggests that one goal of a "queer criminology" is "to advance the field beyond the sexual deviance framework to consider how sexual orientation and gender identity/expression as non-deviant differences—in combination with other differences, such as race/ethnicity, class, and religion—may influence victimization, involvement in crime, and experiences in the criminal justice system more broadly" (Woods, this volume, p. 18).

For Woods, "queer criminology" is largely positioned as a project of producing knowledge about crime and LGBTQ people. "Queer criminology" would provide a space in which LGBTQ people can represent themselves within criminological conversations, be recognized as part of these conversations, and ensure that accurate and appropriate understandings of themselves are furthered. The desire of such a project appears to be to "reorient[…] the focus of criminological inquiry to give due consideration to the relationship between sexual orientation/gender identity differences and victimization and offending" (Woods, this volume, p. 16). Additionally, Woods suggests that a "queer criminology" might also "…further the understanding of how gender norms may lead LGBTQ people… to commit crime" (Woods, this volume, p. 29). Defined along these lines, "queer criminology" is an extension of existing projects of criminological knowledge production concerned with understanding and explaining crime, undertaken to capture new people and their experiences.

This becomes most apparent when Woods draws attention to the production of crime statistics, and the widespread exclusion of sexual orientation and gender identity from many large scale surveys (particularly in the U.S.), as well as the use of a binary understanding of "biological" sex in these instruments (Woods, this volume, p. 18). Woods suggests that the lack of baseline data with which to understand the experiences of LGBTQ people, the effect that this has on targeted programs and interventions, and the ongoing disregard for these issues within criminological thought more generally, are compelling reasons to push for this kind of academic (and, indeed, political) project (Woods, this volume). It is in this respect that the project that Woods proposes differs from those discussed above. Woods's primary (though not exclusive) focus is on incorporating queer populations into criminological knowledge. For Woods, "queer" primarily denotes an identity category or group of shared experiences, and while he provides an initial exploration of the ways that queer theory and criminology could become more closely connected, the primary focus of his discussion is on how a "queer criminology" might contribute to criminological knowledge.

As the above discussion has shown, there are a variety of different ways in which "queer" has been used in criminological work. While the foregoing analysis is not exhaustive, it nevertheless identifies the major themes of such discussions, and suggests that there is indeed much that might be considered to be "queer" about "queer criminology." After all, there are some significant engagements with queer theory within criminological research, and the studies discussed above have made productive contributions to criminology. Each has utilized queer thought in various ways. However, there still remain some aspects of queer theoretical work that have not been widely engaged with in these studies. It is useful to critically examine these other approaches within queer theory, and to use them to reflect on the current state of "queer criminology." In doing this, the chapter will now consider what is *queer* about the various engagements discussed above.

What's Queer About All of This?

While there are many different kinds of engagements between queer theory and criminology, this section will consider whether these engagements align with the positional stance of "queer," such as that outlined by David Halperin (discussed earlier), and connect to the extensive deconstructive projects (regarding knowledge and politics) that "queer" can signify. It will argue that while many of the engagements between queer theory and criminology are productive and positive steps forward, opening up a space for further discussion and addressing gaps in our knowledge base, they can nevertheless perpetuate a number of troubling issues that must be addressed if a "queer criminology" is going to respond to many of the injustices that "queer criminology" itself is posited as a solution to. The critiques that can be made of the engagements discussed above include that they are: invested in a project of knowledge production that often relies on a discursive reversal reproducing the binaries and categories that ought to be the target of deconstruction; tied to a notion of "queer" as primarily signifying sexuality and gender; and connected to or invested in particular forms of politics that may work against some of the reforms sought. Each of these will be discussed in turn below.

"Queer Criminology" as a Project of Knowledge Production

Many of the discussions about the need for a "queer criminology" point to the necessity of producing robust and systematic information about crime and justice issues of relevance to LGBT people. This is clear in the works of (Woods, this volume), as well as in Tomsen's goal to produce a "queered understanding of crime" (2006, p. 403), and Groombridge's desire to know what "explanations" a queer criminology might offer (1999, p. 539). In some cases, "queer criminology" can thereby quickly begin to sound as though it is a project aimed at producing (often, but not exclusively) statistical knowledge about the frequency of particular crimes often overlooked in crime statistics and descriptive accounts of crimes, the motivations of offenders, and the experiences of victims. While producing different kinds of information about the experiences of various groups is not necessarily problematic, it is important to consider the ways that such knowledge can be produced, and the ends to which that knowledge is put.

The production of such knowledge is often justified (though this does not remain unproblematized, as discussed below) as a way of assisting with administrative projects such as the development of crime control policies or responses to offending (see, for example, Tomsen 1997, p. 37; and in this volume, Belknap, Holsinger, and Little; Panfil; Woods). However, these projects cannot always effectively represent the notion of "queer" and the fluidity that it signifies. "Queer" lives and performativities (if taken to refer to a group of people for a moment) are not easily inscribed in a way that would make them measurable (see Johnson, this volume). While multiple identity categories such as gay, lesbian, bisexual, and transgender can be incorporated into a survey in recognition of the diversity of people that might be captured under the umbrella of "queer," this in itself does not *queer* the research. It does not readily allow for the fluidity and complexity of performativities such as queer to be made apparent, and thus the very margins that are of interest to the researchers are effectively "designed out" of the instruments used to gather such information, with flow-on effects for any subsequent analyses and recommendations the researcher seeks to make (Browne 2008, Sects. 1.1, 1.2, 4.11–4.11). For example, Himmelstein and Brückner's (2011) study of criminal justice and school sanctions against non-heterosexual youth categorized same-sex attraction, same-sex romantic relationships, and lesbian, gay, or bisexual self-identification under the label of "non-heterosexual" for the purposes of their analysis, flattening out diversity among these experiences. This is not uncommon. The author also observed an example of these issues recently at a major international conference in a presentation on intimate partner violence in non-heterosexual relationships. In the research that was discussed, transgender respondents (who, of course, may or may not consider their relationships to be non-heterosexual) were excluded from the analysis because there were not enough in the sample to legitimate any statistical analyses of significance, and sexuality was coded according to the binary of heterosexual and non-heterosexual. While the focus of such research was on those that might fall under the large umbrella of "queer," one could argue that there is actually very little that might be considered *queer* about such research.

There is another important reason that queer criminological scholars might wish to be cautious about producing this information, and that is because of the connections between knowledge and institutions of power, and especially the legitimation and, indeed, the *expansion* of, such institutions. While Woods,

Groombridge, and Tomsen, when setting out their views on what "queer criminology" ought to be, each point out that producing such information is dangerous as it can potentially lead to a range of further injustices for LGBT people (Groombridge 1999, p. 540; Tomsen 1997, pp. 33, 43–44; Woods, this volume), it seems that at times they nevertheless imply that the production of such information about these groups of people, and its use in reforming criminal justice institutions can potentially, at some point, be *un*troubling—that it can, in fact, be positive. While producing knowledge about the lives of "queer" populations in order to challenge normative orders is part of a lot of queer work and is valuable for precisely that reason, many queer scholars also caution against (or seek to avoid outright) the desire for this knowledge to be invested in administrative projects (whether criminological or not, and whether they seek to achieve justice or not), the forms of government that they perpetuate, and the institutions that they help legitimize (see Duggan 2003; Johnson, this volume; Puar 2007; Warner 1999). Thus, the production of criminological knowledge that resembles the straightforward inclusion of queer perspectives into positivist, administrative, or explanatory criminological projects cannot automatically be said to align with the notion of queer as a position.

Discursive Reversal

A related critique of these attempts to produce knowledge about crime is that which concerns the discursive reversal that is often implied or involved. As explored above, there is a tendency for calls for a "queer criminology" to push for the inclusion of "queer voices" in criminological discussions. And there are certainly compelling reasons to make such an argument. Criminological knowledge has been used to regulate queer lives in unjust ways, and for many years, queer people were *spoken about* by criminologists, sexologists, and others seeking to "know" about those considered sexually deviant. The development of a "queer criminology" is therefore a tempting opportunity to wrest control from those who have historically been authorized to speak in these ways about queer lives, to allow for homophobic discourses to be made apparent, and to provide a space in which queer people can speak for themselves (Halperin 1995, pp. 52, 56).

Such an approach implies a reversal or shifting of the privilege of heterosexual subjects within criminological discourses, with the queer subject being made as a legitimate position from which to speak.[8] However, these kinds of arguments do not simply *describe* divisions and oversights within criminology, but rather *reiterate* them and the very discourses about sexuality that have contributed to the

---

[8] This is a different kind of discursive reversal to that which is discussed by Groombridge, Tomsen, and Narrain, where the criminological gaze shifts from viewing the "homosexual" as deviant towards seeing the homophobe as deviant (Groombridge 1999, p. 540, 541; Narrain 2008, p. 49; Tomsen 2009, pp. 137–138).

current injustices that queer people experience (Browne 2008, Sects. 4.1–4.2, 4.5–4.8; Butler 1993, p. 2). In such discussions, a distinction is maintained between heterosexual and homosexual, perpetuating the assumption that hetero-sexuality and homosexuality are stable categories, and oppositional (not to men-tion that "queer" refers primarily to sexuality, which will be discussed below) (Corber and Valocchi 2003, p. 3; Jagose 1996, p. 92; Sullivan 2003, p. 45).

By citing these very categories—the same categories that have featured in numerous projects of government over queer lives—in attempts to establish a "queer criminology" and position it somewhat in contrast to mainstream forms of criminology, those seeking to establish a "queer criminology" do not seem to be pushing for a fundamental reformulation of the contours of knowledge production in this context (Halperin 1995, p. 56). While this is not necessarily always a bad thing—as Foucault (1998, p. 101) points out, "...discourse can be both an instrument and an effect of power, but also a hindrance, a stumbling-block, a point of resistance and a starting point for an opposing strategy"—it is important to interrogate the effects of doing this. Not only are these categories lent more weight through this very citation, but the suggestion that one discourse ought to be set up in opposition to a repressive and negating "other" is precisely one of the strategies of power through which the "dominated" discourse can enroll allies and establish its own position of power. Thus, calls to produce queer criminological knowledge *for* queers and in order to address injustice can actually reinscribe the power and knowledge relations that exist (Corber and Valocchi 2003, p. 11; Jagose 1996, p. 81).[9] "Speaking for" queers in these ways can cite identity categories and "...marginalize other ways and modes of inhabiting queer... sexualities" (Douglas et al. 2011, p. 115). One very clear sign of this is the continued citation of the notion of the closet, and the need to "come out of the closet," in criminological and criminal justice discourses of various kinds. While citing the closet and the necessity to "come out" within these discourses and programs might be an effective political strategy in some contexts and for some people, it is also important to be cautious when doing so because the notion of "coming out" can reinforce contingent historical identity categories such as the "homosexual" that are not held by all, and feature as part of the very same regimes of power and knowledge that regulate sexuality and gender identity (Foucault 1998).

Thus, some calls for a "queer criminology" are in what might actually be a rather counterproductive position of seeking to improve the lives of queer people by having them invest themselves in projects of knowledge production in the discipline that has traditionally sought to govern a variety of "deviants," and to do so under the sign of an identity category that has been connected to those very same regulatory projects. It is therefore possible to suggest that if we want to develop a queer project of criminology, we should not seek to engage with the discourse that has disqualified queer lives as part of the strategy to reclaim those

---

[9] In a similar way, struggles to achieve marriage equality or to allow LGBTQ people to serve openly in the military legitimate marriage and the military as social institutions, respectively.

lives from that discourse and its silences, oversights, and other effects (see further Halperin 1995, p. 56). We ought instead to produce more discursive spaces for queer people to inhabit, and seek to fundamentally shift the way we think about, talk about, and research these issues. How we might achieve this is one of the central tasks of future work in this area (for preliminary suggestions, see Ball 2014). However, a first step in doing so would be to interrogate the assumptions that we make and concepts that we use when doing so, because, as Judith Butler (2004, p. 129) points out, "[i]f we engage the terms that these debates supply, then we ratify the frame at the moment in which we take our stand. This signals a certain paralysis in the face of exercising power to change the terms by which such topics are rendered thinkable."

Queer = Sexuality and Gender

While a number of queer theorists have argued for some time that "queer" does not refer solely to sexuality and gender, and that queer research needs to constantly problematize sexuality and gender as its proper objects (Eng et al. 2005, p. 4; Giffney 2004, pp. 73–74), discussions about the connections between queer theory and criminology still focus largely on sexuality. This connection is reinforced by the use of "queer" as an identity category or umbrella category, as well as the criminological research discussed above that uses queer theory in order to effectively represent and understand the lives of those who they are researching—for example by recognizing that identity is fluid and trying to make sure that this is captured accurately in surveys or in other research design, or indeed in our attempts to respond to victimization (see Tomsen 2006). Thus, even those arguing for "queer criminology" can end up essentializing the relationship between "queer" and sexuality or gender diversity. What this means is that the deconstructive potential of the notion of queer is not often used to explore other important concepts.

For example, as discussed above, Chakraborti and Garland's (2009) book on hate crimes discusses queer theory in the chapter on transphobic hate crimes, suggesting that it can assist in understanding those being researched. However, queer theory is not used elsewhere in the book to explore other ways of thinking about hate crime as it is experienced by other people. Similarly, Narrain's (2008, p. 51) discussion of queer theory and criminology largely restricts the focus to gay and lesbian people, also reinforcing the notion that queer still stands for sexuality. This is not to suggest that these uses of queer theory are incorrect. Rather, it is to point out that queer is continually used in these discussions to refer to sexuality and gender, reinforcing the notion that queer refers to *something*—most often an identity—as opposed to being a *position*. This may be, in part, a result of the ongoing association between "queer" and sexuality and/or gender in a variety of cultural contexts, as opposed to the additional ways that "queer" is used in academic analysis.

Emerging strains of queer theory are critical of the tendency to connect "queer" primarily to sexuality and gender, as doing so not only takes sexuality for granted, but often also connects these projects to understandings of identity. Notwithstanding the effectiveness of using the term "queer" to refer to LGBT people generally, using the term in this way can imply some stability to these categories, and maintain the assumption that identities are stable, coherent, and have somewhat fixed boundaries—precisely the approaches that queer theorists seek to move away from in their explorations of identity as provisional and contingent (Corber and Valocchi 2003, pp. 2–3; Jagose 1996, p. 77; Sullivan 2003, p. 41).

As mentioned above, "queer" is a false unifying umbrella (Anzaldúa in Sullivan 2003, p. 44; Giffney 2009, p. 2). There are a variety of experiences and differences even within and between these identity categories, and the use of terms such as LGBT or queer can homogenize people, erase other important differences along the lines of race, for example, and further marginalize those at the borders (Anzaldúa in Sullivan 2003, p. 44). It can also mean that important injustices might be misconstrued as matters of concern for gay and lesbian people, when it might not be possible to categorize them so neatly. This is a point made in Lamble's work on the way that forms of violence are spoken of and memorialized (discussed earlier), where particular aspects of hate crimes have been erased or looked over, the story of the crime retold, and victimization claimed for only one group of people. As Jacob Hale states on this point, "[w]hen a border zone denizen's corpse is claimed by those with firmer categorical location, border zones become less habitable for those who are trying to live in the nearly unspeakable spaces created by overlapping margins of distinct categories" (cited in Lamble 2008, p. 36).

There is some strategic value to adopting such identity categories. For example, if LGBT communities are understood to share similar experiences by virtue of their positions outside social expectations of heterosexuality, binarized understandings of gender, and cisgendered assumptions, then "queer" can be politically convenient and strategic. Tomsen (1997, pp. 43, 44) rightly suggests that such essentialism can be useful in mobilizing political action around important issues. However, he also points out that this simplifies the political ground, and "…forgoes an opportunity to impact upon the wider operation of sexual regimes" (p. 44). Similarly, Judith Butler argues that identity categories are "necessary errors" and instruments of regulatory regimes that should remain problematized in any political campaigns that utilize them (1993, p. 230; Jagose 1996, p. 91). They can be used in ways that render various lives more or less "liveable" (Butler 2004, pp. 8, 29–30).

Ultimately, then, "queer criminology" might be more effective if it were to shift the ground on which knowledge of people, and the politics that seeks to change the conditions of their lives, is built. Doing so would mean that it would not simply focus on representing or speaking for a particular group of people. Opening up the meaning of "queer," so as to prevent sexuality and gender remaining the taken-for-granted objects of queer critique, and moving towards a greater focus on "queer" as signifying a position, would allow "queer criminology" to align more closely with the aspects of queer theory that this chapter suggests can help shape new conversations in this area.

Achieving Justice, Regulatory Projects, and Investments in the State

As mentioned above, some calls for "queer criminology" seem to suggest that much of the work that ought to be carried out in this context should be connected to administrative or governmental criminological projects, such as by improving the interaction between criminal justice institutions and LGBT people. It is suggested that addressing gaps in the knowledge of these issues can lead to the development of specifically targeted responses that would address injustice (Chakraborti and Garland 2009; Dwyer 2008, 2011, 2012; Tomsen 1997; see also, this volume, Belknap et al.; Panfil; Sumner and Jenness; Woods). These works, it might be argued, have various levels of investment in the nation-state and its institutions (though some are often still hesitant about a complete investment in such institutions—see Narrain 2008; Tomsen 2006, 2009).

One example of the connections between a "queer criminology" and projects of regulation of various sorts is also reinforced by Woods's suggestion that a "queer criminology" would make us ask questions about the nature of sexual orientation and gender identity, and whether this is innate, socially constructed, or a combination of both. While he suggests that these are important questions because of the moral and political implications of such a debate (Woods, this volume), doing so takes for granted that this search for the "truth" of sexuality and gender identity necessarily *ought to* feature as a legitimate prop for moral and political projects, and that queer criminologists ought to engage in such a task. As queer theorists trace the genealogies of these categories in order to historicize them, problematize their stability, and identify their connection to a panoply of regulatory projects (Butler 1990; Foucault 1998), a "queer criminology" that sought a "truth" about the nature of sexual orientation and gender identity would work somewhat against these queer tasks, and even allow certain forms of regulation to become instituted on the basis of these "truths."

There is a constant need to interrogate the investments of "queer criminologists" in regulatory projects and justice institutions, as what might appear to be progressive projects that address the various crime- and policing-related injustices faced by queer communities (such as the development of programs to prevent intimate partner violence, the introduction of harsher sentences for those that commit homophobic hate crime, or the expanded use of police liaison programs) can involve particular forms of violence and exclusion, and perpetuate hierarchies (Ball 2013a; Dwyer 2012; Mogul et al. 2011; Moran 2009, p. 311). Some contend that these investments in the justice system involve making a demand for the law's violence (Moran in Narrain 2008, p. 50). As Wendy Brown (1995, p. 27) puts it, this "casts the law in particular and the state more generally as neutral arbiters of injury rather than as themselves invested with the power to injure." It involves having faith in a set of institutions that produces mass incarceration, the over-representation of indigenous people and specific racial groups in prison, and social exclusions (Moran 2009, p. 311). As Mogul et al. (2011, p. 140) suggest, "LGBT people need to deeply question whether institutions rooted in the control and punishment of people of color, poor people, immigrants, and queers can ever be deployed in the service of LGBT interests without abandoning entire segments of queer communities to continuing state violence." A "queer criminology" ought to be wary of such investments.

These investments can also perpetuate further divisions in the form of homo-normativity. Duggan points out that homonormativity refers to the ways that queer politics have often been reformulated in neoliberal terms, particularly "...in narrow terms of privacy, domesticity, and the unfettered ability to consume in the 'free' market..., [which]...collaborates with a mainstreamed nationalist politics of identity, entitlement, inclusion, and personal responsibility while abandoning a more global critique of capitalist exploitation and domination, state violence and expansion, and religious fundamentalisms and hate" (Eng et al. 2005, p. 11). Homonormative politics are those wherein LGBT people seek to share in the "privileges and presumption of normality" (Sedgwick 2011, p. 201). This is an important part of a queer interrogation of the investments in criminal justice institutions, because, as suggested earlier, these also effect divisions *within* queer communities, such as which queer lives are respectable and which ones are not, and thus, who ought to be protected by the law and state institutions and who should not be. In this context, fellow members of the community (however that community might be conceived)—such as those who have sex in public or at beats[10] (Conrad 2009), or those who are visibly "queer" in public space (Dwyer 2012)—can be "othered" in order to achieve a claim to decency. Adopting the notion that "queer" signifies a position would involve a constant questioning of the forms of normalization that are attached to these investments in the state and its institutions.

Queer Theory and Criminological Reluctance

While many of the works discussed above seek to engage in some productive way with elements of queer theory, there remains some reluctance to forging connections between this particular approach within queer theory and criminology, with some authors remaining troubled by the work that might be undertaken along

---

[10] "Beat" is a term used in Australia as a substitute for "cottage" or "tearoom," and generally refers to venues in public places where (usually) men meet to engage in anonymous sexual activity with other men.

these lines. For example, Woods points out that some *feminist* work that deconstructs what he terms the "...heterosexist social order... subordinat[ing] LGBTQ people" is a positive step forward. However, he suggests that such work still operates at a highly abstract level (Woods, this volume, p. 28)—to say nothing of the work of *queer* scholars that might undertake a similar task and work at a similarly "abstract" level. He also suggests that while the use of the term "queer" to signify LGBTQ perspectives may still effect exclusions, using it in a more deconstructive manner could also be problematic because it might risk "...diluting demographically-relevant social differences to the extent that it may discount the experiences of people who identify with, and experience marginalization on the basis of, those differences" (Woods, this volume, p. 30).[11] To some extent, this concern is connected to the idea that deconstructive approaches often seem disconnected from the amelioration of material injustices.

It is important to address these concerns, as they are common critiques directed toward queer work. On the first point—that queer theorizing is abstract and focuses perhaps too much on the discursive, and not lived experiences of injustice—it might be accurate to say that some queer work operates at what seems a more abstract level. However, this does not mean that queer theoretical work is deliberately *obscure*, or that queer theorists are disengaged from real injustices. Many queer theorists explore the discursive because, as their work is informed by poststructural thought, they recognize that discourses mediate the way in which we think about and interact in the world (McLaughlin 2006). As such, they recognize that discourses are necessary targets for achieving fundamental change—as the contestation over identity categories shows. To suggest a separation between the discursive and the material implies that one can have access to the material unmediated by discourse, and overlooks the dense interconnections between them (see Butler 1993). Queer theoretical work can seem abstract because of the significant work that queer theorists do to shift the discursive terrain upon which our discussions about various phenomena take place. And they do this in order to ensure that they push as far as possible away from the terms, categories, and assumptions that are generally used to think about the world, and reformulate the conceptual ground on which such work is carried out. Thus, while it might be accurate to suggest that a lot of queer theoretical work—and especially that which takes queer as a position—reads as abstract, this is not to suggest that it is disengaged, irrelevant, or obscure, which is what is often implied.

On the second point—that queer theory leads to the discounting of the experiences of those who identify using categories such as lesbian, gay, bisexual, and trans*—there is little within queer theoretical work to suggest that a person's experience would be *discounted or marginalized* in this way. Not only is there a body of thought within queer theory that cautions against, or at least seeks to

---

[11] Importantly, I do not want to suggest that Woods argues *against* these deconstructive approaches in "queer criminology" completely. His work has been quoted here simply because he draws attention to these concerns.

grapple with, precisely this (Halperin 1995, p. 65; Lance and Tanesini 2000), but if queer theorists were going to discount or marginalize such experiences, then they would not have spent so much time pointing out the cultural power that attaches to these identities (even to the extent that they feel deeply embedded and one becomes invested in them), and the various ways in which political campaigns employ these categories (see discussions in Jagose 1996; Sullivan 2003). Furthermore, following from the critiques of identity categories above, there are many on the margins of, or outside, these categories that might also benefit from work that draws criminology and this particular approach within queer theory more closely together. So, despite the cultural power of the identities mentioned above, embracing a more deconstructive approach allows the variety of ways of being, relating, forming intimacies, and of thinking about the world to be reflected in criminological work.

Conclusion

By asking what is specifically "queer" about "queer criminology," this chapter has attempted to open a space for critical reflection on current work that argues for, positions itself as, or is positioned as part of, 'queer criminology.' It has interrogated the extent to which "queer criminology" engages with queer theory, and suggested that there are more opportunities to foster such engagement that could be followed in future work. In particular, it has suggested that it is important that "queer criminology" adopt an understanding of "queer" as an attitude or position if it is not only to use the most cutting insights developed within queer theory, but also if the injustices that "queer criminologists" have identified (and which they suggest a "queer criminology" is the answer to) are to be most effectively responded to and avoided.

These analyses are not intended to close down the possibilities of "queer criminology," nor are they intended as an exercise in policing the term "queer." As Judith Butler (1993, p. 230) suggests, "queer" is "...a discursive site whose uses are not fully constrained in advance," and this "...ought to be safeguarded not only for the purposes of continuing to democratize queer politics, but also to expose, affirm, and rework the specific historicity of the term." Rather, this kind of reflection is to open up a space for discussing and considering these issues, and for a more thorough interrogation of the intended and unintended effects of these discourses. While it is desirable to maintain an open stance to the notion of "queer," and a "queer criminology" (in whatever form it takes) can remain open to competing views, it is nevertheless important to, at the same time, explore the unintended consequences of such an open stance. If nothing else, the foregoing analysis hopes to at least encourage a little more critical reflection on the use of the term "queer" in this developing field, because, as Foucault (1983, p. 256) suggests, the "...point is not that everything is bad, but that everything is dangerous, which is not exactly the same as bad. If everything is dangerous, then we always have something to do." Each potential use of "queer" carries its own dangers. It would not be surprising, then, to point out that this chapter has implicitly suggested that establishing "queer criminology" as a sub-discipline within criminology, or embedding it within the concerns of mainstream criminology, is not necessarily desirable. This is the kind of project that Groombridge (1999, p. 543) advocates—the positioning of queer criminology in the mainstream of criminology. While there is certainly an important place for such work, and the work that has done this has been (and will continue to be) productive, these approaches can often mean that "queer" is utilized largely as an identity category, or queer theory is used as a set of theoretical concepts put to work *for criminology*. This can thereby limit the numerous possibilities of "queer," and potentially lead to "...a taming of the critical energy, a domestication, a declawing and detoothing of its sharpest assets" (Kemp 2009, p. 22). This mainstreaming could potentially limit the possibilities of queer critique, and push for some measure of the institutionalization of queer approaches, thereby working against the notion that "queer" gains its greatest potential and strength from its marginal position and its constant push against norms. To avoid this, a "queer criminology" should always sit at an oblique angle to the rest of criminological discourse, remaining in the margins in order for its critical potential to have any impact. If "queer criminology" is to be anything, it should always refer to a disposition or *attitude* of criminologists.

Acknowledgments The author would like to thank the following people for their insightful comments on this chapter: Christian Callisen, Belinda Carpenter, Jo Phoenix, Jordan Blair Woods, Juan Tauri, Liz Morrish, Peter O'Brien, Angela Dwyer, Sharon Hayes, Vanessa Panfil, and Dana Peterson.

References

Backus, M. G. (2009). "Things that have the potential to go terribly wrong": Homosexuality, pedophilia and the Kincora Boys' Home scandal. In N. Giffney & M. O'Rourke (Eds.), *The Ashgate research companion to queer theory* (pp. 237–253). Farnham, UK: Ashgate Publishing.

Ball, M. (2013a). Heteronormativity, homonormativity and violence. In K. Carrington, M. Ball, E. O'Brien, & J. Tauri (Eds.), *Crime, justice and social democracy: International perspectives* (pp. 186–199). Basingstoke, UK: Palgrave Macmillan.

Ball, M. (2013b). The use of "queer" in criminal justice discourses. In K. Richards & J. Tauri (Eds.), *Crime, justice and social democracy: Proceedings of the 2nd international conference, 2013* (Vol. 1, pp. 1–9). Brisbane, QLD: Crime and Justice Research Center, QUT.

Ball, M. (2014). Queer criminology, critique, and the 'art of not being governed'. *Critical Criminology: An International Journal, 22*.

Berlant, L., & Warner, M. (1995). What does queer theory teach us about X? *PMLA, 110*, 343–349.

Brown, W. (1995). *States of injury: Power and freedom in late modernity*. Princeton, NJ: Princeton University Press.

Browne, K. (2008). Selling my queer soul or queerying quantitative research? *Sociological Research Online*, *13*(1), 11. http://www.socresonline.org.uk/13/1/11.html.

Butler, J. (1990). *Gender trouble: Feminism and the subversion of identity*. New York, NY: Routledge.

Butler, J. (1993). *Bodies that matter: On the discursive limits of "sex"*. New York, NY: Routledge.

Butler, J. (2004). *Undoing gender*. New York, NY: Routledge.

Carlen, P. (2011). Against evangelism in academic criminology: For criminology as a scientific art. In M. Bosworth & C. Hoyle (Eds.), *What is criminology?* (pp. 95–108). Oxford, UK: Oxford University Press.

Carline, A. (2006). Resignifications and subversive transformations: Judith Butler's queer theory and women who kill. *Liverpool Law Review*, *27*, 303–335.

Carrington, K. (2002). Feminism and critical criminology: Confronting genealogies. In K. Carrington & R. Hogg (Eds.), *Critical criminology: Issues, debates, challenges* (pp. 114–142). Devon, UK: Willan Publishing.

Chakraborti, N., & Garland, J. (2009). *Hate crime: Impact, causes, and responses*. London, UK: Sage Publications.

Conrad, K. (2009). Nothing to hide… nothing to fear: Discriminatory surveillance and queer visibility in Great Britain and Northern Ireland. In N. Giffney & M. O'Rourke (Eds.), *The Ashgate research companion to queer theory* (pp. 329–346). Farnham, UK: Ashgate Publishing.

Corber, R., & Valocchi, S. (2003). Introduction. In R. Corber & S. Valocchi (Eds.), *Queer studies: An interdisciplinary reader* (pp. 1–19). Oxford, UK: Blackwell Publishing.

Crenshaw, K. (2000). Demarginalizing the intersections of race and sex: A black feminist critique of antidiscrimination doctrine, feminist theory, and antiracist politics. In J. James & T. Sharpley-Whiting (Eds.), *The black feminist reader* (pp. 208–238). Oxford, UK: Blackwell Publishers.

Cunneen, C. (2011). Postcolonial perspectives for criminology. In M. Bosworth & C. Hoyle (Eds.), *What is criminology?* (pp. 249–266). Oxford, UK: Oxford University Press.

Dalton, D. (2006). Surveying deviance, figuring disgust: Locating the homocriminal body in time and space. *Social and Legal Studies*, *15*(2), 277–299.

Dalton, D. (2007). Genealogy of the Australian homocriminal subject: A study of two explanatory models of deviance. *Griffith Law Review*, *16*(1), 83–106.

Douglas, S., Jivraj, S., & Lamble, S. (2011). Liabilities of queer anti-racist critique. *Feminist Legal Studies*, *19*, 107–118.

Duggan, L. (1993). The trials of Alice Mitchell: Sensationalism, sexology, and the lesbian subject in turn-of-the-century America. In R. Corber & S. Valocchi (Eds.), *Queer studies: An interdisciplinary reader* (pp. 73–87). Oxford, UK: Blackwell Publishing.

Duggan, L. (2001). Making it perfectly queer. In A. Herrmann & A. J. Stewart (Eds.), *Theorising feminism: Parallel trends in the humanities and social sciences* (2nd ed., pp. 215–231). Boulder, CO: Westview Press.

Duggan, L. (2003). *The twilight of equality? Neoliberalism, cultural politics, and the attack on democracy*. Boston, MA: Beacon Press.

Duggan, M. (2012). *Queering conflict: Examining lesbian and gay experiences of homophobia in Northern Ireland*. Farnham, UK: Ashgate Publishing.

Dwyer, A. (2008). Policing queer bodies: Focusing on queer embodiment in policing research as an ethical question. *Queensland University of Technology Law and Justice Journal*, *8*(2), 414–428.

Dwyer, A. (2011). Policing lesbian, gay, bisexual and transgender young people: A gap in the research literature. *Current Issues in Criminal Justice*, *22*(3), 415–433.

Dwyer, A. (2012). Policing visible sexual/gender diversity as a program of governance. *International Journal for Crime and Justice*, *1*(1), 17–34.

Eng, D., Halberstam, J., & Muñoz, J. E. (2005). Introduction: What's queer about queer studies now? *Social Text*, *23*(3–4), 1–17.

Ferrell, J., & Sanders, C. R. (1995). Toward a cultural criminology. In J. Ferrell & C. R. Sanders (Eds.), *Cultural criminology* (pp. 297–326). Boston, MA: Northeastern University Press.

Foucault, M. (1983). On the genealogy of ethics: An overview of work in progress. In P. Rabinow (Ed.), *Ethics: Subjectivity and truth. essential works of Foucault 1954–1984: Volume 1* (2000) (pp. 253–280). London, UK: Penguin Books.

Foucault, M. (1998). *The will to knowledge: The history of sexuality volume 1.* London, UK: Penguin Books.

Giffney, N. (2004). Denormatizing queer theory: More than (simply) lesbian and gay studies. *Feminist Theory, 5*(1), 73–78.

Giffney, N. (2009). Introduction: The "q" word. In N. Giffney & M. O'Rourke (Eds.), *The Ashgate research companion to queer theory* (pp. 1–13). Farnham, UK: Ashgate Publishing.

Groombridge, N. (1998). Letter to the editor. *Theoretical Criminology, 2,* 119–120.

Groombridge, N. (1999). Perverse criminologies: The closet of Doctor Lombroso. *Social and Legal Studies, 8,* 531–548.

Halperin, D. (1995). *Saint Foucault: Towards a gay hagiography.* Oxford, UK: Oxford University Press.

Himmelstein, K., & Brückner, H. (2011). Criminal-justice and school sanctions against nonheterosexual youth: A national longitudinal study. *Pediatrics, 127*(1), 49–57.

Jagose, A. (1996). *Queer theory.* Melbourne, VIC: Melbourne University Press.

Johnson, P., & Dalton, D. (Eds.). (2012). *Policing sex.* Oxon, UK: Routledge.

Kemp, J. (2009). Queer past, queer present, queer future. *Graduate Journal of Social Science, 6*(1), 3–23.

Lamble, S. (2008). Retelling racialized violence, remaking white innocence: The politics of interlocking oppressions in transgender day of remembrance. *Sexuality Research and Social Policy, 5*(1), 24–42.

Lamble, S. (2009). Unknowable bodies, unthinkable sexualities: Lesbian and transgender legal invisibility in the Toronto women's bathhouse raid. *Social and Legal Studies, 18*(1), 111–130.

Lance, M. N., & Tanesini, A. (2000). Identity judgments, queer politics. In I. Morland & A. Willox (Eds.), *Queer theory (2005)* (pp. 171–186). Basingstoke, UK: Palgrave Macmillan.

Mason, G. (2001a). Body maps: Envisaging homophobia, violence, and safety. *Social and Legal Studies, 10*(1), 23–44.

Mason, G. (2001b). Not our kind of hate crime. *Law and Critique, 12,* 253–278.

McLaughlin, J. (2006). The return of the material: Cycles of theoretical fashion in Lesbian, Gay and Queer Studies. In D. Richardson, J. McLaughlin, & M. E. Casey (Eds.), *Intersections between feminism and queer theory* (pp. 59–77). Basingstoke, UK: Palgrave MacMillan.

Mogul, J. L., Ritchie, A. J., & Whitlock, K. (2011). *Queer (in)justice: The criminalization of LGBT people in the United States.* Boston, MA: Beacon Press.

Moran, L. J. (2009). What kind of field is "law, gender and sexuality"? Achievements, concerns and possible futures. *Feminist Legal Studies, 17,* 309–313.

Moran, L. J., Monk, D., & Beresford, S. (1998). *Legal queeries: Lesbian, gay, and transgender legal studies.* London, UK: Cassell.

Narrain, A. (2008). "That despicable specimen of humanity": Policing of homosexuality in India. In K. Kananbiran & R. Singh (Eds.), *Challenging the rule(s) of law: Colonialism, criminology, and human rights in India* (pp. 48–77). New Delhi, India: Sage Publications.

Puar, J. K. (2007). *Terrorist assemblages: Homonationalism in queer times.* Durham, NC: Duke University Press.

Ristock, J. (Ed.). (2011). *Intimate partner violence in LGBTQ lives.* New York, NY: Routledge.

Robson, R. (Ed.). (2011). *Sexuality and law. Volume II: Crime and punishment.* Farnham, UK: Ashgate Publishing.

Sedgwick, E. K. (2011). *The weather in Proust.* Durham, NC: Duke University Press.

Sorainen, A. (2003). Queering criminology. Paper presented at *Crime and Control in an Integrating Europe: 3rd Annual Conference of the European Society of Criminology,* Helsinki, Finland.

Stychin, C. (1995). *Law's desire: Sexuality and the limits of justice.* London, UK: Routledge.

Sullivan, N. (2003). *A critical introduction to queer theory*. New York, NY: New York University Press.

Tomsen, S. (1997). Was Lombroso a queer? Criminology, criminal justice, and the heterosexual imaginary. In G. Mason & S. Tomsen (Eds.), *Homophobic violence* (pp. 33–45). Annandale, NSW: Hawkins Press.

Tomsen, S. (2006). Homophobic violence, cultural essentialism and shifting sexual identities. *Social and Legal Studies, 15*, 389–407.

Tomsen, S. (2009). *Violence, prejudice, and sexuality*. New York, NY: Routledge.

Umphrey, M. (1995). The trouble with Harry Thaw. In R. Corber & S. Valocchi (Eds.), *Queer studies: An interdisciplinary reader* (pp. 21–30). Oxford, UK: Blackwell Publishing.

Walklate, S. (2011). *Gender, crime and criminal justice* (3rd ed.). Oxon, UK: Routledge.

Warner, M. (1999). *The trouble with normal: Sex, politics, and the ethics of queer life*. Boston, MA: Harvard University Press.

Wiegman, R. (2012). *Object lessons*. Durham, NC: Duke University Press.

Chapter 25
Hardly Queer, or Very Queer Indeed? Concluding Thoughts about the *Handbook of LGBT Communities, Crime, and Justice*

Vanessa R. Panfil and Dana Peterson

Abstract In this chapter, the *Handbook* editors reflect on the main goals of the volume by revisiting an earlier critique of research with LGBT populations. They synthesize the work in the volume to illustrate how the chapters build on previous work, but expand and clarify central themes within this body of research. They also provide suggestions for the future of queer criminological research.

Keywords LGBT · Lesbian · Gay · Bisexual · Transgender · Trans* · Queer · Criminology · Criminal justice · Queer criminology · Essentializing · Theory · Research · Practice · Heteronormative · Hegemonic · Critical · Critique · Discourse · Victimization · Agency · Resistance

With the Foreword and the preceding 24 chapters, we have collectively attempted to deconstruct assumptions implicit in so much of the existing criminological research: the assumptions of heterosexuality and of normative gender identity. Our volume, then, scratches the surface of what has been "lost," what can be learned, and even how we can learn it. This volume's chapters push further than an overarching critique of criminology and criminal justice's hegemonic history; the chapters dialogue with each other by building on the scant previous research that helped bring these issues to the fore, and also exploring the shortcomings of this previous work to expand our understandings of categorizations, critical perspectives, and cross-cultural differences. In this conclusion, we utilize a prior critique

V. R. Panfil (✉)
School of Criminal Justice, Rutgers University, Center for Law and Justice,
123 Washington Street Room 579B, Newark, NJ 07102, USA
e-mail: vanessa.panfil@rutgers.edu

D. Peterson
School of Criminal Justice, University at Albany, 135 Western Ave.,
DR 219, Albany, NY 12222, USA
e-mail: dpeterson@albany.edu

D. Peterson and V. R. Panfil (eds.), *Handbook of LGBT Communities,*
Crime, and Justice, DOI: 10.1007/978-1-4614-9188-0_25,
© Springer Science+Business Media New York 2014

to frame the arguments presented in the volume, and build on the volume's chapters to advocate for the future of this developing body of scholarship, which is increasingly referred to as "queer criminology."

Revisiting a Critique of Research on Sexual Minority Populations

Over 10 years ago, Savin-Williams (2001) raised several critiques regarding research on sexual minority youth (which also would apply to research on sexual minority adults). These prescient critiques remain salient today, and especially in relation to the topics covered in our volume. One is that extant research focuses on the difficulties sexual minority youth face, with much less attention given to their strength and resiliency. Other critiques raised by Savin-Williams are that assumptions about sexual minority youths' "uniqueness" from heterosexual youth encourages stereotypes about them; that sexual minority youth may be unduly characterized as "at-risk"; that within-group differences likely exist but similar explanations are espoused for the experiences of gay and lesbian youth as a whole; and that "sexual minority" in itself is a problematic differentiation and can be based on vastly different criteria such as attraction, behavior, and/or self-identity. We note that Savin-Williams's critiques can be extended as well to extant research on gender minorities and trans* communities, in that there are similar foci on difference and risk; their experiences are collapsed into categories and explanations based primarily on *sexual* identity and not necessarily gender identity, thus, in many cases, erasing their identities altogether; and "trans*" is itself an umbrella term that may not hold the same meaning for all groups of people categorized as such.

The parallels between the content of this *Handbook* and Savin-Williams's (2001) critiques are patently clear. First, although we want to acknowledge the challenges faced by LGBT populations and bring to light their experiences of victimization (which still remain largely hidden from the public *and* academic audiences), we want to represent the full picture by also critically exploring the ways LGBT people *respond to* exclusion, discriminatory treatment, and victimization. Many of the chapters have focused on LGBT individuals' resistance to their exclusion and on their exercise of agency, including Frederick's work on homeless sexual minority youth; Johnson's work on Dykes Taking Over (DTO); Panfil's work on gay gang- and crime-involved men; and Pearce and Cooper's work on queer equality movements in Southeastern Europe. Of course, many of the difficulties explored throughout the chapters *are* due, in large or small part, to these individuals' sexual and/or gender identities (though perhaps admittedly due to the foci we have stressed to our contributors), but the fact that these individuals find sites of resistance is of paramount importance in light of the criminological literature's traditional focus on LGBT persons as victims of interpersonal violence. The chapters on victimization included herein, such as Messinger's research on same-sex IPV, Stotzer's research on SOGI-based bias crimes, Gillum and

DiFulvio's research on dating violence, and Warbelow and Cobb's research on bullying and anti-bullying legislation, have helped to set the stage for these discussions of agency. They build on impressive traditions of prior work, and are important pieces of the puzzle that help us understand LGBT peoples' resistance. The victim-offender overlap, as reflected in much criminological work, also has its home here and must inform efforts to understand and reduce victimization and crime.

Despite our conscious effort to explore sites of resistance, we may have underestimated the actual nature and quality of resilience and even the current state of affairs. Readers might be surprised, just as we were, for example, that Waldman's chapter on criminalization of HIV transmission focused very little on defendants who engage sexually with members of the same sex, suggesting they are *not* the ones most likely to be swept up by these controversial and inappropriately-applied laws. Or, for example, that Dwyer's work detailed LGBT peoples' partnerships with, not just pain derived from, law enforcement; or perhaps even more striking, that Colvin found that gay and lesbian police officers actually perceive the downsides of closeness with LGBT communities to be more salient than any discernable positives. It was in illuminative instances such as these where we wondered if maybe, in our quest for recognition of and social justice for LGBT populations, we were still unduly subscribing to stereotypes of them as being at risk and/or without agency by assuming certain chapters in our volume would hold several 'truths' to be self-evident. Luckily, our quest for sound historical, theoretical, and empirical work won out, and we celebrate the various competing, but still complementary frameworks (truths) advanced in this volume, including illustrations of both challenge and resilience that serve to break down stereotypes and humanize LGBT populations.

It is also with regard to the issue of categorization and nomenclature where we have struggled to do justice to the many voices in this volume. Even Western notions of "gay" or "transgender" may not be applicable in a global context, as evidenced by Nichols's work on Sri Lankan nachchi. We were also struck by Conover-Williams's revelation that in an often-used and large dataset, a key variable—respondents' sex—was determined based on a visual judgment by the interviewer. It is for these reasons that we all would do well to trouble existing sources' assumptions and data collection methods as they relate to these issues, but also to tread lightly regarding issues of naming and classification. We noted in our introduction (Peterson and Panfil, this volume) that by even employing the "shorthand" term "LGBT people," we are, by strict definition (though not by intention), excluding other diverse identities and representing these heterogeneous people and groups as a homogeneous unit, though we hope our nomenclature of "LGBT communities" has better clarified our intentions. Several authors in this volume question the utility of categories altogether, while others find them to at least be useful and intuitive for various audiences; importantly, respondents themselves may self-identify as and find meaning within categories such as "gay" or "lesbian."

We also made conscious decisions to include some chapters that focus on gay men, on lesbians, on transgender individuals, and so on (instead of the full complement of "LGBT" within a single chapter), to better understand these populations' varied concerns, rather than essentialize or homogenize them. Along these lines, we encourage, as has Savin-Williams, consideration of within-group differences. It is also important to acknowledge that intersections, such as gender and sexuality, in addition to race, socioeconomic status, and other factors structure individuals' experience, and we have attempted to maximize the diversity represented in the volume (though, admittedly, can do only so much in a single collection intended to be broad in nature). While this strategy risks fracturing our understandings of more broadly applicable social phenomena, we do not want to commit errors of exclusion similar to those we critique, and so we have pressed the contributors to consider how individuals' lived realities are affected by other salient social characteristics. In addition, regarding both intersectionalities and categories, we recognize the paralleling pitfalls of grouping people based on sexual identity and race/ethnicity (for example), and have attempted to frame sexual and/or gender identities as critical components of identity, but not at the expense of others. We agree, at least in part, with suggestions made by Ball in this volume regarding deconstructionist sensibility and its efficacy in critically interrogating taken-for-granted categories of identity.

The Way Forward

One common request we gave to *Handbook* authors was to provide suggestions for future theorizing, research, policy, and/or practice, which we often referred to as "the way forward." We encouraged these suggestions with the hope that other *Handbook* authors and our readers could then use these expert pieces of advice in their own research and practice. What, then, is the way forward? This volume has presented diverse and often competing roadmaps for the journey. Although they may disagree on the utility of, for example, big data (e.g., Johnson), hegemonic categories of identity (e.g., Ball), or methods of achieving equality, especially in a global context (e.g., Cobb; Pearce and Cooper), not one author in this *Handbook* was willing to consider that, regarding their topic, the case was closed. A shared sentiment of all authors was the need to keep the conversation going; the cacophony of voices is not as discordant as it may seem. In light of this basic consensus in advocating for further inquiry in one form or another, we do not intend any of the oft-conflicting and sometimes contentious discussions and rec-ommendations presented herein to scare off scholars looking to pursue these lines of inquiry. Indeed, we caution against thinking there is 'one right way' of con-ducting queer criminological research, or research on LGBT populations. For example, Woods's work imparts evidence that there have been many ways and will continue to be; a goal of our volume is to encourage productive dialogue regarding these issues and to provide resources for each of these paths.

We also realize that we are advocating for the hegemonic recommendation of the academic machine in arguing for more research, and in that way, our advice is hardly queer. But we argue, unequivocally, that introducing these concepts and issues into the CCJ discipline's consciousness will ultimately change the discourse, just as feminist scholarship did for issues of gender (and, to a lesser extent, sexuality), as discussed by Miller in the Foreword to this volume. We also hope that Miller's gracious reflection on her own work helps to convince skeptics of how much can be missed when normative assumptions are made in social science research. She asks how *Getting Played* might have been different; we similarly wonder how any other classics might have been different and ultimately, whether this volume would be one of many had the course of CCJ history been charted any differently. Of course, this volume is not one of many; it is one of a handful in good company, but not part of a long-standing tradition (yet). In that regard, this volume is very queer indeed.

Beyond bringing the larger CCJ discipline on board, there is clearly much more work to be done, as evidenced by Dennis's chapter that suggests gay people (gay men, specifically) are still depicted as villains in popular culture; DeJong and Long's research regarding Uganda's proposed legislation that might carry the death penalty for acts of "aggravated homosexuality"; and Levy's work in theorizing how certain individuals are simultaneously the focus of HIV discourse but are excluded from effective treatment. And, of course, the (however-inadequate) protections for LGB people are still light years ahead of protections for transgender and gender non-conforming people, as evidenced by Sumner and Jenness's work on correctional policy and Forbes's work on legislative outcomes. These concerns are related to the quality and competency of treatment for LGBT youth and adults. We need only point to the requests of LGB youth in residential treatment for programming they are not receiving, as described by Belknap, Holsinger, and Little, or to Cannon, Dirks-Linhorst, Cobb, Maatita, Beichner, and Ogle's work on the attitudes of future CJ professionals to get a sense of how underserved LGBT populations may be. These failures of our system responses to adequately serve LGBT populations represent one of the ethical considerations that underlie this volume; failing to recognize and consider gender and sexuality as part of our system responses (or, as part of our response to systems) is, we and others argue, unethical and inhumane. We look eagerly toward the future and provide our support to scholars and activists with social justice goals, as well as all those who seek to improve the lived realities of queer persons globally.

That so much of this course remains yet uncharted is both daunting and exhilarating. A much-beloved paper fortune from a cookie is displayed on the first author's desk, which we decided was applicable in our quest to pursue this program of research and thus, this volume: "Your path is arduous but will be amply rewarding." We trust that this is true.

Reference

Savin-Williams, R. C. (2001). A critique of research on sexual-minority youths. *Journal of Adolescence, 24*, 5–13.

Glossary–Defining Terms and Acronyms

Asexual "An asexual person is a person who does not experience sexual attraction. Unlike celibacy, which is a choice, asexuality is a sexual orientation. Asexual people have the same emotional needs as everybody else and are just as capable of forming intimate relationships." [Source: The Asexual Visibility and Education Network (AVEN), retrieved July 28, 2013 from http://www.asexuality.org/home/].

Bisexual "An individual who is physically, romantically and/or emotionally attracted to men and women. Bisexuals need not have had sexual experience with both men and women; in fact, they need not have had any sexual experience at all to identify as bisexual."[1] "A person emotionally, romantically, sexually and relationally attracted to both men and women, though not necessarily simultaneously; a bisexual person may not be equally attracted to both sexes, and the degree of attraction may vary as sexual identity develops over time."[2]

Cisgender An adjective used to refer to people whose gender identity and/or gender expression is consistent with the sex they were assigned at birth.

FTM Acronym that stands for "female-to-male" transgender (also "transgender man").

Gay "A word describing a man or a woman who is emotionally, romantically, sexually and relationally attracted to members of the same sex" (see footnote 2).

Gender "The activity of managing situated conduct in light of normative conceptions of attitudes and activities appropriate for one's sex category [male or female]" (Source: p. 127 in West, C., & Zimmerman, D. H. (1987). Doing gender. *Gender & Society, 1*(2), 125–151.)

Gender expression "External manifestation of one's gender identity, usually expressed through 'masculine,' 'feminine' or gender-variant behavior, clothing,

---

[1] Gay and Lesbian Alliance Against Defamation (GLAAD). (2010). *GLAAD media reference guide, 8th edn*. Retrieved July 27, 2013 from http://www.glaad.org/reference/transgender

[2] Human Rights Campaign. (2013). HRC's glossary of terms. Retrieved July 27, 2013 from http://www.hrc.org/resources/entry/glossary-of-terms

D. Peterson and V. R. Panfil (eds.), *Handbook of LGBT Communities, Crime, and Justice*, DOI: 10.1007/978-1-4614-9188-0,
© Springer Science+Business Media New York 2014

haircut, voice or body characteristics. Typically, transgender people seek to make their gender expression match their gender identity, rather than their birth-assigned sex" (see footnote 1).

Gender identity "One's internal, personal sense of being a man or a woman (or a boy or a girl). For transgender people, their birth-assigned sex and their own internal sense of gender identity do not match" (see footnote 1).

Gender non-conformity (GNC) Gender expression that does not conform to dominant gender norms of "male" and "female" or "masculine" and "feminine" for one's birth sex.

Hegemony "(1) preponderant influence or authority over others; (2) the social, cultural, ideological, or economic influence exerted by a dominant group." [Source: Merriam-Webster Online Dictionary, retrieved July 29, 2013 from http://www.merriam-webster.com/dictionary/hegemony].

Heteronormativity Pervasive and institutionalized cultural bias in favor of heterosexuality and opposite-sex relationships; cultural assumptions of heterosexuality as the norm.

Heterosexism Assumption that all people are heterosexual; prejudice or discrimination by people who are heterosexual against people who are not heterosexual.

Heterosexual "An adjective used to describe people whose enduring physical, romantic and/or emotional attraction is to people of the opposite sex (also 'straight')" (see footnote 1).

Homophobia "The fear and hatred of or discomfort with people who love and are sexually attracted to members of the same sex" (see footnote 2).

Homosexual "Outdated clinical term considered derogatory and offensive by many gay and lesbian people" (see footnote 1).

Internalized heterosexism (see "Internalized homophobia").

Internalized homophobia "Self-identification of societal stereotypes by an LGBT person, causing them to dislike and resent their sexual orientation or gender identity" (see footnote 2).

Intersex "Describing a person whose biological sex is ambiguous. There are many genetic, hormonal or anatomical variations that make a person's sex ambiguous (e.g., Klinefelter Syndrome). Parents and medical professionals usually assign intersex infants a sex and perform surgical operations to conform the infant's body to that assignment. This practice has become increasingly controversial as intersex adults speak out against the practice. The term *intersex* is **not** interchangeable with or a synonym for *transgender*" (see footnote 1).

IPV (and SSIPV OSIPV) , Acronym for "intimate partner violence" (and "same-sex IPV," "opposite-sex IPV").

Lesbian "A woman whose enduring physical, romantic and/or emotional attraction is to other women. Some lesbians may prefer to identify as gay (adj.) or as gay women" (see footnote 1).

LGBTQIAP Acronym for "lesbian, gay, bisexual, transgender, queer, intersex, asexual, pansexual" (often "LGBT" is used as shorthand to refer to and intended to be inclusive of all persons of non-normative sexual orientation and/ or gender identity).

MSM Acronym for "men who have sex with men."

MTF Acronym that stands for "male-to-female" transgender (also "transgender woman").

Pansexual Refers to someone who is physically, emotionally, and/or romantically attracted to other people regardless of their sex or gender identity. The gender or sex of the other person is insignificant or irrelevant in determining attraction.

Queer "Traditionally a pejorative term, *queer* has been appropriated by some LGBT people to describe themselves. However, it is not universally accepted even within the LGBT community and should be avoided unless quoting or describing someone who self-identifies that way" (see footnote 1).

Sex (Biological sex) "The classification of people as male or female. At birth, infants are assigned a sex based on a combination of bodily characteristics including: chromosomes, hormones, internal reproductive organs, and genitals" (see footnote 1).

Sexual orientation "An inherent or immutable enduring emotional, romantic, sexual and relational attraction to another person; may be a same-sex orientation, opposite-sex orientation or a bisexual orientation" (see footnote 1). "Gender identity and sexual orientation are not the same. Transgender people may be straight, lesbian, gay or bisexual. For example, a man who transitions from male to female and is attracted to other women would be identified as a lesbian or a gay woman" (see footnote 2).

Sex Reassignment Surgery (SRS) Refers to surgical alteration of one's biological sex. Preferred over the term "sex change operation." This is only one small part of a person's transition (see "Transition"). Not all transgender people (see "Transgender") choose to or can afford to have SRS [Definition adapted from GLAAD].

SMS Acronym for "sexual minority status," an umbrella term used to refer to individuals with a sexual orientation other than opposite-sex orientation (see "Sexual orientation").

SOGI Acronym for "sexual orientation and/or gender identity."

Trans* An umbrella term for "non-normative" gender identities (e.g., transgender, transsexual, transvestite, genderqueer, two-spirit, third gender).

Transgender "An umbrella term (adj.) for people whose gender identity and/or gender expression differs from the sex they were assigned at birth. The term may include but is not limited to: transsexuals, cross-dressers and other gender-variant people. Transgender people may identify as female-to-male (FTM) or male-to-female (MTF). Use the descriptive term (*transgender, transsexual, cross-dresser*, FTM or MTF) preferred by the individual. Transgender people may or may not decide to alter their bodies hormonally and/or surgically" (see footnote 1). (see "Sex Reassignment Surgery" and "Transition").

Transition "Altering one's birth sex is not a one-step process; it is a complex process that occurs over a long period of time. Transition includes some or all of the following personal, legal and medical adjustments: telling one's family, friends and/or co-workers; changing one's name and/or sex on legal documents; hormone therapy; and possibly (though not always) one or more forms of surgery" (see footnote 1). [see also "Sex Reassignment Surgery"].

Transsexual (or Transexual) "An older term which originated in the medical and psychological communities. While some transsexual people still prefer to use the term to describe themselves, many transgender people prefer the term *transgender* to *transsexual*. Unlike *transgender*, *transsexual* is not an umbrella term, as many transgender people do not identify as transsexual. It is best to ask which term an individual prefers" (see footnote 1). "A medical term describing people whose gender and sex do not line up, and who often seek medical treatment to bring their body and gender identity into alignment. Avoid using this term unless an individual self-identifies as transsexual" (see footnote 2).

Transvestite An older, derogatory term used to describe a person who occasionally dresses in clothes stereotypically associated with the opposite sex. [Note: "Cross-dressers are usually comfortable with the sex they were assigned at birth and do not wish to change it. 'Cross-dresser' should NOT be used to describe someone who has transitioned to live full-time as the other sex or who intends to do so in the future. Cross-dressing is a form of gender expression and is not necessarily tied to erotic activity. Cross-dressing is not indicative of sexual orientation" (see footnote 1)].

Two-Spirit (also "Third gender") An umbrella term used to refer to multi-gendered, multi-sexed, LGBT, and/or gender-variant Native American or First Nation people.

WSM Acronym for "women who have sex with women."

About the Editors

Dana Peterson received her Ph.D. in Criminal Justice from the University of Nebraska at Omaha and is currently Associate Dean and Associate Professor in the School of Criminal Justice at the University at Albany (New York). She teaches and conducts research primarily on youth gangs and gang prevention, youth violence and juvenile treatment, and the ways in which sex and gender structure each of these. She co-edited (with Frank van Gemert and Inger-Lise Lien) the third Eurogang Network book *Street Gangs, Migration, and Ethnicity* (2008, Willan Publishing); has co-authored numerous articles and book chapters (including a forthcoming chapter on sex, gender, and gangs, co-authored with Vanessa R. Panfil, in *The Oxford Handbook of Gender, Sex, and Crime*, edited by Rosemary Gartner and William McCarthy); and co-authored a book with long-time friends and colleagues Finn-Aage Esbensen, Terrance J. Taylor, and Adrienne Freng titled *Youth Violence: Sex and Race Differences in Offending, Victimization, and Gang Membership* (2010, Temple University Press). And for the past 4 years, she has had the pleasure and honor of serving on the University at Albany Advisory Committee on Lesbian, Gay, Bi-Sexual, Transgender, Queer, Intersexed (LGBTQI) Issues, Co-Chairing the committee for the past 3 years.

Vanessa R. Panfil received her Ph.D. in Criminal Justice from the University at Albany and is currently a post-doctoral associate in the School of Criminal Justice at Rutgers University (Newark, NJ). Her research explores how gender and sexuality shape individuals' experiences with gangs, crime, victimization, and the criminal and juvenile justice systems. For her dissertation, she designed and conducted a partially ethnographic, in-depth interview study of self-identified gay gang members, in order to analyze the complex relationships between crime commission and/or gang membership and the construction of gay and masculine identities. Her published and forthcoming works from that line of inquiry explicitly challenge existing cultural and criminological assumptions regarding gay men. Other forthcoming papers focus on the gendered experiences of both female and male gang members, as well as the promise of qualitative methods for studying queer populations and contributing to criminological theory. She also highly values and has experience with program evaluation. Finally, for over ten years, she has volunteered for LGBTQ advocacy organizations, including those that provide services to at-risk youth and those that seek to improve the quality of life for students, staff, and faculty in higher education.

D. Peterson and V. R. Panfil (eds.), *Handbook of LGBT Communities,*
Crime, and Justice, DOI: 10.1007/978-1-4614-9188-0,
© Springer Science+Business Media New York 2014

Index

0-9

1995 federal Violence Against Women Act (VAWA), 75, 76
2001 National Prosecutor's Survey in the U.S., 47
methodological limitations, 47–48
2004 National Inmate Survey, 97, 98
2007 Law Enforcement Management and Administrative Statistics (LEMAS) survey, 195
2010 National Intimate Partner and Sexual Violence Survey (NISVS), 66, 67
2010 toolkit on LGBT rights, 326
2011 annual meeting of American Society of Criminology (ASC), 4, 6

A

Abject exemptions, 505–506
Abuse, 72, 166, 462, 476
physical, 166, 170
police, 166
sequencing of, 69–70
sexual, 175–178
substance, 70
verbal, 48, 52, 65, 169
Abusers, 68, 70, 71, 72, 73, 74, 75, 79
Accident fallacy
fallacy explained, 367
logical accident, as due process problem, 367–370
Accountability, 155
Accusations of exclusion, 411, 412
Addictions, 89, 95, 485
Administrative segregation, 244
Admiral Duncan bombings, 156
Adolescent dating violence, 438
Africa
politics of sodomy law reform in, 296
sodomy law expansions in, 298

African-Americans
lesbian gang, 109
negative attitudes toward gays and lesbians, 263
Agency, 5, 7, 9, 12, 125, 141, 558, 559
Aggravated assault, HIV-related, 364–367, 369–372
accident fallacy, 367–370
transmitting HIV, 364–367
Aggravated homosexuality, 296, 297, 341
serial offenders for, 343
Aid conditionality, 299, 300, 301, 302, 303
AIDS, 365, 371, 372, 373, 377, 378
and gay people, 92–93
and HIV, 379, 380, 382, 383
AIG (corporation), 113
Air Force Court of Criminal Appeal (AFCCA), 379
Akbam, Zamir (Pakistan's representative to the UN), 295
Albania, 312, 317t, 328, 329, 331
Alcohol, 452, 457t, 468
and substance use, 453, 457t, 469
Aleanca LGBT, 314
All in the Family (television program), 93
Alternative family images, 510
American Medical Association (AMA HOD Resolution 122 2008), 393
American Psychological Association (APA Policy Statement 008), 393
Amnesty International, 158, 286, 296, 297, 320, 322
Anatomical sex segregation, 243
Anatomy-based policies, 231, 242
Androgyny, 88–89
Anomie and strain theories, 26
Anti-discrimination laws, 14, 329, 330
Anti-gay aggression, 56
Anti-gay bullying, 409
Anti-gay harassment, 122, 131

D. Peterson and V. R. Panfil (eds.), *Handbook of LGBT Communities, Crime, and Justice*, DOI: 10.1007/978-1-4614-9188-0,
© Springer Science+Business Media New York 2014

Anti-gay harassment (*cont.*)
    fighting back, 122, 124, 130
    responding with violence, 138–141
Anti-gay violence, 352
Anti-Homosexuality Bill, 11, 296, 297, 298, 299, 340–343.
    See also Uganda Anti-Homosexuality Bill
Anti-lesbian crimes, 57
Anti-lesbian violence, 106
Anti-LGBT laws, 57
Anti-sodomy laws, 10, 11, 17, 24, 26, 27, 345
Anything is possible standard, 368–369, 378, 379, 380, 381
Arizona law, 399
Arrests, 18, 19, 47, 75, 95, 96, 98, 106, 109, 136, 152, 153, 154, 160, 168, 170, 172, 174, 176, 177, 180, 185, 189, 190, 191, 211, 212, 223, 269, 364
Asylum, 324*t*, 325, 329
    gender-based, 326
    phallometric testing, 329
    Turkey's policy, 331, 331n3
Attitudes Toward Lesbians and Gay Men Scale, 266
Audio-CASI (audio computer-aided self interview), 455
Australia, 27n4, 46
    anti-gay bias, 49
    bias crime in, 51
    homosexuality in, 152–154
    LGBT hate crime in, 156–157, 160
    sexual assaults, 53
    transgender respondents, 54

B

BABELNOR, 315
    in Southeast Europe, 316
Banda, Joyce (President of Malawi), 298
Barnes v. City of Cincinnati (2005), 392
Bash Back, 124
Battista v. Clarke (2011), 250n12
Beat, 549n10
Beatie, Thomas (The Pregnant Man), 399
Berisha, Dr. Sali (Albanian Prime Minister), 330
Bias crimes, 20, 45.
    See also Gender identity-based bias crime; Sexual orientation-motivated bias crime; SOGI violence explanation
    basic features, 45–46
    causes of, 46
    consequences of, 58
    definition of, 48

domestic violence, 270
    explanations for, 57–58
    gender identity motivated, 48, 51, 52
    multiple determinism of, 58, 59–60
    perpetrators, 47, 55, 57, 59
    potential for, 269–272
    prosecution rates, 47
    reporting rates, 49
    research issues with, 46, 57
    risk factors, 50–51, 52
    school settings, 271
    sexual orientation motivated, 47, 48–49
Bidirectional IPV, 68
Biomedical technoscience, 514
Biosocial communities, 517
Bipolar societies, 349
Bisexual people, 3, 4, 50, 53, 66–68, 71, 73, 79, 209, 211, 214, 214*t*, 215*t*, 216*f*, 222, 312, 313, 315, 319, 406, 407
Black Feminist Thought, 107
Black lesbian identities, 106
Black Pink Triangle Izmir Association, 315
Blood, 365, 366, 373, 374, 375
Board of Immigration Appeals, 326
Bolivia, 166
Boomerang effect, 322, 326, 327, 332, 333
Boomerang-ricochet dynamics, 323
Boomerangs, 322
(B)ordering, 504, 505, 509, 519
    lives, 507–508
Borders of social normativity, 509–510
Born Free and Equal (U.N. report), 325
Bosnia, 314, 328
Bosnia and Herzegovina (BiH), 312, 317*t*, 328
    homosexuality as disease, 330
Bosnian Genocide, 352, 353
Boyfriends, 98, 133, 441
Boys stroll, 484
Brazil, 52, 166
Bridges v. Wixon (1945), 370
British Crime Survey, 53, 54
Brock v. State (1989), 371, 372
Brooks v. Berg (2003), 241
Bullying, 53, 426, 474
    anti-bullying laws, 406, 410, 411, 421*f*
    anti-bullying policies, 407, 408, 411, 421*f*
    behavior, defining, 408–410
    of LGBT youths, 412, 417, 418, 418, 419
    by peers, 406
    prevalence and consequences of, 406–407
    suicide attempts by victims, 407
Bullying of LGBT youth, federal responses to, 412
    congressional responses, 420

executive branch action, 416–418
legislative proposals, 418–420
leveraging existing legislation, 413–416
tragedy after visible federal response,
    412–413
Bureau of Alcohol, Tobacco, Firearms, and
    Explosives (ATFE), 392
Burundi, homosexuality prohibition, 298

C
California Department of Corrections and
    Rehabilitation (CDCR), 235
California's Administrative Procedure Act,
    242
Cameron, David (British Prime Minister), 299
Canada, 6, 46, 48, 53, 54, 79, 193, 263, 474,
    483, 488, 490
Cancer and AIDS, 520
Capital punishment for homosexuality, 353,
    357
    in African countries, 346
    in Uganda, 340
CD4⁺ cell count, 365, 373.
    See also T-cell count
    basic features, 45, 46
Census of State and Local Law Enforcement
    Departments (CSLLEA), 195
Center for Epidemiologic Studies-Depression
    Scale, 436
Centers for Disease Control and Prevention
    (CDC), 366
    dating violence definition, 432
Central organizing principle of correctional
    systems, 234
Centre for Euro-Atlantic Studies (CEAS), 319
Chicago Alternative Policing Strategy
    (CAPS), 191
Chile, 53
Christian universalism, 344
Chronic offenders, 346
Chronic pain, 433
Cisgender, 389, 390, 394, 397–398, 400, 419,
    479, 484, 488, 547
Citizen rights and LGBT issue, 312
Classical theories of sociology, 26
Clementi, Tyler, 413
Clinton, Hillary, 323
Clothing and adornment, 247, 248–252
Cloud computing, 113
Coercion, 291
Collaboration, 152, 155
Columbus's metropolitan statistical area
    (MSA), 129

Coming out process, 475
Community policing, 150, 154, 183, 187, 188.
    See also Lesbian police officer; Gay police
    officer
    limitations for, 201–202
    measurable outcomes of, 190–191
Comptons Cafeteria raid, 154
Confidentiality Certificate from the U.S.
    National Institute of Health, 128n3
Conflict theory, 95–96
Conflict, power, and resistance in global sod-
    omy law reform, 292–293
Conflict-centred model of the world polity,
    293
Congressional Anti-Bullying Caucus, 420
Continuation program, 240
Convention against Genocide, 357
Convention on the Prevention and Punishment
    of the Crime of Genocide, 339, 348
Cook County jail in Chicago, 230
Correctional mission statements, 234
Correctional Service of Canada, 234
Corrective rape, 13, 57, 346
Council of Europe (COE), 315
The Council of Europe Convention on Pre-
    venting and Combating Violence
    against Women and Domestic Vio-
    lence, 323
Counseling, 213, 214f, 217, 218
    policy implications and recommendations,
    222
    by sexual minority status (SMS), 219t
Court of Appeals for the Armed Forces
    (C.A.A.F.), 376, 379, 380
Crime
    anti-gay bias crimes, 124
    data, in United States, 18–21
    drug selling, 123
    gang activity, 123
    gender, social inequality and, 450–451
    and justice, 542
    sexuality and, 451–452
    violence, 123
Crime-social process theories, 26
Criminal justice, 3, 4, 6, 12, 268, 557
Criminal law, 364, 366, 369–371
    biting cases, 371–375
    sex cases, 375–381
Criminal Man (Lombroso), 22
Criminal offenders. See Villains
Criminal offenses, 517
Criminalization, 150, 152, 153
Criminology and criminal justice (CCJ), 3, 4,
    5, 6, 7, 13, 561

Criminological theory, 17, 20–21
  clinical perspectives on crime, 27–29
  early biological perspectives on crime, 21–22
  feminist criminological perspectives, 28
  psychological perspective on crime, 23–25
  radical (Marxist) perspectives on crime, 28
  sociological perspectives on crime, 25–27
Criminology, 557
  and gay victims, 94–95
  and queer, 534–535
Critical, 557, 560
Critical analysis, 506
Critical ethnography, 522, 523
Critique, 532, 533, 534–535, 537, 538, 540, 542, 544, 547, 549–552
  of criminology, 557
  of research on sexual minority populations, 558–560
Croatia, 50, 312, 317*t*, 318, 328, 329
Crosby v. Reynolds (1991), 244
Crossing borders, 519–521
  distrust of authority, 521
  low socioeconomic status, 521
  for MSM public health outreach projects, 519
  racial discrimination, 521
  social othering, 520
  transnational governmentality, 520
Crown Prosecution Service, United Kingdom, 47
Cruel and unusual punishment, 239, 241, 243
CSR (Classification Staff Representative), 239n7
Cultural clash of civilizations, 290
Culture of control, 231, 232–233, 234, 253
Culture of sexual promiscuity, 350
Current dating violence, 438–439
  univariate analyses of, 439–440
Cyberbullying, 406, 413, 420

D
Darwin's concept of atavism, 22
Data science, 105
  to verify truth, 114
  hygienic categorization of, 116
Date rape laws, 342
Dating relationships
  perpetration in, 435
  victimization in, 435
Dating violence (DV), 434
  future research, 444
  implications for service, 444–445

  prevalence of, 432, 438*t*
  study limitations, 443
Dating violence, demographic questionnaire, 434–435
  Analysis of Variance (ANOVA), 436
  mental health outcomes, 439, 440*t*
  sample demographics, 437*t*
  violence prevalence, 438*t*
Davidson Trauma Scale (DTS), 436
Davis v. Monroe County Board of Education (1999), 409
Death penalty, 153
  de facto death penalty, 354
  for homosexuality, 339, 341, 343, 344, 348
Deblasio v. Johnson (2000), 251
Decided body of case law, 241
Defense of Marriage Act (DOMA), 13, 400
Dehumanization, 351–352
Delinquency, 451, 454, 469
  of sexual minority, 450, 453
  types of, 462, 467
  violent, 465, 466
Delinquent outcomes, 124
Delinquents, 208, 209, 211, 212, 223, 224
Department of Youth Services (DYS) delinquent institutions, 212
Department Operations Manual for the California Department of Corrections and Rehabilitation (CDCR), 238
Department Operations Manual, 250
Depression, 12, 53, 124, 210, 214, 217, 222, 223, 395, 407, 433, 434, 439, 440, 442
Developmental and life course (DLC) theories of crime, 25, 451, 468
Deviance-centered element, 17
Deviant behavior, 27, 186
Deviant family images, 510
Diagnostic and Statistical Manual (DSM), 23, 152, 237, 253, 436, 490
  homosexuality, removal from, 24
"Differential-reinforcement" theory, 26
Disability, 105, 341, 342, 394, 395, 417, 419, 420, 433
Disbordered lives, 508–511
Disclosure, 159, 215, 381
  HIV, 561
  of sexual orientation, 186
  SSIPV, 75
Discrimination, 172, 269, 351, 382, 478, 516
  employment, 184, 270, 390–393, 408
  fighting, 401
  housing, 393–395
  sex-based, 408
  and transgender, 389

Discriminatory interactions, 269–272
Disordered bodies, 508–511
Dittrich, Boris (LGBT rights advocacy director in Skopje), 320–321
Diversity, 184, 185, 190–192, 202
Doe v. Bell (2003), 395
Doe v. United Consumer Financial Services (UCFS) (2001), 391
Doe, and U.S v. Anoka Hennepin School District (2011), 416
Domestic violence, 74, 75, 76, 93, 94, 131, 190, 270, 271, 274, 445
Domestic violence allegations, 270
Don't Ask, Don't Tell (DADT) policy, 13
Don't Say Gay laws, 422–425, 425*f*, 426
Drug and alcohol use, 474
Drug use, 468, 481–482
Drugs, 452, 456*t*
Due process problem, 367–371, 375, 377, 378, 381
Dutch embassy, 320
Dykes and Fags Bash Back, 124
Dykes Taking Over (DTO), 104
  anxiety-fueled crisis, 111
  masculine young women, 112
  same-sex sexual harassment, 111

E
Ecuador, 325
Education, 453, 459, 469
Educational
  attainment, 195, 271
  factors, 262
  independent variables, 457*t*, 458
  leaders, 112
  policy, 284
  protective and risk factors, 461*t*, 465
  responses, 270
  systems, 113
  training, 8, 408, 409
Effeminate homosexuals, 238
Eighth Amendment protections against cruel and unusual punishment, 239
Emotional labor, 188
  and police work, 188–189
Employment discrimination, 388
End of history thesis, 290n4
Endogenous or internally generated changes, 287
Entrapment, 152, 153
Enumeration, 410
Equal Employment Opportunity Commission (EEOC), 392, 408

Essentializing, 9, 12, 560
Ethnography of sexuality, 522–523
European Court of Human Rights (ECHR), 326
European Union (EU), 11, 47, 312, 324*t*
EU Conference of Parliamentary Committees for Union Affairs, 333
Exposing a juvenile to immorality, 90

F
Facebook, 113, 297, 315, 320
Fag/faggot, 128, 133, 138
Fair Housing Act (FHA), 394
Family, 451–453, 458, 468, 469
Family conflict, 474
Farmer v. Brennan (1994), 237, 243
Fatigue, 433
FBI Hate Crime Reports, 94
Federal Bureau of Prisons, 234, 235, 240
Female adolescents, 109
Female inmates, 249, 250
Female sex criminality, 22
Female to male (FTM), 388
Femininity, 167, 169, 173, 178, 180
Feminist criminology, viii, 28, 109, 450, 536n3
Feminist IPV theory, 70
Feminist methodology, 107
Feminist scholarship, 17, 107, 507, 561
Fields v. Smith (2010), 240
Fierce (membership-based organization), 108
Fighting back, 122, 124, 130, 141
  for building reputation, 140
Films
  Aladdin (1992), 91
  Cruising (1980), 92
  Diamonds are Forever (1971), 91
  Gilda (1946), 91
  The Maltese Falcon (1941), 91
  Midnight Cowboy (1969), 92
  My Child, 332
  Paris is Burning (Livingston and Swimar), 484
  Silence of the Lambs(1991), 94
  The Parade, 33
  Zenne Danner, 33
  Peter Pan (1953), 91
  The Powerpuff Girls (1998-2005), 91
  Ratatouille (2007), 91
  Rope (1948), 91
  Silence of the Lambs (1991), 94
  Skyfall (2012), 91
  Strangers on a Train (1951), 91

Films (*cont.*)
  Terry and the Pirates (1936), 91
  The Parade, 331
  Thunderball (1965), 91
  Zenne Dancer, 331
Fines, 153
First Amendment, 250, 410, 424
First gay criminals, 88, 89
First gay victims, 91–93
Five Factor Model (FFM), 24
Former Yugoslav Republic of Macedonia
  (FYR Macedonia), 312, 317*t*
Fostering Connections to Success and
  Increasing Adoptions Act of 2008, 396
Foucault's framework, 114
Fourteenth Amendment, 240
Freeze-frame policies, 240
Freud's concept of sublimation, 23

G
Gallup, 115
Gang violence, 134–136
  Boog's experience with, 136–138
Gangs, 104, 106, 108, 109, 122, 125.
  See also Lesbian gang policing
Gastrointestinal problems, 433
Gathering officer experiences and perceptions,
  192
Gay, 3, 4, 5, 7, 9, 10, 66, 67, 77, 78, 209, 211,
  212, 214, 214*t*, 215*t*, 216*f*, 222, 312,
  383, 406, 407, 412, 415, 419, 424, 558,
  559, 561
  anti-gay harassment, 5, 9, 122
  discrimination against, 220
  men, involvement in violence, 123–125
Gay & Lesbian to Socialize and Rehabilitation, 315
Gay and Lesbian Liaison Unit (GLLU), 194
Gay and lesbian social movement, 114
Gay bashing, 92
Gay disease, 347
Gay identity, 127, 127n1
Gay intersubjectivity, 512
Gay men's violence, 130
  involvement in, 123–125
Gay police officer, 185–187
  conflicting roles in LGBT communities,
  198
  demographic information of respondents,
  195, 195*t*
  focus groups sessions with, 194–195
  hate crime victims, feeling towards, 199
  interpersonal relationships, 200

issue of disclosure of sexual orientation,
  186
in law enforcement environment, 187
responses to more effective policing, 196,
  197*t*
served in silence, 184
sexual orientation demographic information about respondents, 196, 196*t*
socialization of, 201
survey of, 192–194
Gay pride parades, 50, 52, 316–319, 321
Gay villains, 91
Gay/lesbian prisoners, 97–99
  differences in life histories, 99
  fit in with society, 99
Gayborhoods, 51
Gay-rights diplomacy and country report
  cards, 327–330
Gay-straight alliances (GSAs), 418, 468
*Gebser v. Lago Vista Independent School
  District* (1998), 409
Gender, 19, 312, 325, 329, 450–451
  definition, 20
Gender defined models of sexuality, 167
Gender diversity, 150, 155, 160
Gender dysphoria, 237, 238, 398, 490
  treatment, 238, 239
Gender expression, 105–106, 396, 406n1
Gender identity, 6, 8, 9, 10, 13, 304, 313, 315,
  321, 323, 324*t*, 326, 328, 329, 332
  bias crimes based on, 51–52
  measures, 115
  bias, 19
  omission from crime data, 20
  sociological-criminological engagement
  with, 26
Gender Identity Committee, 230
Gender identity disorder (GID), 237, 398, 490
Gender identity-based bias crime, 51–52
  characteristics, 52
  risk factors for, 52
Gender identity-related bullying, 396
Gender inequalities, crime-facilitative features
  of, viii
Gender minorities, 312, 313, 322, 323, 324*t*,
  327, 332
Gender nonconforming (GNC) individuals,
  393, 394, 395, 396
Gender nonconformity, 5, 387, 388, 389, 390,
  475
Gender presentation, 106, 249, 251, 389, 393,
  396, 397
Gender stereotyping, 409, 414–416, 418
"Gender-appropriate" punishment, 231

Gender-based asylum, 324*t*, 326
Gender-based violence, 323, 325
Gender-neutral, 231
Gender-segregated. *See* Sex-segregated
Gender-specific needs, 208
Gendered organization, 231
General strain theory, 208, 215
Genitalia-based approach, 242
Genocide, 339, 340, 357, 358
  definition, 355
  eight stages of, 348–355, 358
  of homosexuals, 339, 348
  prior genocides, 355, 356
Genocide Watch, 348
Ginn v. Georgia (2008), 364
Giraldo v.California Department of Corrections and Rehabilitation (2007), 243, 248
Girlfriends, 98
Global gender/sexuality mainstreaming, 322–327
Global governance, 332
Global obsession with security, 517
Global sodomy law reform
  conflict, power, and resistance in. *See* Conflict, power, and resistance in global sodomy law reform
  and world polity perspective, 285–286
  world polity perspective on, 288–289
Global South, 292, 301, 302, 304
GLSEN (Gay, Lesbian, and Straight Education Network), 115, 406, 407, 411
Google Search, 113, 235
Gossip, 133
Governmentality, 292
Graffiti, 456*t*, 460, 460*t*
Grassroots organizations, 314
Greene v. Bowles (2004), 243
Gross indecency, 88
Grossman v. Bernards Township Board of Education (1975), 391
GSA (Gay Straight Alliance), 418, 468, 469
Guatemala, 325
Gynecological problems, 433

H
Harassment, 151, 154, 157–159, 406, 408, 411–413, 418–421
  discriminatory, 413
  gender-based, 414, 416
  peer-to-peer, 417
  prevent and punish, 410
  same-sex, 409

sexual. *See* Sexual harassment
  teacher-on-student, 410
  verbal, 415, 424
Hard labor, 153
Harff's political model, 355
  autocratic rule, 356
  economic and political interdependence, 357
  exclusionary ideologies, 356
  political upheaval, 355
  prior genocides, 355–356
Harlem, 89
Hate crime legislation, 155
  in Australia, 156
Hate crime paradigms, 537
Hate Crime Statistics Act (1990), 92, 155
Hate Crime: Impact, Causes and Responses (Chakraborti and Garland), 538
Hate crimes, 57, 160, 190, 197*t*, 199
  definition, 327
Health as a human right, 504, 523
Health inequality, 513, 516, 522
Hegemonic history, 557, 560
Hegemonic masculinity, 70, 111
Helsinki Watch, 322
Heteronormative, x, 6
  society, 99, 304, 451
  violence, 6, 12, 87, 247
Heterosexism, 5, 71, 74, 98, 433
Heterosexual, 98
  vs gay men, 98
Highly Active Antiretroviral Therapy (HAART), 365, 366
HIV, 364, 371, 372, 378, 380–382, 515–517
  aggravated assault cases, 368, 369, 374
  and AIDS, 379
  developed in saliva, 374
  knowingly spreading, 342
  related assaults, 380
  transmitting, 364–367, 375, 383
HIV criminalization, 364, 382
HIV transmission, stemming
  criminal conviction, 382
  effective communication, 382
  harsh criminal penalties, 381–382
  stigma and criminalization, 383
HIV/AIDS, 304, 347, 433, 504, 509, 511–515, 516, 517, 520, 521
HIV-negative, 364, 370, 371
HIV-positive, 364, 366, 367, 369–371, 377–383
  blood, 365, 366, 373, 374, 375
  immune system, 366
  needle prick, 373

saliva, 372, 373, 374, 375
HIV-specific RNA, 365
Hollywood, 88–89
Homeless young LGBT people, 12
Homelessness, 480, 481, 482, 483, 484, 486,
    487, 489, 491, 493
  complications, 482–483
  criminalization and social culture, 488–490
  diversity of experience, 483–486
  drug use, mental health, and victimization,
    481–482
  leaving home, 474–477
  legal control of, 488
  social relationships, street culture, and
    belonging, 486–488
  with street prostitution, 485
  subsistence and sex work, 477–481
Homophobia, 87, 91, 94, 95, 96, 156, 158, 272,
    358, 475
  in Africa, 345
  and spread of disease, 350
  in Uganda, 347
  in U.S., 355
  in Western cultures, 349
Homophobia: A Weapon of Sexism (Pharr),
    208
Homophobic attitudes, 152, 157
Homophobic bullying, 109, 112, 124, 125,
    128, 138, 140, 475, 482
Homophobic policing practices, 159
Homosexual advance defense, 269
Homosexual deviancy thesis, 17
Homosexual intent, 90
Homosexual psychopaths, 89
Homosexuality, 17, 150, 152, 156
  definition, 340–341
  evolving conceptions, 22
Homosexuals, 88, 90, 506, 510, 513, 516
  apocalyptic, 511
  behavior, 519
  and HIV/AIDS, 513
  males, 89
  as toxic bodies, 512
Honce v. Vigil (1993), 394
Honduras, 325
Hong Kong, 49, 53, 263
Honor crimes, 321
Hoover, J. Edgar, 89
Hormonal treatment, 231, 237, 239, 240, 249,
    253, 330
Housing assignments, 242, 252
Human Rights Campaign (HRC), 115, 406,
    407, 412
Human Rights Watch, 57, 297, 320

Huntington's clash of civilizations thesis,
    291n6
Hypercriminalization, 518
Hypermasculine, 125, 243
Hypotheses, on risk and protective factors with
    sexual minority, 453

I
IBM data machines, 114
Identity, 4, 5, 6, 7, 12
  confusion, 93
Identity-based approach, 30, 242, 243
IGLYO (International Gay, Lesbian, Bisexual,
    Transgender, Queer Youth, and Student
    Organization), 315, 316
ILGA-Europe, 315
Illinois policy, 237
Immaturity, 133
Impersonal Guilt theory, 368
  guilt is personal, 369–370
Imprisonment, 153, 234, 340, 341, 346, 383
Incarcerated, 208, 209, 211, 212, 213, 214,
    215, 216, 217, 218.
  See also Incarcerated Ohio youth, findings
  counseling by SMS, 219t
  policy implications and recommendations,
    222–224
  by SMS, 220t
Incarcerated Ohio youth, findings
  current analyses regarding SMS youth and
    programming, 217–221
  previously-reported findings on SMS
    youth, 213–217
  self-reported sexual identity by sex/gender
    and race, 215t
  survey options received and desired, 214f
Indecent behavior, 90
Independent Living Program, 218n3
India, 302, 303, 304
Indigenous people, 51
Inductive approach (data analysis), 128
Injury, 433
*Injustice at Every Turn: A Report of the
    National Transgender Discrimination
    Survey*, 236
Institute of Education Sciences (IES), 115
Institutionalized values and myths, 233
Intel, 113
Intergovernmental organizations (IGOs), 288
Internalized homophobia, 53, 54, 216, 222,
    441, 475
International Council on Human Rights Policy,
    516

International Day Against Homophobia, 328
International Day Against Homophobia, Biphobia and Transphobia (IDAHO), 331
International Gay Pride Day, 319
International Lesbian Gay, Bisexual, Trans, and Intersex Association (ILGA), 285–286
International Monetary Fund, 299
International non-governmental organizations (INGOs), 285, 288
Intersectionality, 31, 106–108, 516, 520, 521
Intersex, 77, 312, 328–329
Interviews, 126–128
  gay identity, 127, 127n1
  period of, 127
Intimate partner violence (IPV), 65, 131–132, 432.
  See also Opposite-sex IPV (OSIPV); Same-sex IPV (SSIPV); SSIPV, dynamics
  adverse mental and physical health outcomes, 433
  future directions, 76–79
Intimate Partner Violence in LGBTQ Lives (Ristock), 535
Inverts. *See* Homosexuals
Invisibility element, 17
Islam in the former Yugoslavia, 340
Islamic and Western cultural traditions, 291
Isomorphism, 305
Istanbul Convention, 323
Istanbul Criminal Court, 327
Istanbul, Turkey, 318
It Gets Better Project, 158, 413, 416, 420

J

J.L. v. Mohawk Central School District (2010), 415
Jealousy, 93, 132, 133, 364
The Journal of Interpersonal Violence, 92
Judaism in the Holocaust, 340
Justice, 387–389, 391, 401
Justifiable violence, 130
  for building reputation, 140
  disrespect as recurrent theme, 133–134
  explainable, but not justifiable, 134
  intimate matters, 131–133
  self-defense and the defense of others, 130–131
Juvenile delinquency, 97, 467
Juvenile incarceration facilities, 215
Juvenile justice system, 395, 396
Juveniles, 211, 224

K

Kamanyire, Bishop Eustace, 344
Kantaras v. Kantaras (2004), 398
Kaos GL, 315
Keyword search, 94
Kicked out, 454, 455
"Kill the Gays" Bill. *See* Anti-Homosexuality Bill
Knowledge, 7, 13, 16, 54, 201, 273, 520, 543, 547
Kosilek v. Maloney (2002), 239
Kosilek v. Spencer (2012), 241
Kosovo, 312, 313, 317t
  civil society organizations (CSOs) in, 320
Kowalski v. Berkeley County School District (2011), 410

L

Labeling theory, 208, 215
Lambdaistanbul LGBT Solidarity Association, 315
Law and public policy, ix
Law enforcement, 185–188, 191, 193, 194, 200
Law enforcement agencies, 274
  goal, 271
Law Enforcement Gays and Lesbians International (LEGAL International), 193
Law Reform (Decriminalization of Sodomy) Act of 1989, 27n4
Law-abiding activity, 135
Law-on-the-books and law-in-action, 254
Lawrence v. Texas (2003), 75
Laws
  contracts law, 398
  defining sex, 391
  federal law, 400
  housing discrimination, 394
  preventing discrimination, 389, 390, 391
  protecting civil rights, 387
  specific areas, 388
  transgender equality in, 399
Left-realism, 29
Legacy of colonization, homosexuality and, 344–345
(Legal) self-regulation, 508
Legitimacy, 233–234, 293, 295, 301, 303, 517
Lesbian, 3, 4, 7, 9, 10, 66, 67, 71, 73, 77, 208, 209, 211, 212, 214, 214t, 215t, 216f, 222, 312, 406, 407, 419, 558, 559
  cure lesbianism, 13
  queer landscape of the borderlands, 108–110

threat, 106
Lesbian fusion, 71
Lesbian gang policing, 110–112
Lesbian police officer, 185–187
  conflicting roles in LGBT communities,
    198
  demographic information of respondents,
    195, 195*t*
  focus groups sessions with, 194–195
  hate crime victims, feeling towards, 199
  interpersonal relationships, 200
  issue of disclosure of sexual orientation,
    186
  in law enforcement environment, 187
  responses to more effective policing, 196,
    197*t*
  served in silence, 184
  sexual orientation demographic informa-
    tion about respondents, 196, 196*t*
  socialization of, 201
  survey of, 192–194
Lesbian Youth in Resistance, 104, 105
Lesbian, gay, bisexual, and trans* (LGBT)
  people. *See* LGBT (lesbian, gay,
  bisexual, or transgender)
Lesbian, gay, bisexual, transgender, and queer
  (LGBTQ) populations, 16
  biological degeneracy, 31
  crime data, in United States, 18–21
  criminal victimization, 20
  experiences of crime, 16
  nature-nurture debate, 32
  sexual deviance, 18
Levin & McDevitt's typology of bias crime
  perpetrators, 55, 56
Lexis Nexis Academic, 235
LGB (lesbian, gay, and bisexual), 66
LGB parades, 321
LGB vs LGBT, 262
LGBQ (lesbian, gay, bisexual, and queer), 388
LGBT (lesbian, gay, bisexual, and/or transgender), 3, 4, 5, 262, 406, 414, 532,
  558, 559, 560, 561
  adults, 7
  college students' attitudes toward, 262–264
  communities, 8–12
  criminal justice majors' attitudes toward,
    265–268
  as queer, 547
  rights movement, 284
  thematic panels and roundtables, 6
  violence against, 45
  youths, 7, 11

LGBT activism, 313
LGBT community, 104, 115, 199–200, 269,
  351
LGBT delinquents, 97
LGBT education initiatives, 272–274
LGBT homicides, 49
LGBT human rights, 304
LGBT issues
  bias, potential for, 269–272
  and criminal justice education, 262
  discriminatory interactions, 269–272
  future directions, 274–275
  and status of criminal justice education on,
    268–269
  study limitations, 265
LGBT offenders, 87, 88, 95–97
LGBT organizations, transnational networks,
  332
LGBT police recruitment, 157
LGBT rights, timeline international instru-
  ments addressing, 324*t*
LGBT-police landscapes, 159–161
LGBT-police relations, 150–151
  contemporary moments of, 155–158
  future of, 158–159
  historical painful moments of, 151–155
LGBTQ populations, 541
LGBTQ youth, 111
LGBTT (Lesbian, Gay, Bisexual, Transvestite,
  and Transsexual) 315n2
Liaison officers, 199, 202
License to Bully provisions, 422–425
Life course, 451, 470
LİSTAG (Families of LGBTs in Istanbul), 315
Littleton v. Prange (1999), 399
Long v. Nix (1995), 238
Los Angeles School of Law, 115
Lovins v. Pleasant Hill Public School District
  (2010), 415
Lukšić, Igo (Montenegro's Prime Minister),
  330

M

Macedonian Helsinki Committee of Human
  Rights (MHCHR), 320
Macy v. Holder (2012), 392
Maggert v. Hanks (1997), 237, 241
Malawi, homosexuality prohibition, 298
Male inmates, 249
Male-to-female (MTF), 388
Male-to-female transgender sex workers, 166
Male-to-female transgender youth, 211, 397

Manual for Courts-Martial (MCM), 376, 378
Mardi Gras, 150, 151, 155, 159
Mario v. P&C Food Mkts. (2000), 393
Marked toxicity, 505
Marxist studies of class differences
  in crime, 95
Masculine female adolescent, 105
Masculine games, 125
Masculine women and feminine men
  culture, 89
Masculinity, ix, 111, 154, 179, 211, 442
  performance of, 28, 56, 56, 125
  physical toughness, 131
  protective behaviors, 106, 110, 131, 138,
    263, 346
Mattachine Review, 24
Medical care, 232, 238
  accessing, 239–242, 389
Medical deviance and disease, 517
Medical knowledge, 151, 152, 153, 156
Medicalization, 511
Medina-Tejada v. Sacramento County (2006),
  245
Men who have sex with men (MSM), 52, 347,
  504, 519, 523
Mental health, 481–482, 484, 489, 490
Mental health problems, 474, 475, 477, 481,
  483
Mentors, 452, 453, 455, 458, 469
Meritor Savings Bank v. Vinson (1986), 409
Meriwether v. Faulkner (1987), 239, 240, 244
Meyer, John W., 286
Meyer's world polity perspective, 286–288,
  305
Micro-physics of power, 292
Miles v. New York University (1997), 410
Milk, Harvey (gay politician), 155
Mistrust, 150
Model of the gay criminal, 87
Model of the gay victim, 87
Modern criminology, inception, 16
Modern Homophobia Scale, 267
Modern homosexual identity, 25
Montenegro, 312, 317*t*, 321, 323, 328, 329,
  330
Montgomery v. Indep. Sch. (2000), 409n3
Mortality, 433
Moscone, George (Mayor of San Francisco,
  CA), 155
Movies. *See also* Films
  sexual perversion in, 91
MSM of color, 504, 505, 513, 523
Mudoko dako, 345

Murray v. United States Bureau of Prisons
  (1997), 251
Museveni, Yoweri Kaguta (President of
  Uganda), 298
My Child (documentary), 332
MySpace, 126

N
Nachchi, 5n1, 165, 166, 168
  cross dressing, 168
  gender transgression, 168
  and masculine partners, 167
National Association of Social Workers
  (NASW Policy on Transgender and
  Gender Identity, in Social Work Speaks
  2009), 393
National Crime Victimization Survey (NCVS),
  19
National Health Indicators (NHIS) Survey,
  115
National Longitudinal Study of Adolescent
  Health (Add Health), 67, 454
NATO (North Atlantic Treaty Organization),
  312, 313
Naz Foundation, 302, 303
Naz Foundation v Union of India, 302
Needle prick, 373
Neo-institutionalist world polity perspective,
  284
The Netherlands, 56, 315, 490n11
New phenology, 231, 234
  and culture of control, 232–233
New York City Gay Officers Action League
  (GOAL NY), 192, 194
New York City Police Department (NYPD),
  108, 184
New Zealand, bias crime in, 51
NGO Pink Embassy, 328
NGO TGEU (Transgender Europe), 328
Nigeria, 298, 345, 346
Nominalist rebranding, 533
Non-SMS, 208, 210, 211, 213, 215, 215*t*, 216,
  217, 218, 219*t*, 220*t*, 221, 222, 223
Normative, 557, 561
Normative sex/gender relations, 236
Nuremberg Race Laws, 353

O
Obama, Barack, 76, 210, 343, 412, 415
  2011 directive by, 325
  same-sex marriage rights, 211

Offending, 16, 18, 20, 30, 31, 32
  masculinity in, 28
  motivations for, 29
Office for Democratic Institutions and Human
  Rights (ODIHR), 45, 327
Ohio Office of Criminal Justice Services
  (OCJS), 208
Ohio v. Roberts (2004), 364
Oncale v. Sundowner Offshore Services
  (1998), 409
The Onion (Ugandan tabloid publication), 351
Opposite-sex harassment, 409
Opposite-sex IPV (OSIPV), 65
  relative prevalence of, 66–68
  relative prevalence among bisexuals, 68
Organization for Security and Cooperation in
  Europe (OSCE), 45
Organization of Islamic Cooperation, 293
Organization of the Islamic Conference (OIC),
  294, 303
  act of resistance to the UN HRC resolution,
  295
Orientation. *See* Sexual orientation
Organization Q, 314, 315
Organizational culture, 234
Organizational perviousness, 234n2
Organized deviant group, 27. *See also*
  Homosexuality
Orthodox Church clergy, 316
Othering, 349, 350, 351, 352, 358
Others, 504, 506, 507, 508, 511

P
The Parade (2011 Serbian film), 331
Parent–child relationships, 451, 452, 453, 458,
  468, 469
Paris is Burning (Livingston and Swimar), 484
Partnership, 150, 151, 158, 159, 160
  policing, 155–158
Patriarchal sexual ideology, 22
Pederasts, 22
  insane criminal, 22
Peer dynamics, 56
Personal psychological dysfunction, 480
*Perverse Criminologies: The Closet of Doctor
  Lombroso* (Groombridge), 539
Perversion, 151, 152, 153, 155, 158
Peter meter study, 55, 56
Philadelphia Inquirer, 110
Philippines, 166, 178
*Phillips v. Michigan Department of Correc-
  tions* (1990), 240
Philosophic resonance, 233

Physical abuse, 474
Pillay, Navi (United Nations High Commissioner for Human Rights), 319
Pink Life Association LGBTT Solidarity, 315
Pinkerton v. United States (1946), 370
Police abuses
  failure to protect, 171–172
  false accusations, 172–173
  forced bribes and theft, 170–171
  forced gender behavior, 174–175
  physical abuse, 170
  punishment inequalities, 173–174
  sexual abuse, 175–178
  verbal abuse, 169
Police culture, 160
Police departments in the United States,
  184–185
Police liaison, 157, 158
Police mistreatment, 152
Policing, 104, 105, 108, 114, 116, 117.
  See also Lesbian gang policing
  in lesbian and gay communities, 189–190
Political-economic transformations, 313
Politico-financial neoliberalism, 514
Politics, 158, 290, 542, 547, 549
  inmate, 131
  queer, 115
  racial identity, 108
  sexual, 300
  sexual identity, 301, 521, 533
  of sodomy law, 296, 297
Polluted risk behavior, 508
Ponnaya, 169, 171, 175, 176, 179
Poor pregnancy outcomes, 433
Poststructural theory, 533, 550
Post-traumatic stress disorder (PTSD), 12,
  433, 436, 439, 440, 442, 477, 481
Power differentials, 71
  dependency, 71
  heterosexism, 71–72
  HIV status, 72
  labor, 71
  outness, 71
Practice, 4–10, 13, 560
Pratt v. Indian River Central School District
  (2010), 415, 416
Prejudice-motivated violence, 45
Price Waterhouse v. Hopkins (1989), 390, 391,
  409
Prison policies, 231
  deference toward corrections, 231
Prison systems, 230, 250, 490
Prisons, 89, 94, 98.
  See also Gay/lesbian prisoners

gay female vs heterosexual prisoners, 95
gay male vs heterosexual prisoners, 95
  same-sex practices in, 94
Professionalization, 150, 155, 156
Pronoun use, 247, 248
Prostitution, 22, 27, 88, 94, 167, 484, 485, 490
Protective factors, 452, 463t, 464t, 465t, 466t
  family, 453
  peers and mentors, 453
  religion, 453
  school, 452
  work, 453
Pro-gay civil rights legislation, 57
Psychological distress, 475, 476
Psychopathia Sexualis (Krafft-Ebing), 21, 22
Psychoticism-Extraversion-Neuroticism
  (PEN) model, 24
Public health, 11, 65, 304, 364, 381, 383, 513,
  519
Public inquiries, 153
Punitive panopticism, 518
*Putnam v. Board of Education of Somerset
  Independent Schools* (2000), 415

Q
Q Festival, 318
Quantification of identities, 106–108
Quantitative matrix, 104, 105, 113, 114, 116
Queer, 2, 4, 114, 437, 532, 533–534, 558, 561
  achieving justice, 548–549
  discursive reversal, 544–546
  equality movements in Southeastern Europe, 558
  equals sexuality and gender, 546–548
  features, notion of, 533
  as identity category, 535–536
  investments in the state, 548–549
  regulatory projects, 548–549
*Queer (In)justice: The Criminalization of
  LGBT People in the United States*
  (Mogul et al.), 535, 536
"Queer CCJ" listserv, 6
Queer criminology, vii, 6, 8, 12, 13, 18, 532,
  536n3, 539–542, 539n6, 558
  attitude, 532
  feminist research, 540n7
  pioneers of, 8
  as project of knowledge production,
    542–544
  research work, 560
Queer Nation, 124
Queer recognition in methodological regimes,
  112–114

Queer scholars, 301
Queer theory, 107, 532, 533, 533n1
  concepts of, 534–535
  and criminological reluctance, 549–551
  legitimate and irresponsible citizenship,
    537
  respectable and non-respectable members,
    538
  as set of theoretical tools, 536–539
Queer-bashing, 92
*Queering Conflict: Examining Lesbian and
  Gay Experiences of Homophobia in
  Northern Ireland* (Duggan), 535
Queering criminology, 29–32
  deconstructionist paradigms, 30
  definition conflicts, 30
  diversity, 31
  nature-nurture debate, 32

R
Race, 16, 18, 19, 20, 25, 29, 30, 31, 32, 454,
  464, 469
Race and gender issues, 270, 273
Racialized others vs LGBT communities, 301
Ray v. Antioch Unified Sch. (2000), 409n3
Rehabilitative programming, 231
Religion, 452, 453
Religious knowledge, 151, 152, 153
Research, 3, 4, 5, 6, 7, 8, 9, 13, 557, 558, 559,
  560, 561
Resistance, 558, 559
Revised Conflict Tactics Scale (CTS2), 435
Rhoades v. Iowa (2008), 364
Ricochet process, 322
Rights and Respect of Others, 247
Risk factors, 452, 463t, 464t, 465t, 466t
  alcohol and substance use, 453
  housing stability, 454
  victimization, 454
Rolling Stone (Ugandan tabloid publication),
  350
Romania's sodomy laws, 300
Running away, 454, 465, 466, 467, 469

S
Safe Schools Improvement Act (H.R. 1199),
  412, 419
Safety and security, legitimacy and the centrality of, 233–234
  correctional problem, 233
  organizational culture, 234
  organizational legitimacy, 233

organizational perviousness, 234n2
Sakia Gunn case, viii, 106
Saliva, 372, 373, 374, 375
Same-sex affection, 151, 152, 153, 154, 157, 158
Same-sex behavior, 506, 509, 510, 511, 512, 518, 520, 521
Same-sex harassment, 409
Same-sex IPV (SSIPV), 65, 131–132
   prevalence of bidirectional versus unidirectional, 68
   relative prevalence among bisexuals, 68
   relative prevalence of, 66–68
   relative prevalence of forms of, 66
Same-sex relationships, public attitudes on, 344–345
San Francisco AIDS Foundation (SFAF), 382
Sarajevo, BiH, 318
Sarejevo Open Centre, 314
Savage, Dan (gay writer and activist), 413
Savin-Williams's critiques, 558
Scales v. United States (1961), 370
Schools, 415, 451, 452, 458, 461t, 466, 468, 469
   using bully pulpit, 416
   bullying prevention in, 407, 408, 411
   suicide risk for LGBT students, 407
   Title IX in, 413, 414
Scroggins v. State (1990), 372–373, 374
Second World War, 286, 293, 305
Self-defense, 123, 130
Self-harming behaviors, 210, 224
Serbia, 313, 314, 317t
Severe, Pervasive, and Objectively Offensive Legal Standard, 408
Sex fiend, 89
Sex hierarchy evidences, 511
Sex segregation, 231
Sex presentation. See Gender presentation
Sex reassignment, 94
Sex reassignment surgery, 237, 240, 241
Sex work, 467, 474, 476, 478n3, 485, 486, 493.
   See also Nachchis
   complications, 482
   diversity of experience, 483–486
   involvement in, 481
   male-to-male sexual contact, 167
   nachchi and masculine partners, 167
   practical benefits, 491
   significant diversity in, 484
   social control of, 490
   subsistence and, 477–481
   victimization, 482

Sex workers, 52
Sex-segregated, 10, 230, 231, 232, 245, 252, 253
Sex/gender, 230, 231, 236
Sexology, science of, 21
Sexual abuse, 175–178, 474, 476
   counseling, 219t, 221t
Sexual assault, 455, 458t, 461t, 462, 469
Sexual attraction, 343
Sexual behavior, 504, 507, 508, 509, 510, 515, 516
   medicalization of, 504
Sexual clash of civilizations, 295
Sexual deviance, 18, 150
Sexual disorder, 511–515
Sexual diversity, 157
Sexual diversity training, 157
Sexual exchange, 478n4
Sexual harassment, 414, 415, 417
Sexual identity, 211, 215t, 221t, 223
Sexual identity distress, 475
Sexual immorality, 347
Sexual indecency, 90
Sexual inverts, 88
Sexual minority status (SMS), 208, 213
Sexual minority young people, 441–443, 474, 476, 479, 480, 483, 492
   leaving home, 474, 475
   mental health care system, 490
   peers and, 486
   securing employment, 478
   social control of, 488, 489
   street life for, 477, 482, 491
   street prostitution, 484, 485
   survival sex, 478, 478n3
Sexual orientation, 19, 70, 71, 77, 78, 304, 321, 323, 324t, 326, 328, 329, 330, 332
   bias crimes based on, 48–49
   omission from crime data, 20
   sociological-criminological engagement with, 26
Sexual orientation and/or gender identity (SOGI), 46. See also SOGI-motivated violence
   SO versus GI-related bias crimes, 55
   violence, impacts on well-being, 53–54
   visibility of SOGI identity, 54
Sexual orientation bias, 19
Sexual Orientation Studies Association, 315
Sexual orientation-motivated bias crime, 48–49
   characteristics, 49
   differences between men and women in, 49–50

risk factors for, 50–51
Sexual outlaws, 90
Sexual perversion, 22
Sexual predators, 518
Sexual psychopath laws, 17, 24, 26, 27, 345
Sexual psychopaths, 89, 518
Sexuality, 504, 507–509, 511, 514, 520, 521
  toward critical ethnography of, 522–523
  and dynamics of power, 304
  global cultural conceptions of, 289
  human rights standards on, 303
  queer scholars, 301
  toxic sexuality, 516
  between West and Islam, 295
Sexually disordered bodies, 510
Sexually transmitted infections, 433
Shared perceptions in the workplace, 184, 185,
  192, 193, 194
Sheer amnesia, 345
Shellhammer v. Lewallen (1985), 394
*Shore Regional High School Board of Educa-
  tion v. P.S.* (2004), 397
Silence of the Lambs (1991), 94
Siri, 113
Sleep disturbances, 433
Slovenia, 312n1
Smith v. City of Salem (2004), 392
Smith, Charles E., 90
Snowball sampling design, 126
Social border(s), 523
Social categorization, 507
Social control theories, 26
Social deviance, 508
Social disorganization theories, 26
Social exceptions, 505–506
  and ephemeral rights, 506
Social exemption, 504
Social inequality, 450–451
Social labeling, 507
Social othering, 504, 507, 520, 521
Social Policies Gender Identity and Sexual
  Orientation Studies Association, 315
Social structure theories, 26
Sociological and Criminal Justice Abstracts,
  235
Sodomites, 88
Sodomy, 153, 156, 158
Sodomy law liberalization, demands for, 306
Sodomy law reform, 284
  economy of silence, 284, 284n2
Sodomy laws, 17, 284n1
SOGI violence explanation, 55
  individualistic explanations, 55–56
  interpersonal explanations, 56–57

sociocultural explanations, 57–58
SOGI-motivated violence, 46
  bias crime. *See* Sexual orientation-moti-
    vated bias crime
  explaining, 55–59
  impacts on well-being, 53–54
  prevalence of, 46–48
  visibility, 50
Solidarity
  of gay and lesbian, 154
  of LGBT, 154
South Africa, 47, 49, 53, 303, 342, 346, 513
South Sudan, homosexuality prohibition, 298
Southeast Europe
  LGBT developments in, 317t
  progressive cultural shifts, 330–332
Spade, Dean, 254
Sri Lanka
  male-to-male sexual contact in, 167
  nachchi and masculine partners, 167
  sex industry in, 165
  sexuality and gender in, 166–169
SSIPV, dynamics, 69
  gender performance, 70
  intergenerational transmission of violence,
    69
  outcomes of, 73
  power differentials. *See* Power differentials
  reasons victims stay, 72–73
  sequencing of abuse, 69–70
  substance abuse, 70
SSIPV, future directions
  defining population, 76–77
  future research methodologies, 76–78
  future research topics and policy implica-
    tions, 78–79
  sampling population, 77–78
Stakeholders, 233, 234, 235
Stanton, Gregory, 348
Stanton's eight stages of genocide, 348–349,
  358
  classification, 349–350
  dehumanization, 351–352
  denial, 354–355
  extermination, 354, 358
  organization, 352
  polarization, 352–353, 358
  preparation, 353, 358
  symbolization, 350–351
Star v. Gramley (1993), 250
State and state interventions, 517–519
State initiatives
  anti-bullying laws and policies, 421f
  Don't Say Gay laws, 422–425, 426

State initiatives (*cont.*)
　License to Bully provisions, 422–426
　state safe school legal landscape, 420–422
State of exception, 504, 505
State security, 152
State-sponsored homophobia, 316
Stereotypes, cultural, 125
"Stereotypical" gay men, 51
"Stereotypical" lesbians, 51
Stevens v. Williams (2008), 242, 243, 248
Stewart v. State (1981), 372
STIs (sexually-transmitted infections), 482
Stonewall riots, 154
Stonewall Survey, United Kingdom, 48
StopBullying.gov, 417
Stranger danger hysteria, 90
Street prostitution, 484, 485
Structural isomorphism, 287
The Student Non-Discrimination Act, 418–419
Sub-Saharan Africa, 296, 298
Substance abuse, 70, 433
Suicide, 407, 412, 413, 416
Supportive environment, 407
Surgical castration, 231
Surveillance, 104, 105, 108, 109, 113, 116,
　153
Swedish National Council for Crime Preven-
　tion (SNCCP), 47, 49–50
Sylvia Rivera Law Project, 254
Symbolic toxicity, 505
Symbolic violence, 508, 509

T
Task Force (National Gay and Lesbian Task
　Force), 115
Tates v. Blanas (2002), 244, 245
T-cell count, 365, 373
Teen dating violence, 433
Teletubbies (British television show), 351
Television
　LGBT persons on, 93*t*
　villain to victim on, 93–94
Templeton v. United States (1945), 370
Theoretical Criminology (Vold and Bernard),
　28
Theory, 3, 5, 7, 13, 559, 560, 561
Theory-building, 13
Three-factor (T-3) model, 24
Thrill-seekers, 55, 56
*Tinker v. Des Moines Independent Community
　School District* (1969), 410
Tipping point, 294

Title IX of U.S. Civil Rights Act, 408, 409,
　410, 413, 414, 415, 416, 418, 419, 425,
　426
　enforcement of, 414–416
Title VII, 408, 409
Trade openness, 357
Traditional African heterosexuality, 296
Traditional criminal law, logical accident and
　errors, 371
　biting cases, 371–375
　sex cases, 375–377
Tranny stroll, 484
Trans*, 535, 550, 558
Trans* communities, 77, 533, 558
Trans* individuals, 326
Trans* parades, 317*t*, 318, 321
Trans* people, 154, 157, 160, 532
Trans* persons, 79
Transgender, 3, 4, 10, 11, 312, 406, 559, 561
　basis for victimization, 180, 181
　definition, 236–239
　dressing, 174
　false accusations, 173
　feminine gender identity, 179
　inequality in police response, 172
　ponnaya, 179
　prisoners, 238–239, 252–253
　punishment inequalities, 173
　sex workers, 166
　source of stigma, 178
　unique configuration of abuse, 175, 181
　Western conceptualization, 167
Transgender America, 230
Transgender correctional policy in United
　States, 235–236
　accessing medical care, 239–242
　clothing and adornment, 248–252
　defining transgender, 236–239
　determining housing, 242–246
　displaying gender, 246–247
　names and pronoun use, 247–248
Transgender Day of Remembrance, 537
Transgender individuals
　defining family, 397–400
　employment discrimination, 390–393
　experience, 388–389
　GNC youth, 395–397
　housing discrimination, 393–395
　legal outcomes for, 387–388
　protection for, 395–397
Transgender inmate, 237, 246
　incarceration of, 252
Transgender policy, 253

legitimacy and the centrality of safety and security in organizational policy, 233–234

new penology and culture of control, 232–233

setting stage for, 232

Transmitting HIV, 364–367

blood. *See* Blood

CD4$^+$ cell count, 365

needle prick. *See* Needle prick

saliva. *See* Saliva

viral load test, 365

Transnationalism, 519–521

distrust of authority, 521

low socioeconomic status, 521

for MSM public health outreach projects, 519

racial discrimination, 521

social othering, 520

transnational governmentality, 520

Transphobic bullying, 396

Transsexual, 237, 315n2

Transvestite, 91, 93, 169, 318

Turkey, 317*t*

homosexuality as disease, 330

LGBT rights organizations in, 314

Twitter, 297, 315

Twitter posts, 113

Two-spirit, 474

Tyler Clementi Higher Education Anti-Harassment Act, 419–420, 426

Typology conceptualization of "mission" oriented bias crime, 56

U

UCLA Law Review, 109

Uganda, 345, 355, 356, 357

2007 Anti-Homosexuality Bill in, 340–343, 353, 358

aggravated homosexuality, 339

anti-gay assessment, 344

anti-gay hatred, 339

anti-gay violence, 352

autocratic rule, 356

colonization, 344–345

evidence of symbolization, 351

gay agenda, 350

HIV/AIDS in, 348

homophobia in, 347

homosexuals, 340, 349, 350, 352

inappropriate sexual activity, 354

upheaval, 355

Uganda Anti-Homosexuality Bill, 296–298, 302

Uganda National Liberation Front, 355

Ugandan "Kill the Gays" Bill, genocidal intentions of, 348, 358

Ugandan Penal Code Act, 341

Undergraduate criminal justice majors, 262, 266, 272, 273

Undergraduate education, 273, 275

Undergraduate students, 265

Underground market, 240

Unenumerated laws, 410–411

Uniform Code of Military Justice (UCMJ), 375, 378

Uniform Crime Report (UCR), 18

offenses, 18n1

United Nations (UN), 294, 296, 297

United Nations Human Rights Council (UN HRC), 293, 295, 302

U.S. Agency for International Development (USAID), 324*t*, 325, 327

U.S. Census Bureau, 19

U.S. Christian Evangelical movements, 298

U.S. Christian Right, 298

U.S. Department of Education (USDOE), 408

United States Department of Housing and Urban Development (HUD), 394

U.S. Department of Justice, 19

U.S. Federal Bureau of Investigation (FBI), 89

U.S. Federal Bureau of Prisons, 234

United States Federal government, 113

U.S. National Science Foundation, 113

U.S. Office of Juvenile Justice and Delinquency Prevention (OJJDP), 208

U.S. State Department's Bureau of Population, Refugees, and Migration (PRM), 323

United States v. Corralez (2005), 380

United States v. Dacus (2008), 378–380

United States v. Johnson (1990), 377, 378, 380

United States v. Joseph (1993), 379, 380

United States v. Stewart (1989), 380

United States v. Weatherspoon (1998), 379

United States v. Windsor (2013), 400

United States v. Womack (1989), 380

Universal Declaration of Human Rights, 325

Urban Men's Health Study (UMHS), 78

V

Vaginoplasty, 241

Verbal harassment, 53. *See also* Bullying

Victimization, 16, 18, 20, 30, 31, 152, 558, 559

Victimization (*cont.*)
  LGBTQ, 28
  surveys, 19
Victims helping, 73
  formal help-giving resources, absence of,
    74
  heterosexism among service providers,
    74–75
  legal barriers, 75, 76
Victims of anti-gay bias crimes, 122
Victorian ideology, 21
Villains
  gay villain, 91
  to victim on television, 93–94
Violence, 151, 152, 154, 155, 157, 460
  anti-gay harassment, 122
  gay men's involvement in, 123–125
  against organizing, 316–322
  purposes, 123
  sample characteristics, 129, 129*t*
  young women's experiences of, viii
Violent Crime Control and Law Enforcement
    Act (1994), 92, 187
Viral load test, 365

W
Wallerstein, Immanuel, 292, 301
War on the Sex Criminal, 89
*Was Lombroso a Queer? Criminology, Crim-
  inal Justice, and the Heterosexual
  Imaginary* (Tomsen), 539
Weeks v. State (1992), 374, 375
Welcoming Schools, 417–418
Well-being, 50, 71, 246, 247, 304
  SOGI-motivated violence, impacts on,
    53–54
Western Australia, homosexuality, 27n4
Western neo-colonialism, 304
Western-inspired cultural scripts, 287
When Black + Lesbian + Woman ≠ Black
    Lesbian Woman (Bowleg), 107–108
White House LGBT Conference on Safe
    Schools and Communities in Arlington,
    Virginia, 417
White Night riots, 155

Williams Institute at UCLA School of Law,
    115
Willingness, 266
Winship's due process concern, 369
Wolfenden Report, 155
Women of color, 109
Work, 453
World Bank, 113, 299
World polity perspective
  blind spot, 289–292
  on global sodomy law reform, 288–289
  of neo-institutionalist, 284
Worse overall general health, 433

X
The X-Files: I Want to Believe (2008), 94

Y
Young lesbians, 116
Youngblood v. School Bd. of Hillsborough Cty
    (2002), 397
Youth, 475, 476, 477, 478, 479, 480, 485, 486,
    487, 491, 492, 493
  complications, 482–483
  diversity of experience, 483–486
  drug use, mental health, and victimization,
    481, 482
  homelessness, 480
Youth Risk Behavior Surveillance (YRBS),
    432
Youth, LGBT, 406, 426
  bully pulpit, 416
  bullying, 412, 417, 418, 418, 419
  "It Gets Better" videos, 158, 416, 420
  suicides, 407, 413
  Title IX, fight against harassment, 410,
    413, 414, 415
YouTube, 315

Z
Zagreb, Croatia, 318
Zenne Dancer (film), 331

"Hope" (Photo taken at the 2012 Pride Parade, Belgrade, Serbia. Printed with kind permission from Alex Cooper).

Photographer: Alex Cooper

D. Peterson and V. R. Panfil (eds.), *Handbook of LGBT Communities,*
Crime, and Justice, DOI: 10.1007/978-1-4614-9188-0,
© Springer Science+Business Media New York 2014

CPSIA information can be obtained at www.ICGtesting.com
Printed in the USA
BVOW11s2203090215

387065BV00002B/6/P

9 781493 917